PCI System Architecture, Fourth Edition

MINDSHARE, INC.

Don Anderson
Tom Shanley

ADDISON-WESLEY

An imprint of Addison Wesley Longman, Inc.

Reading, Massachusetts • Menlo Park, California • New York
Don Mills, Ontario • Harlow, England • Amsterdam
Bonn • Sydney • Singapore • Tokyo • Madrid • San Juan
Paris • Seoul • Milan • Mexico City • Taipei

For more information, please contact:
Corporate, Government and Special Sales Group
Addison Wesley Longman, Inc.
One Jacob Way
Reading, Massachusetts 01867
(781) 944-3700

Library of Congress Cataloging-in-Publication Data is available.

ISBN: 0-201-30974-2

Sponsoring Editor: Karen Gettman
Production Coordinator: Jacquelyn Young
Cover Designer: Simone R. Payment
Set in 10 point Palatino by MindShare, Inc.

Text printed on recycled and acid-free paper.
ISBN 0201309742
3 4 5 6 7 8   MA   02 01 00 99
3rd Printing September 1999

PC System Architecture Series

MindShare, Inc.

Please see our web site (http://www.awl.com/cseng/series/mindshare) for more information on these titles.

80486 System Architecture: Third Edition
0-201-40994-1

AGP System Architecture
0-201-37964-3

CardBus System Architecture
0-201-40997-6

EISA System Architecture: Second Edition
0-201-40995-X

FireWire® System Architecture: Second Edition
0-201-48535-4

ISA System Architecture: Third Edition
0-201-40996-8

PCI System Architecture: Fourth Edition
0-201-30974-2

PCMCIA System Architecture: Second Edition
0-201-40991-7

Pentium® Pro and Pentium® II System Architecture: Second Edition
0-201-30973-4

Pentium® Processor System Architecture: Second Edition
0-201-40992-5

Plug and Play System Architecture
0-201-41013-3

Power PC System Architecture
0-201-40990-9

Protected Mode Software Architecture
0-201-55447-X

Universal Serial Bus System Architecture
0-201-46137-4

For my darlin' Nancy

Contents

About This Book

Chapter 1: Intro To PCI

Chapter 2: Intro to PCI Bus Operation

Chapter 3: Intro to Reflected-Wave Switching

Contents

Chapter 4: The Signal Groups

Chapter 5: PCI Bus Arbitration

Contents

Chapter 6: Master and Target Latency

Contents

Chapter 7: The Commands

Contents

Contents

Chapter 11: Fast Back-to-Back & Stepping

Chapter 12: Early Transaction End

Contents

Contents

Contents

Chapter 14: Interrupts

Contents

Chapter 15: The 64-bit PCI Extension

Contents

Chapter 16: 66MHz PCI Implementation

Contents

Chapter 19: Configuration Registers

Contents

Chapter 20: Expansion ROMs

Contents

Chapter 21: Add-in Cards and Connectors

Contents

Chapter 22: Hot-Plug PCI

Contents

Chapter 23: Power Management

Contents

Contents

Chapter 24: PCI-to-PCI Bridge

Contents

Contents

Contents

Contents

Contents

Contents

Figures

Figures

Figures

Tables

Tables

Tables

Tables

Acknowledgments

Thanks to the many thousands of engineers who have attended our PCI classes over the past four years and driven us mad with their endless questions and observations. We've had fun and hope you have as well.

The MindShare Architecture Series

The MindShare Architecture book series currently includes the books listed in Table 1, "PC Architecture Book Series," on page 1. Rather than duplicating common information in each book, the series uses the building-block approach. Generally-speaking, *ISA System Architecture* is the core book upon which the others build. In a sense, it is a PC-compatibility book.

Table 1: PC Architecture Book Series

Category	Title	Edition	ISBN
Processor Architecture	80486 System Architecture	3rd	0-201-40994-1
	Pentium Processor System Architecture	2nd	0-201-40992-5
	Pentium Pro and Pentium II System Architecture	2nd	0-201-30973-4
	PowerPC System Architecture	1st	0-201-40990-9
Bus Architecture	PCI System Architecture	4th	0-201-30974-2
	EISA System Architecture	Out-of-print	0-201-40995-X
	Firewire System Architecture: IEEE 1394	2nd	0-201-48535-4
	ISA System Architecture	3rd	0-201-40996-8
	Universal Serial Bus System Architecture	1st	0-201-46137-4

Table 1: PC Architecture Book Series (Continued)

Category	Title	Edition	ISBN
Other Architectures	PCMCIA System Architecture: 16-Bit PC Cards	2nd	0-201-40991-7
	CardBus System Architecture	1st	0-201-40997-6
	Plug and Play System Architecture	1st	0-201-41013-3
	Protected Mode Software Architecture	1st	0-201-55447-X
	AGP System Architecture	1st	0-201-37964-3

Organization of This Book

The fourth edition of *PCI System Architecture* has been updated to reflect:

- revision 2.2 of the *PCI Local Bus Specification*.
- revision 1.1 of the *PCI-to-PCI Bridge Architecture Specification*.
- revision 1.0 of the *PCI Hot-Plug Specification*.
- revision 1.1 of the *PCI Bus Power Management Interface Specification*.
- revision 2.1 *PCI BIOS Specification*.

It has been completely reorganized and expanded to include more detailed discussions of virtually every topic found in the first three editions. In addition, chapters have been added on other PCI-related subjects such as Hot-Plug, Power Management, and CompactPCI. The book is divided into the following topics:

Chapter 1: Intro To PCI.
Chapter 2: Intro to PCI Bus Operation
Chapter 3: Intro to Reflected-Wave Switching
Chapter 4: The Signal Groups
Chapter 5: PCI Bus Arbitration
Chapter 6: Master and Target Latency
Chapter 7: The Commands
Chapter 8: Read Transfers
Chapter 9: Write Transfers
Chapter 10: Memory and IO Addressing

Designation of Specification Changes

As illustrated in the margin, areas that have changed from the 2.1 PCI spec to **2.2** the 2.2 PCI spec are marked for easy reference.

In addition, areas that have changed from 1.0 PCI-to-PCI Bridge spec to the 1.1 **1.1** spec are also marked for easy reference.

AS ILLUSTRATED IN THE FORMAT OF THIS TEXT, THE AFFECTED TEXT IS PRINTED IN A DIFFERENT FONT AND IS CAPITALIZED. If an entire section of this book reflects a major change area, the 2.2 or 1.1 designator is displayed in the margin adjacent to the section heading, **BUT THE BODY TEXT FONT IS NOT PRINTED LIKE THIS.**

Cautionary Note

The reader of this or any other book that covers an evolving hardware technology should be aware that the official specification should be used during the design process. The specification has the final say of what's right and what's wrong. In addition, the reader must realize that the specification for an emerging technology is rapidly evolving. We make every attempt to produce our books on a timely basis, but the next revision of the specification sometimes outruns us. This version of our PCI book complies with revision 2.2 of the specification, dated 12/18/98.

Who this Book is For

This book is intended for use by hardware and software design and support personnel. Due to the clear, concise explanatory methods used to describe each subject, personnel outside of the design field may also find the text useful.

Prerequisite Knowledge

It is highly recommended that the reader have a good knowledge of PC and processor bus architecture prior to reading this book. The MindShare publications entitled *ISA System Architecture* and *Pentium Pro and Pentium II System Architecture* provide sufficient background for this purpose. Alternately, the reader may substitute *Pentium Processor System Architecture* or *PowerPC System Architecture* in place of *Pentium Pro and Pentium II System Architecture*.

Object Size Designations

The following designations are used throughout this book when referring to the size of data objects:

- A **byte** is an 8-bit object.
- A **word** is a 16-bit, or two byte, object.
- A **doubleword, or dword,** is a 32-bit or four byte, object.
- A **quadword** is a 64-bit, or eight byte, object.
- A **paragraph** is a 128-bit, or 16 byte, object.
- A **page** is a 4K-aligned 4KB area of address space.

The specification frequently uses the processor's cache **line** size as a convenient memory block size in various discussions. Be aware that the cache line size is defined by the processor type utilized in the system. As an example, the current members of the P6 processor family have a cache line size of 32 bytes.

Documentation Conventions

This section defines the typographical convention used throughout this book.

Hex Notation

All hex numbers are followed by an "h". Examples:

```
9A4Eh
0100h
```

Binary Notation

All binary numbers are followed by a "b". Examples:

```
0001 0101b
01b
```

Decimal Notation

Numbers without any suffix are decimal. When required for clarity, decimal numbers are followed by a "d". The following examples each represent a decimal number:

```
16
255
256d
128d
```

Signal Name Representation

Each signal that assumes the logic low state when asserted is followed by a pound sign (#). As an example, the TRDY# signal is asserted low when the target is ready to complete a data transfer.

Signals that are not followed by a pound sign are asserted when they assume the logic high state. As an example, IDSEL is asserted high to indicate that a PCI device's configuration space is being addressed.

Identification of Bit Fields (logical groups of bits or signals)

All bit fields are designated in little-endian bit ordering as follows:

```
[X:Y],
```

where "X" is the most-significant bit and "Y" is the least-significant bit of the field. As an example, the PCI address/data bus consists of AD[31:0], where AD[31] is the most-significant and AD[0] the least-significant bit of the field.

We Want Your Feedback

MindShare values your comments and suggestions. You can contact us via mail, phone, fax or internet email.

Phone: (719) 488-8990
Fax: (719) 488-9855
E-mail: tshanley@interserv.com
Web Site: WWW.MINDSHARE.COM

To obtain information on public or private seminars, go to our web site.

Mailing Address

MindShare, Inc.
615 Beacon Lite Rd.
Monument, CO 80132

Intro To PCI

This Chapter

This chapter provides a brief history of PCI, introduces its major feature set, the concept of a PCI device versus a PCI function, and identifies the specifications that this book is based upon.

The Next Chapter

The next chapter provides an introduction to the PCI transfer mechanism, including a definition of the following basic concepts: burst transfers, the initiator, targets, agents, single and multi-function devices, the PCI bus clock, the address phase, claiming the transaction, the data phase, transaction completion and the return of the bus to the idle state. It defines how a device must respond if the device that it is transferring data with exhibits a protocol violation. Finally, it introduces the "green" nature of PCI—power conservation is stressed in the spec.

PCI Bus History

Intel made the decision not to back the VESA VL standard because the emerging standard did not take a sufficiently long-term approach towards the problems presented at that time and those to be faced in the coming five years. In addition, the VL bus had very limited support for burst transfers, thereby limiting the achievable throughput.

Intel defined the PCI bus to ensure that the marketplace would not become crowded with various permutations of local bus architectures peculiar to a specific processor bus. The first release of the specification, version 1.0, became available on 6/22/92. Revision 2.0 became available in April of 1993. Revision 2.1 was issued in Q1 of 1995. The latest version, 2.2, was completed on December 18, 1998, and became available in February of 1999.

PCI Bus Features

PCI stands for *Peripheral Component Interconnect*. The PCI bus can be populated with adapters requiring fast accesses to each other and/or system memory and that can be accessed by the processor at speeds approaching that of the processor's full native bus speed. It is very important to note that all read and write transfers over the PCI bus can be performed as burst transfers. The length of the burst is determined by the bus master. The target is given the start address and the transaction type at the start of the transaction, but is not told the transfer length. As the master becomes ready to transfer each data item, it informs the target whether or not it's the last one. The transaction completes when the final data item has been transferred.

Figure 1-1 on page 11 illustrates the basic relationship of the PCI, expansion, processor and memory buses.

- The host/PCI bridge, frequently referred to as the North Bridge, connects the host processor bus to the root PCI bus.
- The PCI-to-ISA bridge, frequently referred to as the South Bridge, connects the root PCI bus to the ISA (or EISA) bus. The South Bridge also typically incorporates the Interrupt Controller, IDE Controller, USB Host Controller, and the DMA Controller. The North and South Bridges comprise the chipset.
- One or more PCI-to-PCI bridges (not shown) may be embedded on the root PCI bus, or may reside on a PCI add-in card.
- In addition, a chipset may support more than one North Bridge (not shown).

Table 1-1: Major PCI Features

Feature	Description
Processor Independence	Components designed for the PCI bus are PCI-specific, not processor-specific, thereby isolating device design from processor upgrade treadmill.
Support for up to approximately 80 PCI functions per PCI bus	A typical PCI bus implementation supports approximately ten electrical loads, and each device presents a load to the bus. Each device, in turn, may contain up to eight PCI functions.

Table 1-1: Major PCI Features (Continued)

Feature	Description
Support for up to 256 PCI buses	The specification provides support for up to 256 PCI buses.
Low-power consumption	A major design goal of the PCI specification is the creation of a system design that draws as little current as possible.
Bursts can be performed on all read and write transfers	A 32-bit PCI bus supports a 132Mbytes per second peak transfer rate for both read and write transfers, and a 264Mbytes per second peak transfer rate for 64-bit PCI transfers. Transfer rates of up to 528Mbytes per second are achievable on a 64-bit, 66MHz PCI bus.
Bus speed	Revision 2.0 spec supported PCI bus speeds up to 33MHz. Revision 2.1 adds support for 66MHz bus operation.
64-bit bus width	Full definition of a 64-bit extension.
Access time	As fast as 60ns (at a bus speed of 33MHz when an initiator parked on the PCI bus is writing to a PCI target).
Concurrent bus operation	Bridges support full bus concurrency with processor bus, PCI bus (or buses), and the expansion bus simultaneously in use.
Bus master support	Full support of PCI bus masters allows peer-to-peer PCI bus access, as well as access to main memory and expansion bus devices through PCI-to-PCI and expansion bus bridges. In addition, a PCI master can access a target that resides on another PCI bus lower in the bus hierarchy.
Hidden bus arbitration	Arbitration for the PCI bus can take place while another bus master is performing a transfer on the PCI bus.
Low-pin count	Economical use of bus signals allows implementation of a functional PCI target with 47 pins and an initiator with 49 pins.
Transaction integrity check	Parity checking on the address, command and data.
Three address spaces	Memory, I/O and configuration address space.

Table 1-1: Major PCI Features (Continued)

Feature	Description
Auto-Configuration	Full bit-level specification of the configuration registers necessary to support automatic device detection and configuration.
Software Transparency	Software drivers utilize same command set and status definition when communicating with PCI device or its expansion bus-oriented cousin.
Add-In Cards	The specification includes a definition of PCI connectors and add-in cards.
Add-In Card Size	The specification defines three card sizes: long, short and variable-height short cards.

Figure 1-1: The PCI System

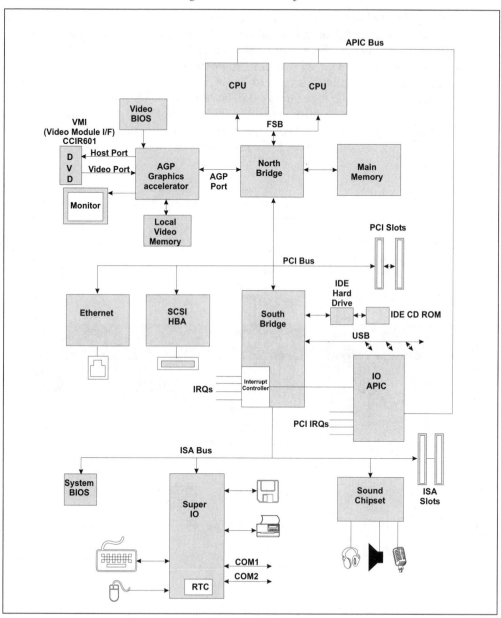

PCI Device vs. Function

The typical PCI device consists of a complete peripheral adapter encapsulated within an IC package or integrated onto a PCI expansion card. Typical examples would be a network, display or SCSI adapter. During the initial period after the introduction of the PCI specification, many vendors chose to interface pre-existent, non-PCI compliant devices to the PCI bus. This was easily accomplished using programmable logic arrays (PLAs). Figure 1-2 on page 12 illustrates ten PCI-compliant devices attached to the PCI bus on the system board. It should also be noted that each PCI-compliant package (embedded component or add-in card) may contain up to eight PCI functions. A function is a logical device.

Figure 1-2: PCI Devices Attached to the PCI Bus

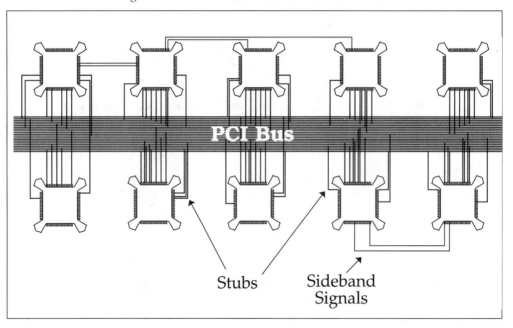

Specifications Book is Based On

This book is based on the documents indicated in Table 1-2 on page 13.

Table 1-2: This Book is Based On The Following Documents

Document Title	Revision
PCI Local Bus Specification	2.2
PCI-to-PCI Bridge Specification	1.1
PCI System Design Guide	1.0
PCI BIOS Specification	2.1
PCI Bus Power Management Interface Specification	1.1
PCI Hot-Plug Specification	1.0

Obtaining PCI Bus Specification(s)

The PCI bus specification, version 1.0, was developed by Intel Corporation. The specification is now managed by a consortium of industry partners known as the PCI Special Interest Group (SIG). MindShare, Inc. is a member of the SIG. The specifications are commercially available for purchase from the SIG. The latest revision of the specification (as of this printing) is 2.2. For information regarding the specifications and/or SIG membership, contact:

PCI Special Interest Group
2575 N.E. Kathryn #17
Hillsboro, Oregon 97124
1-800-433-5177 (USA)
503-693-6232 (International)
503-693-8344 (Fax)
pcisig@pcisig.com
http://www.pcisig.com

2 Intro to PCI Bus Operation

The Previous Chapter

The previous chapter provided a brief history of PCI, introduced it's major feature set, the concept of a PCI device versus a PCI function, and identified the specifications that this book is based upon. It also provided information on contacting the PCI SIG.

In This Chapter

This chapter provides an introduction to the PCI transfer mechanism, including a definition of the following basic concepts: burst transfers, the initiator, targets, agents, single and multi-function devices, the PCI bus clock, the address phase, claiming the transaction, the data phase, transaction completion and the return of the bus to the idle state. It defines how a device must respond if the device that it is transferring data with exhibits a protocol violation. Finally, it introduces the "green" nature of PCI—power conservation is stressed in the spec.

The Next Chapter

Unlike many buses, the PCI bus does not incorporate termination resistors at the physical end of the bus to absorb voltage changes and prevent the wavefront caused by a voltage change from being reflected back down the bus. Rather, PCI uses reflections to advantage. The next chapter provides an introduction to reflected-wave switching.

Burst Transfer

Refer to Figure 2-1 on page 16. A burst transfer is one consisting of a single address phase followed by two or more data phases. The bus master only has to arbitrate for bus ownership one time. The start address and transaction type are issued during the address phase. All devices on the bus latch the address and transaction type and decode them to determine which is the target device. The target device latches the start address into an address counter (assuming it supports burst mode—more on this later) and is responsible for incrementing the address from data phase to data phase.

PCI data transfers can be accomplished using burst transfers. Many PCI bus masters and target devices are designed to support burst mode. It should be noted that a PCI target may be designed such that it can only handle single data phase transactions. When a bus master attempts to perform a burst transaction, the target forces the master to terminate the transaction at the completion of the first data phase. The master must re-arbitrate for the bus to attempt resumption of the burst with the next data item. The target terminates each burst transfer attempt when the first data phase completes. This would yield very poor performance, but may be the correct approach for a device that doesn't require high throughput. Each burst transfer consists of the following basic components:

- The address and transfer type are output during the **address phase**.
- A data object (up to 32-bits in a 32-bit implementation or 64-bits in a 64-bit implementation) may then be transferred during each subsequent **data phase**.

Assuming that neither the initiator (i.e., the master) nor the target device inserts wait states in each data phase, a data object (a dword or a quadword) may be transferred on the rising-edge of each PCI clock cycle. At a PCI bus clock frequency of 33MHz, a transfer rate of 132Mbytes/second may be achieved. A transfer rate of 264Mbytes/second may be achieved in a 64-bit implementation when performing 64-bit transfers during each data phase. A 66MHz PCI bus implementation can achieve 264 or 528Mbytes/second transfer rates using 32- or 64-bit transfers. This chapter introduces the burst mechanism used to performing block transfers over the PCI bus.

Figure 2-1: Example Burst Data Transfer

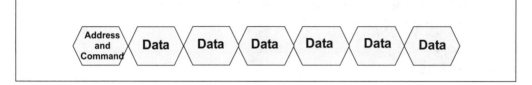

Initiator, Target and Agents

There are two participants in every PCI burst transfer: the initiator and the target. The initiator, or bus master, is the device that initiates a transfer. The terms bus master and initiator can be used interchangeably and frequently are in the PCI specification. The target is the device currently addressed by the initiator for the purpose of performing a data transfer. PCI initiator and target devices are commonly referred to as PCI-compliant agents in the spec.

Single- Vs. Multi-Function PCI Devices

A PCI physical device package may take the form of a component integrated onto the system board or may be implemented on a PCI add-in card. Each PCI package (referred to in the spec as a **device**) may incorporate from one to eight separate functions. A **function** is a logical device. This is analogous to a multi-function card found in any ISA, EISA or Micro Channel machine.

- A package containing one function is referred to as a **single-function** PCI **device**,
- while a package containing two or more PCI functions is referred to as a **multi-function PCI device**.

Each function contains its own, individually-addressable configuration space, 64 dwords in size. Its configuration registers are implemented in this space. Using these registers, the configuration software can automatically detect the function's presence, determine its resource requirements (memory space, IO space, interrupt line, etc.), and can then assign resources to the function that are guaranteed not to conflict with the resources assigned to other devices.

PCI Bus Clock

Refer to the CLK signal in Figure 2-2 on page 19. All actions on the PCI bus are synchronized to the PCI CLK signal. The frequency of the CLK signal may be anywhere from 0MHz to 33MHz. The revision 1.0 specification stated that all devices must support operation from 16 to 33MHz, while recommending support for operation down to 0MHz (in other words, when the clock has been stopped as a power conservation strategy). The revision 2.x (x = 1 or 2) PCI specification indicates that **all** PCI **devices must support** PCI **operation within the 0MHz to 33MHz range**. Support for operation down to 0MHz provides low-power and static debug capability. On a bus with a clock running at 33MHz or slower, the PCI CLK frequency may be changed at any time and may be stopped (but only in the low state). Components integrated onto the system board may be designed to only operate at a single frequency and may require a policy of no frequency change (and the system board designer would ensure that the clock frequency remains unchanged). Devices on add-in cards must support operation from 0 through 33MHz (because the card must operate in any platform that it may be installed in).

The revision 2.1 specification also defined PCI bus operation at speeds of up to 66MHz. The chapter entitled "66MHz PCI Implementation" describes the operational characteristics of the 66MHz PCI bus, embedded devices and add-in cards.

Address Phase

Refer to Figure 2-2 on page 19. Every PCI transaction (with the exception of a transaction using 64-bit addressing) starts off with an address phase one PCI clock period in duration (the only exception is a transaction wherein the initiator uses 64-bit addressing delivered in two address phases and consuming two PCI clock periods—this topic is covered in "64-bit Addressing" on page 287). During the address phase, the initiator identifies the target device (via the address) and the type of transaction (also referred to as the command type). The target device is identified by driving a start address within its assigned range onto the PCI address/data bus. At the same time, the initiator identifies the type of transaction by driving the command type onto the 4-bit wide PCI Command/Byte Enable bus. The initiator also asserts the FRAME# signal to indicate the presence of a valid start address and transaction type on the bus. Since the initiator only presents the start address and command for one PCI clock cycle, it is the responsibility of every PCI target device to latch the address and command on the next rising-edge of the clock so that it may subsequently be decoded.

By decoding the address latched from the address bus and the command type latched from the Command/Byte Enable bus, a target device can determine if it is being addressed and the type of transaction in progress. It's important to note that the initiator only supplies a start address to the target (during the address phase). Upon completion of the address phase, the address/data bus becomes the data bus for the duration of the transaction and is used to transfer data in each of the data phases. It is the responsibility of the target to latch the start address and to auto-increment it (assuming that the target supports burst transfers) to point to the next group of locations (a dword or a quadword) during each subsequent data transfer.

Figure 2-2: Typical PCI Transaction

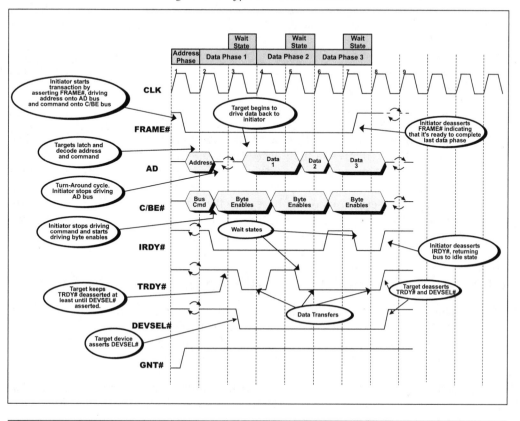

Claiming the Transaction

Refer to Figure 2-2 on page 19. When a PCI target determines that it is the target of a transaction, it must claim the transaction by asserting DEVSEL# (Device Select). If the initiator doesn't sample DEVSEL# asserted within a predetermined amount of time, it aborts the transaction.

Data Phase(s)

Refer to Figure 2-2 on page 19. The data phase of a transaction is the period during which a data object is transferred between the initiator and the target. The number of data bytes to be transferred during a data phase is determined by the number of Command/Byte Enable signals that are asserted by the initiator during the data phase.

Each data phase is at least one PCI clock period in duration. Both the initiator and the target must indicate that they are ready to complete a data phase, or the data phase is extended by a wait state one PCI CLK period in duration. The PCI bus defines ready signal lines used by both the initiator (IRDY#) and the target (TRDY#) for this purpose.

Transaction Duration

The initiator doesn't issue a transfer count to the target. Rather, in each data phase it indicates whether it's ready to transfer the current data item and, if it is, whether it's the final data item. FRAME# is asserted at the start of the address phase and remains asserted until the initiator is ready (asserts IRDY#) to complete the final data phase. When the target samples IRDY# asserted and FRAME# deasserted in a data phase, it realizes that this is the final data phase. However, the data phase will not complete until the target has also asserted the TRDY# signal.

Transaction Completion and Return of Bus to Idle State

Refer to Figure 2-2 on page 19. The initiator indicates that the last data transfer (of a burst transfer) is in progress by deasserting FRAME# and asserting IRDY#. When the last data transfer has been completed, the initiator returns the PCI bus to the idle state by deasserting its ready line (IRDY#).

If another bus master had previously been granted ownership of the bus by the PCI bus arbiter and was waiting for the current initiator to surrender the bus, it can detect that the bus has returned to the idle state by detecting FRAME# and IRDY# both deasserted on the same rising-edge of the PCI clock (on the rising-edge of clock nine in the figure).

Response to Illegal Behavior

The PCI specification does not encourage the device designer to actively check for protocol violations. If a device does detect a violation, however, the following policy is advised.

Upon detection of illegal use of bus protocol, all PCI devices should be designed to gracefully return to the idle state (i.e., cease driving all bus signals and return its target or master state machine to the quiescent state) as quickly as possible. The good device (as opposed to the evil one) should attempt to stay operational so it can participate in future transactions.

The specification is understandably vague on this point. It depends on the nature of the protocol violation as to whether the devices can gracefully return to their idle states and still function properly. As an example, the specification cites the case where the initiator simultaneously deasserts FRAME# and IRDY# (an illegal action). In this case, when the target detects this illegal end to the transaction, it is suggested that the target deassert all target-related signals and return its state machine to the idle state. In the event that a protocol violation leaves a target device questioning its ability to function correctly in the future, it can respond to all future access attempts with a Target Abort (explained in "Target Abort" on page 194). If the target thinks that the protocol violation has not impaired its ability to function correctly, it just surrenders all signals, returns to the idle state, and does not indicate any type of error.

"Green" Machine

In keeping with the goal of low power consumption, the specification calls for low-power, CMOS output drivers and receivers to be used by PCI devices.

The next chapter introduces the reflected-wave switching used in the PCI bus environment to permit low-power, CMOS drivers to successfully drive the bus.

If the address/data bus and command/byte enable signals are permitted to float (around the switching region of the CMOS input buffers which exist in every PCI device) for extended periods of time, the receiver inputs would oscillate and draw excessive current. This is a violation of the spec. To prevent this from happening, it is a rule in PCI that the address/data bus, the command/byte enables, and the parity signal must not be permitted to float for extended periods of time. Since the bus is normally driven most of the time, it may be assumed that the pre-charged bus (precharged by the last entity to drive the bus) will retain its state while not being driven for brief periods of time during turnaround cycles (turnaround cycles are described in the chapter entitled "Read Transfers" on page 123).

"Bus Parking" on page 65 describes the mechanism utilized to prevent the bus from floating when the bus is idle. The chapters entitled "Read Transfers" on page 123 and "Write Transfers" on page 135 describe the mechanism utilized during data phases with wait states. The chapter entitled "The 64-bit PCI Extension" describes the mechanism utilized to keep the upper half of the bus from floating when it's not in use (during a 32-bit transfer).

3 Intro to Reflected-Wave Switching

Prior To This Chapter

The previous chapter provided an introduction to the PCI transfer mechanism, including a definition of the following basic concepts: burst transfers, the initiator, targets, agents, single and multi-function devices, the PCI bus clock, the address phase, claiming the transaction, the data phase, transaction completion and the return of the bus to the idle state. It defined how a device must respond if the device that it is transferring data with exhibits a protocol violation. Finally, it introduced the "green" nature of PCI—power conservation is stressed in the spec.

In This Chapter

Unlike many buses, the PCI bus does not incorporate termination resistors at the physical end of the bus to absorb voltage changes and prevent the wavefront caused by a voltage change from being reflected back down the bus. Rather, PCI uses reflections to advantage. This chapter provides an introduction to reflected-wave switching.

The Next Chapter

The next chapter provides an introduction to the signal groups that comprise the PCI bus.

Each Trace Is a Transmission Line

Refer to Figure 3-1 on page 25. Consider the case where a signal trace is fed by a driver and is attached to a number of device inputs distributed along the signal trace. In the past, in order to specify the strength of the driver to be used, the system designer would ignore the electrical characteristics of the trace itself and only factor in the electrical characteristics of the devices connected to the trace. This approach was acceptable when the system clock rate was down in the 1MHz range. The designer would add up the capacitance of each input connected to the trace and treat it as a lumped capacitance. This value would be used to select the drive current capability of the driver. In high-frequency environments such as PCI, traces must switch state at rates from 25MHz on up. At these bus speeds, traces act as transmission lines and the electrical characteristics of the trace must also be factored into the equation used to select the characteristics of the output driver.

A transmission line presents impedance to the driver attempting to drive a voltage change onto the trace and also imposes a time delay in the transmission of the voltage change along the trace. The typical trace's impedance ranges from 50 to 110 Ohms. The width of the trace and the distance of the trace from a ground plane are the major factors that influence its impedance. A wide trace located close to a ground plane is more capacitive in nature and its impedance is close to 50 Ohms. A narrow trace located far from a ground plane is more inductive in nature and its impedance is in the area of 110 Ohms Each device input attached to the trace is largely capacitive in nature. This has the effect of decreasing the overall impedance that the trace offers to a driver.

Old Method: Incident-Wave Switching

Consider the case where the driver at position one in Figure 3-1 on page 25 must drive the signal line from a logic high to a logic low. Assume that the designer has selected a strong output driver that is capable of driving the signal line from a high to a low at the point of incidence (the point at which it starts to drive). This is referred to as incident-wave switching. As the wavefront propagates down the trace (toward device 10), each device it passes detects a logic low. The amount of time it takes to switch all of the inputs along the trace to a low would be the time it takes the signal to propagate the length of the trace. This would appear to be the best approach because all device inputs are switched in the quickest possible time (one traversal of the trace).

There are negative effects associated with this approach, however. As mentioned earlier, the capacitance of each input along the trace adds capacitance and thus lowers the overall impedance of the trace. The typical overall impedance of the trace would typically be around 30 Ohms. When a 5V device begins to drive a trace, a voltage divider is created between the driver's internal impedance and the impedance of the trace that it is attempting to drive. Assuming that a 20 Ohm driver is attempting to drive a 30 Ohm trace, two of the five volts is dropped within the driver and a three volt incident voltage is propagated onto the trace. Since current = voltage divided by resistance, the current that must be sourced by the driver = 2 volts/20 Ohms, or 100ma.

When considered by itself, this doesn't appear to present a problem. Assume, however, that a device driver must simultaneously drive 32 address traces, four command traces and four other signals. This is not atypical in a 32-bit bus architecture. Assuming that all of the drivers are encapsulated in one driver package, the package must source four Amps of current, virtually instantaneously (in as short a period as one nanosecond). This current surge presents a number of problems:

- extremely difficult to decouple.
- causes spikes on internal bond wires.
- increases EMI.
- causes crosstalk inside and outside of the package.

This is the reason that most strong drivers are available in packages that encapsulate only eight drivers. In addition, 20 Ohm output drivers consume quite a bit of silicon real-estate and become quite warm at high frequencies.

Another side-effect occurs when the signal wavefront arrives at the physical end of the trace (at device 10 in Figure 3-1 on page 25). If the designer does not incorporate a terminating resistor at the end of the trace (and the PCI bus is not terminated), the trace stub presents a very high impedance to the signal. Since the signal cannot proceed, it turns around and is reflected back down the bus. During the return passage of the wavefront, this effectively doubles the voltage change seen on the trace at each device's input and at the driver that originated the wavefront. When an incident-wave driver is used (as in this case), the already high voltage it drives onto the trace is doubled. In order to absorb the signal at the physical end of the trace, the system designer frequently includes a terminating resistor.

The usage of incident-wave switching consumes a significant amount of power and violates the green nature of the PCI bus.

Figure 3-1: Device Loads Distributed Along a Trace

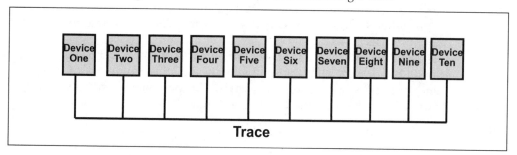

PCI Method: Reflected-Wave Switching

Refer to Figure 3-1 on page 25 and Figure 3-2 on page 27. The PCI bus is unterminated and uses wavefront reflection to advantage. A carefully selected, relatively weak output driver is used to drive the signal line partially towards the desired logic state (as illustrated at point **A** in Figure 3-2 on page 27). The driver only has to drive the signal line partially towards its final state, rather than completely (as a strong incident-wave driver would). No inputs along the trace will sample the signal until the next rising-edge of the clock.

When the wavefront arrives at the unterminated end of the bus, it is reflected back and doubled (see point **B** in Figure 3-2 on page 27). Upon passing each device input again during the wavefront's return trip down the trace, a valid logic level registers at the input on each device. The signal is not sampled, however, until the next rising-edge of the PCI clock (point **C** in the figure). Finally, the wavefront is absorbed by the low-impedance within the driver. This method cuts driver size and surge current in half. There are three timing parameters associated with PCI signal timing:

- **Tval**. PCI devices always start driving a signal on the rising-edge of the PCI clock. Tval is the amount of time it takes the output driver to drive the signal a single-step towards its final logic state. The driver must ensure that its output voltage reaches a specified level (Vtest for 5vdc or Vstep for 3.3vdc switching) to ensure that a valid logic level is detected by the receivers on the next rising edge of the clock.
- **Tprop** (propagation delay). This is the amount of time that it takes the wavefront to travel to the other end of the trace, reflect (thereby doubling the voltage swing), and travel back down the trace.
- **Tsu** (setup time). The signal must have settled in its final state at all inputs at least this amount of time prior to the next rising-edge of the clock (when all receiving devices sample their inputs). The setup times for the REQ# and GNT# signals (these are point-to-point signals; all others are bussed between all devices) deviate from the value illustrated: REQ# setup time is 12ns, while GNT# has a setup time of 10ns. The setup time for all other input signals is 7ns.
- **Th** (hold time). This is the amount of time that signals must be held in their current logic state after the sample point (i.e., the rising-edge of the clock) and is specified as 0ns for PCI signals. This parameter is not illustrated in Figure 3-2 on page 27 and Figure 3-3 on page 28.

Chapter 3: Intro to Reflected-Wave Switching

In many systems, correct operation of the PCI bus relies on diodes embedded within devices to limit reflections and to successfully meet the specified propagation delay. If a system has long trace runs without connection to a PCI component (e.g., a series of unpopulated add-in connectors), it may be necessary to add diode terminators at that end of the bus to ensure signal quality.

The PCI specification states that devices must only sample their inputs on the rising-edge of the PCI clock signal. The physical layout of the PCI bus traces are very important to ensure that signal propagation is within assigned limits. When a driver asserts or deasserts a signal, the wavefront must propagate to the physical end of the bus, reflect back and make the full passage back down the bus before the signal(s) is sampled on the next rising-edge of the PCI clock. At 33MHz, the propagation delay is specified as 10ns, but may be increased to 11ns by lowering the clock skew from component to component. The specification contains a complete description of trace length and electrical characteristics.

Figure 3-2: High-Going Signal Reflects and Is Doubled

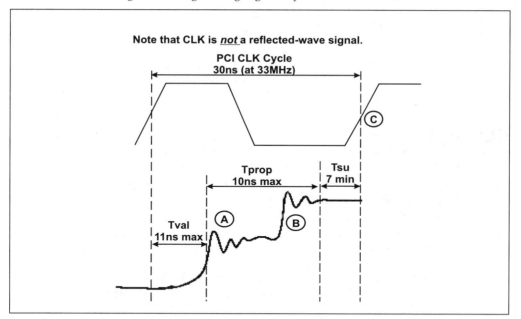

Figure 3-3: Low-Going Signal Reflects and Is Doubled

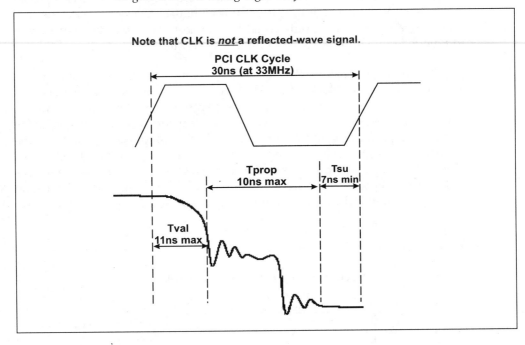

CLK Signal

As illustrated in Figure 3-4 on page 29, the minimum CLK cycle time is 30ns (at 33MHz; 15ns at 66MHz). The maximum skew on the clock when measured on the CLK pin of any two PCI components is 2ns (1ns at 66MHz). The clock frequency can be changed as long as the clock edges remain clean and the T_cyc, T_high and T_low minimums are not violated. The clock may be stopped, but only in the low state.

On a PCI bus with a clock frequency between 33.33MHz and 66.66MHz, the PCI RST# signal must be asserted before a clock frequency change is made.

Figure 3-4: CLK Signal Timing Characteristics

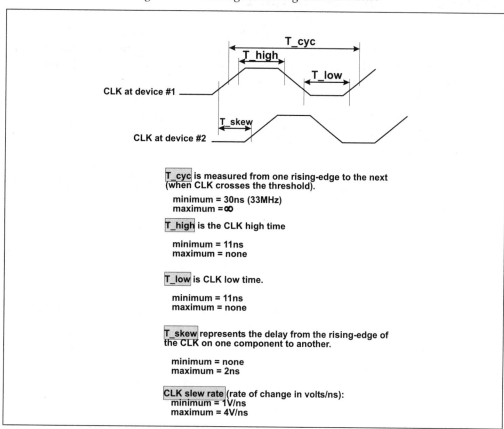

T_cyc is measured from one rising-edge to the next (when CLK crosses the threshold).

minimum = 30ns (33MHz)
maximum =∞

T_high is the CLK high time

minimum = 11ns
maximum = none

T_low is CLK low time.

minimum = 11ns
maximum = none

T_skew represents the delay from the rising-edge of the CLK on one component to another.

minimum = none
maximum = 2ns

CLK slew rate (rate of change in volts/ns):
minimum = 1V/ns
maximum = 4V/ns

RST#/REQ64# Timing

The assertion and deassertion of RST# is asynchronous to the PCI clock signal. If desired, a synchronous reset may be implemented, however. RST# must remain asserted for a minimum of 1ms after the power has stabilized. RST# must remain asserted for a minimum of 100 (s after the CLK has stabilized. When RST# is asserted, all devices must float their output drivers within a maximum of 40ns.

During assertion of RST#, the system board reset logic must assert REQ64# for a minimum of 10 clock cycles. REQ64# may remain asserted for a maximum of 50ns after RST# is deasserted. For a discussion of REQ64# assertion during reset, refer to "64-bit Cards in 32-bit Add-in Connectors" on page 266.

Slower Clock Permits Longer Bus

If the system board designer chooses to run the PCI clock at a rate slower than 33MHz, the physical characteristics of the bus may be altered while still achieving proper operation (i.e., more loads, more connectors, physically longer trace runs).

The Signal Groups

The Previous Chapter

The previous chapter provided an introduction to reflected-wave switching.

This Chapter

This chapter divides the PCI bus signals into functional groups and describes the function of each signal.

The Next Chapter

When a PCI bus master requires the use of the PCI bus to perform a data transfer, it must request the use of the bus from the PCI bus arbiter. The next chapter provides a detailed discussion of the PCI bus arbitration timing. The PCI specification defines the timing of the request and grant handshaking, but not the procedure used to determine the winner of a competition. The algorithm used by a system's PCI bus arbiter to decide which of the requesting bus masters will be granted use of the PCI bus is system-specific and outside the scope of the specification.

Introduction

This chapter introduces the signals utilized to interface a PCI-compliant device to the PCI bus. Figures 2-1 and 3-2 illustrate the required and optional signals for master and target PCI devices, respectively. A PCI device that can act as the initiator or target of a transaction would obviously have to incorporate both initiator and target-related signals. In actuality, there is no such thing as a device that is purely a bus master and never a target. At a minimum, a device must act as the target of configuration reads and writes.

Each of the signal groupings are described in the following sections. It should be noted that some of the optional signals are not optional for certain types of PCI agents. The sections that follow identify the circumstances where signals must be implemented.

Figure 4-1: PCI-Compliant Master Device Signals

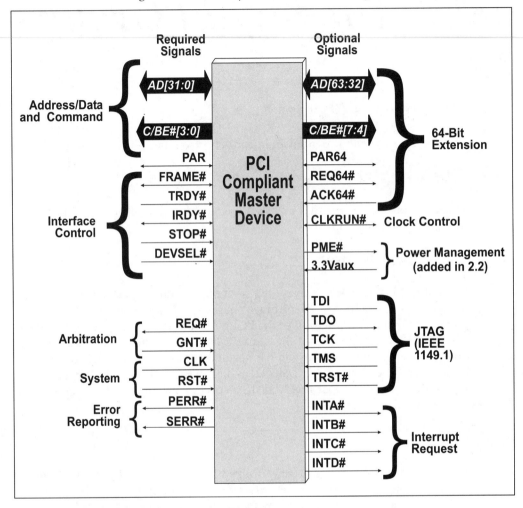

Figure 4-2: PCI-Compliant Target Device Signals

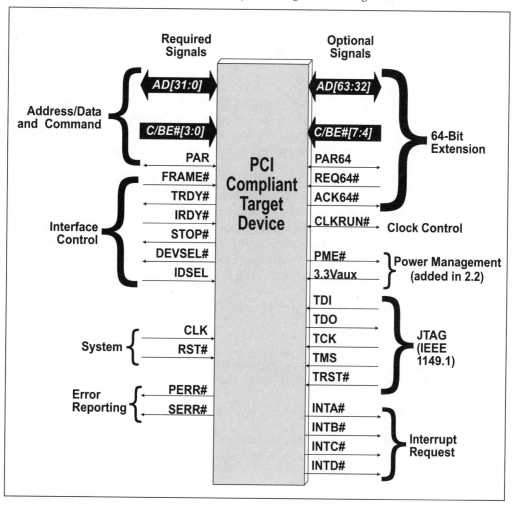

System Signals

PCI Clock Signal (CLK)

The CLK signal is an input to all devices residing on the PCI bus. It is *not* a reflected-wave signal. It provides timing for all transactions, including bus arbitration. All inputs to PCI devices are sampled on the rising edge of the CLK signal. The state of all input signals are don't-care at all other times. All PCI timing parameters are specified with respect to the rising-edge of the CLK signal.

All actions on the PCI bus are synchronized to the PCI CLK signal. The frequency of the CLK signal may be anywhere from 0MHz to 33MHz. The revision 1.0 PCI specification stated that all devices must support operation from 16 to 33MHz and it strongly recommended support for operation down to 0MHz for static debug and low power operation. The revision 2.x PCI specification indicates that **ALL** PCI devices (with one exception noted below) **MUST** support PCI operation within the 0MHz to 33MHz range.

The clock frequency may be changed at any time as long as:

- The clock edges remain clean.
- The minimum clock high and low times are not violated.
- There are no bus requests outstanding.
- LOCK# is not asserted.

The clock may only be stopped in a low state (to conserve power).

As an exception, components designed to be integrated onto the system board may be designed to operate at a fixed frequency (of up to 33MHz) and may only operate at that frequency.

For a discussion of 66MHz bus operation, refer to the chapter entitled "66MHz PCI Implementation" on page 299

CLKRUN# Signal

Description

Refer to Figure 4-3 on page 36. The CLKRUN# signal is optional and is defined for the mobile (i.e., portable) environment. It is not available on the PCI add-in connector. This section provides an introduction to this subject. A more detailed description of the mobile environment and the CLKRUN# signal's role can be found in the document entitled *PCI Mobile Design Guide* (available from the SIG). It should be noted that the CLKRUN# signal is required on a Small PCI card connector. This subject is covered in the *Small PCI Specification* and is outside the scope of this book.

Although the PCI specification states that the clock may be stopped or its frequency changed, it does not define a method for determining when to stop (or slow down) the clock, or a method for determining when to restart the clock.

A portable system includes a central resource that includes the PCI clock generation logic. With respect to the clock generation logic (typically part of the chipset), the CLKRUN# signal is a sustained tri-state input/output signal. The clock generation logic keeps CLKRUN# asserted when the clock is running normally. During periods when the clock has been stopped (or slowed), the clock generation logic monitors CLKRUN# to recognize requests from master and target devices for the PCI clock signal to be restored to full speed. The clock cannot be stopped if the bus is not idle. Before it stops (or slows down) the clock frequency, the clock generation logic deasserts CLKRUN# for one clock to inform PCI devices that the clock is about to be stopped (or slowed). After driving CLKRUN# high (deasserted) for one clock, the clock generation logic tri-states its CLKRUN# output driver. The keeper resistor on CLKRUN# then assumes responsibility for maintaining the deasserted state of CLKRUN# during the period in which the clock is stopped (or slowed).

The clock continues to run unchanged for a minimum of four clocks after the clock generation logic deasserts CLKRUN#. After deassertion of CLKRUN#, the clock generation logic must monitor CLKRUN# for two possible cases:

CASE 1. After the clock has been stopped (or slowed), a master (or multiple masters) may require clock restart in order to request use of the bus. Prior to issuing the bus request, the master(s) must first request clock restart. This is accomplished by assertion of CLKRUN#. When the clock generation logic detects the assertion of CLKRUN# by another party, it turns on (or speeds up) the clock and turns on its CLKRUN# output driver to assert CLKRUN#.

When the master detects that CLKRUN# has been asserted for two rising-edges of the PCI CLK signal, the master may then tri-state its CLKRUN# output driver.

CASE 2. When the clock generation logic has deasserted CLKRUN#, indicating its intention to stop (or slow) the clock, the clock must continue to run for a minimum of four clocks. During this period of time, a target (or master) that requires continued clock operation (e.g., in order to perform internal house-keeping after the completion of a transaction), may reassert CLKRUN# for two PCI clock cycles to request continued generation of CLK. When the clock generation logic samples CLKRUN# reasserted, it reasserts CLK-RUN# and continues to generate the clock (rather than stopping it or slowing it down). The specification doesn't define the period of time that the clock will continue to run after a request for continued operation. The author interprets this as implying that the period is system design-specific.

Achieving CLKRUN# Benefit On Add-In Cards

As mentioned earlier, there isn't a CLKRUN# pin defined on the normal PCI add-in connector. The same basic functionality can be achieved, however, in the following manner. During bus idle time, the chipset could reduce the PCI CLK frequency to 1MHz. The chipset then monitors the bus master request signals (REQ#) and the PCI interrupt traces and returns the CLK to full speed if a bus request or an interrupt request is sensed.

Figure 4-3: CLKRUN# Signal Usage

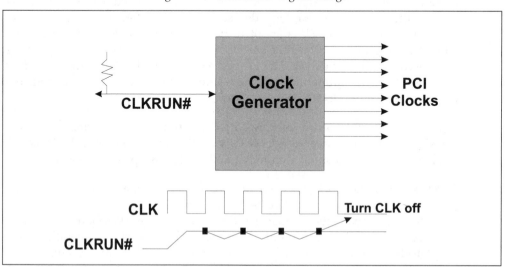

Reset Signal (RST#)

When asserted, the reset signal forces all PCI configuration registers, master and target state machines and output drivers to an initialized state. RST# may be asserted or deasserted asynchronously to the PCI CLK edge. The assertion of RST# also initializes other, device-specific functions, but this subject is beyond the scope of the PCI specification. All PCI output signals must be driven to their benign states. In general, this means they must be tri-stated. Exceptions are:

- SERR# is floated.
- If SBO# and SDONE (*NOTE THAT THESE SIGNALS WERE OBSOLETED IN THE REV 2.2 SPEC*) cannot be tri-stated, they will be driven low.
- To prevent the AD bus, the C/BE bus and the PAR signals from floating during reset, they may be driven low by a central resource during reset.

2.2

Additional definition of the reset signal's behavior can be found in the chapters entitled "Hot-Plug PCI" on page 455 and "Power Management" on page 479.

Refer to "64-bit Cards in 32-bit Add-in Connectors" on page 266 for a discussion of the REQ64# signal's behavior during reset.

Address/Data Bus, Command Bus, and Byte Enables

The PCI bus uses a time-multiplexed address/data bus. During the address phase of a transaction:

- The **AD bus**, AD[31:0], carries the start address. The resolution of this address is on a doubleword boundary (address divisible by four) during a memory or a configuration transaction, or a byte-specific address during an I/O read or write transaction. Additional information on memory and I/O addressing can be found in the chapter entitled "Memory and IO Addressing" on page 143. Additional information on configuration addressing can be found in "Configuration Transactions" on page 317 and "Type 1 Configuration Transactions" on page 620.
- The **Command or Byte Enable bus**, C/BE#[3:0], defines the type of transaction. The chapter entitled "The Commands" on page 99 defines the transaction types.
- The **Parity signal, PAR**, is driven by the initiator one clock after completion of the address phase or one clock after assertion of IRDY# during each data phase of write transactions. It is driven by the currently-addressed target one clock after the assertion of TRDY# during each data phase of read trans-

actions. One clock after completion of the address phase, the initiator drives PAR either high or low to ensure even parity across the address bus, AD[31:0], and the four Command/Byte Enable lines, C/BE#[3:0]. Refer to the chapter entitled "Error Detection and Handling" on page 199 for a discussion of parity.

During each data phase:

- The data bus, **AD[31:0]**, is driven by the initiator (during a write) or the currently-addressed target (during a read).
- **PAR** is driven by either the initiator (during a write) or the currently-addressed target (during a read) one clock after the assertion of IRDY# (on a write) or TRDY# (on a read) during each data phase and ensures even parity across AD[31:0] and C/BE#[3:0]. If all four data paths are not being used during a data phase, the agent driving the data bus (the master during a write or the target during a read) must ensure that valid data is being driven onto all data paths (including those not being used to transfer data). This is necessary because PAR must reflect even parity across the entire AD and C/BE buses.
- The Command/Byte Enable bus, **C/BE#[3:0]**, is driven by the initiator to indicate the bytes to be transferred within the currently-addressed doubleword and the data paths to be used to transfer the data. Table 4-1 on page 38 indicates the mapping of the byte enable signals to the data paths and to the locations within the currently-addressed doubleword. Table 4-2 on page 39 defines the interpretation of the byte enable signals during each data phase. Any combination of byte enables is considered valid and the byte enables may change from data phase to data phase.

Table 4-1: Byte Enable Mapping To Data Paths and To Locations Within the Currently-Addressed Dword

Byte Enable Signal	Maps To
C/BE3#	Data path 3, AD[31:24], and the 4th location in the currently-addressed dword.
C/BE2#	Data path 2, AD[23:16], and the 3rd location in the currently-addressed dword.
C/BE1#	Data path 1, AD[15:8], and the 2nd location in the currently-addressed dword.

Table 4-1: Byte Enable Mapping To Data Paths and To Locations Within the Currently-Addressed Dword (Continued)

Byte Enable Signal	Maps To
C/BE0#	Data path 0, AD[7:0], and the 1st location in the currently-addressed dword.

Table 4-2: Interpretation of the Byte Enables During a Data Phase

C/BE[3:0]# (binary)	Meaning
0000	The initiator intends to transfer all four bytes within the currently-addressed doubleword using all four data paths.
0001	The initiator intends to transfer the upper three bytes within the currently-addressed doubleword using the upper three data paths.
0010	The initiator intends to transfer the upper two bytes and the first byte within the currently-addressed doubleword using the upper two data paths and the first data path.
0011	The initiator intends to transfer the upper two bytes within the currently-addressed doubleword using the upper two data paths.
0100	The initiator intends to transfer the upper byte and the lower two bytes within the currently-addressed doubleword using the upper data path and the lower two data paths.
0101	The initiator intends to transfer the second and the fourth bytes within the currently-addressed doubleword using the second and fourth data paths.
0110	The initiator intends to transfer the first and the fourth bytes within the currently-addressed doubleword using the first and the fourth data paths.
0111	The initiator intends to transfer the upper byte within the currently-addressed doubleword using the upper data path.
1000	The initiator intends to transfer the lower three bytes within the currently-addressed doubleword using the lower three data paths.

Table 4-2: Interpretation of the Byte Enables During a Data Phase (Continued)

C/BE[3:0]# (binary)	Meaning
1001	The initiator intends to transfer the middle two bytes within the currently-addressed doubleword using the middle two data paths.
1010	The initiator intends to transfer the first and third bytes within the currently-addressed doubleword using the first and the third data paths.
1011	The initiator intends to transfer the third byte within the currently-addressed doubleword using the third data path.
1100	The initiator intends to transfer the lower two bytes within the currently-addressed doubleword using the lower two data paths.
1101	The initiator intends to transfer the second byte within the currently-addressed doubleword using the second data path.
1110	The initiator intends to transfer the first byte within the currently-addressed doubleword using the first data path.
1111	The initiator does not intend to transfer any of the four bytes within the currently-addressed doubleword and will not use any of the data paths. This is a null data phase.

Preventing Excessive Current Drain

If the inputs to CMOS input receivers are permitted to float for long periods, the receivers tend to oscillate and draw excessive current. In order to prevent this phenomena and preserve the green nature of the PCI bus, several rules are applied:

RULE 1. When the bus is idle and no bus masters are requesting ownership, either the bus arbiter or a master that has the bus parked on it must enable its AD, C/BE and PAR output drivers and drive a stable pattern onto these signal lines. This issue is discussed in "Bus Parking" on page 65.

RULE 2. During a data phase in a write transaction, the initiator must drive a stable pattern onto the AD bus when it is not yet ready to deliver the next set of data bytes. This subject is covered in the Clock 4 description on page 139.

RULE 3. During a data phase in a read transaction, the target must drive a stable pattern onto the AD bus when it is not yet ready to deliver the next set of data bytes. This subject is covered in the description of Clock 4 on page 128.

RULE 4. A 64-bit card plugged into a 32-bit expansion slot must keep its AD[63:32], C/BE#[7:4] and PAR64 input receivers from floating. This subject is covered in "64-bit Cards in 32-bit Add-in Connectors" on page 266.

Transaction Control Signals

Table 4-3 on page 41 provides a brief description of each signal used to control a PCI transfer.

Table 4-3: PCI Interface Control Signals

Signal	Master	Target	Description
FRAME#	In/Out	In	**Cycle Frame** is driven by the current initiator and indicates the start (when it's first asserted) and duration (the duration of its assertion) of a transaction. In order to determine that bus ownership has been acquired, the master must sample FRAME# and IRDY# both deasserted and GNT# asserted on the same rising-edge of the PCI CLK signal. A transaction may consist of one or more data transfers between the current initiator and the currently-addressed target. FRAME# is deasserted when the initiator is ready to complete the final data phase.
TRDY#	In	Out	**Target Ready** is driven by the currently-addressed target. It is asserted when the target is ready to complete the current data phase (data transfer). A data phase is completed when the target is asserting TRDY# and the initiator is asserting IRDY# at the rising-edge of the CLK signal. During a read, TRDY# asserted indicates that the target is driving valid data onto the data bus. During a write, TRDY# asserted indicates that the target is ready to accept data from the master. Wait states are inserted in the current data phase until both TDRY# and IRDY# are sampled asserted.

Table 4-3: PCI Interface Control Signals (Continued)

Signal	Master	Target	Description
IRDY#	In/Out	In	**Initiator Ready** is driven by the current bus master (the initiator of the transaction). During a write, IRDY# asserted indicates that the initiator is driving valid data onto the data bus. During a read, IRDY# asserted indicates that the initiator is ready to accept data from the currently-addressed target. In order to determine that bus ownership has been acquired, the master must sample FRAME# and IRDY# both deasserted and GNT# asserted on the same rising-edge of the PCI CLK signal. Also refer to the description of TRDY# in this table.
STOP#	In	Out	The target asserts **STOP#** to indicate that it wishes the initiator to stop the transaction in progress. For more information, refer to "Target-Initiated Termination" on page 180.
IDSEL	N/A	In	**Initialization Device Select** is an input to the PCI device and is used as a chip select during an access to one of the device's configuration registers. For additional information, refer to "Type 0 Configuration Transaction" on page 335.
LOCK#	In/Out	In	Used by the initiator to **lock** the currently-addressed target during an atomic transaction series (e.g., during a semaphore read/modify/write operation). Refer to "Resource Locking" on page 48 and to the chapter entitled "Locking" on page 683.
DEVSEL#	In	Out	**Device Select** is asserted by a target when the target has decoded its address. It acts as an input to the current initiator and the subtractive decoder in the expansion bus bridge. If a master initiates a transfer and does not detect DEVSEL# active within six CLK periods, it must assume that the target cannot respond or that the address is unpopulated. A master-abort results.

Arbitration Signals

Each PCI master has a pair of arbitration lines that connect it directly to the PCI bus arbiter. When a master requires the use of the PCI bus, it asserts its device-specific REQ# line to the arbiter. When the arbiter has determined that the requesting master should be granted control of the PCI bus, it asserts the GNT# (grant) line specific to the requesting master. In the PCI environment, bus arbitration can take place while another master is still in control of the bus. This is known as "hidden" arbitration. When a master receives a grant from the bus arbiter, it must wait for the current initiator to complete its transfer before initiating its own transfer. It cannot assume ownership of the PCI bus until FRAME# is sampled deasserted (indicating the start of the last data phase) and IRDY# is then sampled deasserted (indicating the completion of the last data phase). This indicates that the current transaction has been completed and the bus has been returned to the idle state. Bus arbitration is discussed in more detail in the chapter entitled "PCI Bus Arbitration" on page 59.

IF THE ARBITER IS POWERED BY A DIFFERENT SUPPLY VOLTAGE THAN THE BUS MASTER, POWER SEQUENCING REQUIREMENTS DICTATE THAT REQ# AND GNT# ARE TRI-STATE SIGNALS. While RST# is asserted, all masters must tri-state their REQ# output drivers and must ignore their GNT# inputs. In a system with PCI add-in connectors, the arbiter may require a weak pullup on the REQ# inputs that are wired to the add-in connectors. This will keep them from floating when the connectors are unoccupied.

2.2

Interrupt Request Signals

PCI agents that must generate requests for service can utilize one of the PCI interrupt request lines, INTA#, INTB#, INTC# or INTD#. *ALTERNATIVELY, THE DEVICE MAY USE MESSAGE SIGNALED INTERRUPTS (MSI) TO INTERRUPT THE PROGRAM CURRENTLY BEING EXECUTED BY THE PROCESSOR. A DESCRIPTION OF THE INT SIGNALS AS WELL AS MESSAGE SIGNALED INTERRUPTS CAN BE FOUND IN THE CHAPTER ENTITLED "INTERRUPTS" ON PAGE 221.*

2.2

Error Reporting Signals

The sections that follow provide an introduction to the PERR# and SERR# signals. The chapter entitled "Error Detection and Handling" on page 199 provides a more detailed discussion of error detection and handling.

Data Parity Error

The **generation of parity information is mandatory for all PCI devices** that drive address or data information onto the AD bus. This is a requirement because the agent driving the AD bus must assume that the agent receiving the data and parity will check the validity of the parity and may either flag an error or even fail the machine if incorrect parity is received.

The **detection and reporting of parity errors by PCI devices is generally required.** The specification is written this way to indicate that, in some cases, the designer may choose to ignore parity errors. An example might be a video frame buffer. The designer may choose not to verify the correctness of the data being written into the video memory by the initiator. In the event that corrupted data is received and written into the frame memory, the only effect will be one or more corrupted video pixels displayed on the screen. Although this may have a deleterious effect on the end user's peace of mind, it will not corrupt programs or the data structures associated with programs.

Implementation of the PERR# pin is required on all add-in PCI cards (and is generally required on system board devices). The data parity error signal, PERR#, may be pulsed by a PCI device under the following circumstances:

- In the event of a data parity error detected by a PCI target during a write data phase, the target must set the Detected Parity Error bit in its PCI configuration Status register and must assert PERR# (if the Parity Response bit in its configuration Command register is set to one). It may then either continue the transaction or may assert STOP# to terminate the transaction prematurely. During a burst write, the initiator is responsible for monitoring the PERR# signal to ensure that each data item is not corrupted in flight while being written to the target.
- In the event of a data parity error detected by the PCI initiator during a read data phase, the initiator must set the Detected Parity Error bit in its PCI configuration Status register and must assert PERR# (if the Parity Error Response bit in its configuration Command register is set to one). The platform designer may include third-party logic that monitors PERR# or may leave error reporting up to the initiator.

To ensure that correct parity is available to any PCI devices that perform parity checking, all PCI devices must generate even parity on AD[31:0], C/BE#[3:0] and PAR for the address and data phases. PERR# is implemented as an output on targets and as both an input and an output on masters. The initiator of a transaction has responsibility for reporting the detection of a data parity error to software. For this reason, it must monitor PERR# during write data phases to determine if the target has detected a data parity error. The action taken by an initiator when a parity error is detected is design-dependent. It may perform retries with the target or may choose to terminate the transaction and generate an interrupt to invoke its device-specific interrupt handler. If the initiator reports the failure to software, it must also set the Master Data Parity Error bit in its PCI configuration Status register. PERR# is only driven by one device at time.

A detailed discussion of data parity error detection and handling may be found in the chapter entitled "Error Detection and Handling" on page 199.

System Error

The System Error signal, SERR#, may be pulsed by any PCI device to report address parity errors, data parity errors during a Special Cycle, and critical errors other than parity. SERR# is required on all add-in PCI cards that perform address parity checking or report other serious errors using SERR#. This signal is considered a "last-recourse" for reporting serious errors. Non-catastrophic and correctable errors should be signaled in some other way. In a PC-compatible machine, SERR# typically causes an NMI to the system processor (although the designer is not constrained to have it generate an NMI). In a PowerPC, PReP-compliant platform, assertion of SERR# is reported to the host processor via assertion of TEA# or MC# and causes a machine check interrupt. This is the functional equivalent of NMI in the Intel world. If the designer of a PCI device does not want an NMI to be initiated, some means other than SERR# should be used to flag an error condition (such as setting a bit in the device's Status register and generating an interrupt request). SERR# is PCI clock-synchronous signal and is an open-drain signal. It may be driven by more than one PCI agent at a time. When asserted, the device drives it low for one clock and then tri-states its output driver. The keeper resistor on SERR# is responsible for returning it to the deasserted state (this takes two to three clock periods).

A detailed discussion of system error detection and handling may be found in the chapter entitled "SERR# Signal" on page 214.

SERR# is an input to the secondary side of a PCI-to-PCI bridge. This is discussed in "Handling SERR# on Secondary Side" on page 647.

Cache Support (Snoop Result) Signals

2.2

PLEASE BE AWARE THAT SUPPORT FOR THE PCI SNOOP RESULT SIGNALS AND ALL RELATED TOPICS HAS BEEN ELIMINATED IN THE 2.2 SPEC. THIS DESCRIPTION IS ONLY PROVIDED AS A HISTORICAL REFERENCE.

Table 4-4 on page 46 provides a brief description of the now-deleted PCI cache support signals.

Table 4-4: Cache Snoop Result Signals

Signal	Description
SBO#	*Snoop Back Off*. This signal is an output from the PCI cache/bridge and an input to cacheable memory subsystems residing on the PCI bus. It is asserted by the bridge to indicate that the PCI memory access in progress is about to read or update stale information in memory. SBO# is qualified by and only has meaning when the SDONE signal is also asserted by the bridge. When SDONE and SBO# are sampled asserted, the currently-addressed cacheable PCI memory subsystem should respond by signaling a retry to the current initiator.
SDONE	*Snoop Done*. This signal is an output from the PCI cache/bridge and an input to cacheable memory subsystems residing on the PCI bus. It is deasserted by the bridge while the processor's cache(s) snoops a memory access started by the current initiator. The bridge asserts SDONE when the snoop has been completed. The results of the snoop are then indicated on the SBO# signal. SBO# sampled deasserted indicates that the PCI initiator is accessing a clean line in memory and the PCI cacheable memory target is permitted to accept or supply the indicated data. SBO# sampled asserted indicates that the PCI initiator is accessing a stale line in memory and should not complete the data access. Instead, the memory target should terminate the access by signaling a retry to the PCI initiator.

The specification recommends that systems that do not support cacheable memory on the PCI bus should supply pullups on the SDONE and SBO# pins at each add-in connector. Anytime an initiator attempts to access a PCI card with memory, the card will always detect a clean snoop (the system board pullups keep SDONE asserted and SBO# deasserted) and will permit the initiator to access it.

The assertion of RST# at system startup clears the Cache Line Size configuration register to zero. In a system that does not support caching from PCI memory, this register will still contain zero after the configuration software enables the device's memory decoder(s) using the Memory Space bit in the device's PCI configuration Command register. When this is the case, the memory may ignore the snoop result signals and therefore permit slightly faster access. On the other hand, a non-zero value in this register after the device is enabled indicates that the processor's caches do keep copies of information read from this memory. In this case, the memory target is not permitted to respond (i.e., assert TRDY#) until the snoop result is presented to it by the bridge.

64-bit Extension Signals

The PCI specification provides a detailed definition of a 64-bit extension to its baseline 32-bit architecture. Systems that implement the extension support the transfer of up to eight bytes per data phase between a 64-bit initiator and a 64-bit target. The signals involved are defined in Table 4-5 on page 47. A more detailed explanation can be found in the chapter entitled "The 64-bit PCI Extension" on page 265.

Table 4-5: The 64-Bit Extension

Signal	Description
AD[63:32]	**Upper four data lanes.** In combination with AD[31:0], extends the width of the data bus to 64 bits. These pins aren't used during the address phase of a transfer (unless 64-bit addressing is being used).
C/BE#[7:4]	**Byte Enables** for data lanes four-through-seven. Used during the data transfer phase, but not during the address phase (unless 64-bit addressing is being used.)
REQ64#	**Request 64-bit Transfer.** Generated by the current initiator to indicate its desire to perform transfers using one or more of the upper four data paths. REQ64# has the same timing as the FRAME# signal. Refer to the chapter entitled "The 64-bit PCI Extension" on page 265 for more information.
ACK64#	**Acknowledge 64-bit Transfer.** Generated by the currently-addressed target (if it supports 64-bit transfers) in response to a REQ64# assertion by the initiator. ACK64# has the same timing as the DEVSEL# signal.

Table 4-5: The 64-Bit Extension (Continued)

Signal	Description
PAR64	**Parity for the upper doubleword**. This is the even parity bit associated with AD[63:32] and C/BE#[7:4]. For additional information, refer to the chapters entitled "The 64-bit PCI Extension" on page 265 and "Error Detection and Handling" on page 199

Resource Locking

2.2

THE LOCK# SIGNAL MUST ONLY BE UTILIZED BY BRIDGES THAT PERFORM A SERIES OF TWO OR MORE SEPARATE LOCKED TRANSACTIONS. THE INTENDED USE OF THIS FACILITY HAS BEEN CHANGED CONSIDERABLY IN THE 2.2 SPEC AND IS DESCRIBED IN THE CHAPTER ENTITLED "LOCKING" ON PAGE 683. IT IS NOT INTENDED FOR USE OF NON-BRIDGE PCI MASTERS AND MUST NOT BE HONORED BY PCI MEMORY TARGETS.

An initiator requiring exclusive access to a target may use the LOCK# signal if it isn't currently being driven by another initiator. When the target device is addressed and LOCK# is deasserted by the initiator during the address phase and then asserted during the data phase, the target device is reserved for as long as the LOCK# signal remains asserted. If the target is subsequently addressed by another initiator while the lock is still in force, the target issues a retry to the initiator. While a target is locked, other bus masters (that don't require exclusive access to a target) are permitted to acquire the bus to access targets other than the locked target.

JTAG/Boundary Scan Signals

2.2

The designer of a PCI device may optionally implement the IEEE 1149.1 Boundary Scan interface signals to permit in-circuit testing of the PCI device. The related signals are defined in Table 4-6 on page 49. THESE PINS MUST OPERATE AT THE SAME VOLTAGE LEVELS AS THE PCI BUS SIGNALS (I.E., 5V OR 3.3V). A detailed discussion of boundary scan is beyond the scope of this publication.

Table 4-6: Boundary Scan Signals

Signal	Description
TCK	*Test Clock.* Used to clock state information and data into and out of the device during boundary scan.
TDI	*Test Input.* Used (in conjunction with TCK) to shift data and instructions into the Test Access Port (TAP) in a serial bit stream.
TDO	*Test Output.* Used (in conjunction with TCK) to shift data out of the Test Access Port (TAP) in a serial bit stream.
TMS	*Test Mode Select.* Used to control the state of the Test Access Port controller.
TRST#	*Test Reset.* Used to force the Test Access Port controller into an initialized state.

Interrupt Request Pins

The PCI interrupt request signals (INTA#, INTB#, INTC# and INTD#) are discussed in the chapter entitled "Interrupts" on page 221.

PME# and 3.3Vaux

2.2

POWER MANAGEMENT EVENT AND 3.3VAUX ARE WERE ADDED IN THE 2.2. SPEC AND ARE OPTIONAL. A DEVICE THAT IS CAPABLE OF GENERATING PMES WOULD IMPLEMENT THEM. A DETAILED DESCRIPTION CAN BE FOUND IN THE CHAPTER ENTITLED "POWER MANAGEMENT" ON PAGE 479.

Sideband Signals

A sideband signal is defined as a signal that is not part of the PCI bus standard and interconnects two or more PCI agents. This signal only has meaning for the agents it interconnects. The following are some examples of sideband signals:

- A PCI bus arbiter could monitor a "busy" signal from a PCI device (such as an EISA or Micro Channel (expansion bus bridge) to determine if the device is available before granting the PCI bus to a PCI initiator.
- PC compatibility signals like A20GATE, CPU RESET, etc.

Signal Types

Table 4-7 on page 50 defines the PCI signal types. The signals that comprise the PCI bus are electrically defined in one of the following fashions:

- **IN** defines a signal as a standard input-only signal.
- **OUT** defines a signal as a standard output-only signal.
- **T/S** defines a signal as a bi-directional, tri-state input/output signal.
- **S/T/S** defines a signal as a sustained tri-state signal that is driven by only one owner at a time. An agent that drives an s/t/s pin low must actively drive it high for one clock before tri-stating it. A pullup resistor is required to sustain the inactive state until another agent takes ownership of and drives the signal. The resistor is supplied as a central resource in the system design. The next owner of the signal cannot start driving the s/t/s signal any sooner than one clock after it is released by the previous owner.
- **O/D** defines a signal as an open drain. It is wire-ORed with other agents. The signaling agent asserts the signal, but returning the signal to the inactive state is accomplished by a weak pull-up resistor. The deasserted state is maintained by the pullup resistor. The pullup may take two or three PCI clock periods to fully restore the signal to the deasserted state.

Table 4-7: PCI Signal Types

Signal(s)	Type	Note
CLK	IN	
RST#		
AD[31:0]	T/S	
C/BE#[3:0]		
PAR		
FRAME#	S/T/S	Pulled up on system board.
TRDY#		
IRDY#		
STOP#		
LOCK#		

Table 4-7: PCI Signal Types (Continued)

Signal(s)	Type	Note
IDSEL	IN	
DEVSEL#	S/T/S	Pulled up on system board.
REQ#	T/S	If the arbiter is powered by a different supply voltage than the bus master, power sequencing requirements dictate that REQ# and GNT# are tri-state signals.
GNT#		
PERR#	S/T/S	Pulled up on system board.
SERR#	O/D	
SBO#	IN or OUT	
SDONE		
AD[63:32]	T/S	Pulled up on system board.
C/BE#[7:4]		
REQ64#	S/T/S	
ACK64#		
PAR64	T/S	
TCK	IN	
TDI		
TDO	OUT	
TMS	IN	
TRST#		
INTA# - INTD#	O/D	Pulled up on system board. Since this is an open-drain signal, it must be considered indeterminate for a number of cycles after a device ceases to drive it asserted.

Table 4-7: PCI Signal Types (Continued)

Signal(s)	Type	Note
CLKRUN#	S/T/S	Pulled up on system board. CLKRUN# is not present on connector.
PME#	O/D	ADDED IN 2.2 SPEC. POWER MANAGEMENT EVENT. PULLED UP ON SYSTEM BOARD. SINCE THIS IS AN OPEN-DRAIN SIGNAL, IT MUST BE CONSIDERED INDETERMINATE FOR A NUMBER OF CYCLES (TYPICALLY UP TO 100NS) AFTER A DEVICE CEASES TO DRIVE IT ASSERTED.
3.3VAUX	POWER SUPPLY	ADDED IN 2.2 SPEC. SEE "POWER MANAGEMENT" ON PAGE 479 FOR MORE DETAIL.

2.2

Device Cannot Simultaneously Drive and Receive a Signal

THE 2.2 SPEC FORBIDS A DEVICE TO SIMULTANEOUSLY DRIVE AND RECEIVE A SIGNAL. THIS WOULD REQUIRE THAT THE DEVICE CONNECT BOTH A DRIVER AND A RECEIVER TO THE PIN, VIOLATING THE RULE THAT ONLY PERMITS EACH DEVICE TO PLACE ONE LOAD ON EACH PCI SIGNAL.

Central Resource Functions

Any platform that implements the PCI bus must supply a toolbox of support functions necessary for the proper operation of all PCI devices. Some examples would include:

- **PCI bus arbiter.** The arbiter is necessary to support PCI masters. The PCI specification does not define the decision-making process utilized by the PCI bus arbiter. The design of the arbiter is therefore platform-specific.
- **Pullup resistors** on signals that are not always driven to a valid state. This would include: all of the s/t/s signals; INTx# signals; AD[63:32]; C/BE#[7:4]; PAR64; and SERR#.
- **Error logic** responsible for converting SERR# to the platform-specific signal (e.g., NMI in an Intel-based platform or TEA# in a PowerPC(-based platform) utilized to alert the host processor that an error has occurred.

- Central resource to **generate** the proper **IDSEL** signal when a PCI device's configuration space is being addressed (this function is typically performed by the host/PCI bridge).
- System board logic to **assert REQ64# during reset**. A detailed description of this function is provided in "64-bit Cards in 32-bit Add-in Connectors" on page 266.
- **Subtractive decoder**. Each PCI target device must implement positive decode. In other words, it must decode any address placed on the PCI bus to determine if it is the target of the current transaction. Only one agent on the PCI bus may optionally implement subtractive decode. This is typically the expansion bus (e.g., EISA, ISA, or Micro Channel) bridge.
- Additionally, the reset logic, clock generator, power supply and interrupt controller are necessary central resources.

Subtractive Decode (by ISA Bridge)

Background

Refer to Figure 4-4 on page 55. Although we are all striving for its demise in the not too distant future, the ISA bus is still present in the majority of systems on the market (as of this writing on 2/28/99). It is referred to as the expansion bus bridge in the PCI spec and is typically embedded within the South Bridge (along with a multitude of other entities). The ISA bridge can claim transactions in one of two fashions:

METHOD 1. When a PCI master is addressing a device that is embedded within the bridge (e.g., the Real-Time Clock), the bridge knows the addresses associated with these devices and therefore may decode the address quickly and claim the transaction.

METHOD 2. On the other hand, if a master is addressing a device that resides on the ISA bus, the bridge has a problem. It has no idea whether any devices are installed in the ISA expansion slots, and even if it did, it has no way of knowing what IO and/or memory ranges they use.In this case, the bridge performs subtractive decode. When a transaction is not claimed by any other PCI device within a specified period of time, the PCI/expansion bus bridge may assert DEVSEL# and pass the transaction through to the expansion bus. It can determine that no other PCI device has claimed a transaction by monitoring the state of the DEVSEL# signal generated by the other PCI devices. If DEVSEL# is not sampled asserted within four clock periods after the address phase of a transaction, no other PCI device has claimed the transaction. The expansion bus bridge may then claim the transaction by asserting DEVSEL# during the period between the fifth and sixth clocks of the transaction. This is referred to as subtractive decode. Additional information regarding subtractive decode can be found in "Master Abort: Target Doesn't Claim Transaction" on page 176.

The ISA bus environment is one that depends heavily on subtractive decoding to claim transactions. Because most ISA bus devices are not plug and play-capable, the configuration software cannot automatically detect their presence and assign address ranges to their address decoders. The ISA bridge uses subtractive decode to claim all transactions that meet the following criteria:

- No other PCI device has claimed the transaction. By definition, all PCI device address decoders are:
    - **fast** (decodes address and asserts DEVSEL# during the clock cell immediately following completion of the address phase),
    - **medium** (asserts DEVSEL# during the second clock cell after completion of the address phase)
    - or **slow** (asserts DEVSEL# during the third clock after completion of the address phase).

    If the ISA bridge does not detect DEVSEL# asserted by any other PCI device (and the target address "makes sense" for the ISA environment; see next bullet), the bridge asserts DEVSEL# during the fourth clock after completion of the address phase. The transaction is then initiated on the ISA bus.
- The target address is one that falls within the overall ISA memory or I/O address ranges. Any memory address below 16MB that goes unclaimed by PCI devices is claimed and passed through to the ISA bus. Any I/O address in the lower 64KB of I/O space that goes unclaimed by PCI devices is claimed and passed through to the ISA bus.

Figure 4-4: Typically, ISA Bridge Is the Subtractive Decode Agent

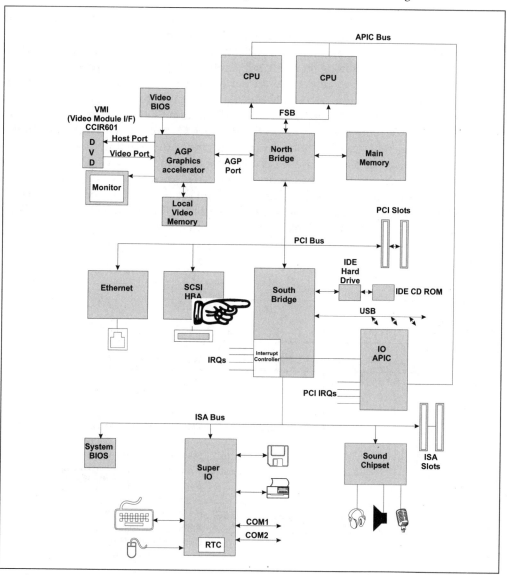

Tuning Subtractive Decoder

This means that a transaction initiated by the host processor (or any other bus master) does not appear on the ISA bus until four or five clocks after the completion of the address phase on the PCI bus. The processor's performance when accessing ISA devices is therefore substantially degraded. In order to minimize the effect of subtractive decode on performance, the ISA bridge designer can permit the subtractive decoder to be "tuned." During the configuration process, the configuration software reads the configuration Status register (see Figure 4-5 on page 56) for every device on the PCI bus. One of the required fields in the Status register is the DEVSEL# timing field, indicating whether the device has a fast, medium or slow address decoder. As an example, if every device on the PCI bus indicates that it has a fast decoder, the software can program the subtractive decoder to assert DEVSEL# and claim the transaction during the second clock after the completion of the address phase (if it doesn't detect DEVSEL# asserted during the first clock after the address phase).

Figure 4-5: Status Register

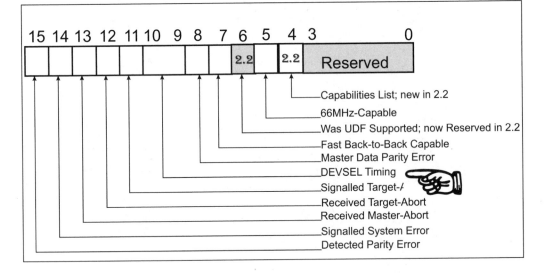

Reading Timing Diagrams

Figure 4-6 on page 58 illustrates a typical PCI timing diagram. When a PCI signal is asserted or deasserted by a PCI device, the output driver utilized is typically a weak CMOS driver. This being the case, the driver isn't capable of transitioning the signal line past the logic threshold for a logic high or low in one step. The voltage change initiated on the signal line propagates down the trace until it hits the physical end of the trace. As it passes the stub for each PCI device along the way, the wavefront has not yet transitioned past the new logic threshold, so the change isn't detected by any of the devices. When reflected back along the trace, however, the reflection doubles the voltage change on the line, causing it to cross the logic threshold. As the doubled wavefront propagates back down the length of the trace, the signal's new state is detected by each device it passes. The time it takes the signal to travel the length of the bus and reflect back is referred to as the Tprop, or propagation delay. This delay is illustrated in the timing diagrams.

As an example, a master samples FRAME# and IRDY# deasserted (bus idle) and its GNT# asserted on the rising-edge of clock one, indicating that it has bus acquisition. The master initiates the transaction during clock cell one by asserting the FRAME# signal to indicate the start of the transaction. In the timing diagram, FRAME# isn't shown transitioning from high-to-low until sometime after the rising-edge of clock one and before the rising-edge of clock two, thereby illustrating the propagation delay. Coincident with FRAME# assertion, the initiator drives the start address onto the AD bus during clock cell one, but the address change isn't valid until sometime after the rising-edge of clock one and before the rising-edge of clock two.

The address phase ends on the rising-edge of clock two and the initiator begins to turn off its AD bus drivers. The time that it takes the driver to actually cease driving the AD bus is illustrated in the timing diagram (the initiator has not successfully disconnected from the AD bus until sometime during clock cell two).

Figure 4-6: Typical PCI Timing Diagram

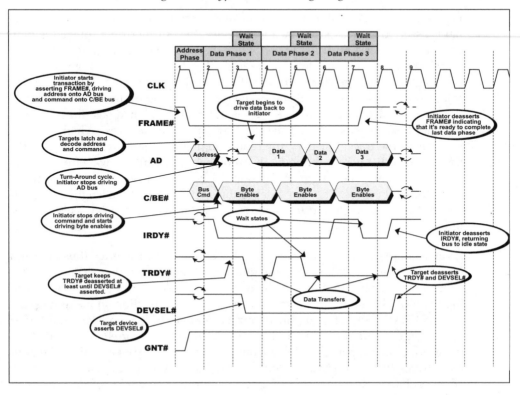

5 PCI Bus Arbitration

The Previous Chapter

The previous chapter provided a detailed description of the PCI functional signal groups.

This Chapter

When a PCI bus master requires the use of the PCI bus to perform a data transfer, it must request the use of the bus from the PCI bus arbiter. This chapter provides a detailed discussion of the PCI bus arbitration timing. The PCI specification defines the timing of the request and grant handshaking, but not the procedure used to determine the winner of a competition. The algorithm used by a system's PCI bus arbiter to decide which of the requesting bus masters will be granted use of the PCI bus is system-specific and outside the scope of the specification.

The Next Chapter

The next chapter describes the rules governing how much time a device may hold the bus in wait states during any given data phase. It describes how soon after reset is removed the first transaction may be initiated and how soon after reset is removed a target device must be prepared to transfer data. The mechanisms that a target may use to meet the latency rules are described: Delayed Transactions, as well as the posting of memory writes.

Arbiter

At a given instant in time, one or more PCI bus master devices may require use of the PCI bus to perform a data transfer with another PCI device. Each requesting master asserts its REQ# output to inform the bus arbiter of its pending request for the use of the bus. Figure 5-1 on page 60 illustrates the relationship of the PCI masters to the central PCI resource known as the bus arbiter. In this example, there are seven possible masters connected to the PCI bus arbiter in the illustration. Each master is connected to the arbiter via a separate pair of REQ#/GNT# signals. Although the arbiter is shown as a separate component, it usually is integrated into the PCI chip set; specifically, it is typically integrated into the host/PCI or the PCI/expansion bus bridge chip.

Figure 5-1: The PCI Bus Arbiter

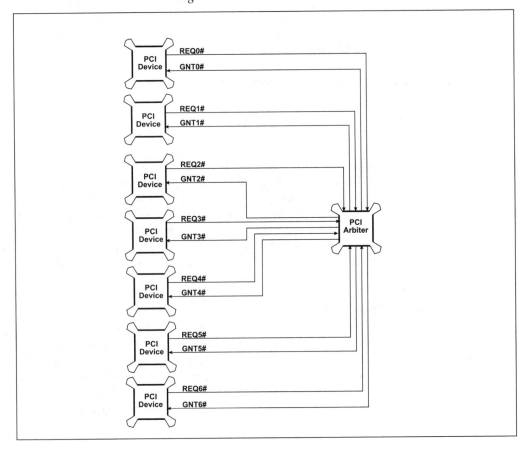

Arbitration Algorithm

As stated at the beginning of this chapter, the PCI specification does not define the scheme used by the PCI bus arbiter to decide the winner of the competition when multiple masters simultaneously request bus ownership. The arbiter may utilize any scheme, such as one based on fixed or rotational priority or a combination of the two (rotational among one group of masters and fixed within another group). The 2.1 specification states that the arbiter is required to implement a fairness algorithm to avoid deadlocks. The exact verbiage that is used is:

> "The central arbiter is required to implement a fairness algorithm to avoid deadlocks. Fairness means that each potential bus master must be granted access to the bus independent of other requests. Fairness is defined as a policy that ensures that high-priority masters will not dominate the bus to the exclusion of lower-priority masters when they are continually requesting the bus. However, this does not mean that all agents are required to have equal access to the bus. By requiring a fairness algorithm there are no special conditions to handle when LOCK# is active (assuming a resource lock) or when cacheable memory is located on PCI. A system that uses a fairness algorithm is still considered fair if it implements a complete bus lock instead of a resource lock. However, the arbiter must advance to a new agent if the initial transaction attempting to establish a lock is terminated with retry."

The specification contains an example arbiter implementation that does clarify the intent of the specification. The example can be found in the next section.

Ideally, the bus arbiter should be programmable by the system. If it is, the startup configuration software can determine the priority to be assigned to each member of the bus master community by reading from the Maximum Latency (Max_Lat) configuration register associated with each bus master (see Figure 5-2 on page 62). The bus master designer hardwires this register to indicate, in increments of 250ns, how quickly the master requires access to the bus in order to achieve adequate performance.

In order to grant the PCI bus to a bus master, the arbiter asserts the device's respective GNT# signal. This grants the bus to the master for one transaction (consisting of one or more data phases).

If a master generates a request, is subsequently granted the bus and does not initiate a transaction (assert FRAME#) within 16 PCI clocks after the bus goes idle, the arbiter may assume that the master is malfunctioning. In this case, the action taken by the arbiter would be system design-dependent.

Figure 5-2: Maximum Latency Configuration Register

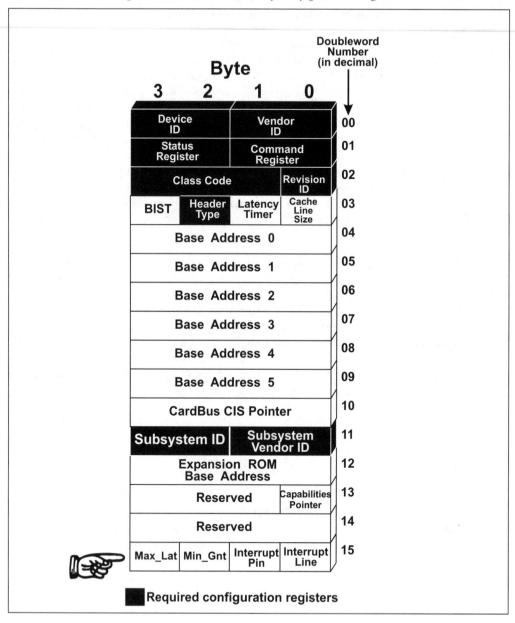

Example Arbiter with Fairness

A system may divide the overall community of bus masters on a PCI bus into two categories:

1. Bus masters that require fast access to the bus or high throughput in order to achieve good performance. Examples might be the video adapter, an ATM network interface, or an FDDI network interface.
2. Bus masters that don't require very fast access to the bus or high throughput in order to achieve good performance. Examples might be a SCSI host bus adapter or a standard expansion bus master.

The arbiter would segregate the REQ#/GNT# signals into two groups with greater precedence given to those in one group. Assume that bus masters A and B are in the group that requires fast access, while masters X, Y and Z are in the other group. The arbiter can be programmed or designed to treat each group as rotational priority within the group and rotational priority between the two groups. This is pictured in Figure 5-3 on page 64.

Assume the following conditions:

- Master A is the next to receive the bus in the first group.
- Master X is the next to receive it in the second group.
- A master in the first group is the next to receive the bus.
- All masters are asserting REQ# and wish to perform multiple transactions (i.e., they keep their respective REQ# asserted after starting a transaction).

The order in which the masters would receive access to the bus is:

1. Master A.
2. Master B.
3. Master X.
4. Master A.
5. Master B.
6. Master Y.
7. Master A.
8. Master B.
9. Master Z.
10. Master A.
11. Master B.
12. Master X, etc.

The masters in the first group are permitted to access the bus more frequently than those that reside in the second group.

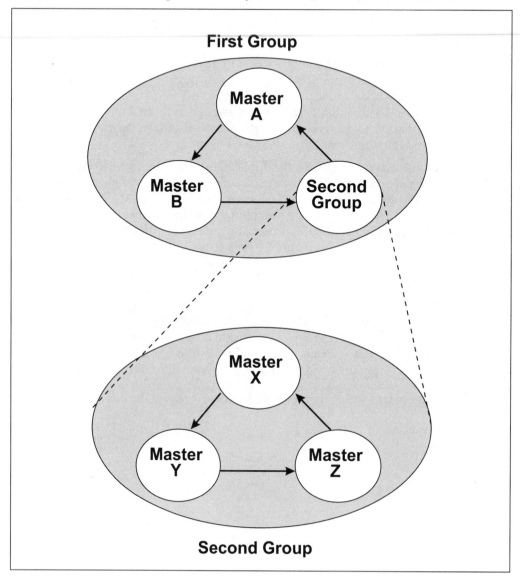

Figure 5-3: Example Arbitration Scheme

Master Wishes To Perform More Than One Transaction

If the master has another transaction to perform immediately after the one it just initiated, it should keep its REQ# line asserted when it asserts FRAME# to begin the current transaction (as an example, refer to clock 2 in Figure 5-4 on page 71). This informs the arbiter of its desire to maintain ownership of the bus after completion of the current transaction. Depending on other pending requests, the arbiter may or may not permit the master to maintain bus ownership after the completion of the current transaction. In the event that ownership is not maintained, the master should keep its REQ# asserted until it is successful in acquiring bus ownership again.

At a given instant in time, only one bus master may use the bus. This means that no more than one GNT# line will be asserted by the arbiter during any PCI clock cycle.

Hidden Bus Arbitration

Unlike some arbitration schemes, the PCI scheme allows bus arbitration to take place while the current initiator is performing a data transfer. If the arbiter decides to grant ownership of the bus for the next transaction to a master other than the initiator of the current transaction, it removes the GNT# from the current initiator (i.e., it preempts it) and issues GNT# to the next owner of the bus. The next owner cannot assume bus ownership, however, until the bus is idled by the current initiator. No bus time is wasted on a dedicated period of time to perform an arbitration bus cycle. This is referred to as hidden arbitration.

Bus Parking

A master must only assert its REQ# output to signal a current need for the bus. In other words, a master must not use its REQ# output to "park" the bus on itself. If a system designer implements a bus parking scheme, the bus arbiter design should indicate a default bus owner by asserting the device's GNT# signal when no request from any bus masters are currently pending. In this manner, a REQ# from the default bus master is granted immediately (if no other bus masters require the use of the PCI bus).

If the bus arbiter is designed to implement bus parking, it asserts GNT# to a default bus master when none of the REQ# lines are active. In this manner, the bus is immediately available to the default bus master if it should require the use of the bus (and no other higher-priority request is pending). If the master that the bus is parked on subsequently requires access to the PCI bus, it needn't assert its REQ#. Upon sampling bus idle (FRAME# and IRDY# deasserted) and its GNT# asserted, it can immediately initiate a transaction. The choice of which master to park the bus on is defined by the designer of the bus arbiter. Any process may be used, such as the last bus master to use the bus or a predefined default bus master.

There are two possible scenarios regarding the method utilized when implementing bus parking:

METHOD 1. The arbiter may monitor FRAME# and IRDY# to determine if the bus is busy before parking the bus. Assume that a master requests the bus, receives its GNT# and starts a multiple data phase burst transaction. If it doesn't have another transaction to run after this one completes, it deasserts its REQ# when it asserts FRAME#. In this case, the arbiter may be designed to recognize that the bus is busy and, as a result, will not deassert the current master's grant to park the bus on another master (it is strongly recommended that this approach be used).

METHOD 2. The arbiter may not monitor for bus idle. Assume that a master requests the bus, receives its GNT# and starts a multiple data phase burst transaction. If it doesn't have another transaction to run after this one completes, it deasserts its REQ# when it asserts FRAME#. In this case, the arbiter may, in the absence of any requests from other masters, take away GNT# from the current master and issue GNT# to the master it intends to park the bus on. When the current master has exhausted its master latency timer and determines that it has lost its grant, it is forced to relinquish the bus, wait two clocks, and then rearbitrate for it again to resume the transaction at the point where it left off.

The specification recommends that the bus be parked on the last master that acquired the bus. In case two, then, the arbiter would continue to issue GNT# to the burst master and it can continue its transaction until either it is completed or until a request is received from another master.

When the arbiter parks the bus on a master (by asserting its grant) and the bus is idle, that master becomes responsible for keeping the AD bus, C/BE bus and PAR from floating (to keep the CMOS input buffers on all devices from oscillating and drawing excessive current). The master must enable its AD[31:0], C/BE#[3:0], and (one clock later) its PAR output drivers. The master doesn't have to turn on all of its output drivers in a single clock (it may take up to eight clocks, but two to three clocks is recommended). This procedure ensures that the bus doesn't float during bus idle periods. If the arbiter is not designed to park the bus, the arbiter itself should drive the AD bus, C/BE# lines and PAR during periods when the bus is idle.

Chapter 5: PCI Bus Arbitration

Request/Grant Timing

When the arbiter determines that it is a master's turn to use the bus, it asserts the master's GNT# line. The arbiter may deassert a master's GNT# on any PCI clock. A master must ensure that its GNT# is asserted on the rising clock edge on which it wishes to start a transaction. If GNT# is deasserted, the transaction must not proceed. Once asserted by the arbiter, GNT# may be deasserted under the following circumstances:

- If GNT# is deasserted and FRAME# is asserted the transfer is valid and will continue. The deassertion of GNT# by the arbiter indicates that the master will no longer own the bus at the completion of the transaction currently in progress. The master keeps FRAME# asserted while the current transaction is still in progress. It deasserts FRAME# when it is ready to complete the final data phase.
- The GNT# to one master can be deasserted simultaneously with the assertion of another master's GNT# **if the bus isn't in the idle state**. The idle state is defined as a clock cycle during which both FRAME# and IRDY# are deasserted. If the bus appears to be idle, the master whose GNT# is being removed may be using stepping to drive the bus (even though it hasn't asserted FRAME# yet; stepping is covered in "Address/Data Stepping" on page 162). The coincidental deassertion of its GNT# along with the assertion of another master's GNT# could result in contention on the AD bus. The other master could immediately start a transaction (because the bus is technically idle). The problem is prevented by delaying grant to the other master by one cycle. Table 5-1 on page 67 defines the bus state as indicated by the current state of FRAME# and IRDY#.
- GNT# may be deasserted during the final data phase (FRAME# is deasserted) in response to the current bus master's REQ# being deasserted.

Table 5-1: Bus State

FRAME#	IRDY#	Description
deasserted	deasserted	Bus Idle.
deasserted	asserted	Initiator is ready to complete the last data transfer of a transaction, but it has not yet completed.
asserted	deasserted	A transaction is in progress and the initiator is not ready to complete the current data phase.

Table 5-1: Bus State (Continued)

FRAME#	IRDY#	Description
asserted	asserted	A transaction is in progress and the initiator is ready to complete the current data phase.

Example of Arbitration Between Two Masters

Figure 5-4 on page 71 illustrates bus usage between two masters arbitrating for access to the PCI bus. The following assumptions must be made in order to interpret this example correctly:

- Bus master **A** requires the bus to perform two transactions. The first consists of a three data phase write and the second transaction type is a single data phase write.
- The arbitration scheme is fixed and bus master **B** has a higher priority than bus master **A**, or the scheme is rotational and it is **B's** turn next.
- Bus master **B** only requires the bus to execute a single transaction consisting of one data phase.

It is important to remember that all PCI signals are sampled on the rising-edge of the PCI CLK signal. If the current owner of the bus requires the bus to perform additional transactions upon completion of the current transaction, it should keep its REQ# line asserted after assertion of FRAME# for the current transaction. If no other bus masters are requesting the use of the bus or the current bus master has the highest priority, the bus arbiter will continue to grant the bus to the current bus master at the conclusion of the current transaction.

The sample arbitration sequence pictured in Figure 5-4 on page 71 proceeds as follows:

CLOCK 1. Prior to clock edge one, bus master **A** asserts its REQ# to request access to the PCI bus.
THE arbiter samples **A's** REQ# active at the rising-edge of clock one.
AT this point, bus master **B** doesn't yet require the bus.
DURING clock cell one, the arbiter asserts GNT# to bus master **A**, granting it ownership of the bus.
DURING the same clock period, bus master **B** asserts its REQ#, indicating its desire to execute a transaction.

CLOCK 2. Bus master **A** samples its GNT# asserted on the rising-edge of clock two.

IT also samples IRDY# and FRAME# deasserted, indicating that the bus is in the idle state.

IN response, bus master **A** initiates the first of its two transactions. It asserts FRAME# and begins to drive the start address onto AD[31:0] and the command onto the Command/Byte Enable bus.

IF master **A** did not have another transaction to perform after this one, it would deassert its REQ# line during clock cell two. In this example, it does have another transaction to perform, so it keeps its REQ# line asserted.

THE PCI bus arbiter samples the requests from bus masters **A** and **B** asserted at the rising-edge of clock two and begins the arbitration process to determine the next bus master.

DURING clock cell two, the arbiter removes the GNT# from master **A**.

CLOCK 3. On the rising-edge of clock three, master **A** determines that it has been preempted, but continues its transaction because its LT (Latency Timer) has not yet expired (the LT is covered later in this chapter).

DURING clock cell three, the arbiter asserts bus master **B's** GNT#.

MASTER A begins to drive the first data item onto the AD bus (this is a write transaction) during clock cell three, asserts the appropriate Command/Byte Enables (to indicate the data lanes to be used for the transfer) and asserts IRDY# to indicate to the target that the data is present on the bus.

CLOCK 4. On the rising-edge of clock four, master **B** samples its GNT# asserted, indicating that it may be the next owner of the bus. It must continue to sample its GNT# on each subsequent rising-edge of the clock until it has bus acquisition. This is necessary because the arbiter may remove its grant and grant the bus to another party with a higher priority before the bus goes idle. Master **B** cannot begin to use the bus until the bus returns to the idle state.

AT the rising-edge of clock four, IRDY# and TRDY# are sampled asserted and the first data transfer takes place.

CLOCK 5. At the rising-edge of clock five, IRDY# and TRDY# are sampled asserted and the second data transfer takes place.

DURING clock cell five, master **A** keeps IRDY# asserted and deasserts FRAME#, indicating that the final data phase is in progress.

CLOCK 6. At the rising-edge of clock six, IRDY# and TRDY# are sampled asserted and the third and final data transfer is completed.

DURING clock cell six, bus master **A** deasserts IRDY#, returning the bus to the idle state.

CLOCK 7. On the rising-edge of clock seven, master **B** samples FRAME# and IRDY# both deasserted and determines that the bus is now idle.

It also samples its GNT# still asserted, indicating that it has bus acquisition. **In** response, it starts its transaction and turns off its REQ# line during clock cell seven (because it only requires the bus to perform this one transaction). **When** it asserts FRAME# during clock cell seven, master **B** also begins driving the address onto the AD bus and the command onto Command/ Byte Enable bus.

Clock 8. At the rising-edge of clock eight, the arbiter samples master **B**'s REQ# deasserted and master **A**'s REQ# still asserted.

In response, the arbiter de-asserts master **B**'s GNT# and asserts master **A**'s GNT# during clock cell eight. Master **A** had kept its REQ# line asserted because it wanted to use the bus for another transaction. Master **A** now samples IRDY# and FRAME# on the rising-edge of each clock until the bus is sensed idle. At that time, it can begin its next transaction.

During clock cell eight, master **B** deasserts FRAME#, indicating that its first (and only) data phase is in progress.

It also begins to drive the write data onto the AD bus and the appropriate setting onto the Command/Byte Enable bus during clock cell eight. It asserts IRDY# to indicate to the target that the data is present on the AD bus.

Clock 9. At the rising-edge of clock nine, IRDY# and TRDY# are sampled asserted and the data transfer takes place.

The initiator, master **B**, then deasserts IRDY# (during clock cell nine) to return the bus to the idle state.

Clock 10. Master **A** samples the bus idle and its GNT# asserted at the rising-edge of clock ten and initiates its second transaction during clock cell ten.

It also deasserts its REQ# when its asserts FRAME#, indicating to the arbiter that it does not require the bus again upon completion of this transaction.

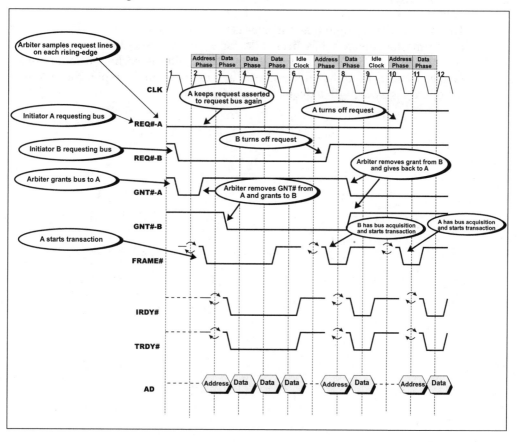

Figure 5-4: PCI Bus Arbitration Between Two Masters

State of REQ# and GNT# During RST#

While RST# is asserted, all masters must tri-state their REQ# output drivers and must ignore their GNT# inputs.

Pullups On REQ# From Add-In Connectors

In a system with PCI add-in connectors, the arbiter may require a weak pullup on the REQ# inputs that are wired to the add-in connectors. This will keep them from floating when the connectors are unoccupied.

Broken Master

The arbiter may assume that a master is broken if the arbiter has issued GNT# to the master, the bus has been idle for 16 clocks, and the master has not asserted FRAME# to start its transaction. The arbiter is permitted to ignore all further requests from the broken master and may optionally report the failure to the operating system (in a device-specific fashion).

6 *Master and Target Latency*

The Previous Chapter

The previous chapter provided a detailed description of the mechanism used to arbitrate for PCI bus ownership.

This Chapter

This chapter describes the rules governing how much time a device may hold the bus in wait states during any given data phase. It describes how soon after reset is removed the first transaction may be initiated and how soon after reset is removed a target device must be prepared to transfer data. The mechanisms that a target may use to meet the latency rules are described: Delayed Transactions, and posting of memory writes.

The Next Chapter

The next chapter describes the transaction types, or commands, that the initiator may utilize when it has successfully acquired PCI bus ownership.

Mandatory Delay Before First Transaction Initiated

The 2.2 spec mandates that the system (i.e., the arbiter within the chipset) must guarantee that the first transaction will not be initiated on the PCI bus for at least five PCI clock cycles after RST# is deasserted. This value is referred to as **Trhff** in the spec (Time from Reset High-to-First-FRAME# assertion).

Bus Access Latency

When a bus master wishes to transfer a block of one or more data items between itself and a target PCI device, it must request the use of the bus from the bus arbiter. Bus access latency is defined as the amount of time that expires from the moment a bus master requests the use of the PCI bus until it completes the first data transfer of the transaction. Figure 6-1 on page 75 illustrates the different components of the access latency experienced by a PCI bus master. Table 6-1 on page 74 describes each latency component.

Table 6-1: Access Latency Components

Component	Description
Bus Access Latency	Defined as the amount of time that expires from the moment a bus master requests the use of the PCI bus until it completes the first data transfer of the transaction. In other words, it is the sum of arbitration, bus acquisition and target latency.
Arbitration Latency	Defined as the period of time from the bus master's assertion of REQ# until the bus arbiter asserts the bus master's GNT#. This period is a function of the arbitration algorithm, the master's priority and whether any other masters are requesting access to the bus.
Bus Acquisition Latency	Defined as the period time from the reception of GNT# by the requesting bus master until the current bus master surrenders the bus. The requesting bus master can then initiate its transaction by asserting FRAME#. The duration of this period is a function of how long the current bus master's transaction-in-progress takes to complete. This parameter is the larger of either the current master's LT value (in other words, its timeslice) or the longest latency to first data phase completion in the system (which is limited to a maximum of 16 clocks).
Initiator and Target Latency	Defined as the period of time from the start of a transaction until the master and the currently-addressed target are ready to complete the first data transfer of the transaction. This period is a function how fast the master is able to transfer the first data item, as well as the access time for the currently-addressed target device (and is limited to a maximum of 8 clocks for the master and 16 clocks for the target).

Figure 6-1: Access Latency Components

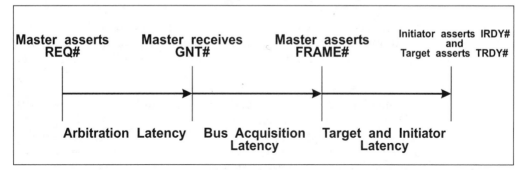

PCI bus masters should always use burst transfers to transfer blocks of data between themselves and a target PCI device (some poorly-designed masters use a series of single-data phase transactions to transfer a block of data). The transfer may consist of anywhere from one to an unlimited number of bytes. A bus master that has requested and has been granted the use of the bus (its GNT# is asserted by the arbiter) cannot begin a transaction until the current bus master completes its transaction-in-progress. If the current master were permitted to own the bus until its entire transfer were completed, it would be possible for the current bus master to starve other bus masters from using the bus for extended periods of time. The extensive delay incurred could cause other bus masters (and/or the application programs they serve) to experience poor performance or even to malfunction (buffer overflows or starvation may be experienced).

As an example, a bus master could have a buffer full condition and is requesting the use of the bus in order to off-load its buffer contents to system memory. If it experiences an extended delay (latency) in acquiring the bus to begin the transfer, it may experience a data overrun condition as it receives more data from its associated device (such as a network) to be placed into its buffer.

In order to insure that the designers of bus masters are dealing with a predictable and manageable amount of bus latency, the PCI specification defines two mechanisms:

- Master Latency Timer (MLT).
- Target-Initiated Termination.

Pre-2.1 Devices Can Be Bad Boys

Prior to the 2.1 spec, there were some rules regarding how quickly a master or target had to transfer data, but they were not complete, nor were they clearly stated. The following list describes the behavior permitted by the pre-2.1 versions of the spec:

- In any data phase, the master could take any amount of time before asserting IRDY# to transfer a data item.
- At the end of the final data phase, the spec didn't say how quickly the master had to return IRDY# to the deasserted state, thereby returning the bus to the idle state so another master could use it.
- There was no 16 clock first data phase completion rule for the target. It could keep TRDY# deasserted forever if it wanted to.
- There was a subsequent data phase completion rule for the target, but it was not written clearly and provided a huge loop hole that permitted the target to insert any number of wait states in a data phase other than the first one. Basically, it said that the target *should* (there's a fuzzy word that should be banned from every spec) be ready to transfer a data item within eight clocks after entering a data phase. If it couldn't meet this eight clock recommendation, however, then whenever it did become ready to transfer the data item (*could be a gazillion clocks later*), it must assert STOP# along with TRDY#.

The bottom line is that pre-2.1 targets and masters can exhibit *very* poor behavior that ties up the PCI bus for awful amounts of time. The 2.1 spec closed these loop holes.

Preventing Master from Monopolizing the Bus

Master Must Transfer Data Within 8 CLKs

Refer to Figure 6-2 on page 77. It is a rule that the initiator must not keep IRDY# deasserted for more than seven PCI clocks during any data phase. In other words, it must be prepared to transfer a data item within eight clocks after entry into any data phase. If the initiator has no buffer space available to store read data, it must delay requesting the bus until is has room for the data. On a write transaction, the initiator must have the data available before it asks for the bus.

Figure 6-2: Longest Legal Deassertion of IRDY# In Any Data Phase Is 8 Clocks

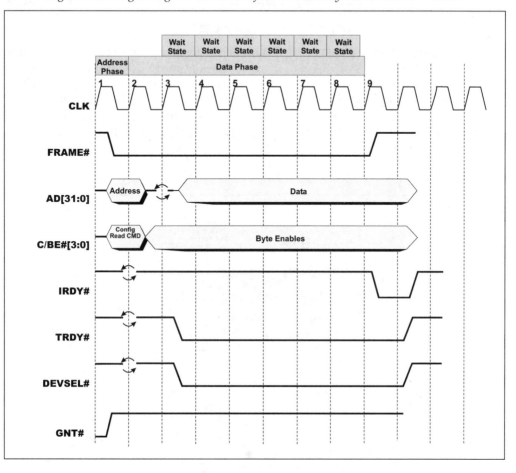

IRDY# Deasserted In Clock After Last Data Transfer   2.2

REFER TO THE END OF CLOCK 9 IN FIGURE 6-2 ON PAGE 77. UPON COMPLETION OF THE FINAL DATA TRANSFER (IRDY# AND TRDY# ASSERTED AND FRAME# DEASSERTED), THE MASTER MUST RELEASE THE IRDY# SIGNAL DURING THE NEXT CLOCK PERIOD. THIS RULE WAS ADDED IN THE 2.2 SPEC.

Latency Timer Keeps Master From Monopolizing Bus

Location and Purpose of Master Latency Timer

The Master Latency Timer, or LT, is implemented as a PCI configuration register in the bus master's configuration space (see byte one of dword three in Figure 6-3 on page 78). It is either initialized by the configuration software at startup time, or contains a hardwired value. The value contained in the LT defines the minimum amount of time (in PCI clock periods) that the bus master is permitted to retain ownership of the bus each time that it acquires bus ownership and initiates a transaction.

Figure 6-3: Master Latency Timer Is a Configuration Register

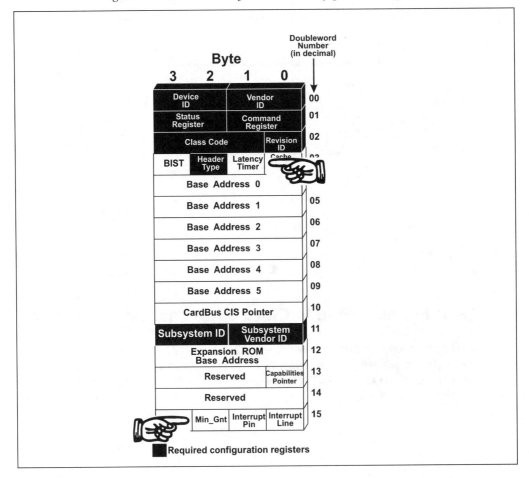

How LT Works

When the bus master detects bus idle (FRAME# and IRDY# deasserted) and its GNT# asserted, it has bus acquisition and may initiate a transaction. Upon initiation of the transaction, the master's LT is initialized to the value written to the LT by the configuration software at startup time (or its hardwired value). Starting on the next rising-edge of the PCI clock and on every subsequent rising-edge, the master decrements its LT by one.

If the master is in the midst of a burst transaction and the arbiter removes its GNT# (in other words, it is preempted), this indicates that the arbiter has detected a request from another master and is granting ownership of the bus for the next transaction to the other master. In other words, the current master has been preempted.

If the current master's LT has not yet been exhausted (decremented all the way down), it has not yet used up its timeslice and may retain ownership of the bus until either:

- it completes its burst transaction or
- its LT expires,

whichever comes first. If it is able to complete its burst before expiration of its LT, the other master that has its GNT# may assume bus ownership when it detects that the current master has returned the bus to the idle state. If the current master is not able to complete its burst transfer before expiration of its LT, it is permitted to complete one more data transfer and must then yield the bus.

If the current master has exhausted its LT, still has its GNT# and has not yet completed it burst transfer, it may retain ownership of the bus and continue to burst data until either:

- it completes its overall burst transfer or
- its GNT# is removed by the arbiter.

In the latter case, the current master is permitted to complete one more data transfer and must then yield the bus.

It should be noted that, when forced to prematurely terminate a data transfer, the bus master must "remember" where it was in the transfer. After a brief period, it may then reassert its REQ# to request bus ownership again so that it may continue where it left off.

Is Implementation of LT Register Mandatory?

It must be implemented as a read/writable register by any master that performs more than two data phases per transaction. This implies that the register is optional and may therefore be hardwired to zero. If you do this, be aware that your master has a timeslice of zero! In other words, if you initiate a transaction and the arbiter immediately removes your GNT# (because another master is requesting the bus), your master can perform one (and only one) data phase and must relinquish the bus.

Can LT Value Be Hardwired?

Yes, for a master that performs one or two data phases per transaction, but the hardwired value may not exceed 16 (and it could be zero). Please refer to the previous sections regarding the implication if you choose to hardwire a value of zero.

How Does Software Determine Timeslice To Be Allocated To Master?

The bus master designer implements a read-only configuration register referred to as the Minimum Grant (Min_Gnt) register (see byte two of dword 15 in Figure 6-3 on page 78). A better name for it might be the Timeslice Request register. A value of zero indicates that the bus master has no specific requirements regarding the setting assigned to its LT. A non-zero value indicates, in increments of 250ns, how long a timeslice the master requires in order to achieve adequate performance. *THE VALUE HARDWIRED INTO THIS REGISTER BY THE BUS MASTER DESIGNER ASSUMES A BUS SPEED OF 33MHZ. WHEN CHOOSING THIS VALUE, THE DESIGNER MUST ASSUME THAT THE TARGET DOESN'T INSERT WAIT STATES INTO DATA PHASES (THIS WAS ADDED IN THE 2.2 SPEC).*

The BIOS determines the timeslice to load into a master's LT register by using the value from the MIN_GNT register in conjunction with the BIOS's knowledge of the PCI bus speed. These factors are used to compute the duration of the requested timeslice (as a number of PCI clock ticks). The timeslice requests from all masters on the bus are evaluated to determine the actual timeslice allocated to each master.

Treatment of Memory Write and Invalidate Command

Any master performing a Memory Write and Invalidate command (see "Memory Write-and-Invalidate Command" on page 117) should not terminate its transfer until it reaches a cache line boundary (even if its LT has expired and it

2.2

has been preempted) unless STOP# is asserted by the target. If it reaches a cache line boundary with its LT expired and its GNT# has been removed by the arbiter, the initiator *must* terminate the transaction. If a memory write and invalidate command is terminated by the target (STOP# asserted by a non-cacheable memory target), the master should complete the line update in memory using the memory write command as soon as it can. Cacheable memory targets must not disconnect a memory write and invalidate command except at cache line boundaries, even if caching is currently disabled. For this reason, the snooper (i.e., the host/PCI bridge) can always assume that the memory write and invalidate command will complete without disconnection if the access is within a memory range designated as cacheable.

If FRAME# is still asserted (i.e., it's not the last data phase of the transaction) when the master's LT expires (it's timeslice has just expired), *and* the command is a memory write and invalidate, *and* the current data phase is transferring the final dword of the current cache line when GNT# is deasserted, the master must terminate the transaction at the end of the next cache line. This is necessary because the master, by keeping FRAME# asserted, committed to transfer at least one more dword to the target (and that is the first dword of the next line).

Preventing Target From Monopolizing Bus

General

The problem of a bus master hogging the bus is solved by:

1. The inclusion of the LT associated with each master.
2. The rule that requires the initiator to keep IRDY# deasserted for no longer than eight PCI clocks during any data phase.

It is also possible, however, for a target with a very slow access time to monopolize the bus while a data item is being transferred between itself and the current master. The target does not assert the target ready signal, TRDY#, until it is ready to complete the transfer of the data item.

Target Must Transfer Data Expeditiously

General

The slow target problem was addressed in the 2.1 PCI specification by requiring a slow target to terminate a transfer prematurely (before all of the intended data has been transferred) if it will tie up the bus for too long. The spec addresses two cases wherein the target could tie up the bus unnecessarily:

CASE 1. The target cannot transfer the first data item within 16 clocks from the assertion of FRAME#.

CASE 2. Although the target can transfer the first data item within 16 clocks from the assertion of FRAME#, it cannot transfer one of the subsequent data items within eight clocks from the start of the respective data phase. Any data phase other than the first one is referred to as a *subsequent data phase.*

The sections that follow describe the rules associated with the first data phase and subsequent data phases.

The First Data Phase Rule

General. If the target cannot complete the first data transfer **within 16 PCI CLKs** (**from** the assertion of **FRAME#**), the target **must** (the revision 2.0 specification used the word "should" rather than "must") immediately issue a **retry** to the master (retry is fully-defined in "Retry" on page 189). In other words, in the first data phase the target:

- asserts DEVSEL# to claim the transaction.
- does not assert TRDY#, thereby indicating its unwillingness to transfer the first data item.
- asserts STOP# to indicate that it wants to terminate the transaction with no data transferred in the first data phase and *therefore no data transferred in the transaction.*

Master's Response To Retry. Receipt of a Retry forces the master to terminate the transaction with no data transferred, thus freeing up the bus for other masters to use. After two PCI clocks have elapsed (recommended), the master can reassert its request and, when it receives its GNT#, reinitiate its transaction again. The transaction **must be retried identically** (this is explained in "Delayed Transactions" on page 86 and in "Retry" on page 189).

A master cannot depend on targets responding to the first data phase within 16 clocks because the 16 clock rule only affects post-2.0 devices. Target devices designed prior to the revision 2.1 specification can take longer than 16 clocks to respond.

***Sometimes* Target Can't Transfer First Data Within 16 CLKs.** If the nature of a target is such that it occasionally cannot complete the first data phase within 16 PCI CLKs from the assertion of FRAME#, the target **must** immediately issue a **Retry** to the master. *It does not, however, have to "memorize" the transaction and process it off-line.* A target is permitted to do this only when there is a high probability the target will be able to complete the transaction when the master repeats the request. Odds are its inability to transfer the first data item expeditiously is due to a temporary condition (such as a temporary logic busy condition) and that it will be prepared to transfer the data within 16 clocks from the assertion of FRAME# the next time that the transaction is repeated.

Target *Frequently* Can't Transfer First Data Within 16 CLKs. If a target frequently cannot transfer the first data item within 16 clocks from the assertion of FRAME#, it not only must issue a retry to the master, but *must also "memorize" the transaction and process it off-line.* In other words:

- If it's a read transaction, issue the retry after memorizing the address and command from the address phase, and the byte enables from the first data phase. It then starts reading the requested data from the slow medium (e.g., from an ISA target).
- If it's a write transaction, issue a retry after memorizing the address and command from the address phase and the byte enables and write data from the first data phase. The target then initiates the write to the slow medium.

This is referred to as a **Delayed Read** or a **Delayed Write**. A detailed description of delayed transactions can be found in "Delayed Transactions" on page 86.

Two Exceptions To First Data Phase Rule. There are only **two exceptions**:

- **During system initialization time** (defined as 2^{25} CLKs after RST# removed), targets do not have to adhere to the 16 clock rule. After initialization time has elapsed, all targets must obey the 16 clock rule for first data phase completion. For more information, refer to "Target Latency During Initialization Time" on page 85.
- A **host/PCI bridge that is snooping** is permitted to exceed the 16 clock limit, but may never exceed **32 clocks**. Assume that a PCI master is accessing main memory. the host/PCI bridge can start inserting wait states in the first data phase while it sends the memory address back to the processors to be snooped in their caches. In the event of a snoop hit on a modified line, the processor with the modified line will transfer the line to the bridge. If the bridge knows that this process can be accomplished within 32 PCI clocks from the start of master's transaction, then it is legal for it to hold the PCI bus in wait states while the snoop and possible memory update takes place.

Subsequent Data Phase Rule

General. If it will take **more than eight PCI clocks to complete a data phase** other than the first (referred to as the **subsequent latency timeout**) and it is not the final data phase (FRAME# is still asserted), the target must force the master to terminate the transaction. There are two cases and each is described in the next two sections.

In Data Phase and Cannot Transfer Data Within 8 Clocks. The target can't transfer the data item in the current data phase within eight clocks after entry into the data phase. In this case, the target had deasserted TRDY# upon entry into the data phase (indicating its unreadiness to transfer the data). The target can handle this scenario in one of two ways:

METHOD 1. Assert STOP# as soon as possible after entry into the data phase (and not later than the eight clock of the data phase). DEVSEL# remains asserted. This signal combination instructs the master to disconnect from the target with no data transferred in the current data phase. This is referred to as a **disconnect without data** transferred. In the author's opinion, this termination method is greatly preferred over the alternative cited in item 2.

METHOD 2. Alternately, the target could signal a **Target Abort** to the master by keeping TRDY# deasserted, asserting STOP# and deasserting DEVSEL#. Target abort is intended to indicate a fatal error or that the target will never be able to complete the request.

OK In This Data Phase, But Can't Meet Rule In Next One. The target can transfer the data item in the current data phase within eight clocks after entry into the data phase. However, it knows that this is not the final data phase (because the master still has FRAME# asserted) and it knows in advance that it cannot transfer the next data item within eight clocks after entry into the next data phase. In the current data phase, it should therefore assert STOP# along with TRDY# when it is ready to transfer the current data item. DEVSEL# remains asserted. This combination instructs the master to disconnect from the target with data transferred in the current data phase. This is referred to as a **disconnect with data** transferred.

Master's Response To a Disconnect. In response to a target disconnect, the master must terminate the transaction and may choose to resume it later at the dword that wasn't transferred (if the master was prefetching, it may choose not to resume the transaction). After two PCI clocks have elapsed, the master that received the disconnect can reassert its request and, when it receives its GNT#, reinitiate its transaction again at the next data item.

Target's Subsequent Latency and Master's Latency Timer. The subsequent latency timeout is completely independent of the master's LT. The target has no visibility to the master's LT (and vice versa) and therefore cannot tell whether it has timed out or not. This means that slow access targets always (before or after LT expiration) disconnect from the master, thereby fragmenting the overall burst transaction into a series of single data phase transactions. Two examples of devices that might perform disconnects are:

- Targets that are very slow all of the time (virtually all ISA bus devices would fall into this category).
- A target that exhibits very slow access sometimes (perhaps because of a buffer full condition or the need for mechanical movement) and would therefore tie up the PCI bus.

Target Latency During Initialization Time

Initialization Time vs. Run Time

Initialization time is the period of time during which the POST (Power-On Self-Test) code executes and the PCI devices are discovered and configured. Run time begins after initialization time completes. The 2.1 spec provided a very fuzzy definition of these two time periods and the 2.2 spec is much more definitive. During initialization time, PCI devices are not required to adhere to the 16 clock rule for first data phase completion.

Definition of Initialization Time and Behavior (Before 2.2)

The following text is reprinted directly from the 2.1 spec:

"All devices are granted two exceptions to the initial latency rule during initialization time. Initialization time begins when RST# is deasserted and completes when the POST code has initialized the system. The time following the completion of the POST code is considered Run-time. The following two exceptions have no upper bound on initial latency and are granted during initialization time only.

- POST code accessing the device's configuration registers.
- POST code copying the expansion ROM image to memory.

The target being accessed after initialization time must adhere to the 16 clock initial latency requirements."

Definition of Initialization Time and Behavior (2.2)

2.2

AS DEFINED IN THE 2.2 SPEC, INITIALIZATION-TIME BEGINS WHEN RST# IS DEASSERTED AND COMPLETES 2^{25} PCI CLOCKS LATER. THIS PARAMETER IS REFERRED TO IN THE SPEC AS TRHFA (TIME FROM RESET HIGH-TO-FIRST-ACCESS). AT A BUS SPEED OF 33MHz, THIS EQUATES TO 1.0066 SECONDS, WHILE IT EQUATES TO .5033 SECONDS AT A BUS SPEED OF 66MHz. RUN-TIME FOLLOWS INITIALIZATION-TIME. IF A TARGET IS ACCESSED DURING INITIALIZATION-TIME, IT IS ALLOWED TO DO ANY OF THE FOLLOWING:

- *IGNORE THE REQUEST (EXCEPT IF IT IS A BOOT DEVICE). A BOOT DEVICE IS ONE THAT MUST RESPOND AS A TARGET IN ORDER TO ALLOW THE PROCESSOR TO ACCESS THE BOOT ROM. IN A TYPICAL PC DESIGN, THIS WOULD BE THE PCI-TO-ISA BRIDGE. DEVICES IN THE PROCESSOR'S PATH TO THE BOOT ROM SHOULD BE PREPARED TO BE THE TARGET OF A TRANSACTION IMMEDIATELY AFTER TRHFF EXPIRES (FIVE CLOCK CYCLES AFTER RST# IS DEASSERTED; SEE "MANDATORY DELAY BEFORE FIRST TRANS-ACTION INITIATED" ON PAGE 73).*
- *CLAIM THE ACCESS AND HOLD IN WAIT STATES UNTIL IT CAN COMPLETE THE REQUEST, NOT TO EXCEED THE END OF INITIALIZATION-TIME.*
- *CLAIM THE ACCESS AND TERMINATE WITH RETRY.*

Delayed Transactions

The Problem

The section entitled "Target Frequently Can't Transfer First Data Within 16 CLKs" on page 83 defined the problem for which delayed transactions provide the solution. It's a rule that a target that can't transfer the first data item within 16 clocks from the assertion of FRAME# must issue a retry to the master. In other words, from the master's point of view, the transaction is rejected and it must retry the transaction on a periodic basis until the target is able to transfer the first data item within 16 clocks. Theoretically, if the target is *always* very slow, the transaction would *never* take place. Obviously, this isn't acceptable.

The Solution

Figure 6-4 on page 87 presents an example scenario. Assume that the processor initiates a transaction to read data from or write data to the target that resides on PCI Bus 1. The numbered steps in the illustration provide a basic description of Delayed Transactions.

Figure 6-4: A Delayed Transaction Example

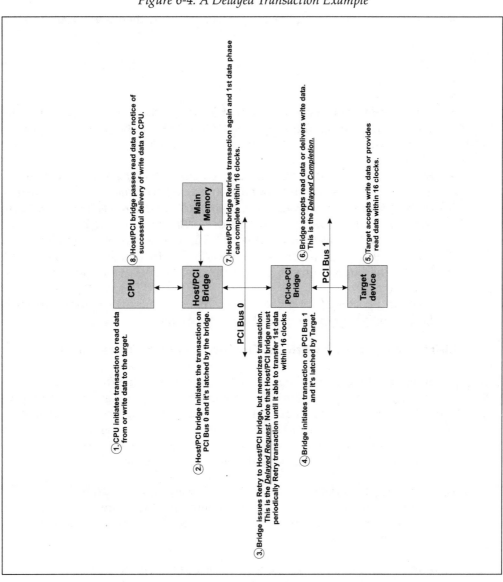

Information Memorized

The target must latch the following information and then issue a retry to the master:

- address.
- command.
- byte enables.
- *ADDRESS AND DATA PARITY, IF THE PARITY ERROR RESPONSE BIT (BIT 6 OF THE COMMAND REGISTER) IS SET. THIS IS MORE STRICT THAN THE 2.1 SPEC WHICH SAID, "PARITY BITS MAY ALSO BE USED IF PARITY CHECKING IS ENABLED."*
- REQ64# (if a 64-bit transfer).
- *FOR WRITE TRANSACTIONS COMPLETED USING DELAYED TRANSACTION TERMINATION, A TARGET MUST ALSO LATCH DATA FROM BYTE LANES FOR WHICH THE BYTE ENABLE IS ASSERTED AND MAY OPTIONALLY LATCH DATA FROM BYTE LANES FOR WHICH THE BYTE ENABLE IS DEASSERTED. THIS IS MUCH MORE DEFINITIVE THAN THE 2.1 SPEC WHICH SAID, "DATA (IF A WRITE TRANSACTION)."* The target knows the write data is present when the master asserts IRDY#. The byte enables are presented immediately upon entry into a data phase, irrespective of the state of the ready signals.
- Refer to "Locking" on page 683 for requirements for a bridge to latch **LOCK#** when completing a Delayed Transaction.

Master and Target Actions During Delayed Transaction

Upon receipt of the Retry, the initiator is forced to end the transaction with no data transferred and is required to retry the transaction again later using precisely the same address phase and first data phase information. If a read request, the target proceeds to fetch the requested data and set it up in a buffer for the master to read later when it retries the transaction. If a write request, the target attempts to deliver the write data to the target device.

When the target sees the master retry the transaction, it attempts to match the second request with the initial request by comparing the address phase and first data phase information to those latched earlier. If they match, the following action is taken:

- If the request was a read, the requested read data is transferred to the master well within the 16 clock limit imposed on the first data transfer.
- If the request was a write, the target asserts TRDY# to indicate that the ultimate target has accepted the write data.

If they aren't an exact match, the target interprets this as a new request and issues a retry to the master again. To summarize, if the master doesn't duplicate the transaction exactly each time it retries the transaction, it will never have its request fulfilled. The target is not required to service retries that aren't exact matches.

Commands That Can Use Delayed Transactions

All transactions that must complete on the destination bus before they can complete on the originating bus may be handled as delayed transactions. This would include:

- Interrupt Acknowledge.
- I/O read.
- I/O write.
- Memory read.
- Memory read line.
- Memory read multiple.
- Configuration read.
- Configuration write.

In other words, everything but the memory write commands. The Memory Write and the Memory Write and Invalidate commands immediately complete on the originating bus because they are posted in a bridge. For a discussion of posted memory writes, refer to "Posting Improves Memory Write Performance" on page 94.

Request Not Completed and Targeted Again

If a different master attempts to access the target and the target can only deal with one latched request at a time, it must issue a retry to the master without latching its transaction information.

Special Cycle Monitoring While Processing Request

If the target is designed to monitor for special cycles (see "Special Cycle Command" on page 107), it must be able to process a special cycle during the same period of time that is processing a previously latched read or write request.

Discard of Delayed Requests

A device that has "memorized" a delayed request and issued a retry to the initiator is permitted to discard the request any time prior to its initiation of the request on the destination bus. This is permitted because the master will retry the transaction again, thereby giving the device the opportunity to "re-memorize" the transaction.

Multiple Delayed Requests from Same Master

A master may be designed to stall on the repeating of a retried transaction until it completes successfully (before proceeding on to another transaction). Alternately, the master may be designed to present additional requests, each of which may receive retries. The master must continue to retry all of these transactions until they each complete. The specification contains the following statement:

> "The repeating of the requests is not required to be equal, but is required to be fair."

The author is not sure if this is a fragment of the Equal Opportunities Act or is actually part of the specification (just kidding). It means that the master must retry each of the transactions on a regular basis, but the order in which they are retried is not important. Just don't "neglect" any of the transactions.

Request Queuing In Target

A target that frequently cannot complete the first data phase within 16 clocks must support Delayed Transactions. At a minimum, it must be capable of latching one transaction request and treating it as a Delayed Transaction Request. If the device is the target of any subsequent transactions before it has completed the currently-latched transaction request, it issues a Retry to the master and does not memorize the transaction. The master is then obliged to repeat the rejected transaction until it is accepted and completed by the target.

Optionally, the target could be designed to accept and queue up multiple transaction requests. Bridges typically support both Delayed Transaction queuing and memory write posting. Posted memory writes are introduced in "Posting Improves Memory Write Performance" on page 94, and a detailed discussion of transaction ordering can be found in the chapter entitled "Transaction Ordering & Deadlocks" on page 649.

Discard of Delayed Completions

Once a delayed request has been completed on the destination bus, it may be discarded under two circumstances.

Read From Prefetchable Memory. A prefetchable memory target is one that is very well behaved in handling reads—any number of reads from the same location doesn't change the contents of the location (see "What Is Prefetchable Memory?" on page 93). If the transaction is a read within a memory region that the bridge knows is prefetchable, or the command was a memory read line or memory read multiple (both of which imply that the originating master "knows" that the memory region is prefetchable), then the bridge may discard the data. This is permissible because the bridge can rememorize the transaction when the master repeats it and can then refetch the data from the prefetchable memory target.

Master Tardy In Repeating Transaction. A bridge must discard data (if a read) and the completion status of a transaction if the master has not retried the transaction within 2^{10} PCI clocks (about 30 µs at 33 MHz). However, it is recommended that the bridge not discard the transaction until 2^{15} PCI clocks (about 983 µs at 33 MHz) after it acquired the data or status. The shorter number is useful in a system where a master designed to a previous version of the specification (before 2.2) fails to repeat a transaction exactly (as defined in the 2.2 spec) as first requested. In this case, the bridge may be programmed to discard the abandoned Delayed Completion early (see the new 2.2 bits in the "Bridge Control Register" on page 560) and allow other transactions to proceed. Normally, however, the bridge would wait the longer time, in case the retry of the transaction is being delayed by another bridge or bridges designed to a previous version of the specification that did not support Delayed Transactions. When this timer (referred to as the **discard timer**) expires, the device is required to discard the data (if a read) and the Completion status.

Reporting Discard of Data On a Read. When the delayed completion is discarded along with read data, the device may take one of two actions:

- When the data was read from a prefetchable region, the specification recommends that the error be ignored (because the data is still correct in the memory location from which it originated).
- WHEN THE DATA WAS READ FROM A NON-PREFETCHABLE MEMORY REGION (E.G., MEMORY-MAPPED I/O), IT IS RECOMMENDED THAT THE ERROR BE REPORTED TO THE DEVICE DRIVER. IF THE MASTER IS A BRIDGE, IT SHOULD IDEALLY SET A STATUS BIT IN A BRIDGE-SPECIFIC STATUS REGISTER TO INDICATE WHAT OCCURRED AND SHOULD GENERATE AN INTERRUPT REQUEST TO INVOKE ITS DRIVER TO COME CHECK ITS STATUS. ALTERNATELY, IT COULD ASSERT SERR# TO THE CHIPSET. FOR MORE INFORMATION, REFER TO "BRIDGE CONTROL REGISTER" ON PAGE 560.

2.2

Handling Multiple Data Phases

When the master is successful in completing the first data phase (in other words, it doesn't receive a retry), it may proceed with more data phases.

- **If** this is a **burst memory read** transaction, the target (assuming that it's a bridge) may have prefetched additional data into a read-ahead buffer and can therefore start streaming data to the master. The bridge could still be reading from the target on the destination bus and a steady data stream could then flow through the bridge until the transfer is complete, the target disconnects, or the master or bridge are preempted on their respective buses.
- **If** this is a **burst memory write** transaction, the earlier retry may have been issued because the target (a bridge) had a temporarily-full posted memory write buffer. Since then, the bridge could have partially or fully emptied the posted memory write buffer and can therefore start accepting multiple dwords into the buffer rapidly.

The target may issue a disconnect on any data phase after the first. In this case, the master is not required to resume the transaction later. Both the master and the target consider the original request fulfilled.

Master or Target Abort Handling

A delayed transaction is also considered completed if it results in a Master Abort or receives a Target Abort rather than a retry on a re-attempt of the retried transaction. The target compares to ensure that the master is the one that originated the request before it issues a Target Abort to it, or lets the transaction end in a Master Abort. This means that the transaction on the destination bus ended in a Master Abort because no target responded or in a Target Abort because the target is broken or does not support the byte enable combination (i.e., it doesn't own all of the addressed 8-bit ports within the dword). In both of these cases, the master is not required to repeat the transaction.

When a Master Abort occurs on the destination bus of a PCI-to-PCI bridge, follow the procedure detailed in "Master Abort on Other Side of PCI-to-PCI Bridge" on page 195.

Chapter 6: Master and Target Latency

What Is Prefetchable Memory?

Memory is defined as prefetchable if it exhibits the following characteristics:

- no side effects on reads (reads do not alter the contents of memory).
- the memory always returns all bytes on reads irrespective of the byte enable settings. This permits the target to exhibit better performance because it doesn't have to wait one clock into each data phase to sample the byte enables before supplying the data.
- bridges can perform byte merging within their posted memory write buffers for writes within this area without causing errors (see "Byte Merging" on page 95).

In a nutshell, regular memory is prefetchable while memory-mapped I/O (or any other badly-behaved memory region) is not. The configuration software can determine that a memory target is prefetchable or not by checking the Prefetchable bit in the memory target's Base Address Register (BAR). For additional information, refer to "Prefetchable Attribute Bit" on page 380.

Delayed Read Prefetch

A delayed read can result in the reading of more data than indicated in the master's initial data phase if the target knows that prefetching data doesn't alter the contents of memory locations (in other words, the memory is prefetchable and prefetches therefore do not change the contents of memory as it would in memory-mapped I/O ports). The target can prefetch more data than initially requested under the following circumstances:

- The master has used the Memory Read Line or Memory Read Multiple command, thereby indicating that it knows the targeted area is prefetchable memory.
- The master used a Memory Read command, but the bridge that accepted the Delayed Request recognizes that the address falls within a range defined as prefetchable.

In all other cases, the target (i.e., the bridge) cannot perform anything other than the single data phase indicated by the originating master.

Posting Improves Memory Write Performance

General

When acting as the target of a memory write transaction, a bridge (PCI-to-PCI bridge or host/PCI) may immediately absorb the address and the data to be written into a posted-write buffer that allows the bus master to complete a memory write quickly. The transaction and the write data are latched within the bridge's posted-write buffer and the master is permitted to complete the transaction.

When a bridge implements a posted-write buffer, a potential problem exists. Another bus master (or the same one) may initiate a memory read from the target of the posted write before the data is actually written to the memory target. If this were permitted, the master performing the read would not receive the freshest copy of the information. In order to prevent this from occurring, before permitting a read to occur on the target bus the bridge designer must first flush all posted writes to their destination memory targets. A device driver can ensure that all memory data has been written to its device by performing a read from the device. This will force the flushing of all posted write buffers in bridges that reside between the master executing the read and the target device before the read is permitted to complete.

It is also a requirement that the bridge must perform all posted writes in the same order in which they were originally posted.

A bridge is only permitted to post writes to memory targets. Software must be assured real-time communication with I/O devices, as well as with configuration registers.

Combining

A bridge may combine posted memory writes to successive dwords into a single burst memory write transaction using linear addressing. This feature is recommended to improve performance. The dwords must be written in the same order in which they were posted. This means that writes posted to dwords 0, 1 and 2 (they were posted in that order) can be combined into a linear burst write, while writes posted to dwords 2, 1, 0 cannot. Instead, these three writes would have to be performed as three separate single data phase memory write transactions. Writes posted to dwords 0, 1, and 3 (in that order) can be combined into a linear burst write with no byte enables asserted in the third data phase. The specification recommends that bridges that permit combining include a control bit to allow this feature to be disabled.

Byte Merging

A bridge may combine writes to a single dword within one entry in the posted-write buffer. This feature is recommended to improve performance and is only permitted in memory address ranges that are designated as prefetchable (for more information on prefetchable memory, refer to "What Is Prefetchable Memory?" on page 93 and to "Prefetchable Attribute Bit" on page 380).

As an example, assume that a bus master performs two memory writes: the first writes to locations 00000100h and 00000101h and the second writes to locations 00000102h and 00000103h. These four locations reside within the same dword. The bridge could absorb the first two-byte write into a dword buffer entry and then absorb the second two byte write into the same dword buffer entry. When the bridge performs the memory write, it can complete it in a single data phase. It is a violation of the specification, however, for a bridge to combine separate byte writes to the same location into a single write on the destination bus. As an example, assume that a bus master performs four separate memory writes to the same dword: the first writes to location zero in the dword, the second to location zero again, the third to location one and the fourth to location two. When the bridge performs the posted writes, it has to perform a single data phase transaction to write the first byte to location zero. It then performs a second single data phase memory write to locations zero (the second byte written to it by the bus master), one and two.

Collapsing Is Forbidden

Multiple writes to the same location(s) cannot be performed as a single write on the other side of the bridge. Collapsing is defined as reducing multiple writes posted to the same location to only one write that delivers the final write's data to the location. Two sequential writes (where at least one of the byte enables was asserted in both writes) posted for writing to the same dword must be performed as two separate transactions on the other bus.

Collapsing of writes is forbidden for any type of write transactions. The specification states that a bridge may allow collapsing within a specific range when a device driver indicates that this will not cause operational problems. How the device driver would indicate this to a bridge is outside the scope of the specification.

2.2 Memory Write Maximum Completion Limit

WHEN DATA IS WRITTEN TO A MEMORY TARGET, THE TARGET CAN HANDLE IT IN ONE OF THREE WAYS:

METHOD 1. THE TARGET CAN IMMEDIATELY ACCEPT THE DATA AND WRITE IT INTO MEMORY. HOW FAST THIS CAN BE ACCOMPLISHED IS DEPENDENT ON THE WRITE LATENCY OF THE MEMORY BEING WRITTEN TO (BUT IT SHOULD BE ABLE TO ACCOMPLISH THE WRITE WITH 16 CLOCKS).

METHOD 2. THE TARGET CAN IMMEDIATELY ACCEPT THE DATA INTO A POSTED MEMORY WRITE BUFFER.

METHOD 3. IF THE TARGET HAS A TEMPORARY CONDITION THAT PREVENTS IT FROM ACCEPTING THE DATA WITHIN 16 CLOCKS, IT CAN ISSUE A RETRY TO THE MASTER. THE KEY WORD HERE IS TEMPORARY. THE TARGET IS NOT ALLOWED TO ISSUE RETRIES INDEFINITELY TO THE MASTER ATTEMPTING THE WRITE. THE MAXIMUM COMPLETION LIMIT ON MEMORY WRITES APPLIES TO THIS CASE.

AFTER A TARGET TERMINATES A MEMORY WRITE TRANSACTION WITH A RETRY, IT MUST COMPLETE AT LEAST ONE DATA PHASE OF A MEMORY WRITE WITHIN:

- 334 CLOCKS FROM THE FIRST RETRY TERMINATION FOR SYSTEMS RUNNING AT 33 MHz OR SLOWER.
- 668 CLOCKS FROM THE FIRST RETRY TERMINATION FOR SYSTEMS RUNNING AT 66 MHz.

THIS 10 MICROSECOND (AT BOTH 33 MHz AND 66 MHz) TIME LIMIT IS CALLED THE MAXIMUM COMPLETION TIME. IF A TARGET IS PRESENTED WITH MULTIPLE MEMORY WRITES, THE MAXIMUM COMPLETION TIME IS MEASURED FROM THE TIME THE FIRST MEMORY WRITE TRANSACTION IS TERMINATED WITH RETRY UNTIL THE TIME THE FIRST DATA PHASE OF ANY MEMORY WRITE TO THE TARGET COMPLETES WITH SOMETHING OTHER THAN RETRY.

WHEN A TERMINATION OTHER THAN A RETRY OCCURS, THE TIME LIMIT STARTS OVER AGAIN WITH THE NEXT RETRY ON A MEMORY WRITE. THE ACTUAL TIME THAT THE DATA PHASE COMPLETES ALSO DEPENDS UPON WHEN THE MASTER REPEATS THE TRANSACTION. TARGETS MUST BE DESIGNED TO MEET THE MAXIMUM COMPLETION TIME REQUIREMENTS ASSUMING THE MASTER WILL REPEAT THE MEMORY WRITE TRANSACTION PRECISELY AT THE LIMIT OF THE MAXIMUM COMPLETION TIME.

DEVICES ARE NOT REQUIRED TO HONOR THIS TIME LIMIT DURING TRHFA (I.E., FOR 225 CLOCK CYCLES AFTER RST# IS DEASSERTED). FOR MORE INFORMATION, REFER TO "INITIALIZATION TIME VS. RUN TIME" ON PAGE 85.

Transaction Ordering and Deadlocks

This chapter described delayed transactions as well as the posting of memory writes. It should be fairly obvious that there must be some rules regarding the relationships between different transactions initiated on the various buses in the system. The chapter entitled "Transaction Ordering & Deadlocks" on page 649 describes the ordering rules, the model that they are based upon, and a number of deadlock scenarios that can arise and how they are avoided.

The Commands

The Previous Chapter

The previous chapter described the rules governing how much time a device may hold the bus in wait states during any given data phase. It described how soon after reset is removed the first transaction may be initiated and how soon after reset is removed a target device must be prepared to transfer data. The mechanisms that a target may use to meet the latency rules were described: Delayed Transactions, and posting of memory writes.

In This Chapter

This chapter defines the types of commands (i.e., transaction types) that a bus master may initiate when it has acquired ownership of the PCI bus.

The Next Chapter

Using timing diagrams, the next chapter provides a detailed description of PCI read transactions. It also describes the treatment of the Byte Enable signals during both reads and writes.

Introduction

When a bus master acquires ownership of the PCI bus, it may initiate one of the types of transactions listed in Table 7-1 on page 100. During the address phase of a transaction, the Command/Byte Enable bus, C/BE#[3:0], is used to indicate the command, or transaction, type. Table 7-1 on page 100 provides the setting that the initiator places on the Command/Byte Enable lines to indicate the type of transaction in progress. The sections that follow provide a description of each of the command types.

Table 7-1: PCI Command Types

C/BE[3:0]# (binary)	Command Type
0000	Interrupt Acknowledge
0001	Special Cycle
0010	I/O Read
0011	I/O Write
0100	Reserved
0101	
0110	Memory Read
0111	Memory Write
1000	Reserved
1001	
1010	Configuration Read
1011	Configuration Write
1100	Memory Read Multiple
1101	Dual Address Cycle
1110	Memory Read Line
1111	Memory Write-and-Invalidate

Interrupt Acknowledge Command

Introduction

In a PC-compatible system, interrupts can be delivered to the processor in one of three ways:

METHOD 1. In a single processor system (see Figure 7-1 on page 103), the interrupt controller asserts **INTR** to the x86 processor. In this case, the processor responds with an Interrupt Acknowledge transaction. This section describes that transaction.

METHOD 2. In a multi-processor system, interrupts can be delivered to the array of processors over the **APIC** (Advanced Programmable Interrupt Controller) bus in the form of message packets. For more information, refer to the MindShare book entitled *Pentium Processor System Architecture* (published by Addison-Wesley).

METHOD 3. In a system that supports **Message Signaled Interrupts**, interrupts can be delivered to the host/PCI bridge in the form of memory writes. For more information, refer to "Message Signaled Interrupts (MSI)" on page 252.

In response to an interrupt request delivered over the INTR signal line, an Intel x86 processor issues two Interrupt Acknowledge transactions (note that the P6 family processors only issues one) to read the interrupt vector from the interrupt controller. The interrupt vector tells the processor which interrupt service routine to execute.

Background

In an Intel x86-based system, the processor is usually the device that services interrupt requests received from subsystems that require servicing. In a PC-compatible system, the subsystem requiring service issues a request by asserting one of the system interrupt request signals, IRQ0 through IRQ15. When the IRQ is detected by the interrupt controller within the South Bridge (see Figure 7-1 on page 103), it asserts INTR to the host processor. Assuming that the host processor is enabled to recognize interrupt requests (the Interrupt Flag bit in the EFLAGS register is set to one), the processor responds by requesting the interrupt vector from the interrupt controller. This is accomplished by the processor performing the following sequence:

1. **The processor generates an Interrupt Acknowledge bus cycle.** *Please note that a P6 family processor does not generate this first Interrupt Acknowledge bus cycle.* No address is output by the processor because the address of the target device, the interrupt controller, is implicit in the bus cycle type. The purpose of this bus cycle is to **command the interrupt controller to prioritize** its **currently-pending requests** and select the request to be processed. The processor doesn't expect any data to be returned by the interrupt controller during this bus cycle.

2. **The processor generates a second Interrupt Acknowledge bus cycle to request the interrupt vector** from the interrupt controller. If this is a P6 family processor, this is the only Interrupt Acknowledge transaction it generates. BE0# is asserted by the processor, indicating that an 8-bit vector is expected to be returned on the lower data path, D[7:0]. To state this more precisely, the processor requests that the interrupt controller return the index into the interrupt table in memory. This tells the processor which table entry to read. The table entry contains the start address of the device-specific interrupt service routine in memory. In response to the second Interrupt Acknowledge bus cycle, the interrupt controller must drive the interrupt table index, or vector, associated with the highest-priority request currently pending back to the processor over the lower data path, D[7:0]. The processor reads the vector from the bus and uses it to determine the start address of the interrupt service routine that it must execute.

Figure 7-1: Typical PC Block Diagram—Single Processor

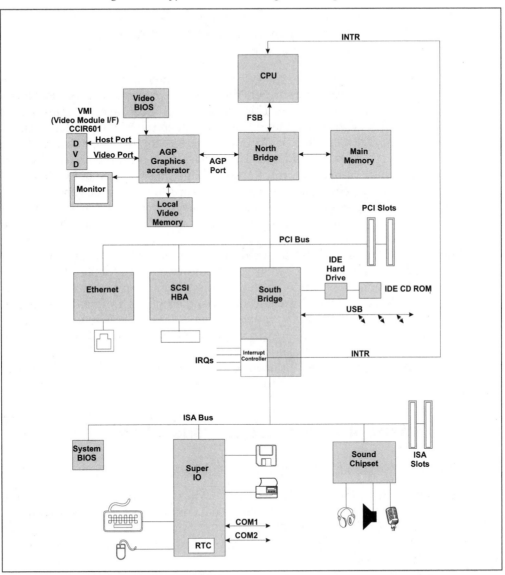

Host/PCI Bridge Handling of Interrupt Acknowledge

The following description assumes that the processor belongs to the P6 processor family and therefore only generates one Interrupt Acknowledge transaction in response to the assertion of INTR.

When the host/PCI bridge detects the start of an Interrupt Acknowledge on the host side, the bridge acquires ownership of the PCI bus and initiates a PCI Interrupt Acknowledge transaction. This transaction is illustrated in Figure 7-2 on page 106 and is described in the next section. When the PCI target that contains the interrupt controller (the South Bridge) detects the Interrupt Acknowledge transaction, it asserts DEVSEL# to claim the transaction. It then internally generates two, back-to-back interrupt acknowledge pulses to the 8259A interrupt controller, thereby emulating the double Interrupt Acknowledge generated by a pre-P6 Intel x86 processor. In response, the interrupt controller drives the interrupt vector onto the lower data path and asserts TRDY# to indicate the presence of the vector to the initiator (the host/PCI bridge). When the host/PCI bridge samples TRDY# and IRDY# asserted, it reads the vector from the lower data path and terminates the PCI Interrupt Acknowledge transaction. During this period, the bridge was either inserting wait states into the processor's Interrupt Acknowledge transaction, or could have handled it as a Deferred Transaction (refer to MindShare's *Pentium Pro and Pentium II System Architecture* book, published by Addison-Wesley). It then drives the 8-bit interrupt vector onto the processor's lower data path and the processor reads the vector from the bus. It then uses it to index into the memory-based interrupt table to get the start address of the interrupt service routine to execute.

PCI Interrupt Acknowledge Transaction

Figure 7-2 on page 106 illustrates the PCI interrupt acknowledge transaction.

CLOCK 1. The bridge does not drive an address onto the AD bus during the address phase, but must drive stable data onto the AD bus along with correct parity on the PAR line.
    THE C/BE bus contains the Interrupt Acknowledge command during the address phase.
CLOCK 2. The host/PCI bridge asserts IRDY# to indicate that it's ready to read the vector.
    IT simultaneously deasserts FRAME# to signal that this is final data phase.
    DURING the clock two, the target holds off the assertion of TRDY# and

DEVSEL# to force a wait state into the first data phase. This is necessary to permit the bridge sufficient time to turn off its AD bus output drivers before the target (the interrupt controller) begins to drive the requested interrupt vector back to the bridge on the AD bus. Clock two is referred to as the turnaround cycle.

CLOCK 3. The target (the South Bridge) has completed decoding the address phase information (address and command) and asserts DEVSEL# to claim the transaction.

THE host/PCI bridge samples DEVSEL# still deasserted on the rising-edge of clock three, indicating that the target has not yet claimed the transaction. As a result, the data phase is extended by an extra clock (clock three), a wait state tagged onto the data phase.

DURING the wait state (clock three) the target then drives the vector onto the data path(s) indicated by the byte enable settings on the C/BE bus (just BE0# asserted in an x86 environment, but a different processor type might ask for a 32-bit vector) and asserts TRDY# to indicate the presence of the requested vector.

THE byte enables are a duplicate of the byte enables asserted by the host processor during its second interrupt acknowledge bus cycle.

CLOCK 4. The host/PCI bridge samples DEVSEL# asserted on the rising-edge of clock 4, indicating that the target has claimed the transaction.

THE host/PCI bridge also samples IRDY# and TRDY# asserted on the rising-edge of clock four, indicating that the data is present (TRDY# asserted). It reads the vector from the AD bus.

THE target samples IRDY# asserted and FRAME# deasserted on the rising-edge of clock four, indicating that then initiator is ready to complete the final data phase (in fact, the only one) of the transaction.

Since the one and only data phase completed on the rising-edge of clock four, the initiator ceases to drive the byte enables and deasserts the IRDY# signal to return the bus to the idle state.

THE target deasserts TRDY# and DEVSEL# and ceases to drive the interrupt vector.

CLOCK 5. The bus returns to the idle state (FRAME# and IRDY# both deasserted) on the rising-edge of clock five.

The host/PCI bridge passes the vector back to the processor which then reads the vector off its data bus and terminates the Interrupt Acknowledge transaction.

Figure 7-2: PCI Interrupt Acknowledge Transaction

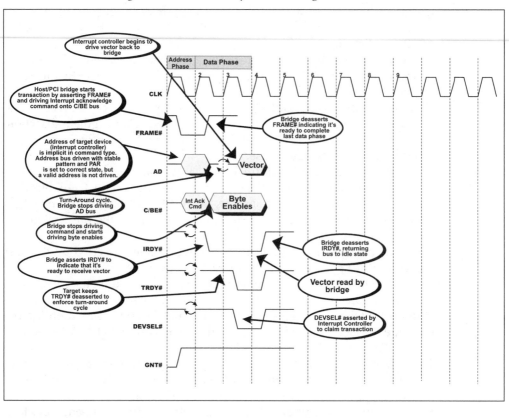

PowerPC PReP Handling of INTR

In a PowerPC PReP-compliant platform, the programmer performs a one to four byte memory read from memory location BFFFFFF0h. When the host/PCI bridge detects this read, it acquires ownership of the PCI bus and initiates the PCI Interrupt Acknowledge transaction. When the interrupt controller supplies the requested vector to the host/PCI bridge, the bridge in turn supplies it to the processor and asserts TA# (Transfer Acknowledge) to indicate its presence. The processor reads the vector and places it into the GPR (General Purpose Register) indicated by the load instruction being executed. The programmer then uses the vector as an index into the interrupt table.

In a system based on a processor other than an x86, the interrupt vector requested by the processor may be four bytes rather one byte wide. If this were the case, the host/PCI bridge would assert all four byte enables to request a 32-bit vector.

Special Cycle Command

General

The Special Cycle command is issued by an initiator to broadcast a message to one or more targets residing on a target PCI bus. Each target on the PCI bus must examine the message to determine whether the message applies to it (a target may be designed not to recognize any messages or to recognize only specific messages; most targets don't pay any attention to messages delivered via Special Cycle). Via its the Special Cycles bit in its configuration Command register (see Figure 7-3 on page 109), a target's ability to monitor Special Cycle messages can be enabled or disabled. As an example of message passing using the Special Cycle, Intel x86 processors use the Special Cycle to indicate when they are going into a Halt or Shutdown condition.

During the address phase, a valid address is not driven onto the AD bus (because Intel x86 processors do not supply a valid address when they initiate a Special Cycle transaction). The AD bus must be driven with a stable pattern, however, so that the parity of the AD bus (the PAR signal) and the command bus content can be checked for correctness. In the address phase, the initiator uses C/BE#[3:0] to indicate that this is a Special Cycle transaction.

During the data phase, the initiator broadcasts the message type on AD[15:0] and an optional, message-dependent data field may be presented on AD[31:16]. The message and associated data are only valid during the clock when IRDY# is asserted. The data contained in and the timing of subsequent data phases is message dependent (the subject of multiple data phase Special Cycles is discussed in "Multiple Data Phase Special Cycle Transaction" on page 112). If necessary, the initiator may insert wait states into the transaction by deasserting IRDY#, but targets cannot insert wait states. In addition, no target should assert DEVSEL# when it recognizes a message. Since multiple targets can recognize the message type, there would be contention on the DEVSEL# line if they all tried to claim the transaction by asserting DEVSEL#. The targets must watch IRDY# to determine the presence of the message being sent by the initiator. Since all Special Cycles are intended to pass messages only to PCI targets, a subtractive decode bridge should not pass the transaction onto an expansion bus (such as ISA or EISA) when it doesn't see any target claim the transaction by asserting DEVSEL#.

Since no target is permitted to respond to the Special Cycle transaction (DEVSEL# is not asserted), another means must be used to end the transaction. The initiator must perform a Master Abort to end the transaction (in other words, return the bus to the idle state in a graceful fashion). Master Abort is explained in "Master Abort: Target Doesn't Claim Transaction" on page 176. It must be noted that when the initiator terminates the transaction with a Master Abort (because DEVSEL# was not asserted by a target), it must not set the Received Master Abort bit in its configuration Status register. That bit should only be set in a transaction wherein DEVSEL# is expected but not received.

Table 7-2 on page 108 provides the message types currently defined in the specification. The first two message codes, 0000h and 0001h, are defined as Shutdown and Halt. Message code 0002h is reserved for use by Intel x86 processors to broadcast x86-specific messages that may be defined in the future. In that case, during the data phase AD[15:0] would contain 0002h, while AD[31:16] would contain the x86-specific message. The x86-specific message codes are defined by Intel in product-specific documentation. Message codes 0003h through FFFFh are reserved for future use. Allocation of new message codes is handled through the SIG and requests for allocation of new message codes should be submitted to the SIG in writing.

During system design, each PCI device that is capable of recognizing or broadcasting message types must be hardwired with the message types it recognizes or broadcasts. Upon recognition of any of its assigned message types, a PCI target should take the application-specific action defined by the message type received.

Table 7-2: Message Types Defined In the Specification

Message Code (on AD[15:0])	Message Type
0000h	**Shutdown**. Processor is going into a Shutdown condition due to a severe, unrecoverable software problem.
0001h	**Halt**. The processor has fetched and is executing a Halt instruction. In response, the processor issues the Halt message using the Special Cycle transaction to indicate to all external devices that it is going to cease fetching and executing instructions.

Table 7-2: Message Types Defined In the Specification (Continued)

Message Code (on AD[15:0])	Message Type
0002h	**x86-specific message**. AD[31:16] contains the Intel device-specific message. None are currently defined.
0003h-FFFFh	**Reserved**.

The Special Cycle command takes a minimum of six clocks to complete (more if the initiator inserts wait states by delaying the presentation of the message and the assertion of IRDY#). One additional clock is required for the turn-around cycle before the next transaction is initiated on the bus. Therefore, assuming that the master immediately outputs the message upon entry to the data phase, a total of seven clock cycles are required from the start of the Special Cycle to the start of the next cycle.

Figure 7-3: Command Register Bit Assignment

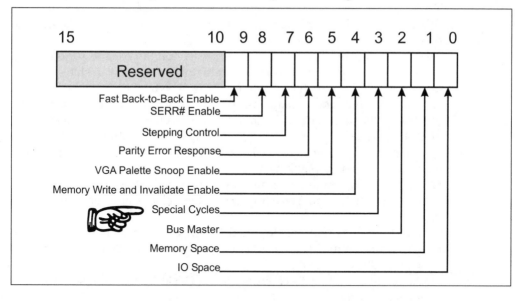

Special Cycle Generation Under Software Control

Host/PCI bridges are not required to provide a mechanism that permits Special Cycles to be generated under software control. If the bridge does provide this capability, however, a detailed description of a mechanism can be found in

"Software Generation of Special Cycles" on page 329 and "Special Cycle Trans-actions" on page 619. Additional information can also be found in "PCI BIOS Present Call" on page 680.

Special Cycle Transaction

Single-Data Phase Special Cycle Transaction

Figure 7-4 on page 111 illustrates the special cycle transaction timing.

CLOCK 1. During the address phase, the initiator drives a stable pattern onto the AD bus and PAR. This is only for parity checking purposes. No actual address is driven. In addition, the initiator drives the special cycle command onto the C/BE bus during the address phase.

CLOCK 2. At the end of the address phase, the data phase begins. The initiator drives the message code onto AD[15:0] and any optional, message-related data onto AD[31:16].

THE initiator also asserts the appropriate byte enable lines (i.e., just C/BE#[1:0] if the message is Halt or Shutdown, or C/BE#[3:0] if it's message type two).

THE message is only guaranteed to be present on the AD bus for one clock when the initiator asserts IRDY#. The initiator can insert wait states into the data phase by delaying the assertion of IRDY#. When the message is driven onto the AD bus, the initiator asserts IRDY# to indicate its presence. As illustrated, the message may or may not be driven for more than one clock.

WHEN the initiator asserts IRDY# to indicate it's presenting the message, it simultaneously deasserts FRAME# to indicate that this is the one and only data phase of this transaction.

IT is legal for the initiator to delay assertion of IRDY# (and therefore the presentation of the message) for up to seven clocks after entering a data phase.

CLOCK 3. The targets that are designed to recognize special cycles latch the message information from the AD bus when IRDY# is sampled asserted on the rising-edge of clock three.

No target is permitted to claim a Special Cycle transaction, so DEVSEL# remains deasserted.

CLOCK 4. See Clock 7.
CLOCK 5. See Clock 7.
CLOCK 6. See Clock 7.

CLOCK 7. Once the initiator presents the message and asserts IRDY# to indicate its presence, it must keep IRDY# asserted for four additional clocks to provide four clocks of guaranteed processing to time to the targets to process the message. If it were to deassert IRDY# sooner than this, the bus would return to the idle state and another master could start a transaction targeting one of the targets that just received the message. The target might not be able to handle this gracefully. On the flip-side of the coin, the targets that received the message must be done processing it and be prepared to deal with another transaction that might be initiated four clocks after message delivery.

As a variation, assume that the initiator did not assert IRDY# until clock cycle four. The initiator must then keep IRDY# asserted until clock nine, thereby prolonging the transaction to permit the targets a total of four clock from the delivery of the message (on clock five) to process it.

Figure 7-4: Special Cycle Transaction

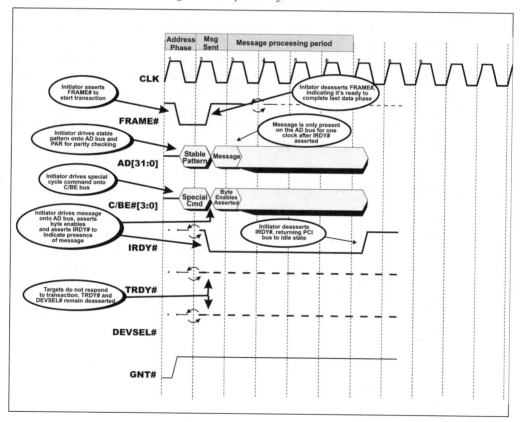

Multiple Data Phase Special Cycle Transaction

It is permissible for an initiator to deliver multiple packets of message information during the special cycle. No messages are currently defined that provide this capability, however. The target(s) latch the first message packet on the rising-edge of the clock when IRDY# is first sampled asserted. In each data phase, FRAME# would be kept asserted when IRDY# is asserted, indicating that there is at least one more data phase. FRAME# would remain asserted until IRDY# is asserted for the transmission of the last message data packet. It is deasserted simultaneously with the final IRDY# assertion. The message type encoded on AD[15:0] may imply the number of additional message packets to be delivered or the data field encoded on AD[31:16] may state the number of packets. The second data phase starts during the clock cell immediately following the first assertion of IRDY#.

Although the specification doesn't clearly state so, the author interprets the specification as indirectly stating that the initiator can deassert IRDY# during the second (and any subsequent) data phase until it has placed the next message packet on the AD bus. Each additional data phase completes when IRDY# is sampled asserted. During the final data phase, the initiator deasserts FRAME# when it asserts IRDY#, indicating that this is the last data phase. When the final data transfer completes, the initiator must keep IRDY# asserted for at least four additional clocks before performing a Master Abort to return the bus to the idle state. As previously stated, this time period is required to give the target(s) sufficient time to "process" the message. The specification does not explain what form this "processing" might take (because it would be subsystem specific).

IO Read and Write Commands

The IO read and write commands are used to transfer data between the initiator and the currently-addressed I/O target (a device's IO register set). The target must decode the entire 32-bit address. For a detailed description of IO addressing refer to "PCI IO Addressing" on page 146. For a detailed description of read and write transactions, refer to "Read Transfers" on page 123 and "Write Transfers" on page 135.

Accessing Memory

The PCI specification defines five commands utilized to access memory:

- Memory Read command, frequently abbreviated as MR.
- Memory Write command, frequently abbreviated as MW.
- Optional **bulk memory commands** are performance enhancement tools:
  - Memory Read Multiple command, frequently abbreviated as MRM.
  - Memory Read Line command, frequently abbreviated as MRL.
  - Memory Write-and-Invalidate command, frequently abbreviated as MWI.

Target Support For Bulk Commands Is Optional

It is optional whether or not a memory target supports the bulk commands. If it doesn't, it must alias them to the respective basic memory access command:

- The MRL and MRM should be aliased to (i.e., be treated the same as) the Memory Read command.
- The MWI should be aliased to the Memory Write command.

Cache Line Size Register And the Bulk Commands

Refer to Figure 7-5 on page 114. The specification says that the Cache Line Size configuration register (described in "Cache Line Size Register" on page 376) must be implemented by bus masters that utilize the Memory Write-and-Invalidate command (described in "Memory Write-and-Invalidate Command" on page 117). It also strongly recommends that this register be implemented for bus masters that utilize the Memory Read (MR), Memory Read Line (MRL) and Memory Read Multiple (MRM) commands.

If the Cache Line Size configuration register is implemented, the initiator should follow the usage guidelines outlined in Table 7-3 on page 115 in deciding which form of the memory read command to use when reading from memory reads. If an initiator accesses memory and does not implement the Cache Line Size configuration register, it should follow the same guidelines, assuming a cache line size of 16 or 32 bytes.

Figure 7-5: Cache Line Size Configuration Register

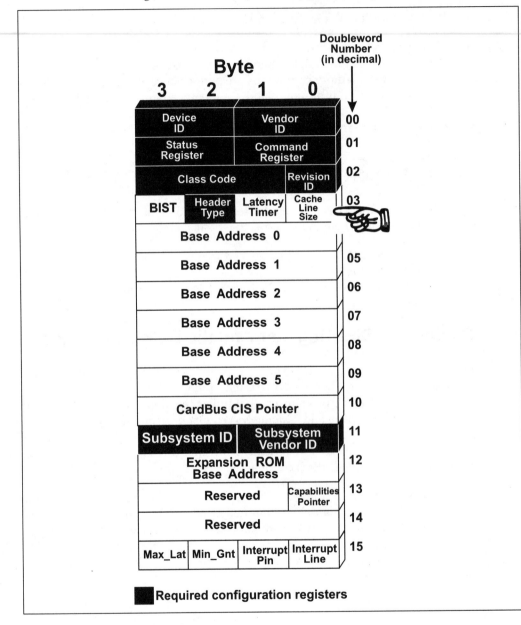

Bulk Commands Are Optional Performance Enhancement Tools

When a bus master uses the Memory Read Line or the Memory Read Multiple commands, it is indicating that it knows that the target memory is well-behaved (in other words, it's Prefetchable memory, not a memory-mapped I/O device). Prefetchable memory is defined in "What Is Prefetchable Memory?" on page 93. A master should use the Memory Read command when reading from memory-mapped I/O. If the read traverses a bridge, use of the bulk read commands (Memory Read Line or Memory Read Multiple) gives the bridge permission to prefetch ahead of the master's transaction to boost performance. This would permit the bridge to establish a buffered link through the bridge between the initiator and the target, with the bridge loading the prefetch buffer from the memory on the destination bus and the initiator reading the data from the other end of the buffer on the originating bus. This would result in a dramatic improvement in performance.

The specification strongly recommends that the bulk read/write commands be used when transferring large blocks of data to or from memory. Once again, these commands are Memory Write-and-Invalidate, Memory Read Line and Memory Read Multiple (the unspoken word here is "line").

Table 7-3: Preferred Use of Read Commands

Read Command Type	To Be Used When
Memory Read (MR)	Use when reading data from non-prefetchable memory (e.g., memory-mapped I/O), or if the characteristics of the memory target aren't known, or if reading a single dword.
Memory Read Line (MRL)	Use when reading more than one dword but no more than a cache line in Prefetchable memory space. By using this command, the bus master is indicating that it has specific knowledge that starting at the start address issued and up to the next cache line boundary minus one is well-behaved, Prefetchable memory. This gives limited prefetching permission (up to the next line boundary) to any bridges that the read has to traverse.

Table 7-3: Preferred Use of Read Commands (Continued)

Read Command Type	To Be Used When
Memory Read Multiple (MRM)	Use when a read crosses a cache line boundary in a Prefetchable memory range. By using this command, the bus master is indicating that it has specific knowledge that starting at the start address issued and up to the end of the next cache line (after this one) is well-behaved, Prefetchable memory. This gives less-constrained prefetching permission to any bridges that the read has to traverse.

Bridges Must Discard Prefetched Data Not Consumed By Master

The revision 1.1 *PCI-to-PCI Bridge Architecture Spec* states that a bridge that has prefetched memory read data for a master must discard any prefetched read data that the master doesn't actually end up reading. The spec poses the following example scenario as a demonstration of a problem that will result if a bridge doesn't discard prefetched data that wasn't consumed.

STEP 1 The processor has two buffers in main memory that occupy adjacent memory regions.

STEP 2. The processor writes data into the first memory buffer and then instructs a bus master beyond a PCI-to-PCI bridge to read and process the data.

STEP 3. The bus master starts its memory read using one of the bulk memory read commands, thus giving the bridge permission to prefetch ahead of the master while reading from main memory. The bridge ends up prefetching past the end of the first memory buffer into the second one, but the bus master only actually reads the data from the first buffer area.

STEP 4. The bridge does not discard the unused data that was prefetched from the second buffer.

STEP 5. The processor writes data into the second memory buffer and then instructs a bus master (the same master or a different one) beyond the same PCI-to-PCI bridge to read and process the data.

STEP 6. The bus master starts its memory read at the start address of the second buffer. The bridge delivers the data that it prefetched from the beginning of the second buffer earlier. *This is stale data and doesn't reflect the latest data written into the second memory buffer.*

Writing Memory

The initiator may use the Memory Write or the Memory Write-and-Invalidate command to update data in memory.

Memory Write Command

This command is used to transfer one or more data items (dwords or quadwords) to memory. As the target asserts TRDY# in each data phase, it has assumed responsibility for maintaining the coherency of the data. This can be accomplished by ensuring that any software-transparent posting buffer is flushed prior to synchronization events such as interrupts, or the updating of an IO status register or memory flag being passed through the device that contains the posted-write buffer (i.e., a bridge).

Memory Write-and-Invalidate Command

Problem. Refer to Figure 7-6 on page 120. Assume that a PCI master initiates a Memory Write to main memory.

The host/PCI bridge initiates a transaction on the processor bus to allow the processor's cache(s) to snoop the transaction. One of the processors experiences a snoop hit on a modified line. This means that the initiator is about to update a stale line in memory. One option is that the cache could invalidate the cache line. This, however, would be a mistake. The fact that the line is marked modified indicates that some or all of the information in the line is more current than the corresponding line in memory that the master is attempting to write to. The Memory Write being performed by the current initiator is updating all or a subset of the memory line (using the Memory Write command doesn't indicate how much data will be written), making the data it will supply even more current than that already in the corresponding locations of the processor's modified line. Trashing the line from the cache may trash some data that is more current than that in the memory line and that the PCI master may not end up writing to.

If the host/PCI bridge permits the PCI master to complete the Memory Write to main memory and then the processor flushes the modified cache line to main memory, the data just written by the initiator is over-written by the data in the cache line (some of which is older than the bytes just written by the master). This obviously isn't acceptable. There are **three possible courses** of action.

1. One course of action would be to force the PCI master that is attempting the write to surrender the bus (issue it a Retry). The host/PCI bridge then allows the processor to transfer, or flush, the modified cache line to main memory. The processor invalidates its copy of the cache line because the master will subsequently update all or a subset of the memory line immediately after the cache line is flushed to memory. The next time that the master retries the Memory Write, it will be snooped in the processor caches again, this time resulting in a snoop miss. The master is therefore permitted to write data into the line in memory. The memory line now contains the most current data.

2. An alternate course of action would be for the host/PCI bridge to accept the first line written by the PCI master (or, if it's a short write, a subset thereof) into a buffer in the bridge. Meanwhile, the bridge sends the snoop back to the processor and, if there's a hit on a modified line, the processor writes the modified line into another buffer within the bridge. The bridge then merges the master's write data into the modified line supplied by the processor and then writes the resultant line into memory.

3. A third course of action would be to insert wait states into the first data phase of the master's transaction (the host/PCI bridge is permitted to keep TRDY# deasserted for up to 32 PCI clocks from the master's assertion of FRAME#). Meanwhile, the bridge sends the snoop back to the processor and, if there's a hit on a modified line, the processor writes the modified line into a buffer within the bridge. The bridge can then start accepting write data from the master and merges the master's write data into the modified line supplied by the processor and then writes the resultant line into memory.

Any way you look at it, this is not a great scenario from a performance perspective. Option 1 is better than options 2 and 3, but delays can still be incurred. If the master's write crosses a cache line boundary and the processing of the first line is not yet complete, the bridge would have to insert wait states in the first data phase of the second line until it catches up.

Description of Memory Write-and-Invalidate Command. The Memory Write-and-Invalidate command is identical to the Memory Write command except that it guarantees the transfer of a complete cache line (or multiple cache lines) during the current transaction. This implies that the Cache Line Size configuration register must be implemented in the master so that it can make the determination that the write starts on a cache line boundary and an entire cache line (or multiple cache lines) will be written.

When the host/PCI detects a Memory Write-and-Invalidate transaction initiated, it starts a snoop transaction on the processor bus. Even if it then detects a processor snoop hit on a modified line, the host/PCI bridge can immediately (even before the snoop result is seen) accept the master's line into memory. This is possible because the initiator has indicated that it is updating the entire memory line and all of the data in the modified cache line is therefore stale (because the processor's updates to that line occurred earlier in time then the PCI master's write of the entire line with new data). The processor that experienced the hit on the modified line may or may not flush it to the bridge. If it does, the bridge just throws it away. This increases performance by eliminating the requirement for the delay for snoop and line flush.

It is a requirement that the initiator must assert all of the byte enable signals during each data phase of the Memory Write-and-Invalidate transaction. It is also required that linear addressing be used. For information on the byte enables, refer to "Address/Data Bus, Command Bus, and Byte Enables" on page 37. For information on linear addressing, refer to "Linear (Sequential) Mode" on page 144.

More Information On Memory Transfers

For a detailed description of read and write transactions, refer to the chapters entitled "Read Transfers" on page 123 and "Write Transfers" on page 135.

PCI System Architecture

Figure 7-6: Example System Block Diagram

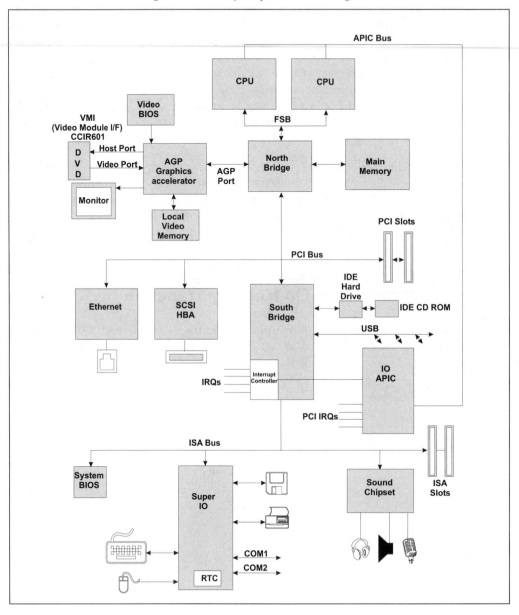

Configuration Read and Write Commands

Each PCI logical device (i.e., function) may implement up to 64 dwords of configuration registers that are used during system initialization to configure the logical device for proper operation in the system. To access a logical device's configuration registers, a configuration read or write command must be initiated and the device must sense its IDSEL input asserted during the address phase. IDSEL acts as a chip-select, AD[10:8] select the function (i.e., the logical device) within the package and the contents of AD[7:2] (during the address phase) are used to select one of the target function's 64 dwords of configuration space.

The x86 processor family implements two address spaces: memory and I/O. PCI requires the implementation of a third address space: configuration space. The mechanism used to generate configuration transactions is described in "Intro to Configuration Mechanisms" on page 321.

Dual-Address Cycle

The initiator uses the Dual-Address Cycle (DAC) command to indicate that it is using 64-bit memory addressing to address a memory target that resides above the 4GB boundary. This subject is covered in "64-bit Addressing" on page 287.

Reserved Bus Commands

Targets must not respond (must not assert DEVSEL#) in response to reserved bus commands. This means that use of a reserved bus command will result in the initiator experiencing a Master Abort.

8 *Read Transfers*

The Previous Chapter

The previous chapter defined the types of commands (i.e., transaction types) that a bus master may initiate when it has acquired ownership of the PCI bus.

This Chapter

Using timing diagrams, this chapter provides a detailed description of PCI read transactions. It also describes the treatment of the Byte Enable signals during both reads and writes.

The Next Chapter

The next chapter describes write transactions using example timing diagrams.

Some Basic Rules For Both Reads and Writes

The ready signal (IRDY# or TRDY#) from the device sourcing the data must be asserted when it starts driving valid data onto the data bus, while the device receiving the data keeps its ready line deasserted until it is ready to receive the data. Once a device's ready signal is asserted, it must remain so until the end of the current data phase (i.e., until the data is transferred).

A device must not alter its control line settings once it has indicated that it is ready to complete the current data phase. Once the initiator has asserted IRDY# to indicate that it's ready to transfer the current data item, it may not change the state of IRDY# or FRAME# regardless of the state of TRDY#. Once a target has asserted TRDY# or STOP#, it may not change TRDY#, STOP# or DEVSEL# until the current data phase completes.

Parity

Parity generation, checking, error reporting and timing is not discussed in this chapter. This subject is covered in detail in the chapter entitled "Error Detection and Handling" on page 199.

Example Single Data Phase Read

Refer to Figure 8-1 on page 126. Each clock cycle is numbered for easy reference and begins on its rising-edge. It is assumed that the bus master has already arbitrated for and been granted access to the bus. The bus master then must wait for the bus to become idle. This is accomplished by sampling the state of FRAME# and IRDY# on the rising-edge of each clock (along with GNT#). When both are sampled deasserted (along with GNT# still asserted), the bus is idle and a transaction may be initiated by the bus master.

CLOCK 1. On detecting bus idle (FRAME# and IRDY# both deasserted), the initiator starts the transaction on the rising-edge of clock one.

THE initiator drives out the address on AD[31:0] and the command on C/BE#[3:0].

THE initiator asserts FRAME# to indicate that the transaction has started and that there is a valid address and command on the bus.

CLOCK 2. All targets on the bus sample the address, command and FRAME# on the rising-edge of clock two, completing the address phase.

THE targets begin the decode to determine which of them is the target of the transaction.

THE initiator asserts IRDY# to indicate that is ready to accept the first read data item from the target.

THE initiator also deasserts FRAME# when it asserts IRDY#, thereby indicating that it is ready to complete the final data phase of the transaction.

THE initiator stops driving the command onto C/BE#[3:0] and starts driving the byte enables to indicate which locations it wished to read from the first dword.

No target asserts DEVSEL# in clock two to claim the transaction.

CLOCK 3. On the rising-edge of clock three, the initiator samples DEVSEL# deasserted indicating that the transaction has not yet been claimed by a target. The first (and only) data phase therefore cannot complete yet. It is extended by one clock (a wait state) in clock three.

DURING the wait state, the initiator must continue to drive the byte enables and to assert IRDY#. It must continue to drive them until the data phase completes.

A target asserts DEVSEL# to claim the transaction.

THE target also asserts TRDY# to indicate that it is driving the first dword onto the AD bus.

CLOCK 4. Both the initiator and the target sample IRDY# and TRDY# asserted on the rising-edge of clock four. The initiator also latches the data and the assertion of TRDY# indicates that the data is good. The first (and only) data item has been successfully read.

IF the target needed to sample the byte enables, it would sample them at this point. In this example, however, the target already supplied the data to the master without consulting the byte enables. This behavior is permitted if it's a well-behaved memory target (one wherein a read from a location doesn't change the content of the location). This is referred to as Prefetchable memory and is described in "What Is Prefetchable Memory?" on page 93.

THE target samples FRAME# deasserted, indicating that this is the final data phase.

BECAUSE the transaction has been completed, the initiator deasserts IRDY# and ceases to drive the byte enables.

THE target deasserts TRDY# and DEVSEL# and stops driving the data during clock four.

CLOCK 5. The bus returns to the idle state on the rising-edge of clock five.

Figure 8-1: Example Single Data Phase Read

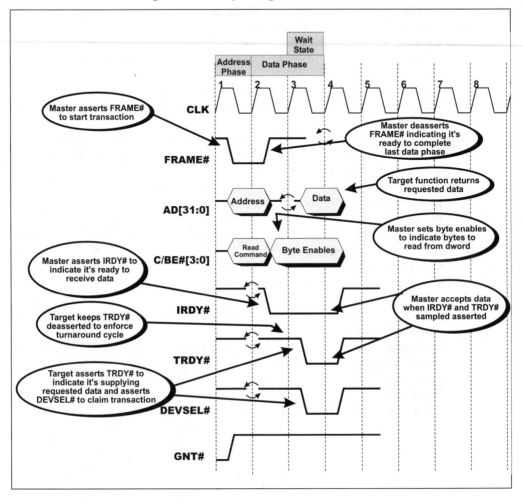

Example Burst Read

During the following description of an example burst read transaction, refer to Figure 8-2 on page 130.

CLOCK 1. At the start of clock one, the initiator asserts FRAME#, indicating that the transaction has begun and that a valid start address and command are on the bus. FRAME# must remain asserted until the initiator is ready to complete the last data phase.

AT the same time that the initiator asserts FRAME#, it drives the start address onto the AD bus and the transaction type onto the Command/Byte Enable lines, C/BE[3:0]#. The address and transaction type are driven onto the bus for the duration of clock one.

DURING clock one, IRDY#, TRDY# and DEVSEL# are not driven (in preparation for takeover by the new initiator and target). They are kept in the deasserted state by keeper resistors on the system board (required system board resource).

CLOCK 2. At the start of clock two, the initiator ceases driving the AD bus. A turn-around cycle (i.e., a dead cycle) is required on all signals that may be driven by more than one PCI bus agent. This period is required to avoid a collision when one agent is in the process of turning off its output drivers and another agent begins driving the same signal(s). The target will take control of the AD bus to drive the first requested data item (between one and four bytes) back to the initiator. During a read, clock two is defined as the turn-around cycle because ownership of the AD bus is changing from the initiator to the addressed target. It is the responsibility of the addressed target to keep TRDY# deasserted to enforce this period.

ALSO at the start of clock two, the initiator ceases to drive the command onto the Command/Byte Enable lines and uses them to indicate the bytes to be transferred in the currently-addressed dword (as well as the data paths to be used during the data transfer). Typically, the initiator will assert all of the byte enables during a read.

THE initiator also asserts IRDY# to indicate that it is ready to receive the first data item from the target.

UPON asserting IRDY#, the initiator does not deassert FRAME#, thereby indicating that this is not the final data phase of the example transaction. If this were the final data phase, the initiator would assert IRDY# and deassert FRAME# simultaneously to indicate that it is ready to complete the final data phase.

IT should be noted that the initiator does not have to assert IRDY# immediately upon entering a data phase. It may require some time before it's ready to receive the first data item (e.g., it has a buffer full condition). However, the initiator may not keep IRDY# deasserted for more than seven PCI clocks during any data phase. This rule was added in version 2.1 of the specification.

CLOCK 3. During clock cycle three, the target asserts DEVSEL# to indicate that it has recognized its address and will participate in the transaction.

THE target also begins to drive the first data item (between one and four bytes, as requested by the setting of the C/BE lines) onto the AD bus and asserts TRDY# to indicate the presence of the requested data.

CLOCK 4. When the initiator and the currently-addressed target sample TRDY# and IRDY# both asserted at the rising-edge of clock four, the first data item is read from the bus by the initiator, completing the first data phase. The first data phase consisted of clock cycle two and the wait state (turnaround cycle) inserted by the target (clock cycle three).

AT the start of the second data phase (clock edge four), the initiator sets the byte enables to indicate the bytes to be transferred within the next dword. It is a rule that the initiator must immediately output the byte enables for a data phase upon entry to the data phase. If for some reason the initiator doesn't know what the byte enable settings will be for the next data phase, it should keep IRDY# deasserted and not let the current data phase end until it knows what they will be.

IN this example, the initiator keeps IRDY# asserted upon entry into the second data phase, but does not deassert FRAME#. This indicates that the initiator is ready to read the second data item, but this is not the final data phase.

IN a multiple-data phase transaction, it is the responsibility of the target (if it supports bursting) to latch the start address into an address counter and to manage the address counter from data phase to data phase. As an example, upon completion of one data phase, the target would increment the latched address by four to point to the next dword (or by eight to point to the next quadword if it's a 64-bit transfer). It then examines the initiator's byte enable settings to determine the bytes to be transferred within the currently-addressed dword. Address counter management is covered in "Memory and IO Addressing" on page 143.

IN this example, the target is going to need some time before it can provide the second data item requested, so it deasserts TRDY# to insert a wait state (clock cycle five is the wait state) into the second data phase. In order to keep the data paths from floating, the target must continue to drive a stable data pattern, usually consisting of the last data item, onto the AD bus until it starts driving the second requested data item. This is illustrated in clock four. It is necessary to keep the AD bus from floating in order to prevent all of the CMOS input buffers connected to the AD bus from oscillating and drawing excessive current. Mentioned earlier in the book, this is one of the measures taken to conserve power.

CLOCK 5. At the rising-edge of clock five, the initiator samples TRDY# deasserted and, recognizing that the target is requesting more time for the transfer of the second data item, it inserts a wait state into the second data phase (clock cycle five).

DURING the wait state, the target begins to drive the second data item onto the AD bus and asserts TRDY# to indicate its presence.

CLOCK 6. When the initiator samples both IRDY# and TRDY# asserted on the rising-edge of clock six, it reads the second data item from the bus. This completes the second data phase. The second data phase consisted of clock cycles four and five.

AT the start of the third data phase, the initiator sets the byte enables to indicate the bytes to be transferred in the next dword. It also deasserts IRDY#, indicating that it requires more than one clock cycle before it will be ready to receive the data.

DURING clock cycle six, the target keeps TRDY# asserted, indicating that it is immediately driving the third requested data item onto the AD bus. In this example, however, the initiator requires more time before it will be able to read the data item (probably because it has a temporary buffer-full condition). This causes a wait state (clock cycle seven) to be inserted into data phase three.

CLOCK 7. The target must continue to drive the third data item onto the AD bus during the wait state (clock cycle seven).

DURING clock cycle seven, the initiator asserts IRDY#, indicating its willingness to accept the third data item on the next rising clock edge. It also deasserts FRAME#, indicating that this is the final data phase.

CLOCK 8. Sampling both IRDY# and TRDY# asserted at the rising-edge of clock eight, the initiator reads the third data item from the bus. The third data phase consisted of clocks six and seven. Sampling FRAME# deasserted on the rising-edge of clock eight instructs the target that this is the final data item.

THE overall burst transfer consisting of three data phases has been completed. The initiator deasserts IRDY#, returning the bus to the idle state (on the rising-edge of clock nine), and the target deasserts TRDY# and DEVSEL#.

CLOCK 9. The bus returns to the idle state (IRDY# and FRAME# both deasserted).

Figure 8-2: Read Transaction

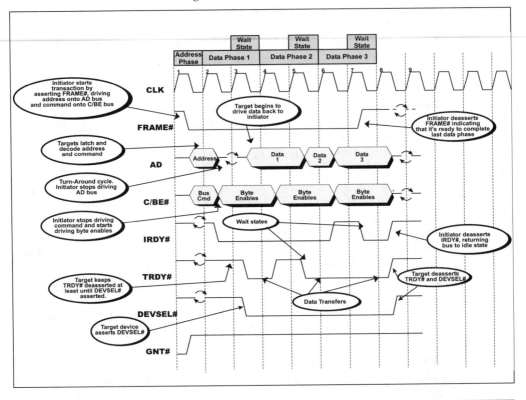

Treatment of Byte Enables During Read or Write

Byte Enables Presented on Entry To Data Phase

Immediately upon entry into a data phase, the initiator must present the proper byte enables to indicate which bytes are to be transferred within the current dword (or quadword). This is true even if the initiator deasserts IRDY# on entry to the data phase to indicate that it's not yet ready to transfer (read or write) the current data item. This means that the initiator should have extended the previous data phase (by keeping IRDY# deasserted) if it did not yet know which bytes were to be transferred in the current data phase.

The byte enable settings for a data phase must be presented unchanged for the duration of the data phase (i.e., until the data item transfers).

Byte Enables May Change In Each Data Phase

PCI permits burst transactions where the byte enables change from one data phase to the next. Furthermore, the initiator may use any byte enable setting, consisting of contiguous or non-contiguous byte enables. During a read transaction, the initiator will typically assert all of the byte enables during each data phase (because burst reads are typically reading a stream of dwords or quadwords), but it may use any combination.

It should be noted that every target may not be capable of handling non-contiguous byte enables. An example would be a PCI/ISA bridge. In this case, the target could take one of the following actions:

- assert SERR#.
- break the transaction into two 16-bit transfers.

Data Phase with No Byte Enables Asserted

As stated in the previous paragraph, any combination of byte enables is valid in any data phase. This includes a data phase with no byte enables asserted (a null data phase). This can occur for a number of reasons. Some examples would be:

- During a burst transfer, the **programmer may wish to "skip" a dword**. This would be accomplished by keeping all byte enables deasserted during that data phase. This method of skipping a dword is infinitely preferable to ending the transaction, rearbitrating for bus ownership, and resuming the transaction at the next dword to be transferred.
- At the initiation of a **64-bit transfer**, the initiator does not yet know whether the target device is a 64- or a 32-bit device. In certain cases, if a 32-bit device responds, this can result in the first data phase being null. This case is described in "Null Data Phase Example" on page 280.
- There are cases where the **last data phase** of a block transfer may not have any of the byte enables asserted. Assume that an expansion bus master (EISA or Micro Channel) has initiated a series of accesses with a PCI target. The bridge between the expansion and PCI buses will frequently packetize this series of bus master accesses into a PCI burst transfer. When the expansion bus master has completed its last data transfer to the bridge, the bridge signals this to the target by asserting IRDY# and deasserting FRAME#. This informs the target that the last data transfer is in progress. Since the bus master has already transferred all of the data, however, the bridge will not assert any of the byte enables during this last data phase.

When none of the byte enables are asserted, the target must react as follows:

- **On a read**: the target must ensure that no data or status is destroyed or altered as a result of this data transfer. The target must supply a stable pattern on all data paths and must generate the proper parity (for the AD and C/BE buses) on the PAR bit.
- **On a write**: the target must not store any data and the initiator must supply a stable pattern on all data paths and ensure that PAR is valid for the AD and C/BE buses.

Target with Limited Byte Enable Support

IO and memory targets may support restricted byte enable settings and may respond with Target Abort (see "Unsupported Byte Enable Combination Results in Target Abort" on page 148) for any other pattern. All devices must support any byte enable combination during configuration transactions.

Rule for Sampling of Byte Enables

If the target requires sampling of the byte enables (in order to precisely determine which bytes are to be transferred within the currently-addressed dword) during each data transfer, it must wait for the byte enables to be valid during each data phase (one clock into the data phase) before completing the transfer. An example of a device that requires sampling of byte enables would be a memory-mapped IO device. It should not accept a write to or a read from 8-bit registers within the currently-addressed dword until it has verified (via the byte enables) that the initiator is in fact addressing those ports.

If a target does not require examination of the byte enables on a read, the target must supply all four bytes. An example of a device that would not have to wait to sample the byte enables would be a Prefetchable memory target. Well-behaved memory yields the same data from a location no matter how many times the location is read from. In other words, performing a speculative read from the memory does not alter the data stored in the location. This type of memory target is designed to supply all four bytes in every data phase of a read burst. The initiator only take the bytes it's addressing (as indicated by the byte enable settings) and ignores the others.

Cases Where Byte Enables Can Be Ignored

If the target **memory is Prefetchable**, it ignores the byte enable settings in each data phase of a read and returns all four bytes (or eight bytes, if it's a 64-bit transfer) during each read data phase.

Performance During Read Transactions

As described earlier, a turn-around cycle must be included in the first data transfer of a read transaction. This being the case, a single data phase read from a target always consists of at least three clock cycles (one clock cycle for the address phase and two clock cycles for the data phase). At a clock rate of 33MHz, a read transaction consisting of a single data transfer would take 90ns to complete. An idle cycle (30ns in duration at 33MHz) must be included between transactions, resulting in 120ns per transaction. Using back-to-back single data phase read transfers, the data throughput would be 8.33 million transfers per second. If each transfer involved four bytes, the resultant transfer rate would be 33.33Mbytes per second.

In actual practice however, most read transactions involve a burst transfer of multiple objects (dwords or quadwords) between the initiator and the currently-addressed target. The read transaction involving multiple data phases only requires the turn-around cycle during the first data phase. The second through the last data phases can each be accomplished in a single clock cycle (if both the initiator and the currently-addressed target are capable of zero wait state transfers). The achievable transfer rate during the second through the last data phases is thus one transfer every 30ns (at a PCI bus speed of 33MHz), or 33 million transfers per second. If each data phase involves the transfer of four bytes, the resultant data transfer rate is 132Mbytes per second. Figure 8-3 on page 134 illustrates a read transaction consisting of three data phases, the second two of which complete with zero wait states.

Figure 8-3: Optimized Read Transaction (no wait states)

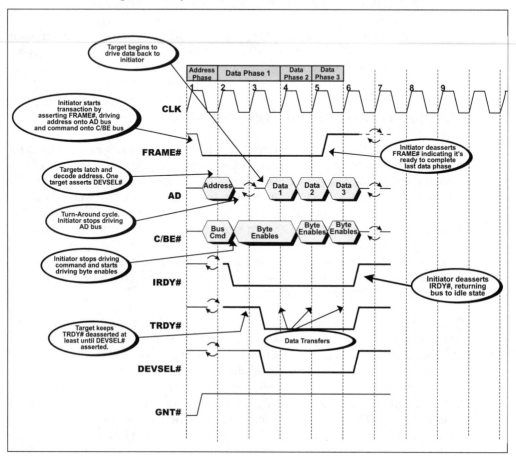

Write Transfers

The Previous Chapter

Using timing diagrams, the previous chapter provided a detailed description of PCI read transactions. It also described the treatment of the Byte Enable signals during both reads and writes.

In This Chapter

This chapter describes write transactions using example timing diagrams.

The Next Chapter

The next chapter describes the differences between the memory and IO addresses issued during the address phase.

Example Single Data Phase Write Transaction

Refer to Figure 9-1 on page 137. Each clock cycle is numbered for easy reference and begins and ends on the rising-edge. It is assumed that the bus master has already arbitrated for and been granted access to the bus. The bus master then must wait for the bus to become idle. This is accomplished by sampling the state of FRAME# and IRDY# on the rising-edge of each clock (along with GNT#). When both are sampled deasserted (clock edge one), the bus is idle and a transaction may be initiated by the bus master.

CLOCK 1. On detecting bus idle (FRAME# and IRDY# both deasserted), the initiator starts the transaction on the rising-edge of clock one.
THE initiator drives out the address on AD[31:0] and the command on C/BE#[3:0].
THE initiator asserts FRAME# to indicate that the transaction has started and that there is a valid address and command on the bus.

CLOCK 2 All targets on the bus sample the address, command and FRAME# on the rising-edge of clock two, completing the address phase.

THE targets begin the decode to determine which of them is the target of the transaction.

THE initiator asserts IRDY# to indicate that is driving the first write data item to the target over the AD bus. As long as the initiator asserts IRDY# within seven clocks after entering a data phase, it is within spec.

THE initiator also deasserts FRAME# when it asserts IRDY#, thereby indicating that it is ready to complete the final data phase of the transaction.

THE initiator stops driving the command onto C/BE#[3:0] and starts driving the byte enables to indicate which locations it wished to write to in the first dword.

THE target asserts DEVSEL# in clock two to claim the transaction.

THE target also asserts TRDY# to indicate its readiness to accept the first write data item.

CLOCK 3 The master samples DEVSEL# asserted, indicating that the target has claimed the transaction.

THE target samples IRDY# and the data on the AD bus. The asserted state of IRDY# indicates that it has just latched the first valid write data item.

THE asserted state of TRDY# indicates to the initiator that the target was ready to accept it, so both parties now know that the first data item has been transferred.

THE target also sampled FRAME# deasserted, indicating that this is the final data phase of the transaction.

BECAUSE the transaction has been completed, the initiator deasserts IRDY# and ceases to drive the byte enables and the data.

THE target deasserts TRDY# and DEVSEL# during clock four.

CLOCK 4 The bus returns to the idle state on the rising-edge of clock five.

Figure 9-1: Example Single Data Phase Write Transaction

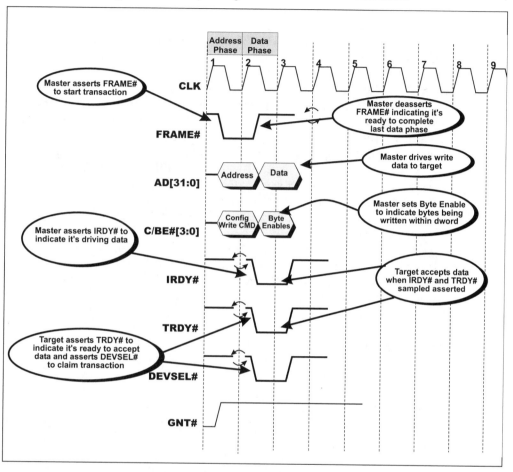

Example Burst Write Transaction

During the following description of the write transaction, refer to Figure 9-2 on page 141.

CLOCK 1. When both IRDY# and FRAME# are sampled deasserted (on the rising-edge of clock one), the bus is idle and a transaction may be initiated by the bus master whose GNT# signal is currently asserted by the bus arbiter. **AT** the start of clock cycle one, the initiator asserts FRAME# to indicate that the transaction has begun and that a valid start address and command are present on the bus. FRAME# remains asserted until the initiator is ready (has asserted IRDY#) to complete the last data phase. At the same time that the initiator asserts FRAME#, it drives the start address onto the AD bus and the transaction type onto C/BE#[3:0]. The address and transaction type are driven onto the bus for the duration of clock one.

DURING clock cycle one, IRDY#, TRDY# and DEVSEL# are not driven (in preparation for takeover by the new initiator and target). They are maintained in the deasserted state by the pullups on the system board.

CLOCK 2. At the start of clock cycle two, the initiator stops driving the address onto the AD bus and begins driving the first write data item. Since it doesn't have to hand off control of the AD bus to the target (as it does during a read), a turn-around cycle is unnecessary. The initiator may begin to drive the first data item onto the AD bus immediately upon entry to clock cycle two. Remember, though, that the initiator is still in spec as long as it presents the data within eight clocks after entering a data phase.

DURING clock cycle two, the initiator stops driving the command and starts driving the byte enables to indicate the bytes to be written to the currently-addressed dword.

THE initiator drives the write data onto the AD bus and asserts IRDY# to indicate the presence of the data on the bus. The initiator doesn't deassert FRAME# when it asserts IRDY# (because this is not the final data phase). Once again, it should be noted that the initiator does not have to assert IRDY# immediately upon entering a data phase. It may require some time before it's ready to source the first data item (e.g., it has a buffer empty condition). However, the initiator may not keep IRDY# deasserted for more than seven clocks during any data phase. This rule was added in version 2.1 of the specification.

DURING clock cycle two, the target decodes the address and command and asserts DEVSEL# to claim the transaction.

IN addition, it asserts TRDY#, indicating its readiness to accept the first data item.

CLOCK 3. At the rising-edge of clock three, the initiator and the currently-addressed target sample both TRDY# and IRDY# asserted, indicating that they are both ready to complete the first data phase. This is a zero wait state transfer (i.e., a one clock data phase). The target accepts the first data item from the bus on the rising-edge of clock three (and samples the byte enables in order to determine which bytes are being written), completing the first data phase.

THE target increments its address counter by four to point to the next dword.

DURING clock cycle three, the initiator drives the second data item onto the AD bus and sets the byte enables to indicate the bytes being written into the next dword and the data paths to be used during the second data phase.

THE initiator also keeps IRDY# asserted and does not deassert FRAME#, thereby indicating that it is ready to complete the second data phase and that this is not the final data phase. Assertion of IRDY# indicates that the write data is present on the bus.

CLOCK 4. At the rising-edge of clock four, the initiator and the currently-addressed target sample both TRDY# and IRDY# asserted, indicating that they are both ready to complete the second data phase. This is a zero wait state data phase. The target accepts the second data item from the bus on the rising-edge of clock four (and samples the byte enables to determine which data lanes contain valid data), completing the second data phase.

THE initiator requires more time before beginning to drive the next data item onto the AD bus (it has a buffer-empty condition). It therefore inserts a wait state into the third data phase by deasserting IRDY# at the start of clock cycle four. This allows the initiator to delay presentation of the new data, but it must set the byte enables to the proper setting for the third data phase immediately upon entering the data phase.

IN this example, the target also requires more time before it will be ready to accept the third data item. To indicate the requirement for more time, the target deasserts TRDY# during clock cycle four.

THE target once again increments its address counter to point to the next dword.

DURING clock cycle four, although the initiator does not yet have the third data item available to drive, it must drive a stable pattern onto the data paths rather than let the AD bus float (required power conservation measure). The specification doesn't dictate the pattern to be driven during this period. It is usually accomplished by continuing to drive the previous data item. The target will not accept the data being presented to it for two reasons:

- By deasserting TRDY#, it has indicated that it isn't ready to accept data.
- By deasserting IRDY#, the initiator has indicated that it is not yet presenting the next data item to the target.

CLOCK 5. When the initiator and target sample IRDY# and TRDY# deasserted at the rising-edge of clock five, they insert a wait state (clock cycle five) into the third data phase.

DURING clock cycle five, the initiator asserts IRDY# and drives the final data item onto the AD bus.

THE initiator also deasserts FRAME# to indicate that this is the last data phase.

THE initiator must continue to drive the byte enables for the third data phase until it completes.

THE target keeps TRDY# deasserted, indicating that it is not yet ready to accept the third data item.

CLOCK 6. At the rising-edge of clock six, the initiator samples IRDY# asserted indicating that it is presenting the data, but TRDY# is still deasserted (because the target is not yet ready to accept the data item).

THE target also samples FRAME# deasserted, indicating that the final data phase is in progress. The only thing impeding the completion of the final data phase now is the target (by keeping TRDY# deasserted until it is ready to accept the final data item).

IN response to sampling TRDY# deasserted on clock edge six, the target and initiator insert a second wait state (clock cycle six) into the third data phase. During the second wait state, the initiator continues to drive the third data item onto the AD bus and maintains the setting on the byte enables. The target keeps TRDY# deasserted, indicating that is not ready to accept the third data item yet.

CLOCK 7. At the rising-edge of clock seven, the target and initiator sample IRDY# asserted, indicating that the initiator is still presenting the data, but TRDY# is still deasserted. In response, the target and initiator insert a third wait state (clock cycle seven) into the third data phase.

DURING the third wait state, the initiator continues to drive the third data item onto the AD bus and maintains the setting on the byte enables.

THE target now asserts TRDY#, indicating that it is ready to complete the final data phase.

CLOCK 8. At the rising-edge of clock eight, the target and initiator sample both IRDY# and TRDY# asserted, indicating that both the initiator and the target are ready to end the third and final data phase. In response, the third data phase is completed on the rising-edge of clock eight. The target accepts the third data item from the AD bus. The third data phase consisted of four clock periods (the first clock cycle of the data phase, clock cycle four, plus three wait states).

DURING clock cycle eight, the initiator ceases to drive the data onto the AD bus, stops driving the C/BE bus, and deasserts IRDY# (returning the bus to the idle state). The target deasserts TRDY# and DEVSEL#.

Figure 9-2: PCI Write Transaction

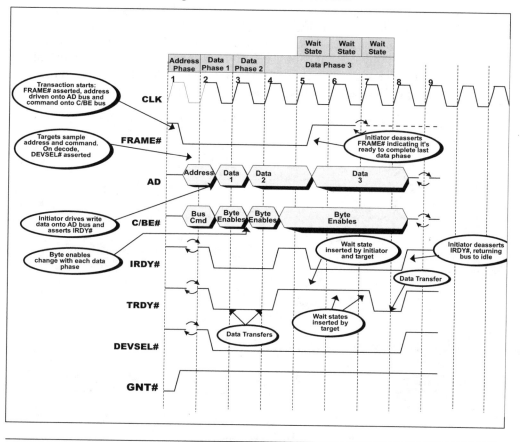

Performance During Write Transactions

Transactions wherein an initiator performs a single data phase write to a target consist of at least two cycles of the PCI clock (the address phase and a one clock data phase). An idle cycle (at 33MHz, 30ns in duration) must be included between transactions. At a clock rate of 33MHz, a single data phase write transaction takes 90ns to complete. Using back-to-back single data phase write transfers, the data throughput would be 11.11 million transfers per second. If each transfer involved four bytes, the resulting transfer rate would be 44.44Mbytes per second.

The first through the last data transfer of a burst write transaction can each be accomplished in a single clock cycle (if both the initiator and the currently-addressed target are capable of zero wait state data phases). The achievable transaction rate during the first through the last data phases is thus one transfer every 30ns (at a PCI bus speed of 33MHz), or 33 million transfers per second. If each transfer involves the transfer of four bytes, the data transfer rate is 132Mbytes per second. Figure 9-3 on page 142 illustrates a write transaction consisting of three zero wait state data phases.

Figure 9-3: Optimized Write Transaction (no wait states)

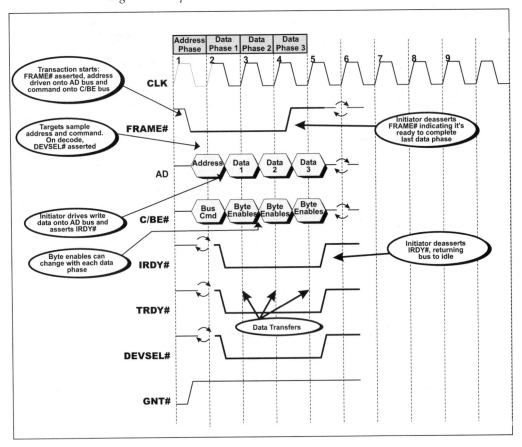

10 Memory and IO Addressing

The Previous Chapter

The previous chapter described write transactions using example timing diagrams.

In This Chapter

This chapter describes the differences between the memory and IO addresses issued during the address phase.

The Next Chapter

The next chapter provides a detailed description of Fast Back-to-Back transactions and address/data Stepping.

Memory Addressing

The Start Address

The start address issued during any form of memory transaction is a dword-aligned address presented on AD[31:2] during the address phase. It is a quad-word-aligned address if the master is starting a 64-bit transfer, but this subject is covered in "The 64-bit PCI Extension" on page 265.

Addressing Sequence During Memory Burst

The following discussion assumes that the memory target supports bursting. The memory target latches the start address into an address counter and uses it for the first data phase. Upon completion of the first data phase and assuming that it's not a single data phase transaction, the memory target must update its address counter to point to the next dword to be transferred.

On a memory access, the memory target must check the state of address bits one and zero (AD[1:0]) to determine the policy to use when updating its address counter at the conclusion of each data phase. Table 10-1 on page 144 defines the addressing sequences defined in the revision 2.2 specification and encoded in the first two address bits. Only two addressing sequences are currently defined:

- Linear (sequential) Mode.
- Cache Line Wrap Mode.

Table 10-1: Memory Burst Address Sequence

AD1	AD0	Addressing Sequence
0	0	**Linear**, or sequential, addressing sequence during the burst.
0	1	**Reserved**. Prior to revision 2.1, this indicated Intel Toggle Mode addressing. When detected, the memory target should signal a Disconnect with data transfer during the first data phase or a disconnect without data transfer in the second data phase.
1	0	**Cache Line Wrap** mode. First defined in revision 2.1.
1	1	**Reserved**. When detected, the memory target should signal a Disconnect with data transfer during the first data phase or a disconnect without data transfer in the second data phase.

Linear (Sequential) Mode

All memory devices that support multiple data phase transfers must support linear addressing. When the Memory Write-and-Invalidate command is used, the start address must be aligned on a cache line boundary and it must indicate (on AD[1:0]) linear addressing. At the completion of each data phase, (even if the initiator isn't asserting any Byte Enables in the next data phase) the memory target increments its address counter by four to point to the next sequential dword for the next data phase (or the next sequential quadword if performing 64-bit transfers)

Cache Line Wrap Mode

Support for Cache Line Wrap Mode is optional and is only used for memory reads. A memory target that supports this mode must implement the Cache Line Size configuration register (so it knows when the end of a line has been reached). The start address can be any dword within a line. At the start of each data phase of the burst read, the memory target increments the dword address in its address counter. When the end of the current cache line is encountered and assuming that the master continues the burst, the target starts the transfer of the next cache line at the same relative start position (i.e., dword) as that used in the first cache line.

Implementation of Cache Line Wrap Mode is optional for memory and meaningless for IO and configuration targets.

The author is not aware (some people, mostly my friends, would agree with that) of any bus masters that use Cache Line Wrap Mode when performing memory reads. It would mainly be useful if the processor were permitted to cache from memory targets residing on the PCI bus. This is no longer supported, but was in the 2.1 spec. The following explanation is only presented as background to explain the inclusion of Cache Line Wrap Mode in the earlier spec.

When a processor has a cache miss, it initiates a cache line fill transaction on its external bus to fetch the line from memory. If the target memory is not main memory, the host/PCI bridge starts a burst memory read from the PCI memory target using Cache Line Wrap Mode. Most processors (other than x86 processors) use Wrap addressing when performing a cache line fill. The processor expects the memory controller to understand that it wants the critical quadword first (because it contains the bytes that caused the cache miss), followed by the remaining quadwords that comprise the cache line. The transfer sequence of the remaining quadwords is typically circular (which is what Wrap Mode is all about).

The Intel x86 processors do not use wrap addressing (they use Toggle Mode addressing). The PowerPC 601, 603 and 604 processors use Wrap addressing. For a detailed description of the 486 cache line fill addressing sequence, refer to the Addison-Wesley publication entitled *80486 System Architecture*. For that used by the Pentium processor, refer to the Addison-Wesley publication entitled *Pentium Processor System Architecture*. For that used by the P6-family processors, refer to the Addison-Wesley publication entitled *Pentium Pro and Pentium II System Architecture*. For that used by the PowerPC 60x processors, refer to the Addison-Wesley publication entitled *PowerPC System Architecture*.

When Target Doesn't Support Setting on AD[1:0]

Although a memory target may support burst mode, it may not implement the addressing sequence indicated by the bus master during the address phase. When the master uses a pattern on AD[1:0] that the target doesn't support (Reserved or Cache Line Wrap), the target must respond as follows:

- The target must either issue a **Disconnect with data transfer** on the transfer of the first data item,
- or a **Disconnect without data transfer** during the second data phase.

This is necessary because the initiator is indicating an addressing sequence the target is unfamiliar with and the target therefore doesn't know what to do with its address counter.

There are two scenarios where the master may use a bit pattern not supported by the target:

- The master was built to a different rev of the spec. and is using a pattern that was reserved when the target was designed.
- The master indicates Cache Line Wrap addressing on a burst, but the target only supports Linear addressing.

PCI IO Addressing

Do Not Merge Processor IO Writes

To ensure that IO devices function correctly, bridges must never merge sequential IO accesses into a single data phase (merging byte accesses performed by the processor into a single-dword transfer) or a multiple data phase transaction. Each individual IO transaction generated by the processor must be performed on the PCI bus as it appears on the host bus. This rule includes accesses to both IO space and memory-mapped IO space (non-Prefetchable memory). Bridges are not permitted to perform byte merging in the their posted memory write buffers when writes are performed to non-Prefetchable memory (see "Byte Merging" on page 95 and "What Is Prefetchable Memory?" on page 93.

General

During an IO transaction, the start IO address placed on the AD bus during the address phase has the following format:

- AD[31:2] identify the target dword of IO space.
- AD[1:0] identify the least-significant byte (i.e., the start byte) within the target dword that the initiator wishes to perform a transfer with (00b = byte 0, 01b = byte 1, etc.).

At the end of the address phase, all IO targets latch the start address and the IO read or write command and begin the address decode.

Decode By Device That Owns Entire IO Dword

An IO device that only implements 32-bit IO ports can ignore AD[1:0] when performing address decode. In other words, it decodes AD[31:2] plus the command in deciding whether or not to claim the transaction by asserting DEVSEL#. It then examines the byte enables in the first data phase to determine which of the four locations in the addressed IO dword are being read or written.

Decode by Device With 8-Bit or 16-Bit Ports

An IO device may not implement all four locations within each dword of IO space assigned to it. As an example, within a given dword of IO space it may implement locations 0 and 1, but not 2 and 3. This type of IO target claims the transaction based on the *byte-specific* start address that it latched at the end of the address phase. In other words, it must decode the full 32-bit IO address consisting of AD[31:0]. If that 8-bit IO port is implemented in the target, the target asserts DEVSEL# and claims the transaction.

The byte enables asserted during the data phase identify the least-significant byte within the dword (the same one indicated by the setting of AD[1:0]) as well as any additional bytes (within the addressed dword) that the initiator wishes to transfer. It is illegal (and makes no sense) for the initiator to assert any byte enables of lesser significance than the one indicated by the AD[1:0] setting. If the initiator does assert any of the illegal byte enable patterns, the target must terminate the transaction with a Target Abort. Table 10-2 on page 147 contains some examples of valid IO addresses.

Table 10-2: Examples of IO Addressing

AD[31:0]	C/BE3#	C/BE2#	C/BE1#	C/BE0#	Description
00001000h	1	1	1	0	just location 1000h
000095A2h	0	0	1	1	95A2 and 95A3h
00001510h	0	0	0	0	1510h-1513h
1267AE21h	0	0	0	1	1267AE21h-1267AE23h

Unsupported Byte Enable Combination Results in Target Abort

If an IO target claims a transaction (asserts DEVSEL#) based on the byte-specific start address issued during the address phase, then subsequently examines the byte enables (issued during the data phase) and determines that it cannot fulfill the initiator's request, the target must respond by indicating a Target Abort (STOP# asserted, TRDY# and DEVSEL# deasserted) to the initiator. The Target Abort is covered in "Target Abort" on page 194. A typical example wherein the target must abort the transaction could result from the execution of the following x86 instruction:

```
IN    AX, 60 ;read 2 bytes from IO starting at Port 60h
```

When executed by a P6 family processor, quadword address 00000060h is driven onto the processor's byte enables during the processor's resultant IO read transaction and the processor asserts BE#[1:0], but not BE#[7:2]. This indicates to the host/PCI bridge that the processor is addressing locations 00000060h and 00000061h within the IO quadword starting at port 00000060h. Assuming that the host/PCI bridge doesn't incorporate either of these IO port addresses (it typically doesn't in a PC chipset), it arbitrates for ownership of the PCI bus and initiates a PCI IO read transaction.

During the address phase, the host/PCI bridge drives the address of the least-significant IO port to be read by the processor, 00000060h, onto the AD bus. The bridge determined this is the least-significant port to be read by examining the processor's byte enable settings and testing for the least-significant byte enable asserted by the processor. In this case, it is BE0#, corresponding to the first location in the currently-addressed quadword, 00000060h-00000067h.

In a PC-compatible machine, this is the address of the keyboard data port. Assuming that the keyboard controller resides on the PCI bus (e.g., embedded within or closely-associated with the PCI/ISA bridge), the keyboard controller would assert DEVSEL# to claim the transaction. Subsequently, when the processor's byte enables are presented during the data phase and are sampled by the target, C/BE#[1:0] are asserted, but not C/BE#[3:2]. This identifies IO addresses 60h and 61h as the target locations within the IO dword that starts at IO address 00000060h.

IO Port 61h has nothing to do with the keyboard interface (it is System Control Port B, a general IO status port on the system board). Assuming that IO Port 61h is not implemented in the same device that claimed the transaction, the device that claimed the transaction cannot service the request. It could supply the contents of Port 60h, but not that of Port 61h. Since there is no way to indicate partial fulfillment of desire in PCI, the target device must issue a Target Abort to the host/PCI bridge (STOP# asserted, TRDY# and DEVSEL# deasserted) and terminate the transaction with no data transferred. As a result, the initiator sets its Received Target Abort status bit and the target sets its Signaled Target Abort status bit (in their respective PCI configuration Status registers). The initiator reports this error back to the software in a device-specific fashion (e.g., by generating an interrupt to the processor).

An ISA expansion bus bridge doesn't have specific knowledge regarding all of the IO ports that exists on the ISA bus. It therefore claims IO transactions that are not claimed by PCI IO devices. Since it doesn't "know" what IO ports exists behind it, it can not judge whether to Target Abort the transaction based on the byte enable settings.

Null First Data Phase Is Legal

In the address phase, the master could supply a byte-specific start IO address addressing any of the bytes with an IO dword and then deassert all of the byte enables in the first data phase. This is legal.

IO Address Management

X86 Processor Cannot Perform IO Burst

Although burst IO transactions are legal in PCI, IO transactions are typically initiated by the processor and x86 processors cannot perform burst IO transactions. At the time of this writing, the author is unaware of any currently-existing processor that is capable of performing burst IO write transactions. An IN instruction (and IO read) or an OUT instruction (an IO write) specifies the AL, AH, or AX register as the source register for an IO write or the destination register for an IO read. This means that an IO read or write transaction initiated by the processor will have one, two, or four byte enables asserted, and can there only transfer a byte, word, a dword in each IO transaction.

It's easy to assume that the Intel x86 INS (input string) and OUTS (output string) instructions cause the processor to generate a burst IO read or write series, but this isn't so. When an INS (IN String) instruction is executed by the x86 processor, it results in a series of back-to-back IO read/memory write transaction pairs. The OUTS (Out String) instruction results in a string of back-to-back memory read and IO write bus cycles.

Burst IO Address Counter Management

As in any PCI read/write transaction, it is the responsibility of the IO target to latch the start address delivered by the initiator. It then assumes responsibility for managing the address for each subsequent data phase that follows the first data phase. Unlike memory address management, in PCI there is no explicit or implicit IO address sequencing from one data phase to the next. The initiator and the target must both understand and utilize the same IO address management. Two examples would be:

- Both the initiator and the target understand that the dword address (on AD[31:2]) delivered by the initiator is to be incremented by four at the completion of each data phase. In other words, the read or write transaction proceeds sequentially through the target's IO address space a dword at a time.
- Both the initiator and the target understand that the target doesn't increment the dword address for each subsequent data phase. This is how a designer would implement a 32-bit FIFO buffer front-end.

When IO Target Doesn't Support Multi-Data Phase Transactions

Many PCI IO targets are not designed to handle multi-data phase transactions. A target can determine that the initiator intends to perform a second data phase upon completion of the first by checking the state of FRAME# when IRDY# is sampled asserted in the first data phase. If IRDY# has been asserted by the initiator and it still has FRAME# asserted, this indicates that this is not the final data phase in the transaction.

If an IO target doesn't support multi-data phase transactions and the initiator indicates that a second data phase is forthcoming, the target must respond in one of two ways:

- When it's ready to transfer the first data item, **terminate the first data phase with a disconnect with data transfer** (STOP# and TRDY# asserted). The first data item is transferred successfully, but the initiator is forced to terminate the transaction at that point. It must then re-arbitrate for bus ownership and resume the transaction at the point of disconnection.
- **Terminate the second data phase with a disconnect without data transfer** (STOP# asserted, TRDY# deasserted). The first data phase completes normally. The initiator is then forced to terminate the transaction during the

second data phase without transferring any additional data. The initiator then re-arbitrates for bus ownership and resume the transaction at the point of disconnection.

Legacy IO Decode

2.2

LEGACY PC-COMPATIBLE DEVICES SUCH AS VGA AND IDE CONTROLLERS FREQUENTLY EXPECT TO BE LOCATED WITHIN FIXED LEGACY IO RANGES. SUCH DEVICES DO NOT IMPLEMENT BASE ADDRESS REGISTERS. INSTEAD, THE CONFIGURATION SOFTWARE IDENTIFIES IT AS A LEGACY DEVICE VIA ITS CLASS CODE REGISTER AND THEN ENABLES ITS IO DECODER(S) BY SETTING THE IO SPACE BIT IN ITS COMMAND REGISTER TO ONE.

A LEGACY IO DEVICE MAY OR MAY NOT OWN ALL OF THE BYTE LOCATIONS WITHIN A DWORD OF IO SPACE.

When Legacy IO Device Owns Entire Dword

A LEGACY IO DEVICE THAT DOES OWN ALL OF THE BYTES WITHIN THE CURRENTLY-ADDRESSED DWORD CAN PERFORM ITS DECODE USING THE DWORD-ALIGNED ADDRESS LATCHED FROM AD[31:2] AT THE END OF ADDRESS PHASE. IT DOES NOT HAVE TO USE AD[1:0].

When Legacy IO Device Doesn't Own Entire Dword

A LEGACY IO DEVICE THAT DOES NOT OWN ALL OF THE BYTE LOCATIONS WITHIN A DWORD MUST DECODE ALL 32 ADDRESS BITS LATCHED AT THE END OF THE ADDRESS PHASE TO DETERMINE IF IT OWNS THE BYTE-SPECIFIC START LOCATION BEING ADDRESSED AND ASSERTS DEVSEL# TO CLAIM THE TRANSACTION IF IT DOES. IT MUST THEN EXAMINE THE BYTE ENABLES TO DETERMINE IF THE INITIATOR IS ADDRESSING ADDITIONAL BYTE LOCATIONS WITHIN THE TARGET IO DWORD. IF IT OWNS ALL OF THE ADDRESSED IO PORTS, THE DEVICE CAN HONOR THE REQUEST. IF, HOWEVER, IT DOESN'T OWN THEM ALL, IT MUST ISSUE A TARGET ABORT TO THE INITIATOR. FOR MORE INFORMATION, REFER TO "UNSUPPORTED BYTE ENABLE COMBINATION RESULTS IN TARGET ABORT" ON PAGE 148.

THE EXCEPTION IS A BRIDGE THAT PERFORMS SUBTRACTIVE DECODE (SEE "SUBTRACTIVE DECODE (BY ISA BRIDGE)" ON PAGE 53). A SUBTRACTIVE DECODE BRIDGE DOES NOT HAVE TO CHECK THE STATE OF AD[1:0] BEFORE CLAIMING THE TRANSACTION (SUBTRACTIVELY) AND PASSING IT THROUGH TO THE ISA BUS.

11 *Fast Back-to-Back & Stepping*

The Previous Chapter

The previous chapter described the differences between the memory and IO addresses issued during the address phase.

This Chapter

This chapter provides a detailed description of Fast Back-to-Back transactions and address/data Stepping.

The Next Chapter

The next chapter describes the early termination of a transaction before all of the intended data has been transferred between the master and the target. This includes descriptions of Master Abort, the preemption of a master, Target Retry, Target Disconnect, and Target Abort.

Fast Back-to-Back Transactions

Assertion of its grant by the PCI bus arbiter gives a PCI bus master access to the bus for a single transaction consisting of one or more data phases. If a bus master desires another access, it should continue to assert its REQ# after it has asserted FRAME# for the first transaction. If the arbiter continues to assert GNT# to the master at the end of the first transaction, the master may then immediately initiate a second transaction. However, a bus master attempting to perform two, back-to-back transactions usually must insert an idle cycle between the two transactions. This is illustrated in clock 6 of Figure 11-1 on page 154. If all of the required criteria are met, the master can eliminate the idle cycle between the two bus transactions. These are referred to as Fast Back-to-Back transactions. This can only occur if there is a guarantee that there will not be contention (on any signal lines) between the masters and/or targets involved in the two transactions. There are two scenarios where this is the case.

CASE 1. In the first case, the master guarantees that there will be no contention. It's optional whether or not a master implements this capability, but it's mandatory that targets support it.

CASE 2. In the second case, the master and the community of PCI targets collectively provide the guarantee.

The sections that follow describe these two scenarios.

Figure 11-1: Back-to-Back Transactions With an Idle State In-Between

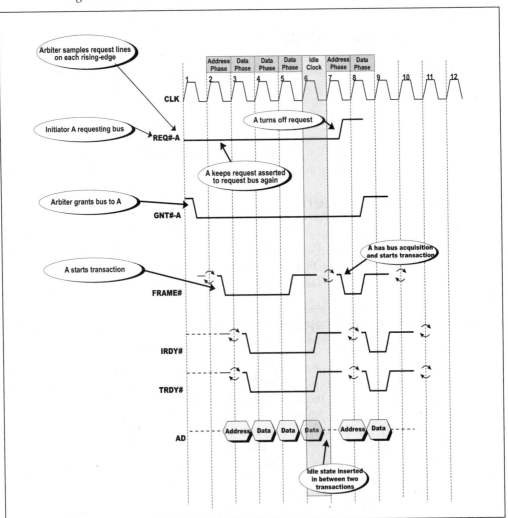

Decision to Implement Fast Back-to-Back Capability

The subsequent two sections describe the rules that permit deletion of the idle state between two transactions. Since they represent a fairly constraining set of rules, the designer of a bus master should make an informed decision as to whether or not it's worth the additional logic it would take to implement it.

Assume that the nature of a particular bus master is such that it typically performs long burst transfers whenever it acquires bus ownership. A SCSI Host Bus Adapter would be a good example. In this case, including the extra logic to support Fast Back-to-Back transactions would not be worth the effort. Percentage-wise, you're only saving one clock tick of latency in between each pair of long transfers.

Assume that the nature of another master is such that it typically performs lots of small data transfers. In this case, inclusion of the extra logic may result in a measurable increase in performance. Since each of the small transactions typically only consists of a few clock ticks and the master performs lots of these small transactions in rapid succession, the savings of one clock tick in between each transaction pair can amount to the removal of a fair percentage of overhead normally spent in bus idle time.

Scenario 1: Master Guarantees Lack of Contention

In this scenario (defined in revision 1.0 of the specification and still true in revision 2.x), the master must ensure that, when it performs a pair of back-to-back transactions with no idle state in between the two, there is no contention on any of the signals driven by the bus master or on those driven by the target. An idle cycle is required whenever AD[31:0], C/BE#[3:0], FRAME#, PAR and IRDY# are driven by different masters from one clock cycle to the next. The idle cycle allows one cycle for the master currently driving these signals to surrender control (cease driving) before the next bus master begins to drive these signals. This prevents bus contention on the bus master-related signals.

1st Must Be Write, 2nd Is Read or Write, But Same Target

The master must ensure that the same set of output drivers are driving the master-related signals at the end of the first transaction and the start of the second. This means that the master must ensure that it is driving the bus at the end of the first transaction and at the start of the second.

To meet this criteria, the first transaction must be a write transaction so the master will be driving the AD bus with the final write data item at the end of the transaction. The second transaction can be either a read or a write but must be initiated by the same master. This means that the master must keep its REQ# asserted to the arbiter when it starts the first transaction and must check to make sure that the arbiter leaves its GNT# asserted at the end of the first transaction. Whether or not the arbiter leaves the GNT# on the master is dependent on whether or not the arbiter receives any bus requests from other masters during this master's first transaction. Refer to Figure 11-2 on page 158.

CLOCK 1. When the master acquires bus ownership and starts the first transaction (on the rising-edge of clock one), it drives out the address and command and asserts FRAME#. The transaction must be a write.

THE initiator continues to assert its REQ# line to try and get the arbiter to leave the GNT# on it so it can immediately start the second transaction of the Fast Back-to-Back pair after the final data phase of the first transaction completes.

CLOCK 2. When the address phase is completed (on the rising-edge of clock two), the master drives the first data item onto the AD bus and sets the byte enables to indicate which data paths contain valid data bytes.

THE master asserts IRDY# to indicate the presence of the write data on the AD bus.

THE master simultaneously deasserts FRAME#, indicating that this is the final data phase of the write transaction.

THE target asserts DEVSEL# to claim the transaction.

THE target also asserts TRDY# to indicate its readiness to accept the first write data item.

CLOCK 3. At the conclusion of the first data phase (on the rising-edge of clock three) and each subsequent data phase (there aren't any in this example), the bus master is driving write data onto the AD bus and is also driving the byte enables.

THE master samples DEVSEL# asserted on the rising-edge of clock three indicating that the target has claimed the transaction.

THE target samples IRDY# asserted and FRAME# deasserted on the rising-edge of clock three, indicating that the master is ready to complete the final data phase.

BOTH parties sample IRDY# and TRDY# asserted on the rising-edge of clock three, indicating that the target has latched the final data item.

THE master samples its GNT# still asserted by the arbiter, indicating that it has retained bus ownership for the next transaction. *If GNT# were sampled deasserted at this point, the master has lost ownership and cannot proceed with the second transaction. It would have to wait until ownership passes back to it and then perform the second transaction.*

CLOCK three would normally be the idle clock during which the master and target would ceasing driving their respective signals. However, the master has retained bus ownership and will immediately start a new transaction (either a write or a read) during clock three. It *must ensure that it is addressing the same target*, however, so that there isn't any contention on the target-related signals (see Clock Four).

THE master stops driving the final write data item and the byte enables and immediately starts driving the start address and command for the second transaction.

THE master immediately reasserts FRAME# to indicate that it is starting a new transaction. It should be noted that *the bus does not return to the idle state* (FRAME# and IRDY# both deasserted). *It is a rule that targets must recognize a change from IRDY# asserted and FRAME# deasserted on one clock edge to IRDY# deasserted and FRAME# asserted on the next clock edge as the end of one transaction and the beginning of a new one.*

THE master deasserts its REQ# to the arbiter (unless it wishes to perform another transaction immediately after the new one it's just beginning).

CLOCK 4. When the targets on the bus detect FRAME# reasserted, this qualifies the address and command just latched as valid for a new transaction. They begin the decode.

THE target of the previous transaction had actively-driven TRDY# and DEVSEL# back high for one clock starting on the rising-edge of clock three and continuing until the rising-edge of clock four. That target is just beginning to back its DEVSEL# and TRDY# output drivers off those two signals starting on the rising-edge of clock four. If a different target were addressed in the second transaction and it had a fast decoder, it would turn on its DEVSEL# output driver starting on the rising-edge of clock four to assert DEVSEL#. In addition, if the second transaction were a write, the target of the second transaction might also turn on its TRDY# output driver to indicate its readiness to accept the first data item. In summary, if the master were to address different targets in the first and second transactions, there might be a collision on the target-related signals. *This is why it's a rule that the master must address the same target in both transactions.* In this way, the same target output drivers that just drove both lines high can now drive them low.

Since the configuration PCI software dynamically assigns address ranges to a device's programmable PCI memory and IO decoders each time the machine is powered up, it can be a real challenge for the master to "know" that it is addressing the same target in the first and second transactions.

Figure 11-2: Arbitration For Fast Back-To-Back Accesses

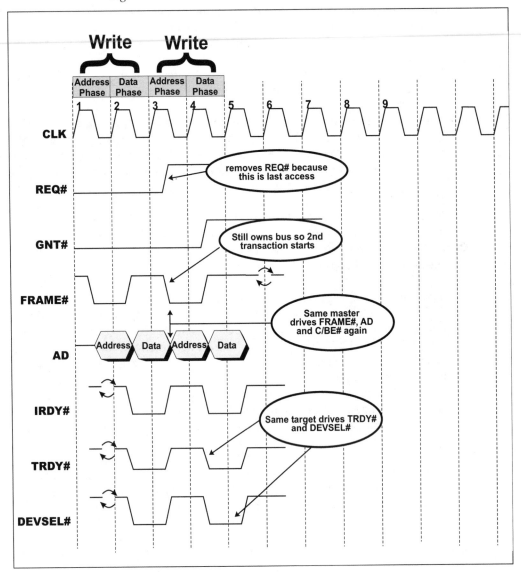

How Collision Avoided On Signals Driven By Target

The signals asserted by the target of the first transaction at the completion of the final data phase (clock edge three) are TRDY# and DEVSEL# (and, possibly, STOP#). Two clocks after the end of the data phase, the target may also drive PERR#. As it is a rule in this scenario that the same target must be addressed in the second transaction, the same target again drives these signals. Even if the target has a fast address decoder and begins to assert DEVSEL# (and TRDY# if it is a write) during clock cycle four in the second transaction, the fact that it is the same target ensures that there is not a collision on TRDY# and DEVSEL# (and possibly STOP# and PERR#) between output drivers associated with two different targets.

How Targets Recognize New Transaction Has Begun

It is a rule that all PCI targets must recognize either of the following conditions as the start of a new transaction:

- **Normal Start**: Bus idle (FRAME# and IRDY# deasserted) detected on one rising-edge of the PCI clock followed on the next rising-edge by address phase-in-progress (FRAME# asserted and IRDY# deasserted).
- **Fast Start**: Final data phase in progress (FRAME# deasserted and IRDY# asserted) detected on one rising-edge of the PCI clock, followed on the next rising-edge by address phase-in-progress (FRAME# asserted and IRDY# deasserted).

Implementation of support for this type of Fast Back-to-Back capability is optional for an initiator, but all targets must be able to decode them.

Fast Back-to-Back and Master Abort

When a master experiences a Master Abort on a transaction during a Fast Back-to-Back series, it may continue performing fast transactions (as long as it still has its GNT#). No target responded to the aborted transaction, thereby ensuring that there will not be a collision on the target-related signals. If the transaction that ended with a Master Abort was a Special Cycle transaction, the target(s) that received the message were already given sufficient time (by the master) to process the message and should be prepared to recognize another transaction.

Scenario Two: Targets Guarantee Lack of Contention

In the second scenario (defined in revision 2.0 of the specification and still true in revision 2.x), the entire community of PCI targets that reside on the PCI bus as well as the bus master collectively guarantee lack of contention during fast back-to-back transactions. A constraint incurred when using the master-guaranteed method (see "Scenario 1: Master Guarantees Lack of Contention" on page 155) is that the master can only perform Fast Back-to-Back transactions if both transactions access the same target and the first transaction is a write. The tricky part for the master is knowing the address boundaries of various targets. A master doesn't typically have this kind of knowledge. That's why an additional method was introduced in the 2.0 spec.

The reason that scenario one states that the target of the first and second transactions must be the same target is to prevent the possibility of a collision on the target-related signals: TRDY#, DEVSEL# and STOP# (and, possibly, PERR#). This possibility can be avoided if:

1. All targets have medium or slow address decoders. Alternatively, a target might normally perform a fast decode, but adjust its decode timing to the medium decode time slot when it detects a master initiating the second transaction of a Fast Back-to-Back pair. Note that this target would still indicate its normal decode speed (fast) in the DEVSEL# Timing field of its Status register. Targets with Medium or Slow decoders, or targets that are normally fast but will adjust their decode timing to avoid a collision will hardwire the Fast Back-to-Back Capable bit in their Status registers to a one.
2. It is a requirement that all targets must be capable of discerning that a new transaction has begun without a transition through the bus idle state and are capable of latching the address and command associated with the second transaction.

During system configuration (at power-up), software polls each device's configuration Status register (see Figure 11-4 on page 162) and checks the state of its Fast Back-to-Back Capable bit. If all devices indicate support for this anti-collision mechanism, then the configuration software can set each bus master's Fast Back-to-Back Enable bit (see Figure 11-3 on page 161) in its configuration Command register. When this bit is set, a master is enabled to perform Fast Back-to-Back transactions with different targets in the first and second transactions. This bit, and therefore this capability is optional for a bus master.

If the full suite of targets on a PCI bus meet both of these requirements, then any bus master that is Fast Back-to-Back Capable can perform Fast Back-to-Back transactions without worrying about which targets it addresses in the first and second transactions. If so much as one target indicates to the configuration software that it cannot guarantee that a collision won't occur, then the configuration software cannot set the Fast Back-to-Back Capable bit to one in the Command registers of masters that support this feature.

There are two scenarios when a target with a fast address decoder doesn't have to insert this one clock delay:

SCENARIO 1. The current transaction was preceded by a bus idle state (FRAME# and IRDY# deasserted).

SCENARIO 2. The currently-addressed target was also addressed in the previous transaction. This ensures a lack of contention on TRDY#, STOP# and DEVSEL# (because it was driving these signals during the previous transaction).

To prevent collisions on the master-related signals, the first transaction must still be a write, and the second transaction must be performed by the same master.

Figure 11-3: Command Register Bit Assignment

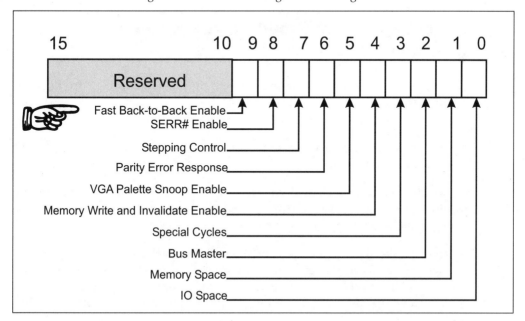

Figure 11-4: Status Register Bit Assignment

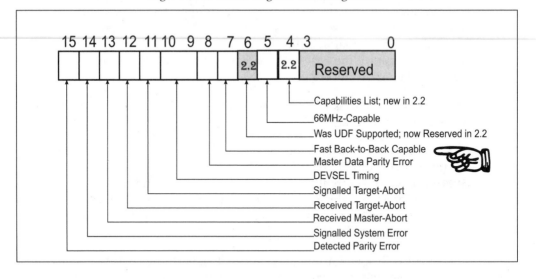

Address/Data Stepping

Advantages: Diminished Current Drain and Crosstalk

Turning on a large number of output drivers simultaneously (e.g., driving a 32-bit address onto the AD bus) can result in:

- a large spike of current drain.
- a significant amount of crosstalk within the driver chip and on adjacent external signal lines.

Optionally, the designer could choose to alleviate both of these problems by turning on the drivers associated with non-adjacent signal drivers in groups over a number of steps, or clock periods.

As an example, assume that the system board designer lays out the 32 AD lines as adjacent signal traces in bit sequential order. By simultaneously driving all 32 lines, crosstalk would be generated on the traces (and within the driver chip). Now assume that there are four 8-bit groups of signal drivers connected as follows:

- driver group one is connected to AD lines 0, 4, 8, 12, 16, 20, 24, 28.
- driver group two is connected to AD lines 1, 5, 9, 13, 17, 21, 25, 29.
- driver group three is connected to AD lines 2, 6, 10, 14, 18, 22, 26, 30.
- driver group four is connected to AD lines 3, 7, 11, 15, 19, 23, 27, 31.

The initiator could turn on the first driver group in clock cycle one of a transaction, followed by group two in clock cycle two, group three in clock cycle three, and group four in clock cycle four. Using this sequence, non-adjacent signal lines are being switched during each clock cycle, reducing the interaction and crosstalk.

Why Targets Don't Latch Address During Stepping Process

Since the entire address is not present on the bus until clock cycle four in the example cited in the previous section, the initiator must delay assertion of the FRAME# signal until clock cycle four when the final group driver is switched on. Because the assertion of FRAME# qualifies the address (and command) as being valid, no targets latch and use the address and command until FRAME# is sampled asserted.

Data Stepping

The data presented by the initiator during each data phase of a write transaction is qualified by the assertion of the IRDY# signal by the initiator. The data presented by the target during each data phase of a read transaction is qualified by the assertion of the TRDY# signal by the target. In other words, data can be stepped onto the bus, as well as address.

How Device Indicates Ability to Use Stepping

A DEVICE INDICATES ITS ABILITY TO PERFORM STEPPING VIA THE STEPPING CONTROL BIT (THIS BIT'S NAME CHANGED FROM THE WAIT CYCLE CONTROL BIT IN REV 2.2 OF THE SPEC) IN ITS CONFIGURATION COMMAND REGISTER. There are three possible cases:

CASE 1. If the device is not capable of stepping, the bit is hardwired to zero.
CASE 2. If the device always using stepping, the bit is hardwired to one.

Case 3. If the device's ability to use stepping can be enabled and disabled via software, the bit is implemented as a read/writable bit, and reset sets it to one (i.e., Stepping is enabled). A device with this flexibility could be programmed to use stepping in a laptop to conserve power, and to not use stepping when in a high-performance machine.

Designer May Step Address, Data, PAR (and PAR64) and IDSEL

The address may be stepped onto the AD bus (including the 64-bit extension) because it is qualified by FRAME#. PAR (and PAR64) may also be stepped because they are guaranteed qualified one clock after the end of the address phase and one clock after the assertion of IRDY# or TRDY# during each data phase. IDSEL can be stepped because it is qualified by the FRAME# signal (refer to "Resistive-Coupling Means Stepping In Type 0 Transactions" on page 341). Data can be stepped onto the AD bus during each data phase because it is qualified by the assertion of IRDY# (on a write) or TRDY# (on a read).

Table 11-1 on page 164 defines the relationship of the AD bus, PAR, PAR64, IDSEL and DEVSEL# and the conditions that qualify them as valid.

Table 11-1: Qualification Requirements

Signal(s)	Qualifier
AD bus during address phase	Qualified when FRAME# signal sampled asserted at the end of the address phase.
AD bus during data phase on read	Qualified when TRDY# signal sampled asserted on a rising clock edge during the data phase.
AD bus during data phase on write	Qualified when IRDY# signal sampled asserted on a rising clock edge during the data phase.
PAR and PAR64	Implicitly qualified on rising clock edge after address phase, or one clock after IRDY# (on a write) or TRDY# (on a read).

Table 11-1: Qualification Requirements (Continued)

Signal(s)	Qualifier
IDSEL	Qualified when FRAME# sampled asserted at the end of the address phase and a Type Zero configuration command is present on the C/BE bus.

Continuous and Discrete Stepping

The initiator (or the target) may use one of two methods to step a valid address or data onto the AD bus, or a valid level onto the PAR and PAR64 signal lines, or IDSEL:

METHOD 1. If the device driving the AD bus and the parity pins or IDSEL, either initiator or target (but note that the target doesn't drive IDSEL), **uses** *very* **weak output drivers**, it may take several clocks for it to produce a valid level on these bus signals (i.e., the propagation delay may be lengthy because it may take several reflections, with the resultant voltage-doubling effect, before the address (or data) is in the correct state on the bus). This is known as **continuous stepping**. When using this approach, care must be taken to avoid coupling between control signals that are sampled on the clock's rising-edge (e.g., FRAME#) and signals that are being stepped and are transitioning on that clock edge.

METHOD 2. The device driving the AD bus and the parity pins or IDSEL, either initiator or target (once again, note that the target doesn't drive IDSEL), may have **strong output drivers** and may drive a subset of them on each of several clock edges until all of them have been driven. This is known as **discrete stepping**. It only takes one reflection for these signals to achieve the appropriate state.

Disadvantages of Stepping

There are two disadvantages associated with stepping:

- Due to the prolonged period it takes to set up the address or data on the bus, there is a **performance penalty** associated in any address or data phase where stepping is used.
- In the midst of stepping the address onto the bus, the **arbiter may remove** the **grant** from the stepping master. This subject is covered in the next section.

Preemption While Stepping in Progress

When the PCI bus arbiter grants the bus to a bus master, the master then waits for bus idle before initiating its transaction. If, during this period of time, the arbiter detects a request from a higher-priority master, it can remove the grant from the first master before it begins a transaction (i.e., before it asserts FRAME#).

Assuming that this doesn't occur, the master retains its grant and awaits bus idle. Upon detection of the bus idle state, the master begins to step the address onto the AD bus, but delays the assertion of FRAME# for several clocks until the address is fully driven. During this period of time, the arbiter may still remove the grant from the master. The arbiter hasn't detected FRAME# asserted and may therefore assume that the master hasn't yet started a transaction. If the arbiter receives a request from a higher-priority master, it may remove the grant from the master that is currently engaged in stepping an address onto the AD bus. In response to the loss of grant, the stepping master must immediately tri-state its output drivers.

It is a rule that the arbiter cannot deassert one master's grant and assert grant to another master during the same clock cycle if the bus appears to be idle. The bus may not, in fact, be idle. A master may not have asserted FRAME# yet because it is in the act of stepping the address onto the AD bus.

If the arbiter were to simultaneously remove the stepping master's GNT# and issue GNT# to another master, the following problem would result. On the next rising-edge of the clock, the stepping master detects removal of its GNT# and begins to turn off its address drivers (which takes time). At the same time, the other master detects its GNT# and bus idle (because the stepping master had not yet asserted FRAME#) and initiates a transaction. This results in a collision on the AD bus.

When the bus appears to be idle, the arbiter must remove the grant from one master, wait one clock cycle, and then assert grant to the other master. This provides a one clock cycle buffer zone for the stepping master to back off its output drivers completely before the other master detects its grant plus bus idle and starts its transaction.

It is permissible for the arbiter to simultaneously remove one master's grant and assert another's during the same clock cycle if the bus isn't idle (i.e., a transaction is in progress). There is no danger of a collision because the master that has just received the grant cannot start driving the bus until the current master idles the bus.

Broken Master

The arbiter may assume that a master is broken if the arbiter has issued GNT# to the master, the bus has been idle for 16 clocks, and the master has not asserted FRAME# to start its transaction. The arbiter is permitted to ignore all further requests for bus ownership from the broken master and may optionally report the failure to the OS (in a device-specific fashion).

Stepping Example

Figure 11-5 on page 168 provides an example of an initiator using stepping over a period of three clocks to drive the address onto the AD bus.

CLOCK 3. The initiator can start the transaction on clock three (GNT# sampled asserted and bus idle—FRAME# and IRDY# sampled deasserted). It then begins to drive part of the address onto the AD bus and the command onto the C/BE bus.

CLOCK 4. During clock cycle four, it continues to drive the first part of the address and starts to drive another portion of the address onto the AD bus.

CLOCK 5. During the clock cycle five, it drives the final portion of the address and asserts FRAME#, indicating the presence of the full address and command.

CLOCK 6. When the targets sample FRAME# asserted on the rising-edge of clock six (the end of the address phase), they latch the address and command and begin the address decode.

SINCE this is an example of a write transaction, the initiator begins to drive the data onto the AD bus at the start of the data phase (clock six). In this example, it uses stepping, asserting the write data over a period of two clocks. It withholds the assertion of IRDY# until the data has been fully driven.

Figure 11-5: Example of Address and Data Stepping

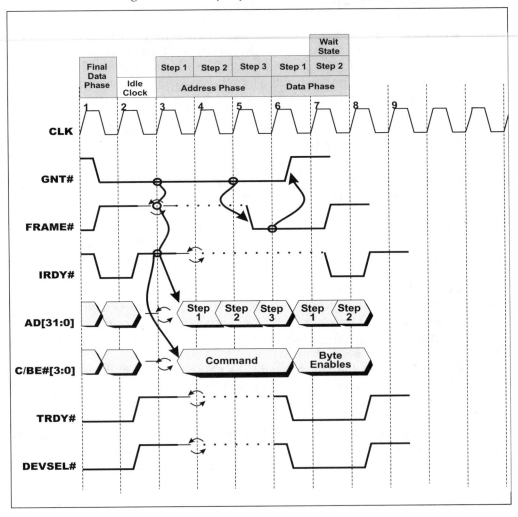

When Not to Use Stepping

Stepping must not be utilized when using 64-bit addressing because targets that respond to 64-bit addressing expect the upper 32 bits of the address to be presented one tick after FRAME# is sampled asserted. For more information, refer to "64-bit Addressing" on page 287.

Who Must Support Stepping?

All PCI devices must be able to handle address and data stepping performed by the other party in a transaction. The ability to use stepping, however, is optional.

12 Early Transaction End

The Previous Chapter

The previous chapter provided a detailed description of Fast Back-to-Back transactions and address/data Stepping.

In This Chapter

This chapter describes the early termination of a transaction before all of the intended data has been transferred between the master and the target. This includes descriptions of Master Abort, the preemption of a master, Target Retry, Target Disconnect, and Target Abort.

The Next Chapter

The next chapter describes error detection, reporting and handling.

Introduction

In certain circumstances, a transaction must be prematurely terminated before all of the data has been transferred. Either the initiator or the target makes the determination to prematurely terminate a transaction. The following sections define the circumstances requiring termination and the mechanisms used to accomplish it. The first half of this chapter discusses situations wherein the master makes the decision to prematurely terminate a transaction. The second half discusses situations wherein the target makes the decision.

Master-Initiated Termination

The initiator terminates a transaction for one of four reasons:

1. The **transaction has completed normally**. All of the data that the master intended to transfer to or from the target has been transferred. This is a normal, rather than a premature transaction termination.
2   The **initiator has already used up its time slice and has been living on borrowed time and is then preempted** by the arbiter (because one or more other bus masters are requesting the bus) before it completes its burst transfer. In other words, the initiator's Latency Timer expired some time ago and the arbiter has now removed the initiator's bus grant signal (GNT#).
3   The initiator is **preempted during** its **time slice and** then **uses up** its allotted **time slice** before completing its overall transfer.
4   The initiator has aborted the transaction because **no target has responded** to the address. This is referred to as a Master Abort.

Normal transaction termination is described in the chapters entitled "Read Transfers" on page 123 and "Write Transfers" on page 135. The second and third scenarios are described in this chapter.

Master Preempted

Introduction

Figure 12-1 on page 175 illustrates two cases of preemption. In the first case (the upper part of the diagram), the arbiter removes GNT# from the initiator, but the initiator's LT (Latency Timer; see "Latency Timer Keeps Master From Monopolizing Bus" on page 78) has not yet expired, indicating that its timeslice has not yet been exhausted. It may therefore continue to use the bus either until it has completed its transfer, or until its timeslice is exhausted, whichever comes first.

In the second case, the initiator has already used up its timeslice but has not yet lost its GNT# (referred to as preemption). It may therefore continue its transaction until it has completed its transfer, or until its GNT# is removed, whichever comes first. The following two sections provide a detailed description of the two scenarios illustrated.

Chapter 12: Early Transaction End

Preemption During Timeslice

In the upper example in Figure 12-1 on page 175, the current initiator initiated a transaction at some earlier point in time.

CLOCK 1. The master is preempted on the rising-edge of clock one (GNT# has been removed by the arbiter), indicating that the arbiter has detected a request from another master and is instructing the current master to surrender the bus.

AT the point of preemption, however, the master's LT has not yet expired (i.e., its timeslice has not been exhausted). The master may therefore retain bus ownership until it has either completed its overall transfer or until its timeslice is exhausted, which ever comes first.

CLOCK 2. Data transfers occur on the rising-edge of clocks two through five (because IRDY# and TRDY# are both sampled asserted) and the master also decrements its LT on the rising-edge of each clock (the LT register is of course not visible in the timing diagram).

CLOCK 3. See Clock Two.

CLOCK 4. See Clock Two.

CLOCK 5. On the rising-edge of clock five, a data item is transferred (IRDY# and TRDY# sampled asserted) and the master decrements its LT again and it's exhausted (transferring data can be very tiring). The rule is that if the master has used up its timeslice (i.e., LT value) and has lost its grant, the initiator can perform one final data phase and must then surrender ownership of the bus.

IN what it now knows is the final data phase, the initiator keeps IRDY# asserted and deasserts FRAME#, indicating that it's ready to complete the final data phase.

CLOCK 6. The target realizes that this is the final data phase because it samples FRAME# deasserted and IRDY# asserted on clock six.

THE final data item is transferred on the rising-edge of clock six.

THE initiator then deasserts IRDY#, returning the bus to the idle state.

CLOCK 7. The bus is idle (FRAME# and IRDY# deasserted).

THE master that has its GNT# and has been testing for bus idle on each clock can now assume bus ownership on the rising-edge of clock seven.

Timeslice Expiration Followed by Preemption

The lower half of Figure 12-1 on page 175 illustrates the case where the master started a transaction at some earlier point in time, used up its timeslice, and is then preempted at some later point in time.

CLOCK 1. The initiator determines that its LT has expired at the rising-edge of clock one, and a data transfer occurs at the same time (IRDY# and TRDY# sampled asserted). The initiator doesn't have to yield the bus yet because the arbiter hasn't removed its GNT#. It may therefore retain bus ownership until it either completes its overall data transfer or until its GNT# is removed by the arbiter, which ever occurs first.

CLOCK 2. A data transfer takes place on the rising-edge of clock two (because IRDY# and TRDY# are sampled asserted).

CLOCK 3. No data transfer takes place on the rising-edge of clock three (because the initiator wasn't ready (IRDY# deasserted).

CLOCK 4. A data transfer takes place on the rising-edge of clock four.

CLOCK 5. A data transfer takes place on the rising-edge of clock five (because IRDY# and TRDY# are sampled asserted).

ON the rising-edge of clock five, the initiator detects that its GNT# has been removed by the arbiter, indicating that it must surrender bus ownership after performing one more data phase.

IN clock five, the initiator keeps IRDY# asserted and removes FRAME#, indicating that the final data phase is in progress.

CLOCK 6. The final data item is transferred on the rising-edge of clock six. The initiator then deasserts IRDY# in clock six, returning the bus to the idle state.

CLOCK 7. The bus has returned to the idle state (FRAME# and IRDY# sampled deasserted on the rising-edge of clock seven.

THE master that has its GNT# and has been testing for bus idle on each clock can now assume bus ownership on clock seven.

Figure 12-1: Master-Initiated Termination Due to Preemption and Master Latency Timer Expiration

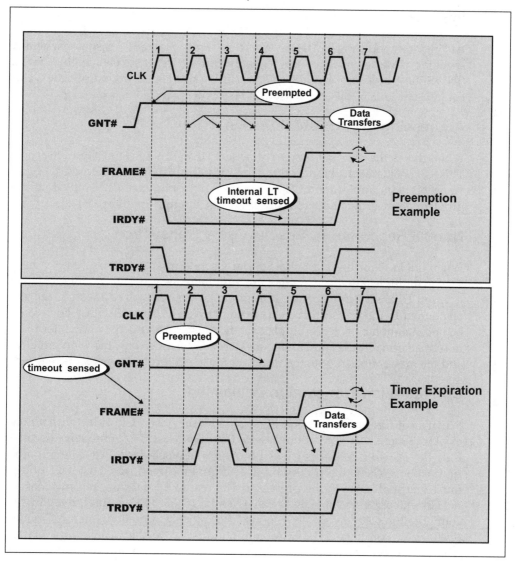

Master Abort: Target Doesn't Claim Transaction

Introduction

An initiator performs a Master Abort for one of several reasons. Generally speaking, a Master Abort occurs when the transaction is not claimed by a target (DEVSEL# is not sampled asserted within a pre-defined period of time). This could occur for a number of reasons. The following are some examples:

Addressing Non-Existent Device

When this is the case, no target will assert DEVSEL# to claim the transaction. This is considered to be an error. The master must set the Received Master Abort bit in its configuration Status register. It should then alert software that a problem has been encountered (usually, by generating an interrupt).

Normal Response To Special Cycle Transaction

When the initiator has started a **Special Cycle** transaction to broadcast a message to multiple targets on a target bus simultaneously, it is illegal for any target to assert DEVSEL# in response. If multiple targets recognized the message and responded to the transaction by asserting DEVSEL#, the DEVSEL# line would be in contention between multiple drivers. Master Abort is the normal termination of a special cycle and is not considered to be an error. This is not an error and the master does not set the Received Master Abort bit in its Status register.

Configuration Transaction Unclaimed

When a **configuration access** is attempted by the host/PCI bridge **with a non-existent target**, DEVSEL# is not asserted by any target. The subtractive decoder (i.e., the PCI-to-ISA bridge) will not claim an unclaimed PCI configuration transaction. When this occurs on a configuration read, the host/PCI bridge must return all ones to the processor. The reason all ones are returned for an unclaimed configuration read is that a Vendor ID of FFFFh is interpreted by the configuration software as "no response" (for more information, refer to "Vendor ID Register" on page 354). On a configuration write that results in a Master Abort, the processor write is permitted to terminate normally (i.e., as if the data were successfully written).

A configuration read or write that results in a Master Abort is considered to be an error and the master must set the Received Master Abort bit in its Status register.

Chapter 12: Early Transaction End

No Target Will Claim Transaction Using Reserved Command

When a bus master initiates a transaction **using a reserved command,** no target responds and it results in a Master Abort. This is considered to be an error and the master must set the Received Master Abort bit in its Status register.

Master Abort On Single vs. Multiple-Data Phase Transaction

There are two possible cases to consider:

CASE 1. The initiator starts a single data phase transaction and aborts it due to DEVSEL# not detected. This case is illustrated in Figure 12-2 on page 178.

CASE 2. The initiator starts a multi-data phase transaction and aborts it due to DEVSEL# not detected. This case is illustrated in Figure 12-3 on page 179.

The following two sections describe these two cases.

Master Abort on Single Data Phase Transaction

Refer to Figure 12-3 on page 179.

CLOCK 1. The initiator starts the transaction at the start of clock one by asserting FRAME# and driving the address onto the AD bus and the command type onto the Command/Byte Enable lines.

CLOCK 2. Because it is not yet ready to transfer the first data item, the initiator doesn't assert IRDY# in clock two.

CLOCK 3. During clock three, the master asserts IRDY# to indicate its readiness to transfer the first (and only) data item.

AT the same time, it deasserts FRAME#, indicating to the target that this is the final data phase.

ON the rising-edge of clock three, the master samples DEVSEL# deasserted, indicating that the transaction has not been claimed by any target with a *Fast* PCI decoder.

CLOCK 4. On the rising-edge of clock four, the master samples DEVSEL# deasserted again, indicating that the transaction has not been claimed by any target with a *Medium* PCI decoder.

CLOCK 5. On the rising-edge of clock five, the master samples DEVSEL# deasserted again, indicating that the transaction has not been claimed by any target with a *Slow* PCI decoder.

CLOCK 6. The initiator then samples DEVSEL# a final time on the rising-edge of clock six to determine if the subtractive decoder in the ISA bridge has claimed the transaction. In the example, the transaction has not been claimed by any target, so the initiator must Master Abort the transaction and return the bus to the idle state in a graceful fashion. This is accomplished by deasserting IRDY# during clock six. FRAME# was already deasserted when the initiator asserted IRDY# in the final data phase.

CLOCK 7. The bus is idle on the rising-edge of clock seven and is available for use by another master.

Figure 12-2: Example of Master Abort on Single-Data Phase Transaction
(note: this is not a special cycle)

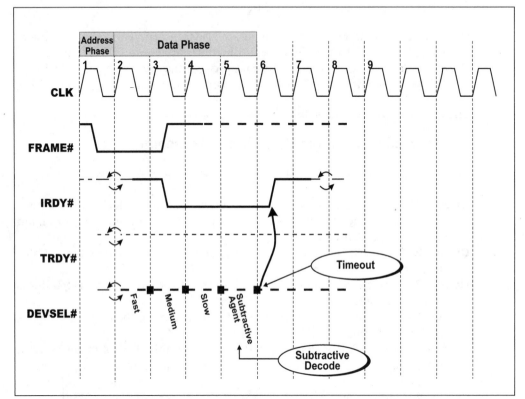

Master Abort on Multi-Data Phase Transaction

Figure 12-3 on page 179 illustrates an example of a multiple data phase transaction that results in a Master Abort. During the data phase, the initiator asserts IRDY# (during clock three in this example; it could be asserted earlier or later) when it is ready to complete the first data phase, but keeps FRAME# asserted to indicate its intention to perform a second data phase upon the completion of this one.

The initiator samples DEVSEL# on the rising-edge of clocks three through five to determine if a PCI target with a fast, medium or slow decoder has claimed the transaction. In this example, DEVSEL# is sampled deasserted each time. The initiator then samples DEVSEL# a final time on the rising-edge of clock six to determine if the subtractive decoder in the PCI/expansion bus bridge has claimed the transaction. In the example, the transaction has not been claimed by any target, so the initiator must Master Abort the transaction and return the bus to the idle state in a graceful fashion. This is accomplished by deasserting FRAME# in clock six and then IRDY# in clock seven. This returns the bus to the idle state on clock eight.

Figure 12-3: Example of Master Abort on Multiple Data Phase Transaction

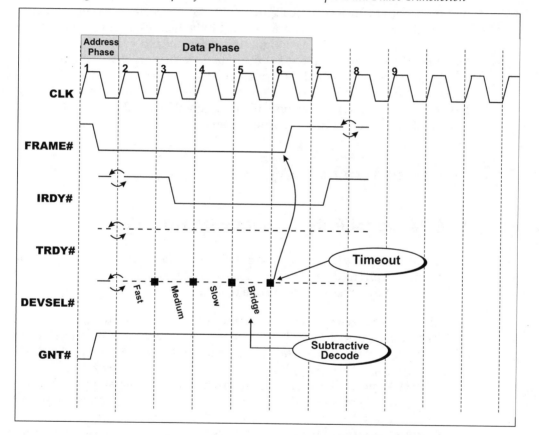

Action Taken by Master in Response to Master Abort

General. When the initiator experiences a Master Abort, it must set the Received Master Abort bit in its configuration Status register and report the error back to the device driver (typically, via an interrupt request).

Master Abort On Special Cycle Transaction. The Received Master Abort status bit should not be set, however, if the abort was experienced during a Special Cycle transaction (because Master Abort is the normal end to the Special Cycle transaction). No target is expected to assert DEVSEL# during a Special Cycle and it would be a protocol violation if one did.

Master Abort On Configuration Access. As stated earlier, when a Master Abort occurs on a configuration read, the host/PCI bridge must return all ones to the processor. On a configuration write, the processor write is permitted to terminate normally (i.e., as if the data were successfully written). This is considered to be an error and the master must set the Received Master Abort bit in its Status register. Therefore, if all ones are received when attempting to read the Vendor ID from a PCI function, the programmer should clear the Received Master Abort bit in the bridge's Status register (by writing a one to it).

Target-Initiated Termination

STOP# Signal Puts Target In the Driver's Seat

For various reasons, a target may use STOP# to tell the initiator to end the transaction on the current data phase. Using DEVSEL# and TRDY# in conjunction with STOP#, the target can indicate one of the following to the initiator:

- **Disconnect With Data Transfer**: The target is ready and willing to transfer the current dword, but instructs the master to Disconnect upon completion of the current data phase (current dword is transferred). This is referred to as a Disconnect With Data Transfer. There are **two variants: Disconnect A and B**. The initiator may continue the transfer (starting with next dword) at a later time, or may choose not to resume the transaction (this might occur if it were prefetching and did not really need the data).
- **Disconnect Without Data Transfer**: The target refuses to transfer the current dword and instructs the master to disconnect from it without transferring the dword. This is referred to as a Disconnect Without Data Transfer. There are **two variants: Disconnect 1 and Disconnect 2 Without Data**

Transfer. The initiator may choose to continue the transfer (starting with the current dword) at a later time, or may choose not to resume the transaction (this might occur if it were prefetching and did not really need the data).

- **Retry**: Issue a Retry during the first data phase. No data is transferred during the transaction and the initiator is obliged to Retry the transaction later.
- **Target Abort:** Target Abort the transaction and do not Retry (no data is transferred).

STOP# Not Permitted During Turn-Around Cycle · 2.2

STOP# MUST NOT BE ASSERTED DURING THE TURNAROUND CYCLE THAT IMMEDIATELY FOLLOWS THE ADDRESS PHASE OF A READ TRANSACTION.

Disconnect

Resumption of Disconnected Transaction Is Optional

Unlike a Retry, upon receipt of a Disconnect the master may or may not choose to rearbitrate for the bus and continue the transaction at the point of disconnection. As an example, a bridge might continue a memory read transaction past the first data phase to fill up a read-ahead buffer (i.e., a prefetch buffer) in case the originating master on the other side of the bridge wanted to read additional information. If the memory target that it's reading from disconnects from it at some point, the master would probably choose not to resume the transaction at the point of disconnection.

Reasons Target Issues Disconnect

Target Slow to Complete Subsequent Data Phase. Assume that the target determines that the **latency to complete a data phase** (except the first, which must adhere to the 16 clock rule) will be **longer than eight PCI clocks.** There are two cases:

CASE 1. The target determines that it can transfer the current data item within eight clocks and also knows that the master intends to perform another data phase (the master kept FRAME# asserted when it asserted IRDY#). The target has determined that it will not be able to transfer the next data item within eight clocks after entering the next data phase. The target must assert TRDY# and STOP#, thereby forcing the master to disconnect from it upon completing the transfer of the current data item.

CASE 2. In this case, the target enters a data phase before determining that it cannot transfer a data item within eight clocks. The target must keep TRDY# deasserted and assert STOP# as soon as it determines that it cannot meet the eight clock rule. This forces the master to disconnect from the target without transferring the current data item.

It should be noted that this rule was added in revision 2.1 of the specification. The target used to be permitted to take as long as it needed to transfer a data item and would then issue a Disconnect A or B (i.e., a Disconnect With Data Transfer) to the initiator. In essence, the old wording of this rule permitted a target to tie up the bus for long periods of time. This rule ensures that a slow target will not tie up the bus for extended periods of time. This subject is covered in "Subsequent Data Phase Rule" on page 84.

Target Doesn't Support Burst Mode. If a target doesn't support burst mode and it detects that the master intends to perform a second data phase (FRAME# is still asserted when IRDY# is asserted), the target must force the master to disconnect from it. This can be handled in two ways:

METHOD 1. The target can assert TRDY# and STOP# in the first data phase, instructing the master to transfer the first data item and then disconnect. This method is preferred over the one below because it returns the bus to the idle state more quickly so another transaction can be initiated by the next bus owner.

METHOD 2. Alternately, the target could just assert TRDY# in the first data phase, thereby permitting the master to transfer the first data item and move into the second data phase. Upon entry into the second data phase, the target deasserts TRDY# and asserts STOP#, instructing the master to disconnect without transferring the second data item.

Memory Target Doesn't Understand Addressing Sequence. If a memory target doesn't understand the addressing sequence (see "Memory Addressing" on page 143 for more information) indicated by the initiator via AD[1:0] during the address phase, the target must disconnect from the master. It has two options:

OPTION 1. The target can assert TRDY# and STOP# in the first data phase, instructing the master to transfer the first data item and then disconnect. This method is preferred over the one below because it returns the bus to the idle state more quickly so another transaction can be initiated by the next bus owner.

OPTION 2. Alternately, the target could just assert TRDY# in the first data phase, thereby permitting the master to transfer the first data item and move into the second data phase. Upon entry into the second data phase, the target deasserts TRDY# and asserts STOP#, instructing the master to disconnect without transferring the second data item.

This forces the initiator to fragment a burst transaction into single data phase transactions that the target can handle. The initiator may be using an AD[1:0] pattern defined in a later revision of the specification than the target was designed to.

Transfer Crosses Over Target's Address Boundary. If a target determines during the current data phase that the initiator intends to perform another data phase (FRAME# is still asserted) and that the **current data item is the last within its address boundaries**, the target must disconnect from the master. It has two options:

OPTION 1. The target can assert TRDY# and STOP# in the current data phase, instructing the master to transfer the current data item and then disconnect. This method is preferred over the one below because it returns the bus to the idle state more quickly so another transaction can be initiated by the next bus owner.

OPTION 2. Alternately, the target could just assert TRDY# in the current data phase, thereby permitting the master to transfer the first data item and move into the next data phase. Upon entry into the next data phase, the target deasserts TRDY# and asserts STOP#, instructing the master to disconnect without transferring the next data item.

The master then waits two PCI clocks and reasserts its REQ# to request ownership of the bus again. When it has re-acquired bus ownership, it resumes its transaction using the next dword address. This gives an opportunity to another target that implements the next sequential dword address to claim the transaction, thereby permitting the transfer to continue across target boundaries.

Burst Memory Transfer Crosses Cache Line Boundary. BE AWARE THAT THE 2.2 SPEC HAS DELETED THIS REQUIREMENT (AND GOOD RIDDANCE). THE FOLLOWING DISCUSSION IS ONLY INCLUDED AS HISTORICAL INFORMATION. 2.2

During a memory burst transaction, a cacheable PCI memory target detects that the initiator intends to perform another data phase (FRAME# is still asserted) after completion of the current data phase and is transferring the last dword within the current cache line in the current data phase. In order to force the bus master to generate the start address of the next cache line to be snooped by the host/PCI bridge, the target must issue a Disconnect With Data Transfer when it is ready to transfer the last dword of the current line. This forces the bus master to yield bus ownership, re-arbitrate for ownership again, and then initiate a new memory transaction starting at the first dword of the next cache line. This permits the snooper (the host/PCI bridge) to snoop the next line address in the processor's L1 and L2 caches.

Disconnect With Data Transfer (A and B)

The target indicates that it wants to transfer the current data item and then disconnect by asserting TRDY# and STOP# while keeping DEVSEL# asserted. This tells the initiator that the target is ready to transfer the current data item (TRDY# asserted) and wishes to stop the transfer (STOP# asserted). DEVSEL# remaining asserted gives the initiator permission to resume the transaction at a later time (if so desired; resumption is not mandatory) at the point where it was disconnected (on the dword that would have been transferred in the next data phase). Disconnect A and B differ from each other by the state of IRDY# at the point where the Disconnect is signaled.

Disconnect A. Refer to clock one in Figure 12-5 on page 186. It is a Disconnect A if IRDY# has not yet been asserted by the initiator when STOP# and TRDY# are asserted by the target. The current dword cannot be transferred until the initiator asserts IRDY#. When IRDY# is asserted (during clock two), the initiator also deasserts FRAME# (because it was instructed to disconnect), indicating that this is the final data phase. The current dword is transferred and the transaction ends. In clock three, the target deasserts STOP#, TRDY# and DEVSEL#, and the master deasserts IRDY#, returning the bus to the idle state on the rising-edge of clock four.

Disconnect B. Refer to Figure 12-5 on page 186. A Disconnect With Data Transfer—type B is indicated if IRDY# has already been asserted by the initiator when STOP# and TRDY# are asserted by the target. In this case, the current dword is transferred on that clock (clock two) and no more data is transferred. FRAME# is still asserted. Normally, the initiator deasserts FRAME# when it asserts IRDY# for the last data phase, but in this case the initiator did not know this was the last data phase when it asserted IRDY#. For this reason, the initiator keeps IRDY# asserted in clock two and deasserts FRAME#, indicating that it is ready to complete the final data phase. Both the initiator and the target know that no data will be transferred in this "dummy" data phase, however. The target deasserts TRDY# to enforce this fact. In clock three, IRDY# is deasserted to return the bus to the idle state. The target deasserts STOP# and DEVSEL# (the target is not permitted to deassert them until it samples FRAME# deasserted).

Assuming that the master decides to resume the transfer, after keeping its REQ# deasserted for two PCI clocks, the master should then reassert its REQ# and re-arbitrate for bus ownership. When it has successfully re-acquired bus ownership, the initiator should re-initiate the transaction using the dword address of the next data item that would have been transferred if the Disconnect had not occurred. In other words, the initiator should resume the transfer where it left off. This implies that the master must "remember" the address to resume at.

Figure 12-4: Disconnect A With Data Transfer—IRDY# Still Deasserted When Disconnect Issued

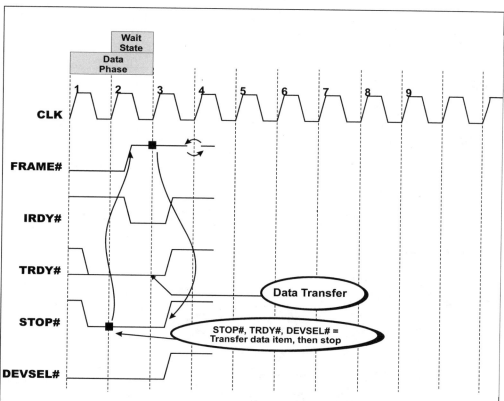

Figure 12-5: Disconnect B With Data Transfer—IRDY# Already Asserted When Disconnect Issued

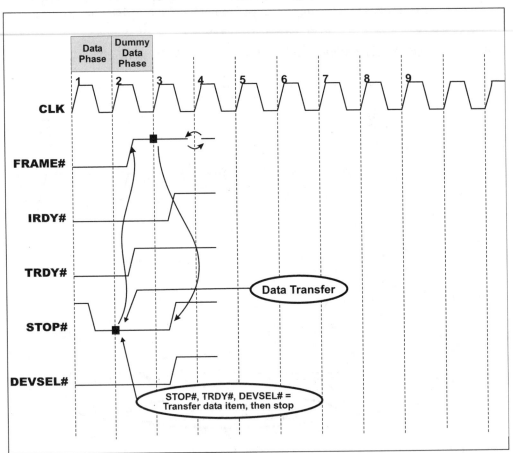

Disconnect Without Data Transfer

Disconnect Without Data Transfer—Type 1. Refer to Figure 12-6 on page 188. Assume that at least one data phase has completed (on the rising-edge of clock one) and at least one dword has therefore been transferred. When the initiator completed the previous data phase and entered the current one (in clock one), it kept IRDY# asserted to indicate that it is ready to complete the current data phase. It did not, however, deassert FRAME# because this isn't the final data phase. In this data phase, the target asserts STOP# (during clock one) and deasserts TRDY#, indicating that it wants the initiator to terminate the transaction on this data phase with no data transferred. In response, the initiator keeps IRDY# asserted (in clock two) and deasserts FRAME#, indicating that the final data phase is in progress. No data is transferred in this last "dummy" data phase, however, because the target has TRDY# deasserted. In clock three, the initiator deasserts IRDY#, returning the bus to the idle state. The target deasserts STOP# and DEVSEL#.

Disconnect Without Data Transfer—Type 2. Figure 12-7 on page 189 also illustrates a Disconnect Without Data Transfer, but the initiator deasserted IRDY# upon entry to the current data phase (indicating that it isn't ready to transfer the current data item). When the initiator discovers (on the rising-edge of clock two) that the target wants it to stop on this data phase without transferring the current dword, it responds by asserting IRDY# and deasserting FRAME#. This signals the final "dummy" data phase. The initiator deasserts IRDY# one clock later to return the bus to the idle state and the target deasserts STOP# and DEVSEL#.

Upon receipt of a Disconnect Without Data Transfer, the initiator has the option of resuming the transaction later or not. If it was prefetching data that wasn't explicitly required, it may choose not to.

Figure 12-6: Disconnect 1—When Target Asserts STOP# and Deasserts TRDY#, IRDY# Is Already Asserted

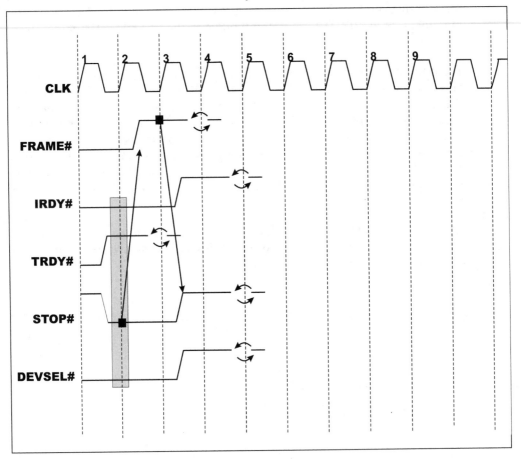

Figure 12-7: Disconnect 2—When Target Asserts STOP# and Deasserts TRDY#, IRDY# Has Not Been Asserted

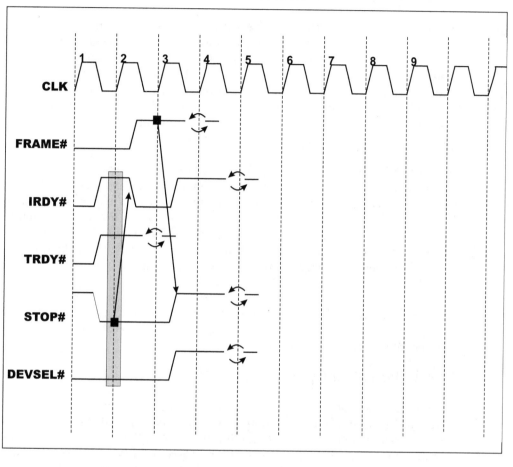

Retry

Reasons Target Issues Retry

Target Very Slow to Complete First Data Phase. If the latency to first data phase completion will be longer than 16 PCI clocks, the target must issue a Retry to the initiator. The only exception to the 16 clock rule is granted to the host/PCI bridge. It is permitted 32 clocks to complete the first data phase (for more information, refer to "Two Exceptions To First Data Phase Rule" on page 83). The 16 clock target first data phase latency rule prevents a target with a very long latency to first data phase completion from monopolizing the bus. This subject is covered in "The First Data Phase Rule" on page 82.

Snoop Hit on Modified Cache Line. When a PCI master is performing an access to main memory, the host/PCI bridge has to send a snoop transaction to the processors to determine if the master is accessing a stale line in main memory. In the event the snoop results in a hit on modified cache line, the bridge may choose to issue a Retry to the master while the processor transfers the modified line to the memory controller in the bridge. For additional information, refer to "Memory Write-and-Invalidate Command" on page 117. Also refer to "Two Exceptions To First Data Phase Rule" on page 83.

Resource Busy. If a target recognizes that a resource necessary for it to transfer the first data item is currently busy, it should immediately issue a Retry to the initiator. An example would be an attempt by a PCI master to access an EISA target while the EISA bus is currently owned by an EISA bus master. In that case, the PCI/EISA bridge should immediately issue a Retry to the PCI master to force it to free the PCI bus for use by other masters. This subject is covered in "Sometimes Target Can't Transfer First Data Within 16 CLKs" on page 82.

Bridge Locked. A locked bridge must issue a Retry when a master other than the one that locked it attempts to access it. This subject is covered in the chapter entitled "Locking" on page 683.

Description of Retry

A target only issues Retry to the initiator if it cannot permit any data to be transferred during the current transaction. In other words, it is a rule that if a target is going to issue a Retry to the initiator, it must do it in the first data phase. The signaling for a Retry is identical as that for a Disconnect Without Data Transfer except that it occurs in the first data phase. Unlike the Disconnect Without Data Transfer, however, the initiator is required to re-attempt the transaction at a later time (while resumption of the transaction is optional if disconnected).

Retry is indicated to the initiator (by the target) by keeping TRDY# deasserted while asserting STOP# and DEVSEL#. This tells the initiator that the target does not intend to transfer the current (the first) data item (TRDY# deasserted) and that the initiator must stop the transaction on this data phase (STOP# asserted). The transaction must be retried periodically and must be retried identically each time. Identically means it must repeat the transaction using the same:

- address.
- command.
- byte enables.
- *ADDRESS AND DATA PARITY, IF THE PARITY ERROR RESPONSE BIT (BIT 6 OF THE COMMAND REGISTER) IS SET. THIS IS MORE STRICT THAN THE 2.1 SPEC WHICH SAID, "PARITY BITS MAY ALSO BE USED IF PARITY CHECKING IS ENABLED."* **2.2**
- REQ64# (if a 64-bit transfer).
- *FOR WRITE TRANSACTIONS COMPLETED USING DELAYED TRANSACTION TERMINATION, A TARGET MUST ALSO LATCH DATA FROM BYTE LANES FOR WHICH THE BYTE ENABLE IS ASSERTED AND MAY OPTIONALLY LATCH DATA FROM BYTE LANES FOR WHICH THE BYTE ENABLE IS DEASSERTED. THIS IS MUCH MORE DEFINITIVE THAN THE 2.1 SPEC WHICH SAID, "DATA (IF A WRITE TRANSACTION)."* The target knows the write data is present when the master asserts IRDY#. The byte enables are presented immediately upon entry into a data phase, irrespective of the state of the ready signals. **2.2**
- Refer to "Locking" on page 683 for requirements for a bridge to latch LOCK# when completing a Delayed Transaction.

This rule is unconditional. The access must be retried as many times as it takes to complete the transfer. If the master also has target capability, it must respond to accesses to it by other masters that occur in between its attempts to Retry the transaction.

The specification cites the example of a multi-function device with three functions. More than one function in a multi-function device may have bus master capability. Assume that the device has three functions all having bus master capability. Such a device only has one pair of REQ#/GNT# signals, however. Assume that function zero initiates a transaction and receives a Retry. It must try the transaction again later. If the GNT# line is still asserted, function one can perform a transaction, and, when it's finished, function three can perform a transaction. Assume that function one's transaction completes, but function two's transaction receives a Retry. Both function zero and function two must periodically re-attempt their retried transactions until they are able to complete them.

Figure 12-8 on page 192 and Figure 12-9 on page 193 illustrate two variants on the Retry.

Retry Issued and IRDY# Already Asserted

In Figure 12-8 on page 192 the initiator had already asserted IRDY# when the target issues the Retry. When the Retry is detected (on the rising-edge of clock four), the initiator responds by keeping IRDY# asserted (in clock four) and deasserting FRAME#. One clock later it deasserts IRDY# to return the bus to the idle state. The target deasserts STOP# and DEVSEL#.

Retry Issued and IRDY# Not Yet Asserted

In Figure 12-9 on page 193 the initiator has not yet asserted IRDY# when it receives the Retry from the target (on the rising-edge of clock four). In response, the initiator asserts IRDY# (in clock four) and deasserts FRAME#. One clock later, it deasserts IRDY# to return the bus to the idle state. The target deasserts STOP# and DEVSEL#.

Figure 12-8: Retry Received with IRDY# Asserted

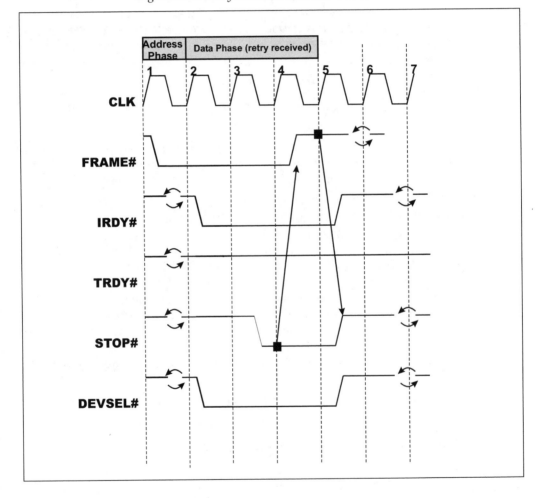

Figure 12-9: Retry Received without IRDY# Asserted

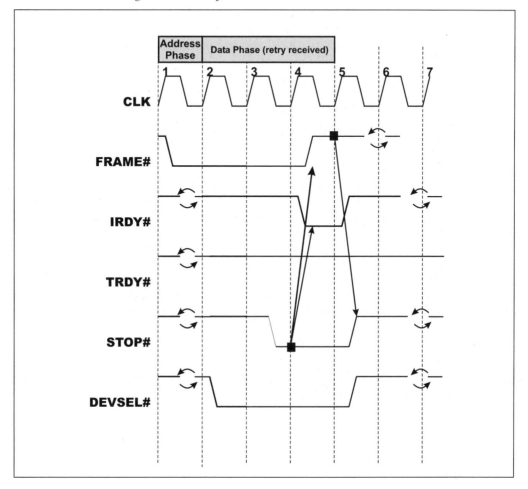

Host Bridge Retry Counter

The author must stress that the feature described in this section is *not* in the spec. It was in the spec up to and including the 2.1 draft spec and it disappeared in the 2.1 final spec. It is included because in the author's opinion it was and is a *very* good idea.

The spec says that it's a hard, fast rule that, upon receipt of a Retry, a master must Retry the transaction on a periodic basis until it is able to transfer the first data item successfully. No exceptions!

As stated at the beginning of this section, the earlier spec recommended that the host/PCI bridge implement a Retry counter. The counter is set to initial count whenever the bridge successfully transfers data during a transaction. Each time that the bridge experiences a Retry during a specific transaction, the counter is decremented (or incremented). When the Retry count limit (implementation-specific) has been reached, the bridge should discontinue retries of the transaction and should permit the host processor to complete the transaction in progress. On a read, the bridge should supply dummy data (all ones) to the processor. On a write, the bridge should pretend that the write completed with no problems. After permitting the processor to complete the transaction, the bridge would then generate an interrupt to alert the processor that a problem exists.

This recommendation existed for the following reason. Assume that the host processor initiates a transaction to perform a read from a PCI target device. The bridge arbitrates for ownership of the PCI bus and initiates the transaction. In response, the addressed target issues a Retry, causing the bridge to terminate the PCI transaction without transferring the requested data to the processor. After two PCI clocks, the bridge re-arbitrates for ownership of the PCI bus, retries the read transaction and again receives a Retry in response.

The bridge keeps inserting wait states into the host processor's bus transaction while it awaits the requested data. If the target continues to issue retries for an extended period, the host processor cannot recognize an external interrupt that is awaiting servicing during this period (the interrupt the host/PCI bridge generates to signal the excessive Retry condition). The processor cannot recognize the interrupt and use its bus to fetch and execute the interrupt service routine until the current bus cycle is permitted to complete.

Target Abort

Description

If a target detects a fatal error or will never be able to respond to the transaction for some other reason, it may signal a Target Abort. It can occur in the first or any other data phase of the transaction. This instructs the initiator to end the transaction and indicates that the target does not want the transaction resumed. It also means that any data already transferred during this transaction may be corrupted. The initiator must set the Received Target Abort bit in its configuration Status register and the target must set the Signaled Target Abort bit in its configuration Status register.

Target Abort is indicated to the initiator by simultaneously asserting STOP# and deasserting TRDY# and DEVSEL#. This tells the initiator that the target will not transfer the current data item (TRDY# deasserted) and that the initiator must stop the transaction on the current data phase (STOP# asserted). The early deassertion of DEVSEL# instructs the initiator not to re-attempt the transaction and differentiates Target Abort from Disconnect Without Data Transfer.

Some Reasons Target Issues Target Abort

Broken Target. If a target is broken and unable to transfer data, it may indicate this by issuing a Target Abort to the master.

I/O Addressing Error. The byte enable combination is not one supported by the target (in other words, it doesn't "own" all of the addressed locations within the current dword). This subject is covered in "Unsupported Byte Enable Combination Results in Target Abort" on page 148.

Address Phase Parity Error. If a target appears to be addressed in a transaction but there is a address phase parity error, the target may end the transaction by issuing a Target Abort to the master (as well as asserting SERR#).

Master Abort on Other Side of PCI-to-PCI Bridge. When a PCI-to-PCI bridge passes a transaction through the bridge for an initiator and the transaction is not claimed by a target on the other bus:

- the bridge experiences a Master Abort on the destination bus and sets the Received Master Abort bit in the status register that is associated with the destination bus (a bridge has two status registers; one for each side).
- the bridge then issues a Target Abort to the originating master and sets the Signaled Target Abort bit in its status register that is associated with the originating bus.
- The originating master sets the Received Target Abort bit in its Status register and generates an interrupt to have its driver check its status.

For more information, refer to "Handling Master Abort" on page 641.

Master's Response to Target Abort

In response to a Target Abort, the initiator takes one of the following actions:

- Generates an **interrupt** to alert its related device driver to check its status.
- Generates **SERR#** (assuming the master's SERR# Enable bit is set to one in its PCI configuration Command register). For more information on SERR#, refer to "SERR# Signal" on page 214.

Target Abort Example

Figure 12-10 on page 196 illustrates a target signaling a Target Abort. To indicate that it wishes to abort the transaction, the target simultaneously asserts STOP# and deasserts TRDY# (if it wasn't already deasserted) and DEVSEL#. This instructs the initiator to stop on the current data phase (STOP# asserted) with no data transferred (TRDY# deasserted) and not to reattempt the transaction again (DEVSEL# deasserted early).

The initiator samples the state of STOP#, TRDY# and DEVSEL# on the rising-edge of clock two and responds by deasserting FRAME# and asserting IRDY# (if it wasn't already asserted) during clock cycle two. This indicates that the initiator is ready to complete the final data phase (a "dummy" data phase). During clock three, the target deasserts STOP# (in response to sampling FRAME# deasserted). At the same time, the initiator deasserts IRDY#, returning the bus to the idle state on the rising-edge of clock four.

Figure 12-10: Target Abort Example

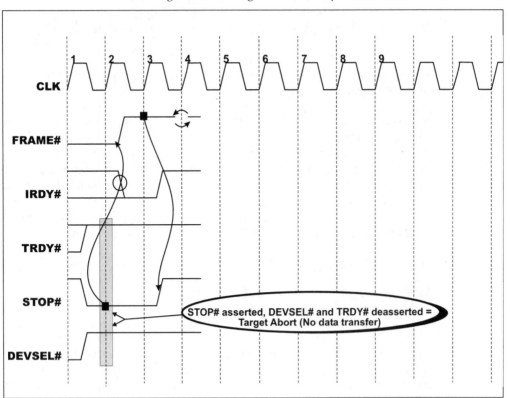

After Retry/Disconnect, Repeat Request ASAP

General

In the event of a Retry, the initiator **must** repeat the transaction again. Resumption of a transaction terminated with a Disconnect is optional (because the master may have been prefetching at the time it was disconnected). The initiator must deassert its REQ# line for a minimum of two PCI clocks: one when the bus goes idle (FRAME# and IRDY# deasserted) and another either the clock immediately before or after the return to idle. This provides lower-priority bus masters with an opportunity to gain bus ownership. If the initiator intends to complete the data transfer that was Disconnected, it must reassert its REQ# again after its two clock deassertion (or it may experience starvation).

If a target memorizes a transaction request (i.e., it treats it as a Delayed Request) and issues a Retry, the master must repeat the transaction identically within 2^{15} clocks, or the target will discard the completion. For more information, refer to "Discard of Delayed Completions" on page 91. The spec recommends that the transaction be repeated as soon as possible, preferably within 33 PCI clocks.

Behavior of Device Containing Multiple Masters

A PCI device may contains more than one device capable of initiating PCI transactions. All of the devices within this package then share the REQ#/GNT# signal pair associated with that device position on the bus. The package will incorporate logic to arbitrate between the master-capable devices within the package.

As long as the arbiter leaves the GNT# on the package, the master-capable devices within the package may take turns using the bus to initiate transactions and REQ# does not have to be deasserted between the transaction attempts (even if an access attempt is terminated with a Retry or a Disconnect). Before the package re-attempts a transaction that received a Retry or a Disconnect, however, it must deassert REQ# for two clocks (one of which is the idle clock between transactions).

Target-Initiated Termination Summary

Table 12-1 on page 198 summarizes the three cases of target-initiated termination.

Table 12-1: Target-Initiated Termination Summary

Termination Type	TRDY#	STOP#	DEVSEL#	Data Transfer?	Comments
Disconnect With Data Transfer	asserted	asserted	asserted	some data transferred, including current dword	If master wants to transfer more data, transaction will be re-initiated using next dword address.
Disconnect Without Data Transfer	deasserted	asserted	asserted	some data transferred, but not current dword	Occurs in a data phase other than the first. The master may resume the transaction or not. If resumed, it will start on the same dword.
Retry	deasserted	asserted	asserted	no	Occurs in first data phase. Master is obliged to Retry the transaction identically.
Target Abort	deasserted	asserted	deasserted	perhaps	Fatal error; no Retry.

13 Error Detection and Handling

Prior To This Chapter

The previous chapter described the early termination of a transaction before all of the intended data has been transferred between the master and the target. This included descriptions of Master Abort, the preemption of a master, Target Retry, Target Disconnect, and Target Abort.

In This Chapter

The PCI bus architecture provides two error reporting mechanisms: one for reporting data parity errors and the other for reporting more serious system errors. This chapter provides a discussion of error detection, reporting and handling using these two mechanisms.

The Next Chapter

The next chapter provides a discussion of interrupt-related issues.

Status Bit Name Change

Please note that the **Master Data Parity Error bit** in the Status register (see Figure 13-4 on page 211) was named Data Parity Reported in the 1.0 and 2.0 specs. Its name changed to the Data Parity Error Detected bit the 2.1 spec. Its name has changed yet again in the 2.2 spec to Master Data Parity Error. Although its name has changed over time, its meaning has remained the same.

Introduction to PCI Parity

The PCI bus is parity-protected during both the address and data phases of a transaction. A single parity bit, PAR, protects AD[31:0] and C/BE#[3:0]. If a 64-bit data transfer is in progress, an additional parity bit, PAR64, protects

AD[63:32] and C/BE#[7:4]. 64-bit parity has the same timing as 32-bit parity and is discussed in "64-bit Parity" on page 297.

The PCI device driving the AD bus during the address phase or any data phase of a transaction must always drive a full 32-bit pattern onto the AD bus (because parity is always based on the full content of the AD bus and the C/BE bus). This includes:

- Special Cycle and Interrupt Acknowledge transactions where the address bus doesn't contain a valid address, and during Type Zero Configuration transactions where AD[31:11] do not contain valid information.
- Data phases where the device supplying data isn't supplying all four bytes (all four byte enables are not asserted).

The PCI device driving the AD bus during the address phase or any data phase of a transaction is responsible for calculating and supplying the parity bit for the phase. The parity bit must be driven one clock after the address or data is first driven onto the bus (when TRDY# is asserted during a read data phase to indicate the presence of the read data on the bus, or when IRDY# is asserted during a write data phase to indicate the presence of the write data on the bus) and must continue to be driven until one clock after the data phase completes. Even parity is used (i.e., there must be an even number of ones in the overall 37-bit pattern). The computed parity bit supplied on PAR must be set (or cleared) so that the 37-bit field consisting of AD[31:0], C/BE#[3:0] and PAR contains an even number of one bits.

During the clock cycle immediately following the conclusion of the address phase or any data phase of a transaction, the PCI agent receiving the address or data computes expected parity based on the information latched from AD[31:0] and C/BE#[3:0]. The agent supplying the parity bit must present it:

- on the rising-edge of the clock that immediately follows the conclusion of the address phase.
- one clock after presentation of data (IRDY# assertion on a write or TRDY# assertion on a read) during a data phase.

The device(s) receiving the address or data expect the parity to be present and stable at that point. The computed parity bit is then compared to the parity bit actually received on PAR to determine if address or data corruption has occurred. If the parity is correct, no action is taken. If the parity is incorrect, the error must be reported. This subject is covered in the sections that follow.

During a read transaction where the initiator is inserting wait states (by delaying assertion of IRDY#) because it has a buffer full condition, the initiator can optionally be designed with a parity checker that:

- samples the target's data (when TRDY# is sampled asserted),
- calculates expected parity,
- samples actual parity (on the clock edge after TRDY# sampled asserted)
- and asserts PERR# (if the parity is incorrect).

In this case, the initiator must keep PERR# asserted until one clock after the completion of the data phase.

The same is true in a write transaction. If the target is inserting wait states by delaying assertion of TRDY#, the target's parity checker can optionally be designed to:

- sample the initiator's data (when IRDY# is sampled asserted),
- calculate expected parity,
- sample actual parity (on the clock edge after IRDY# sampled asserted)
- and assert PERR# (if the parity is incorrect).

In this case, the target must keep PERR# asserted until two clocks after the completion of the data phase.

PERR# Signal

PERR# is a sustained tri-state signal used to signal the detection of a parity error related to a data phase. There is one exception to this rule: a parity error detected on a data phase during a Special Cycle is reported using SERR# rather than PERR#. This subject is covered later in this chapter in "Special Case: Data Parity Error During Special Cycle" on page 213.

PERR# is implemented as an output on targets and as an input/output on masters. Although PERR# is bussed to all PCI devices, it is guaranteed to be driven by only one device at a time (the initiator on a read, or the target on a write).

Data Parity

Data Parity Generation and Checking on Read

Introduction

During each data phase of a read transaction, the target drives data onto the AD bus. It is therefore the target's responsibility to supply correct parity to the initiator on the PAR signal starting one clock after the assertion of TRDY#. At the conclusion of each data phase, it is the initiator's responsibility to latch the contents of AD[31:0] and C/BE#[3:0] and to calculate the expected parity during the clock cycle immediately following the conclusion of the data phase. The initiator then latches the parity bit supplied by the target from the PAR signal on the next rising-edge of the clock and compares computed vs. actual parity. If a miscompare occurs, the initiator then asserts PERR# during the next clock (if it's enabled to do so by a one in the Parity Error Response bit in its Command register). The assertion of PERR# lags the conclusion of each data phase by two PCI clock cycles.

The platform design (in other words, the chipset) may or may not include logic that monitors PERR# during a read and takes some system-specific action (such as asserting NMI to the processor in an Intel x86-based system; for more information, refer to "Important Note Regarding Chipsets That Monitor PERR#" on page 210) when it is asserted by a PCI master or a target that has received corrupted data. The master may also take other actions in addition to the assertion of PERR#. "Data Parity Reporting" on page 209 provides a detailed discussion of the actions taken by a bus master upon receipt of bad data.

Example Burst Read

Refer to the read burst transaction illustrated in Figure 13-1 on page 204 during this discussion.

CLOCK 1. The initiator drives the address and command onto the bus during the address phase (clock one).

CLOCK 2. The targets latch the address and command on clock two and begin address decode. In this example, the target has a fast address decoder and asserts DEVSEL# during clock two.

ALL targets that latched the address and command compute the expected parity based on the information latched from AD[31:0] and C/BE#[3:0].

THE initiator sets the parity signal, PAR, to the appropriate value to force even parity.

THE target keeps TRDY# deasserted to insert the wait state necessary for the turnaround cycle on the AD bus.

CLOCK 3. On clock three, the targets latch the PAR bit and compare it to the expected parity computed during clock two. If any of the targets have a miscompare, they assert SERR# (if the Parity Error Response and SERR# Enable bits in their respective configuration Command registers are set to one) within two clocks (recommended) after the error was detected. This subject is covered in "Address Phase Parity" on page 215.

THE target begins to drive the first data item onto the AD bus and asserts TRDY# to indicate its presence.

Chapter 13: Error Detection and Handling

CLOCK 4. The initiator latches the data on clock four (IRDY# and TRDY# are sampled asserted).

THE second data phase begins during clock four. The target drives the second data item onto the bus and keeps TRDY# asserted to indicate its presence.

DURING clock four, the target drives the PAR signal to the appropriate state for first data phase parity. The initiator computes the expected parity.

CLOCK 5. The initiator latches PAR on clock five and compares it to the expected parity. If the parity is incorrect, the initiator asserts PERR# during clock five.

THE initiator latches the data on the rising-edge of clock five (IRDY# and TRDY# sampled asserted).

DURING clock five, the initiator computes the expected parity.

The third data phase begins on clock five. The target drives the third data item onto the AD bus and keeps TRDY# asserted to indicate its presence.

THE initiator deasserts IRDY# to indicate that it is not yet ready to accept the third data item (e.g., it has a buffer full condition).

CLOCK 6. The actual parity is latched from PAR on clock six and checked against the expected parity. If an error is detected, the initiator asserts PERR# during clock six.

WHEN the initiator samples TRDY# asserted on clock six, this qualifies the presence of the third data item on the bus. The initiator's parity checker can be designed to sample the data (along with the byte enables) at this point.

CLOCK 7. Assuming that it is designed this way, the initiator can latch the PAR bit from the bus on clock seven (it's a rule that the target must present PAR one clock after presenting the data).

AT the earliest, then, the initiator could detect a parity miscompare during clock seven and assert PERR#. It must keep PERR# asserted until two clocks after completion of the data phase. *IN THE EVENT THAT THE INITIATOR ASSERTS PERR# EARLY IN THIS MANNER, THE 2.2 SPEC HAS ADDED A RULE THAT THE INITIATOR MUST EVENTUALLY ASSERT IRDY# TO COMPLETE THE DATA PHASE. THE TARGET IS NOT PERMITTED TO END THE DATA PHASE WITH A RETRY, DISCONNECT WITHOUT DATA, OR A TARGET ABORT.* **2.2**

DURING the third data phase, the initiator re-asserts IRDY# during clock seven and deasserts FRAME# to indicate that it is ready to complete the final data phase.

CLOCK 8. The final data phase completes on clock eight when IRDY# and TRDY# are sampled asserted. The initiator reads the final data item from the bus at that point.

CLOCK 9. At the latest (if early parity check wasn't performed), the initiator must sample PAR one clock afterwards, on clock nine, and, in the event of an error, must assert PERR# during clock nine.

Figure 13-1: Parity on Read Transaction

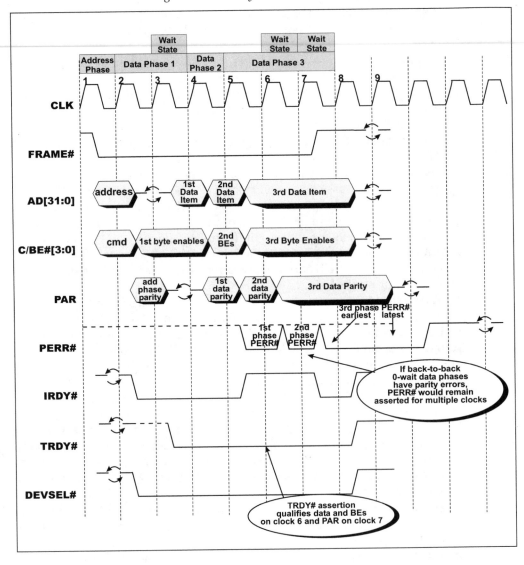

Data Parity Generation and Checking on Write

Introduction

During each data phase of a write transaction, the initiator drives data onto the AD bus. It is therefore the initiator's responsibility to supply correct parity to the target on PAR during the clock immediately following the assertion of IRDY#. At the conclusion of each data phase, it is the target's responsibility to latch the contents of AD[31:0] and C/BE#[3:0] and to calculate the expected parity during the clock cycle immediately following the conclusion of the data phase. The target then latches the PAR bit supplied by the initiator on the next rising-edge of the clock and compares the computed parity to the actual parity. If a miscompare occurs, the target then asserts PERR# to the master during the next clock. The assertion of PERR# lags the conclusion of each data phase by one PCI clock cycle. During a burst write, it is the initiator's responsibility to sample the state of the PERR# signal on the second rising-edge of the PCI clock after the conclusion of each data phase. If it samples PERR# asserted by the target, this indicates that the last data item written to the target was corrupted in flight. "Data Parity Reporting" on page 209 provides a detailed discussion of the actions taken by a bus master upon detection of a data phase parity error.

Example Burst Write

Refer to the write burst transaction illustrated in Figure 13-2 on page 208 during the following discussion.

CLOCK 1. The address phase starts on the rising-edge of clock one and completes on clock two.

CLOCK 2. All targets latch the address and command.
    DURING clock two, all targets compute the expected address phase parity.
    THE initiator supplies the address phase parity bit on the PAR signal.
    THE first data phase starts on the rising-edge of clock two. The initiator supplies the first data item on the AD bus and asserts IRDY# to indicate its presence.

CLOCK 3. All targets latch PAR on clock three. They then compare expected vs. actual parity. If an error were detected, the target(s) that detected the miscompare would assert SERR# (if the Parity Error Response and SERR# Enable bits in their respective configuration Command registers are set to one) within two clocks (recommended).
    THE first data item is latched by the target on the rising-edge of clock three (IRDY# and TRDY# sampled asserted).

THE initiator supplies the parity bit on PAR.

THE target computes the expected parity.

THE second data phase starts during clock three. The initiator drives the second data item onto the AD bus and the second set of byte enables onto the C/BE bus.

CLOCK 4. The actual parity for the first data phase is latched on the rising-edge of clock four and is compared to the expected parity. In the event of an error, the target asserts PERR# in clock four (if the Parity Error Response bit in its configuration Command register is set to one) back to the initiator to indicate that the first data item was corrupted in flight.

THE target latches the second data item on the rising-edge of clock four when it samples IRDY# and TRDY# both asserted.

THE third data phase starts during clock four. The initiator drives the third data item onto the AD bus and the third set of byte enables onto the C/BE bus.

THE target deasserts TRDY#, indicating that it isn't yet ready to accept the third data item (e.g., it has a buffer full condition).

THE initiator keeps IRDY# asserted to indicate that it is presenting the third data item.

THE initiator also deasserts FRAME#, indicating that this is the final data phase.

CLOCK 5. The initiator samples PERR# on clock five to determine if the first data item transferred with no errors.

THE initiator and target sample IRDY# asserted and TRDY# deasserted on the rising-edge of clock five, causing a wait state to be inserted in the third data phase during clock five.

THE target keeps TRDY# deasserted to indicate that it still isn't ready to transfer the third data item.

THE initiator must keep IRDY# asserted until the third data phase completes.

THE target samples PAR (the actual parity for the second data item) on the rising-edge of clock five. If the actual parity isn't the same as the parity bit computed during clock four, the target will assert PERR# to the initiator in clock six.

THE target could be designed to optionally check parity and report a parity error while it's still inserting wait states in the data phase. In this example, the target's parity checker could latch the data and byte enables on clock five (because IRDY# is asserted, indicating that the data is present) and submit them to its parity generator to compute the expected parity during clock five.

ALSO during clock five, the initiator must begin (one clock after it started driving the third data item) to drive the parity bit onto PAR.

CLOCK 6. The initiator and target sample IRDY# asserted but TRDY# still deasserted on the rising-edge of clock six, causing a second wait state to be inserted in the third data phase during clock six.

THE initiator samples PERR# to see if the second data item was received correctly by the target.

THE target's parity latches PAR on clock six and compares the third data phase's actual parity to the expected parity. In the event of an error, the target asserts PERR# during clock six. If the target performs this early parity check and asserts PERR#, it must keep PERR# asserted until two clocks after completion of the data phase. In the event that the target asserts PERR# early in this manner, the 2.2 spec has added a rule that the target must eventually assert TRDY# to complete the data phase. It is not permitted to end the data phase with a Retry, Disconnect Without Data, or a Target Abort.

DURING the third data phase, the target re-asserts TRDY# during clock six to indicate that it is ready to complete the data phase.

CLOCK 7. The final data phase completes on the rising-edge of clock seven when IRDY# and TRDY# are sampled asserted. The target latches the final data item from the bus at that point.

CLOCK 8. At the latest (if early parity check wasn't performed), the target must sample PAR one clock afterwards, on clock eight, and, in the event of an error, must assert PERR# during clock eight.

Figure 13-2: Parity on Write Transaction

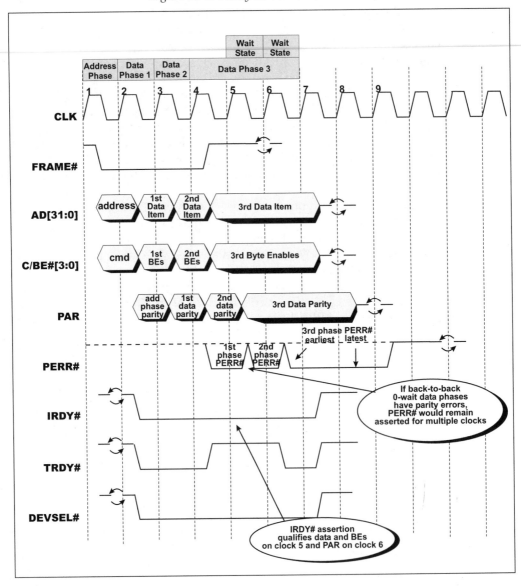

Data Parity Reporting

General

Upon detection of a data phase parity error, the device that checked the parity is responsible for asserting the Detected Parity Error bit in its PCI configuration Status register (see Figure 13-4 on page 211). It also asserts PERR# if the Parity Error Response bit in its PCI configuration Command register (see Figure 13-3 on page 211) is set to one. Only two categories of devices are excluded from the requirement to implement the PERR# signal and the Parity Error Response bit. They are described in "Devices Excluded from PERR# Requirement" on page 213.

If a data phase parity error is detected, PERR# must be asserted (at the latest) in the second clock after completion of the data phase (i.e., one clock after PAR is latched). Once PERR# is asserted, it must not be deasserted until during the third clock after the data phase completes. Figure 13-1 on page 204 and Figure 13-2 on page 208 both illustrate examples where the devices receiving the data checked parity and asserted PERR# before the completion of the data phase.

Master Can Choose Not To Assert PERR#

The master of a transaction that has a data phase parity error could choose not to assert PERR#. Rather, it could choose to attempt error recovery on its own or to invoke its driver (by generating an interrupt) so that it may attempt error recovery.

Parity Error During Read

During a read transaction, the target sources the data and the parity. The initiator receives the data and parity and checks the parity for correctness. If the data is incorrect, the initiator must set the Detected Parity Error bit in its PCI configuration Status register (irrespective of the state of its Parity Error Response bit). Assuming that the initiator's Parity Error Response bit is set to one, the initiator asserts PERR# in the second clock following completion of the data phase and sets the Master Data Parity Error bit in its configuration Status register.

Whether or not the bus master continues the transaction or terminates it is master design-dependent. The specification recommends that the transaction be continued to completion. In addition to the assertion of PERR#, the bus master is required to report the parity error to the system software. The specification recommends utilization of an interrupt or the setting of a bit in a device-specific status register that is polled by the device driver. Alternately, the designer can assert SERR#, but this approach should not be used lightly. It will more than likely result in a system shutdown.

Important Note Regarding Chipsets That Monitor PERR#

In many platform designs (i.e., chipset designs), the chip set logic converts any assertion of PERR# by anyone into SERR#. This means that if either the master (on a read) or the target (on a write) asserts PERR#, the chipset may very well either assert SERR# or just take the same action that it normally does when it detects SERR# asserted. Typically, this results in the generation of a fatal interrupt to the processor (such as NMI or Machine Check).

Parity Error During Write

During a write transaction, the initiator sources the data and the parity. The target receives the data and parity and checks the parity for correctness. If the data is incorrect, the target must set its Detected Parity Error bit to one (irrespective of the state of its Parity Error Response bit). Assuming that the target's Parity Error Response bit is set to one, the target asserts PERR# in the second clock following completion of the data phase. The initiator samples PERR# on the second clock after completion of the data phase. If PERR# has been asserted by the target, the initiator sets the Master Data Parity Error bit in its PCI configuration Status register. Targets never set this bit because only the bus master reports the error to software.

Whether or not the bus master continues the transaction or terminates it is master design-dependent. The specification recommends that the transaction be continued to completion. In addition to the assertion of PERR#, the bus master is required to report the parity error to the system software. The specification recommends utilization of an interrupt or the setting of a bit in a device-specific status register that is polled by the device driver. Alternately, the designer can assert SERR#, but this approach should not be used lightly. It will more than likely result in a system shutdown. In a particular platform design, the chip set logic may convert any assertion of PERR# into SERR#.

Figure 13-3: PCI Device's Configuration Command Register

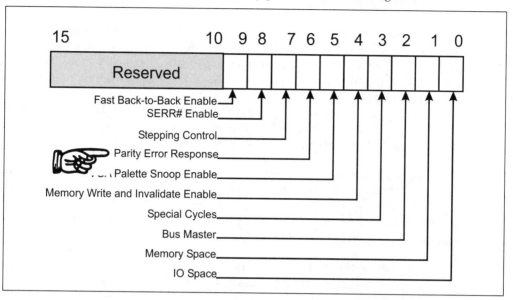

Figure 13-4: PCI Device's Configuration Status Register

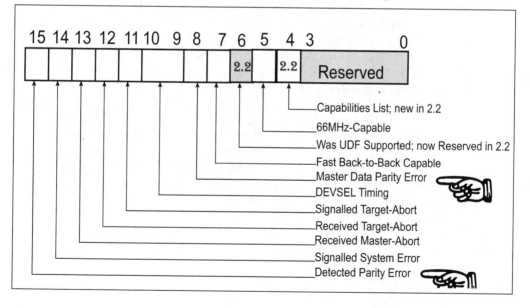

Data Parity Error Recovery

The PCI specification permits recovery from data phase parity errors but does not require it. The specification recommends that recovery be attempted at the lowest possible level (i.e., by the bus master). Ideally, the master should attempt error recovery without involving software. If the master cannot perform an action or actions to recover from the error, it should report the error to its device driver and possibly the driver can perform error recovery. The error should only be reported to the OS if neither the master nor its driver can recover from the error. How the OS responds to the error is OS-specific.

If the device reports the error by asserting SERR#, error recovery cannot be attempted (because assertion of SERR# causes the chipset to issue a fatal interrupt to the processor and the OS will shut down; see "Important Note Regarding Chipsets That Monitor PERR#" on page 210). Examples of recovery by the master, device driver and the OS are listed below:

- **Recovery by the bus master.** The master may attempt recovery by re-attempting the transaction if it knows that it will have no side effects (e.g., if the target device is a FIFO buffer, the access should not be re-attempted). If the re-attempt of the access completes with no errors, the master does not have to report an error to the system. If the attempt (or, perhaps several attempts) is unsuccessful, then the master must report the error. If there is a device driver associated with the master, the master alerts the driver to the error by generating an interrupt, setting a status bit, or some similar method. If there isn't a device driver associated with the master, the master may report the error by asserting SERR#.
- **Recovery by the device driver.** Assuming that the bus master reported the error to its device driver (e.g., by setting a device-specific status bit and generating an interrupt), the driver may instruct the bus master to re-attempt the transaction (once again, the driver must know that the re-attempt will not cause side effects). If the access completes with no errors, the device driver does not have to report the error to the OS. If the access error cannot be recovered from, the driver must report the error to the OS.
- **Recovery by the operating system.** How the OS responds to the report of a data parity error is OS-specific.

Special Case: Data Parity Error During Special Cycle

A master can use a Special Cycle transaction to broadcast a message (during the data phase) to the entire community of targets on a specific PCI bus (for more information, see "Special Cycle Command" on page 107 and "Special Cycle Transactions" on page 619). In the event that any target(s) detects a parity error related to the data phase, this indicates that the message was corrupted in flight. Since messages are used to issue instructions to subsystems, a corrupted message might place a subsystem in a state never intended. The PCI specification considers this to be a destabilizing event (like an address phase parity error). SERR# is used as the reporting mechanism.

The target(s) that detected the parity error must assert SERR# if all of the following conditions are true:

- the SERR# Enable bit in its PCI configuration Command register is set to one, and
- the Special Cycles bit is set in the device's Command register, and
- the Parity Error Response bit is also set to one in its Command register.

The target(s) must set the Detected Parity Error bit in its configuration Status registers. Any PCI device that signals SERR# is required to set the Signaled System Error bit in its PCI configuration Status register.

Devices Excluded from PERR# Requirement

The PCI specification excludes two types of devices from the requirement to implement the PERR# signal and the Parity Error Response bit in the configuration Command register. The following two sections describe these device categories.

Chipsets

In a PC, the chipset is embedded on the system board and typically consists of the host/PCI bridge and the PCI/expansion bus bridge. These two entities can be designed without the PERR# pin. Consider the following example.

When the host/PCI bridge initiates a PCI read transaction for the host processor, it receives a data item from the target at the completion of each data phase. One clock after the receipt of each data item it latches the parity bit(s) (PAR and possibly PAR64) and compares the received parity to that it computed. If the expected vs. received parity miscompares, the host/PCI bridge doesn't have to generate PERR# (because the bridge is frequently the device that monitors PERR# and reports its assertion to the OS). Instead, it can alert the processor that a parity error was received in a host bus-specific fashion. For example, in a PowerPC-based system, it could generate Machine Check interrupt to the processor.

Assume that a machine has been designed as a completely embedded environment: all devices are integrated onto the PCI bus and there are no PCI expansion slots. Also assume that none of the embedded devices checks the integrity of data written to them over the PCI bus. In this case, no device will ever assert PERR# upon receipt of a corrupted data item. There is therefore no requirement for PERR# to be implemented as an input pin on the host/PCI bridge.

Devices That Don't Deal with OS/Application Program or Data

An ideal example would be a video frame buffer. It is legal to build a video frame buffer that doesn't check the integrity of data written into its memory buffer. In the event that one or more data items are corrupted while being written into the buffer, the only effect is "wild and crazy" pictures on the screen. While this may be destabilizing to the end user's state of mind, it is not corrupting programs or data in memory or on permanent storage (e.g., hard drives).

SERR# Signal

SERR# is a required output from all PCI devices and is an input to the platform support logic (i.e., the chipset). A PCI device is not permitted to assert SERR# unless the SERR# Enable bit in its configuration Command register is set to one. SERR# is implemented as an open-drain, shared signal because multiple PCI devices may assert SERR# simultaneously. The system designer must provide a pull-up resistor on the SERR# signal line. When any (or all) PCI devices that are asserting SERR# cease driving it, the pull-up is responsible for returning SERR# to the deasserted state. This can take several PCI clocks.

When asserted, SERR# is asserted starting on the rising-edge of the PCI clock and is asserted for one clock and then tri-stated. It may be asserted at any time (i.e., its assertion is not tied to any type or phase of a PCI transaction). The specification suggests that SERR# should be asserted as quickly as possible (within two clocks of detecting an error condition is recommended).

Chapter 13: Error Detection and Handling

The SERR# signal is used to signal the following types of conditions:

- parity error on the address phase of a transaction.
- parity error on the data phase of a Special Cycle transaction.
- **ERROR WHEN ATTEMPTING A MEMORY WRITE TO DELIVER A MESSAGE SIGNALED 2.2 INTERRUPT (MSI).**
- serious problems other than parity detected by a PCI device.
- critical system failures detected by system board logic.

Before deciding to assert SERR# for an error, the designer should always consider that assertion of SERR# is considered an indication of a very serious problem. As examples, upon detection of SERR# assertion, the platform logic may assert NMI in an Intel system or TEA# or MC# in a PowerPC system. The NMI or Machine Check interrupt handler is invoked and will almost certainly halt the machine. The PCI specification does not dictate the action to be taken by the system logic when SERR# assertion is detected. As indicated earlier, it could result in a high-priority interrupt, or in the setting of a status bit to be polled by system software, etc.

Once the system logic detects SERR# asserted, it must sample SERR# deasserted on two successive clock edges before assuming that it has been deasserted. This requirement is because open-drain signaling cannot guarantee stable signals on every clock edge (the signal is pulled up to the logic high slowly by the weak pullup and then rings for a while before settling).

The sections that follow provide additional discussion of SERR# usage.

Address Phase Parity

Address Phase Parity Generation and Checking

Refer to Figure 13-5 on page 217 during the following discussion.

CLOCK 1. Every PCI transaction starts with the address phase (clock one in the figure). During the address phase, the initiator drives the start address onto AD[31:0] and the command (transaction type) onto C/BE#[3:0]. It also asserts FRAME# to indicate the presence of a valid start address and transaction type on the bus.

CLOCK 2. At the end of the address phase (on the rising-edge of clock two), the community of targets latch the address, command and the state of the FRAME# signal. Sampling FRAME# asserted at this point qualifies the address and command as valid. All targets then begin address decode during clock two.

THE targets calculate the expected parity to determine the value they expect to latch from the PAR signal on clock three.

THE initiator drives PAR to either a one or a zero to force even parity on the 37-bit field consisting of AD[31:0], C/BE#[3:0] and PAR.

CLOCK 3. On the rising-edge of clock three, the targets latch the state of the PAR signal.

DURING clock three the targets compare the expected parity they computed to the actual parity bit supplied by the initiator on the PAR signal. If it results in a good compare, the targets take no action. If, however, it results in a miscompare by any (or all) of the targets, the address and/or command were corrupted in flight. This is considered to be a destabilizing event in the PCI environment. The initiator is reaching out and addressing someone it never meant to or is accessing it in a way it never meant to. SERR# is the reporting mechanism. The next section describes error reporting of address phase parity errors.

Figure 13-5: Address Parity Generation/Checking

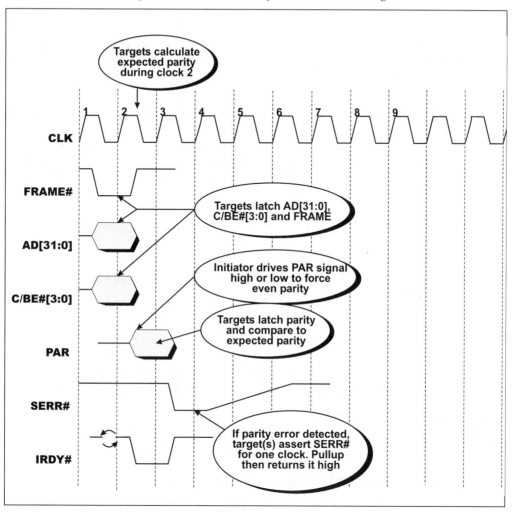

Address Phase Parity Error Reporting

Each target that detects an address phase parity miscompare must assert SERR# for one clock (if the device's SERR# Enable bit is set to one in its configuration Command register). Any devices that assert SERR# must also set the Signaled System Error bit in their configuration Status registers to one. The device's Detected Parity Error bit must also be set to one (even if SERR# isn't signaled by a device due to the state of its SERR# Enable bit). The PCI configuration Command register is pictured in Figure 13-3 on page 211. The Status register is pictured in Figure 13-4 on page 211.

As stated earlier, the specification recommends that SERR# be asserted within two PCI clocks of error detection. The earliest that SERR# would therefore be asserted would be during clock three, but it could be during clock four, five, or later (although not recommended).

In addition to the assertion of SERR#, the target device that is apparently addressed in a corrupted address phase can react in one of the following ways:

METHOD 1. assert DEVSEL# and complete the transaction normally.
METHOD 2. assert DEVSEL# and terminate the transaction with a Target Abort.
METHOD 3. not assert DEVSEL# and let the master time out and execute a Master Abort.

The target is not permitted to terminate the transaction with a Retry or a Disconnect.

System Errors

General

The following sections outline the various causes of SERR# assertion. In all cases, a device is not enabled to assert SERR# unless the SERR# Enable bit in its configuration Command register is set to one.

Address Phase Parity Error

This subject is discussed in "Address Phase Parity" on page 215.

Data Parity Error During Special Cycle

This subject is discussed in "Special Case: Data Parity Error During Special Cycle" on page 213.

Master of MSI Receives an Error

IF A MASTER GENERATES A MEMORY WRITE TRANSACTION TO SIGNAL A MESSAGE SIGNALED INTERRUPT (MSI) AND ONE OF THE FOLLOWING OCCURS, THE MASTER MUST ASSERT SERR# (ASSUMING THAT THE SERR# ENABLE BIT IN ITS COMMAND REGISTER IS SET TO ONE).

- *TARGET SIGNALS A TARGET ABORT.*
- *MASTER EXPERIENCES A MASTER ABORT.*
- *MASTER SAMPLES PERR# ASSERTED.*

Target Abort Detection

A master that doesn't have a mechanism (such as an interrupt line) to report receipt of a Target Abort to system software may assert SERR# to alert system software. The master must also set the Received Target Abort bit in its Status register.

Other Possible Causes of System Error

When any PCI device suffers a serious failure that impairs its ability to operate correctly, it may assert SERR# (if its SERR# Enable bit is set to one) to inform system software of the failure. It must also set the Signaled System Error status bit in its configuration Status register.

Devices Excluded from SERR# Requirement

The exceptions stated for PERR# implementation in "Devices Excluded from PERR# Requirement" on page 213 are also exceptions for SERR#.

Interrupts

Prior To This Chapter

The PCI bus architecture provides two error reporting mechanisms: one for reporting data parity errors and the other for reporting more serious system errors. The previous chapter provided a discussion of error detection, reporting and handling using these two mechanisms.

In This Chapter

This chapter provides a discussion of issues related to interrupt routing, generation and servicing.

The Next Chapter

The next chapter describes the 64-bit extension that permits PCI agents to perform eight byte transfers in each data phase. It also describes 64-bit addressing used to address memory targets that reside above the 4GB boundary.

Three Ways To Deliver Interrupts To Processor

There are three ways in which interrupt requests may be issued to a processor by a hardware device:

METHOD 1. **The Legacy method** delivers interrupt requests to the processor by asserting its INTR input pin. This method is frequently used in single processor Intel x86-based systems (e.g., Celeron-based systems).

METHOD 2. In **multiprocessor systems**, the interrupt request lines are tied to inputs on the IO **APIC** (Advanced Programmable Interrupt Controller) and the IO APIC delivers interrupt message packets to the array of processors via the APIC bus. This method is described in the MindShare book entitled *Pentium Processor System Architecture* (published by Addison-Wesley).

METHOD 3. THE 2.2 PCI SPECIFICATION DEFINES A NEW METHOD FOR DELIVERING INTER- **2.2** RUPT REQUESTS TO THE PROCESSORS BY PERFORMING MEMORY WRITE TRANSACTIONS. THIS METHOD ELIMINATES THE NEED FOR INTERRUPT REQUEST PINS AND SIGNAL TRACES AND IS DESCRIBED IN *"MESSAGE SIGNALED INTERRUPTS (MSI)"* ON PAGE 252.

Using Pins vs. Using MSI Capability

If a PCI function generates interrupt requests to request servicing by its device driver, the designer has **two choices**:

2.2

1. As described in the sections that follow, the device designer can use a **pin** on the device to signal an interrupt request to the processor.

2. ALTERNATIVELY, THE DESIGNER CAN IMPLEMENT MESSAGE SIGNALED INTERRUPT (MSI) CAPABILITY AND USE IT TO SIGNAL AN INTERRUPT REQUEST TO THE PROCESSOR. THIS METHOD ELIMINATES THE NEED FOR AN INTERRUPT PIN AND TRACE AND IS DESCRIBED IN THE SECTION ENTITLED "MESSAGE SIGNALED INTERRUPTS (MSI)" ON PAGE 252.

THE SPEC RECOMMENDS THAT A DEVICE THAT IMPLEMENTS MSI CAPABILITY ALSO IMPLEMENT AN INTERRUPT PIN TO ALLOW USAGE OF THE DEVICE IN A SYSTEM THAT DOESN'T SUPPORT MSI CAPABILITY. SYSTEM CONFIGURATION SOFTWARE MUST NOT ASSUME, HOWEVER, THAT AN MSI-CAPABLE DEVICE HAS AN INTERRUPT PIN.

With exclusion of the section entitled "Message Signaled Interrupts (MSI)" on page 252, the remainder of this chapter assumes that MSI is not being used by a device.

Single-Function PCI Device

A single-function PCI device is a physical package (add-in board or a component embedded on the PCI bus) that embodies one and only one function (i.e., logical device). If a single-function device generates interrupt requests to request servicing by its device driver, the designer must bond the device's interrupt request signal to the INTA# pin on the package (component or add-in board). A single-function PCI device must only use INTA# (never INTB#, INTC# or INTD#) to generate interrupt requests. In addition, the designer must hardwire this bonding information into the device's read-only, Interrupt Pin configuration register. Table 14-1 on page 223 indicates the value to be hardwired into this register (01h for INTA# for a single-function PCI device). The Interrupt Pin register resides in the second byte of configuration dword number 15d in the device's configuration Header space. The configuration Header space (the first 16d dwords of its configuration space) is illustrated in Figure 14-1 on page 223. It should be stressed that the format illustrated is for that used for PCI device's other than PCI-to-PCI or CardBus bridge devices and is referred to as Header Type Zero. The layout of the Header space for a PCI-to-PCI bridge can be found in "Configuration Registers" on page 552, while the Header layout for a CardBus bridge can be found in the CardBus spec.

Table 14-1: Value To Be Hardwired Into Interrupt Pin Register

Interrupt Signal Bonded To	Value Hardwired In Pin Register
Device doesn't generate interrupts.	00h
INTA# pin	01h
INTB# pin	02h
INTC# pin	03h
INTD# pin	04h

Figure 14-1: PCI Logical Device's Configuration Header Space Format

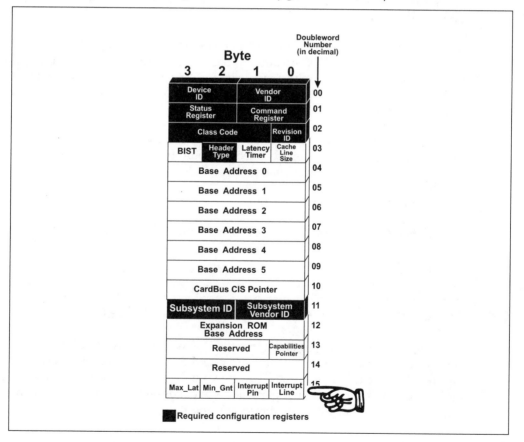

Multi-Function PCI Device

A multi-function PCI device is a physical package (add-in board or a component embedded on the PCI bus) that embodies between two and eight PCI functions. An example might be a card with a high-speed communications port and a parallel port implemented in the same package. There is no conceptual difference between a multi-function PCI device and a multi-function ISA, EISA or Micro Channel card.

The device designer may implement up to four interrupt pins on a multi-function device: INTA#, INTB#, INTC# and INTD#. Each function within the package is only permitted to use one of these interrupt pins to generate requests. Each function's Interrupt Pin register indicates which of the package's interrupt pins the device's internal interrupt request signal is bonded to (refer to Table 14-1 on page 223).

If a package implements one pin, it must be called INTA#. If it implements two pins, they must be called INTA# and INTB#, etc. All functions embodied within a package may be bonded to the same pin, INTA#, or each may be bonded to a dedicated pin (this would be true for a package with up to four functions embodied within it).

Groups of functions within the package may share the same pin. As some examples, a package embodying eight functions could bond their interrupt request signals in any of the following combinations:

*   all eight bonded to the INTA# pin.
*   four bonded to INTA# and four to INTB#.
*   two bonded to INTA#, two to INTB#, two to INTC# and two to INTD#.
*   seven to INTA# and one to INTB#.
*   etc.

Connection of INTx# Pins To System Board Traces

The temptation is great to imagine that the INTA# pin on every PCI package is connected to a trace on the system board called INTA#, and that the INTB# pin on every PCI package is connected to a trace on the system board called INTB#, etc. While this may be true in a particular system design, it's only one of many different scenarios permitted by the specification.

The system board designer may route the PCI interrupt pins on the various PCI packages to the system board interrupt controller in any fashion. As examples:

- They may all be tied to one trace on the system board that is hardwired to one input on the system interrupt controller.
- They may each be connected to a separate trace on the system board and each of these traces may be hardwired to a separate input on the system interrupt controller.
- They may each be connected to a separate trace on the motherboard. Each of these traces may be connected to a separate input of a programmable interrupt routing device. This device can be programmed at startup time to route each individual PCI interrupt trace to a selected input of the system interrupt controller.
- All of the INTA# pins can be tied together on one trace. All of the INTB# pins can be tied together on another trace, etc. Each of these traces can, in turn, be hardwired to a separate input on the system interrupt controller or may be hardwired to separate inputs on a programmable routing device.
- Etc.

The exact verbiage used in this section of the specification is:

"The system vendor is free to combine the various INTx# signals from PCI connector(s) in any way to connect them to the interrupt controller. They may be wire-ORed or electronically switched under program control, or any combination thereof."

Interrupt Routing

General

Ideally, the system configuration software should have maximum flexibility in choosing how to distribute the interrupt requests issued by various devices to inputs on the interrupt controller. The best scenario is pictured in Figure 14-2 on page 227. In this example, each of the individual PCI interrupt lines is provided to the programmable router as a separate input. In addition, the ISA interrupt request lines are completely segregated from the PCI lines. The ISA lines are connected to the master and slave 8259A interrupt controllers. In turn, the interrupt request output of the master interrupt controller is connected to one of the inputs on the programmable interrupt routing device. The router could be implemented using an Intel IO APIC module. The APIC I/O module can be programmed to assign a separate interrupt vector (interrupt table entry number) for each of the PCI interrupt request lines. It can also be programmed so that it realizes that one of its inputs is connected to an Intel 8259A interrupt controller.

Whenever any of the PCI interrupts request lines is asserted, the IO APIC module supplies the vector associated with that input to the processor's embedded local APIC module. Whenever the 8259A master interrupt controller generates a request, the APIC IO informs the processor that it must poll the 8259As to get the vector. In response, Intel processors that predate the P6 family processors generate two back-to-back Interrupt Acknowledge transactions. P6 family processors only generate a single Interrupt Acknowledge transaction. The first Interrupt Acknowledge forces the 8259As to prioritize their pending ISA requests, while the second Interrupt Acknowledge requests that the interrupt controller send the vector to the processor. For a detailed discussion of APIC operation, refer to the MindShare book entitled *Pentium Processor System Architecture* (published by Addison-Wesley). For a detailed description of 8259A operation, refer to the MindShare book entitled *ISA System Architecture* (published by Addison-Wesley).

Figure 14-2: Preferred Interrupt Design

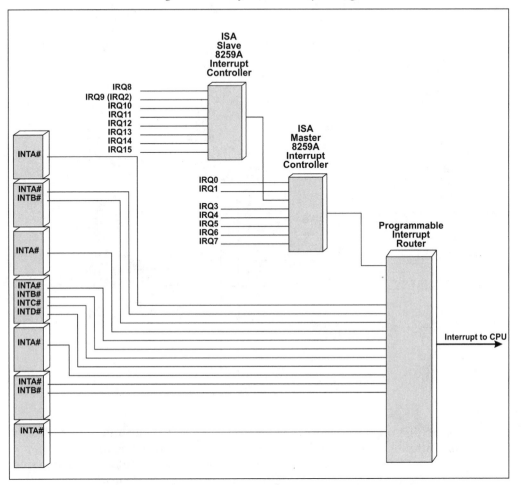

Figure 14-3 on page 228 illustrates another approach. Each of the PCI interrupt request lines is connected to a separate input of a programmable router. The router is programmed at startup time to route each of the PCI interrupt requests onto selected ISA interrupt request lines. This is a more limiting approach because ISA interrupt request lines are positive edge-triggered and are not shareable, while PCI interrupt request lines are active low, level-sensitive, shareable request lines. The PCI interrupts can only be routed onto ISA interrupt request lines that are not in use by ISA devices.

Figure 14-3: Alternative Interrupt Layout

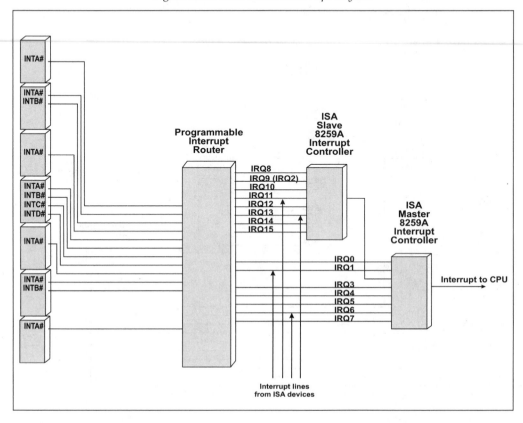

Figure 14-4 on page 229 and Figure 14-5 on page 230 illustrate typical designs for platforms implemented in the 1993/1999 timeframe using the most common chipsets. Of these two designs, Figure 14-5 on page 230 would be preferred over Figure 14-4 on page 229. The programmable router is built into the PCI/ISA bridge chip and provides four inputs to connect PCI interrupt request signal lines to. The router can be programmed to route each PCI interrupt request signal to any of the ISA interrupt request lines that are not being used by ISA devices. As mentioned earlier, ISA interrupt request lines are positive edge-triggered and are not shareable. As you can see in Figure 14-4 on page 229, the INTA# request line is heavily-weighted (seven devices). By laying out the PCI interrupt traces as illustrated in Figure 14-5 on page 230, the interrupts are spread more evenly (only three devices per line) across the four inputs of the router.

Figure 14-4: Typical Design In Some Older Machines (1993/1994)

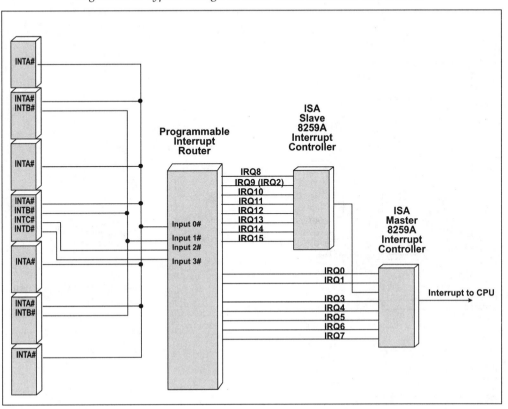

Figure 14-5: Recommended PCI Interrupt Line Routing (when router only has four input pins)

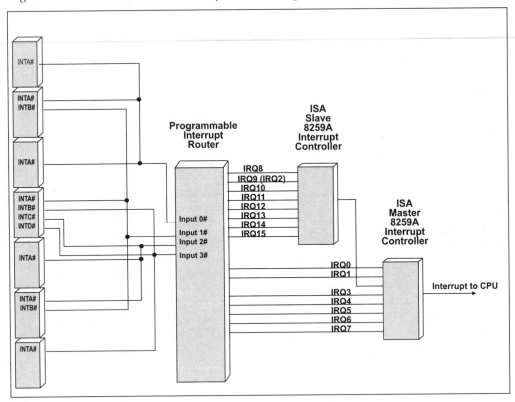

Routing Recommendation In PCI Specification

Refer to Figure 14-5 on page 230. In many of today's PC systems, the programmable router embedded within the PCI/ISA bridge has four inputs for connection to PCI interrupt traces. In addition, most current PCI devices are single-function devices. If they are interrupt-driven, they must therefore use the INTA# pin on the package. Recognizing that it would be best to "spread" the interrupts from the various single-function devices across the interrupt router's four inputs, the specification writers recommend the interconnect of the INTA# outputs to the system board traces and the trace connection to the router's four inputs such that they are evenly spread across the four pins.

BIOS "Knows" Interrupt Trace Layout

The platform startup software (in the BIOS) is platform-specific and "knows" how the PCI interrupt traces are connected between PCI devices, card slots, and the interrupt router (or the interrupt controller if there is no router). As an example, it might know that:

- the INTA# pin on the SCSI host bus adapter integrated onto the PCI bus is physically connected to input pin 13 on the router.
- the INTA# pin on PCI expansion slot one is physically connected to input pin 14 on the router.
- the INTB# pin on the embedded Ethernet controller is physically connected to input pin 15 on the router.

Well-Designed Chipset Has Programmable Interrupt Router

A well-designed chipset incorporates a software-programmable interrupt routing device. The startup configuration software attempts to program the router to distribute the PCI interrupts in an optimal fashion. Using Figure 14-5 on page 230 as an example, the startup configuration software can program the router to route each of these PCI interrupts to an interrupt controller input that isn't used by an ISA device.

Each IRQ input of the interrupt controller that is connected to a single ISA device is programmed for positive-edge triggered, non-shareable operation, while those connected to PCI interrupt lines must be programmed as active low, level-sensitive, shareable inputs.

It must be recognized that the startup configuration software is typically not very intelligent and may not make the best possible routing decisions. The router can be reprogrammed after system startup by a user running a configuration utility and making more informed selections, or by a Plug-and-Play OS such as Windows 98 or Windows 2000. "PCI Interrupts Are Shareable" on page 238 provides a detailed discussion of the issues related to interrupt routing and performance implications. The section entitled "Interrupt Routing Table" on page 233 describes how a Plug-and-Play OS can discover the type of router and how the PCI devices are attached to the router.

Interrupt Routing Information

Once the startup configuration software has programmed the router, the routing information (the system IRQ line the device's PCI interrupt pin is routed to) must then be saved in the Interrupt Line register in the PCI function's configuration Header space (refer to Figure 14-1 on page 223). The definition of the routing information is machine architecture-specific. The specification dictates the definition for x86-based PCs. Table 14-2 on page 232 indicates the values to be written into the Interrupt Line register in an Intel x86-based PC. The values 16d - 254 are reserved, while the value 255d indicates routing "unknown" or "no connection." Although it doesn't state this in the specification, it is the author's opinion that RST# should initialize the Interrupt Line register to a value of FFh, thereby indicating that a system IRQ line has not yet been assigned to the device's interrupt pin.

Table 14-2: Interrupt Line Register Values for x86 PC Platforms

System IRQ Line Interrupt Routed To	Value To Be Written In Line Register
IRQ0	0d
IRQ1	1d
IRQ2	2d
IRQ3	3d
IRQ4	4d
IRQ5	5d
IRQ6	6d
IRQ7	7d
IRQ8	8d
IRQ9	9d
IRQ10	10d
IRQ11	11d
IRQ12	12d
IRQ13	13d

Table 14-2: Interrupt Line Register Values for x86 PC Platforms (Continued)

System IRQ Line Interrupt Routed To	Value To Be Written In Line Register
IRQ14	14d
IRQ15	15d

Interrupt Routing Table

General

In a PC-compatible platform, the Plug-and-Play OS must have the ability to learn how each PCI function's interrupt pin (assuming that the function generates interrupts using an interrupt pin) is connected to a selected input on the interrupt router. It must also have the ability to program the router. In order to do this, the OS must have access to the following information:

- Whether or not the chipset has a programmable interrupt router.
- If there is a router, an entry in the table identifies the bus, device and function number within which the router resides.
- Another entry identifies whether or not the router's control register interface complies with a specific, standard chipset register interface (e.g., the Intel 440BX chipset). Assuming that the OS has a driver available that understands that interface standard, this gives the OS the ability to program the router and thereby select which IRQ input on the interrupt controller is associated with the interrupt trace coming from the function.
- Identifies which IRQ inputs on the interrupt controller are connected to the outputs of the router. In other words, it identifies the IRQs that are tied exclusively to the outputs of the router and therefore may only be assigned to PCI functions (as opposed to devices other than PCI functions such as ISA devices).
- In addition to the information already listed, the table contains one entry for each embedded PCI device as well one for each PCI add-in card connector. These are referred to as Slot entries.

It is the responsibility of the system board vendor to embed a table (referred to as the Interrupt Routing Table) in the BIOS ROM. This table contains the information listed in Table 14-3 on page 234.

Finding the Table

The PCI Interrupt Routing Table can be detected by searching system memory from F0000h to FFFFFh at every 16-byte boundary for the table's signature ("$PIR"). Once the signature is found, the following items need to be validated:

- **Version**. Must be 1.0.
- **Table size**. Must be larger than 32 and must be a multiple of 16.
- **Checksum**. The entire structure's checksum must be 0.

Table 14-3: PCI Interrupt Routing Table

Byte Offset from Table Start	Size (bytes)	Description
0	4	**Signature**. The signature for this table is the ASCII string "$PIR". Byte 0 is a 24h, byte 1 a 50h, byte 2 is a 49h, and byte 3 is 52h.
4	2	**Version**. The version consists of a Minor version byte followed by a Major version byte. Since this specification describes the Version 1.0 table format, byte 4 of the table is a 00h and byte 5 is a 01h.
6	2	**Table Size**. The size of the PCI Interrupt Routing Table in bytes. The table consists of 32 bytes of general info followed by a 16 byte entry for each embedded PCI device and add-in card slot. As an example, if there were five slot entries in the table, the table size would be 32 + (5 * 16) = 112 bytes.
8	1	**PCI Interrupt Router's Bus**. This contains the number of the PCI bus that the PCI Interrupt Router resides on.
9	1	**PCI Interrupt Router's DevFunc**. This contains the Device and Function number wherein resides the PCI Interrupt Router device. The Device is in the upper five bits and the Function in the lower three.
10	2	**PCI Exclusive IRQs**. This is an 16-bit IRQ bitmap that indicates which IRQ inputs on the interrupt controller are devoted exclusively for PCI usage. Bit 15 corresponds to IRQ15, while bit 0 corresponds to IRQ0. As an example, if IRQ11 is devoted exclusively to PCI and cannot be assigned to an ISA device, then bit 11 of this 16-bit field should be set to 1. If there are no IRQs devoted exclusively to PCI, then this value should be 0.

Table 14-3: PCI Interrupt Routing Table (Continued)

Byte Offset from Table Start	Size (bytes)	Description
12	4	**Compatible PCI Interrupt Router.** This field contains the Vendor ID (bytes 12 and 13) and Device ID (bytes 14 and 15) of a compatible PCI Interrupt Router, or zero if there is none. A compatible PCI Interrupt Router is one that uses the same method (i.e., the same register set layout) for mapping PCI interrupt traces (also referred to as **links**) to IRQs, and for controlling the edge/level triggering of IRQs. Using this Vendor and Device ID, an OS can load the driver for the compatible PCI chipset router.
16	4	**Miniport Data.** This dword is passed directly to the IRQ Miniport's Initialize() function. If an IRQ Miniport does not need any additional information, this field should be set to zero.
20	11	Reserved.
31	1	**Checksum.** This byte should be set such that the sum of all of the bytes in the PCI Interrupt Routing Table, including the checksum and all of the slot entries (modulo 256) is zero.
32	16	**First Slot Entry.** Each slot entry is 16-bytes long and describes how a slot's PCI interrupt pins are wire OR'd to the interrupt pins on other slots and to the chipset's router input pins. Each entry has the format illustrated in Table 14-4 on page 235.
48	16	**Second Slot Entry.** See *First Slot Entry.*
(N + 1) * 16	16	**nth Slot Entry.** See *First Slot Entry.*

Table 14-4: Format of Slot Entry in PCI Interrupt Routing Table

Byte Offset from Table Start	Size (bytes)	Description
0	1	**PCI Bus Number.** The bus number that the slot resides on.
1	1	**PCI Device Number** (in upper five bits). The device number of the slot.

Table 14-4: Format of Slot Entry in PCI Interrupt Routing Table (Continued)

Byte Offset from Table Start	Size (bytes)	Description
2	1	**Link Value for INTA#.** • **00h**: Indicates that the INTA# interrupt pin at this device position is not connected to any other device's interrupt pins and is not connected to any of the Interrupt Router's interrupt pins. • **non-zero**: The choice of a non-zero link value is specific to a chipset and decided by the chip-set vendor. A suggested implementation follows. **Example**: The interrupt pins on PCI devices are connected to traces on the system board and each of those traces is connected to an input on the chipset's interrupt router. The number of input pins on a specific chipset's interrupt router is chipset-specific. A value in this field between one and the number of interrupt pins on the Interrupt Router means the pin is connected to that pin of the Interrupt Router. A value larger than the number of interrupt pins on the Interrupt Router means the pin is wire OR'd together with other slot interrupt pins, but the group is not connected to any input pin on the Interrupt Router. In other words, that trace bypasses the router and is connected directly to an input on interrupt controller. Other interpretations of the link values are possible. For instance, the link value may indicate which byte of Configuration Space or which IO Port to access for the link. The specific interpretation of the link value is decided by the manufacturer of the Interrupt Router and is supported by the driver for that router.

Table 14-4: Format of Slot Entry in PCI Interrupt Routing Table (Continued)

Byte Offset from Table Start	Size (bytes)	Description
3	2	**IRQ Bitmap for INTA#.** This value indicates which of the IRQ inputs on the interrupt controller this PCI device's interrupts can be routed to. This provides the routing options for one particular PCI interrupt pin. In this bitmap, bit 0 corresponds to IRQ0, bit 1 to IRQ1, and so on. A 1 bit in this bitmap indicates that routing is possible; a 0 bit indicates that no routing is possible. This bitmap must be the same for all pins that have the same link number (because their INTx# pins are all tied to the same trace and therefore to the same input on the router).
5	1	**Link Value for INTB#.** See *Link Value for INTA#*.
6	2	**IRQ Bitmap for INTB#.** See *IRQ Bitmap for INTA#*.
8	1	**Link Value for INTC#.** See *Link Value for INTA#*.
9	2	**IRQ Bitmap for INTC#.** See *IRQ Bitmap for INTA#*.
11	1	**Link Value for INTD#.** See *Link Value for INTA#*.
12	2	**IRQ Bitmap for INTD#.** See *IRQ Bitmap for INTA#*.

Table 14-4: Format of Slot Entry in PCI Interrupt Routing Table (Continued)

Byte Offset from Table Start	Size (bytes)	Description
14	1	**Slot Number.** Indicates whether the table entry is for a PCI device embedded on the system-board or for an add-in slot. • 00h = embedded system board devices. • non-zero = the physical placement of an add-in card slot on the system board. This provides a way to correlate physical slots with PCI device numbers (see "Definition of a Chassis" on page 595). Values (with the exception of zero) are OEM-specific. For end-user ease-of-use, slots in the system should be clearly labeled (via solder mask, back panel labels, etc.) with the same value indicated in this field. It should be noted that the format of the slot entries in the PCI Interrupt Routing Table are compatible with the format of the IRQ Routing Options Buffer table returned when a Get PCI Interrupt Routing Options call is made to the PCI BIOS (see Table 26-2 on page 681). This makes it possible to support both the PCI Interrupt Routing Table and the PCI BIOS specification with only one table in ROM.
15	1d	Reserved.

PCI Interrupts Are Shareable

The PCI interrupt request signals are open-drain. Multiple devices connected to the same PCI interrupt request signal line can assert it simultaneously without damage. The net result is that the line is driven low. The system board designer provides a pullup resistor on each of the lines, so that their native state (when no device is asserting a request) is deasserted.

Hooking the Interrupt

After the system startup configuration software executes (typically from firmware), the system initialization begins. The system or the OS must provide a device-specific interrupt service routine for each interrupt-driven device in the system. Furthermore, the startup and OS software must build an interrupt table in memory. Each entry in the interrupt table must contain the start address (i.e., the entry point) of the device-specific interrupt service routine associated with a particular device.

When the system is first powered up, system main memory contains junk. Since the interrupt table resides in DRAM in a PC, the interrupt table must be built prior to enabling interrupt-driven devices to generate interrupt requests. Placing the start address of a device's interrupt service routine into the correct entry in the interrupt table is commonly referred to as "hooking" the interrupt. The next section provides a detailed discussion of how the interrupt table is built during system startup in a PC environment.

Interrupt Chaining

General

As stated earlier, when the system first starts up, the processor has interrupt recognition disabled and the interrupt table has not yet been built in memory. There are basically two categories of interrupt-driven devices that will have to have entries made in the interrupt table:

- embedded devices that the system already knows about.
- devices discovered during the startup and auto-config process.

The interrupt handler for each interrupt driven device is implemented within the device's device driver. The driver can be found in one of three places:

- **within** the **system BIOS ROM**. The drivers for some or all of the embedded devices (embedded on the PCI bus and/or the ISA bus) are typically found within the system BIOS ROM. The startup POST/BIOS code knows the entry points of these handlers and the entries in the interrupt table that they are associated with.

- **within** a **device ROM** associated with the interrupt-driven device itself. These device ROMs are "discovered" during the bus scan (enumeration) process at startup, the drivers are loaded into main memory, and the initialization code within them is automatically executed.
- **on disk** as a loadable device driver loaded by the OS during the OS load and initialization process. As the OS loads each loadable driver into memory, it calls the initialization code within the driver. The initialization code calls the PCI BIOS to determine if its associated device exists in the system. If found and the device is interrupt-driven, the driver contains the device's interrupt handler. The driver initialization code is responsible for placing the start address of the interrupt handler into the proper entry within the interrupt table.

The following sections provide an example of the sequence of actions taken to build the interrupt table in memory.

Step 1: Initialize All Entries To Point To Dummy Handler

Initially, the interrupt table in main memory contains junk. The startup firmware stores the entry point of a dummy interrupt service routine into each entry. This routine contains the following instructions:

- If this handler is associated with one of the IRQ lines on the master 8259A interrupt controller, it contains an IO write instruction that writes a Non-Specific **EOI** (End-of-Interrupt) command **to the master interrupt controller**. When executed, this clears the highest bit currently set to one in the controller's In-Service register.
- If this handler is associated with one of the IRQ lines on the slave 8259A interrupt controller, it contains an IO write instruction that writes a Non-Specific **EOI** command **to the master** interrupt controller, **and** an additional IO write that writes a Non-Specific EOI command **to the slave interrupt controller**. When executed, this clears the highest bit currently set to one in both of the controllers' In-Service registers.
- The final instruction in the dummy handler is an **IRET** (interrupt return).

Step 2: Initialize All Entries For Embedded Devices

As stated earlier, the system designer usually includes the device drivers for embedded devices in the system POST/BIOS firmware. These devices may already be hardwired to pre-defined interrupt request lines and each of these lines is associated with a pre-defined vector, or entry, in the interrupt table. For each embedded device, the startup firmware stores the start address of the embedded device's interrupt handler into the associated table entry in memory.

Step 3: Hook Entries For Embedded Device BIOS Routines

The system firmware usually contains a series of BIOS routines used to communicate with IO devices. In an Intel x86 machine, the INT (software interrupt) instruction is used to call a BIOS routine. The parameter supplied with the INT instruction (INT xx) is the interrupt table entry that contains the pointer to the routine to be called. As an example, INT 21h causes the processor to call the interrupt service routine pointed to by entry 21h in the interrupt table.

During system startup, the system firmware stores the pointers to these routines into the appropriate entries in the table (after first saving the pointers previously stored in those entries).

Step 4: Perform Expansion Bus ROM Scan

The system firmware then scans the expansion bus (e.g., ISA bus) for device ROMs associated with devices residing on that bus. At 2KB intervals starting at memory address 00C0000h and proceeding through memory address 00DFFFFh, the first two bytes are read. A value of 55h in the first location and AAh in the second is the signature of a device ROM. When a device ROM is discovered, the system firmware calls the device's initialization code within the ROM just discovered (by calling location three within the ROM).

ISA bus devices typically have their interrupt lines assigned via DIP switches on the card. Assuming that a device is interrupt-driven, the device's initialization code hooks the appropriate entry in the interrupt table. Since ISA IRQ lines are not shared with other devices, it does this by storing the start address of its own interrupt handler routine in the entry. When the device's initialization routine completes execution, it returns control to the system firmware. The system firmware then continues scanning the 00C0000h through 00DFFFFh (or 00EFFFFh in some systems) memory range (on 2KB address boundaries) for more ROMs.

Step 5: Perform PCI Device Scan

The firmware-based configuration software attempts to read the Vendor ID from function zero at each physical PCI device position on the PCI bus. Any position that returns a Vendor ID of FFFFh is unoccupied (see "Vendor ID Register" on page 354). Those that return values other than FFFFh are occupied by a single- or a multi-function device. For each occupied position, the firmware takes the following actions:

STEP 1. Reads function zero's configuration Header registers to determine the needs and requirements of the device.

STEP 2. Allocates memory space to the device's memory address decoder(s) (i.e., its memory BAR registers), IO space to its IO address decoder(s) (IO BAR registers), etc.

STEP 3. Reads from the device's Interrupt Pin register to determine if the function is interrupt driven. A value of zero indicates that it isn't, while a value of 01h, 02h, 03h, or 04h indicates that it is and which of the device's PCI interrupt pins (INTA#, INTB#, INTC#, or INTD#) the device uses to generate interrupt requests.

STEP 4. Programs the interrupt router to route interrupts generated by the device to a specific system interrupt line (IRQ line).

STEP 5. Writes the routing information into the device's Interrupt Line (routing) register. As an example, if it is routed to IRQ3, the value 03h is written to its Interrupt Line register.

STEP 6. Probes the device's Expansion ROM Base Address register to determine if the device has an embedded device ROM. If it does, the ROM Base Address Register is programmed with a start memory address and its memory address decoder is enabled. For more information, refer to "Expansion ROMs" on page 411.

STEP 7. The ROM code image (a device driver) is copied into main memory (it's a rule in PCI that ROM code is never executed in place). The ROM address decoder is disabled.

STEP 8. The system firmware then calls the initialization routine (at location three) embedded in the driver. If the device is interrupt driven, the device-specific handler is embedded within the driver. The driver reads the Interrupt Line register to determine the routing information. This is used to determine the entry in the interrupt table to be hooked. This entry may have already been previously-hooked to point to an embedded PCI device's interrupt handler. The current contents of the entry is saved in the body of the device's handler and then the start address of the device's handler is stored in the entry. In this way, the interrupt table entry now points to this device's handler and the handler "remembers" the pointer to the previous device's handler. A linked list of interrupt service routines is being created.

STEP 9. If the ROM image contains a device-specific BIOS routine, the start address of the routine is stored in the appropriate interrupt table entry (after first saving the pointer previously stored in that entry).

STEP 10. Upon completion of the device driver's initialization code, program execution is returned back to the system firmware which then checks bit seven of function zero's Header Type configuration register to determine if this is a multi-function device. If cleared to zero, the device is a single function device, so the configuration software continues scanning (enumerating) the PCI bus. The next physical device position is probed on the PCI bus to determine if it's occupied.

STEP 11. However, if bit seven is set to one, this is a multi-function device. The software then probes functions one through seven within the PCI device to determine which additional functions are implemented. The process described above is repeated for each device discovered.

Step 6: Load OS

After both the PCI and expansion bus scans have been completed, the system firmware begins to read the OS startup code into memory and then cedes control to it. The actions taken by the OS are specific to that OS. The discussion that follows is generic in nature.

Step 7: OS Loads and Call Drivers' Initialization Code

At some point, the OS initialization code processes the CONFIG.SYS file (or its equivalent, such as the Windows 95 Registry). Each time that a "DEVICE=" statement is encountered, the following actions are taken:

STEP 1. The indicated device driver is loaded into memory and the OS calls its initialization code.

STEP 2. The device driver's initialization code determines if its associated device is present in the machine. For a device driver associated with an ISA device, this is accomplished by probing IO ports associated with the device to see if it's present. For a driver associated with a PCI device, this is accomplished by issuing a PCI BIOS call (see Table 26-2 on page 681), or a HAL call in Windows NT, supplying the device's Vendor and Device ID or its Class Code as search parameters. The BIOS checks CMOS RAM or walks the PCI bus to determine if the device is present. If present, the driver's initialization code then reads the Interrupt Line register to obtain the interrupt routing information. In the case of an ISA device, the interrupt controller input number is typically supplied as a parameter on the "DEVICE=" command line in CONFIG.SYS.

STEP 3. Having determined the interrupt controller input associated with the device, the driver first reads and saves the pointer previously residing in the corresponding interrupt table entry. It then replaces it with the pointer to the device-specific interrupt service routine embedded within the device driver body. The driver's initialization code then returns control to the OS initialization code which then continues processing CONFIG.SYS (or whatever mechanism that OS uses to identify drivers that need to be loaded).

Linked-List Has Been Built for Each Interrupt Level

The OS load process has now completed and the machine is operational. The interrupt table has been completely initialized. The interrupt service routine currently pointed to by an interrupt table entry is associated with the last device "discovered" during the bus scan that uses that interrupt level.

In turn, that interrupt service routine "remembers" the start address of the interrupt service routine associated with the device that had previously hooked the same interrupt. Likewise, the previous device's interrupt service routine "remembers" the start address of the interrupt service routine associated with the device that hooked the same interrupt before it had, etc. A linked list has been established for each interrupt level.

Servicing Shared Interrupts

Example Scenario

Refer to Figure 14-6 on page 245 during the discussion that follows. This figure illustrates two devices, an Ethernet controller and communications port two, that both generate interrupt requests using the same PCI interrupt request line (e.g., two devices in the same package that both share INTA#, or two devices in separate packages that share the same interrupt request signal trace on the system board). Assume that no other drivers had hooked the interrupt prior to the COM port and the Ethernet controller. In other words, the entry in the interrupt table contains a pointer to the dummy interrupt handler (see "Step 1: Initialize All Entries To Point To Dummy Handler" on page 240) and that the COM port hooked the interrupt first, followed by the Ethernet controller.

Each device has an open-collector driver that it uses to assert an interrupt request. This is accomplished when the device's logic asserts its internal IRQ# signal, providing an enable to the output driver. This creates a path to ground and the external request line is driven low. The interrupt signal trace on the system board has a pullup resistor on it, thereby keeping the request line deasserted when none of the devices connected to that line are generating a request. When one or more devices are generating a request on the line, the external interrupt request line is low. In other words, a low on the request line indicates to the interrupt controller that one or more devices are generating a request.

In addition to driving the request line low, a device also sets an interrupt pending bit in a device-specific IO status port known to its interrupt service routine.

Figure 14-6: Shared Interrupt Model

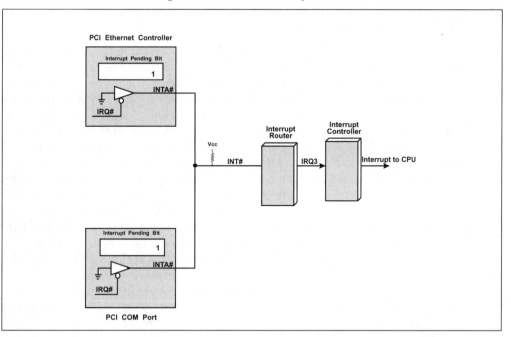

Both Devices Simultaneously Generate Requests

Referring to Figure 14-6 on page 245, both devices sharing the same interrupt request signal (the Ethernet controller and the COM port) assert a request simultaneously. Each of them sets their respective interrupt pending bits to one and both turn on their respective interrupt request output drivers, resulting in a low on the interrupt request line (INT#). In this example, assume that the interrupt routing device routes the PCI interrupt request line onto system interrupt line IRQ3.

Processor Interrupted and Requests Vector

Refer to Figure 14-7 on page 248. This example scenario assumes that this is a single processor system. The IRQs are tied to the master and slave 8259A interrupt controllers within the PCI-to-ISA bridge (the South Bridge). When it detects one or more inputs asserted, it asserts its INTR output to the processor.

Assuming that the processor is enabled to recognize external interrupts (Interrupt Flag bit set to one in the x86's EFLAGS register, or EE bit set to one in a PowerPC processor's MSR register), the processor recognizes the interrupt on the next instruction boundary.

The processor automatically saves its place in the interrupted program. Assuming that it's an Intel x86 processor, this is accomplished by pushing the contents of the CS, IP and EFLAG registers into stack memory. The processor (assuming it's a P6-family processor) then generates one Interrupt Acknowledge transaction (for more information, see "Interrupt Acknowledge Command" on page 100). The transaction is propagated to the PCI bus and is visible to the South Bridge (which contains the interrupt controller). This commands the interrupt controller to prioritize its pending requests and then provide the processor with the vector associated with the highest-priority interrupt currently pending. In this case, assuming that IRQ3 is the highest pending request, the processor receives the vector associated with IRQ3. The vectors are programmed into the interrupt controller during startup time and are listed in Table 14-5 on page 247. The vector, or table entry, for IRQ3 is 0Bh. When the processor receives vector 0Bh it multiplies it by four (if in real mode; by eight if in protected mode) because each entry in the interrupt table contains the four byte start address of an interrupt service routine (or an 8-byte Interrupt Descriptor in Protected Mode). This yields the start memory address of the table entry, 0000002Ch. The processor then reads the contents of memory locations 0000002Ch through 0000002Fh to obtain the start address of the interrupt service routine to execute.

Table 14-5: ISA Interrupt Vectors

IRQ Number	Vector (Table Entry)
IRQ0	08h
IRQ1	09h
IRQ2	0Ah
IRQ3	0Bh
IRQ4	0Ch
IRQ5	0Dh
IRQ6	0Eh
IRQ7	0Fh
IRQ8	70h
IRQ9	71h
IRQ10	72h
IRQ11	73h
IRQ12	74h
IRQ13	75h
IRQ14	76h
IRQ15	77h

Figure 14-7: Single Processor PC

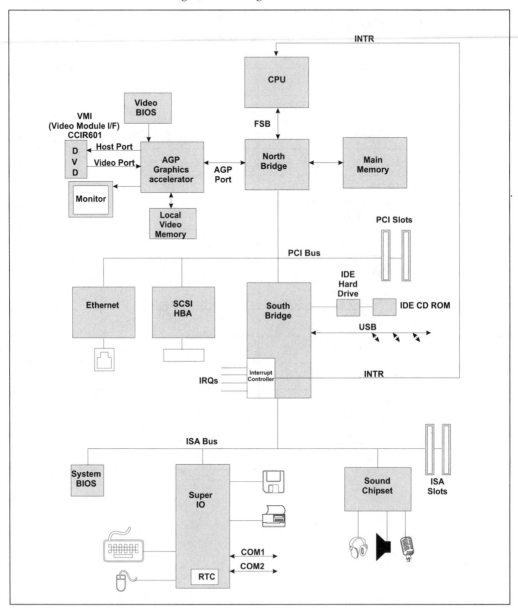

First Handler Executed

In this example, the COM port had hooked the interrupt first, followed by the Ethernet controller. This means that entry 0Bh in the table currently points to the Ethernet controller's interrupt service routine and the entry point of the COM port's interrupt service routine is known to the Ethernet controller's routine.

The processor jumps to the Ethernet controller's interrupt service routine. At the front end of this routine, the programmer reads the Ethernet controller's interrupt pending bit from an IO status port implemented in the Ethernet controller to determine if the Ethernet controller is currently generating a request. In this case it is, so the body of the Ethernet controller's interrupt service routine is therefore executed and its request is serviced. The act of servicing the interrupt clears the interrupt request within the device. The Ethernet controller clears its interrupt pending bit and deasserts its local IRQ# signal. This disables the open-collector driver and removes the path to ground from the external interrupt request signal line. The line remains low, however, because the COM port is still generating a request.

Jump to Next Driver in Linked List

The last instruction in the Ethernet controller's interrupt service routine jumps to the entry point of the COM port's interrupt service routine. The device-specific COM port interrupt service routine checks the COM port's interrupt pending bit to determine if it requires servicing. Since its bit is set to one, the body of the interrupt service routine is executed. Once again, the act of servicing an interrupt clears the request. The COM port clears its interrupt pending bit and disables its open-collector driver, removing the path to ground from the external interrupt request signal line. The pullup resistor on the line automatically desasserts it. All interrupts on that line have been serviced.

Jump to Dummy Handler: Control Passed Back to Interrupted Program

The last instruction in the COM port's interrupt service routine jumps to the entry point of the dummy interrupt handler which only contains the following instructions:

- If this handler is associated with one of the IRQ lines on the master 8259A interrupt controller, an IO write instruction is executed to write a non-specific **EOI** (End-of-Interrupt) command **to** the **master** interrupt controller. This has the effect of clearing the highest bit currently set to one in the controller's In-Service register.
- If this handler is associated with one of the IRQ lines on the slave 8259A interrupt controller, an IO write instruction is executed to write a non-specific **EOI** command **to** the **master** interrupt controller. An **additional** IO write is executed to write a non-specific **EOI** command **to** the **slave** interrupt controller. This has the effect of clearing the highest bit currently set to one in both of the controllers In-Service registers.
- After the EOI(s) have been sent, the final instruction in the dummy handler, an **IRET** (interrupt return), is executed, causing the processor to resume execution of the interrupted program.

Implied Priority Scheme

Any architecture that utilizes a shared interrupt scheme (e.g., PCI, EISA, and Micro Channel) has an explicit and an implicit interrupt priority scheme. In EISA, ISA and Micro Channel, the interrupt controllers are programmed at startup time to use an explicit, fixed-priority scheme (see Table 14-6 on page 250).

Table 14-6: Interrupt Priority Scheme

PC Interrupt Priority (highest to lowest)
IRQ0
IRQ1
IRQ8
IRQ9
IRQ10
IRQ11
IRQ12
IRQ13
IRQ14
IRQ15

Table 14-6: Interrupt Priority Scheme (Continued)

PC Interrupt Priority (highest to lowest)
IRQ3
IRQ4
IRQ5
IRQ6
IRQ7

If an interrupt line is shared by multiple devices, as they are in PCI, there is also an implied priority scheme among the devices that share an interrupt request line. In the Ethernet/COM port example just covered, whenever an interrupt occurs on IRQ3, the processor always jumps to the Ethernet controller's interrupt service routine first. Control is only passed to the COM port's interrupt service routine by the Ethernet controller's interrupt service routine when the Ethernet controller's service routine completes execution. If the Ethernet controller were to generate interrupt requests at a high frequency, the COM port might starve while awaiting servicing (because it must await the completion of the execution of the Ethernet driver's interrupt service routine before it is called).

Assuming that both devices have loadable device drivers, a fix for this problem would be to change the order in which the drivers are loaded. This will change the order in which the interrupt table entry is hooked by the two devices.

Interrupts and PCI-to-PCI Bridges

Refer to "Interrupt Support" on page 624 and "Interrupt-Related Registers" on page 593 for a description of interrupts and PCI-to-PCI bridges.

2.2 Message Signaled Interrupts (MSI)

Introduction

A PCI function that generates interrupt requests to request servicing by its device driver can do so using one of **two methods**:

METHOD 1. As described in the earlier parts of this chapter, the device designer can use a **pin** on the device to signal an interrupt request to the processor.

METHOD 2. Alternatively, the designer can implement Message Signaled Interrupt, or **MSI**, capability and use it to signal an interrupt request to the processor. This method eliminates the need for an interrupt pin and trace and is described in this section.

The spec recommends that a device that implements MSI capability also use an interrupt pin to allow usage of the device in a system that doesn't support MSI capability. System configuration software cannot assume that an MSI-capable device has an interrupt pin.

Advantages of MSI Interrupts

The advantages of MSI interrupt generation versus using an interrupt pin are as follows:

- eliminates the need for interrupt traces.
- eliminates multiple PCI functions sharing the same interrupt request input on the interrupt controller.
- eliminates the chaining of device drivers.
- eliminates the need to perform a dummy read from a device in its interrupt service routine to force all posted memory writes to be flushed to memory.

Basics of MSI Configuration

Refer to Figure 14-8 on page 254.

STEP 1. At startup time, the configuration software scans the PCI bus(es) (referred to as bus enumeration) and discovers devices (i.e., it performs configuration reads for valid Vendor IDs).

STEP 2. When a PCI function is discovered, the configuration software checks the Capabilities List bit in the device's PCI Status register and determines that the device incorporates one or more new capabilities. For more information about New Capabilities, refer to "New Capabilities" on page 390.

STEP 3. The software then traverses the New Capabilities list and discovers (via a Capability ID of 05h) that the device can use MSI to issue interrupt requests.

STEP 4. The software assigns a dword-aligned memory address to the device's Message Address register. This is the address that the device performs a memory write to when it must generate a request.

STEP 5. The software checks the Multiple Message Capable field in the device's Message Control register to determine how many event-specific messages the device would like assigned to it).

STEP 6. The software then allocates the device a number of messages equal to or less than that requested. At a minimum, one message will be allocated to the device.

STEP 7. The software writes the base message data pattern into the device's Message Data register.

STEP 8. Finally, the software sets the MSI Enable bit in the device's Message Control register, thereby enabling it to generate interrupts using MSI memory writes.

Figure 14-8: Device MSI Configuration Process

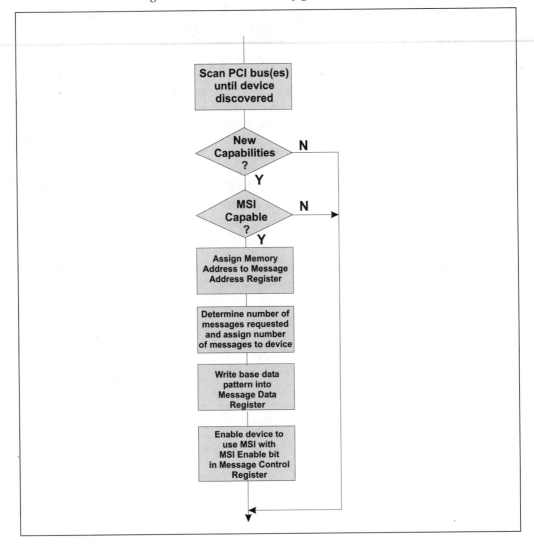

Basics of Generating an MSI Interrupt Request

When a PCI function supports MSI and it is enabled to do so, it generates an interrupt request to the processor by writing a pre-defined data item (a message) to a predefined memory address. As described earlier, the configuration software is responsible for priming the function's MSI Address and Data registers with the appropriate memory address and the data to be written to that address when generating a request. It also primes a field in the Message Control register with the number of messages that have been allocated to the device.

When the device must generate an interrupt request, it writes the Message Data register contents to the memory address specified in its Message Address register. If the system software allocated more than one message to the device, it is permitted to modify the lower bits of the assigned Message Data value to send a different message for each device-specific event type that requires servicing by the device driver.

As an example, assume the following:

- Four messages have been allocated to a device.
- A data value of 0500h has been assigned to the device's Message Data register.
- Memory address 0A000000h has been written into the device's Message Address register.

When any one of four different device-specific events occurs, the device generates a request by performing a dword write to memory address 0A000000h with a data value of 00000500h, 00000501h, 00000502h, or 00000503h. In other words, the device automatically appends the value 0000h to the upper part of its assigned message data value (to make a 32-bit value) and modifies the lower two bits of the value to indicate the specific message type.

How Is the Memory Write Treated by Bridges?

It's treated like any other write. It is posted by any bridges it encounters on its way to the host/PCI bridge. When it finally arrives at the host/PCI bridge, it's chipset-specific how the host/PCI bridge converts the message into an interrupt to one or more of the processors on the host bus.

As an example, a host/PCI bridge could implement a 32-bit memory-mapped IO port that receives MSI memory writes and converts them into interrupts to the processor. When a 32-bit data item is written into the port from the PCI side of the bridge, the bridge can then convert the data value into a specific interrupt vector to deliver to the processor (in a processor-specific fashion). As an example, the processor bus may support an "interrupt" transaction that delivers the appropriate interrupt vector (the one associated with the message type) to a processor.

Memory Already Sync'd When Interrupt Handler Entered

The Problem

Assume that a PCI device performs one or more memory write transactions to write data into main memory. If there are any bridges between the device and main memory, the writes are posted and are actually performed at some later time. Assume that the writes have not yet arrived at main memory and the device now generates an interrupt request to inform its driver that the data is in memory ready to be processed. The device generates its request using its interrupt request pin rather than MSI. The hardware interrupt request is delivered to the processor over the INTR signal line or the APIC bus and does not cause bridges to flush their posted writes buffers. The currently-executing program is suspended and the processor executes the interrupt handler within the device's device driver. The driver then reads the data from main memory and processes it. **Oops!** All of the memory writes may not have arrived in main memory yet, so **the driver is not processing the correct data**.

The Old Way of Solving the Problem

The driver can solve this problem by **performing** a **read from** a **location within its device before processing** the **data**. The read has to traverse the same bridge (or bridges) that the memory writes from the device have to traverse to get to main memory. The ordering rules for bridges dictate that the bridge must flush its posted write buffers before permitting a read to traverse the bridge. As a result, by the time the read data is returned to the driver, all of the posted writes have been flushed to memory. Performing this extra read from the device is a clunky extra step that it would be nice to eliminate.

How MSI Solves the Problem

Once again assume that a PCI device performs one or more memory write transactions to write data into main memory. If there are any bridges between the device and main memory, the writes are posted and are actually performed at some later time. Assume that the writes have not yet arrived at main memory and the device generates an interrupt request to inform its driver that the data is in memory ready to be processed. However, this time the device generates its request using MSI. In other words, it performs a memory write to write the Message Data to the memory address specified in the Message Address register. This address is typically a memory-mapped IO port within the host/PCI bridge. Also keep in mind that the host/PCI bridge is the gateway to the main memory controller. This means that the message memory write is in the posted write buffers and was posted after the writes that the device previously performed to update the buffer in main memory. A *key ingredient* here is that it's a rule that *bridges must perform posted writes in the same order that they were received*. This means that by the time the write to the MSI memory address arrives at the host/PCI bridge, main memory has already received all of the writes to the device's buffer in main memory. Upon receipt of the MSI write, the host/PCI bridge then generates the interrupt request to the processor, the currently-executing program is suspended and the processor executes the interrupt handler within the device's device driver. The driver then reads the data from main memory and processes it—and it's the correct data. The programmer doesn't have to perform the artificial step of reading from its device to force the posted writes to be flushed to memory.

Interrupt Latency

The time from signaling an interrupt request until software services the device is referred to as its interrupt latency. As with the other interrupt request delivery mechanisms mentioned in the section entitled "Three Ways To Deliver Interrupts To Processor" on page 221, the **MSI capability doesn't provide interrupt latency guarantees**.

MSI Are Non-Shared

When using a PCI interrupt pin to generate interrupts requests, it's highly probable that a linked list of device drivers are executed (because multiple devices share the same interrupt trace). For more information, refer to "Interrupt Chaining" on page 239. The driver for the device may not be the first one in the list and may not be executed until the handlers for several other device drivers have completed execution. This injects additional latency into the process of serving a device.

It is the intent of the spec that the system software and the host/PCI bridge will treat each interrupt message (delivered via MSI memory writes) as a separate interrupt level and that no two events will be assigned the same level. In other words, only one driver hooks each entry in the interrupt table in memory. This can substantially decrease the interrupt latency for a device.

MSI Is a New Capability Type

A PCI function indicates its support for MSI as a New Capability. For a primer on the New Capabilities, refer to the section entitled "New Capabilities" on page 390. The following are rules related to MSI implementation:

- Each PCI function that supports MSI must implement its own MSI register set within its own configuration space.
- Each function may only implement one MSI register set.

Figure 14-9 on page 258 and Figure 14-10 on page 258 illustrate the two possible formats of the MSI Capability registers. Later sections will clarify why there are two possible formats (but only one will be implemented in a given device).

Figure 14-9: 32-bit MSI Capability Register Set Format

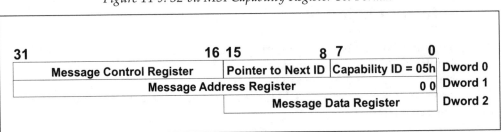

Figure 14-10: 64-bit MSI Capability Register Format

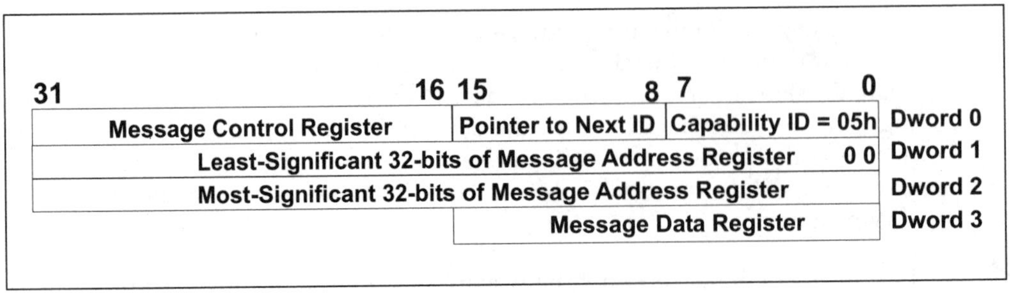

Description of the MSI Capability Register Set

Refer to Figure 14-9 on page 258 and Figure 14-10 on page 258.

Capability ID

The Capability ID that identifies the MSI register set is **05h**. This is a hardwired, read-only value.

Pointer To Next New Capability

The second byte of the register set either points to the next New Capability's register set or contains 00h if this is the end of the New Capabilities list. This is a hardwired, read-only value. If non-zero, it must be a dword-aligned value.

Message Control Register

Figure 14-11 on page 259 and Table 14-7 on page 260 illustrate the layout and usage of the Message Control register.

Figure 14-11: Message Control Register

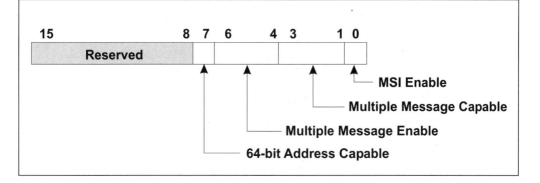

Table 14-7: Format and Usage of Message Control Register

Bit(s)	Field Name	Description
15:8	Reserved	Read-Only. Always zero.
7	64-bit Address Capable	Read-Only. • 0 = Function does not implement the upper 32-bits of the Message Address register and is incapable of generating a 64-bit memory address. • 1 = Function implements the upper 32-bits of the Message Address register and is capable of generating a 64-bit memory address.
6:4	Multiple Message Enable	Read/Write. After system software reads the Multiple Message Capable field (see next row in this table) to determine how many messages are requested by the device, it programs a 3-bit value into this field indicating the actual number of messages allocated to the device. The number allocated can be equal to or less than the number actually requested. The state of this field after reset is 000b. The field is encoded as follows: **Value** **Number of Messages Requested** 000b 1 001b 2 010b 4 011b 8 100b 16 101b 32 110b Reserved 111b Reserved

Table 14-7: Format and Usage of Message Control Register (Continued)

Bit(s)	Field Name	Description
3:1	Multiple Message Capable	Read-Only. System software reads this field to determine how many messages the device would like allocated to it. The requested number of messages is a power of two, therefore a device that requests three messages must request that four messages be allocated to it. The field is encoded as follows: **Value** **Number of Messages Requested** 000b 1 001b 2 010b 4 011b 8 100b 16 101b 32 110b Reserved 111b Reserved
0	MSI Enable	Read/Write. State after reset is 0, indicating that the device's MSI capability is disabled. ***Device drivers are not allowed to clear this bit*** to disable the device's MSI capability. If the driver did clear this bit after system software had set it, the device would then begin using its PCI interrupt pin. This would result in the processor jumping through the entry in the interrupt table associated with whatever IRQ the pin is routed to, ***and that entry is not pointing to the device's driver.*** • **0** = Function is **disabled** from using **MSI**. It must use its interrupt pin to request service. • **1** = Function is **enabled** to use **MSI** to request service and is forbidden to use its interrupt pin.

Message Address Register

The lower two bits of the 32-bit Message Address register are hardwired to zero and cannot be changed. In other words, the address assigned by system software is always aligned on a dword address boundary.

The upper 32-bits of the Message Address register (see dword two in Figure 14-10 on page 258) are optional and are only present if bit 7 of the Message Control register (see Figure 14-11 on page 259), the 64-Bit Address Capable bit, is a one. If present, it is a read/write register and it is used in conjunction with the Message Address register to assign a 32-bit or a 64-bit memory address to the device:

- If the upper 32-bits of the Message Address register are set to a non-zero value by the system software, then a 64-bit message address has been assigned to the device using both the upper and lower halves of the register.
- If the upper 32-bits of the Message Address register are set to zero by the system software, then a 32-bit message address has been assigned to the device using both the upper and lower halves of the register.

Message Data Register

The system software assigns the device a base message data pattern by writing it into this 16-bit, read/write register. When the device must generate an interrupt request, it writes a 32-bit value to the memory address specified in the Message Address register. The data written has the following format:

- The upper 16 bits are always set to zero.
- The lower 16 bits are supplied from the Message Data register. If more than one message has been assigned to the device, the device modifies the lower bits (the number of modifiable bits depends on how many messages have been assigned to the device by the configuration software) of the data from the Message Data register to form the appropriate message for the event it wishes to report to its driver. For an example, refer to the example cited in "Basics of Generating an MSI Interrupt Request" on page 254.

Message Write Can Have Bad Ending

Retry or Disconnect

If the target terminates the memory write with a Retry or a Disconnect, the master must behave normally (as defined in "Disconnect" on page 181 and "Retry" on page 189).

Master or Target Abort Received

If the MSI write transaction is terminated with a Master Abort or a Target Abort, the master that originated the MSI memory write transaction is required to report the error by asserting SERR# (assuming that the SERR# Enable bit is set in its configuration Command register) and must set the Signaled System Error as well as the Received Master Abort or Received Target Abort bits in its configuration Status register. The MSI write transaction is ignored by the target when terminated with a Master Abort or Target Abort. If the MSI memory write has to traverse one or more bridges to get to the host/PCI bridge and it experiences an abort before it arrives at the host/PCI bridge, then it never gets to the host/PCI bridge at all. The target must set the Signaled Target Abort bit in its configuration Status register if it responded to the write with a Target Abort.

Write Results In Data Parity Error

If the MSI memory write transaction results in a data parity error, the master that originated the MSI write transaction is required to assert SERR# (assuming that the SERR# Enable bit is set in its configuration Command register) and set the Signaled System Error bit as well as the Master Data Parity Error bit (bit 8) in its configuration Status register. The erroneous interrupt may be delivered to the processor and can jeopardize system integrity. For example, the erroneous message may result in an apparent interrupt from a device that did not request service.

Some Rules, Recommendations, etc.

1. It is the spec's intention that mutually-exclusive messages will be assigned to devices by the system software and that each message will be converted to an exclusive interrupt level upon delivery to the processor.
2. The spec recommends that a device that implements MSI capability also implement an interrupt pin to allow usage of the device in a system that doesn't support MSI capability. System configuration software must not assume that an MSI-capable device has an interrupt pin.
3. More than one MSI capability register set per function is prohibited.
4. A read from Message Address register produces undefined results.
5. Reserved registers and bits are read-only and always return zero when read.
6. System software can modify Message Control register bits, but the device is prohibited from doing so. In other words, it's not permitted to modify the bits via the "back door."
7. At a minimum, a single message will be assigned to device.
8. System software must not write to the upper half of the dword that contains the Message Data register.
9. When MSI capability is enabled, the device must not use its interrupt pin.
10. If the device writes the same message multiple times, only one of those

messages is guaranteed to be serviced. If all of them must be serviced, the device must not generate the same message again until the driver services the earlier one.

11. If a device has more than one message assigned, and it writes a series of different messages, it is guaranteed that all of them will be serviced.

15 *The 64-bit PCI Extension*

The Previous Chapter

The previous chapter provided a discussion of issues related to interrupt routing, generation and servicing.

In This Chapter

This chapter describes the 64-bit extension that permits masters and targets to perform eight byte transfers during each data phase. It also describes 64-bit addressing used to address memory targets that reside above the 4GB boundary.

The Next Chapter

The next chapter describes the implementation of a 66MHz bus and components.

64-bit Data Transfers and 64-bit Addressing: Separate Capabilities

The PCI specification provides a mechanism that permits a 64-bit bus master to perform 64-bit data transfers with a 64-bit target. At the beginning of a transaction, the 64-bit bus master automatically senses if the responding target is a 64-bit or a 32-bit device. If it's a 64-bit device, up to eight bytes (a quadword) may be transferred during each data phase. Assuming a series of 0-wait state data phases, throughput of 264Mbytes/second can be achieved at a bus speed of 33MHz (8 bytes/transfer x 33 million transfers/second) and 528Mbytes/second at 66MHz. If the responding target is a 32-bit device, the bus master automatically senses this and steers all data to or from the target over the lower four data paths (AD[31:0]).

The specification also defines 64-bit memory addressing capability. This capability is only used to address memory targets that reside above the 4GB address boundary. Both 32- and 64-bit bus masters can perform 64-bit addressing. In addition, memory targets (that reside over the 4GB address boundary) that respond to 64-bit addressing can be implemented as either 32- or 64-bit targets.

It is important to note that 64-bit addressing and 64-bit data transfer capability are two features, separate and distinct from each other. A device may support one, the other, both, or neither.

64-Bit Extension Signals

In order to support the 64-bit data transfer capability, the PCI bus implements an additional thirty-nine pins:

- **REQ64#** is asserted by a 64-bit bus master to indicate that it would like to perform 64-bit data transfers. REQ64# has the same timing and duration as the FRAME# signal. The REQ64# signal line must be supplied with a pullup resistor on the system board. REQ64# cannot be permitted to float when a 32-bit bus master is performing a transaction.
- **ACK64#** is asserted by a target in response to REQ64# assertion by the master (if the target supports 64-bit data transfers). ACK64# has the same timing and duration as DEVSEL# (but ACK64# must not be asserted unless REQ64# is asserted by the initiator). Like REQ64#, the ACK64# signal line must also be supplied with a pullup resistor on the system board. ACK64# cannot be permitted to float when a 32-bit device is the target of a transaction.
- **AD[63:32]** comprise the upper four address/data paths.
- **C/BE#[7:4]** comprise the upper four command/byte enable signals.
- **PAR64** is the parity bit that provides even parity for the upper four AD paths and the upper four C/BE signal lines.

The following sections provide a detailed discussion of 64-bit data transfer and addressing capability.

64-bit Cards in 32-bit Add-in Connectors

A 64-bit card installed in a 32-bit expansion slot automatically only uses the lower half of the bus to perform transfers. This is true because the system board designer connects the REQ64# output pin and the ACK64# input pin on the connector to individual pullups on the system board and to nothing else.

When a 64-bit bus master is installed in a 32-bit card slot and it initiates a transaction, its assertion of REQ64# is not visible to any of the targets. In addition, its ACK64# input is always sampled deasserted (because it's pulled up on the system board). This forces the bus master to use only the lower part of the bus during the transfer. Furthermore, if the target addressed in the transaction is a 64-bit target, it samples REQ64# deasserted (because it's pulled up on the system board), forcing it to only utilize the lower half of the bus during the transaction and to disable its ACK64# output.

The 64-bit extension signal lines on the card itself cannot be permitted to float when they are not in use. The CMOS input receivers on the card would oscillate and draw excessive current, thus violating the "green" aspect of the specification. When the card is installed in a 32-bit slot, it cannot use the upper half of the bus. The manner in which the card detects the type of slot (REQ64# sampled deasserted at startup time) is described in the next section.

Pullups Prevent 64-bit Extension from Floating When Not in Use

If the 64-bit extension signals (AD[63:32], C/BE#[7:4] and PAR64) are permitted to float when not in use, the CMOS input buffers on the card will oscillate and draw excessive current. In order to prevent the extension from floating when not in use, the system board designer is required to include pullup resistors on the extension signals to keep them from floating. Because these pullups are guaranteed to keep the extension from floating when not in use, 64-bit devices that are embedded on the system board and 64-bit cards installed in 64-bit PCI add-in connectors don't need to take any special action to keep the extension from floating when they are not using it.

The 64-bit extension is not in use under the following circumstances:

1. The PCI bus is idle.
2. A 32-bit bus master is performing a transaction with a 32-bit target.
3. A 32-bit bus master is performing a transaction with a 64-bit target. Upon detecting REQ64# deasserted at the start of the transaction, the target will not use the upper half of the bus.
4. A 64-bit bus master addresses a target to perform 32-bit data transfers (REQ64# deasserted) and the target resides below the 4GB address boundary (the upper half of the bus is not used during the address phase and is also not used in the data phases). Whether the target is a 32-bit or a 64-bit target, the upper half of the bus isn't used during the data phases (because REQ64# is deasserted).

5. A 64-bit bus master attempts a 64-bit data transfer (REQ64# asserted) with a 32-bit memory target that resides below the 4GB boundary. In this case, the initiator only uses the lower half of the bus during the address phase (because it's only generating a 32-bit address). When it discovers that the currently-addressed target is a 32-bit target (ACK64# not asserted when DEVSEL# asserted), the initiator ceases to use the upper half of the bus during the data phases.

Problem: a 64-bit Card in a 32-bit PCI Connector

Refer to Figure 15-1 on page 269. Installation of a 64-bit card in a 32-bit card connector is permitted. The main (32-bit) portion of the connector contains all of the 32-bit PCI signals, while an extension to the connector contains the 64-bit extension signals (with the exception of REQ64# and ACK64# which are located on the 32-bit portion of the connector).

When a 64-bit device is installed in a 32-bit PCI expansion slot, the system board pullups on AD[63:32], C/BE#[7:4] and PAR64 are not available to the add-in card. This means that the add-in card's input buffers that are connected to the extension signal pins will float, oscillate, and draw excessive current.

The specification states that the add-in card designer must *not* solve this problem by supplying pullup resistors on the extension lines on the add-in card. Using this approach would cause problems when the card is installed in a 64-bit expansion slot. There would then be two sets of pullup resistors on these signal lines (the ones on the card plus the ones on the system board). If all designers solved the problem in this manner, a machine with multiple 64-bit cards inserted in 64-bit card connectors would have multiple pullups on the extension signals, resulting in pullup current overload.

The specification provides a method for a 64-bit card to determine at startup time whether it's installed in a 32-bit or a 64-bit connector. If the card detects that it is plugged into a 64-bit connector, the pullups on the system board will keep the input receivers on the card from floating when the extension is not in use. On the other hand, if a 64-bit card detects that it is installed in a 32-bit card connector, the logic on the card must keep the input receivers from switching. The specification states that an approach similar to one of the following should be used:

*   Biasing the input buffer to turn it off.
*   Actively driving the outputs continually (since they aren't connected to anything).

Chapter 15: The 64-bit PCI Extension

Figure 15-1: 64- and 32- Bit Connectors

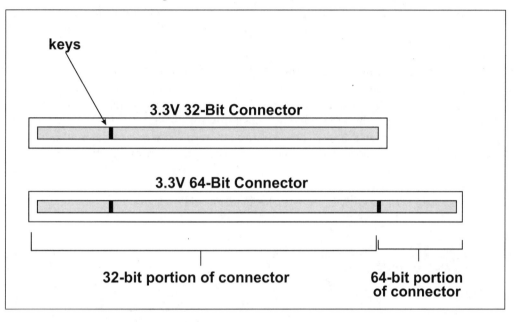

How 64-bit Card Determines Type of Slot Installed In

Refer to Figure 15-2 on page 270. When the system is powered up, the reset signal is automatically asserted. During this period of time, the logic on the system board must assert the REQ64# signal as well as RST#. REQ64# has a single pullup resistor on it and is connected to the REQ64# pin on all 64-bit devices integrated onto the system board and on all 64-bit PCI expansion slots. The specification states that the REQ64# signal line on each 32-bit PCI expansion slot (REQ64# and ACK64# are located on the 32-bit portion of the connector), however, each has its own independent pullup resistor.

During reset time, the system board reset logic initially asserts the PCI RST# signal while the POWERGOOD signal from the power supply is deasserted. During the assertion of RST#, the system board logic asserts REQ64# and keeps it asserted until after it removes the RST# signal. When POWERGOOD is asserted by the power supply logic, the system board reset logic deasserts the PCI RST# signal. On the trailing-edge of RST# assertion, all 64-bit devices are required to sample the state of the REQ64# signal.

All 64-bit devices that are embedded on the system board or that are installed in 64-bit expansion slots sample REQ64# asserted on the trailing-edge of RST#. This informs them that they are connected to the extension pullups on the system board and need take no special action to keep the extension from floating when not using it.

All 64-bit devices that are installed in 32-bit card slots, however, detect REQ64# deasserted on the trailing-edge of RST#. This informs them that they are not connected to the system board-resident pullups on the extension signals. The card logic must therefore take responsibility for the state of its own on-card 64-bit extension signal lines. The card must therefore use one of the methods cited in the previous section to prevent excessive current draw by the card's input receivers.

Figure 15-2: REQ64# Signal Routing

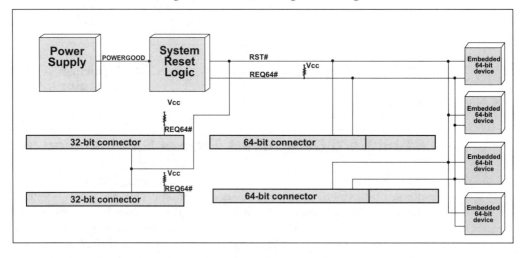

64-bit Data Transfer Capability

The agreement to perform 64-bit transfers is established by a handshake between the initiator and the target. When the initiator supports 64-bit transfers and wishes to perform 64-bit transfers, it asserts REQ64# along with FRAME# during the address phase. If the currently-addressed target supports 64-bit data transfers, it replies with ACK64#. Because they are both pulled high, the quiescent state of REQ64# and ACK64# is deasserted. If either the master or the target, or both, do not support 64-bit data transfers, 32-bit data transfers are used instead.

During 64-bit transfers, all transfer timing during data phases is identical to that used during 32-bit data transfers. One to eight bytes may be transferred between the initiator and the target during each data phase and all combinations of byte enables are valid (including none asserted; an example is provided later in this chapter). The setting on the byte enable lines may be changed with each data phase. The following sections provide examples of:

- 64-bit initiator performing a transfer with a 64-bit target.
- 64-bit initiator performing a transfer with a 32-bit target.
- 32-bit initiator performing a transfer with a 64-bit target.

Only Memory Commands May Use 64-bit Transfers

Only memory commands may utilize 64-bit data transfer capability. The specification provides the following arguments for not implementing support for 64-bit data transfers for the other types of commands:

- During the special cycle transaction, no target responds with DEVSEL#. ACK64#, therefore, is also not asserted.
- Configuration transactions do not require the level of throughput achievable with 64-bit data transfers and therefore do not justify the added complexity and cost necessary to support 64-bit data transfer capability. The author has heard arguments from some designers (of large mainframes and supercomputers) that devices that require large streams of configuration information would benefit from 64-bit configuration support.
- As with configuration transactions, IO transactions do not require a high level of throughput and therefore do not justify the added complexity and cost necessary to support 64-bit data transfer capability.
- By definition, the Interrupt Acknowledge command only performs a single data phase consisting of a one, two, three or four byte transfer.

Start Address Quadword-Aligned

When a bus master starts a transfer and asserts REQ64#, the start address it issues is quadword-, not dword-, aligned (e.g., address 00000100h, 00000108h, 00000110h, etc.). This means that AD[2] must be set to zero. AD[1:0] still convey the addressing sequence (for more information see "Memory Addressing" on page 143).

64-bit Target's Interpretation of Address

Assuming that the target supports 64-bit data transfers (it asserts ACK64#), the target latches the start **quadword-aligned address** into its address counter (if it supports burst mode). If the addressing sequence indicated by the bus master on AD[1:0] is sequential (Linear) addressing, the target increments the address in its address counter by eight at the completion of each data phase to point to the next sequential quadword. If Cache Line Wrap addressing is indicated, it will increment through the cacheline quadword-by-quadword and then wrap to the start of the line when it hits the end of the line. The target samples the eight byte enables, C/BE#[7:0], during each data phase to determine which of the eight bytes within the currently-addressed quadword is to be transferred (and therefore which of the eight data paths are to be used).

32-bit Target's Interpretation of Address

If the target that responds to the transaction is a 32-bit target (ACK64# not asserted), it treats the **start** address as a **dword-aligned address** and latches it into its address counter. If the addressing sequence indicated by the bus master on AD[1:0] is sequential (Linear) addressing, the target increments the address in its address counter by four at the completion of each data phase to point to the next sequential dword. If Cache Line Wrap addressing is indicated, it will increment through the cacheline dword-by-dword and then wrap to the start of the line when it hits the end of the line. The target samples the four lower byte enables, C/BE#[3:0], during each data phase to determine which of the four bytes within the currently-addressed dword is to be transferred and which of the four data paths (on the AD[31:0] portion of the bus) are to be used.

64-bit Initiator and 64-bit Target

Figure 15-3 on page 275 illustrates a 64-bit master performing a 64-bit read data transfer with a 64-bit memory target. The master is not using 64-bit addressing (it's not necessary because the target in the example does not reside over the 4GB address boundary). The following numbered sequence describes this transaction.

CLOCK 1. On the rising-edge of clock one, the initiator asserts FRAME# to indicate the start of the transfer and REQ64# to indicate its desire to perform 64-bit transfers.

IT also drives the quadword-aligned start address onto the AD bus and sets C/BE#[3:0] to indicate that it is performing a memory read transaction (MR, MRL, or MRM).

AD[63:32] and C/BE#[7:4] aren't used during the address phase. The system board designer is required to include pullups on AD[63:32], C/BE#[7:4] and PAR64 so that these signal lines do not float when they aren't in use (e.g., during the address phase of this transaction). Additional information regarding the pullup requirement can be found in "Pullups Prevent 64-bit Extension from Floating When Not in Use" on page 267.

Clock 2. The targets latch the address, command and REQ64# on the rising-edge of clock two and begin the decode process.

The initiator ceases to drive the AD bus so that the target can begin to drive the first requested data item onto the AD bus.

The initiator also ceases to drive the read command onto the C/BE bus and sets C/BE#[7:0] to indicate which bytes are to be transferred within the first quadword during the first data phase.

The initiator asserts IRDY# to indicate that is ready to receive the first data item.

The initiator also keeps FRAME# asserted, indicating that this is not the final data phase.

The target asserts DEVSEL# to claim the transaction and also asserts ACK64#, indicating that it is capable of using all eight data paths.

The target leaves TRDY# deasserted to enforce the turn-around cycle.

Clock 3. During clock three, the target asserts TRDY# to indicate the presence of the first data item on the AD bus and it begins to drive the requested data onto AD[63:0].

Clock 4. At the rising-edge of clock four, TRDY# and IRDY# are sampled asserted and the first data is transferred. This completes the first data phase.

The second data phase starts during clock four.

The target increments its address counter by eight (assuming that Linear addressing was indicated during the address phase).

The initiator drives the next data request onto the byte enables.

The initiator keeps IRDY# asserted and does not deassert FRAME#, indicating that it is ready to complete the second data phase and that it is not the final data phase.

The target deasserts TRDY#, indicating that it requires a wait state inserted into data phase two in order to fetch the next requested data item.

Clock 5. On the rising-edge of clock five, TRDY# is sampled deasserted, resulting in a delay of the second data transfer and the conversion of clock five into a wait state.

During the wait state (clock five), the target begins to drive the requested data onto the data bus and asserts TRDY# to indicate its presence on the bus.

Clock 6. On the rising-edge of clock six, IRDY# and TRDY# are sampled asserted and the requested data is transferred, completing the second data phase.

THE third data phase begins during clock six.

THE initiator drives the next data request onto the byte enables, but deasserts IRDY#, indicating that it isn't ready to accept the third data item yet (e.g., it has a buffer full condition). In other words, the initiator requires a wait state inserted into data phase three.

THE target increments its address counter by eight to point to the next quadword and begins to drive the requested data onto the data bus.

CLOCK 7. On the rising-edge of clock seven, IRDY# is sampled deasserted, resulting in a delay of the third data transfer and the conversion of clock seven into a wait state.

DURING the wait state, the initiator asserts IRDY# to indicate that it is now ready to accept the data. It also deasserts FRAME# and REQ64# to indicate that this is the last data phase.

CLOCK 8. On the rising-edge of clock eight, IRDY# and TRDY# are sampled asserted and the last data item is transferred.

THE initiator deasserts IRDY#, indicating the conclusion of the last data phase.

DURING clock eight, the target deasserts TRDY#, DEVSEL# and ACK64# and ceases to drive the last data item onto the data bus.

THE initiator ceases to drive the byte enables.

CLOCK 9. The bus returns to the idle state on clock nine.

Figure 15-3: Transfer Between a 64-bit Initiator and 64-bit Target7

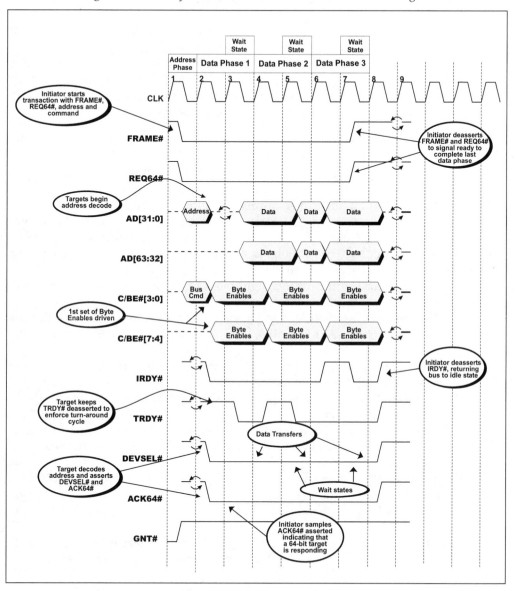

64-bit Initiator and 32-bit Target

Figure 15-4 on page 279 illustrates a 64-bit PCI initiator performing a 64-bit write data transfer with a 32-bit PCI target. The start address is 00000100h, Linear addressing is indicated (AD[1:0] are set to 00b), and the initiator will attempt to transfer eight bytes per data phase (all eight byte enables will be asserted in the first data phase and eight bytes will be driven onto AD[63:0]]). The following numbered sequence describes this data transfer.

CLOCK 1. On the rising-edge of clock one, the initiator starts the transaction by asserting FRAME# and REQ64#.

IT drives the quadword-aligned address, 00000100h, onto the AD bus and the memory write command onto C/BE#[3:0].

C/BE#[7:4] are not driven during the address phase.

CLOCK 2. On the rising-edge of clock two, the targets sample the address, command and REQ64# and begin the address decode. The 32-bit target treats the start address, 00000100h, as a dword-aligned address identifying the block of four locations from 00000100h through 00000103h.

THE initiator begins to drive eight bytes of write data onto the eight data paths and asserts all eight byte enables, C/BE#[7:0].

THE initiator asserts IRDY# to indicate the presence of the data on the bus and does not deassert FRAME#, thereby indicating that this is not the final data phase.

THE addressed target does a fast address decode during clock two and asserts DEVSEL# to claim the transaction.

THE target simultaneously asserts TRDY#, indicating that it is ready to receive the first data item.

THE target does not assert ACK64#, indicating that it can only perform data transfers over the lower four data paths (and that it is not connected to C/BE#[7:4]).

CLOCK 3. On the rising-edge of clock three, the initiator samples DEVSEL#, IRDY# and TRDY# asserted and ACK64# deasserted.

DEVSEL# asserted indicates that the addressed target has claimed the transaction.

THE deasserted state of ACK64# indicates that the target can only transfer data over the lower four data paths and cannot see the C/BE#[7:4] lines.

IRDY# and TRDY# asserted indicates that the initiator is presenting the data (eight bytes) and the target is ready to accept it (four bytes), but only over the lower four data paths.

THE target latches the four bytes destined for memory locations 00000100h through 00000103h from the lower four data paths on the rising-edge of clock three. The fact that this is a 32-bit target means that the start address that it latched into its address counter during the address phase, 00000100h, is treated as a dword-aligned address, not quadword-aligned.

UPON completion of the first data phase on the rising-edge of clock three, the target increments its address counter by four to point to the next dword, 00000104h.

AT the start of the second data phase (during clock three), the initiator copies the settings on the upper byte enables, C/BE#[7:4], to the lower byte enables, C/BE#[3:0], and copies the data that had been driven onto the upper four data paths (destined for memory locations 00000104h through 00000107h) onto the lower four data paths. The example shows this occurring in one clock, but the initiator can legally deassert IRDY# for up to seven clocks in a data phase.

THE initiator ceases to drive C/BE#[7:4] and AD[63:32], but these signal lines are prevented from floating by the required pullups on the system board.

THE initiator keeps IRDY# asserted, indicating the presence of the next four bytes on the lower part of the data bus.

THE initiator does not deassert FRAME#, indicating that this is not the final data phase.

CLOCK 4. On the rising-edge of clock four, IRDY# and TRDY# are sampled asserted and the four bytes on the lower four data paths are written into memory locations 00000104h through 00000107h. This completes the second data phase.

DURING clock four, the initiator asserts all four of the lower four byte enables, but deasserts IRDY# to indicate that it is not yet ready to drive the third data item onto the data paths (e.g., it has a buffer dry condition). Although it's not yet ready to deliver the third data item, the initiator is responsible for keeping the AD bus driven with a stable pattern. The designer typically just continues to drive the previous data item until ready to start driving the new one.

ALSO during clock four, the target increments its address counter to point to dword-aligned address 00000108h, but deasserts TRDY# to indicate that it is not yet ready to accept data.

CLOCK 5. On the rising-edge of clock five, IRDY# and TRDY# are sampled deasserted, forcing clock five to become a wait state in the third data phase.

DURING clock five (the wait state), the initiator then asserts IRDY# and begins to drive the data onto the data bus.

AT the same time, the initiator deasserts FRAME# and REQ64#, indicating that this is the last data phase.

CLOCK 6. see Clock 7.

CLOCK 7. TRDY# is sampled deasserted on the rising-edge of clocks six and seven, indicating that the target is not yet ready to accept the last data item. Clocks six and seven are therefore wait states in data phase three.

THE initiator must continue to drive the byte enables and the data until the target accepts the data.

DURING clock seven, the target asserts TRDY# to indicate that it is ready to accept the last data item.

CLOCK 8. On the rising-edge of clock eight, TRDY# and IRDY# are sampled asserted and the last data item is transferred. The four bytes on AD[31:0] are written into memory locations 00000108h through 0000010Bh.

THE target samples IRDY# asserted and FRAME# deasserted, indicating that this is the final data phase.

THE initiator then ceases to drive the AD and C/BE buses and IRDY#, returning the bus to the idle state.

THE target deasserts TRDY# and DEVSEL#.

Figure 15-4: Transfer Between a 64-bit Initiator and a 32-bit Target

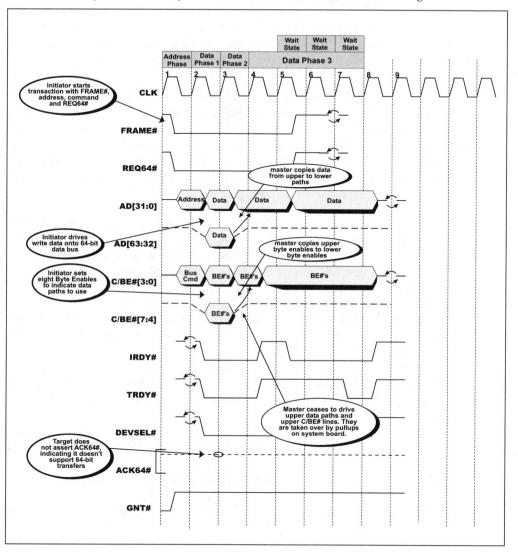

Null Data Phase Example

In the previous section, the 64-bit bus master attempted to perform a burst write with a 32-bit target. It started the transaction on a quadword-aligned address (00000100h) and wanted to transfer eight bytes in the first and all subsequent data phases.

Now consider the case where the master starts the transfer on a misaligned address (not a quadword-aligned address). In this example, the master starts the transfer with the last four bytes in the first quadword, 00000104h through 00000107h, but wants to transfer eight bytes in every subsequent data phase. The start address issued is 00000100h, but only C/BE#[7:4] are asserted during the first data phase (not C/BE#[3:0]). This example uses the same timing diagram as the previous section (Figure 15-4 on page 279).

CLOCK 1. On the rising-edge of clock one, the initiator starts the transaction by asserting FRAME# and REQ64#. It drives quadword-aligned address 00000100h onto the AD bus and the memory write command onto C/BE#[3:0]. C/BE#[7:4] are not driven during the address phase.

CLOCK 2. On the rising-edge of clock two, the targets sample the address, command and REQ64# and begin the address decode.

THE 32-bit target treats the start address, 00000100h, as a dword-aligned address identifying the block of four locations from 00000100h through 00000103h.

THE initiator begins to drive four bytes of write data onto AD[63:32] and asserts the upper four byte enables, C/BE#[7:4]. It does not assert the lower four byte enables because it isn't writing to locations 00000100h-through-00000103h.

THE initiator asserts IRDY# to indicate the presence of the data on the bus. However, it does not deassert FRAME#, indicating that this is not the final data phase.

THE addressed target does a fast address decode during clock two and asserts DEVSEL# to claim the transaction.

THE target simultaneously asserts TRDY#, indicating that it is ready to receive the first data item.

THE target does not assert ACK64#, indicating that it can only perform data transfers over the lower four data paths (and that it is not connected to C/BE#[7:4]).

CLOCK 3. On the rising-edge of clock three, the initiator samples DEVSEL#, IRDY# and TRDY# asserted and ACK64# deasserted.

DEVSEL# asserted indicates that the addressed target has claimed the transaction.

THE deasserted state of ACK64# indicates that the target can only transfer data over the lower four data paths and cannot see the C/BE#[7:4] lines.

IRDY# and TRDY# asserted indicates that the initiator is ready to complete the write (of the upper four bytes) and the target is ready to accept write data, but only over the lower four data paths (ACK64# was not asserted). Because none of the lower four byte enables, C/BE#[3:0], are asserted, the target treats this as a null data phase and doesn't accept any write data. The fact that this is a 32-bit target means that the start address that it latched into its address counter during the address phase, 00000100h, is treated as a dword-aligned address, not quadword-aligned.

UPON completion of the null data phase on the rising-edge of clock three, the target increments its address counter by four to point to the next dword, 00000104h.

AT the start of the second data phase (during clock three), the initiator copies the settings on the upper byte enables, C/BE#[7:4], to the lower byte enables, C/BE#[3:0], and copies the data that had been driven onto the upper four data paths (destined for memory locations 00000104h through 00000107h) onto the lower four data paths. It could legally take up to eight clocks to do this.

THE initiator ceases to drive C/BE#[7:4] and AD[63:32], but these signal lines are prevented from floating by the required pullups on the system board.

THE initiator keeps IRDY# asserted, indicating the presence of the next four bytes on the lower part of the data bus. It does not deassert FRAME#, however, indicating that this is not the final data phase.

CLOCK 4. On the rising-edge of clock four, IRDY# and TRDY# are sampled asserted and the four bytes on the lower four data paths are written into memory locations 00000104h through 00000107h. This completes the second data phase.

DURING clock four, the initiator asserts all four of the lower four byte enables, but deasserts IRDY# to indicate that it is not yet ready to drive the third data item onto the data paths (e.g., it has a buffer dry condition).

ALTHOUGH it's not yet ready to deliver the third data item, the initiator is responsible for keeping the AD bus driven with a stable pattern. The designer typically just continues to drive the previous data item until it's ready to start driving the new one.

THE target increments its address counter to point to dword-aligned address 00000108h, but deasserts TRDY# to indicate that it is not yet ready to accept data.

CLOCK 5. On the rising-edge of clock five, IRDY# and TRDY# are sampled deasserted, forcing clock five to become a wait state in the third data phase. **DURING** clock five (the wait state), the initiator then asserts IRDY# and begins to drive the data onto the data bus.

AT the same time, the initiator deasserts FRAME# and REQ64#, indicating that the last data transfer is in progress.

CLOCK 6. See Clock 7.

CLOCK 7. TRDY# is sampled deasserted on the rising-edge of clocks six and seven, indicating that the target is not yet ready to accept the last data item. Clocks six and seven are therefore wait states in data phase three.

THE initiator must continue to drive the byte enables and the data until the target accepts the data.

DURING clock seven, the target asserts TRDY# to indicate that it is ready to accept the last data item.

CLOCK 8. On the rising-edge of clock eight, TRDY# and IRDY# are sampled asserted and the last data item is transferred. The four bytes on AD[31:0] are written into memory locations 00000108h through 0000010Bh.

THE initiator ceases to drive the AD and C/BE buses and IRDY#, returning the bus to the idle state.

THE target deasserts TRDY# and DEVSEL#.

32-bit Initiator and 64-bit Target

If the initiator is a 32-bit bus master, it never asserts REQ64# when it starts a transaction (it's not even connected to REQ64#). If it addresses a 64-bit target during the transaction, the target does not assert ACK64# along with DEVSEL# when it decodes the address (because the initiator didn't assert REQ64#). The target recognizes that the initiator is only using 32-bit transfer capability and therefore recognizes that the start address is dword-aligned and that it should increment by four rather than by eight.

Performing One 64-bit Transfer

The specification contains the following statement: "Using a single data phase with 64-bit transfers may not be very effective." The discussion that follows illustrates the rationale for this statement.

Assume that an initiator starts a transaction in order to perform a write consisting of eight bytes (one quadword). Assuming that an initiator wants to write one quadword-aligned group of eight bytes, it cannot be assumed that this will result in only one data phase. The currently-addressed target may be either a 32- or 64-bit target. If it turns out to be a 64-bit target, then it can accept all of the data in one data phase. On the other hand, if it turns out to be a 32-bit target, it's only capable of accepting 32-bits per data phase. This means that two data phases must be performed by the initiator when a 32-bit target claims the transaction.

The initiator does not know the size (32- or 64-bits) of the target until the target has decoded the address and command and asserted DEVSEL#. The initiator then samples ACK64# to make the size determination. When attempting the transfer of a single 64-bit data item, the initiator must defer the assertion of IRDY# and the simultaneous deassertion of FRAME# until it determines whether one (for a 64-bit target) or two phases (for a 32-bit target) will be necessary. Since the protocol dictates that FRAME# must be deasserted when the initiator is ready to complete the final data phase (i.e., when it asserts IRDY#), this situation affects the timing of IRDY# as well. The initiator cannot assert IRDY# during the first data phase until it determines whether or not this is the final data phase (and therefore whether to deassert FRAME# or not).

In summary, if the designer uses 64-bit capability to transfer a single eight byte object, it requires additional design complexity to handle the atypical IRDY#/ FRAME# timing. In addition, it would not result in a faster transfer than could be accomplished using 32-bit transfers. In fact, using 32-bit transfer capability would be equally efficient and less complex.

With 64-bit Target

Figure 15-5 on page 285 illustrates the case where the 64-bit initiator attempts the transfer of a 64-bit data item using 64-bit transfer capability (REQ64# is asserted) and a 64-bit target claims the transaction. Even though it has started driving the write data, the initiator cannot assert IRDY# during clock two because it hasn't yet determined if this is the only data phase or the first of two. It therefore has not yet determined whether or not to deassert FRAME# with the assertion of IRDY#.

At the rising-edge of clock three, it samples DEVSEL# and ACK64# asserted, indicating that a 64-bit target has claimed the transaction. Since this means that only one data phase is necessary, the initiator can deassert FRAME# and assert IRDY# during clock three, indicating that it is ready to complete the final (and only) data phase of the transaction.

The data transfer occurs on the rising-edge of clock four when IRDY# and TRDY# are sampled asserted. The transaction takes three clocks to complete and requires atypical IRDY#/FRAME# timing.

With 32-bit Target

Figure 15-6 on page 286 illustrates the case where the 64-bit initiator attempts the transfer of a 64-bit data item using 64-bit transfer capability (REQ64# is asserted) and a 32-bit target claims the transaction. During clock two, even though it has started driving the write data, the initiator can't assert IRDY# yet because it hasn't yet determined whether this is the only data phase or the first of two data phases.

At the rising-edge of clock three, the initiator samples DEVSEL# asserted and ACK64# deasserted, indicating that a 32-bit target has claimed the transaction. Since this means that this is the first of two data phases, the initiator asserts IRDY# during clock three, but doesn't deassert FRAME#. IRDY# asserted indicates the presence of the lower 32-bits of write data on AD[31:0]. The transfer of the first 32-bits occurs on the rising-edge of clock four when IRDY# and TRDY# are sampled asserted. This completes the first data phase and the second data phase then begins.

The initiator then copies the bytes from the upper four data paths, AD[63:32], to the lower four data paths and the upper byte enables, C/BE#[7:4], to the lower byte enables, C/BE#[3:0]. It keeps IRDY# asserted to indicate the presence of the data and also deasserts FRAME#, indicating its readiness to complete the last data phase. The second data transfer occurs on the rising-edge of clock five when IRDY# and TRDY# are sampled asserted. The transaction takes four clocks to complete (perhaps more if it takes multiple clocks to copy the second data item from the upper to the lower half of the bus) and requires the atypical IRDY#/FRAME# timing.

Simpler and Just as Fast: Use 32-bit Transfers

When performed without asserting REQ64#, the same transaction can be accomplished in three clocks (assuming 0-wait state operation on the part of both the master and the target) using normal IRDY#/FRAME# timing. The transaction would consist of the address phase plus one clock for the transfer of each of the two 32-bit objects.

With Known 64-bit Target

If the 64-bit master knows in advance that the target it's addressing is a 64-bit target (via a device-specific configuration register or some other mechanism), it doesn't need to wait for DEVSEL# and ACK64# to assert IRDY# and deassert FRAME#. It can assert IRDY# and deassert FRAME# immediately upon entering the first data phase (assuming that it's ready to transfer the data immediately). When dealing with 0-wait state memory, the transfer could then be accomplished in two clocks (one for the address phase and one for the data phase).

Figure 15-5: Single Data Phase 64-bit Transfer With a 64-bit Target

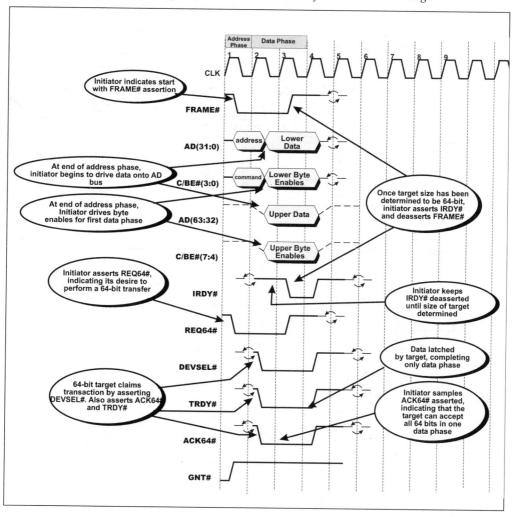

Figure 15-6: Dual-Data Phase 64-bit Transfer With a 32-bit Target

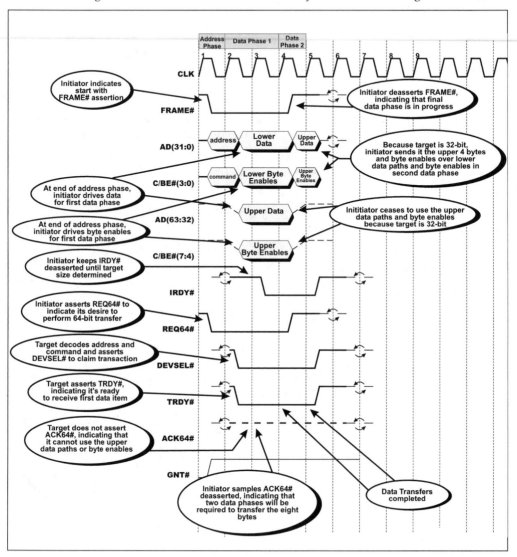

Disconnect on Initial Data Phase

Assume that a master starts a multiple-data phase read transaction and asserts REQ64#. The quadword-aligned start address is 00000100h and all eight byte enables are asserted during the first data phase. Also assume that the target is a 32-bit target and is not capable of handling a multiple-data phase transaction. This has the following effects:

1. The target does not assert ACK64#.
2. The target only transfers locations 00000100h through 00000103h during the first data phase and terminates the transaction by asserting STOP# along with TRDY#.
3. The master accepts the four bytes and ends the transaction.
4. The master re-arbitrates for the bus and then initiates the read again. It asserts FRAME# and REQ64# again. This time, the quadword-aligned start address is once again 00000100h, but only the upper four byte enables are asserted during the first data phase (because 00000100h through 00000103h have already been transferred).
5. The 32-bit target doesn't assert ACK64# and doesn't transfer any data (because the lower four byte enables are deasserted) and terminates the transaction with a Disconnect With Data Transfer (TRDY# and STOP# asserted).
6. Recognizing that the upper four bytes in the quadword still haven't been transferred, the master re-arbitrates for the bus and tries it again. It will never be successful in transferring the upper four bytes.

The **solution** to this dilemma is as follows: **when** the master was **disconnected** after the first dword transfer, it should **restart** the transaction **as a 32-bit transfer** (i.e., do not assert REQ64#, and output the dword-aligned address of the next four bytes to be transferred: 00000104h).

64-bit Addressing

Used to Address Memory Above 4GB

Bus masters are only permitted to use 64-bit addressing when communicating with memory that resides above the 4GB address boundary. Standard 32-bit addressing (in other words, a single address phase) must be used if the start address resides below this boundary (i.e., the upper 32 bits of the address are all zero).

Introduction

Using the basic command set, the PCI address bus, AD[31:0], permits the initiator to address devices that reside within the first 4GB of address space (using a single address phase; any command that uses a single address phase is referred to as a Single Address Command, or SAC).

Without the addition of any signals, the PCI specification also provides support for addressing memory devices that reside above the 4GB boundary. The Dual Address Cycle, or DAC, is used by an initiator to inform the community of targets that it is broadcasting a 64-bit memory address in two, back-to-back address phases. 64-bit addressing capability is not restricted to 64-bit initiators. Initiators fall into two categories:

- Those that are capable of generating only 32-bit addresses over AD[31:0] using a single address phase.
- Those that are capable of generating 32- and 64-bit addresses.

The sections that follow discuss the methods used by both 32-bit and 64-bit initiators in presenting a 64-bit address to the community of targets. Targets fall into two categories:

- Those that recognize the 64-bit addressing protocol (i.e., they have memory that resides above the 4GB address boundary).
- Those that only recognize the 32-bit addressing protocol (i.e., they do not have any memory that resides above the 4GB address boundary).

64-bit Addressing Protocol

64-bit Addressing by 32-bit Initiator

Figure 15-7 on page 291 illustrates a 32-bit initiator performing a burst memory read access from above the 4GB boundary. The target in this example is a 32-bit target, although a 64-bit target would respond exactly the same way to a 64-bit address generated by a 32-bit initiator (because it would not see REQ64# asserted).

CLOCK 1. The initiator begins the transaction on the rising-edge of clock one by asserting FRAME#, placing the lower 32 bits of the address on AD[31:0], and placing the Dual Address Cycle, or DAC, on C/BE#[3:0].

CLOCK 2. On the rising edge of clock two, all targets latch the lower 32 bits of the address and the Dual Address Cycle. All targets that support 64-bit addressing (in other words, memory targets that reside above 4GB) recognize the DAC and expect a second address phase to deliver the upper 32 bits of the address. All non-memory targets (i.e., I/O targets, configuration space and the interrupt controller) ignore the transaction after detecting the Dual Address Cycle. In this example, the initiator is not a 64-bit device, so it doesn't assert REQ64#.

THE second address phase is begun during clock two. The initiator drives the upper 32 bits of the address onto AD[31:0] and one of the memory read commands onto C/BE#[3:0].

CLOCK 3. On the rising-edge of clock three, the memory targets that reside above 4GB latch the upper 32 bits of the address from AD[31:0], the memory read command from C/BE#[3:0], and begin the address decode process.

THE first data phase begins during clock three. The initiator ceases to drive the upper part of the address onto AD[31:0] (in preparation for the target driving the requested data onto the AD bus).

THE initiator asserts IRDY# to indicate that it is ready to receive the requested data and also sets the byte enables to indicate the bytes to be transferred and the data paths to be used.

FRAME# is not deasserted when IRDY# is asserted, indicating that this is not the final data phase.

THE target has a fast address decoder and asserts DEVSEL# during clock three, but not ACK64# (because it's a 32-bit target).

CLOCK 4. On the rising-edge of clock four, TRDY# is sampled deasserted. The target has kept TRDY# deasserted to enforce the turn-around cycle necessary between the address phase and the first data phase of a read.

THE target then asserts TRDY# during clock four (a wait state), indicating the presence of the first data item on the bus.

CLOCK 5. On the rising-edge of clock five, the requested data is transferred (because TRDY# and IRDY# are sampled asserted). This completes the first data phase.

DURING clock five, the initiator changes the setting on the byte enables to request the next set of bytes, but deasserts IRDY# to indicate that it will not be ready to accept the requested data on the next rising-edge of the clock (a wait state must be inserted).

THE target keeps TRDY# asserted and begins to drive the second data item onto the AD bus.

CLOCK 6. On the rising-edge of clock six, IRDY# is sampled deasserted, so no data transfer takes place.

CLOCK six is a wait state.

THE initiator asserts IRDY# to indicate that it will be ready to transfer the data on the next rising-edge of the clock and also deasserts FRAME# to indicate that the last data phase is in progress.

CLOCK 7. On the rising-edge of clock seven, IRDY# and TRDY# are sampled asserted and the last data phase completes.

THE target samples IRDY# asserted and FRAME# deasserted, indicating that the initiator is ready to complete the last data phase.

THE initiator then deasserts IRDY#, returning the bus to the idle state. It also ceases to drive the C/BE# bus.

THE target ceases to drive the data onto the AD bus and deasserts TRDY# and DEVSEL#.

Figure 15-7: 32-bit Initiator Reading From Address at or Above 4GB

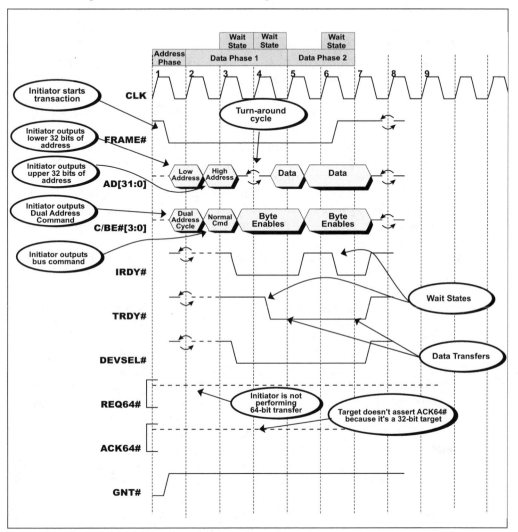

64-bit Addressing by 64-bit Initiator

Figure 15-8 on page 294 illustrates a 64-bit initiator performing a burst memory read access from an address above the 4GB boundary. In addition to using 64-bit addressing, the initiator asserts REQ64# to indicate that it wishes to perform 64-bit data transfers. The target of this transaction is a 64-bit target. If the target were a 32-bit device, it would not assert ACK64#, thereby indicating that it could not handle 64-bit data transfers. The initiator would then copy the byte enables from the upper lines, C/BE#[7:4], to the lower lines, C/BE#[3:0]. This subject is covered in the earlier part of this chapter. Since the target would only have access to AD[31:0] and C/BE#[3:0], it would handle the 64-bit address as discussed in the section preceding this one.

CLOCK 1. The initiator starts the transaction on the rising-edge of clock one by asserting FRAME# and REQ64#, and driving the Dual Address Cycle onto C/BE#[3:0].

THE initiator also drives the lower 32-bits of the address onto AD[31:0], the upper 32-bits of the address onto AD[63:32], and the memory read command onto C/BE#[7:4]. It continues to drive the upper part of the address onto AD[63:32] and the memory read command onto C/BE#[7:4] for the duration of both address phases.

REQ64# is asserted, indicating that the initiator is using the entire 64-bit bus for address output (during the first address phase) and that the initiator wishes to perform 64-bit data transfers (if the addressed target is a 64-bit device).

CLOCK 2. On the rising-edge of clock two, the community of 32-bit targets latch the DAC (Dual Address Cycle) from C/BE#[3:0] and the lower 32 bits of the address from AD[31:0].

THE community of 64-bit memory targets that reside above the 4GB boundary latch the entire 64-bit address from AD[63:0] and the memory read command from C/BE#[7:4].

DURING clock two, all 32-bit targets other than memory targets that reside above the 4GB address boundary quit listening to the transaction. All 64-bit memory targets that reside below the 4GB boundary also quit listening.

THE initiator starts the second address phase by driving the upper part of the address onto AD[31:0] (in case the currently-addressed target is not a 64-bit device) and the memory read command onto C/BE#[3:0].

CLOCK 3. On the rising-edge of clock three, all 32-bit memory targets that reside above the 4GB address boundary latch the upper 32 bits of the address from AD[31:0] and the memory read command from C/BE#[3:0]. They begin the address decode during clock three.

THE initiator asserts IRDY# to indicate that it is ready to receive the requested data and keeps FRAME# asserted, indicating that this is not the final data phase.

THE initiator ceases to drive address information onto both halves of the AD bus so the bus is free to be driven by the target during the data phase.

THE initiator sets C/BE#[7:0] to indicate which bytes to transfer during the first data phase.

THE target asserts DEVSEL# to claim the transaction and ACK64# to indicate that it is capable of performing 64-bit data transfers.

Clock 4. On the rising-edge of clock four, TRDY# is sampled deasserted, enforcing the insertion of the turn-around cycle.

During clock four, the target starts to drive the requested data onto the AD bus and asserts TRDY# to indicate its presence on the bus.

Clock 5. On the rising-edge of clock five, IRDY# and TRDY# are sampled asserted and the first data item is transferred. This completes the first data phase.

The initiator sets C/BE#[7:0] to indicate which bytes to transfer during the second data phase and deasserts IRDY# to indicate that it will not be ready to accept the requested data on the next rising-edge of the clock.

The target increments its address counter by eight to point to the next quadword.

The target keeps TRDY# asserted and begins to drive the second data item onto the AD bus.

Clock 6. On the rising-edge of clock six, IRDY# is sampled deasserted and the data is not transferred.

During the inserted wait state (clock six) the initiator asserts IRDY# to indicate that it will be ready to transfer the data on the next rising-edge of the clock.

The initiator also deasserts FRAME# and REQ64# to indicate that the last data transfer is in progress.

Clock 7. On the rising-edge of clock seven, IRDY# and TRDY# are sampled asserted and the final data item is transferred.

The target samples IRDY# asserted and FRAME# deasserted, indicating that this is the final data phase.

The initiator then deasserts IRDY#, returning the bus to the idle state and ceases to drive C/BE#[7:0].

The target ceases to drive the final data item onto the AD bus and deasserts TRDY#, DEVSEL# and ACK64#.

A 64-bit target with a fast address decoder could assert DEVSEL# during clock two, but must insert two wait states to account for the second address phase and the turn-around cycle (on a read).

A 64-bit target with a medium-speed address decoder could assert DEVSEL# during clock three, but must insert one wait state to account for the turn-around cycle (on a read).

A 64-bit target with a slow address decoder could assert DEVSEL# during clock four. The address decode latency accounts for the second address phase and the turn-around cycle (on a read), so the target need not insert wait states to account for them.

The only advantage that a 64-bit target has (over a 32-bit target) during 64-bit addressing is a one clock jump on address decode.

Figure 15-8: 64-bit Initiator Reading From Address
Above 4GB With 64-Bit Data Transfers

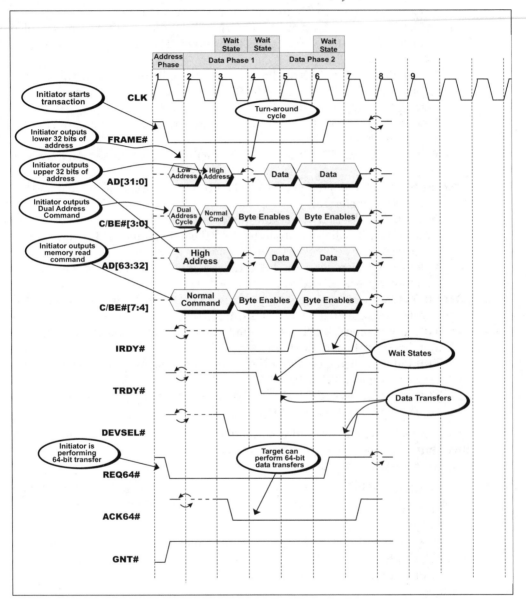

32-bit Initiator Addressing Above 4GB

An initiator that is only connected to AD[31:0] can communicate with memory above 4GB in two ways:

- The 64-bit memory target can alias all or some of its memory above 4GB into an address range in the lower 4GB. In other words, the configuration programmer could set up two address decoders (Base Address registers) for the same block of memory: one that responds to addresses above 4GB and one that recognizes addresses below 4GB. The master can then use SAC (single address phase command) memory commands to transfer data into/out of the memory above 4GB (using the window below 4GB).
- The master can use the DAC (Dual Address Cycle) to communicate directly with the memory above 4GB.

The specification also contains the following statement: "Another alternative is for the master to support only 32-bit addressing and the device driver moves the data from 32-bit address space to the 64-bit address space." The 32-bit bus master transfers a data block into a memory buffer below the 4GB address boundary and generates an interrupt to inform its driver that the data is present in memory. The device driver then moves the data to memory above the 4GB address boundary.

Subtractive Decode Timing Affected

If an expansion bus bridge located on the PCI bus employs subtractive decode (in other words, the ISA bridge), the expansion bus on the other side of the bridge either supports 64-bit addressing or it doesn't. As two examples, the ISA bus does not support 64-bit addressing, while the 64-bit Micro Channel does (but it's typically not a subtractive bridge).

An ISA bridge that incorporates subtractive decode capability (virtually all implementations do) ignores any PCI transaction that uses 64-bit addressing (because there are no memory targets on the ISA bus that reside above 4GB).

A bridge to an expansion bus that supports 64-bit addressing and that incorporates a subtractive decoder operates in the following manner:

- starting one clock after the end of the second address phase, it samples DEVSEL# on three successive rising-edges of the clock to determine that the transaction isn't claimed by any PCI memory targets.
- If none claim it (by asserting DEVSEL#), the bridge's subtractive decoder asserts DEVSEL# during the next clock to claim the transaction. It then ini-

tiates the memory transaction on the expansion bus to make it visible to all memory targets that reside above the 4GB address boundary on the expansion bus.

During a single address phase transaction, starting one clock after the end of the one and only address phase, a subtractive decoder samples DEVSEL# on three successive rising-edges of the clock to determine that the transaction isn't claimed by any PCI memory targets.

Master Abort Timing Affected

Normally, a bus master samples DEVSEL# at the end of the second, third, fourth and fifth clocks of the transaction and then Master Aborts if DEVSEL# was not sampled asserted. When the master is using 64-bit addressing, it samples DEVSEL# at the end of the third, fourth, fifth and sixth clocks of the transaction and then aborts if DEVSEL# was not sampled asserted.

Address Stepping

A bus master that uses stepping (see "Address/Data Stepping" on page 162) to gradually place the full address on the bus keeps FRAME# deasserted until the full address is present and stable on the bus. When the targets sample FRAME# asserted, the address is decoded.

The specification says that **stepping cannot be used for 64-bit addressing**. Although the master could keep FRAME# deasserted for several clocks while it gradually built the lower 32 bits of the address on AD[31:0], 32-bit memory targets then expect the upper 32 bits of the address to be present and stable on AD[31:0] on the next rising-edge of the clock. The upper 32 bits of the address therefore cannot be stepped onto AD[31:0]. It must be presented in one clock.

Although the specification specifically states that stepping cannot be used for 64-bit addressing, the author would note that it's technically possible to step the lower 32-bit of the address onto AD[31:0] and then present the upper 32-bits in one clock. The author cannot think of any side effects stemming from this approach, but would also question the value in it.

FRAME# Timing in Single Data Phase Transaction

If the initiator were using 64-bit addressing to perform a single data phase transaction, FRAME# is asserted at the start of the first address phase and must be kept asserted until IRDY# is asserted in the data phase. It cannot be removed during the second address phase.

Chapter 15: The 64-bit PCI Extension

64-bit Parity

Address Phase Parity

PAR64 Not Used for Single Address Phase

When the initiator is not using 64-bit addressing, there is a single address phase and a 32-bit address is generated by the initiator. In this case, address phase parity is supplied solely over the PAR signal. The 64-bit extension, consisting of AD[63:32], PAR64, and C/BE#[7:4], is not in use during the address phase of the transaction.

PAR64 Not Used for Dual-Address Phases by 32-bit Master

When a 32-bit bus master is performing 64-bit addressing, it is only using AD[31:0] and C/BE#[3:0]. The 64-bit extension is not in use. The PAR64 signal is therefore not used to supply parity on the upper half of the bus.

PAR64 Used for DAC by 64-bit Master When Requesting 64-bit Transfers

When a 64-bit bus master is performing 64-bit addressing and has asserted REQ64#, it is required to drive the upper 32 bits of the address onto AD[63:32] and the memory command onto C/BE#[7:4] during the first address phase. It is also required to supply even parity for this information on the PAR64 signal on the next rising-edge of the clock. During the second address phase, the initiator is required to continue driving the same information on AD[63:32], and C/BE#[7:4]. The initiator must once again supply even parity on PAR64 on the rising-edge of the clock that follows completion of the second address phase. A 64-bit target may be designed to latch the entire address and command and begin the decode at the end of either the first or the second address phase. The target then latches the state of PAR64 on the rising-edge of the clock that follows.

Data Phase Parity

Parity works the same for 32- and 64-bit transfers. For a detailed discussion of 32-bit parity, refer to the chapter entitled "Error Detection and Handling" on page 199. In a 64-bit implementation, an additional parity signal, PAR64, is added. It's timing and function are identical to that of the PAR signal. PAR64 must be implemented by all 64-bit agents.

PAR64 must be set to the appropriate state (to force even parity) one clock after the completion of each address phase and one clock after the data is presented (IRDY# asserted on a write, or TRDY# asserted on a read) in each data phase. Usage of PAR64 is qualified by the assertion of REQ64# (indicating that the initiator wants to perform 64-bit data transfers) and ACK64# (the target supports 64-bit data transfers). If either REQ64# or ACK64# is deasserted, only the lower half of the bus is in use and PAR64 is not used.

16 *66MHz PCI Implementation*

Prior To This Chapter

The previous chapter described the 64-bit extension that permits masters and targets to perform eight byte transfers during each data phase. It also described 64-bit addressing used to address memory targets that reside above the 4GB boundary.

In This Chapter

This chapter describes the implementation of a 66MHz bus and components.

The Next Chapter

The next chapter provides an introduction to PCI configuration address space. The concept of single- and multi-function devices is described. The configuration space available to the designer of a PCI device is introduced, including the device's configuration Header space and its device-specific configuration register area.

Introduction

The PCI specification defines support for the implementation of buses and components that operate at speeds of up to 66MHz. This chapter covers the issues related to this topic. Note that all references to 66MHz in this chapter indicate a frequency within the range from 33.33MHz to 66.66MHz.

66MHz Uses 3.3V Signaling Environment

66MHz components only operate correctly in a 3.3V signaling environment (see "3.3V, 5V and Universal Cards" on page 449). The 5V environment is not supported. This means that 66MHz add-in cards are keyed to install only in 3.3V connectors and cannot be installed in 5V card connectors.

How Components Indicate 66MHz Support

The 66MHz PCI component or add-in card indicates its support in two fashions: programmatically and electrically.

66MHz-Capable Status Bit

The 66MHz-Capable bit has been added to the Status register (see Figure 16-1 on page 302). The designer hardwires a one into this bit if the device supports operation from 0 through 66.66MHz. A 66MHz-capable device hardwires this bit to one. For all 33MHz devices, this bit is reserved and is hardwired to zero. Software can determine the speed capability of a PCI bus by checking the state of this bit in the Status register of the bridge to the bus in question (host/PCI or PCI-to-PCI bridge). Software can also check this bit in the Status register of each additional device discovered on the bus in question to determine if all of the devices on the bus are 66MHz-capable. If just one device returns a zero from this bit, the bus runs at 33MHz (or slower), not 66MHz. Table 16-1 on page 300 defines the combinations of bus and device capability that may be detected.

Table 16-1: Combinations of 66MHz-Capable Bit Settings

Bridge's 66MHz-Capable Bit	Device's 66MHz-Capable Bit	Description
0	0	Bus is a 33MHz bus, so all devices operate at 33MHz.
0	1	66MHz-capable device located on 33MHz bus. Bus and all devices operate at 33MHz. If the device is an add-in device and requires the throughput available on a 66MHz bus, the configuration software may prompt the user to install the card in an add-in connector on a different bus.
1	0	33MHz device located on 66MHz-capable bus. Bus and all devices operate at 33MHz. The configuration software should prompt the user to install the card in an add-in connector on a different bus.

Table 16-1: Combinations of 66MHz-Capable Bit Settings (Continued)

Bridge's 66MHz-Capable Bit	Device's 66MHz-Capable Bit	Description
1	1	66MHz-capable device located on 66MHz-capable bus. If status check of all other devices on the bus indicates that all of the devices are 66MHz-capable, the bus and all devices operate at 66MHz.

M66EN Signal

Refer to Figure 16-2 on page 302. A 66MHz PCI bus includes a newly-defined signal, M66EN. This signal must be bussed to the M66EN pin on all 66MHz-capable devices embedded on the system board and to a redefined pin (referred to as M66EN) on any 3.3V connectors that reside on the bus. The system board designer must supply a single pullup on this trace. The redefined pin on the 3.3V connector is B49 and is attached to the ground plane on 33MHz PCI cards. Unless grounded by insertion of a PCI device, the natural state of the M66EN signal is asserted (due to the pullup). 66MHz embedded devices and cards either use M66EN as an input or don't use it at all (this is discussed later in this chapter).

The designer must include a 0.01uF capacitor located within .25" of the M66EN pin on each add-in connector in order to provide an AC return path and to decouple the M66EN signal to ground.

It is advisable to attach M66EN to a bit in a machine-readable port to allow software to determine if the bus is currently operating at high or low speed. Refer to "66MHz-Related Issues" on page 476.

How Clock Generator Sets Its Frequency

PCI devices embedded on a 66MHz PCI bus are all 66MHz devices. A card installed in a connector on the bus may be either a 66MHz or a 33MHz card. If the card connector(s) isn't populated, M66EN stays asserted (by virtue of the pullup) and the Clock Generator produces a high-speed clock. If any 33MHz component is installed in a connector, however, the ground plane on the 33MHz card is connected to the M66EN signal, deasserting it. This causes the Clock Generator to drop the clock frequency to 33MHz (or lower). A typical implementation would divide the high-speed clock by two to yield the new, lower clock frequency.

Figure 16-1: Configuration Status Register

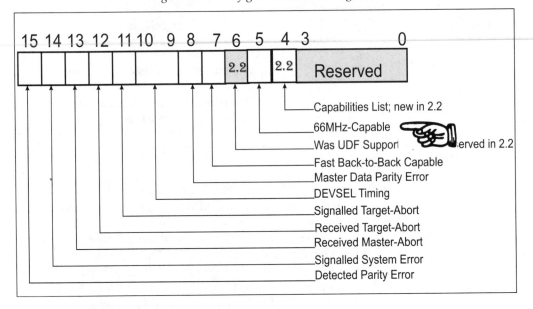

Figure 16-2: Relationship of M66EN Signal and the PCI Clock Generator

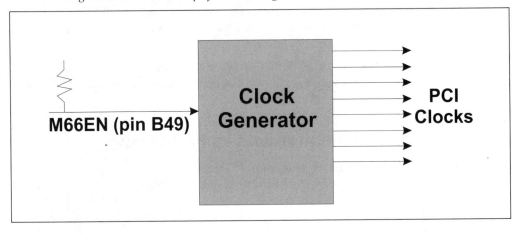

Does Clock Have to be 66MHz?

As defined in revision 1.0 and 2.0 of the specification, the PCI bus does not have to be implemented at its top rated speed of 33MHz. Lower speeds are acceptable. The same is true of the 66MHz PCI bus description found in revision 2.x of the specification. All 66MHz-rated components are required to support operation from 0 through 66.66MHz. The system designer may choose to implement a 50MHz PCI bus, a 60MHz PCI bus, etc.

Clock Signal Source and Routing

The specification recommends that the PCI clock be individually-sourced to each PCI component as a point-to-point signal from separate, low-skew clock drivers. This diminishes signal reflection effects and improves signal integrity. In addition, the add-in card designer must adhere to the clock signal trace length (defined in revision 2.0) of 2.5 inches.

Stopping Clock and Changing Clock Frequency

The 66MHz specification states that the clock frequency may be changed at any time as long as the clock edges remain clean and the minimum high and low times are not violated. Unlike the 33MHz specification, however, the clock frequency may not be changed except in conjunction with assertion of the PCI RST# signal. Components designed to be integrated onto the system board may be designed to operate at a fixed frequency (up to 66MHz) and may require that no clock frequency changes occur.

The clock may be stopped (to conserve power), but only in the low state.

How 66MHz Components Determine Bus Speed

When a 66MHz-capable device senses M66EN deasserted (at reset time), this automatically disables the device's ability to perform operations at speeds above 33MHz. If M66EN is sensed asserted, this indicates that no 33MHz devices are installed on the bus and the clock circuit is supplying a high-speed PCI clock.

A 66MHz device uses the M66EN signal in one of two fashions:

- The device is not connected to M66EN at all (because the device has no need to determine the bus speed in order to operate correctly).
- The device implements M66EN as an input (because the device requires knowledge of the bus speed in order to operate correctly).

System Board with Separate Buses

Refer to Figure 16-3 on page 304. The system board designer can partition the board into two or more PCI buses. A 66MHz bus can be populated with devices that demand low-latency and high throughput, while a separate 33MHz PCI bus is populated only with 33MHz devices. As an example, in the illustration PCI Bus 0 could be a 33MHz PCI bus while PCI Bus 4 is a 66MHz PCI bus.

Figure 16-3: System With Dual Host Bridges

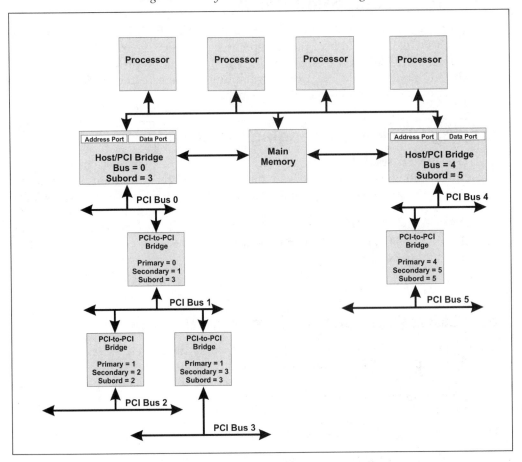

Maximum Achievable Throughput

The theoretical maximum achievable throughput on a 66MHz PCI bus would be:

- 4 bytes per data phase * 66 million data phases per second = 264MB/second. This would be a 32-bit bus master bursting with a 32-bit target.
- 8 bytes per data phase * 66 million data phases per second = 528MB/second. This would be a 64-bit bus master bursting with a 64-bit target.

Electrical Characteristics

To ensure compatibility when operating in a 33MHz PCI bus environment, 66MHz PCI drivers must meet the same DC characteristics and AC drive points as 33MHz bus drivers. However, 66MHz PCI bus operation requires faster timing parameters and redefined measurement conditions. Because of this, a 66MHz PCI bus may require less loading (i.e., fewer devices) and shorter trace lengths than the 33MHz PCI bus environment.

Figure 16-4 on page 305 illustrates the differences in timing between 33 and 66MHz component operation. The chapter entitled "Intro to Reflected-Wave Switching" provides an introduction to 33MHz bus timing and the various timing components (e.g., Tval, Tprop, etc.).

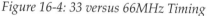

Figure 16-4: 33 versus 66MHz Timing

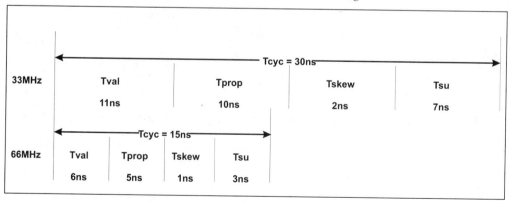

33MHz drivers are specified by their V/I curves, while 66MHz drivers are specified in terms of their AC and DC drive points, timing parameters, and slew rate. The specification defines the following parameters:

- The minimum AC drive point defines an acceptable first step voltage and must be reached within the maximum Tval time.
- The maximum AC drive point limits the amount of overshoot and undershoot in the system.
- The DC drive point specifies steady-state conditions.
- The minimum slew rate and the timing parameters guarantee 66MHz operation.
- The maximum slew rate minimizes system noise.

66MHz PCI designers must design drivers that launch sufficient energy into a 25 Ohm transmission line so that correct input levels are guaranteed after the first reflection.

At 66MHz, the clock cycle time is 15ns (vs. 30ns at 33MHz), while the minimum clock high and low times are 6ns each (vs. 11ns at 33MHz). The clock slew rate has a minimum specification of 1.5 Volts/ns and a maximum of 4 Volts/ns (same as 33MHz specification). Table 16-2 on page 306 defines the 66MHz timing parameters and provides a side-by-side comparison with the 33MHz timing parameters. The following exception applies to the 66MHz values in the table: REQ# and GNT# are point-to-point signals and have different setup times than do bussed signals. They have a setup time of 5ns.

Table 16-2: 66MHz Timing Parameters

Symbol	Description	66MHz		33MHz	
		Min	Max	Min	Max
Tval	CLK to signal valid delay, bussed signals	2ns	6ns	2ns	11ns
Tval (ptp)	CLK to signal valid delay, point-to-point signals	2ns	6ns	2ns	12ns
Ton	Float to active delay	2ns		2ns	
Toff	Active to float delay		14ns		28ns
Tsu	Input setup time to CLK, bussed signals	3ns		7ns	

Table 16-2: 66MHz Timing Parameters (Continued)

Symbol	Description	66MHz		33MHz	
		Min	Max	Min	Max
Tsu (ptp)	Input setup time to CLK, point-to-point signals	5ns		10 or 12ns	
Th	Input hold time from CLK	0ns		0ns	
Trst	Reset active time after power stable	1ms		1ms	
Trst-clk	Reset active time after CLK stable	100us		100us	
Trst-off	Reset active to output float delay		40ns		40ns
Trrsu	REQ64# to RST# setup time	10Tcyc		10Tcyc	
Trrh	RST# to REQ64# hold time	0ns	50ns	0ns	50ns

When computing the 66MHz bus loading model, a maximum pin capacitance of 10pF must be assumed for add-in boards, whereas the actual pin capacitance may be used for devices embedded on the system board.

Latency Rule

Common sense says that devices residing on the 66MHz PCI bus should all be fast access devices. The PCI 2.1 specification requires that, on a read transaction, the time from assertion of FRAME# to the completion of the first data phase not exceed 16 PCI clocks.

THE 2.2 SPEC IMPOSES THIS RESTRICTION ON BOTH READS AND WRITES.   2.2

66MHz Component Recommended Pinout

The revision 2.0 specification suggested a recommended PCI component pinout wherein the signals wrapped around the component in the same order as the pin sequence on the add-in connector. The revision 2.1 and 2.2 specifications states that "the designer may modify the suggested pinout...as required" to meet the 66MHz electrical specification.

Adding More Loads and/or Lengthening Bus

Running the PCI bus at 66MHz imposes tighter constraints on trace length and the number of loads the bus supports. The system board designer may choose to run the bus at a lower speed (e.g., 50MHz), thereby permitting longer traces and/or additional loads.

Number of Add-In Connectors

As a general rule, there is only one add-in connector on a 66MHz bus, but the specification does not preclude the inclusion of additional connectors (as long as the electrical integrity of the bus is maintained).

17 *Intro to Configuration Address Space*

The Previous Chapter

The previous chapter described the implementation of a 66MHz bus and components.

This Chapter

As the chapter title states, this chapter provides an introduction to PCI configuration address space. The concept of single- and multi-function devices is described. The configuration space available to the designer of a PCI device is introduced, including the device's configuration Header space and its device-specific configuration register area.

The Next Chapter

The next chapter provides a detailed discussion of the methods utilized to access PCI configuration registers. The methods described include the standard configuration mechanism, the legacy method that is no longer permitted, and the usage of memory-mapped configuration registers (as implemented in the PowerPC PREP platforms). The Type Zero and Type One configuration read and write transactions that are used to access configuration registers are described in detail.

Introduction

When the machine is first powered on, the configuration software must scan the various buses in the system (PCI and others) to determine what devices exist and what configuration requirements they have. This process is commonly referred to as:

- scanning the bus
- walking the bus

- probing the bus
- the discovery process
- bus enumeration.

The program that performs the PCI bus scan is frequently referred to as the PCI bus enumerator.

In order to facilitate this process, each PCI function must implement a base set of configuration registers defined by the PCI specification. Depending on its operational characteristics, a function may also implement other required or optional configuration registers defined by the specification. In addition, the specification sets aside a number of additional configuration locations for the implementation of function-specific configuration registers.

The configuration software reads a subset of a device's configuration registers in order to determine the presence of the function and its type. Having determined the presence of the device, the software then accesses the function's other configuration registers to determine how many blocks of memory and/or IO space the device requires (in other words, how many programmable memory and/or IO decoders it implements). It then programs the device's memory and/or IO address decoders to respond to memory and/or IO address ranges that are guaranteed to be mutually-exclusive from those assigned to other system devices.

If the function indicates usage of a PCI interrupt request pin (via one of its configuration registers), the configuration software programs it with routing information indicating what system interrupt request (IRQ) line the function's PCI interrupt request pin is routed to by the system.

If the device has bus mastering capability, the configuration software can read two of its configuration registers to determine how often it requires access to the PCI bus (an indication of what arbitration priority it would like to have) and how long it would like to maintain ownership in order to achieve adequate throughput. The system configuration software can utilize this information to program the bus master's Latency Timer (or timeslice) register and the PCI bus arbiter (if it's programmable) to provide the optimal PCI bus utilization.

PCI Device vs. PCI Function

A physical PCI device (e.g., a PCI component embedded on the system board or a PCI expansion board) may contain one or more (up to eight) separate PCI functions (i.e., logical devices). This is not a new concept. Multi-function boards were used in PCs for years prior to the advent of PCI.

Chapter 17: Intro to Configuration Address Space

In order to access a function's configuration registers, a PCI device (i.e., package) needs to know that it is the target of a configuration read or write, the identity of the target function within it, the dword of its configuration space (1-of-64), the bytes within that dword, and whether it's a read or a write. The method that the host/PCI bridge uses to identify the target PCI device, PCI function, etc., is discussed in the chapter entitled "Configuration Transactions" on page 317.

A PCI device that contains only one function is referred to as a single-function device. A PCI device that contains more than one function is referred to as a multi-function device. A bit in one of a function's configuration registers defines whether the package contains one function or more than one. For the configuration process, a device's PCI functions are identified as functions zero-through-seven. From a configuration access standpoint, the function contained in a single-function device must respond as function zero when addressed in a Type 0 PCI configuration read or write transaction.

In a multi-function device, the first function must be designed to respond to configuration accesses as function zero, while additional functions may be designed to respond as any function between one and seven. There is no requirement for multiple functions to be implemented sequentially. As an example, a card may be sold with minimal functionality and the customer may purchase additional functions as upgrades at a later time. These functions could be installed into any of several daughter-card connectors on the card or may be installed as snap-in modules on the card. As an example, a card could have functions zero, three and six populated, but not the others.

Three Address Spaces: I/O, Memory and Configuration

Intel x86 and PowerPC 60x processors possess the ability to address two distinct address spaces: IO and memory (although most system designs do not support processor-generated IO transactions in a PowerPC environment). PCI bus masters (including the host/PCI bridge) use PCI IO and memory transactions to access PCI IO and memory locations, respectively. In addition, a third access type, the configuration access, is used to access a device's configuration registers. A function's configuration registers must be initialized at startup time to configure the function to respond to memory and/or IO address ranges assigned to it by the configuration software.

The PCI memory space is either 4GB or 2^{64} locations in size (if 64-bit addressing is utilized). PCI IO space is 4GB in size (although Intel x86 processors cannot generate IO addresses above the first 64KB of IO space). PCI configuration space is divided into a separate, dedicated configuration address space for each function contained within a PCI device (i.e., in a chip or on a card). Figure 17-1 on page 313 illustrates the basic format of a PCI function's configuration space. The first 16 dwords of a function's configuration space is referred to as the function's configuration Header space. The format and usage of this area are defined by the specification. Three Header formats are currently defined:

- **Header Type Zero** (defined in "Intro to Configuration Header Region" on page 351) for all devices other than PCI-to-PCI bridges.
- **Header Type One** for PCI-to-PCI bridges (defined in "Configuration Registers" on page 552).
- **Header Type Two** for CardBus bridges (defined in the CardBus spec).

The system designer must provide a mechanism that the host/PCI bridge will use to convert processor-initiated accesses with certain pre-defined memory or IO addresses into configuration accesses on the PCI bus. The mechanism defined in the specification is described in "Intro to Configuration Mechanisms" on page 321.

Chapter 17: Intro to Configuration Address Space

Figure 17-1: PCI Function's Basic Configuration Address Space Format

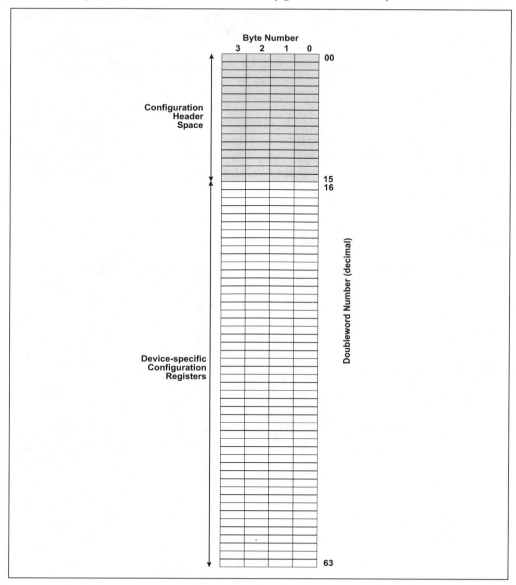

2.2 Host Bridge Needn't Implement Configuration Space

THE 2.1 SPEC STATED THAT ALL PCI DEVICES MUST IMPLEMENT PCI CONFIGURATION SPACE. THE 2.2 PCI SPEC SAYS:

"EVERY DEVICE, OTHER THAN HOST BUS BRIDGES, MUST IMPLEMENT CONFIGURATION ADDRESS SPACE. HOST BUS BRIDGES MAY OPTIONALLY IMPLEMENT CONFIGURATION ADDRESS SPACE."

IF THE HOST/PCI BRIDGE DOESN'T IMPLEMENT ITS CONFIGURATION REGISTERS IN PCI CONFIGURATION SPACE (BUT IT SHOULD BE NOTED THAT MOST DESIGNS DO), ITS CONFIGU-RATION REGISTERS MAY BE IMPLEMENTED IN EITHER IO OR MEMORY-MAPPED IO SPACE. MEMORY-MAPPED IO SPACE WOULD BE BETTER BECAUSE X86 IO SPACE IS SOOOOO SMALL (64KB TOTAL) AND SOOOOO CROWDED.

System with Single PCI Bus

Figure 17-2 on page 315 illustrates a typical system incorporating a single PCI bus. The interface between the host processor bus and the PCI bus is referred to as the host/PCI bridge. The bus directly on the other side of the bridge is always designated (for configuration purposes) as *PCI Bus 0*. If one or more of the functions on PCI Bus 0 are PCI-to-PCI bridges, the two PCI buses connected to a PCI-to-PCI bridge are referred to as the bridge's *primary* (the PCI bus closer to the host processor) and *secondary* buses (the bus further away from the host processor). The chapter entitled "Configuration Transactions" on page 317 provides a detailed description of configuration read and write transactions that target functions residing on PCI Bus 0. "Type 1 Configuration Transactions" on page 620 describes how the processor accesses configuration registers within functions residing on subordinate PCI buses (PCI buses residing beneath PCI Bus 0).

Figure 17-2: System With a Single PCI Bus

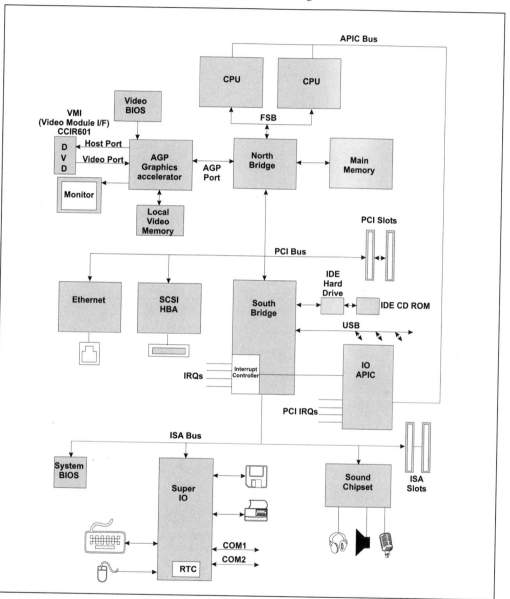

18 Configuration Transactions

The Previous Chapter

The previous chapter provided an introduction to PCI configuration address space. The concept of single- and multi-function devices was described. The configuration space available to the designer of a PCI device was introduced, including the device's configuration Header space and its device-specific configuration register area.

This Chapter

This chapter provides a detailed discussion of the method utilized to access PCI configuration registers. The methods described include the standard configuration mechanism, the legacy method that is no longer permitted, and the usage of memory-mapped configuration registers (as implemented in the PowerPC PReP platforms). The Type Zero configuration read and write configuration transactions that are used to access configuration registers are described in detail. The Type One configuration transactions, used to access configuration registers on the secondary side of a PCI-to-PCI bridge, are also described.

The Next Chapter

Once this chapter has described how the registers are accessed, the next chapter provides a detailed description of the configuration register format and usage for all PCI devices other than PCI-to-PCI bridges and CardBus bridges.

Who Performs Configuration?

Initially, the BIOS code performs device configuration. Once a Plug-and-Play OS (such as Windows 98 or Windows 2000) has been booted and control is passed to it, the OS takes over device management. Additional information regarding PCI device configuration in the Windows environment can be found in "PCI Bus Driver Accesses PCI Configuration and PM Registers" on page 489.

In any case, it is a configuration program executing on the processor that performs system configuration. This means that the host processor must have some way to instruct the host/PCI bridge to perform configuration read and write transactions on the PCI bus.

Bus Hierarchy

Introduction

This chapter focuses on the configuration of systems with one PCI bus (see Figure 18-1 on page 320). Assuming that the system has one or more PCI expansion connectors, however, a card may be installed at any time (perhaps more than one card) that incorporates a PCI-to-PCI bridge. The card has another PCI bus on it, and one or more PCI devices reside on that PCI bus. The configuration software executing on the host processor must be able to perform configuration reads and writes with the functions on each PCI bus that lives beyond the host/PCI bridge.

This highlights the fact that the programmer must supply the following information to the host/PCI bridge when performing a configuration read or write:

- target PCI bus.
- target PCI device (i.e., package) on the bus.
- target PCI function within the device.
- target dword within the function's configuration space.
- target byte(s) within the dword.

These parameters must be supplied to the host/PCI bridge. The bridge must then determine if the target PCI bus specified is:

- the bus immediately on the other side of the host/PCI bridge (in other words, Bus 0)
- a bus further out in the bus hierarchy
- none of the buses behind the bridge.

This implies that the host/PCI bridge has some way of identifying its PCI bus and the range of PCI buses residing beyond its bus. The bus on the other side of the host/PCI bridge is always bus 0 (unless there are more than one host/PCI bridge on the processor bus; for more information, refer to "Multiple Host/PCI Bridges" on page 327). The bridge either implicitly knows this or implements a *Bus Number register* that contains zero after RST# is deasserted. The bridge also incorporates a *Subordinate Bus Number register* that it uses to identify the bus furthest away from the host processor beyond this bridge. The bridge compares the target bus number specified by the programmer to the range of buses that exists beyond the bridge. There are three possible cases:

CASE 1. The target bus is bus 0.

CASE 2. The target bus isn't bus 0, but is less than or equal to the value in the Subordinate Bus Number register. In other words, the transaction targets a device on a subordinate bus.

CASE 3. The target bus doesn't fall within the range of buses that exists beyond this bridge.

In Cases 1 and 2, the bridge will initiate a PCI configuration read or write on the PCI bus in response to the processor's request. In the third case, however, the bridge doesn't respond to the processors' request to perform a PCI configuration transaction at all (because the target bus is not behind it).

Case 1: Target Bus Is PCI Bus 0

If the target bus is bus 0 (the first case), the bridge must initiate a PCI configuration transaction and in some way indicate to the devices on Bus 0 that one of them is the target of this configuration transaction. This is accomplished by setting AD[1:0] to 00b during the address phase of the configuration transaction. This identifies the transaction as a **Type 0** configuration transaction targeting one of the devices on this bus. This bit pattern tells the community of devices on the PCI bus that the bridge that "owns" that bus has already performed the bus number comparison and verified that the request targets a device on its bus. A detailed description of the Type 0 configuration transaction can be found in "Type 0 Configuration Transaction" on page 335.

Case 2: Target Bus Is Subordinate To Bus 0

If, on the other hand, the target bus is a bus that is subordinate to PCI bus 0 (the second case), the bridge still must initiate the configuration transaction on bus 0, but must indicate in some manner that none of the devices on this bus is the target of the transaction. Rather, only PCI-to-PCI bridges residing on the bus should pay attention to the transaction because it targets a device on a bus further out in the hierarchy beyond a PCI-to-PCI bridge that is attached to Bus 0. This is accomplished by setting AD[1:0] to 01b during the address phase of the configuration transaction. This pattern instructs all functions other than PCI-to-PCI bridges that the transaction is not for any of them and is referred to as a **Type 1** configuration transaction. A detailed description of the Type 1 configuration access can be found in "Type 1 Configuration Transactions" on page 344.

Figure 18-1: Typical PC System Block Diagram

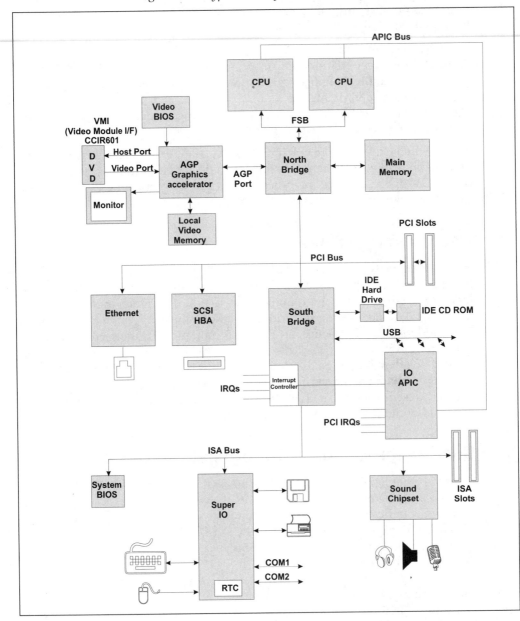

Must Respond To Config Accesses Within 2^{25} Clocks After RST#

2.2

AS DEFINED IN THE 2.2 SPEC, INITIALIZATION-TIME BEGINS WHEN RST# IS DEASSERTED AND COMPLETES 2^{25} PCI CLOCKS LATER. AT A BUS SPEED OF 33MHz, THIS EQUATES TO 1.0066 SECONDS, WHILE IT EQUATES TO .5033 SECONDS AT A BUS SPEED OF 66MHz. DURING THIS PERIOD OF TIME:

- THE SYSTEM'S POWER-ON SELF-TEST (POST) CODE IS EXECUTING.
- PCI SUBSYSTEMS (I.E., FUNCTIONS) ARE TAKING WHATEVER ACTIONS ARE NECESSARY TO PREPARE TO BE ACCESSED.

IF A TARGET IS ACCESSED DURING INITIALIZATION-TIME, IT IS ALLOWED TO DO ANY OF THE FOLLOWING:

- IGNORE THE REQUEST (UNLESS IT IS A DEVICE NECESSARY TO BOOT THE OS).
- CLAIM THE ACCESS AND HOLD IN WAIT STATES UNTIL IT CAN COMPLETE THE REQUEST, NOT TO EXCEED THE END OF INITIALIZATION-TIME.
- CLAIM THE ACCESS AND TERMINATE WITH RETRY.

RUN-TIME FOLLOWS INITIALIZATION-TIME. DEVICES MUST COMPLY WITH THE LATENCY RULES (SEE "PREVENTING TARGET FROM MONOPOLIZING BUS" ON PAGE 81) DURING RUN-TIME.

Intro to Configuration Mechanisms

This section describes the methods used to stimulate the host/PCI bridge to generate PCI configuration transactions. A subsequent section in this chapter provides a detailed description of Type 0 configuration transactions. The section entitled "Type 1 Configuration Transactions" on page 344 provides a detailed description of the Type 1 configuration transactions.

As mentioned earlier in this book, Intel x86 and PowerPC processors (as two examples processor families) do not possess the ability to perform configuration read and write transactions. They use memory and IO (IO is only in the x86 case) read and write transactions to communicate with external devices. This means that the host/PCI bridge must be designed to recognize certain IO or memory accesses initiated by the processor as requests to perform configuration accesses.

2.2

For PC-AT compatible systems (other than PC-compatible PowerPC-based systems), the 2.1 PCI spec defined two methods (one which was only included in the spec as a historical reference) that utilized processor-initiated IO accesses to instruct the host/PCI bridge to perform PCI configuration accesses. *PRIOR TO THE 2.2 PCI SPEC, THESE TWO MECHANISMS WERE DESIGNATED AS CONFIGURATION MECHANISM #1 AND CONFIGURATION MECHANISM #2. THE PCI 2.2 SPEC HAS REMOVED ALL MENTION OF CONFIGURATION MECHANISM #2. IN ADDITION, IT NOW REFERS TO CONFIGURATION MECHANISM #1 AS THE CONFIGURATION MECHANISM (IN OTHER WORDS, THE ONLY MECHANISM).* As historical information only, this chapter does contain a section describing Configuration Mechanism #2. To differentiate it from the mechanism #2, the current Configuration Mechanism is referred to as Configuration Mechanism #1.

Configuration mechanism #2 was only defined in the 2.0 and 2.1 specifications for backward compatibility. This was the mechanism defined in the revision 1.0 specification. The revision 2.0 and 2.1 specifications both contained the following text:

> "**Configuration mechanism #1 is the preferred implementation** and must be provided by all future host bridges (and existing bridges should convert if possible). Configuration mechanism #2 is defined for backward compatibility and must not be used by new designs. Host bridges implemented in PC-AT compatible systems must implement at least one of these mechanisms."

The specification does not define a configuration mechanism to be used in systems other than PC-AT compatible systems.

Although PowerPC 60x processors are capable of performing IO transactions, the PowerPC PReP specification forbids the generation of IO transactions by the processor (the chipset generates a Machine Check to the processor if the processor initiates one). Instead, all PCI IO and configuration registers are accessed by performing accesses to memory-mapped IO locations defined in the PReP specification. "PowerPC PReP Configuration Mechanism" on page 335 provides a basic description of this mechanism.

Configuration Mechanism #1 (The _Only_ Mechanism!)

2.2

REMEMBER THAT THIS IS NOW THE ONLY MECHANISM DEFINED IN THE 2.2 SPEC AND ALL NEW HOST/BRIDGES ARE REQUIRED TO USE THIS METHOD. ALSO KEEP IN MIND THAT IT'S NO LONGER REFERRED TO AS CONFIGURATION MECHANISM #1, BUT ONLY AS THE CONFIGURATION MECHANISM.

Background

The x86 processor family is capable of addressing up to, but no more than, 64KB of IO address space. In the EISA PC environment, the usage of this IO space was defined as indicated in Table 18-1 on page 323. The only IO address ranges available for the implementation of the PCI Configuration Mechanism (without conflicting with an ISA or EISA device) were 0400h - 04FFh, 0800h - 08FFh, and 0C00h - 0CFFh. Many EISA system board controllers already reside within the 0400h - 04FFh address range, making it unavailable.

Consider the following:

- As with any other PCI function, a host/PCI bridge may implement up to 64 dwords of configuration registers.
- Each PCI function on each PCI bus requires 64 dwords of dedicated configuration space.

Due to the lack of available IO real estate within the 64KB of IO space, it wasn't feasible to map each configuration register directly into the processor's IO address space. Alternatively, the system designer could implement the configuration registers within the processor's memory space. This approach may consume a considerable amount (well, it's not *that* considerable) of memory space (for example, twenty-five PCI functions would require 6KB of memory space). The amount of memory space consumed aside, the address range utilized would be unavailable for allocation to regular memory. This would limit the system's flexibility regarding the mapping of real memory.

Table 18-1: EISA PC IO Space Usage

IO Address Range	Reserved For
0000h - 00FFh	PC/AT-compatible system board IO devices
0100h - 03FFh	ISA-compatible IO cards
0400h - 04FFh	EISA system board IO devices
0500h - 07FFh	unusable due to conflict with ISA IO cards
0800h - 08FFh	EISA system board IO devices
0900h - 0BFFh	unusable due to conflict with ISA IO cards
0C00h - 0CFFh	EISA system board IO devices

Table 18-1: EISA PC IO Space Usage (Continued)

IO Address Range	Reserved For
0D00h - 0FFFh	unusable due to conflict with ISA IO cards
1000h - 1FFFh	EISA IO card installed in EISA slot 1
2000h - 2FFFFh	EISA IO card installed in EISA slot 2
3000h - 3FFFh	EISA IO card installed in EISA slot 3
4000h - 4FFFh	EISA IO card installed in EISA slot 4
5000h - 5FFFh	EISA IO card installed in EISA slot 5
6000h - 6FFFh	EISA IO card installed in EISA slot 6
7000h - 7FFFh	EISA IO card installed in EISA slot 7
8000h - 8FFFh	EISA IO card installed in EISA slot 8
9000h - 9FFFh	EISA IO card installed in EISA slot 9
A000h - AFFFh	EISA IO card installed in EISA slot 10
B000h - BFFFh	EISA IO card installed in EISA slot 11
C000h - CFFFh	EISA IO card installed in EISA slot 12
D000h - DFFFh	EISA IO card installed in EISA slot 13
E000h - EFFFh	EISA IO card installed in EISA slot 14
F000h - FFFFh	EISA IO card installed in EISA slot 15

Configuration Mechanism #1 Description

General

Configuration Mechanism #1 utilizes two 32-bit IO ports located at addresses 0CF8h and 0CFCh. These two ports are:

- The 32-bit **Configuration Address Port**, occupying IO addresses 0CF8h through 0CFBh.
- The 32-bit **Configuration Data Port**, occupying IO addresses 0CFCh through 0CFFh.

Chapter 18: Configuration Transactions

Accessing one of a PCI function's configuration registers is a two step process:

STEP 1. Write the target bus number, device number, function number and dword number to the Configuration Address Port and set the Enable bit in it to one.

STEP 2. Perform a one-byte, two-byte, or four-byte IO read from or an write to the Configuration Data Port.

In response, the host/PCI bridge compares the specified target bus to the range of buses that exist on the other side of the bridge and, if the target bus resides beyond the bridge, it initiates a PCI configuration read or write (based on whether the processor is performing an IO read or write with the Configuration Data Port).

Configuration Address Port

Refer to Figure 18-2 on page 326. The Configuration Address Port only latches information when the processor performs a full 32-bit write to the port. A 32-bit read from the port returns its contents. The assertion of reset clears the port to all zeros. Any 8- or 16-bit access within this IO dword is passed directly onto the PCI bus as an 8- or 16-bit PCI IO access. The 32-bits of information written to the Configuration Address Port must conform to the following template (illustrated in Figure 18-2 on page 326):

- bits **[1:0]** are hard-wired, read-only and must return **zeros** when read.
- bits **[7:2]** identify the **target dword** (1-of-64) within the target function's configuration space.
- bits **[10:8]** identify the **target function** number (1-of-8) within the target PCI device.
- bits **[15:11]** identify the target PCI device number (1-of-32).
- bits **[23:16]** identifies the **target PCI bus** number (1-of-256).
- bits **[30:24]** are **reserved** and must be zero.
- bit **31 must be** set to a **one**, enabling the translation of a subsequent processor IO access to the Configuration Data Port into a configuration access on the PCI bus. If bit 31 is zero and the processor initiates an IO read from or IO write to the Configuration Data Port, the transaction is passed through to the PCI bus as a PCI IO transaction.

Figure 18-2: Configuration Address Port at 0CF8h

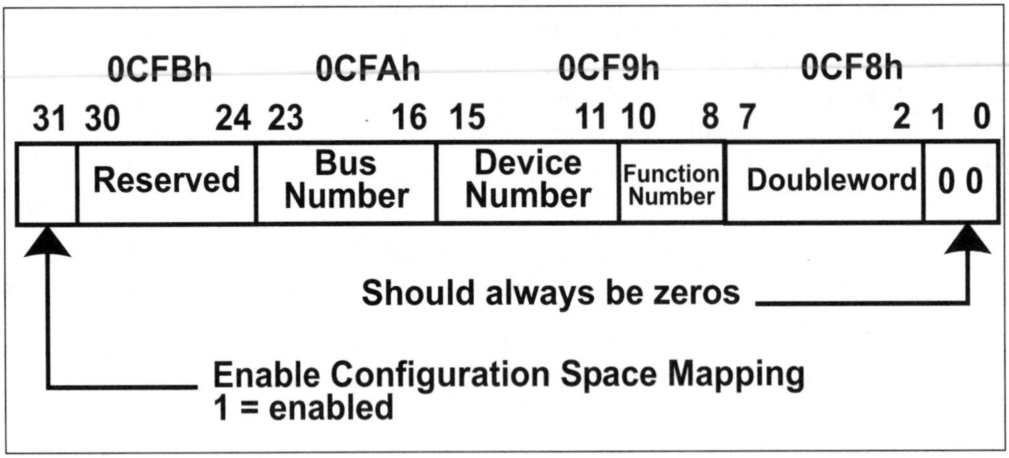

0CFBh	0CFAh	0CF9h	0CF8h

```
 31 30        24 23      16 15        11 10   8 7             2 1  0
```

	Reserved	Bus Number	Device Number	Function Number	Doubleword	0 0

Should always be zeros

Enable Configuration Space Mapping
1 = enabled

Bus Compare and Data Port Usage

Each host/PCI bridge implements a Bus Number register (in a chipset that only supports one host/PCI bridge, the bridge may have a bus number register that is hardwired to 0, a read/write register that reset forces to 0, or it just implicitly knows that it is the bridge to PCI bus 0) and a Subordinate Bus Number register. If bit 31 in the Configuration Address Port (see Figure 18-2 on page 326) is enabled (set to one), the bridge compares the target bus number to the range of buses that exists beyond the bridge. If the target bus is the same as the value in the Bus Number register, this is a request to perform a configuration transaction on PCI bus 0. A subsequent IO read from or write to the bridge's Configuration Data Port at 0CFCh causes the bridge to generate a Type 0 configuration read or write transaction. When devices that reside on a PCI bus detect a Type 0 configuration transaction in progress, this informs them that one of them is the target device.

If the target bus specified in the Configuration Address Port does not compare with the value in the bridge's Bus Number register, but is equal to or less than the value in the bridge's Subordinate Bus Number register, the bridge converts the subsequent processor IO access to its Configuration Data Port into a Type 1 configuration transaction on its PCI bus. When devices that reside on a PCI bus (other than PCI-to-PCI bridges) detect a Type 1 configuration access in progress, they ignore the transaction.

The only devices on a PCI bus that pay attention to the Type 1 configuration transaction are PCI-to-PCI bridges. Each of them must determine if the target bus number is within the range of PCI buses that reside behind them.

- If the target bus is not within range, then a PCI-to-PCI bridge ignores the Type 1 access (i.e., it doesn't assert DEVSEL# to claim the transaction).
- If it's in range, the access is passed through the PCI-to-PCI bridge as either a Type 0 configuration transaction (if the target bus compares to the bridge's Secondary Bus Number register), or as
- a Type 1 transaction (the target bus number is equal to or less than the value in the bridge's Subordinate Bus Number register).

The subject of Type 0 configuration accesses is covered in detail in subsequent sections in this chapter. The subject of Type 1 configuration accesses is covered in detail in "Type 1 Configuration Transactions" on page 620.

Single Host/PCI Bridge

Refer to Figure 18-1 on page 320. The information written to the Configuration Address Port is latched by the host/PCI bridge. If bit 31 is set to one and the target bus number compares to the bridge's PCI Bus Number register (or is equal to or less than the value in the bridge's Subordinate Bus Number register), the bridge is enabled to convert a subsequent processor access targeting its Configuration Data Port into a PCI configuration access. The processor then initiates a one-byte, two-byte, or four-byte (indicated by the processor's byte enable signals; or, if a PowerPC 60x processor, by A[29:31] and TSIZ[0:2]) IO read or write transaction to the Configuration Data Port at 0CFCh. This stimulates the bridge to arbitrate for ownership of the PCI bus and then to perform a configuration read (if the processor is reading from the Configuration Data Port) or a configuration write (if the processor is writing to the Configuration Data Port). It will be a Type 0 configuration transaction if the target bus is PCI bus 0, or a Type 1 configuration transaction if the target bus is further out in the bus hierarchy beyond Bus 0.

"Type 0 Configuration Transaction" on page 335 provides a detailed description of the Type 0 configuration read and write transactions.

Multiple Host/PCI Bridges

If there are multiple host/PCI bridges present on the PROCESSOR bus (refer to Figure 18-3 on page 329), the Configuration Address and Data ports are duplicated at the same IO addresses in each of the host/PCI bridges. In order to prevent contention on the processor's bus signals, only one of the bridges responds to the processor's accesses to the configuration ports.

Step 1. When the processor initiates the IO write to the Configuration Data Port, only one of the host/PCI bridges (typically, the bridge to PCI bus 0) actively participates in the transaction. The other bridge quietly snarfs the data as it's written to the active participant.

Step 2. Both bridges then compare the target bus number to their respective Bus Number and Subordinate Bus Number registers. If the target bus doesn't reside behind a particular host/PCI bridge, that bridge doesn't convert the subsequent access to its Configuration Data Port into a PCI configuration access on its PCI bus (in other words, it ignores the transaction).

Step 3. A subsequent read or write access to the Configuration Data Port is only accepted by the host/PCI bridge that is the gateway to the target bus. This bridge responds to the processor's transaction and the other ignores it.

Step 4. When the access is made to the Configuration Data Port, the bridge with a bus compare tests the state of the Enable bit in its Configuration Address Port. If enabled, the bridge converts the processor's IO access into a PCI configuration access.

- If the target bus is the PCI bus immediately on the other side of the host/PCI bridge, the bridge converts the access to a Type 0 configuration access on its PCI bus.
- Otherwise, it converts it into a Type 1 configuration access.

Figure 18-3: Peer Host/PCI Bridges

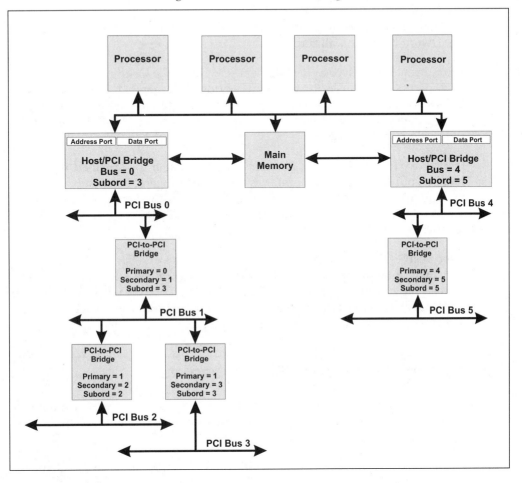

Software Generation of Special Cycles

Host/PCI bridges are not required to provide a means that allows software to initiate a Special Cycle transaction on a target PCI bus. If this capability is provided by the bridge, however, this section describes how it must be implemented.

To prime the host/PCI bridge to generate a PCI Special Cycle transaction, the host processor must write a 32-bit value with the following content to the Configuration Address Port at IO address 0CF8h:

- Bus Number = the target PCI Bus that the Special Cycle transaction is to be performed on.
- Device Number = all ones (31d, or 1Fh).
- Function Number = all ones (7d).
- Dword Number = all zeros.

After this has been accomplished, the next write to the Configuration Data Port at IO port 0CFCh causes the target bus's bridge to generate a PCI Special Cycle transaction on its secondary PCI bus. The data written to the host/PCI bridge's Configuration Data Port is supplied as the message on AD[31:0] during the transaction's data phase.

If the host/PCI bridge's Bus Number does not match the specified target bus number, but the target bus number is within the range of buses subordinate to the bridge's bus, the bridge passes the transaction through as a Type 1 configuration write (so that it can be submitted to PCI-to-PCI bridges further out in the hierarchy).

If the host/PCI bridge has been primed to generate a PCI Special Cycle transaction (by writing the appropriate data to the Configuration Address Port) and an IO read is performed from the Configuration Data Port, the result is undefined. The bridge may pass it through as a Type 0 configuration read (which will result in a Master Abort with all ones returned as data).

Configuration Mechanism #2 (*is obsolete*)

As stated in "Intro to Configuration Mechanisms" on page 321, configuration mechanism #2 has been eliminated in the 2.2 spec. This section is only provided as historical background.

The following quote from the 2.0 specification was cited earlier in this chapter:

"Configuration mechanism #1 is the preferred implementation and must be provided by all future host bridges (and existing bridges should convert if possible). **Configuration mechanism #2 is defined for backward compatibility and must not be used by new designs.** Host bridges implemented in PC-AT compatible systems must implement at least one of these mechanisms."

The 2.2 spec removed all reference to Mechanism #2. Early PCI chipsets implemented this configuration mechanism. The following sections describe Configuration Mechanism #2.

Chapter 18: Configuration Transactions

Basic Configuration #2 Mechanism

The bridge implements the following two single-byte IO ports:

- **Configuration Space Enable, or CSE, register** at IO port 0CF8h.
- **Forward register** at IO port 0CFAh.

To cause the host/PCI bridge to generate a PCI configuration transaction, the programmer performs the following actions:

- Write the target bus number (00h through FFh) into the forward register.
- Write a one byte value to the CSE register at 0CF8h. The bit pattern written to this register has three effects: disables the generation of Special Cycles; enables the generation of configuration transactions; specifies the target PCI function.
- Perform a one, two or four byte IO read or write transaction within the IO range C000h through CFFFh.

The 4KB IO address range from C000h through CFFFh is divided into sub-ranges as indicated in Table 18-2 on page 332. The upper digit of the IO address set to Ch maps the access into PCI configuration space. The third digit of the IO address, x in Cxyzh, identifies the target physical package and is used by the bridge to select an IDSEL signal line to activate. The upper six bits of the first two digits in the IO address, yz in Cxyzh, identifies the target configuration dword. The least-significant two bits of the first digit in the IO address are not used by the bridge.

To summarize, the target bus is specified in the forward register. The target physical device is specified by the third digit of the IO address. The target function within the target physical device is specified by the function field in the CSE register. The target configuration dword within the target function's configuration space is specified by the upper six bits of the least-significant two digits of the IO address. As the following list indicates, the bridge uses this information to determine what type of PCI configuration access to perform.

- The target bus in the forward register selects whether the bridge performs a Type 0 or a Type 1 configuration access.
- The third digit of the IO address selects which IDSEL to assert (if it's a Type 0 access).
- During a Type 0 access, the function number from the CSE register and the dword number from the least-significant two digits of the IO address are placed on the AD bus.

- The setting on the host processor's byte enables during the access within the CXXXh range is used as the byte enable setting during the data phase of the configuration access.
- An IO read (within the CXXXh range) by the host processor is converted into a configuration read and an IO write into a configuration write.

Table 18-2: Sub-Ranges Within C000h through CFFFh IO Range

IO Sub-Range	Targets Physical PCI Package
C000h - C0FFh	0d
C100h - C1FFh	1d
C200h - C2FFh	2d
C300h - C3FFh	3d
C400h - C4FFh	4d
C500h - C5FFh	5d
C600h - C6FFh	6d
C700h - C7FFh	7d
C800h - C8FFh	8d
C900h - C9FFh	9d
CA00h - CAFFh	10d
CB00h - CBFFh	11d
CC00h - CCFFh	12d
CD00h - CDFFh	13d
CE00h - CEFFh	14d
CF00h - CFFFh	15d

Configuration Space Enable, or CSE, Register

Figure 18-4 on page 333 illustrates the format of the configuration space enable register. As stated earlier, the CSE register is an 8-bit register residing at IO port 0CF8h. The assertion of reset clears this register to all zeros. A read from this register returns the last value written to it. When the SCE (Special Cycle Enable) bit is cleared to zero, the host/PCI bridge cannot generate Special Cycles on the PCI bus. A section later in this chapter describes the generation of Special Cycles using configuration mechanism two.

The programmer writes the target function number into bits [3:1] of the CSE register. Setting the key field to a non-zero value enables (turns the key, if you will) the bridge's ability to convert host processor IO accesses within the C000h through CFFFh range into PCI configuration accesses. The fact that reset clears the CSE register to zeros disables the bridge's ability to generate PCI configuration (key field cleared to zero) or Special Cycle (SCE bit cleared to zero) transactions.

Figure 18-4: Configuration Space Enable, or CSE, Register

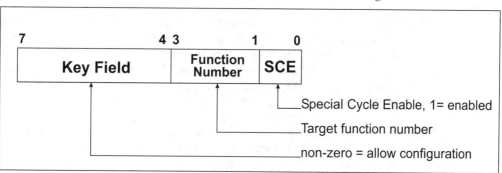

Forward Register

The forward register is a read/write register located at IO port 0CFAh. Reset clears it to zero and a read returns the last value written to it. It is an 8-bit register, permitting the specification of one of 256 possible PCI buses.

It is used to specify the target bus prior to enabling PCI configuration accesses via the CSE register.

Support for Peer Bridges on Host Bus

Configuration mechanism two does not support peer bridges on the host bus.

Generation of Special Cycles

Provision of the mechanism that permits software to generate Special Cycles is optional. The text that follows describes how it is implemented. The host/PCI bridge is enabled to generate Special Cycles in the following manner:

- The SCE bit in the CSE register is set to one.
- The function field is set to all ones.
- The key field is set a non-zero value.

This pattern in the CSE register also permits the programmer to instruct the host/PCI bridge to generate Type 1 configuration accesses. The following text describes how to force the bridge to generate Special Cycle and Type 1 configuration accesses.

Clearing the forward register to zero (and setting the CSE register to the pattern described earlier) permits the bridge to generate Special Cycles. When the processor performs an IO write to port CF00h, the bridge acquires PCI bus ownership and initiates a Special Cycle. A dummy pattern is driven onto the AD bus during the address phase. During the data phase the data written to IO port CF00h is driven onto the AD bus as the message (two or four byte message).

Setting the forward register to a non-zero value (and setting the CSE register to the pattern described earlier) permits the bridge to generate Type 1 configuration accesses. AD[1:0] are set to 01b during the address phase and the bus number specified in the forward register is driven onto AD[23:16]. The physical device number and function number fields (AD[15:11] and AD[10:8], respectively) are set to all ones, while the configuration dword field, AD[7:2], is cleared to zeros.

Host processor reads from IO addresses in the range C000h through CFFFh have undefined results. With the exception of IO address CF00h, write accesses within this range also have undefined results. Setting the SCE bit in the CSE register to one and the function number field to zero has undefined results.

PowerPC PReP Configuration Mechanism

In a PowerPC-based, PReP-compliant chipset, the host/PCI bridge uses the same methodology as Configuration Mechanism #1 (with a slight twist). The Configuration Address Port and Configuration Data Port are implemented as two, 32-bit *memory-mapped* IO ports, rather than as ports mapped into processor IO space.

Type 0 Configuration Transaction

Address Phase

During any PCI transaction, all PCI devices on the bus latch the following information at the end of the address phase:

- The contents of the AD bus. In a configuration transaction, this consists of the target function, configuration dword and 00b on the least-significant two bits if it's a Type 0 configuration transaction, or the target bus number, device number, function number, dword number and 01b on the least-significant two bits if it's a Type 1 configuration transaction.
- The state of the FRAME# signal (asserted, indicating that a valid address and command have been latched from the bus).
- The state of the IDSEL signal (only has meaning if this is a Type 0 configuration transaction). The PCI device (i.e., package) that samples its IDSEL asserted is the target PCI device. The bridge implements a separate IDSEL signal for each PCI device implemented on its secondary bus (see Figure 18-5 on page 337).
- The command on C/BE#[3:0]. In this case, it indicates that this is a configuration read or write transaction. The command type is derived from the type of access the processor is performing with the host/PCI bridge's Configuration Data Port. An IO read converts to a configuration read and an IO write converts to a configuration write.

00b on AD[1:0] indicates that this is a Type 0 configuration transaction targeting one of the devices on this PCI bus. In essence, the 00b is a shorthand way of indicating that the bridge has already done the target bus comparison and established that the transaction is targeting a device on this bus.

The PCI device that samples its IDSEL asserted is the target device. The AD bus information presented during a Type 0 configuration transaction indicates the following:

- **AD[1:0]** are 00b, indicating that this is a **Type 0** transaction targeting one of the devices on this bus.
- **AD[7:2]** indicates the **target** configuration **dword**.
- **AD[10:8]** indicates the **target function** within the physical device.
- **AD[31:11]** are **reserved** and must not be interpreted by any devices.

The target device number specified in bits [15:11] in the Configuration Address Port are decoded within the bridge (see Figure 18-5 on page 337) and the decoder asserts the appropriate IDSEL output signal during the transaction's address phase. If the bridge's device decoder determines that there is no device (or card slot) implemented at the target device position on its secondary bus, it will not assert any IDSEL outputs during the transaction's address phase. The transaction will end up experiencing a Master Abort because no target will assert DEVSEL# to claim the transaction.

Since the Device Number field within the Configuration Address Port is a 5-bit field, the programmer can specify any device number from 0-through-31d as the target device. Obviously, a PCI bus with 32 devices implemented on it (each one presenting a load to the bus) is not going to function correctly. In reality, a 33MHz PCI bus typically supports no more than 10 devices on the bus. Furthermore, each card connector counts as a load, each card as a load, and each embedded PCI device as a load. The bottom line is that most of the 32d possible device positions on any PCI bus are going to be unoccupied. There is no rule, however, that dictates which device position each device must occupy. They don't even have to be implemented as contiguous device numbers, but that wouldn't make a lot of sense. As some examples, the system board designer could attach devices to the following IDSEL signals (which correlate to device numbers):

- 0-through-8.
- 4-through-9.
- 16-through-25.
- 19-through-26.

In other words, the configuration programmer typically has no idea which of the 32 possible device positions are occupied versus unoccupied, so the programmer must look at all of them at startup time in order to determine the full complement of devices that are present. For this reason, if you use a logic analyzer to capture all of the initial configuration reads that the configuration program generates at startup time, you will typically see a lot of them ending in Master Aborts (because no device is present at that position).

Figure 18-5: Bridge's Device Decoder

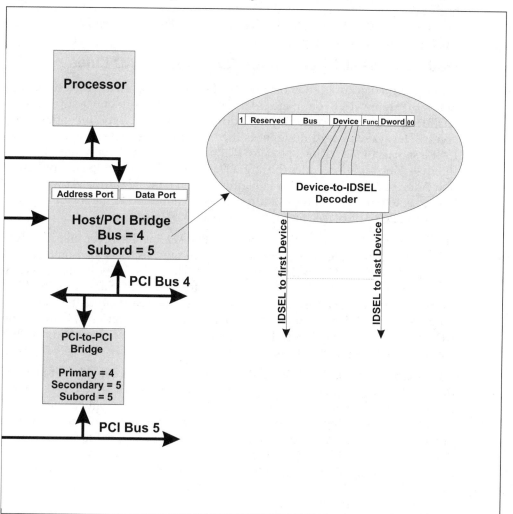

Implementation of IDSEL

The IDSEL outputs can be implemented in one of two ways by the host/PCI bridge designer. These two methods are described in the two sections that follow. Be aware that PCI-to-PCI bridges must use the first method (see "Type 0 Configuration Access" on page 620).

Method One—IDSELs Routed Over Unused AD Lines

This is the method used by most host/PCI bridge and system board designers. Refer to Figure 18-8 on page 342. The upper twenty-one address lines, AD[31:11], are not used during the address phase of a Type 0 configuration access. The system board designer is therefore free to use these signal lines as IDSEL signals to the various physical PCI packages (up to twenty-one of them). Internally, the bridge decodes the target Device number contained in Configuration Address Port bits [15:11] (see Figure 18-2 on page 326) to select which AD line to set to one. Each of these address lines is connected to the IDSEL input of a separate PCI device (see Figure 18-6 on page 339).

This approach places an additional load on the AD line, however, and it's a rule that each PCI device is only permitted to place one electrical load on each PCI bus signal. Refer to Figure 18-7 on page 340. This effect may be mitigated by resistively-coupling the device's IDSEL pin to the appropriate AD pin at the embedded device or at the connector on the system board. Note that resistive-coupling is recommended and not required and a direct connection between the AD line and IDSEL may be used if the system board designer has validated that the additional load does not cause a problem.

As an example of upper AD line-to-IDSEL mapping, AD11 could be set to one if the target device is device zero (the first PCI device); AD12 set to one if the target device is device one, etc. The specification suggests (it's only a suggestion) the following mapping. The bridge internally decodes the device number field in the Configuration Address Port and selects an IDSEL signal to assert. Rather than implementing IDSEL output pins, the IDSEL signals internal to the bridge are directed to AD[31:16] in the following manner:

- The IDSEL associated with device 0 is connected to AD16.
- The IDSEL associated with device 1 is connected to AD17.
- The IDSEL associated with device 2 is connected to AD18, etc.
- The IDSEL associated with device 15 is connected to AD31.
- For devices 16 through 31, none of the upper AD lines should be asserted when the Type 0 configuration transaction is performed. Since no device detects its IDSEL asserted, none respond, resulting in a Master Abort by the bridge.

This approach supports the implementation of 16 devices on a PCI bus (from a configuration standpoint; from a realistic electrical loading standpoint, you're only going to place 10 to 11 loads on a 33MHz bus and have it work correctly).

As illustrated in Figure 18-7 on page 340, many current host/PCI bridge designs map AD16 to device 0, AD17 to device 1, etc. This method saves pins on the bridge and traces on the system board. There isn't a danger of a device misinterpreting the information on the upper part of the address (AD[31:11]) because no devices look at those address bits during a Type 0 configuration access.

Figure 18-6: Direct Connection of Device IDSEL Pins To Upper AD Lines

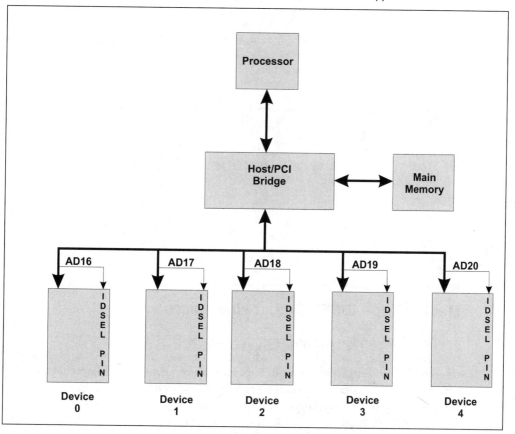

Figure 18-7: Resistive-Coupling Device IDSEL Pins To Upper AD Lines

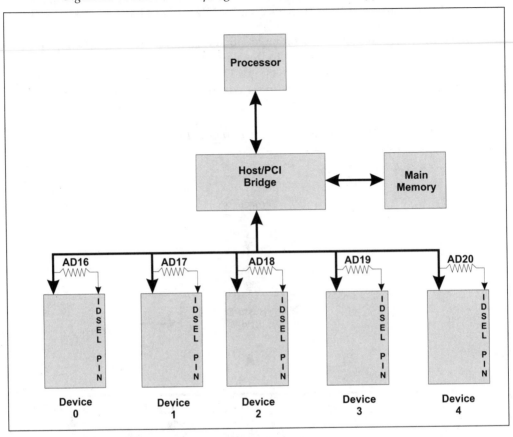

Method Two—IDSEL Output Pins/Traces

The host/PCI bridge designer can decode bits [15:11] (target physical Device number) in the Configuration Address Port and assert the target physical device's IDSEL output signal line. This method requires the implementation of a separate IDSEL output pin on the bridge for each physical package on the PCI bus and a separate point-to-point IDSEL trace on the system board between the bridge and each physical PCI device or connector. Most host/PCI bridge designs don't implement IDSEL output pins because it is a pin- and trace-intensive solution.

Resistive-Coupling Means Stepping In Type 0 Transactions

When the IDSELs are resistively-coupled to upper AD lines, it takes some time for the ones or zeros on the upper AD lines to traverse the resistors and arrive at the correct value at each device's IDSEL input pin. For this reason, the host/PCI bridge must use address stepping (see "Designer May Step Address, Data, PAR (and PAR64) and IDSEL" on page 164), but only for Type 0 configuration transactions.

The host/PCI bridge initiates the Type 0 configuration transaction by driving out the target function and dword number on the AD bus with AD[1:0] set to 00b to indicate that this is a Type 0 configuration transaction. It also outputs its internal device decoder's IDSEL output signals onto the upper AD lines. The configuration read or write command is driven onto C/BE#[3:0].

However, the bridge doesn't assert FRAME# yet. It delays a sufficient number of clocks to let the bits on the upper AD lines propagate through the resistors to the IDSEL pins at the devices and settle to the correct state and then asserts FRAME#. No devices will pay any attention to the transaction until FRAME# is asserted.

Data Phase Entered, Decode Begins

As the data phase is entered, the bridge sets C/BE#[3:0] to indicate which bytes it wishes to transfer within the currently-addressed configuration dword. It gets this information from the processor's access to the bridge's Configuration Data Port which is a one-byte (so just assert C/BE0#), two-byte (assert C/BE#[1:0]), or four-byte (assert all four C/BE lines) read or write.

As the data phase is entered, the PCI devices are performing the address decode to determine which of them is the target of the transaction (00b on AD[1:0] indicates it is for one of them). Devices that sampled their IDSEL inputs deasserted at the end of the address phase ignore the transaction. When a device detects its IDSEL pin was asserted at the end of the address phase, it must determine whether or not to claim the transaction. How it does this depends on whether it is a single- or multi-function device:

- THE 2.2 SPEC STATES THAT A SINGLE-FUNCTION DEVICE CAN EITHER: **2.2**
  - DECODE THE FUNCTION NUMBER AND ONLY ASSERT DEVSEL# FOR FUNCTION ZERO,
  - OR MAY RESPOND TO ALL FUNCTION NUMBERS OTHER THAN ZERO BY NOT ASSERTING DEVSEL# AND ALLOWING THE TRANSACTION TO TERMINATE VIA A MASTER ABORT.

- *IF IT'S A MULTI-FUNCTION DEVICE, IT MUST IMPLEMENT A FUNCTION DECODER AND IT MUST DECODE THE FUNCTION NUMBER DELIVERED ON AD[10:8] DURING THE ADDRESS PHASE. IF THE TARGET FUNCTION IS IMPLEMENTED, THE DEVICE ASSERTS DEVSEL# AND CLAIMS THE TRANSACTION. OTHERWISE, IT IGNORES THE TRANSACTION (BECAUSE THE TARGET FUNCTION IS NOT IMPLEMENTED IN THIS DEVICE).*

Assuming that the device claimed the transaction, the remainder of the transaction is identical to any other read or write transaction.

Type 0 Configuration Transaction Examples

The Type 0 configuration access is used to access a configuration register within a PCI device on the same PCI bus on which the access is performed.

Figure 18-8 on page 342 illustrates the contents of the AD bus during the address phase of the Type 0 configuration access. During the address phase of the transaction, the bridge places the configuration address information on the AD bus and the configuration command on the C/BE bus. Figures 18-11 and 19-12 are timing diagrams of Type 0 read and write configuration accesses.

Figure 18-8: Contents of the AD Bus During Address Phase of a Type 0 Configuration Access

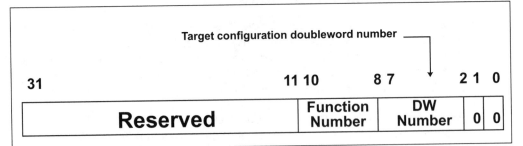

Address bits [10:8] identify the target function and bits AD[7:2] select one of 64 configuration dwords within the target function's configuration space. The command on the C/BE bus during the address phase identifies it as a configuration read or write. During the data phase, the four byte enables, C/BE#[3:0], are used to select the bytes within the currently-addressed configuration dword. The data to be transferred between the bridge and the target configuration location(s) is transferred during the data phase. Once the target function claims the transaction, it is identical to any other read or write transaction.

Figure 18-9: Type 0 Configuration Read Access

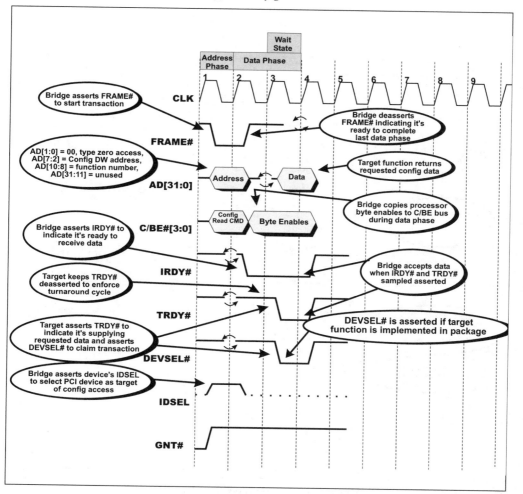

Figure 18-10: Type 0 Configuration Write Access

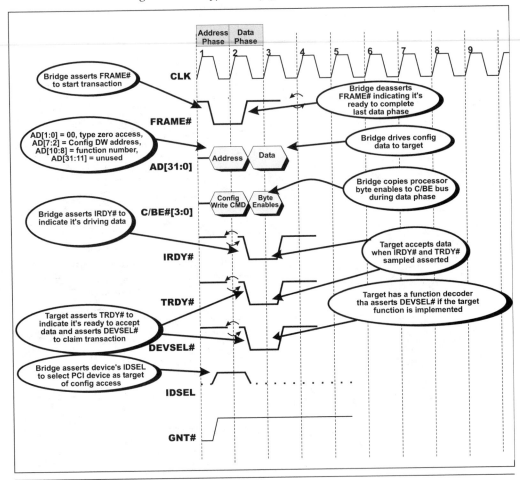

Type 1 Configuration Transactions

Description

When a bridge initiates a configuration access on a PCI bus, it places the configuration address information on the AD bus and the configuration command on the C/BE bus. Figure 18-11 on page 345 illustrates the contents of the AD bus during the address phase of the Type 1 configuration access. Figure 18-12 on page 347 and Figure 18-13 on page 348 are timing diagrams of Type 1 configuration read and write accesses, respectively.

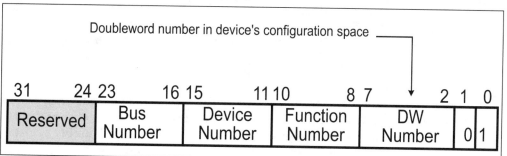

*Figure 18-11: Contents of the AD Bus During Address Phase of a
Type 1 Configuration Access*

During the address phase of a Type 1 configuration access, the information on the AD bus is formatted as follows:

- AD[1:0] contain a 01b, identifying this as a Type 1 configuration access.
- AD[7:2] identifies one of 64 configuration dwords within the target device's configuration space.
- AD[10:8] identifies one of eight functions within the target physical device.
- AD[15:11] identifies one of 32 physical devices. This field is used by the bridge to select which device's IDSEL line to assert.
- AD[23:16] identifies one of 256 PCI buses in the system.
- AD[31:24] are reserved and are cleared to zero.

The configuration read or write command is presented on the C/BE bus during the address phase. During a Type 1 configuration access, PCI devices ignore the state of their IDSEL inputs. When any PCI-to-PCI bridge latches a Type 1 configuration access (command = configuration read or write and AD[1:0] = 01b) on its primary side, it must determine which of the following actions to take:

ACTION 1. If the bus number field on the AD bus doesn't match the number of its secondary bus and isn't within the range of its subordinate buses, the bridge should **ignore** the access.

ACTION 2. If the bus number field matches the bus number of its secondary bus, it should claim and pass the configuration access onto its secondary bus as a **Type 0 configuration access**. AD[1:0] on the secondary bus are set to 00b (indicating a Type 0 access), AD[10:2] (target function and dword) are passed as is to its secondary AD bus. The device number field is decoded within the bridge to select one of the IDSEL lines to assert on the secondary bus. The configuration command is passed from the primary to the secondary C/BE bus.

ACTION 3. If the bus number field isn't equal to its secondary bus, but is within the range of buses that are subordinate to the bridge, the bridge claims and passes the access through as a **Type 1 access**. AD[31:0] (target bus, device, function and dword) are passed to the secondary AD bus as is. AD[1:0] are set to 01b, indicating that a Type 1 access is in progress on the secondary bus. The configuration command is passed from the primary to the secondary C/BE bus.

This implies that, like the host/PCI bridge, PCI-to-PCI bridges must incorporate a Bus Number register and a Subordinate Bus Number register. In fact, each PCI-to-PCI bridge is required to implement a **Primary Bus Number register**, a **Secondary Bus Number register**, and a **Subordinate Bus Number register**. PCI-to-PCI bridges on PCI bus 0 are discovered and numbered during the configuration process. This procedure is covered in the chapter entitled "Bus Number Registers" on page 556.

Special Cycle Request

A Type 1 configuration write detected on the secondary side that specifies

- device = 31d
- function = 7
- dword = 0

is a Special Cycle Request. Upon receiving a Special Cycle Request, a bridge has three choices:

- If the specified target bus matches the bridge's Primary Bus Number register, the transaction must be **passed through as** a **Special Cycle**.
- If the target bus is within the range of buses specified by the bridge's Secondary and Subordinate Bus Number registers, the transaction must be **ignored**.
- If the target bus is outside the range of buses specified by the bridge's primary, secondary, and subordinate bus number registers, the transaction must be **passed through as** a **Type 1 configuration write** (i.e., **unchanged**).

Figure 18-12: Type 1 Configuration Read Access

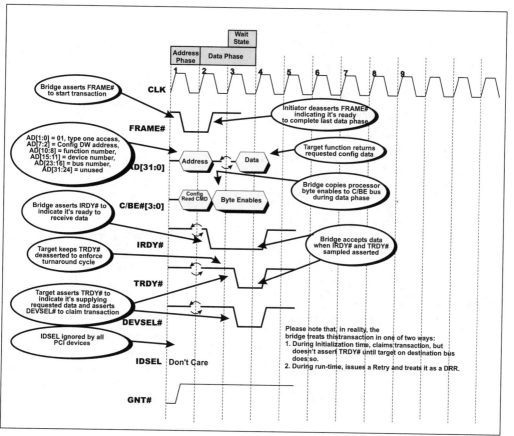

Figure 18-13: Type 1 Configuration Write Access

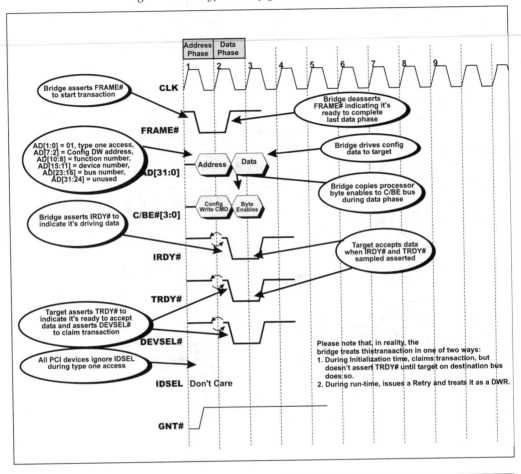

Target Device Doesn't Exist

If the target of a configuration read transaction doesn't exist, DEVSEL# isn't asserted by any PCI function. Note that the subtractive decoder in the expansion bus bridge (i.e., the ISA bridge) does not claim unclaimed PCI configuration transactions. When DEVSEL# remains deasserted, the host/PCI bridge Master Aborts the transaction and sets the Received Master Abort bit in its configuration Status register (see Figure 18-14 on page 349).

- On a read that receives a Master Abort, the bridge returns all ones to the processor as the read data.
- On a write that experiences a Master Abort, the bridge acts as if the write completed OK.

The way that software determines that a PCI device doesn't exist is to read the device's Vendor ID configuration register and check for all ones returned (because a Master Abort occurred and the bridge returned all ones). The Vendor ID of all ones (FFFFh) is reserved for this reason and is not assigned to any vendor by the SIG.

Figure 18-14: Status Register

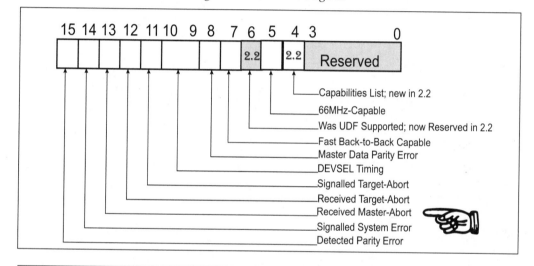

Configuration Burst Transactions Permitted

Although virtually all configuration transactions today are single data phase transactions, the specification permits burst configuration transactions. Linear addressing (see "Linear (Sequential) Mode" on page 144) is implied in a multiple data phase configuration burst transaction. As each data phase completes and the next begins, the target device increments the configuration dword address in its address counter by four and then examines the byte enables to determine which bytes within the currently-addressed configuration dword are to be transferred.

If the target doesn't support burst configuration transactions, it will issue a Disconnect in or immediately after the first data phase (see "Target Doesn't Support Burst Mode" on page 182). This forces the host/PCI bridge to rearbitrate for bus ownership and then explicitly address the next configuration dword.

64-Bit Configuration Transactions Not Permitted

The specification states:

> "The bandwidth requirements for IO and configuration commands cannot justify the added complexity and, therefore, only memory commands support 64-bit data transfers."

19 Configuration Registers

The Previous Chapter

The previous chapter provided a detailed discussion of the mechanisms used to generate configuration transactions as well as a detailed discussion of the Type Zero and Type One configuration read and write transactions.

This Chapter

This chapter provides a detailed description of the configuration register format and usage for all PCI devices other than PCI-to-PCI bridges and CardBus bridges.

The Next Chapter

The next chapter provides a detailed description of device ROMs associated with PCI devices. This includes the following topics:

- device ROM detection.
- internal code/data format.
- shadowing.
- initialization code execution.
- interrupt hooking.

Intro to Configuration Header Region

WITH THE POSSIBLE EXCEPTION OF THE HOST/PCI BRIDGE, every PCI function must **2.2** implement PCI configuration space within which its PCI configuration registers reside. The host/PCI bridge could implement these registers, in PCI configuration space (this is most often the case), in IO space (much too crowded), or in memory space.

Each PCI function possesses a block of 64 configuration dwords reserved for the implementation of its configuration registers. The format and usage of the first 16 dwords is predefined by the PCI specification. This area is referred to as the device's Configuration Header Region (or Header Space). The specification currently defines three Header formats, referred to as Header Types Zero, One and Two.

- **Header Type One** is defined for PCI-to-PCI bridges. A full description of Header Type One can be found in "Configuration Registers" on page 552.
- **Header Type Two** is defined for PCI-to-CardBus bridges and is fully-defined in the PC Card spec.
- **Header Type Zero** is used for all devices other than PCI-to-PCI and cardBus bridges. This chapter defines Header Type Zero.

Figure 19-1 on page 353 illustrates the format of a function's Header region (for functions other than PCI-to-PCI bridges and CardBus bridges). The registers marked in black are always mandatory. Note that although many of the configuration registers in the figure are not marked mandatory, a register may be mandatory for a particular type of device. The subsequent sections define each register and any circumstances where it may be mandatory.

As noted earlier, this format is defined as Header Type Zero. The registers within the Header are used to identify the device, to control its PCI functionality and to sense its PCI status in a generic manner. The usage of the device's

2.2

remaining 48 dwords of configuration space is device-specific, *BUT IT IS NOW ALSO USED AS AN OVERFLOW AREA FOR SOME NEW REGISTERS DEFINED IN THE 2.2. PCI SPEC (FOR MORE INFORMATION, REFER TO "NEW CAPABILITIES" ON PAGE 390).*

Figure 19-1: Format of a PCI Function's Configuration Header

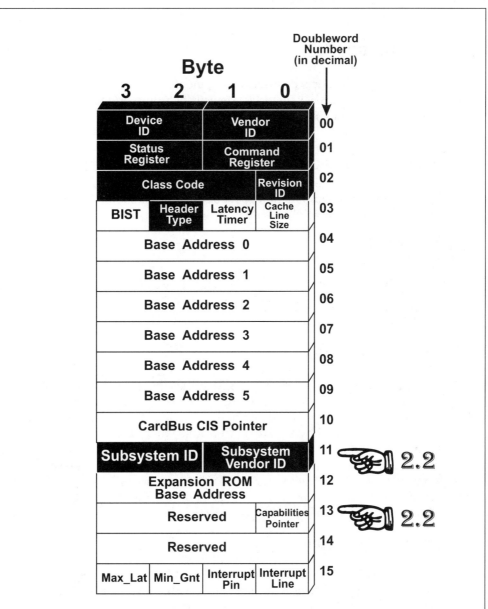

Mandatory Header Registers

Introduction

The following sections describe the mandatory configuration registers that must be implemented in every PCI device, including bridges. The registers are illustrated (in black) in Figure 19-1 on page 353.

Registers Used to Identify Device's Driver

The OS uses some combination of the following mandatory registers to determine which driver to load for a device:

- Vendor ID.
- Device ID.
- Revision.
- Class Code.
- SubSystem Vendor ID.
- SubSystem ID.

Vendor ID Register

Always mandatory. This 16-bit register identifies the manufacturer of the device. The value hardwired in this read-only register is assigned by a central authority (the PCI SIG) that controls issuance of the numbers. The value FFFFh is reserved and must be returned by the host/PCI bridge when an attempt is made to perform a configuration read from a non-existent device's configuration register. The read attempt results in a Master Abort and the bridge must respond with a Vendor ID of FFFFh. The Master Abort is not considered to be an error, but the specification says that the bridge must none the less set its Received Master Abort bit in its configuration Status register.

Device ID Register

Always mandatory. This 16-bit value is assigned by the device manufacturer and identifies the type of device. In conjunction with the Vendor ID and possibly the Revision ID, the Device ID can be used to locate a device-specific (and perhaps revision-specific) driver for the device.

Subsystem Vendor ID and Subsystem ID Registers

Mandatory. This register pair was added in revision **2.1** of the specification and **2.2**
was optional. THE 2.2 SPEC HAS MADE THEM MANDATORY EXCEPT FOR THOSE THAT
HAVE A BASE CLASS OF 06H (A BRIDGE) WITH A SUB CLASS OF 00H-04H (REFER TO
TABLE 19-8 ON PAGE 360), OR A BASE CLASS OF 08H (BASE SYSTEM PERIPHERALS) WITH
A SUB CLASS OF 00H-03H (SEE TABLE 19-10 ON PAGE 363). THIS EXCLUDES BRIDGES OF
THE FOLLOWING TYPES:

- HOST/PCI
- PCI-TO-EISA
- PCI-TO-ISA
- PCI-TO-MICRO CHANNEL
- PCI-TO-PCI

IT ALSO EXCLUDES THE FOLLOWING GENERIC SYSTEM PERIPHERALS:

- INTERRUPT CONTROLLER
- DMA CONTROLLER
- PROGRAMMABLE TIMERS
- RTC CONTROLLER

The Subsystem Vendor ID is obtained from the SIG, while the vendor supplies
its own Subsystem ID (the full name of this register is really "Subsystem Device
ID", but the "device" is silent). A value of zero in these registers indicates there
isn't a Subsystem Vendor and Subsystem ID associated with the device.

Purpose of This Register Pair. A PCI function may reside on a card or
within an embedded device. Two cards or subsystems that are designed around
the same PCI core logic (produced by a third-party) may have the same Vendor
and Device IDs (if the core logic vendor hardwired their own IDs into these registers). If this is the case, the OS would have a problem identifying the correct
driver to load into memory for the device.

These two mandatory registers (Subsystem Vendor ID and Subsystem ID) are
used to uniquely identify the add-in card or subsystem that the device resides
within. Using these two registers, the OS can distinguish the difference between
cards or subsystems manufactured by different vendors but designed around
the same third-party core logic. This permits the Plug-and-Play OS to locate the
correct driver to load into memory.

Must Contain Valid Data When First Accessed. These two registers must contain their assigned values before the system first accesses them. If software attempts to access them before they have been initialized, the device must issue a Retry to the master. The values in these registers could be hardwired, loaded from a serial EEPROM, determined from hardware strapping pins, etc.

Revision ID Register

Always mandatory. This 8-bit value is assigned by the device manufacturer and identifies the revision number of the device. If the vendor has supplied a revision-specific driver, this is handy in ensuring that the correct driver is loaded by the OS.

Class Code Register

General. *Always mandatory.* The Class Code register is pictured in Figure 19-2 on page 357. It is a 24-bit, read-only register divided into three fields: base **Class**, **Sub Class**, and **Programming Interface**. It identifies the basic function of the device (e.g., a mass storage controller), a more specific device sub-class (e.g., IDE mass storage controller), and, in some cases, a register-specific programming interface (such as a specific flavor of the IDE register set).

- The upper byte defines the base Class of the function,
- the middle byte defines a sub-class within the base Class,
- and the lower byte defines the Programming Interface.

The values currently-defined as base Class codes are listed in Table 19-1 on page 357. Table 19-2 on page 358 through Table 19-20 on page 367 define the Subclasses within each base Class. For many Class/SubClass categories, the Programming Interface byte is hardwired to return zeros (in other words, it has no meaning). For some, such as VGA-compatible devices and IDE controllers, it does have meaning.

Purpose of Class Code Register. This register is useful when the OS is attempting to locate a device that a Class driver can work with. As an example, assume that a particular device driver has been written to work with any display adapter that is 100% XGA register set-compatible. If the OS can locate a function with a Class of 03h (see Table 19-1 on page 357) and a Sub Class of 01h (see Table 19-5 on page 359), the driver will work with that device. A Class driver is more flexible than a driver that has been written to work only with a specific device from a specific vendor.

Programming Interface Byte. For some devices (such as the XGA display adapter used as an example in the previous section) the combination of the Class Code and Sub Class Code is sufficient to fully-define its level of register set compatibility. The register set layout for some device types, however, can vary from one implementation to another. As an example, there are a number of flavors of IDE mass storage controllers, so it's not sufficient to identify yourself as an IDE mass storage controller. The Programming Interface byte value (see Table 19-20 on page 367) provides the final level of granularity that identifies the exact register set layout of the device.

Figure 19-2: Class Code Register

23	16	15	8	7	0
Class Code		Sub-Class Code		Prog. I/F	

Table 19-1: Defined Class Codes

Class	Description
00h	Devices built before class codes defined (in other words: before rev 2.0 of the spec).
01h	Mass storage controller.
02h	Network controller.
03h	Display controller.
04h	Multimedia device.
05h	Memory controller.
06h	Bridge device.
07h	Simple communications controllers.
08h	Base system peripherals.
09h	Input devices.
0Ah	Docking stations.

Table 19-1: Defined Class Codes (Continued)

Class	Description
0Bh	Processors.
0Ch	Serial bus controllers.
0DH	**WIRELESS CONTROLLERS.**
0EH	**INTELLIGENT IO CONTROLLERS.**
0FH	**SATELLITE COMMUNICATIONS CONTROLLERS.**
10H	**ENCRYPTION/DECRYPTION CONTROLLERS.**
11H	**DATA ACQUISITION AND SIGNAL PROCESSING CONTROLLERS.**
12h-FEh	Reserved.
FFh	Device does not fit any of the defined class codes.

Table 19-2: Class Code 0 (rev 1.0)

Sub-Class	Prog. I/F	Description
00h	00h	All devices other than VGA.
01h	01h	VGA-compatible device.

Table 19-3: Class Code 1: Mass Storage Controllers

Sub-Class	Prog. I/F	Description
00h	00h	SCSI controller.
01h	xxh	IDE controller. See Table 19-20 on page 367 for definition of Programming Interface byte.
02h	00h	Floppy disk controller.
03h	00h	IPI controller.
04h	00h	RAID controller.
80h	00h	Other mass storage controller.

Table 19-4: Class Code 2: Network Controllers

Sub-Class	Prog. I/F	Description
00h	00h	Ethernet controller.
01h	00h	Token ring controller.
02h	00h	FDDI controller.
03h	00h	ATM controller.
04H	**00H**	**ISDN CONTROLLER.**
80h	00h	Other network controller.

2.2

Table 19-5: Class Code 3: Display Controllers

Sub-Class	Prog. I/F	Description
00h	00h	VGA-compatible controller, responding to memory addresses 000A0000h through 000BFFFFh (Video Frame Buffer), and IO addresses 03B0h through 3BBh, and 03C0h-through-03DFh and all aliases of these addresses.
	01h	8514-compatible controller, responding to IO address 02E8h and its aliases, 02EAh and 02EFh.
01h	00h	XGA controller.
02H	**00H**	**3D CONTROLLER.**
80h	00h	Other display controller.

2.2

Table 19-6: Class Code 4: Multimedia Devices

Sub-Class	Prog. I/F	Description
00h	00h	Video device.
01h	00h	Audio device.
02H	**00H**	**COMPUTER TELEPHONY DEVICE.**
80h	00h	Other multimedia device.

2.2

Table 19-7: Class Code 5: Memory Controllers

Sub-Class	Prog. I/F	Description
00h	00h	RAM memory controller.
01h	00h	Flash memory controller.
80h	00h	Other memory controller.

Table 19-8: Class Code 6: Bridge Devices

Sub-Class	Prog. I/F	Description
00h	00h	Host/PCI bridge.
01h	00h	PCI/ISA bridge.
02h	00h	PCI/EISA bridge.
03h	00h	PCI/Micro Channel bridge.
04h	00h	PCI/PCI bridge.
	01H	**SUBTRACTIVE DECODE PCI-TO-PCI BRIDGE. SUPPORTS SUBTRACTIVE DECODE IN ADDITION TO NORMAL PCI-TO-PCI FUNCTIONS. SEE "PCI-TO-PCI BRIDGE WITH SUBTRACTIVE DECODE FEATURE" ON PAGE 622.**
05h	00h	PCI/PCMCIA bridge.

2.2

Table 19-8: Class Code 6: Bridge Devices (Continued)

Sub-Class	Prog. I/F	Description
06h	00h	PCI/NuBus bridge.
07h	00h	PCI/CardBus bridge.
08H	**XXH**	**RACEWAY BRIDGE. RACEWAY IS AN ANSI STANDARD (ANSI/VITA 5-1994) SWITCHING FABRIC. BITS 7:1 OF THE INTERFACE BITS ARE RESERVED, READ-ONLY AND RETURN ZEROS. BIT 0 IS READ-ONLY AND, IF 0, INDICATES THAT THE BRIDGE IS IN TRANSPARENT MODE, WHILE 1 INDICATES THAT IT'S IN END-POINT MODE.**
80h	00h	Other bridge type.

Table 19-9: Class Code 7: Simple Communications Controllers

Sub-Class	Prog. I/F	Description
00h	00h	Generic XT-compatible serial controller.
	01h	16450-compatible serial controller.
	02h	16550-compatible serial controller.
	03H	**16650-COMPATIBLE SERIAL CONTROLLER.**
	04H	**16750-COMPATIBLE SERIAL CONTROLLER.**
	05H	**16850-COMPATIBLE SERIAL CONTROLLER.**
	06H	**16950-COMPATIBLE SERIAL CONTROLLER.**
01h	00h	Parallel port.
	01h	Bi-directional parallel port.
	02h	ECP 1.X-compliant parallel port.
	03H	**IEEE 1284 CONTROLLER.**
	FEH	**IEEE 1284 TARGET DEVICE (NOT A CONTROLLER).**

Table 19-9: Class Code 7: Simple Communications Controllers (Continued)

	Sub-Class	Prog. I/F	Description
2.2	02H	00H	MULTIPORT SERIAL CONTROLLER.
2.2	03H	00H	GENERIC MODEM.
2.2		01H	HAYES-COMPATIBLE MODEM, 16450-COMPATIBLE INTERFACE. BAR 0 MAPS THE MODEM'S REGISTER SET. THE REGISTER SET CAN BE EITHER MEMORY- OR IO-MAPPED (AS INDICATED BY THE TYPE OF BAR).
2.2		02H	HAYES-COMPATIBLE MODEM, 16550-COMPATIBLE INTERFACE. BAR 0 MAPS THE MODEM'S REGISTER SET. THE REGISTER SET CAN BE EITHER MEMORY- OR IO-MAPPED (AS INDICATED BY THE TYPE OF BAR).
2.2		03H	HAYES-COMPATIBLE MODEM, 16650-COMPATIBLE INTERFACE. BAR 0 MAPS THE MODEM'S REGISTER SET. THE REGISTER SET CAN BE EITHER MEMORY- OR IO-MAPPED (AS INDICATED BY THE TYPE OF BAR).
2.2		04H	HAYES-COMPATIBLE MODEM, 16750-COMPATIBLE INTERFACE. BAR 0 MAPS THE MODEM'S REGISTER SET. THE REGISTER SET CAN BE EITHER MEMORY- OR IO-MAPPED (AS INDICATED BY THE TYPE OF BAR).
	80h	00h	Other communications device.

Table 19-10: Class Code 8: Base System Peripherals

Sub-Class	Prog. I/F	Description
00h	00h	Generic 8259 programmable interrupt controller (PIC).
	01h	ISA PIC.
	02h	EISA PIC.
	10H	**IO APIC. BASE ADDRESS REGISTER 0 IS USED TO REQUEST A MINIMUM OF 32 BYTES OF NON-PREFETCHABLE MEMORY. TWO REGISTERS WITHIN THAT SPACE ARE LOCATED AT BASE + 00H (IO SELECT REGISTER) AND BASE + 10H (IO WINDOW REGISTER). FOR A FULL DESCRIPTION OF THE USE OF THESE REGISTERS, REFER TO THE DATA SHEET FOR THE INTEL 8237EB IN THE 82420/82430 PCISET EISA BRIDGE DATABOOK #290483-003.**
	20H	**IO(x) APIC INTERRUPT CONTROLLER.**
01h	00h	Generic 8237 DMA controller.
	01h	ISA DMA controller.
	02h	EISA DMA controller.
02h	00h	Generic 8254 timer.
	01h	ISA system timers.
	02h	EISA system timers.
03h	00h	Generic RTC controller.
	01h	ISA RTC controller.
04H	**00H**	**GENERIC PCI HOT-PLUG CONTROLLER.**
80h	00h	Other system peripheral.

2.2

2.2

2.2

Table 19-11: Class Code 9: Input Devices

Sub-Class	Prog. I/F	Description
00h	00h	Keyboard controller.
01h	00h	Digitizer (pen).
02h	00h	Mouse controller.
03H	00H	SCANNER CONTROLLER.
04H	00H	GENERIC GAMEPORT CONTROLLER.
	10H	GAMEPORT CONTROLLER. A GAMEPORT CONTROLLER WITH A PROGRAMMING INTERFACE = 10H INDICATES THAT ANY BASE ADDRESS REGISTERS IN THIS FUNCTION THAT REQUEST/ASSIGN IO ADDRESS SPACE, THE REGISTERS IN THAT IO SPACE CONFORM TO THE STANDARD "LEGACY" GAME PORTS. THE BYTE AT OFFSET 00H IN AN IO REGION BEHAVES AS A LEGACY GAMEPORT INTERFACE WHERE READS TO THE BYTE RETURN JOYSTICK/GAMEPAD INFORMATION AND WRITES TO THE BYTE START THE RC TIMER. THE BYTE AT OFFSET 01H IS AN ALIAS OF THE BYTE AT OFFSET 00H. ALL OTHER BYTES IN AN IO REGION ARE UNSPECIFIED AND CAN BE USED IN VENDOR UNIQUE WAYS.
80h	00h	Other input controller.

Table 19-12: Class Code A: Docking Stations

Sub-Class	Prog. I/F	Description
00h	00h	Generic docking station.
80h	00h	Other type of docking station.

Table 19-13: Class Code B: Processors

Sub-Class	Prog. I/F	Description
00h	00h	386.
01h	00h	486.
02h	00h	Pentium.
10h	00h	Alpha.
20h	00h	PowerPC.
30H	*00H*	*MIPS*
40h	00h	Co-processor.

2.2

Table 19-14: Class Code C: Serial Bus Controllers

Sub-Class	Prog. I/F	Description	
00h	00h	Firewire (IEEE 1394).	
	10H	*IEEE 1394 USING 1394 OPENHCI SPEC.*	2.2
01h	00h	ACCESS.bus.	
02h	00h	SSA (Serial Storage Architecture).	
03H	*00H*	*USB (UNIVERSAL SERIAL BUS) CONTROLLER USING UNIVERSAL HOST CONTROLLER SPEC.*	2.2
	10H	*USB (UNIVERSAL SERIAL BUS) CONTROLLER USING OPEN HOST CONTROLLER SPEC.*	2.2
	80H	*USB (UNIVERSAL SERIAL BUS) CONTROLLER WITH NO SPECIFIC PROGRAMMING INTERFACE.*	2.2
	FEH	*USB DEVICE (NOT HOST CONTROLLER).*	2.2
04H	00H	FIBRE CHANNEL.	
05H	*00H*	*SMBUS (SYSTEM MANAGEMENT BUS).*	2.2

2.2

TABLE 19-15: CLASS CODE D: WIRELESS CONTROLLERS

Sub-Class	Interface	Meaning
00	00H	IRDA COMPATIBLE CONTROLLER
01H	00H	CONSUMER IR CONTROLLER
10H	00H	RF CONTROLLER
80H	00H	OTHER TYPE OF WIRELESS CONTROLLER

2.2

TABLE 19-16: CLASS CODE E: INTELLIGENT IO CONTROLLERS

Sub-Class	Interface	Meaning
00H	XXH	INTELLIGENT IO CONTROLLER ADHERING TO THE I2O ARCHITECTURE SPEC. THE SPEC CAN BE DOWNLOADED FROM FTP.INTEL.COM/PUB/IAL/I2O/.
	00H	MESSAGE FIFO AT OFFSET 40H.

2.2

TABLE 19-17: CLASS CODE F: SATELLITE COMMUNICATIONS CONTROLLERS

Sub-Class	Interface	Meaning
01H	00H	TV
02H	00H	AUDIO
03H	00H	VOICE
04H	00H	DATA

TABLE 19-18: CLASS CODE 10H: ENCRYPTION/DECRYPTION CONTROLLERS   2.2

Sub-Class	Interface	Meaning
00H	00H	NETWORK AND COMPUTING ENCRYPT/DECRYPT.
10H	00H	ENTERTAINMENT ENCRYPT/DECRYPT.
80H	00H	OTHER ENCRYPT/DECRYPT.

TABLE 19-19: CLASS CODE 11H: DATA ACQUISITION AND SIGNAL PROCESSING CONTROLLERS   2.2

Sub-Class	Interface	Meaning
00H	00H	DPIO MODULES.
80H	00H	OTHER DATA ACQUISITION AND SIGNAL PROCESSING CONTROLLERS.

Table 19-20: Definition of IDE Programmer's Interface Byte Encoding

Bit(s)	Description
0	Operating mode (primary).
1	Programmable indicator (primary).
2	Operating mode (secondary).
3	Programmable indicator (secondary).
6:4	Reserved. Hardwired to zero.
7	Master IDE device.

Note: The SIG document *PCI IDE Controller Specification* completely describes the layout and meaning of bits 0 through 3 in the Programming Interface byte. The document *Bus Master Programming Interface for IDE ATA Controllers* describes the meaning of bit 7 in the Programming Interface byte. This document can be obtained via FAX by calling (408)741-1600 and requesting document 8038.

Command Register

Always mandatory. This register provides basic control over the device's ability to respond to and/or perform PCI accesses. It's a 16-bit register with bits [9:0] currently defined. Bits [15:10] are reserved for future use and must return zero. The bits are described in Table 19-21 on page 369 and the register is illustrated in Figure 19-3 on page 368. The designer only implements the bits that make sense for the device. As an example, a device with an IO register set but no memory requires bit zero, but not bit one.

After reset, bits [2:0] in this register are cleared to zero (except for a device that must be enabled at startup time because it's used during the raw boot process). This effectively disables the device (with the exception that it remains responsive to configuration accesses) until it is configured and enabled by the configuration software. Devices that must be accessible at boot time through fixed addresses must provide an enable/disable bit to control the recognition of its fixed address ranges. This would permit the configuration software to turn off the recognition of the fixed ranges after boot up and to reconfigure the address range(s) the device responds to.

Figure 19-3: Command Register Bit Assignment

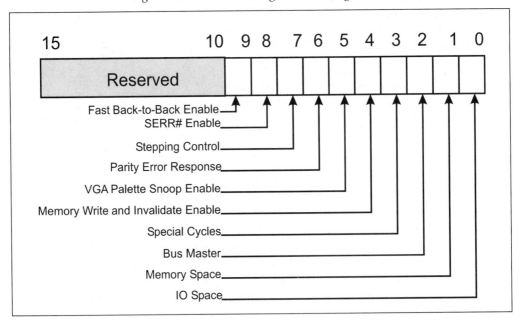

Table 19-21: Command Register Bit Assignment

Bit	Function
0	**IO Space**. When this bit is set to a one, the device's IO address decoder(s) (if any are implemented) responds to PCI IO accesses. Zero disables it. **Required?** Only if function implements any IO decoders. **Default setting:** zero.
1	**Memory Space**. When this bit is set to a one, the device responds to PCI memory accesses (if it implements any memory address decoders). Zero disables it. **Required?** Only if function implements any memory decoders. **Default setting**: zero.
2	**Bus Master**. When set to a one, enables the device to act as a bus master (if it has bus master capability). Zero disables it. Configuration software uses this bit to determine whether a device has bus master capability or not. **Required?** Only for bus masters. **Default setting:** zero.
3	**Special Cycles**. When set to a one, the device is enabled to monitor for PCI Special Cycles (if it's designed to monitor Special Cycles). Zero causes it to ignore Special Cycles. **Required?** Only for devices that recognize messages delivered via the Special Cycle transaction. **Default setting:** zero.
4	**Memory Write and Invalidate Enable**. When set to a one, the device can generate the Memory Write-and-Invalidate command. When set to zero, the device uses Memory Write commands instead. Software should not enable this bit until the device's Cache Line Size configuration register is initialized with the system cache line size. In conjunction with bit 2, Bus Master, the configuration software uses this bit to detect if a master is capable of using the Memory Write and Invalidate command. If it is, the cache line size will be written to the master's Cache Line Size configuration register. **Required?** For bus masters that perform the Memory Write-and-Invalidate transaction. **Default setting:** zero.

Table 19-21: Command Register Bit Assignment (Continued)

Bit	Function
5	**VGA Palette Snoop.** Set to a one, this bit instructs its VGA-compatible device to perform snooping of IO writes to the VGA's Color Palette registers. This function is described in "Display Configuration" on page 608. **Required?** Only for display devices. **Default setting:** In a non-VGA graphics device, reset sets this bit to one, enabling palette snooping. Reset clears this bit in a VGA-compatible controller.
6	**Parity Error Response.** When set to a one, the device can report parity errors (by asserting PERR#). When cleared to a zero, the device does not assert PERR# in the event of a parity error. However, it still must set the Detected Parity Error status bit in its Status register. **Required?** For all devices except those cited in "Devices Excluded from PERR# Requirement" on page 213. **Default setting:** zero.
7	**Stepping Control.** Controls whether the device is enabled to perform address/data stepping. Devices that never use stepping must hardwire this bit to a zero. Devices that always use stepping must hardwire this bit to a one. Devices that can work both ways must implement this bit as read/writable and initialize it to one after reset. Additional information regarding stepping can be found in "Address/Data Stepping" on page 162. **Required?** Only for devices that perform address or data stepping. **Default setting:** See description above.
8	**SERR# Enable.** When set a one, the device can drive the SERR# line. A zero disables the device's SERR# output driver. This bit and bit 6 (Parity Error Response) must be set to report address phase parity errors. **Required?** For all devices with the exception noted in "Devices Excluded from SERR# Requirement" on page 219. **Default setting:** zero.

Table 19-21: Command Register Bit Assignment (Continued)

Bit	Function
9	**Fast Back-to-Back Enable**. If a bus master is capable of performing Fast Back-to-Back transactions with different targets in the first and second transaction, this bit is used to enable or disable this functionality. If all targets on the PCI bus that the master resides on are Fast Back-to-Back capable, configuration software can set this bit to enable this master's ability to perform Fast Back-to-Back transactions without worrying about whether or not the same target is being addressed in the first and second transaction. A complete description of Fast Back-to-Back transactions can be found in "Fast Back-to-Back Transactions" on page 153. **Required?** Only for bus master capable of performing Fast Back-to-Back transactions. **Default setting:** zero.
15:10	Reserved

Status Register

Always mandatory. The Status register tracks the function's status as a PCI entity. A function must implement the bits that relate to its functionality. This register can be read from, but writes are handled as follows. On a write, a bit that is currently set to one can be cleared to zero by writing a one to it. Software cannot set a bit that is current zero to a one. This method was chosen to simplify the programmer's job. After reading the Status and ascertaining the error bits that are set, the programmer clears the bits by writing the value that was read back to the register.

Table 19-22 on page 372 describes the Status register bits and Figure 19-4 on page 372 illustrates its bit assignment. THE 2.2 SPEC HAS MADE THE FOLLOWING 2.2 CHANGES TO THE STATUS REGISTER:

- BIT 4 IS NO LONGER RESERVED. IT IS REFERRED TO AS THE CAPABILITIES LIST BIT.
- THE UDF BIT (BIT 6) AND FEATURE HAS BEEN DELETED AND THE BIT IS NOW RESERVED.
- BIT 8 HAS BEEN RENAMED AS THE MASTER DATA PARITY ERROR BIT.

Figure 19-4: Status Register Bit Assignment

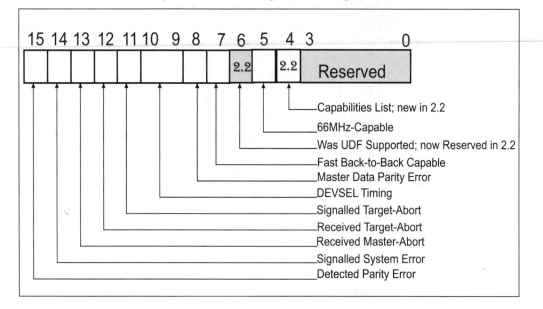

Table 19-22: Status Register Bit Assignment

Bit	R/W	Function
3:0	R	**Reserved**. Hardwired to zero.
4	R	CAPABILITIES LIST. THIS BIT WAS RESERVED IN THE EARLIER SPECS AND IS NEWLY-DEFINED AS THE CAPABILITIES LIST BIT IN THE 2.2 SPEC. IT IS A HARDWIRED, READ-ONLY BIT. IF SET TO ONE, IT INDICATES THAT THE NEW CAPABILITIES LIST POINTER CONFIGURATION REGISTER (SEE FIGURE 19-1 ON PAGE 353) IS IMPLEMENTED IN DWORD 13 OF THE DEVICE'S CONFIGURATION SPACE. IN THIS CASE, THE CONFIGURATION PROGRAMMER SHOULD READ THE POINTER REGISTER TO DETERMINE WHERE THE NEW CAPABILITIES LIST STARTS IN THE DEVICE'S LOWER 48 DWORDS OF CONFIGURATION SPACE. THE PROGRAMMER MAY THEN PARSE THE LIST TO DETERMINE THE ADDITIONAL CAPABILITIES SUPPORTED BY THE DEVICE (AGP, VPD, ETC.) AND MAY USE THEIR RESPECTIVE CONFIGURATION REGISTERS TO CONFIGURE THEM. A DETAILED DESCRIPTION OF THE NEW CAPABILITIES CAN BE FOUND IN "NEW CAPABILITIES" ON PAGE 390. A ZERO IN THIS BIT INDICATES THAT THE DEVICE DOES NOT IMPLEMENT THE NEW CAPABILITIES LIST POINTER CONFIGURATION REGISTER AND THEREFORE THERE ISN'T A LIST TO PARSE. REQUIRED? NO.

Table 19-22: Status Register Bit Assignment (Continued)

Bit	R/W	Function
5	R	**66MHz-Capable.** 1 = device is capable of running at 66MHz. 0 = capable of running at 33MHz. Value hardwired by designer. For more information, refer to the chapter entitled "66MHz PCI Implementation". **Required?** For 66MHz-capable devices, including a bridge with a 66MHz secondary bus.
6	R	RESERVED. PRIOR TO THE 2.2 SPEC, THIS WAS THE UDF SUPPORTED BIT. 1 = DEVICE SUPPORTED USER DEFINABLE FEATURES. 0 = DEVICE DID NOT SUPPORT UDFS. THE VALUE WAS HARDWIRED BY THE DESIGNER. THIS FEATURE BIT WAS ADDED IN THE 2.1 SPEC AND WAS SUBSEQUENTLY DELETED IN THE 2.2 SPEC. FOR MORE INFORMATION, REFER TO THE SECTION "USER-DEFINABLE FEATURES (UDF)" ON PAGE 408 IN THIS CHAPTER.
7	R	**Fast Back-to-Back Capable.** This read-only bit indicates whether or not the target device supports fast back-to-back transactions with different targets. It must be hardwired to zero if the device does not support this feature and to a one if it does. A complete description of Fast Back-to-Back transactions can be found in "Fast Back-to-Back & Stepping" on page 153. Also refer to the description of the Fast Back-to-Back Enable bit in the Command register (see "Command Register" on page 368). **Required?** Yes.
8	R/W	MASTER DATA PARITY ERROR. THIS BIT IS ONLY IMPLEMENTED BY BUS MASTERS AND IS SET ONLY IF THE FOLLOWING CONDITIONS ARE MET: • THE REPORTING BUS MASTER WAS THE INITIATOR OF THE TRANSACTION. • IT SET PERR# ITSELF (DURING A READ) OR DETECTED IT ASSERTED BY THE TARGET (DURING A WRITE). • THE PARITY ERROR RESPONSE BIT IN THE MASTER'S COMMAND CONFIGURATION REGISTER IS SET TO A ONE. PLEASE NOTE THAT THIS BIT WAS NAMED DATA PARITY REPORTED IN THE 1.0 AND 2.0 SPECS. ITS NAME CHANGED TO THE DATA PARITY ERROR DETECTED BIT THE 2.1 SPEC. ITS NAME HAS CHANGED YET AGAIN IN THE 2.2 SPEC TO MASTER DATA PARITY ERROR. ALTHOUGH ITS NAME HAS CHANGED OVER TIME, ITS MEANING HAS REMAINED THE SAME. REQUIRED? FOR MASTERS.

Table 19-22: Status Register Bit Assignment (Continued)

Bit	R/W	Function
10:9	R	**Device Select (DEVSEL#) Timing**. These bits are read-only and define the slowest DEVSEL# timing for a target device (except configuration accesses). 00b = fast 01b = medium 10b = slow 11b = reserved **Required?** For targets. Since all functions have target capability to support accesses to their configuration registers, this means that this bit is **required for all functions**.
11	R/W	**Signaled Target Abort**. Set by the target device whenever it terminates a transaction with a Target Abort. A device that is incapable of signaling Target Abort does not need to implement this bit. **Required?** For targets that are capable of terminating a transaction with Target Abort.
12	R/W	**Received Target Abort**. This bit is set by a bus master whenever its transaction is terminated by a Target Abort from the currently-addressed target. All bus masters must implement this bit. **Required?** For masters.
13	R/W	**Received Master Abort**. This bit should be set by a master whenever its transaction (except for a Special Cycle) is terminated due to a Master Abort. All bus masters must implement this bit. **Required?** For masters.
14	R/W	**Signaled System Error** (SERR#). This bit should be set whenever a device generates a System Error on the SERR# line. If incapable of generating SERR#, it need not implement this bit. **Required?** For all functions, with the exceptions of those noted in "Devices Excluded from SERR# Requirement" on page 219.
15	R/W	**Detected Parity Error.** This bit should be set by a device whenever it detects a parity error (even if parity error reporting is disabled by the Parity Error Response bit in its Command register). **Required?** For all functions, with the exception of those noted in "Devices Excluded from PERR# Requirement" on page 213.

Chapter 19: Configuration Registers

Header Type Register

Always mandatory. Figure 19-4 on page 372 illustrates the format of the Header Type register. Bits [6:0] of this one byte register define the format of dwords 4-through-15 of the device's configuration Header (see Figure 19-1 on page 353). In addition, bit seven defines the device as a single- (bit 7 = 0) or multi-function (bit 7 = 1) device. During configuration, the programmer determines if there are any other functions in this package that require configuration by testing the state of bit seven.

Currently, the only Header formats defined other than the one pictured in Figure 19-1 on page 353 (**Header Type Zero**) are:

- **Header Type One** (PCI-to-PCI bridge Header format; description can be found in "Configuration Registers" on page 552).
- AND HEADER TYPE TWO (CARDBUS BRIDGE; DETAIL CAN BE FOUND IN THE PC CARD 2.2 SPECIFICATION).

Future versions of the specification may define other formats.

Figure 19-5: Header Type Register Bit Assignment

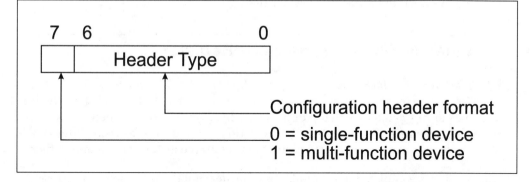

Other Header Registers

Introduction

The configuration registers described in the following paragraphs pertain to device's with Header Type Zero. These registers may be optional or mandatory depending on the device type. They only need to be implemented if a device supports the affected functionality.

Cache Line Size Register

*Mandatory for a **master that uses Memory Write-and-Invalidate command** (see "Memory Write-and-Invalidate Command" on page 117). Also mandatory for **memory targets that support Cacheline Wrap addressing** (see "Cache Line Wrap Mode" on page 144).*

This read/write configuration register specifies the system cache line size in dword increments (e.g., a P6-based system would store the value 08h, indicating a cache line size of eight dwords, or 32 bytes). The register must be implemented by bus masters that implement the Memory Write-and-Invalidate command. Because it must know the cache line size in order to ensure that it starts transactions on a cache line boundary and keeps its promise to write an entire line into memory, the bus master may not use the Memory Write-and-Invalidate command when this register is set to zero (which indicates that the configuration software hasn't yet told it the cache line size). In this case, the master should only use Memory Write transactions to update memory.

A device may limit the number of cache line sizes that it supports. If an unsupported value is written to the register by the configuration software, the device behaves as if the value zero was written.

Latency Timer: "Timeslice" Register

Mandatory (read/writable) for masters that perform burst transactions. The Latency Timer defines the minimum amount of time, in PCI clock cycles, that the bus master can retain ownership of the bus whenever it initiates a new transaction. The bus master decrements its Latency Timer by one on each rising-edge of the clock after it initiates a transaction. It may continue its transaction until either:

- it has completed the overall burst transfer (if it doesn't lose its grant), or
- the target asserts STOP# to prematurely terminate the transaction, or
- it has exhausted its timeslice (LT value) and it has been preempted (lost its GNT# to another PCI master),

whichever comes first.

If a bus master ever performs a burst of more than two data phases it must implement the Latency Timer register as a read/writable register. It *may be implemented as a hardwired, read-only register by masters that never perform more than two data phases, but the hardwired value returned must not exceed sixteen (PCI clock cycles)*. This means that a hardwired value of zero is permitted if the master never performs more than two data phases. A timeslice of zero means the master has a null timeslice. The net effect would be that the master would have to yield the bus after the first data phase if it immediately lost its GNT# to another master. Target devices do not implement this register.

In a typical implementation of a programmable LT register, the low-order three bits are hardwired to zero and the programmer can program any value into the high-order five bits. This permits the programmer to specify the timeslice with a granularity of eight PCI clocks. If the register is programmable, reset clears it. More information on the Latency Timer can be found in "Latency Timer Keeps Master From Monopolizing Bus" on page 78.

Optimally, every bus master should implement this as a read/writable register, thereby permitting the configuration software maximum flexibility when it divides up the available bus time among the community of bus masters. The configuration software determines the bus master's desired timeslice by reading from the function's Min_Gnt (Minimum Grant) register. The designer indicates the desired timeslice by hardwiring the value, in increments of 250ns, into this register. **WHEN CALCULATING THIS VALUE, THE DESIGNER ASSUMES A BUS SPEED OF 33MHz AND ZERO WAIT STATE OPERATION ON THE PART OF THE TARGET.** If the bus master has no stringent requirement regarding its timeslice, the designer hardwires zero into this register.

2.2

BIST Register

Optional. This register may be implemented by both master and target devices. If a device implements a Built-In Self-Test (BIST) it must implement this register as illustrated in Figure 19-6 on page 378. Table 19-23 on page 378 describes each bit's function. If the device doesn't support a BIST, this register must return zeros when read. The device's BIST is invoked by setting bit six to one. The device resets bit six upon completion of the BIST. Configuration software must fail the device if it doesn't reset bit six within two seconds. At the conclusion of the BIST, the test result is indicated in the lower four bits of the register. A completion code of zero indicates successful completion. A non-zero value represents a device-specific error code.

The time limit of two seconds may not be sufficient time to test a very complex device or one with an extremely large buffer that needs to be tested. In that case, the remainder of the test could be completed in the initialization portion of the device's device driver when the OS loads it into memory and calls it.

Figure 19-6: BIST Register Bit Assignment

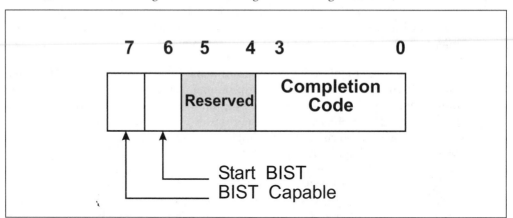

Table 19-23: BIST Register Bit Assignment

Bit	Function
3:0	**Completion Code**. A value of zero indicates successful completion, while a non-zero result indicates a device-specific error.
5:4	Reserved.
6	**Start BIST**. Writing a one into this bit starts the device's BIST. The device resets this bit automatically upon completion. Software should fail the device if the BIST does not complete within two seconds.
7	**BIST Capable**. Should return a one if the device implements a BIST, a zero if it doesn't.

Base Address Registers (BARs)

Required if a device implements memory and/or IO decoders. Virtually all devices implement some memory, and/or a device-specific register set to control the device. Some examples are:

- A parallel port's Status, Command and Data registers could reside in IO or memory-mapped IO space.

- A network interface's control registers (Command/Status, etc.) could reside in IO or memory-mapped IO space.
- The network interface may also incorporate a RAM memory buffer that must be mapped into the system's memory space.
- In addition, a device ROM containing the device's BIOS and interrupt service routine may be present in a device.

On power-up, the system must be automatically configured so that each device's IO and memory functions occupy mutually-exclusive address ranges. In order to accomplish this, the system must be able to detect how many memory and IO address ranges a device requires and the size of each. Obviously, the system must then be able to program the device's address decoders in order to assign non-conflicting address ranges to them.

The Base Address Registers (BARs), located in dwords 4-through-9 of the device's configuration Header space (see Figure 19-1 on page 353), are used to implement a function's programmable memory and/or IO decoders. Each register is 32-bits wide (or 64-bits wide if it's a memory decoder and its associated memory block can be located above the 4GB address boundary). Figure 19-7 on page 382 and Figure 19-8 on page 383 illustrate the two possible formats of a Base Address Register. Bit 0 is a read-only bit and indicates whether it's a memory or an IO decoder:

- Bit 0 = 0, the register is a memory address decoder.
- Bit 0 = 1, the register is an IO address decoder.

The 2.1 spec stated:

"The first Base Address register is always located at offset 10h."

THE 2.2 SPEC CHANGED THIS. DECODERS MAY BE IMPLEMENTED IN ANY OF THE BASE ADDRESS REGISTER POSITIONS. IF MORE THAN ONE DECODER IS IMPLEMENTED, THERE MAY BE HOLES. DURING CONFIGURATION, THE CONFIGURATION SOFTWARE MUST THEREFORE LOOK AT ALL SIX OF THE POSSIBLE BASE ADDRESS REGISTER POSITIONS IN A DEVICE'S HEADER TO DETERMINE WHICH REGISTERS ARE ACTUALLY IMPLEMENTED.

2.2

Memory-Mapping Recommended

In a PC environment, IO space is densely populated and will only become more so in the future. For this reason and because some processors are only capable of performing memory transactions, the specification strongly recommends that the device designer provide only a Memory Base Address Register that maps a device's register set into memory space. Optionally, an IO Base Address Register may also be included to map it into IO space, but this is not recommended.

This gives the configuration software the flexibility to map the device's register set at into memory space and, if an IO Base Address Register is also provided, into IO space as well. If both are implemented, the device driver associated with the device can then choose whether to communicate with its device's register set through memory or IO space.

Memory Base Address Register

This section provides a detailed description of the bit fields within a Memory Base Address Register. The section entitled "Determining Block Size and Assigning Address Range" on page 384 describes how the register is probed to determine its existence, the size of the memory associated with the decoder, and the assignment of the base address to the decoder.

Decoder Width Field. In a Memory Base Address Register (see Figure 19-7 on page 382), bits [2:1] define whether the decoder is 32- or 64-bits wide:

- 00b = it's a **32-bit register**. The configuration software therefore will write a 32-bit start memory address into it specifying any address in the first 4GB of memory address space.
- 10b = it's a **64-bit register**. The configuration software therefore writes a 64-bit start memory address into it that specifies a start address in a 2^{64} memory address space. This means that the device supports the Dual-Address Command (DAC) that is used to address memory above the 4GB address boundary. It also means that this **Base Address Register consumes two dwords** of the configuration Header space. The first dword is used to set the lower 32-bits of the start address and the second dword is completely read/writable and is used to specify the upper 32-bits of the start address.

2.2

PLEASE NOTE THAT THE 2.2 SPEC NO LONGER PERMITS THE PATTERN THAT INDICATES THE DEVICE'S MEMORY MUST BE MAPPED INTO THE FIRST MB OF MEMORY SPACE. THIS PATTERN IS NOW RESERVED.

Prefetchable Attribute Bit. Bit three defines the block of memory as Prefetchable or not. A block of memory space may be marked as Prefetchable only if it can guarantee that:

- there are **no side effects from reads** (e.g., the read doesn't alter the contents of the location or alter the state of the device in some manner). It's permissible for a bridge that resides between a master and a memory target to prefetch read data from memory that has this characteristic. If the master doesn't end up asking for all of the data that the bridge read into a read-ahead buffer, the bridge must discard the data (see "Bridges Must Discard Prefetched Data Not Consumed By Master" on page 116). The data remains unchanged in the target's memory locations.

- on a read, it **always returns all bytes** irrespective of the byte enable settings. This yields better performance because the memory target doesn't have to wait one clock into each data phase to sample the byte enables before providing the data. It can immediately supply the full dword (or quadword, if it's a 64-bit transfer) in the first clock of each data phase (assuming that it's capable of 0-wait state reads).
- the memory device **continues to function correctly if** a bridge that resides between the master and the memory target performs **byte merging** (for more information, refer to "Byte Merging" on page 95) in its posted memory write buffer when memory writes are **performed** within the memory target's range.

As an example, the address decoder for a block of memory-mapped IO ports would hardwire the Prefetchable bit to zero, while the address decoder for well-behaved memory would hardwire it to one.

The configuration software checks this bit to determine a memory target's operational characteristics, assigns a memory range to its decoder (i.e., its Memory Base Address Register), and then backtracks to all bridges between the memory target and the processor and configures the bridges to treat the assigned memory range in the appropriate manner:

- If it's Prefetchable memory, it's permissible to perform read prefetching to yield better performance, and it's also permissible to perform byte merging in its posted memory write buffer for writes performed to the memory.
- If it's non-Prefetchable memory, read prefetching and byte merging are not allowed within the assigned region of memory space. This will not allow bridges to optimize accesses to the device, but you're assured the device will function correctly (and that's pretty important!).

Base Address Field. This field consists of bits [31:4] for a 32-bit memory decoder and bits [63:4] for a 64-bit memory decoder. It is used:

- to determine the size of the memory associated with this decoder, and
- to assign a start (i.e., base) address to the decoder.

Programming of an example Memory Base Address Register is provided in "Determining Block Size and Assigning Address Range" on page 384.

If a memory device requires less than 4KB of memory space, the specification suggests that the memory range be set at 4KB (to minimize the number of bits to be checked by the address decoder). It should be noted that the Hot-Plug PCI spec has a problem with this (see "Efficient Use of Memory and/or IO Space" on page 469).

Figure 19-7: Memory Base Address Register Bit Assignment

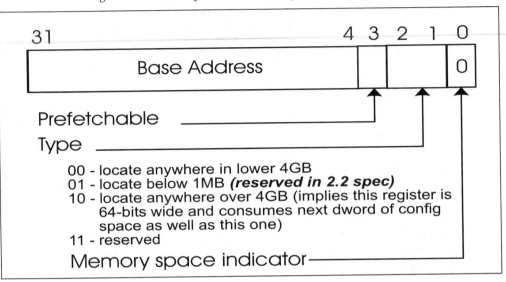

IO Base Address Register

Introduction. This section provides a detailed description of the bit fields within an IO Base Address Register. The section entitled "Determining Block Size and Assigning Address Range" on page 384 describes:

- how the register is probed to determine its existence,
- how to determine the size of the IO register set associated with the decoder and therefore the amount of IO space that must be assigned to it, and
- how to assign the base address to the decoder.

Description. Refer to Figure 19-8 on page 383. Bit zero returns a one, indicating that this is an IO, rather than a memory, decoder. Bit one is reserved and must always return zero. Bits [31:2] is the Base Address field and is used to:

- determine the size of the IO block required and
- to set its start address.

The specification requires that a device that maps its control register set into IO space must not request more than 256 locations per IO Base Address Register.

2.2   **PC-Compatible IO Decoder.** THE UPPER 16-BITS OF THE IO BAR MAY BE HARDWIRED TO ZERO WHEN A DEVICE IS DESIGN SPECIFICALLY FOR A PC-COMPATIBLE, X86-BASED MACHINE (BECAUSE INTEL X86 PROCESSORS ARE INCAPABLE OF GENERATING IO ADDRESSES OVER 64KB). THE DEVICE MUST STILL PERFORM A FULL 32-BIT DECODE OF THE IO ADDRESS, HOWEVER.

Legacy IO Decoders. Legacy PC-compatible devices such as VGA and IDE controllers frequently expect to be located within fixed legacy IO ranges. Such devices do not implement Base Address Registers. Instead, the configuration software identifies them as legacy devices via their respective Class Code and then enables their IO decoder(s) by setting the IO Space bit in its Command register to one.

A legacy IO device may or may not own all of the byte locations within a dword of IO space:

- A legacy IO device that does own all of the bytes within the currently-addressed dword can perform its decode using the dword-aligned address latched from AD[31:2] at the end of address phase. It does not have to use AD[1:0].
- A legacy IO device that does not own all of the byte locations within a dword must decode all 32 address bits latched at the end of the address phase to determine if it owns the byte-specific location being addressed and asserts DEVSEL# to claim the transaction if it does. It must then examine the byte enables to determine if the initiator is addressing additional, higher byte locations within the target IO dword (identified via AD[31:2]). If it owns all of the addressed IO ports, the device can honor the request. However, if it doesn't own them all it must issue a Target Abort to the initiator. For more information, refer to "Unsupported Byte Enable Combination Results in Target Abort" on page 148.

The exception is a bridge that performs subtractive decode (see "Subtractive Decode (by ISA Bridge)" on page 53). It does not have to check the state of AD[1:0] before claiming the transaction (subtractively) and passing it through to the ISA bus.

Figure 19-8: IO Base Address Register Bit Assignment

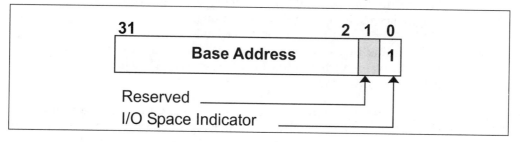

Determining Block Size and Assigning Address Range

How It Works. The configuration program must probe each of a function's possible Base Address Registers to determine:

- Is the Base Address Register implemented?
- Is it a memory or an IO address decoder?
- If it's a memory decoder, is it a 32- or 64-bit Base Address Register?
- If it's a memory decoder, is the memory associated with the register Prefetchable or non-Prefetchable?
- How much memory or address space does it require and with what alignment?

All of this information can be ascertained simply by writing all ones to the Base Address Register and then reading it back. A return value of zero indicates that the Base Address Register isn't implemented. Assuming that the value read is non-zero, scanning the returned value (assuming its non-zero) upwards starting at the least-significant bit of the Base Address field, the programmer determines the size of the required memory or the IO space by finding the first bit that was successfully set to one. Assuming that bit zero of the register has a binary-weighted value of one, bit one a value of two, bit two a value of four, etc., the binary-weighted value of the first one bit found in the Base Address field indicates the required amount of space. This is also the first read/writable bit in the register and all of the bits above it are by definition read/writable. After discovering this information, the program then writes a 32- or 64-bit start memory address, or the 32-bit IO address into the Base Address Register.

A Memory Example. As an example, assume that FFFFFFFFh is written to the Base Address Register at configuration dword 04d and the value read back is FFF00000h. The fact that any bits could be changed to one indicates that the Base Address Register is implemented.

- Bit 0 = 0, indicating that this is a memory address decoder.
- Bits [2:1] = 00b, indicating that it's a 32-bit memory decoder.
- Bit 3 = 0, indicating that it's not Prefetchable memory.
- Bit 20 is the first one bit found in the Base Address field. The binary-weighted value of this bit is 1,048,576, indicating that this is an address decoder for 1MB of memory.

The programmer then writes a 32-bit base address into the register. However, only bits [31:20] are writable. The decoder accepts bits [31:20] and assumes that bits [19:0] of the assigned base address are zero. This means that the base address is divisible by 1MB, the size of the requested memory range. It is a characteristic of PCI decoders that the assigned start address is always divisible by the size of requested range.

As an example, it is possible to program the example memory address decoder for a 1MB block of memory to start on the one, two, or three meg boundary, but it is not possible to set its start address at the 1.5, 2.3, or 3.7 meg boundary.

An IO Example. As a second example, assume that FFFFFFFFh is written to a function's Base Address Register at configuration dword address 05d and the value read back is FFFFFF01h. Bit 0 is a one, indicating that this is an IO address decoder. Scanning upwards starting at bit 2 (the least-significant bit of the Base Address field), bit 8 is the first bit that was successfully changed to one. The binary-weighted value of this bit is 256, indicating that this is IO address decoder is requesting 256 bytes of IO space.

The programmer then writes a 32-bit base IO address into the register. However, only bits [31:20] are writable. The decoder accepts bits [31:8] and assumes that bits [7:0] of the assigned base address are zero. This means that the base address is divisible by 256, the size of the requested IO range.

Smallest/Largest Decoder Sizes

Smallest/Largest Memory Decoders. The smallest memory address decoder would be implemented as a Base Address Register that permitted bits [31:4] to be written. Since the binary-weighted value of bit four is 16, 16 bytes is the smallest memory block a PCI memory decoder can be designed for.

The largest memory decoder would permit only bit 31 to be written. The binary-weighted value of this bit is 2GB and this is therefore the largest range that a PCI memory decoder can request. Note that if the Decoder Size field indicates that this is a 64-bit memory decoder, this BAR consumes two dwords of configuration space (this one the one immediately following it). It also means that, in the second dword, all 32-bits are read/writable and it is used to set the upper 32-bits of the 64-bit start address.

Smallest/Largest IO Decoders. The smallest IO decoder would be implemented as a Base Address Register that permitted bits [31:2] to be programmed. Since the binary-weighted value of bit four is 4, 4 bytes (a dword) is the smallest IO block a PCI IO decoder can be designed for.

The largest IO decoder would permit bits [31:8] to be written. The binary-weighted value of bit 8 is 256 and this is therefore the largest range that a PCI IO decoder can request.

Expansion ROM Base Address Register

Required if a device incorporates a device ROM. Many PCI devices incorporate a device ROM (the spec refers to it as an expansion ROM) that contains a device driver for the device. The expansion ROM start memory address and size is specified in the Expansion ROM Base Address Register at configuration dword 12d in the configuration Header region. As previously described in the section entitled "Base Address Registers", on power-up the system must be automatically configured so that each device's IO and memory decoders recognize mutually-exclusive address ranges. The configuration software must be able to detect how much memory space an expansion ROM requires. In addition, the system must have the capability of programming a ROM's address decoder in order to locate its ROM in a non-conflicting address range.

When the start-up configuration program detects that a device has an Expansion ROM Base Address Register implemented (by writing all ones to it and reading it back), it must then check the first two locations in the ROM for an Expansion ROM signature to determine if a ROM is actually installed (i.e., there may be an empty ROM socket). If installed, the configuration program must shadow the ROM and execute its initialization code. This process is described in "Expansion ROMs" on page 411.

The format of the expansion ROM Base Address Register is illustrated in Figure 19-9 on page 387:

- A one in bit zero enables the device's ROM address decoder (assuming the Memory Space bit in the Command register is also set to one).
- Bits [10:1] are reserved.
- Bits [31:11] are used to specify the ROM's start address (starting on an address divisible by the ROM's size).

As an example, assume that the programmer writes FFFFFFFEh to the ROM's Base Address Register (bit 0, the Expansion ROM Enable bit, is cleared so as not to enable the ROM address decoder until a start memory address has been assigned). A subsequent read from the register yields FFFE0000h. This indicates the following:

- Bit 0 is a zero, indicating that the ROM address decoder is currently disabled.
- Bits [10:1] are reserved.

- In the Base Address field (bits [31:11]), bit 17 is the least-significant bit that the programmer was able to set to one. It has a binary-weighted value of 128K, indicating that the ROM decoder requires 128KB of memory space. The programmer then writes a 32-bit start address into the register to assign the ROM start address on a 128K address boundary.

The spec recommends that the designer of the Expansion ROM Base Address Register should request a memory block slightly larger than that required by the current revision ROM to be installed. This permits the installation of subsequent ROM revisions that occupy more space without requiring a redesign of the logic associated with the device's Expansion ROM Base Address Register. The specification sets a limit of 16MB as the maximum expansion ROM size.

The Memory Space bit in the Command register has precedence over the Expansion ROM Enable bit. The device's expansion ROM should respond to memory accesses only if both its Memory Space bit (in its Command register) and the Expansion ROM Enable bit (in its expansion ROM register) are both set to one.

In order to minimize the number of address decoders that a device must implement, one address decoder can be shared between the Expansion ROM Base Address Register and one of the device's Memory Base Address Registers. The two Base Address Registers must be able to hold different values at the same time, but the address decoder will not decode ROM accesses unless the Expansion ROM Enable bit is set in the Expansion ROM Base Address Register.

A more detailed description of expansion ROM detection, shadowing and usage can be found in "Expansion ROMs" on page 411.

Figure 19-9: Expansion ROM Base Address Register Bit Assignment

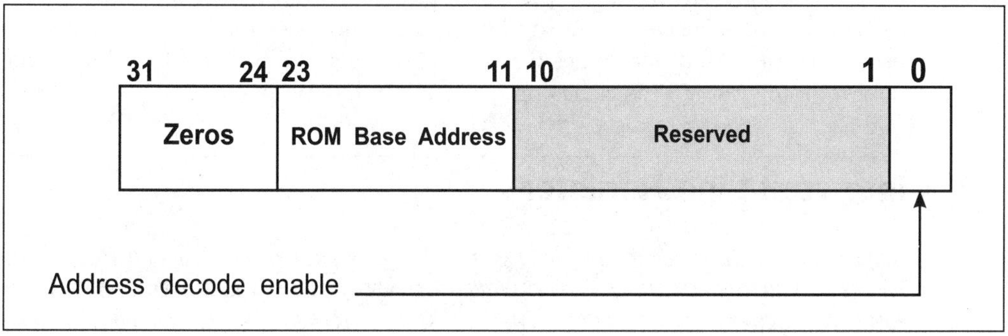

CardBus CIS Pointer

Optional. This optional register is implemented by devices that share silicon between Cardbus and PCI. This field points to the Card Information Structure (CIS) the CardBus card. The register is read-only and contains the offset of the CIS in one of the following places:

- Offset within the function's device-specific configuration space (after dword 15 in the function's configuration space).
- Offset from the start address indicated in one of the device's Memory Base Address Registers.
- Offset within a code image in the device's expansion ROM.

The format of the CardBus CIS Pointer register is defined in the revision 3.0 PC Card specification. A detailed description of the CIS can be found in the Mind-Share architecture series book entitled *CardBus System Architecture*.

Interrupt Pin Register

2.2

Required if a PCI function is capable of generating interrupt requests via an INTx# pin. THIS IS DIFFERENT THAN THE 2.1 SPEC WHICH DEFINED THIS AS A REQUIRED REGISTER IF A FUNCTION GENERATED INTERRUPTS. THE 2.2 SPEC ALLOWS A FUNCTION TO GENERATE INTERRUPTS EITHER USING AN INTERRUPT PIN, OR USING MSI-CAPABILITY (FOR MORE INFORMATION, SEE "MESSAGE SIGNALED INTERRUPTS (MSI)" ON PAGE 252).

The read-only Interrupt Pin register defines which of the four PCI interrupt request pins, INTA#-through-INTD#, a PCI function is connected (i.e., bonded) to. The values 01h-through-04h correspond to PCI interrupt request pins INTA#-through-INTD#. A return value of zero indicates that the device doesn't use interrupts. All other values (05h-FFh) are reserved. For additional information, refer to "Using Pins vs. Using MSI Capability" on page 222.

Interrupt Line Register

2.2

Required if a PCI device is capable of generating interrupt requests via an INTx# pin. THIS IS DIFFERENT THAN THE 2.1 SPEC WHICH DEFINED THIS AS A REQUIRED REGISTER IF A FUNCTION GENERATED INTERRUPTS. THE 2.2 SPEC ALLOWS A FUNCTION TO GENERATE INTERRUPTS EITHER USING AN INTERRUPT PIN, OR USING MSI-CAPABILITY (FOR MORE INFORMATION, SEE "MESSAGE SIGNALED INTERRUPTS (MSI)" ON PAGE 252).

The read/writable Interrupt Line register is used to identify which input on the interrupt controller the function's PCI interrupt request pin (as specified in its Interrupt Pin register) is routed to. For example, in a PC environment the values 00h-through-0Fh in this register (refer to Table 14-2 on page 232) correspond to the IRQ0-through-IRQ15 inputs on the interrupt controller. The value 255d (FFh) indicates "unknown" or "no connection." The values from 10h-through-FEh, inclusive, are reserved. Although it doesn't state this in the specification, it is the author's opinion that RST# should initialize the Interrupt Line register to a value of FFh, thereby indicating that interrupt routing has not yet been assigned to the function.

The OS or device driver can examine a device's Interrupt Line register to determine which system interrupt request line the device uses to issue requests for service (and, therefore, which entry in the interrupt table to "hook"). For additional information, refer to "Hooking the Interrupt" on page 239.

In a non-PC environment, the value written to this register is architecture-specific and therefore outside the scope of the specification.

Min_Gnt Register: Timeslice Request

Optional for a bus master and not applicable to non-master devices. This read-only register is implemented by bus master devices and not by target devices. The value hardwired into this register indicates how long the master would like to retain PCI bus ownership (in order to attain good performance) whenever it initiates a transaction. The value indicates how long a burst period the device needs (in increments of 1/4 of a microsecond, or 250ns). A value of zero indicates the device has no stringent requirement in this area.

The Max_Lat register (see next section) and this register and are information-only registers used by the configuration software to determine:

- how often a bus master typically requires access to the PCI bus and
- the duration of a typical transfer when it does acquire the bus.

The Max_Lat value is useful in programming the PCI bus arbiter (assuming that it's programmable), and the Min_Gnt value in determining the value to be programmed into a bus master's Latency Timer.

THE **2.2** SPEC INDICATES THAT THE VALUE HARDWIRED INTO THIS REGISTER SHOULD ASSUME **2.2** THAT THE DEVICE DOESN'T INSERT ANY WAIT STATES INTO DATA PHASES.

For more information, refer to "Latency Timer Keeps Master From Monopolizing Bus" on page 78.

Max_Lat Register: Priority-Level Request

Optional for a bus master and not applicable to non-master devices. The specification states that this read-only register specifies "how often" the device needs access to the PCI bus (in increments of 1/4 of a microsecond, or 250ns). A value of zero indicates the device has no stringent requirement in this area.

The Max_Lat register value indicates how often the master would like to have access to the bus (i.e., receive its GNT# from the arbiter). The value hardwired into this register is used by the configuration software to determine the priority-level (and possible the arbitration scheme the arbiter uses) the bus arbiter assigns to the master (assuming that the arbiter is programmable). Please note that if the arbiter is not programmable, the configuration software shouldn't waste any time reading this register.

2.2 THE 2.2 SPEC INDICATES THAT THE VALUE HARDWIRED INTO THIS REGISTER SHOULD ASSUME THAT THE DEVICE DOESN'T INSERT ANY WAIT STATES INTO DATA PHASES.

2.2 New Capabilities

Configuration Header Space Not Large Enough

The 2.1 spec defined the first 16 dwords of a function's configuration space as its configuration Header space. It was originally intended that all of the function's PCI spec-defined configuration registers would reside within this region and that all of its function-specific configuration registers would reside within its lower 48 dwords of configuration space. Unfortunately, they ran out of space when defining new configuration registers in the 2.2 spec. For this reason, the spec now permits certain spec-defined registers to overflow into the lower 48 dwords of configuration space.

Discovering That New Capabilities Exist

If the Capabilities List bit in the Status register (see Figure 19-10 on page 391) is set to one, the function implements the New Capabilities List Pointer register in byte zero of dword 13 in its configuration space (see Figure 19-11 on page 392). This implies that the pointer contains the dword-aligned start address of the New Capabilities List within the function's lower 48 dwords of configuration space. It is a rule that the two least-significant bits must be hardwired to zero and must be ignored (i.e., masked) by software when reading the register. The upper six bits represents the upper six bits of the 8-bit, dword-aligned start address of the new registers implemented in the function's lower 48 dwords of configuration space. The two least-significant bits are assumed to be zero.

Figure 19-10: PCI Status Register

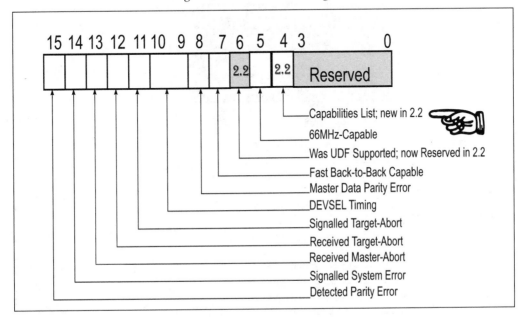

Figure 19-11: New Capabilities Pointer Register

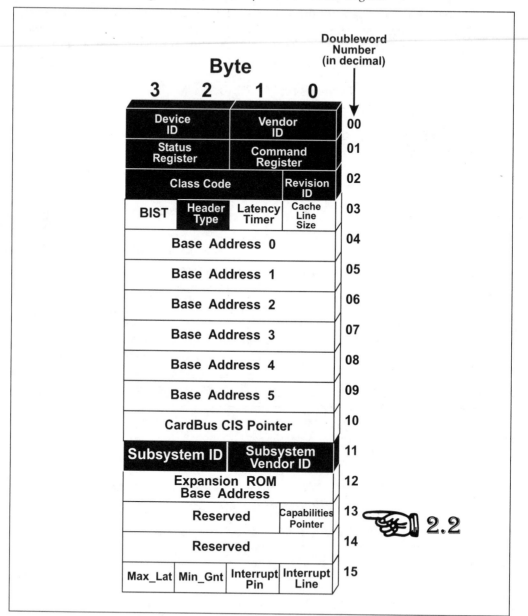

What the New Capabilities List Looks Like

The location pointed to by the Capabilities Pointer register is the first entry in a linked series of one or more configuration register sets, each of which supports a new feature. Each entry has the general format illustrated in Figure 19-12 on page 394. The first byte is referred to as the Capability ID (assigned by the PCI SIG) and identifies the feature associated with this register set (e.g., 2 = AGP), while the second byte either points to the another feature's register set, or indicates that there are no additional register sets (with a pointer value of zero) associated with this function. In either case, the least-significant two bits must return zero. If a pointer to the next feature's register set is present in the second byte, it points to a dword within the functions lower 48 dwords of configuration space (it can point either forward or backward in the function's lower 48 dwords of configuration space). A feature's register set always immediately follows the first two bytes of the entry, and its length and format are defined by what type of feature it is. The New Capabilities currently defined in the 2.2 spec are those listed in Table 19-24 on page 393.

Table 19-24: Currently-Assigned Capability IDs

ID	Description
00h	Reserved.
01h	**PCI Power Management Interface**. Refer to "Power Management" on page 479.
02h	**AGP**. Refer to "AGP Capability" on page 394. Also refer to the MindShare book entitled *AGP System Architecture* (published by Addison-Wesley).
03h	**VPD**. Refer to "Vital Product Data (VPD) Capability" on page 397.
04h	**Slot Identification**. This capability identifies a bridge that provides external expansion capabilities (i.e., an expansion chassis containing add-in card slots). Full documentation of this feature can be found in the revision 1.1 *PCI-to-PCI Bridge Architecture Specification*. For a detailed description, refer to "Introduction To Chassis/Slot Numbering Registers" on page 566 and "Chassis and Slot Number Assignment" on page 594.
05h	**Message Signaled Interrupts**. Refer to "Message Signaled Interrupts (MSI)" on page 252.
06h	**CompactPCI Hot Swap**. Refer to "CompactPCI and PMC" on page 699.
7-255d	Reserved.

Figure 19-12: General Format of a New Capabilities List Entry

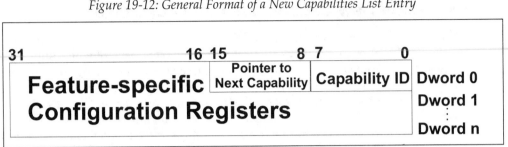

AGP Capability

The 2.2 spec assigns the Capability ID of 02h to AGP. The remainder of this section is only included as an example of a New Capability.

Refer to Figure 19-13 on page 394.

- The AGP's Capability ID is 02h.
- The second byte is the register that points to the register set associated with the next New Capability (if there is one).
- Following the pointer register are two, 4-bit read-only fields designating the major and minor rev of the AGP spec that the AGP device is built to (at the time of this writing, the major rev is 2h and the minor is 0h).
- The last byte of the first dword is reserved and must return zero when read.
- The next two dwords contain the AGP device's AGP Status and AGP Command registers.

The sections that follow define these registers and the bits within them.

For a detailed description of AGP, refer to the MindShare book entitled *AGP System Architecture* (published by Addison-Wesley).

Figure 19-13: Format of the AGP Capability Register Set

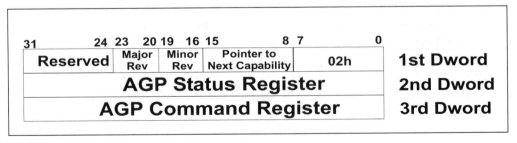

AGP Status Register

The AGP Status register is defined in Table 19-25 on page 395. This is a read-only register. Writes have no affect. Reserved or unimplemented fields or bits always return zeros when read.

Table 19-25: AGP Status Register (Offset CAP_PTR + 4)

Bits	Field	Description
31:24	RQ	The RQ field contains the maximum depth of the AGP request queue. Therefore, this number is the maximum number of transaction requests this device can manage. A "0" is interpreted as a depth of one, while FFh is interpreted as a depth of 256.
23:10	Reserved	Writes have no affect. Reads return zeros.
9	SBA	If set, this device supports Sideband Addressing.
8:6	Reserved	Writes have no affect. Reads return zeros.
5	4G	If set, this device supports addresses greater than 4GB.
4	FW	If set, this device supports Fast Write transactions.
3	Reserved	Writes have no affect. Reads return a zero
2:0	RATE	The RATE field is a bit map that indicates the data transfer rates supported by this device. AGP devices must report all that apply. The RATE field applies to AD, C/BE#, and SBA busses. **Bit Set** **Transfer Rate** 0 1X 1 2X 2 4X

AGP Command Register

The AGP Command register is defined in Table 19-26 on page 396. This is a read/writable register, with reserved fields hard-wired to zeros. All bits in the AGP Command register are cleared to zero after reset. This register is programmed during configuration. With one exception, the behavior of a device if this register is modified during runtime is not specified. If the AGP_Enable bit is cleared, the AGP master is not allowed to initiate a new request.

Table 19-26: AGP Command Register (Offset CAP_PTR + 8)

Bits	Field	Description
31:24	RQ_Depth	**Master**: The RQ_DEPTH field must be programmed with the maximum number of transaction requests the master is allowed to enqueue into the target. The value programmed into this field must be equal to or less than the value reported by the target in the RQ field of its AGP Status Register. A "0" value indicates a request queue depth of one entry, while a value of FFh indicates a request queue depth of 256. **Target**: The RQ_DEPTH field is reserved.
23:10	Reserved	Writes have no affect. Reads return zeros.
9	SBA_Enable	When set, the Sideband Address mechanism is enabled in this device.
8	AGP_Enable	**Master**: Setting the AGP_Enable bit allows the master to initiate AGP operations. When cleared, the master cannot initiate AGP operations. Also when cleared, the master is allowed to stop driving the SBA port. If bits 1 or 2 are set, the master must perform a re-synch cycle before initiating a new request. **Target**: Setting the AGP_Enable bit allows the target to accept AGP operations. When cleared, the target ignores incoming AGP operations. The target must be completely configured and enabled before the master is enabled. The AGP_Enable bit is the last to be set. Reset clears this bit.
7:6	Reserved	Writes have no affect. Reads return zeros.

Table 19-26: AGP Command Register (Offset CAP_PTR + 8) (Continued)

Bits	Field	Description
5	4G	**Master**: Setting the 4G bit allows the master to initiate AGP requests to addresses at or above the 4GB address boundary. When cleared, the master is only allowed to access addresses in the lower 4 GB of addressable space. **Target**: Setting the 4G bit enables the target to accept AGP DAC (Dual-Address Commands) commands, when bit 9 is cleared. When bits 5 and 9 are set, the target can accept a Type 4 SBA command and utilize A[35:32] of the Type 3 SBA command.
4	FW_Enable	When this bit is set, memory write transactions initiated by the core logic will follow the fast write protocol. When this bit is cleared, memory write transactions initiated by the core logic will follow the PCI protocol.
3	Reserved	Writes have no affect. Reads return zeros.
2:0	Data_Rate	No more than one bit in the Data_Rate field must be set to indicate the maximum data transfer rate supported. The same bit must be set in both the master and the target. **Bit Set** **Transfer Rate** 0 1X 1 2X 2 4X

Vital Product Data (VPD) Capability

Introduction

As explained in "Vital Product Data (VPD)" on page 431, the 2.1 spec defined the optional Vital Product Data as residing in a PCI function's expansion ROM.

THE 2.2 SPEC HAS DELETED THIS INFORMATION FROM THE ROM AND INSTEAD PLACES THE **2.2** VPD (IF PRESENT) IN A FUNCTION'S PCI CONFIGURATION REGISTER SPACE (SEE "NEW CAPABILITIES" ON PAGE 390). THIS SECTION DESCRIBES THE 2.2 IMPLEMENTATION OF THE VPD AND PROVIDES AN EXAMPLE FROM THE 2.2 SPEC.

It's Not Really Vital

It's always brought a smile to my face that despite its name, the VPD has never been vital. It's always been named "Vital" in the spec, but its *content* was *not initially defined*. Then in the 2.1 spec, although *vital*, it was defined as residing in a function's ROM, but its inclusion was *optional*. The 2.2 spec has now moved it from the ROM to the configuration space, but it's still *optional*.

What Is VPD?

The configuration registers present in a PCI function's configuration Header region (the first 16 dwords of its configuration space) provide the configuration software with quite a bit of information about the function. However, additional useful information such as

- a board's part number
- the EC (Engineering Change) level of a function
- the device's serial number
- an asset tag identifier

could be quite useful in a repair, tech support or asset management environments. If present, the VPD list provides this type of information.

Where Is the VPD Really Stored?

It is intended that the VPD would reside in a device such as a serial EEPROM associated with the PCI function. The configuration access mechanism described in the next section defines how this information would be accessed via the PCI function's VPD feature registers.

VPD On Cards vs. Embedded PCI Devices

Each add-in card may optionally contain VPD. If it's a multi-function card, only one function may contain VPD or each function may implement it. Embedded functions may or may not contain VPD.

How Is VPD Accessed?

Figure 19-14 on page 400 illustrates the configuration registers that indicate the presence of VPD information and permit the programmer to access it. The Capability ID of the VPD registers is 03h, while the registers used to access to the VPD data consists of the VPD Address and Data registers in conjunction with the one-bit Flag register. The programmer accesses the VPD information using the procedures described in the following two sections.

Reading VPD Data. Use the following procedure to read VPD data:

STEP 1. Using a PCI configuration write, write the dword-aligned VPD address into the Address register and simultaneously set the Flag bit to zero.

STEP 2. Hardware then reads the indicated dword from VPD storage and places the four bytes into the Data register. Upon completion of the operation, the hardware sets the Flag bit to one.

STEP 3. When software sees the Flag bit set to one by the hardware, it can then perform a PCI configuration read to read the four VPD bytes from the Data register.

If either the Address or Data registers are written to prior to hardware setting the Flag bit to one, the results of the read are unpredictable.

Writing VPD Data. Use the following procedure to write VPD data. Please note that only Read/Write VPD Data items may be written to.

STEP 1. Write four bytes of data into the Data register.

STEP 2. Write the dword-aligned VPD address into the Address register and simultaneously set the Flag bit to one.

STEP 3. When software detects that the Flag bit has been cleared to zero by hardware, the VPD write has been completed.

If either the Address or Data registers are written to prior to hardware clearing the Flag bit to zero, the results of the VPD write are unpredictable.

Rules That Apply To Both Read and Writes. The following rules apply to both VPD data reads and writes:

RULE 1. Once a VPD read or write has been initiated, writing to either the Address or Data registers prior to the point at which the hardware changes the state of the Flag bit yields unpredictable results.

RULE 2. Each VPD data read or write always encompasses all four bytes within the VPD dword indicated in the Address register.

RULE 3. The least-significant byte in the Data register corresponds to the least-significant byte in the indicated VPD dword.

RULE 4. The initial values in the Address and Data registers after reset are indeterminate.

RULE 5. Reading or writing data outside the scope of the overall VPD data structure is not allowed. The spec doesn't say what the result will be if you do it, so it is hardware design-specific.

RULE 6. The values contained in the VPD are only stored information and have no effect upon the device.

RULE 7. The two least-significant bits in the Address register must always be zero (i.e., it is illegal to specify an address that is not aligned on a dword address boundary).

Figure 19-14: VPD Capability Registers

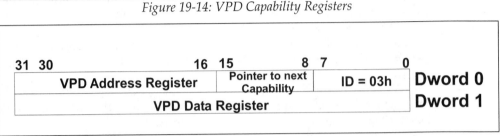

VPD Data Structure Made Up of Descriptors and Keywords

As mentioned earlier, the VPD actually consists of a data structure accessed using the VPD Address and Data registers. The individual data items that comprise the VPD data structure are themselves small data structures known as descriptors. The basic format of two of the descriptors used in the VPD was first defined in the version 1.0a *ISA Plug and Play* spec. For more information about this spec, refer to the MindShare book entitled *Plug and Play System Architecture* (published by Addison-Wesley). The two ISA-like descriptor types are:

- **Identifier String descriptor.** This descriptor contains the alphanumeric name of the card or embedded device. If the VPD is implemented, this descriptor is mandatory and is always the first one in the VPD. It is illustrated in Table 19-28 on page 402.
- **End Tag descriptor.** If the VPD is implemented, this descriptor is mandatory and is used to identify the end of VPD data structure. It's value is always 78h.

In addition to these two descriptors, the 2.2 spec has defined two new descriptor types referred to as:

- **VPD-R descriptor.** This descriptor type identifies the **start and** overall **length of** a **series of** one or more **read-only keywords** within the VPD data structure. The last keyword in the list of read-only keywords must be the Checksum keyword. This checksum encompasses the VPD from its first location to the end of the read-only area. A detailed description of this descriptor can be found in "VPD Read-Only Descriptor (VPD-R) and Keywords" on page 402.

- **VPD-W descriptor**. If used, this optional descriptor type is used to identify the **start and** overall **length of** the **read/write** descriptors within the VPD data structure. A detailed description of this descriptor can be found in "VPD Read/Write Descriptor (VPD-W) and Keywords" on page 405.

The basic format of the overall VPD data structure is illustrated in Table 19-27 on page 401. It has the following characteristics:

1. The VPD always **starts with** an **Identifier String descriptor**, followed by an optional list of one or more read-only VPD keywords.
2. The **list of read-only keywords** always begins with the VPD-R descriptor and ends with the Checksum keyword.
3. Immediately following the list of read-only keywords is an **optional list of read/write keywords**. If present, the read-write keyword list is prefaced with the VPD-W descriptor. Because the VPD read-write keywords can be altered, there is no checksum at the end of the read/write keywords.
4. The overall **VPD** data structure is **always terminated by** a special descriptor known as the **End Tag**. Its value is always 78h.

Table 19-27: Basic Format of VPD Data Structure

Typical Descriptor List	Comments
String Identifier Descriptor	Always the first entry.
Read-Only Descriptor	Heads the list of read-only keywords.
Read-Only Keyword	List of Read-Only keywords.
Read-Only Keyword	
Read-Only Keyword	
Checksum Keyword	
Read/Write Descriptor	Heads the list of read-write keywords.
Read/Write Keyword	List of Read/Write keywords.
Read/Write Keyword	
End Tag descriptor	Always used to indicate the end of the VPD. It's value is always 78h.

Table 19-28: Format of the Identifier String Tag

Byte	Description
0	Must be 82h.
1	Least-significant byte of identifier string length (the length encompasses bytes 3-through-n).
2	Most-significant byte of identifier string length (the length encompasses bytes 3-through-n).
3-through-n	ASCII name of function.

VPD Read-Only Descriptor (VPD-R) and Keywords

Table 19-29 on page 402 illustrates the format of the VPD-R descriptor. As mentioned earlier, this descriptor begins the list of one or more read-only keywords and indicates the length of the list. Each keyword is a minimum of four bytes in length and has the format illustrated in Table 19-30 on page 403. The read-only keywords currently-defined are listed in Table 19-31 on page 403.

Table 19-29: Format of the VPD-R Descriptor

Byte	Description
0	Must be 90h.
1	Least-significant byte of read-only keyword list length (the length encompasses bytes 3-through-n).
2	Most-significant byte of read-only keyword list length (the length encompasses bytes 3-through-n).
3-through-n	List of Read-Only keywords.

Table 19-30: General Format of a Read or a Read/Write Keyword Entry

Byte(s)	Description
0 and 1	ASCII Keyword (see Table 19-31 on page 403 and Table 19-35 on page 405).
2	Length of Keyword field (encompassing bytes 3-through-n).
3-through-n	Keyword data field.

Table 19-31: List of Read-Only VPD Keywords

ASCII Read-Only Keyword	Description of Keyword Data Field
PN	Device Part Number in ASCII.
EC	Engineering Change level (alphanumeric) of device in ASCII.
MN	Manufacturer ID in ASCII.
SN	Serial Number (alphanumeric) in ASCII.
Vx	Vendor-Specific field (alphanumeric) in ASCII. "x" can be any value 0-through-Z.
CP	Extended Capability. If present, this keyword indicates that the function implements an additional New Capability within its IO or memory space. See Table 19-32 on page 404 for a complete description.
RV	Checksum. See Table 19-33 on page 404 for complete description.

Table 19-32: Extended Capability (CP) Keyword Format

Byte	Description
0	New Capability ID.
1	Index of Base Address Register (value between 0 and 5) that points to space containing this capability.
2	Least-significant byte of offset within BAR's range where this New Capability's register set begins.
3	Most-significant byte of offset within BAR's range where this New Capability's register set begins.

Table 19-33: Format of Checksum Keyword

Byte	Description
0	Checksum from start of VPD up to and including this byte. Checksum is correct if sum of all bytes equals zero.
1	Reserved.
2	Reserved.
3-through-n	Reserved read-only space (as much as desired).

Is Read-Only Checksum Keyword Mandatory?

The spec doesn't say if the Checksum is mandatory, but it is the author's opinion that it is. In other words, even if the VPD contained no other read-only keywords, it must contain the VPD-R descriptor followed by the Checksum keyword. This provides the programmer with the checksum for the portion of the VPD that encompasses the String Identifier descriptor, the VPD-R descriptor and the Checksum keyword itself. In other words, it provides the checksum for everything other than the read-write portion of the VPD. It stands to reason the portion of the VPD that can be written to should not be included within the checksummed area.

VPD Read/Write Descriptor (VPD-W) and Keywords

The VPD may optionally contain a list of one or more read/write keyword fields. If present, this list begins with the VPD-W descriptor which indicates the start and length of the read/write keyword list. There is no checksum stored at the end of the read-write keyword list.

Table 19-34 on page 405 illustrates the format of the VPD-W descriptor and Table 19-35 on page 405 provides a list of the currently-defined read/write keyword fields.

Table 19-34: Format of the VPD-W Descriptor

Byte(s)	Description
0	Must be 91h
1	Least-significant byte of read/write keyword list length (the length encompasses bytes 3-through-n).
2	Most-significant byte of read/write keyword list length (the length encompasses bytes 3-through-n).
3-through-n	List of Read/Write keywords.

Table 19-35: List of Read/Write VPD Keywords

ASCII Read/Write Keyword	Description of Keyword Data Field
Vx	Vendor-Specific (alphanumeric in ASCII). "x" may be any character from 0-through-Z.
YA	Asset Tag Identifier. ASCII alphanumeric code supplied by system owner.
Yx	System-specific alphanumeric ASCII item. "x" may be any character from 0-through-9 and B-through-Z.
RW	Remaining read/write area. Identifies the unused portion of the r/w space. The description in the spec is very confusing and defies interpretation by the author (maybe I'm just being thick-headed).

Example VPD List

Table 19-36 on page 406 contains the sample VPD data structure provided in the spec. The author has made a few minor corrections, so it doesn't match the one in the spec exactly. In the draft version of the spec, the 3rd row, last column contained "ABC Super..." etc. and the offset in VPD-R Tag row was wrong. I fixed it by adjusting the offsets in the 1st column. It was fixed in the final version of the 2.2 spec by changing the Product Name to "ABCD Super...".

Table 19-36: Example VPD List

Offset (decimal)	Item	Value
0	String ID Tag	82h
1-2	String length (32d)	0020h (32d)
3-34	Product name in ASCII	"ABC Super-Fast Widget Controller"
	Start of VPD Read-Only Keyword Area	
35	VPD-R Tag. Identifies start and length of read-only keyword area within VPD.	90h
36-37	Length of read-only keyword area.	5Ah (90d)
38-39	Read-only Part Number keyword.	"PN"
40	Length of Part Number data field.	08h (8d)
41-48	Part Number in ASCII.	"6181682A"
49-50	Read-Only Engineering Change (EC) level keyword.	"EC"
51	Length of EC data field.	0Ah (10d)
52-61	EC data field.	"4950262536"
62-63	Read-only Serial Number keyword.	"SN"
64	Serial Number length field.	08h (8d)
65-72	Serial Number data field.	"00000194"

Table 19-36: Example VPD List (Continued)

Offset (decimal)	Item	Value
73-74	Read-only Manufacturer ID keyword.	"MN"
75	Manufacturer ID length field.	04h (4d)
76-79	Manufacturer ID	"1037"
80-81	Read-only Checksum keyword.	"RV"
82	Length of reserved read-only VPD area.	2Ch (44d)
83	Checksum for bytes 0-through-83.	Checksum.
84-127	Reserved read-only area.	
Start of VPD Read/Write Keyword Area		
128	VPD-W Tag	91h
129-130	Length of read/write keyword area.	007Eh (126d)
131-132	Read/Write Vendor-Specific Keyword.	"V1"
133	Vendor-specific data field length.	05h (5d)
134-138	Vendor-specific data field.	"65A01"
139-140	System-specific keyword.	"Y1"
141	System-specific data field length.	0Dh (13d)
142-154	System-specific data field.	"Error Code 26"
155-156	Remaining Read/Write area keyword.	"RW"
157	Length of remaining read/write area.	61h (97d)
158-254	Remainder of read/write area.	reserved.
255	End Tag	78h

User-Definable Features (UDF)

THE UDF WAS ADDED IN THE 2.1 SPEC AND HAS BEEN DELETED IN THE 2.2 SPEC. THE FOLLOWING DESCRIPTION IS ONLY INCLUDED AS HISTORICAL INFORMATION.

One of the major goals of PCI is to provide automatic detection and configuration of any new subsystem installed in the system. The configuration software has no problem detecting a function and in allocating system resources to it (memory space, IO space, Interrupt Line, Latency Timer, arbitration priority level, etc.). However, some configurable aspects of certain subsystems cannot be automatically configured when the subsystem is first detected. It is necessary to provide the end user with a list of questions to be answered by the end user. An example would be a network controller card that must be assigned a network node ID. Another would be a token ring card that must be told what the token ring speed is. When the subsystem is first installed in the system, the end user must be provided with a menu of these selectable options and the user choices must then be saved in non-volatile memory to be used at startup time. Each time the machine is restarted, the configuration software reads the selections from non-volatile memory and writes them into function-specific configuration registers associated with the function.

The user choices are supplied in a file stored in the root directory of a 1.44MB DOS-formatted diskette. The file is referred to as a PCI configuration file, or PCF. Please note that PCF files have been deleted along with the UDF in the 2.2 spec. The file name takes the form XXXXYYYY.PCF and adheres to the following format:

- **XXXX** is either the subsystem Vendor ID from the function's subsystem Vendor ID configuration register, or, if the subsystem Vendor ID register isn't implemented, the Vendor ID from the Vendor ID configuration register.
- **YYYY** is either the subsystem ID from the function's subsystem ID configuration register, or, if the subsystem ID register isn't implemented, the Device ID from the Device ID configuration register.

The PCI function indicates to the configuration software that it has a PCF by hardwiring the UDF Supported bit in its PCI configuration Status register to one. When the configuration software detects the new subsystem and recognizes that PCF has been supplied on diskette, it prompts the end user to insert the diskette into the system. The PCF is then read by the system-specific configuration utility (e.g., the EISA configuration utility). The end user is presented with a series of one or more menus related to the User Definable Features listed in the file. After the user has made the appropriate selections, the selections are stored in non-volatile memory along with the function-specific configuration registers they must be written to each time the system is powered up.

The specification recommends that the system designer supply sufficient non-volatile memory to store 32 bytes of user-defined configuration bytes for each function that could be added to the system. The number of bytes of storage is calculated by multiplying the number of add-in card connectors (system-dependent) times the maximum number of functions per card (eight) times 32 bytes of configuration information per function. Conversely, subsystem designers should design a function so as to require no more than 32 bytes of user-definable configuration data.

The PCF is in ASCII text. The format of the information in the PCF is defined in the 2.1 specification and bears a striking resemblance to the macro language used to write EISA configuration files (the author hasn't compared all aspects of the language, but at first glance it looks identical). The specification contains a definition of the language and the author will not duplicate this information here. It would be a gratuitous use of white space to fatten a book I'm only too glad to finish.

The specification contains the following rules/guidelines regarding the PCF:

- All selections cited in the PCF must target function-specific configuration registers, not registers in the function's configuration Header.
- The PCF cannot be used to select system resources (e.g., Interrupt Line, memory or IO assignments, expansion ROM assignments).
- The function can use the information written to its function-specific configuration registers directly, or may require that the device driver associated with the function copy the contents of the function-specific configuration registers into IO or memory-mapped IO registers associated with the function.
- The function can alias its function-specific configuration registers into its IO or memory-mapped IO registers.
- If any of the configuration information must be accessible after configuration completes, the information must be available through a mechanism other than the configuration registers (e.g., from IO or memory-mapped IO registers).

20 *Expansion ROMs*

The Previous Chapter

The previous chapter provided a detailed description of the configuration register format and usage for all PCI devices other than PCI-to-PCI bridges and CardBus bridges.

This Chapter

This chapter provides a detailed description of device ROMs associated with PCI devices. This includes the following topics:

- device ROM detection.
- internal code/data format.
- shadowing.
- initialization code execution.
- interrupt hooking.

The Next Chapter

The next chapter provides an introduction to the PCI expansion card and connector definition. It covers card and connector types, 5V and 3.3V operability, shared slots, and pinout definition.

ROM Purpose—Device Can Be Used In Boot Process

In order to boot the OS into memory, the system needs three devices:

- A mass storage device to load the OS from. This is sometimes referred to as the **IPL** (Initial Program Load) **device** and is typically an IDE or a SCSI hard drive.
- A display adapter to enable progress messages to be displayed during the boot process. In this context, this is typically referred to as the **output device**.
- A keyboard to allow the user to interact with the machine during the boot process. In this context, this is typically referred to as the **input device**.

The OS must locate three devices that fall into these categories and **must also locate a device driver associated with each of the devices**. Remember that the OS hasn't been booted into memory yet and therefore hasn't loaded any loadable device drivers into memory from disk! This is the main reason that device ROMs exist. It contains a device driver that permits the device to be used during the boot process.

ROM Detection

When the configuration software is configuring a PCI function, it determines if a function-specific ROM exists by checking to see if the designer has implemented an Expansion ROM Base Address Register (refer to Figure 20-2 on page 414).

As described in "Base Address Registers (BARs)" on page 378, the programmer writes all ones (with the exception of bit zero, to prevent the enabling of the ROM address decoder; see Figure 20-1 on page 413) to the Expansion ROM Base Address Register and then reads it back. If a value of zero is returned, then the register is not implemented and there isn't an expansion ROM associated with the device.

On the other hand, the ability to set any bits to ones indicates the presence of the Expansion ROM Base Address Register. This may or may not indicate the presence of a device ROM. Although the address decoder and a socket may exist for a device ROM, the socket may not be occupied at present. The programmer determines the presence of the device ROM by:

- assigning a base address to the register's Base Address field,
- enabling its decoder (by setting bit 0 in the register to one),
- setting the Memory Space bit in the function's Command register,
- and then attempting to read the first two locations from the ROM.

If the first two locations contain the ROM signature—AA55h—then the ROM is present.

Figure 20-1 on page 413 illustrates the format of the Expansion ROM Base Address Register. Assume that the register returns a value of FFFE0000h when read back after writing all ones to it. Bit 17 is the least-significant bit that was successfully changed to a one and has a binary-weighted value of 128K. This indicates that it is a 128KB ROM decoder and bits [24:17] within the Base Address field are writable. The programmer now writes a 32-bit start address into the register and sets bit zero to one to enable its ROM address decoder. In addition to setting this bit to one, the programmer must also set the Memory Space bit in the function's configuration Command register to a one. The function's ROM address decoder is then enabled and the ROM (if present) can be accessed. The maximum ROM decoder size permitted by the specification is 16MB, dictating that bits [31:25] must be hardwired to one.

The programmer then performs a read from the first two locations of the ROM and checks for a return value of AA55h. If this pattern is not received, the ROM is not present. The programmer disables the ROM address decoder (by clearing bit zero of the Expansion ROM Base Address Register to zero). If AA55h is received, the ROM exists and a device driver code image must be copied into main memory and its initialization code must be executed. This topic is covered in the sections that follow.

Figure 20-1: Expansion ROM Base Address Register Bit Assignment

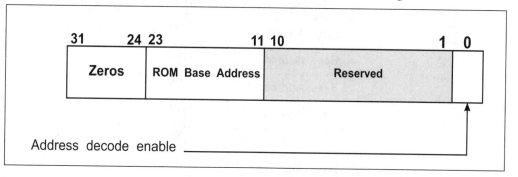

Figure 20-2: Header Type Zero Configuration Register Format

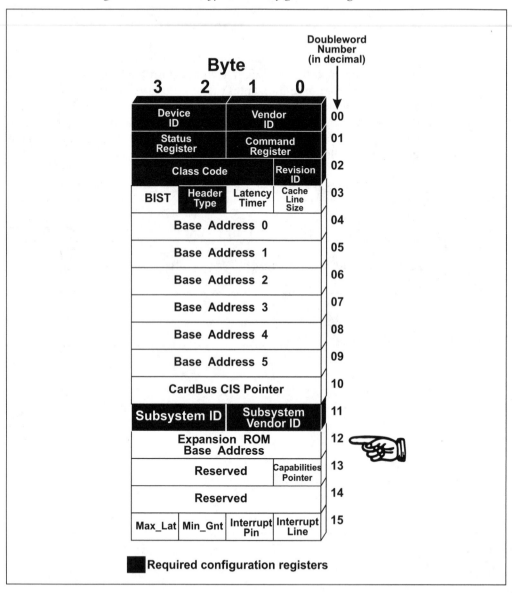

ROM Shadowing Required

The PCI specification requires that device ROM code is never executed in place (i.e., from the ROM). It must be copied to main memory. This is referred to as "shadowing" the ROM code. This requirement exists for two reasons:

- ROM access time is typically quite slow, resulting in poor performance whenever the ROM code is fetched for execution.
- Once the initialization portion of the device driver in the ROM has been executed, it can be discarded and the code image in main memory can be shortened to include only the code necessary for run-time operation. The portion of main memory allocated to hold the initialization portion of the code can be freed up, allowing more efficient use of main memory.

Once the presence of the device ROM has been established (see the previous section), the configuration software must copy a code image into main memory and then disable the ROM address decoder (by clearing bit zero of the Expansion ROM Base Address Register to zero). In a non-PC environment, the area of memory the code image is copied to could be anywhere in the 4GB space. The specification for that environment may define a particular area.

In a PC environment, the ROM code image must be copied into main memory into the range of addresses historically associated with device ROMs: 000C0000h through 000DFFFFh. If the Class Code indicates that this is the VGA's device ROM, its code image must be copied into memory starting at location 000C0000h.

The next section defines the format of the information in the ROM and how the configuration software determines which code image (yes, there can be more than one device driver) to load into main memory.

ROM Content

Multiple Code Images

The PCI specification permits the inclusion of more than one code image in a PCI device ROM. Each code image would contain a copy of the device driver in a specific machine code, or in interpretive code (explained later). The configuration software can then scan through the images in the ROM and select the one best suited to the system processor type. The ROM might contain drivers for various types of devices made by this device's vendor. The code image copied into main memory should match up with the function's ID. To this end, each code image also contains:

- the Vendor ID and Device ID. This is useful for matching up the driver with a function that has a vendor/device match.
- the Class Code. This is useful if the driver is a Class driver that can work with any compatible device within a Class/SubClass. For more information, see "Class Code Register" on page 356.

Figure 20-3 on page 417 illustrates the concept of multiple code images embedded within a device ROM. Each image must start on an address evenly-divisible by 512. Each image consists of two data structures, as well as a run-time code image and an initialization code image. The configuration software interrogates the data structures in order to determine if this is the image it will copy to main memory and use. If it is, the configuration software:

STEP 1. Copies the image to main memory,

STEP 2. Executes the initialization code,

STEP 3. If the initialization code shortens the length indicator in the data structure, the configuration software deallocates the area of main memory that held the initialization portion of the driver (in Figure 20-4 on page 419, notice that the initialization portion of the driver is always at the end of the image).

STEP 4. The area of main memory containing the image is write-protected.

The sections that follow provide a detailed discussion of the code image format and the initialization process.

Figure 20-3: Multiple Code Images Contained In One Device ROM

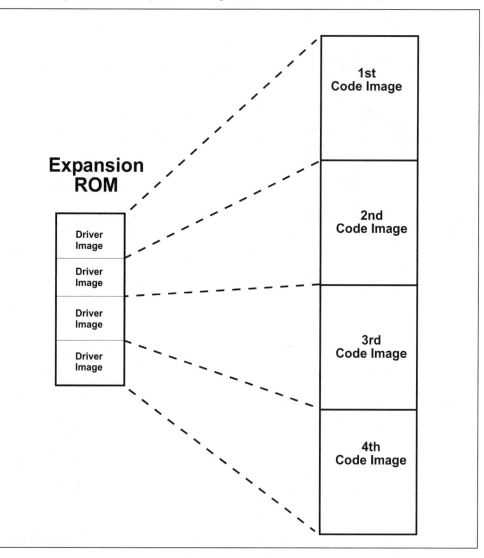

Format of a Code Image

General

Figure 20-4 on page 419 illustrates the format of a single code image. The image consists of the following components:

- **ROM Header.** Described in "ROM Header Format" on page 419. Also contains a 16-bit pointer to the ROM data structure.
- **ROM Data Structure.** Described in "ROM Data Structure Format" on page 421. Contains information about the device and the image.
- **Run-time code.** This is the portion of the device driver that remains in main memory after the OS loads and that remains available for execution on an on-going basis.
- **Initialization code.** This is the portion of the device driver that is called and executed immediately after loading the driver into main memory. It completes the setup of the device and enables it for normal operation. It must always reside at the end of the image so it can be abbreviated or discarded after its initial execution at system startup.

Figure 20-4: Code Image Format

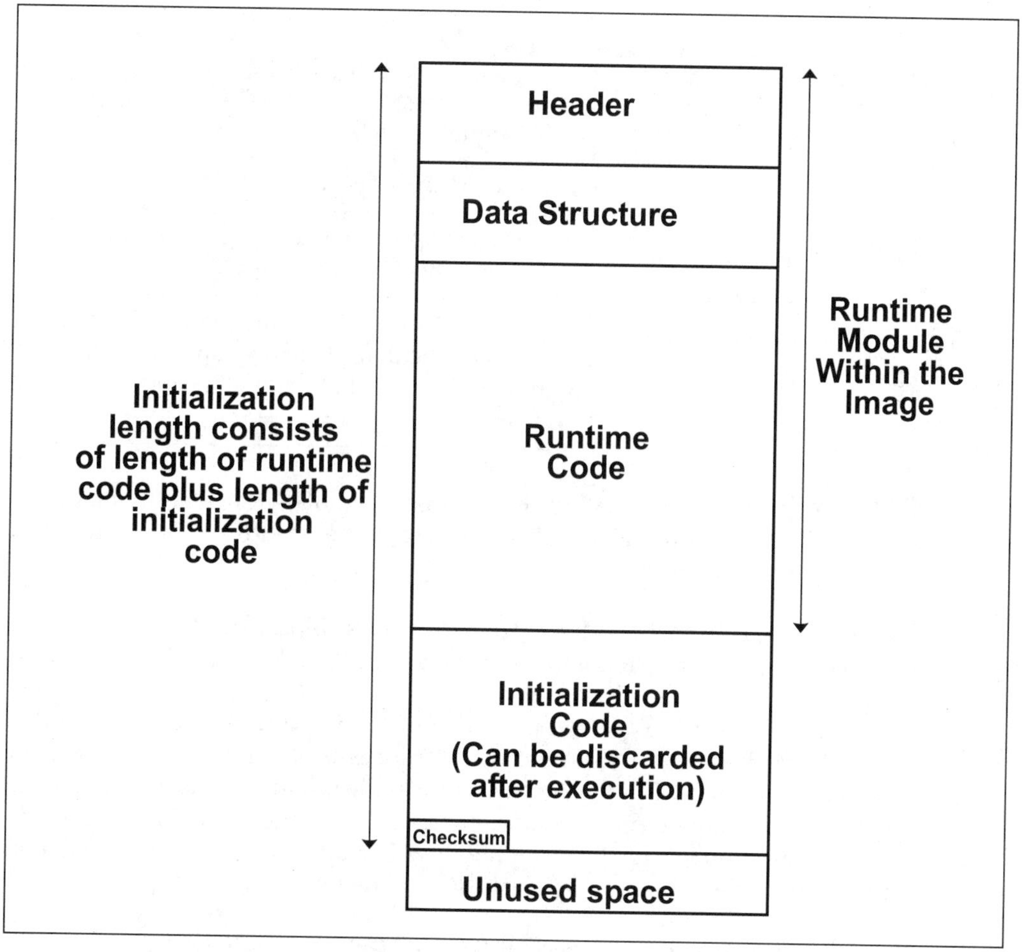

ROM Header Format

The ROM Header must be located at the very start of each image within the ROM (so a better name for it might be the Code Image Header). Table 20-1 on page 420 defines the format of the Header and the purpose of each field is further defined in the paragraphs that follow. The offset specified in the table is the offset from the first location in this ROM code image.

Table 20-1: PCI Expansion ROM Header Format

Offset	Length (bytes)	Value	Description
00h	1d	55h	ROM signature byte one.
01h	1d	AAh	ROM signature byte two.
02h - 17h	22d	n	Reserved for processor architecture unique data. See Table 20-2 on page 420.
18h - 19h	2d	n	Pointer to PCI Data Structure. Since this is a 16-bit pointer, the data structure can be anywhere within 64K forward of the first location in this code image.

ROM Signature. The first two bytes must contain AA55h, identifying this as a device ROM. This has always been the signature used for a device ROM in any PC-compatible machine.

Processor/Architecture Unique Data. This block of 22d locations is reserved for processor/architecture unique data. For PC-compatible environments and images that identify the code as Intel x86-compatible in the Code Type field (see "Code Type" on page 424) of the ROM data structure, the PCI specification defines the structure of the processor/architecture unique data area in the image Header. For non-PC compatible environments, the content of this structure is architecture-specific. Table 20-2 on page 420 defines the fields that must be supplied for PC-compatibility. The offset specified in the table is the offset from the first location of this ROM code image.

Table 20-2: PC-Compatible Processor/Architecture Data Area In ROM Header

Offset	Length (in bytes)	Description
02h	1	Overall size of the image (in 512 byte increments).
03h-05h	3	Entry point for the initialization code. Contains a three-byte, x86 short jump to the initialization code entry point. The POST performs a far call to this location to initialize the device.

Table 20-2: PC-Compatible Processor/Architecture Data Area In ROM Header (Continued)

Offset	Length (in bytes)	Description
06h-17h	18d	Reserved (for application-unique data, such as the copyright notice).

Pointer to ROM Data Structure. This is the 16-bit offset (in little-endian format) to the ROM data structure within this code image. It is an offset from the start address of this code image. Because this is only a 16-bit offset from the first location of this code image, the data structure must reside within 64KB forward of the first location of this code image.

ROM Data Structure Format

As stated earlier, the ROM Data Structure associated with each code image must reside within the first 64KB of each code image. The Data Structure must reside within the run-time code (assuming there is one). It's possible that a ROM may not contain a device driver for the device, but only an initialization module that tests the device and gets it ready for normal operation. If there isn't a run-time code module, the Data Structure must reside within the initialization code. The Data Structure's format is defined in Table 20-3 on page 421 and the purpose of each field is further defined in the sections that follow the table.

Table 20-3: PCI Expansion ROM Data Structure Format

Offset	Length	Description
00h	4	**Signature** consisting of the ASCII string "PCIR" (PCI ROM).
04h	2	**Vendor ID.** This is a duplication of the Vendor ID found in the function's configuration Vendor ID register (see "Vendor ID Register" on page 354). The ROM may contain multiple code images of the desired Code Type (e.g., x86 code), but they may be for different devices produced by the same (or a different) vendor. In order to ensure that it loads the correct one, the configuration software compares the Vendor ID, Device ID, and Class Code values contained in this Data Structure to those found in the function's Vendor ID, Device ID, and Class Code configuration registers.

Table 20-3: PCI Expansion ROM Data Structure Format (Continued)

	Offset	Length	Description
	06h	2	**Device ID.** This is a duplication of the Device ID found in the function's configuration Device ID register (see "Device ID Register" on page 354). See explanation of Vendor ID field in this table.
2.2	08h	2	*POINTER TO VITAL PRODUCT DATA. THE POINTER TO THE OPTIONAL VPD IS PROVIDED AS AN OFFSET FROM THE START LOCATION OF THE CODE IMAGE. THE 2.2 SPEC HAS REDEFINED THIS AS A RESERVED BIT FIELD AND THE OPTIONAL VPD (IF PRESENT) HAS BEEN MOVED TO THE DEVICE'S CONFIGURATION REGISTERS. REFER TO "VITAL PRODUCT DATA (VPD) CAPABILITY" ON PAGE 397.*
	0Ah	2	PCI **Data Structure Length** in bytes, little-endian format.
	0Ch	1	PCI **Data Structure Revision.** The Data Structure format shown in this table is revision zero (in both revision 2.0 and 2.1).
	0Dh	3	**Class Code.** This is a duplication of the Class Code found in the function's configuration Class Code register (see "Class Code Register" on page 356). See explanation of Vendor ID field in this table.
	10h	2	**Image length.** Code image length in increments of 512 bytes (little-endian format).
	12h	2	**Revision level of code/data** in this code image.
2.2	14h	1	*CODE TYPE. SEE "CODE TYPE" ON PAGE 424.*
	15h	1	**Indicator byte.** Bit 7 indicates whether this is the last code image in the ROM (1 = last image). Bits [6:0] are reserved and must be zero.
	16h	2	**Reserved.**

ROM Signature. This unique signature identifies the start of the PCI Data Structure. The "**P**" is stored at offset 00h, the "**C**" at offset 01h, etc. "**PCIR**" stands for PCI ROM.

Vendor ID field in ROM data structure. As stated in Table 20-3 on page 421, the configuration software does not select a code image to load into system memory unless it is the correct Code Type and the Vendor ID, Device ID, and Class Code in the image's Data Structure match the function's respective configuration registers. The ROM may contain code images for variations on the device, either from the same vendor or supplied by different vendors.

Device ID in ROM data structure. Refer to the description of the Vendor ID field in the previous section.

Pointer to Vital Product Data (VPD). THE 2.2 SPEC DEFINES THIS AS A RESERVED FIELD AND THE OPTIONAL VPD (IF PRESENT) HAS BEEN MOVED TO THE DEVICE'S CONFIGURATION REGISTERS. REFER TO "VITAL PRODUCT DATA (VPD) CAPABILITY" ON PAGE 397. THE FOLLOWING DESCRIPTION IS ONLY PROVIDED AS HISTORICAL INFORMATION.

2.2

The offset (from the start of the code image) of the Vital Product Data area. The offset is stored in little-endian format. Because the offset is only 16-bits in size, the Vital Product Data area must reside within the first 64KB of the image. A value of zero indicates that the image contains no Vital Product Data. The revision 2.0 specification said that the pointer is required, but the 2.1 specification has removed that requirement. If no device ROM is present on a device other than the one containing the VPD, there is only one image and it contains the VPD. If multiple code images are present, each image will contain VPD for that device. The VPD data that describes the device may be duplicated in each code image, but the VPD that pertains to software may be different for each code image.

A description of the pre-2.2 method can be found in "Vital Product Data (VPD)" on page 431.

PCI Data Structure Length. This 16-bit value is stored in the little-endian format. It defines the length (in bytes) of the PCI Data Structure for this image.

PCI Data Structure Revision. This 8-bit field reflects the revision of the image's Data Structure. The currently-defined data structure format (as of revision 2.2 of the spec) is revision zero.

Class Code. The 24-bit class code field contains the same information as the Class Code configuration register within the device's configuration header. The configuration software examines this field to determine if this is a VGA-compatible interface. If it is, the ROM code image must be copied into system memory starting at location 000C0000h (for compatibility). Otherwise, it will typically be copied into the C0000h-through-DFFFFh region in a PC-compatible machine. Also refer to "Vendor ID field in ROM data structure" on page 423.

Image Length. This two-byte field indicates the length of the entire code image (refer to Figure 20-4 on page 419) in increments of 512 bytes. It is stored in little-endian format.

Revision Level of Code/Data. This two-byte field reflects the revision level of the code within the image.

Code Type. This one-byte field identifies the type of code contained in this image as either executable machine language for a particular processor/architecture, or as interpretive code.

- Code Type 00h = Intel **x86** (IBM PC-AT compatible) executable code.
- Code Type 01h = **OpenBoot** interpretive code. The Open Firmware standard (reference IEEE standard 1275-1994) defines the format and usage of the interpretive code. A basic description of the Open Firmware standard can be found in "Introduction to Open Firmware" on page 427.
- *02H INDICATES HP PA/RISC EXECUTABLE CODE (ADDED IN 2.2 SPEC).*

2.2

The values from 03h-through-FFh are reserved.

Indicator Byte. Only bit seven is currently defined.

- 0 = not last code image in ROM.
- 1 = last code image in ROM.

Bits [6:0] are reserved.

Execution of Initialization Code

Prior to discovery of the device's ROM the configuration software has accomplished the following:

- Assigned one or more memory and/or IO ranges to the function by programming its Base Address Registers (see "Base Address Registers (BARs)" on page 378).

- If the device is interrupt-driven, the interrupt routing information has been programmed into the device's Interrupt Line register (see "Interrupt Line Register" on page 388).
- In addition, if the UDF bit (*THIS BIT WAS IN THE 2.1 SPEC AND HAS BEEN DELETED FROM THE 2.2 SPEC*) was set in the device's configuration Status register, the user has been prompted to insert the diskette containing the PCI configuration file, or PCF, and the user selected any configuration options available from the file.
- Finally, the configuration software copied a code image from the ROM into RAM memory.

2.2

After the appropriate code image has been copied into system memory, the device ROM's address decoder is disabled. The configuration software must keep the area of RAM (the image resides in) read/writable. The configuration software then executes the following sequence:

STEP 1. Refer to Figure 20-5 on page 427. The software calls the initialization module within the image (through location 3h in the image), supplying it with three parameters in the AX register: the bus number, device number and function number of the function associated with the ROM:

- The 8-bit bus number is supplied in AH,
- the device number is supplied in the upper five bits of AL,
- and the function number in the lower three bits of AL.

It's necessary to supply the initialization code with this information so that it can determine how the function has been configured. For example, what IO and/or memory address range the configuration software has allocated to the device (via its base address registers), what input on the interrupt controller the function's interrupt pin has been routed to, etc.

STEP 2. The initialization code then issues a call to the PCI BIOS (see "Calling PCI BIOS" on page 680), supplying the bus number, device number, and function number as input parameters and requesting the contents of the function's Base Address Registers. Armed with this information, the initialization code can now communicate with the function's IO register set to initialize the device and prepare it for normal operation.

STEP 3. If the ROM image has a device-specific Interrupt Service Routine embedded within the run-time module, it reads from the device's Interrupt Line configuration register to determine which system interrupt request input on the interrupt controller the function's PCI interrupt pin has been routed to by the configuration software. Using this routing information, the initialization code knows which entry in the interrupt table in memory must be hooked (for more information, refer to "Hooking the Interrupt" on page 239). It first reads the pointer currently stored in that interrupt table entry and saves it within the body of the run-time portion of the image. It then stores the pointer to the interrupt service routine embedded within the run-time module of the code image into that interrupt table entry. In this way, it maintains the integrity of the interrupt chain. Since the area of system memory it has been copied into must be kept read/writable until the initialization code completes execution, the initialization code has no problem saving the pointer that it read from the interrupt table entry before hooking it to its own service routine.

STEP 4. The ROM image may also have a device-specific BIOS routine embedded within the run-time module of the code image. In this case, it needs to hook another interrupt table entry to this BIOS routine. Once again, it reads and saves the pointer currently stored in that interrupt table entry and then stores the pointer to the BIOS routine embedded within the run-time module of the code image. In this way, it maintains the integrity of the interrupt chain.

STEP 5. Since the area of system memory it resides in must be kept read/writable until the initialization code completes execution, the initialization code can adjust the code image length (in location 2h of the image). Very typically, at the completion of initialization code execution the programmer will adjust the image length field to encompass the area from the image's start through the end of the run-time code. The initialization code is only typically only executed once and is then discarded. It must also recompute a new Checksum and store it at the end of the run-time code. If it sets the image length to zero, it doesn't need to recompute the image checksum and update it. When it returns control to the configuration software, a length of zero would indicate that the driver will not be used for some reason (perhaps a problem was detected during the setup of the device) and all of the memory it occupies can be deallocated and reused for something else.

STEP 6. Once the initialization code has completed execution, it executes a return to the system software that called it.

The configuration software then takes two final actions:

STEP 1. It interrogates the image size (at offset 2h in the image) to determine if it was altered. If it has, the configuration software adjusts the amount of memory allocated to the image to make more efficient use of memory. The image is typically shorter than it was.

STEP 2. Write-protects the area of main memory the image resides in. This will keep the OS from using the area after it takes control of the machine.

The *ISA Plug-and-Play* specification refers to the PCI method of writing device ROM code and handling its detection, shadowing, and initialization, as the *DDIM (Device Driver Initialization Model)*. That specification stresses that this is the model that all new device ROMs for other buses (e.g., ISA, EISA, Micro Channel, etc.) should adhere to.

Figure 20-5: AL Contents On Entry To Initialization Code

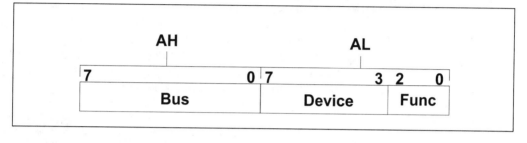

Introduction to Open Firmware

Introduction

The IEEE standard 1275-1994 entitled *Standard for Boot (Initialization, Configuration) Firmware Core Requirements and Practices* addresses two areas of concern regarding the boot process:

- The very first section in this chapter described the basic rationale for including a device ROM in the design of a device—it provides a **device driver** that allows the OS boot program **to use** the device **during** the **OS boot** process. That raises the question of what language to write device driver in. This is one of the two major areas addressed by the OpenBoot standard. It is the one that the PCI spec is concerned with.
- After the OS is booted into memory, the BIOS passes control to it. If it's a Plug-and-Play capable OS, it would be nice if the BIOS would **pass** a **pointer to** the OS that points to a **data structure** that defines all of the devices that the OS has at its disposal. The OS could then traverse this data structure, determine the current state of all devices, and manage them for the remainder of the power-up session. In order for this to work, the exact format of this data structure must be standardized and understood by both the BIOS that builds it and the OS that subsequently takes ownership of it. This is the other major area addressed by the OpenBoot standard.

These two areas are discussed in more detail in the two sections that follow. It should be noted that this is only intended as an introduction to this standard. There's a lot more to it than is covered here: the standard is approximately 300 pages in length, 8.5" x 11" in size. A detailed discussion of Open Firmware is outside the scope of this book.

Universal Device Driver Format

Historically, all of the PC-compatible machines marketed in the past have been based on Intel x86 processors. When writing ROM code for an add-in subsystem on an ISA, EISA or Micro Channel card, it was a simple decision that the device driver image to be stored in the ROM would be an x86 machine language code image.

A number of system vendors have created systems incorporating PCI and based on processors other than the x86 processor family. These machines would take a substantial performance hit when executing expansion ROM code that isn't written in the processor's native machine language (i.e., x86 code is "foreign" to PowerPC and other types of non-Intel compatible processors). They would be forced to emulate the x86 code, an inherently inefficient solution.

Rather than writing an add-in device's ROM code in machine language native to a particular processor, the subsystem designer can write the ROM code in Fcode (tokenized Forth code) based on the Open Firmware specification, IEEE 1275-1994. In other words, the device driver is written in the high-order language Forth.

The Open Firmware would consist of two main components:

- The system BIOS contains the Fcode interpreter and possibly an individual Fcode device driver associated with each of the embedded subsystems that the system Open Firmware is already cognizant of.
- Each add-in subsystem would hopefully contain an Open Firmware Fcode image.

The Open Firmware language is based on the Forth programming language. The ROM code would be written in Forth source code (in ASCII text). The ASCII-based source code is then supplied as input to a "tokenizer" program. The tokenizer processes the ASCII source code into a series of compressed commands, known as Fcode. As an example, an entire line of ASCII source code might be reduced to a single byte that represents the Forth command, only in a much more compact form.

The system BIOS that "discovered" the ROM (as described earlier in this chapter), incorporates an interpreter that converts the Fcode byte stream read from the ROM into machine language instructions specific to the system's processor.

The programmer only has to write this one universal version of the driver and any machine with an Fcode interpreter built into the system BIOS can then utilize this driver with the device during the boot process (allowing the device to be selected as the Input, Output, or IPL boot device). Obviously, executing a driver written in interpretive code would yield less than optimum performance. However, once the OS is booted into memory it then loads native code drivers for the three boot devices to replace the Fcode drivers. Performance of the devices is then optimized.

The 2.2 PCI specification refers the reader to another document, *PCI Bus Binding to IEEE 1275-1994*, for implementation of Open Firmware in a PCI-based machine. This document is available using anonymous FTP to the machine playground.sun.com with the file name

/pub/p1275/bindings/postscript/PCI.ps.

Passing Resource List To Plug-and-Play OS

BIOS Calls Bus Enumerators For Different Bus Environments

A machine architecture can contain many different device environments. Examples would be PCI, CardBus, EISA, Plug-and-Play ISA, etc. The methods that must be used to access the configuration registers associated with each of these different device types are very different from each other. In addition, the layout and format of their configuration registers are quite different as well.

The BIOS includes a separate, bus-specific program for each of these environments. This program is frequently referred to as a **Bus Enumerator**. The Bus Enumerator knows:

- how to access the configuration registers within devices of its specific type (e.g., PCI devices).
- how to "discover" devices within its environment. For example, in a PCI environment, the programmer reads the Vendor ID from a PCI function's Vendor ID register. Any value other than FFFFh represents a valid ID, while FFFFh indicates that no function resides at the currently-addressed location.
- how to probe the device's configuration registers to discover the device's resource requirements.
- how to allocate selected resources to the device.

The system BIOS must call the Bus Enumerators for each of the bus environments supported in the platform. When a specific Enumerator is called, it discovers all of the devices within its target environment, discovers the resources each requires, and allocates non-conflicting resources to each. It does not, however, enable the devices. The Enumerator builds a data structure in memory that list all devices of its type that were found. It then passes a pointer to the start of that data structure back to the system BIOS.

When the system BIOS has called each of the Bus Enumerators for the different environments, it now has a list of pointers to the various, bus-specific data structures that list all of the devices that it has to work with.

BIOS Selects Boot Devices and Finds Drivers For Them

The system BIOS would then scan the data structures to locate an Input device, an Output device, and an IPL device to use in booting the OS into memory. In order to use each of these devices during the boot process, it would also require a device driver for each of them. The drivers would either be embedded within the BIOS itself or within device ROMs discovered with each of the devices.

For each of the three boot devices, the BIOS would then:

- call the initialization code within the device driver. The initialization code would then complete the preparation of the device for use.
- The BIOS would then set the appropriate bits in its configuration Command register (e.g., Memory Space, IO Space, Bus Master, etc.) to enable the device and bring it on-line.

BIOS Boots Plug-and-Play OS and Passes Pointer To It

The system BIOS then uses the three devices to boot the OS into memory and passes control to the OS. It also passes the OS a pointer that points to the head of the list of data structures that identify all of the devices that the OS has to work with.

OS Locates and Loads Drivers and Calls Init Code In each

Note that *Init code* refers to the Initialization code portion of the driver. The OS then locates the disk-based drivers for each device and loads them into memory one-by-one. As it loads each driver, it then calls its initialization code entry point and the driver completes the device-specific setup of the device and brings the device on-line. The machine is now up and running and the OS manages the system devices from this point forward.

Vital Product Data (VPD)

Moved From ROM to Configuration Space in 2.2   2.2

PRIOR TO THE 2.2 SPEC, THE VPD INFORMATION (IF PRESENT) WAS LOCATED WITHIN THE PCI DEVICE'S DEVICE ROM. THE 2.2 SPEC HAS REDEFINED THE LOCATION AND FORMAT OF THE VPD. A COMPLETE DESCRIPTION OF THE NEW LOCATION AND FORMAT CAN FOUND IN "VITAL PRODUCT DATA (VPD) CAPABILITY" ON PAGE 397.

The following section is only provided as historical background and describes how VPD was implemented in 2.1-compliant devices.

VPD Implementation in 2.1 Spec

If present, the VPD is a data structure that identifies items such as hardware, software, and microcode within a system. It provides the configuration software and/or operating system with information on field replaceable units (FRUs), such as part number, serial number, etc. The VPD also provides a method for storing performance and failure data related to a device that is being monitored. Although the VPD is optional, designers are urged to implement it. The presence of the VPD permits a system vendor to implement processes to verify the completeness of a hardware order (in a build-to-order manufacturing environment). The presence of the VPD also permits the device vendor to obtain performance and failure analysis data on their product in the field. VPD also enhances the ability of technical support to ascertain the products that populate a machine.

There are three types of fields within the VPD: recommended, conditionally recommended, and additional fields. If VPD is included, the recommended fields should be included. The conditionally recommended and additional fields may be present (based on the type of device).

Data Structure

The VPD consists of large and small resource descriptors as defined in the version 1.0a Plug and Play specification (refer to the MindShare book entitled *Plug and Play System Architecture*). The VPD therefore consists of a series of tagged data structures (i.e., descriptors).

The Plug and Play descriptor types that are used in the VPD are:

- small Compatible Device ID descriptor
- small Vendor-Defined descriptor
- small End descriptor
- large Identifier String descriptor
- large Vendor-Defined descriptor

The 2.1 PCI specification defines a new large descriptor type for the VPD and it is called the VPD descriptor. It has the format defined in Table 20-4 on page 432:

Table 20-4: VPD Descriptor Format

Byte	Description
0	90h (bit 7=1 indicates large descriptor type, 10h in [6:0] indicates start of the VPD).
0 to1	Overall length of the VPD in bytes.
2 to n	Body of the VPD. Consists of one or more VPD keyword fields, such as part number, serial number, etc. The recommended, conditionally recommended, and additional fields are defined in tables 18-5, 18-6, and 18-7.
n + 1	checksum on entire VPD structure

Table 20-5: Recommended Fields

ASCII Name	Description
PN	Part number.
FN	**FRU part number.**
EC	**Engineering change** level of assembly.
MN	**Manufacturer** ID.
SN	**Serial number.**

Table 20-6: Conditionally Recommended Fields

ASCII Name	Description
LI	**Load ID**. This is a part of the name of the software download code module that may be required by a device to make it a functional.
RL	**ROM level**. Revision level of any non-alterable (as opposed to flash-programmable) ROM code on the function.
RM	**Alterable ROM level**. Revision level of any alterable ROM code (flash-programmable ROM) on the function.
NA	**Network Address**. Needed by network adapters that require a unique network address (e.g., token ring, Baseband, or Ethernet).
DD	**Device driver level**. The minimum device driver level required for proper operation of the function.
DG	**Diagnostic level**. The minimum diagnostic software level required for testing the function.
LL	**Loadable microcode level**. If not present, level zero is implied. If a function uses loadable microcode (firmware), indicates the microcode level required for proper function operation. This field is associated with card ID, rather than the part number or EC level. As changes are made to a card, a new level of microcode may be required.
VI	**Vendor ID/Device ID**. Same as that found in the function's configuration header space.
FU	**Function number**. In a multifunction device, indicates the function that the VPD is associated with. Only one FU field is permitted within the extent of each VPD descriptor.
SI	**Subsystem Vendor ID/Subsystem ID**. Same as that found in the function's configuration header space.

Table 20-7: Additional Fields

ASCII Name	Description
ZO-ZZ	**User/Product-specific fields**. Available for function-specific data for which no keyword has been defined.

Table 20-8 on page 434 is the example VPD supplied in the specification. It actually consists of two VPDs: one for the function and one for its associated diagnostic software.

Table 20-8: Example VPD Data Structure

Offset	Value	Item/Description
0	82h	Identification String descriptor.
1	0021h	descriptor length
3	"ABC Super-Fast Widget Controller"	Identification string
36	90h	VPD start
37	0033h	length
39	"PN"	part number field
41	08h	length
42	"6181682A"	part number
50	"EC"	engineering change (EC) field
52	0Ah	length
53	"4950262536"	EC number
63	"SN"	serial number field
65	08h	length
66	"00000194"	serial number

Table 20-8: Example VPD Data Structure (Continued)

Offset	Value	Item/Description
74	"FN"	FRU number field
76	06h	length
77	"135722"	FRU number
83	"MN"	manufacturer number field
85	04h	length
86	"1037"	manufacturer number
90	90h	VPD start
91	000Ah	length
93	"DG"	diagnostic level field
95	02h	length
96	"01"	diagnostic level
98	"DD"	device driver level field
100	02h	length
101	"01"	device driver level
103	79h	End tag
104	Checksum	checksum of entire VPD (the checksum is correct if the sum of all bytes, including checksum, equal zero).

21 Add-in Cards and Connectors

The Previous Chapter

The previous chapter provided a detailed description of device ROMs associated with PCI devices. This included the following topics:

- device ROM detection.
- internal code/data format.
- shadowing.
- initialization code execution.
- interrupt hooking.

In This Chapter

This chapter provides an introduction to the PCI expansion card and connector definition. It covers card and connector types, 5V and 3.3V operability, shared slots, and pinout definition. For a detailed description of electrical and mechanical issues, refer to the latest version of the PCI specification (as of this printing, revision 2.2).

The Next Chapter

The next chapter describes the Hot-Plug PCI capability defined by the revision 1.0 PCI Hot-Plug spec. A Hot-Plug capable system permits cards to be removed and installed without powering down the system.

Add-In Connectors

32- and 64-bit Connectors

The PCI add-in card connector was derived from the Micro Channel connector. There are two basic types of connectors: the 32- and the 64-bit connector. A basic representation can be found in Figure 21-1 on page 438. Table 21-1 on page 439 illustrates the pinout of 32-bit and 64-bit cards (note that the 64-bit connector is a superset of the 32-bit connector). **THE FOLLOWING PINOUT CHANGES WERE MADE IN THE 2.2 SPEC:** 2.2

- PIN A14 WAS RESERVED AND IS NOW DEFINED AS THE 3.3VAUX PIN (SEE "PME# AND 3.3VAUX" ON PAGE 449).
- PIN A19 WAS RESERVED AND IS NOW DEFINED AS THE PME# PIN (SEE "PME# AND 3.3VAUX" ON PAGE 449).
- PIN A40 WAS THE SDONE PIN AND IS NOW DEFINED AS A RESERVED PIN. THIS WAS THE SNOOP DONE SIGNAL, BUT ALL SUPPORT FOR CACHEABLE MEMORY AND CACHING ENTITIES ON THE PCI BUS HAS BEEN REMOVED.
- PIN A41 WAS THE SBO# PIN AND IS NOW DEFINED AS A RESERVED PIN. THIS WAS THE SNOOP BACKOFF SIGNAL, BUT ALL SUPPORT FOR CACHEABLE MEMORY AND CACHING ENTITIES ON THE PCI BUS HAS BEEN REMOVED.

The table shows the card pinout for three types of cards: 5V, 3.3V, and Universal cards (the three card types are defined in "3.3V and 5V Connectors" on page 445). The system board designer must leave all reserved pins unconnected. The table illustrates the pinouts and keying for 3.3V and 5V connectors. In addition, a Universal card can be installed in either a 3.3V or a 5V connector. There is no such thing as a Universal connector, only Universal cards. Additional information regarding 3V, 5V and Universal cards can be found in this chapter in the section "3.3V and 5V Connectors" on page 445.

Figure 21-1: 32- and 64-bit Connectors

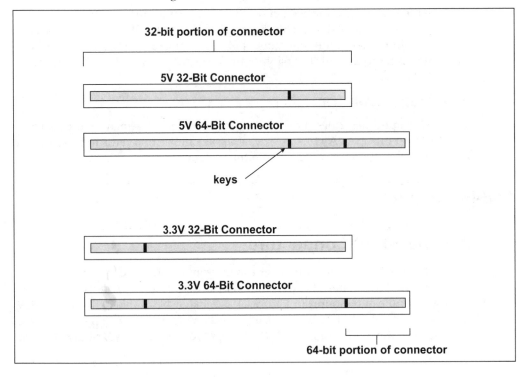

Table 21-1: PCI Add-In Card Pinouts

Pin	5V Card Side B	5V Card Side A	Universal Card Side B	Universal Card Side A	3.3V Card Side B	3.3V Card Side A	Comment
1	-12V	TRST#	-12V	TRST#	-12V	TRST#	32-bit connector start
2	TCK	+12V	TCK	+12V	TCK	+12V	
3	Ground	TMS	Ground	TMS	Ground	TMS	
4	TDO	TDI	TDO	TDI	TDO	TDI	
5	+5V	+5V	+5V	+5V	+5V	+5V	
6	+5V	INTA#	+5V	INTA#	+5V	INTA#	
7	INTB#	INTC#	INTB#	INTC#	INTB#	INTC#	
8	INTD#	+5V	INTD#	+5V	INTD#	+5V	
9	PRSNT1#	Reserved	PRSNT1#	Reserved	PRSNT1#	Reserved	
10	Reserved	+5V	Reserved	*+Vi/o*	Reserved	+3.3V	
11	PRSNT2#	Reserved	PRSNT2#	Reserved	PRSNT2#	Reserved	
12	Ground	Ground					
13	Ground	Ground	Key				3.3V key
14	Reserved	**3.3V**$_{AUX}$	Reserved	**3.3V**$_{AUX}$	Reserved	**3.3V**$_{AUX}$	
15	Ground	RST#	Ground	RST#	Ground	RST#	
16	CLK	+5V	CLK	*+Vi/o*	CLK	+3.3V	
17	Ground	GNT#	Ground	GNT#	Ground	GNT#	
18	REQ#	Ground	REQ#	Ground	REQ#	Ground	
19	+5V	**PME#**	*+Vi/o*	**PME#**	+3.3V	**PME#**	
20	AD[31]	AD[30]	AD[31]	AD[30]	AD[31]	AD[30]	
21	AD[29]	+3.3V	AD[29]	+3.3V	AD[29]	+3.3V	
22	Ground	AD[28]	Ground	AD[28]	Ground	AD[28]	
23	AD[27]	AD[26]	AD[27]	AD[26]	AD[27]	AD[26]	
24	AD[25]	Ground	AD[25]	Ground	AD[25]	Ground	
25	+3.3V	AD[24]	+3.3V	AD[24]	+3.3V	AD[24]	

2.2

2.2

Table 21-1: PCI Add-In Card Pinouts (Continued)

Pin	5V Card Side B	5V Card Side A	Universal Card Side B	Universal Card Side A	3.3V Card Side B	3.3V Card Side A	Comment
26	C/BE#[3]	IDSEL	C/BE#[3]	IDSEL	C/BE#[3]	IDSEL	
27	AD[23]	+3.3V	AD[23]	+3.3V	AD[23]	+3.3V	
28	Ground	AD[22]	Ground	AD[22]	Ground	AD[22]	
29	AD[21]	AD[20]	AD[21]	AD[20]	AD[21]	AD[20]	
30	AD[19]	Ground	AD[19]	Ground	AD[19]	Ground	
31	+3.3V	AD[18]	+3.3V	AD[18]	+3.3V	AD[18]	
32	AD[17]	AD[16]	AD[17]	AD[16]	AD[17]	AD[16]	
33	C/BE#[2]	+3.3V	C/BE#[2]	+3.3V	C/BE#[2]	+3.3V	
34	Ground	FRAME#	Ground	FRAME#	Ground	FRAME#	
35	IRDY#	Ground	IRDY#	Ground	IRDY#	Ground	
36	+3.3V	TRDY#	+3.3V	TRDY#	+3.3V	TRDY#	
37	DEVSEL#	Ground	DEVSEL#	Ground	DEVSEL#	Ground	
38	Ground	STOP#	Ground	STOP#	Ground	STOP#	
39	LOCK#	+3.3V	LOCK#	+3.3V	LOCK#	+3.3V	
40	PERR#	*RESERVED*	PERR#	*RESERVED*	PERR#	*RESERVED*	
41	+3.3V	*RESERVED*	+3.3V	*RESERVED*	+3.3V	*RESERVED*	
42	SERR#	Ground	SERR#	Ground	SERR#	Ground	
43	+3.3V	PAR	+3.3V	PAR	+3.3V	PAR	
44	C/BE[1]#	AD[15}	C/BE[1]#	AD[15}	C/BE[1]#	AD[15}	
45	AD[14]	+3.3V	AD[14]	+3.3V	AD[14]	+3.3V	
46	Ground	AD[13]	Ground	AD[13]	Ground	AD[13]	
47	AD[12]	AD[11]	AD[12]	AD[11]	AD[12]	AD[11]	
48	AD[10]	Ground	AD[10]	Ground	AD[10]	Ground	
49	Ground	AD[09]	Ground	AD[09]	Ground **	AD[09]	** see note
50	Keyway				Ground	Ground	5V key
51					Ground	Ground	5V key

2.2

Table 21-1: PCI Add-In Card Pinouts (Continued)

Pin	5V Card Side B	5V Card Side A	Universal Card Side B	Universal Card Side A	3.3V Card Side B	3.3V Card Side A	Comment
52	AD[08]	C/BE#[0]	AD[08]	C/BE#[0]	AD[08]	C/BE#[0]	
53	AD[07]	+3.3V	AD[07]	+3.3V	AD[07]	+3.3V	
54	+3.3V	AD[06]	+3.3V	AD[06]	+3.3V	AD[06]	
55	AD[05]	AD[04]	AD[05]	AD[04]	AD[05]	AD[04]	
56	AD[03]	Ground	AD[03]	Ground	AD[03]	Ground	
57	Ground	AD[02]	Ground	AD[02]	Ground	AD[02]	
58	AD[01]	AD[00]	AD[01]	AD[00]	AD[01]	AD[00]	
59	+5V	+5V	*+Vi/o*	*+Vi/o*	+3.3V	+3.3V	
60	ACK64#	REQ64#	ACK64#	REQ64#	ACK64#	REQ64#	
61	+5V	+5V	+5V	+5V	+5V	+5V	
62	+5V	+5V	+5V	+5V	+5V	+5V	32-bit connector end
	keyway						64-bit spacer
							64-bit spacer
63	Reserved	Ground	Reserved	Ground	Reserved	Ground	64-bit start
64	Ground	C/BE#[7]	Ground	C/BE#[7]	Ground	C/BE#[7]	
65	C/BE#[6]	C/BE#[5]	C/BE#[6]	C/BE#[5]	C/BE#[6]	C/BE#[5]	
66	C/BE#[4]	+5V	C/BE#[4]	*+Vi/o*	C/BE#[4]	+3.3V	
67	Ground	PAR64	Ground	PAR64	Ground	PAR64	
68	AD[63]	AD[62]	AD[63]	AD[62]	AD[63]	AD[62]	
69	AD[61]	Ground	AD[61]	Ground	AD[61]	Ground	
70	+5V	AD[60]	*+Vi/o*	AD[60]	+3.3V	AD[60]	
71	AD[59]	AD[58]	AD[59]	AD[58]	AD[59]	AD[58]	
72	AD[57]	Ground	AD[57]	Ground	AD[57]	Ground	
73	Ground	AD[56]	Ground	AD[56]	Ground	AD[56]	
74	AD[55]	AD[54]	AD[55]	AD[54]	AD[55]	AD[54]	
75	AD[53]	+5V	AD[53]	*+Vi/o*	AD[53]	+3.3V	

Table 21-1: PCI Add-In Card Pinouts (Continued)

Pin	5V Card Side B	5V Card Side A	Universal Card Side B	Universal Card Side A	3.3V Card Side B	3.3V Card Side A	Comment
76	Ground	AD[52]	Ground	AD[52]	Ground	AD[52]	
77	AD[51]	AD[50]	AD[51]	AD[50]	AD[51]	AD[50]	
78	AD[49]	Ground	AD[49]	Ground	AD[49]	Ground	
79	+5V	AD[48]	+Vi/o	AD[48]	+3.3V	AD[48]	
80	AD[47]	AD[46]	AD[47]	AD[46]	AD[47]	AD[46]	
81	AD[45]	Ground	AD[45]	Ground	AD[45]	Ground	
82	Ground	AD[44]	Ground	AD[44]	Ground	AD[44]	
83	AD[43]	AD[42]	AD[43]	AD[42]	AD[43]	AD[42]	
84	AD[41]	+5V	AD[41]	+Vi/o	AD[41]	+3.3V	
85	Ground	AD[40]	Ground	AD[40]	Ground	AD[40]	
86	AD[39]	AD[38]	AD[39]	AD[38]	AD[39]	AD[38]	
87	AD[37]	Ground	AD[37]	Ground	AD[37]	Ground	
88	+5V	AD[36]	+Vi/o	AD[36]	+3.3V	AD[36]	
89	AD[35]	AD[34]	AD[35]	AD[34]	AD[35]	AD[34]	
90	AD[33]	Ground	AD[33]	Ground	AD[33]	Ground	
91	Ground	AD[32]	Ground	AD[32]	Ground	AD[32]	
92	Reserved	Reserved	Reserved	Reserved	Reserved	Reserved	
93	Reserved	Ground	Reserved	Ground	Reserved	Ground	
94	Ground	Reserved	Ground	Reserved	Ground	Reserved	64-bit end

Note: pin B49 on 3.3V connectors is ground on a 33MHz PCI card, but is called M66EN on a 66MHz PCI card. For more information, refer to "How Clock Generator Sets Its Frequency" on page 301.

32-bit Connector

The 32-bit connector contains all of the PCI signals for the implementation of 32-bit PCI. In addition, it contains two of the 64-bit extension signals, REQ64# and ACK64#, and the two card present signals, PRSNT1# and PRSNT2#.

Card Present Signals. Refer to Figure 21-2 on page 444. The Card Present signals are required for add-in cards, but are optional on the system board.

It must be noted, however, that they are required on a system board that supports Hot-Plug PCI (see "Slot Power Requirements" on page 476). The system board designer must decouple both of the Card Present pins to ground through a 0.01uF high-speed capacitor because one or both of these pins also provide an AC return path. These two card pins must not be bussed together or otherwise connected to each other on the system board. In addition to following these implementation rules, the system board designer may optionally permit software to access the state of the card present signals through a machine-readable port. If they are used in this manner, the system board designer must place a separate pullup resistor on each of these signal lines.

The PCI card designer encodes the maximum power requirements of the card (if it should be configured and brought on-line) on the Card Present signals. When the card is installed in a PCI connector, it grounds one, the other, or both of the Card Present signals. At a minimum, the add-in card must ground one of these two pins.

Table 21-2 on page 443 defines the value encoded on these two signals. The encoded value must indicate the total maximum consumption of the card when it is fully-configured and fully-operational *AND MAY NOT EXCEED 25 WATTS*. The indicated total consumption must include all four power rails, but all of the power may be drawn from either the 5V or 3.3V rail if it's the only one used. When interrogating this value to determine if the system's power supply and cooling will support the card, the system software should assume that the indicated power could be drawn from either the 3.3V or the 5V power rail.

2.2

Table 21-2: Card Power Requirement Indication On Card Present Signals

Description	PRSNT1#	PRSNT2#
Slot empty	1	1
Card present and will draw a maximum of 25W if it's configured and brought on-line.	0	1
Card present and will draw a maximum of 15W if it's configured and brought on-line.	1	0
Card present and will draw a maximum of 7.5W if it's configured and brought on-line.	0	0

Figure 21-2: Card Present Signals

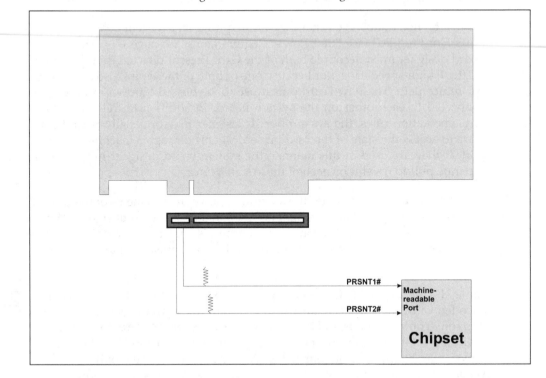

REQ64# and ACK64#. In order to support 64-bit cards installed in 32-bit slots, the REQ64# and ACK64# signals are located on the 32-bit portion of the connector. On 32-bit connectors:

- The system board designer must implement a separate pullup resistor on each connector's REQ64# pin. Nothing else should be connected to these pins.

- THE ACK64# PIN MAY EITHER BE BUSSED TO THE ACK64# SIGNAL LINE USED BY THE 64-BIT DEVICES (IF THERE ARE ANY), OR MAY BE CONNECTED TO A SEPARATE PULLUP RESISTOR ON THE SYSTEM BOARD.

If a 64-bit bus master is installed in a 32-bit card slot and it initiates a transaction, its assertion of REQ64# is not visible to any of the targets. In addition, its ACK64# input is always sampled deasserted. This forces the bus master to use only the lower part of the bus during the transfer. Furthermore, if the target addressed in the transaction is a 64-bit target, it samples REQ64# deasserted, forcing it to only utilize the lower half of the bus during the transaction.

Chapter 21: Add-in Cards and Connectors

As just explained, a 64-bit card installed in a 32-bit connector cannot use the upper half of the bus. This means that the signals related to the upper half of the bus will float on the card unless some special action is taken by the on-card logic. This subject is covered in "Pullups Prevent 64-bit Extension from Floating When Not in Use" on page 267.

64-bit Connector

A 64-bit PCI connector consists of the 32-bit connector plus a 64-bit extension to the connector (refer to Figure 21-1 on page 438 and to Table 21-1 on page 439). The extension contains all of the 64-bit extension signals (with the exception of REQ64# and ACK64#). For a discussion of 64-bit extension operation, refer to the chapter entitled "The 64-bit PCI Extension" on page 265. REQ64# and ACK64# are handled as follows:

- The REQ64# pins on all embedded 64-bit devices and all 64-bit connectors are bussed together with a single pullup on the trace.
- THE ACK64# PINS ON ALL EMBEDDED 64-BIT DEVICES AND ALL 64-BIT CONNECTORS ARE BUSSED TOGETHER WITH A SINGLE PULLUP ON THE TRACE. THIS REQUIREMENT WAS ADDED IN THE 2.2 SPEC. **2.2**

3.3V and 5V Connectors

A PCI system board is implemented around a PCI chipset. The buffer/driver logic that the chipset uses to interface to the PCI bus is implemented as either 5V or 3.3V logic. The chipset design therefore defines the PCI bus signaling environment as either 3.3V or 5V. In order for an add-in PCI card to operate correctly, its buffer/driver logic must match the system board's PCI signaling environment.

As illustrated in Figure 21-1 on page 438, 3.3V and 5V card connectors are keyed 180 degrees out from each other. A card that implements its buffer/driver logic using purely 5V logic is keyed to plug only into a 5V connector, while a card with 3.3V buffer/driver logic is keyed so as to install only in a 3.3V connector. It should be noted that a 5V card can incorporate a mix of 3.3V and 5V logic residing behind its buffer/drivers. Likewise, a 3.3V card can also incorporate a logic mix behind its front-end logic.

Universal Card

A card that implements its buffer/drivers with logic that can operate at either 3.3V or 5V is referred to as a Universal card. It is keyed so as to install in either a 3.3V or a 5V card connector. Its buffer/driver logic receives power from a special set of pins referred to as Vio pins (see Table 21-1 on page 439). The system board designer connects the Vio pins to the voltage rail corresponding to the PCI chipset signaling environment. Figure 21-3 on page 446 illustrates the relationship of the 3.3V, 5V and Universal cards to the 5V and 3.3V connectors.

2.2 *ALL NEW COMPONENT DESIGNS ARE RECOMMENDED TO USE THE DUAL-VOLTAGE BUFFERS AND IT IS RECOMMENDED THAT ALL NEW CARDS BE IMPLEMENTED AS UNIVERSAL CARDS.*

Figure 21-3: 3.3V, 5V and Universal Cards

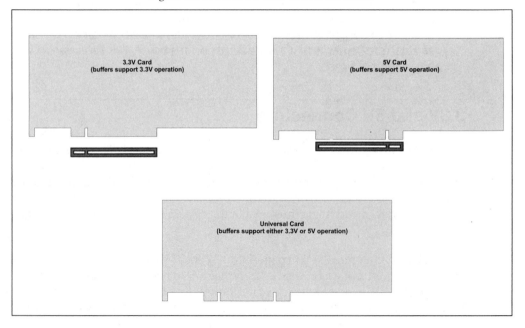

Shared Slot

The machine may incorporate various types of add-in connectors (e.g., ISA and PCI connectors). On the system board, a certain amount of real estate is allocated for each add-in connector and each connector is associated with a rear-panel mounting-bracket area.

Optionally, the system board designer may implement one PCI and one other type of add-in connector in very close proximity to each other (see Figure 21-4 on page 447). This is referred to as the **shared slot**. They share the same rear-panel mounting bracket area and only one of these connectors may therefore be populated. It should also be noted that the component side of a PCI add-in card is the opposite of that for ISA, EISA and Micro Channel add-in cards. This is another reason why both connectors could not be populated. The components of one card would over-hang the other connector. If present, the shared slot is implemented as the last slot in the series of E/ISA or Micro Channel slots. Figure 21-4 on page 447 illustrates a machine with PCI expansion slots and either ISA or EISA expansion slots. Figure 21-5 on page 448 illustrates a unit with PCI and Micro Channel expansion slots. The purpose of the shared slot is to maximize usage of system board real estate.

Figure 21-4: ISA/EISA Unit Expansion Slots

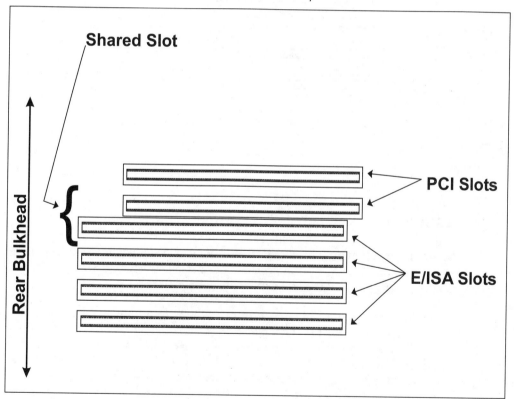

Figure 21-5: Micro Channel Unit Expansion Slots

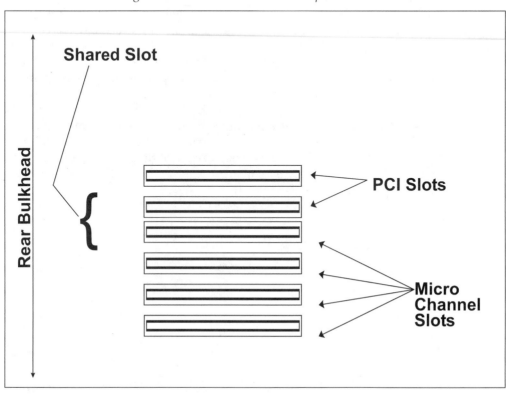

Riser Card

The 2.1 specification only provided illustrations of systems with the PCI expansion connectors located on the system board itself. Designers were, however, permitted to implement the PCI expansion connectors on a riser card.

- As specified in the 2.1 specification, when designing a riser card, "*the designer must ensure that the PCI electrical specification is not violated*". Other than that statement, designers were on their own as to how to accomplish this goal.

2.2
- THE 2.2 SPECIFICATION HAS ADDED EIGHT NEW ILLUSTRATIONS STRICTLY DEFINING THE METHODOLOGY WHEN IMPLEMENTING A PCI RISER CARD. SINCE THIS IS STRICTLY A MECHANICAL ISSUE, IT IS NOT COVERED IN THIS BOOK AND THE SPEC SHOULD BE REFERENCED.

Snoop Result Signals on Add-in Connector

THESE SIGNALS HAVE BEEN DELETED IN THE 2.2 SPEC.

2.2

PME# and 3.3Vaux

2.2

THESE TWO PINS WERE ADDED TO THE CONNECTOR DEFINITION IN THE 2.2 SPEC. POWER MANAGEMENT EVENT AND 3.3VAUX ARE OPTIONAL SIGNALS USED BY A CARD THAT SUPPORTS THE PCI BUS POWER MANAGEMENT INTERFACE SPEC. FOR A DETAILED DESCRIPTION, REFER TO "POWER MANAGEMENT" ON PAGE 479.

Add-In Cards

3.3V, 5V and Universal Cards

"3.3V and 5V Connectors" on page 445 and "Universal Card" on page 446, found earlier in this chapter, provides a description of 3.3V, 5V and Universal cards.

Long and Short Form Cards

In addition to defining the 32- and 64-bit card types, the specification also defines three physical card sizes. They are described in the specification as:

- the standard, or long, cards. The standard card measures 12.283" by 4.2".
- fixed-height short cards. The fixed-height short card measures 4.2" by 6.875".
- variable-height short cards. The variable-height short card can be anywhere from 1.42" to 4.2" in height.

The fixed- and variable-height short cards provide less surface area but are well-suited for small-footprint machines. The reader should refer to the 2.1 specification for a detailed description of the mechanical design.

Small PCI (SPCI)

The version 1.5a *Small PCI Specification* defines a very small card format applicable to highly-integrated portable applications (e.g., laptops). From a configuration, electrical, and protocol perspective, SPCI is identical to normal PCI. It does not, however, support the 64-bit extension nor does it support the JTAG interface (see "JTAG/Boundary Scan Signals" on page 48). CLKRUN# ("CLKRUN# Signal" on page 35) is included on the SPCI connector (it is not included on the normal PCI add-in connector).

Component Layout

In order to meet the PCI signal propagation delay specification, it is critical that the length of PCI signal lines be kept as short as possible. Towards this end, the PCI specification strongly recommends that the pinout sequence on PCI components be exactly aligned with the PCI edge connector pin ordering (as illustrated in Figure 21-6 on page 451). If implemented, the 64-bit extension signals should continue wrapping around the component in a counter-clockwise direction in the same order as they appear on the 64-bit connector.

The placement of IDSEL in close physical proximity to the upper AD lines facilitates resistively-coupling IDSEL to one of them. This subject is covered in "Method One—IDSELs Routed Over Unused AD Lines" on page 338.

Figure 21-6: Recommended PCI Component Pinout Ordering

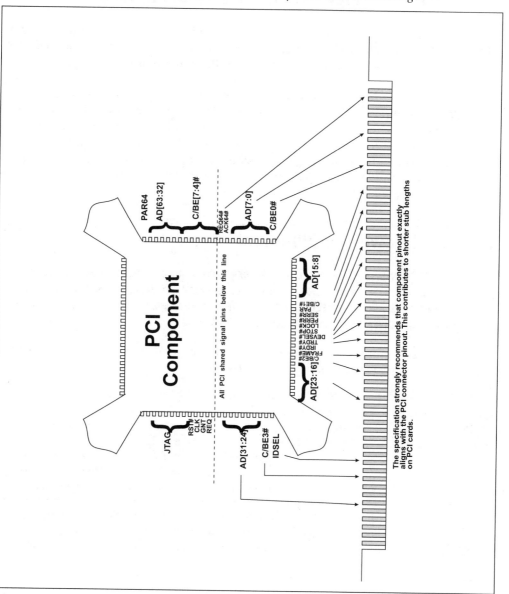

Maintain Integrity of Boundary Scan Chain

Some system board designers may choose to include the PCI add-in connectors in the boundary scan test chain. To ensure that the integrity of the TDI/TDO chain remains intact, cards designed without boundary scan capability must bus the TDI and TDO edge connector pins together. For the reader who isn't familiar with boundary scan testing, TDI and TDO are the serial test data in and test data out pins. Using the TCK (test clock) signal, commands and requests can be shifted to or from the device in a serial fashion. The TDO from one device is connected to the TDI on the next device in the boundary scan test chain. A discussion of boundary scan is outside the scope of this book. The major audience for boundary scan, test engineers, already know this subject. Any who do not had better not let their bosses find out.

Card Power Requirement

2.2

THE 2.2 SPEC HAS CHANGED THE POWER SUPPLY RULES. THE SYSTEM BOARD IS NOW REQUIRED TO SUPPLY ALL FOUR POWER RAILS TO EACH CONNECTOR. IN ADDITION, EXPANSION CARDS ARE NOW REQUIRED TO LIMIT THE TOTAL POWER DRAWN COLLECTIVELY FROM ALL FOUR POWER RAILS TO NO MORE THAN 25 WATTS.

Table 21-3 on page 452 defines the required current sourcing capability for the four power rails (on a per-connector basis).

Table 21-3: Required Power Supply Current Sourcing Capability (per connector)

Power Rail	Tolerance	Current Sourcing Capability
5V	+/- 5%	5A maximum per connector (system design-dependent; in other words, there is no specific requirement for current-per-connector).
3.3V	+/- 0.3V	7.6A maximum per connector (system design-dependent; in other words, there is no specific requirement for current-per-connector).
12V	+/- 5%	500mA per connector.
-12V	+/- 10%	100mA per connector.

The maximum power requirement per card is specified at 25 Watts. This value includes the summary power consumption on all four rails. PCI cards that consume more than 10 watts should power up and reset to a state that consumes 10 watts or less (if possible). While in this state, the card must permit access to its configuration registers. If the card is required for the raw boot process (POST and OS boot), it must be capable of performing its bootstrap functions (e.g., text mode video) while in diminished power mode. After configuration, the card can be placed in full-power mode.

Maximum Card Trace Lengths

The list that follows defines the maximum trace length for PCI signal lines on PCI add-in cards:

- All signals that comprise the **32-bit** portion of the PCI bus must be limited to a maximum trace length of **1.5 inches**.
- All signals that comprise the **64-bit** extension signals must be limited to a maximum trace length of **2 inches**.

The PCI **CLK** signal trace length **must be 2.5 inches** (+/- 0.1") and it must be connected to only one load on the card.

One Load per Shared Signal

It is a strict rule that each PCI device (embedded or on an add-in card) may place only one load on each shared (i.e., bussed) PCI signal line. The following list illustrates PCI add-in card design scenarios that would violate this rule:

- A device ROM attached directly to the PCI bus signals.
- Two or more PCI devices connected to the shared signals. In this case, a PCI-to-PCI bridge should be the only device connected to the system board PCI bus signals. The on-card PCI devices can then be connected to the PCI bus on the card itself.
- Two or more devices that snoop the same PCI signal(s) (in other words, two or more devices with a PCI signal connected to their input buffers).
- On-card chipsets that place more than one load on each pin.
- A card that has more than 10pF capacitance per pin.
- A card that places pullups or other discrete devices on shared PCI signals. Any system board shared PCI bus signals that require pullups already have them on the system board. Placing pullups on these signal lines on an expansion card would result in pullup current overload.

22 *Hot-Plug PCI*

The Previous Chapter

The previous chapter provided an introduction to the PCI expansion card and connector definition. It covered card and connector types, 5V and 3.3V operability, shared slots, and pinout definition.

This Chapter

This chapter describes the Hot-Plug PCI capability defined by the revision 1.0 PCI Hot-Plug spec. A Hot-Plug capable system permits cards to be removed and installed without powering down the system.

The Next Chapter

The next chapter provides a detailed description of PCI power management as defined in the revision 1.1 *PCI Bus PM Interface Specification*. In order to provide an overall context for this discussion, a description of the OnNow Initiative, ACPI (Advanced Configuration and Power Interface), and the involvement of the Windows OS is also provided.

The Problem

In an environment where high-availability is desired, it would be a distinct advantage not to have to shut the system down before installing a new card or removing a card.

As originally designed, the PCI bus was not intended to support installation or removal of PCI cards while power is applied to the machine. This would result in probable damage to components, as well as a mightily confused OS.

The Solution

The solution is defined in the revision 1.0 *PCI Hot-Plug spec* and gives the chipset the ability to handle the following software requests:

- Selectively **assert and deassert** the **PCI RST# signal** to an specific Hot-Plug PCI card connector. As stated in the PCI spec, the card must tri-state its output drivers within 40ns after the assertion of RST#.
- Selectively **isolate** a **card** from the logic on the system board.
- Selectively **remove or apply power** to a specific PCI card connector.
- Selectively **turn on or turn off** an **Attention Indicator** associated with a specific card connector to draw the users attention to the connector.

Hot-Plug PCI is basically a "**no surprises**" Hot-Plug methodology. In other words, the user is not permitted to install or remove a PCI card without first warning the software. The software then performs the necessary steps to prepare the card connector for the installation or removal of a card and finally indicates to the end user (via a visual indicator) when the installation or removal may be performed.

No Changes To Adapter Cards

One of the major goals of the Hot-Plug PCI spec was that PCI add-in cards designed to the PCI spec require no changes in order to be Hot-Pluggable.

Changes are required, however, to the chipset, system board, OS and driver design.

Software Elements

General

Table 22-1 on page 457 describes the major software elements that must be modified to support Hot-Plug capability. Also refer to Figure 22-1 on page 459.

Table 22-1: Introduction to Major Hot-Plug Software Elements

Software Element	Supplied by	Description
User Interface	OS vendor	An OS-supplied utility that permits the end-user to request that a card connector be turned off in order to remove a card or turned on to use a card that just been installed.
Hot-Plug Service	OS vendor	A service that processes requests (referred to as Hot-Plug Primitives) issued by the OS. This includes requests to: • provide slot identifiers • turn card On or Off • turn Attention Indicator On or Off • return current state of slot (On or Off) The Hot-Plug Service interacts with the Hot-Plug System Driver to satisfy the requests. The interface (i.e., API) with the Hot-Plug System Driver is defined by the OS vendor, not by this spec.
Hot-Plug System Driver	System Board vendor	Receives requests (aka Hot-Plug Primitives) from the Hot-Plug Service within the OS. Interacts with the hardware Hot-Plug Controller to accomplish requests. The interface (i.e., API) with the Hot-Plug Service is defined by the OS vendor, not by this spec. A system board may incorporate more than one Hot-Plug Controller, each of which controls a subset of the overall slots in the machine. In this case, there would be one Hot-Plug System Driver for each Controller.

Table 22-1: Introduction to Major Hot-Plug Software Elements (Continued)

Software Element	Supplied by	Description
Device Driver	Adapter card vendor	Some special, Hot-Plug-specific capabilities must be incorporated in a Hot-Plug capable device driver. This includes: • support for the **Quiesce** command. • optional implementation of the **Pause** command. • Possible replacement for device's ROM code. • Support for **Start** command or optional **Resume** command.

System Start Up

A Hot-Plug-capable system may be loaded with an OS that doesn't support Hot-Plug capability. In this case, although the system BIOS would contain some Hot-Plug-related software, the Hot-Plug Service and Hot-Plug System Driver would not be present. Assuming that the user doesn't attempt hot insertion or removal of a card, the system will operate as a standard, non-Hot-Plug system.

- The system startup firmware must ensure that all Attention Indicators are Off.
- The spec also states: "the Hot-Plug slots must be in a state that would be appropriate for loading non-Hot-Plug system software." The author is unclear as to what this means.

Figure 22-1: Hot-Plug Hardware/Software Elements

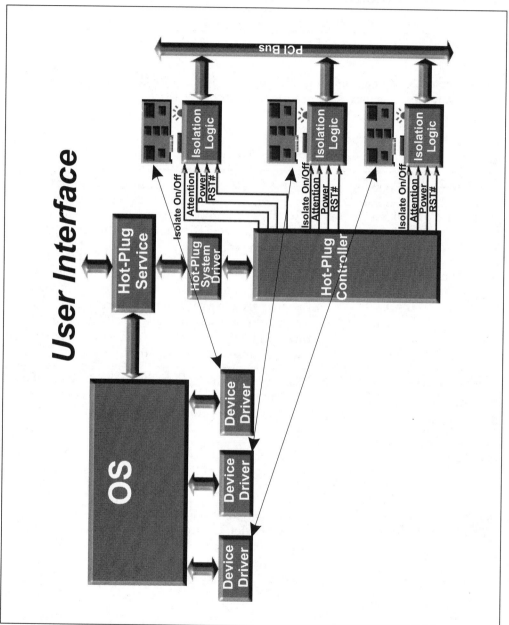

Hardware Elements

General

Table 22-2 on page 460 and Figure 22-1 on page 459 illustrate the major hardware elements necessary to support Hot-Plug PCI.

Table 22-2: Major Hot-Plug Hardware Elements

Hardware Element	Description
Hot-Plug Controller	Receives and processes commands issued by the Hot-Plug System Driver. The Controller is typically part of the chipset on the system board.
Card Connector Isolation Logic	Controlled by the chipset under the direction of the Hot-Plug System Driver. Located on the system board between a card connector and the PCI bus, it permits a card slot to be electrically isolated from the PCI bus under software control in preparation for card installation or removal.
Card Connector Power Switching Logic	Controlled by the chipset under the direction of the Hot-Plug System Driver. Permits the power supply voltages to a slot to be turned on or off under program control.
Card Reset Logic	Controlled by the chipset under the direction of the Hot-Plug System Driver. Permits the selective assertion or deassertion of the PCI RST# signal to a specific slot under program control.
Attention Indicators	One per slot. Controlled by the chipset under the direction of the Hot-Plug System Driver. The Attention Indicator is used to draw the attention of the end user to the slot.

Table 22-2: Major Hot-Plug Hardware Elements (Continued)

Hardware Element	Description
Card Present/Power Requirement Indication	The two Card Present signals defined by the PCI spec, PRSNT#[2:1], must indicate the maximum amount of power required by the card if it should be configured and enabled. The card must have one, the other, or both of these pins grounded. See Table 21-2 on page 443 for encoding. If not grounded, the respective PRSNT#[x] signal must be left open on the card. On the system board, these two signal lines from each slot must be connected to a port that can be read by software, irrespective of whether the slot is On or Off, connected or isolated.
Ability of software to read the state of the M66EN signal as applied to the PCI Clock generator.	For background on M66EN, refer to "How Components Indicate 66MHz Support" on page 300. By reading this bit, software (i.e., the Hot-Plug System Driver) can determine if a PCI bus is running at high speed (above 33.33MHz but not above 66.66MHz).
Ability of software to read the state of the M66EN signal from each slot.	On the system board, the M66EN signal lines from each slot must be connected to a port that can be read by software, irrespective of whether the slot is On or Off, connected or isolated. This gives the Hot-Plug System Driver the ability to determine if a card is 66MHz-capable *before* connecting it to a 66MHz PCI bus.
Correct implementation of the 66MHz Capable bit in the adapter card's PCI configuration Status register.	Used by the Hot-Plug System Driver as an alternative means of determining if the card supports a 66MHz bus speed.

Attention Indicator and Optional Slot State Indicator

As mentioned in Table 22-2 on page 460, the system vendor is required to include one Attention Indicator in close proximity to each Hot-Plug slot. The Attention Indicator is used to draw the attention of the end user to the slot. The

Hot-Plug spec does not define the circumstances under which the Hot-Plug Service would illuminate the Attention Indicator. It might be used to indicate a problem associated with the slot, or to aid in locating a particular slot.

The system vendor may also include an optional, Slot State Indicator that indicates whether the slot is currently on or off.

The Attention and Slot State Indicators might be combined into a single indicator. In this case, the Attention state must take precedence over the slot's On/Off state. The example given in the spec says that the LED might be steady "on" to indicate that the slot is in the On state, steady "off" to indicate that it is in the Off state, and flashing to indicate Attention, irrespective of whether the slot is currently in the On or Off state.

Option—Power Fault Detector

If included, the power fault detection logic associated with a slot would detect if the card exceeds the power limits of the slot and turn the slot off.

Option—Tracking System Power Usage

The system may optionally track system power usage and use this information to decide whether or not it's safe to turn on a newly-installed card.

Card Removal and Insertion Procedures

The descriptions of typical card removal and insertion that follow are intended to be introductory in nature. Additional detail can be found later in this chapter.

It should be noted that the procedures described in the following sections assume that the OS, rather than the Hot-Plug System Driver, is responsible for configuring a newly-installed device. If the Hot-Plug System Driver has this responsibility, the Hot-Plug Service will call the Hot-Plug System Driver and instruct it to configure the newly-installed device.

On and Off States

Definition of On and Off

A slot in the On state has the following characteristics:

- Power is applied to the slot.
- The slot is not electrically isolated from the PCI bus. In other words, it is connected to the bus.
- The PCI RST# signal is deasserted.

A slot in the Off state has the following characteristics:

- Power to the slot is turned off.
- The slot is electrically isolated from the PCI bus. In other words, it is disconnected from the bus.
- The PCI RST# signal is asserted.

Turning Slot On

To turn on a slot that is currently in the off state:

STEP 1. Apply power to the slot.
STEP 2. Deassert the PCI RST# signal to the slot. The system must meet the setup and hold timing requirements (specified in the PCI spec) relative to the rising edge of RST#.
STEP 3. Turn off the isolation logic between the slot and the PCI bus. In other words, connect the slot to the bus. This includes the PCI clock signal.

Note that steps 2 and 3 may be reversed.

In order to ensure that connecting the slot to the PCI bus does not in any way interfere with a PCI transaction in progress, the system hardware may optionally control the PCI bus when connecting the slot and removing RST#. As an example, the arbiter within the chipset could wait until the PCI bus is idle and not grant the PCI bus to any master until the connection is complete.

Turning Slot Off

To turn off a slot that is currently in the On state:

STEP 1. Turn on the isolation logic between the slot and the PCI bus. In other words, disconnect the slot from the bus. This includes the PCI clock signal.

STEP 2. Assert the PCI RST# signal to the slot. The system must meet the setup and hold timing requirements (specified in the PCI spec) relative to the rising edge of RST#.

STEP 3. Remove power from the slot.

Note that steps 1 and 2 may be reversed.

Basic Card Removal Procedure

When a card will be removed from the system, the following steps occur:

STEP 1. Via the Hot-Plug Service utility, the end user **inform**s the **OS** that a card will be removed.

STEP 2. The **Hot-Plug Service** utility **commands** the device's **driver to quiesce**. In other words, the driver must stop using (i.e., issuing requests to) the card.

STEP 3. The Hot-Plug Service utility issues a request to the Hot-Plug System Driver to command the chipset to **assert RST#** only **to** the **specified card connector**. Other PCI device's continue to operate normally.

STEP 4. The Hot-Plug Service utility issues a request to the Hot-Plug System Driver to command the chipset to **enable** the **isolation logic** that resides between the connector and the PCI bus (see Figure 22-1 on page 459). This electrically isolates the card from the PCI bus.

STEP 5. The Hot-Plug Service utility issues a request to the Hot-Plug System Driver to command the chipset to **remove** all **operating voltages** from the specified card connector.

STEP 6. The Hot-Plug Service utility issues a request to the Hot-Plug System Driver to command the chipset to **set** the connector's associated visual **Attention Indicator** to show that the card may be safely removed from the system. Note that this is an example. The spec does not define under what circumstances a slot's Attention indicator is used.

STEP 7. The end user **remove**s the **card** from the system and indicates to the Hot-Plug Service utility that this has been accomplished.

STEP 8. The OS **deallocates** the **memory space, IO space, interrupt line, etc.** that had been assigned to the device and makes these resources available for assignment to other devices in the future.

Basic Card Insertion Procedure

The procedure for installing a new card basically reverses the steps listed for card removal. The following steps *assume that the card connector was left in the same state that it was in immediately after a card was removed from the connector (in other words, the Off state)*:

STEP 1. The end user **informs** the **Hot-Plug Service** utility that a new card will be installed in an empty card connector.

STEP 2. The Hot-Plug Service utility issues a request to the Hot-Plug System Driver commanding the chipset to **set** the connector's associated visual **Attention Indicator** to show that the card may be safely installed in the connector.

STEP 3. The user **installs** the **card** in the connector.

STEP 4. The user **informs** the **Hot-Plug Service** utility that the **card** has been **installed**.

STEP 5. The Hot-Plug Service utility issues a request to the Hot-Plug System Driver commanding the chipset to **set** the connector's **Attention Indicator** to inform the user that the card must not be taken out.

STEP 6. The Hot-Plug Service utility issues a request to the Hot-Plug System Driver commanding the chipset to **reapply power** to the connector.

STEP 7. If the connector's **RST#** signal is not still asserted to the connector, the Hot-Plug Service utility issues a request to the Hot-Plug System Driver commanding the chipset to **assert** it.

STEP 8. The Hot-Plug Service utility issues a request to the Hot-Plug System Driver commanding the chipset to **turn off** the **isolation logic** between the connector and the PCI bus.

STEP 9. The Hot-Plug Service utility issues a request to the Hot-Plug System Driver commanding the chipset to **remove** the **RST#** signal from the connector.

STEP 10. The OS commands the Platform Configuration Routine to interrogate the card to **discover** the **function** or functions (if it's a multi-function card) that reside on the card **and** to determine the **resources** that each function **requires**. This is accomplished by causing the host/PCI Bridge to perform PCI configuration accesses to the device.

STEP 11. The Platform Configuration Routine uses PCI configuration writes to **allocate resources** to the device's configuration registers.

STEP 12. The OS **locates** the appropriate **driver**(s) (using the Vendor ID and Device ID, or the Class Code, or the Subsystem Vendor ID and Subsystem ID configuration register values as search criteria) for the function(s) within the PCI device and loads it (or them) into memory.

STEP 13. The OS then **calls** the **driver's initialization code** entry point, causing the processor to execute the driver's initialization code. This code finishes the setup of the device and then **sets** the appropriate **bits in** the device's PCI configuration **Command register** to enable the device.

Quiescing Card and Driver

General

Prior to removing a card from the system, two things must occur:

1. The device's driver must cease accessing the card.
2. If the card has interrupt or bus master capability, the card must cease generating interrupts and cease initiating bus transactions.

How this is accomplished is OS-specific, but the following must take place:

- The OS must stop issuing new requests to the device's driver or must instruct the driver to stop accepting new requests (from the OS or possibly from other bus masters).
- The driver must terminate or complete all outstanding requests.
- The card must be disabled from generating interrupts or acting as a bus master.

When the OS commands the driver to quiesce itself and its device, the OS must not expect the device to remain in the system (in other words, it could be removed and not replaced with a similar card).

Pausing a Driver (Optional)

Optionally, an OS could implement a "Pause" capability to temporarily stop driver activity in the expectation that the same card or a similar card will be reinserted. If the card is not reinstalled within a reasonable amount of time, however, the driver must be quiesced and then removed from memory.

A card may be removed and an identical card installed in its place. As an example, this could be because the currently-installed card is bad or is being replaced with a later revision as an upgrade. If it is intended that the operation appear seamless from a software and operational perspective, the driver would have to quiesce, save the current device's context (i.e., the contents of all of its registers, etc.). The new card would then be installed, the context restored, and normal operation would resume. It should be noted that if the old card had failed, it may or may not be possible to have the operation appear seamless.

Shared Interrupt Must Be Handled Correctly

It is very important that a driver not access its device after it has been quiesced (because the device may have been removed and the access attempt would result in an error). If the device shares an interrupt request line with one or more other PCI functions, one of those devices might generate a request on the shared interrupt signal line. This could cause the quiesced driver's interrupt handler to be executed. Ordinarily, the handler would poll its device's interrupt pending bit to determine if the device generated an interrupt request, but it must not do so if the driver (and its device) has been quiesced.

Quiescing a Driver That Controls Multiple Devices

If a driver controls multiple cards and it receives a command from the OS to quiesce its activity with respect to a specific card, it must only quiesce its activity with that card as well as quiescing the card itself.

Quiescing a Failed Card

If a card has failed, it may not be possible for the driver to complete requests previously issued to the card. In this case, the driver must detect the error and must terminate the requests without completion and attempt to reset the card.

Driver's Initial Accesses To Card

THE 2.2 SPEC DICTATES THAT SOFTWARE MUST NOT EXPECT TO SUCCEED IN PERFORMING A TRANSFER WITH A CARD FOR AT LEAST 2^{25} PCI CLKs AFTER RST# HAS BEEN DEASSERTED. FOR MORE INFORMATION, REFER TO "TARGET LATENCY DURING INITIALIZATION TIME" ON PAGE 85.

Treatment of Device ROM

A PCI device newly installed in a PCI slot may contain a PCI device ROM (actually it may contain more than one if it's a multi-function card). Normally, when the system is powered up and reset is removed, the BIOS loads the driver from the device's ROM into system memory and executes the initialization code within the driver to finish setting up the device (for more information, refer to "Execution of Initialization Code" on page 424). This occurs before the OS is loaded into memory.

Upon a hot-insertion of the device, the policy with regard to the ROM driver is OS-specific. There are two possible scenarios:

- The OS may permit the driver to be loaded into system memory from ROM and then its init (i.e., initialization) code may be executed. This would not be true in an x86, PC-compatible machine, but might be in some other environment.
- The OS may require that the actions normally taken by the ROM driver to finish setting up the device be taken by the some other piece of software, typically the device's driver. This would be true in an x86, PC-compatible machine. The required actions could also be performed by a device-specific program that calls the device's driver to accomplish the actions normally performed by the ROM code.

Who Configures the Card?

The spec refers to the entity responsible for setting up a newly-installed device's PCI configuration Header registers as the **Platform Configuration Routine**. It is OS-specific whether the Platform Configuration Routine resides within the OS or within the platform-specific software such as the Hot-Plug System Driver.

CASE 1. If the **Platform Configuration Routine** is **part of** the **OS**, then the OS is responsible for interrogating the configuration registers within the function or functions on the card to determine what resources it requires. Examples of resources would be memory space and IO space allocated to memory and IO decoders (i.e., Base Address Registers, or BARs), interrupt lines, etc.

CASE 2. If the **Platform Configuration Routine** is not part of the OS but **resides within** the **platform-specific software**, then the OS will call it to configure the device. As an example, the Configuration Routine **may reside within** the **Hot-Plug System Driver** (this program is always platform-specific). In this case, the OS calls the Hot-Plug System Driver with a command for it to configure the device and it must supply the Hot-Plug System Driver with the following information:

- whether or not the OS requires **full or partial configuration** of the device. An example of partial configuration would be the assignment of memory space but not IO space to a device that requests both.
- The OS must also specify the **state** that the **card** must be **left in** (On or Off) **if** there is an **error** during configuration.
- An adapter card that has **no configuration Header registers** (see "Card Sets" on page 471 for a possible example) must be treated as if all resource requests have been satisfied.

Efficient Use of Memory and/or IO Space

The PCI spec recommends that, even if a device's memory decoder requires less than 4KB of memory space, it should request a 4KB block of space (to minimize the number of address bits that need to be decoded). The largest block of IO space that a device's IO decoder can request is 256 bytes.

The Hot-Plug spec, however, strongly recommends that the device designer only ask for the amount of memory or IO space that the device's memory or IO register set actually needs. After the system has booted the OS and the platform is up and running, memory and IO space has already been allocated to the devices that were resident in the machine at boot-up time. A Hot-Plug card will have a far greater chance of successfully receiving the memory and/or IO space it requests if the size requested is kept to a minimum.

Slot Identification

Refer to Table 22-3 on page 471.

Physical Slot ID

When the user wishes to prepare a slot for card removal or insertion, he or she must use the system vendor's nomenclature in order to properly identify the slot. This is referred to as the Physical Slot ID.

Logical Slot ID

The Hot-Plug Service program in turn must issue a request (i.e., a primitive) to the Hot-Plug System Driver and must include the Slot ID in some form. This parameter, referred to as the Logical Slot ID, may be the same as the Physical Slot ID or may be presented in some other, OS-specific form. As an example, the slot could be identified by the number of the PCI bus that it resides on and its PCI device number on that bus.

PCI Bus Number, Device Number

In order to perform some operations, the Hot-Plug System driver must stimulate the host/PCI Bridge to perform a PCI configuration read or write transaction on the appropriate PCI bus. To do this, it must translate the Logical Slot ID into the PCI bus number and device number. For more information on performing PCI configuration transactions, refer to "Configuration Mechanism #1 (The Only Mechanism!)" on page 322.

Translating Slot IDs

It is the responsibility of the platform vendor to supply the OS (specifically, the Hot-Plug Service) with the Physical Slot IDs and specify how they map to PCI bus number and device number. This information could be:

- supplied in the system BIOS ROM.
- read from a port in the Hot-Plug Controller.
- contained within the Hot-Plug System Driver.
- found within some other platform-specific element of software or hardware.

In an x86, PC-compatible machine, this information is supplied in the Interrupt Routing Table in system ROM. For a detailed description of this table, refer to "Interrupt Routing Table" on page 233. This table contains one entry per slot and each entry contains the slot number (i.e., the Physical Slot ID) and its respective PCI bus number and device number.

Table 22-3: Slot Identifiers

Identifier	Usage	Description
Physical Slot ID	Used in Hot-Plug Service's User Interface to identify slots.	**Supplied by the system vendor** (via the Hot-Plug System Driver), this number **uniquely identifies** the **slot**. In a system with a single chassis containing PCI slots, this could simply be a slot number. In a system with multiple chassis, this could consist of a chassis number and the number of a slot within that chassis. For more information regarding Chassis, refer to "Chassis and Slot Number Assignment" on page 594.
Logical Slot ID	Used to identify the target slot when communicating requests between the Hot-Plug Service and the Hot-Plug System driver.	This ID is OS-specific. As examples, the OS could dictate that the Logical Slot ID could take the form of the PCI bus number and device number, or the Physical Slot ID.
PCI Bus Number, Device Number	Hot-Plug System Driver and host/PCI Bridge	The Hot-Plug System Driver must supply the host/PCI Bridge with the number of the target PCI bus as well as the target device on that bus (i.e., physical device position) when requesting that a PCI configuration read or write be performed by the bridge.

Card Sets

A card set is defined as any set **of cards that must be installed or removed together.** The cards that comprise the set may appear to be multiple PCI functions from a configuration standpoint, or may appear as a single PCI function (e.g., if one or more of the cards are only using the slot to gain access to power and are not connected to the PCI bus). The cards may be interconnected via sideband cables. A card set that does not require that the cards be turned on and off together doesn't require any special care on the part of the Hot-Plug environment to support them. This spec doesn't cover the case wherein the set requires that all cards within the set must be turned on or off simultaneously. A specific OS/platform combination may or may not support this capability.

The Primitives

This section discusses the hot-plug software elements and the information passed between them. For a review of the software elements and their relationships to each other, refer to Figure 22-1 on page 459 and to Table 22-1 on page 457. Communications between the Hot-Plug Service within the OS and the platform-specific Hot-Plug System Driver is in the form of requests. The spec doesn't define the exact format of these requests, but does define the basic request types and their content. Each request type issued to the Hot-Plug System Driver by the Hot-Plug Service is referred to as a *primitive*. They are listed and described in Table 22-4 on page 472.

Table 22-4: The Primitives

Primitive	Parameters	Description
Query Hot-Plug System Driver	**Input**: None	Requests that the Hot-Plug System Driver return a set of Logical Slot IDs for the slots it controls.
	Return: Set of Logical Slot IDs for slots controlled by this driver.	

Table 22-4: The Primitives (Continued)

Primitive	Parameters	Description
Set Slot Status	**Inputs:** • Logical Slot ID • New slot state (on or off). • New Attention Indicator state. **Return:** Request completion status: • status change successful • fault—wrong frequency • fault—insufficient power • fault—insufficient configuration resources • fault—power fail • fault—general failure	This request is used to control the slots and the Attention Indicator associated with each slot. Note that the Hot Plug System Driver must be prepared to wait at least 2^{25} PCI CLKs after RST# is removed before it succeeds in accessing the card or completes a request to turn the card on. Good completion of a request is indicated by returning the Status Change Successful parameter. If a fault is incurred during an attempted status change, the Hot-Plug System Driver should return the appropriate fault message (see middle column). Unless otherwise specified, the card should be left in the off state.

Table 22-4: The Primitives (Continued)

Primitive	Parameters	Description
Query Slot Status	**Input**: Logical Slot ID **Return**: • Slot state (on or off) • Card power requirement (not present, low, medium, high) • Card frequency capability (33MHz, 66MHz, insufficient power) • Slot frequency (33MHz, 66MHz)	This request returns the state of the indicated slot (if a card is present). The Hot-Plug System Driver must return the encoding of the PRSNT#[2:1] pins even if the slot is off. To determine the card's frequency capability, the Hot-Plug System Driver reads the state of the M66EN pin (if it is readable through a port) or the function's 66MHz-Capable bit in its configuration Status register. Determination of the card's speed capability is made independent of whether the card is currently off or on, and independent of whether the bus is operating at 33MHz or 66MHz. If the Driver must read the function's 66MHz-Capable bit but cannot turn the slot on due to the power requirements of the card, then the Driver must indicate that there is insufficient power available to determine the card's frequency capability. Obviously, the card's frequency capability is meaningless if no card is present. The slot frequency parameter indicates the current operating frequency of the bus that the slot resides on.

Table 22-4: The Primitives (Continued)

Primitive	Parameters	Description
Async Notice of Slot Status Change	**Input**: Logical Slot ID **Return**: none	This is the only primitive (defined by the spec) that is issued to the Hot-Plug Service by the Hot-Plug System Driver. It is sent when the Driver detects an unsolicited change in the state of a slot. Examples would be a run-time power fault or card installed in a previously-empty slot with no warning.

Issues Related to PCI RST#

The PCI RST# signal has the following effects on a device:

1. When RST# is asserted, a device must tri-state all of its bus outputs and float its open-drain outputs within 40ns.
2. The device's PCI target and bus master state machines must be held in their reset state as long as RST# remains asserted.
3. When RST# is deasserted, the device's PCI target and bus master state machines must remain in the Idle state until the device is addressed in a PCI transaction.
4. To avoid "misinterpreting" the contents of the bus if RST# is removed in the midst of a transaction currently in progress, a device should not leave the reset state until RST# has been deasserted AND the bus is idle (FRAME# and IRDY# sampled deasserted).
5. The device must not depend on the PCI CLK signal exhibiting any particular characteristics prior to the deassertion of RST#.
6. The PCI spec requires that the operating frequency of a 66MHz bus may not be changed without asserting RST#.
7. *THE 2.2 SPEC DICTATES THAT THE HOT-PLUG SYSTEM DRIVER MUST BE PREPARED TO WAIT AT LEAST 225 PCI CLKs AFTER RST# HAS BEEN DEASSERTED BEFORE IT SUCCEEDS IN ACCESSING THE CARD OR COMPLETES A REQUEST FROM THE HOT-PLUG SERVICE TO TURN THE CARD ON.* **2.2**

66MHz-Related Issues

The Hot-Plug System Driver must ensure that a slot containing a 33MHz card is never connected to a bus operating above 33.33MHz. This can be accomplished in the following manner:

- The software can establish if the card is a 33 or 66MHz card by reading the M66EN bit supplied from the card's connector.
- It can establish if the bus is a 66MHz bus by reading the 66MHz-Capable bit from the bridge's Status register. The bridge could be either a host/PCI bridge or a PCI-to-PCI bridge.
  - If the bridge is a host/PCI bridge, software should check the 66MHz-Capable bit in the bridge's PCI configuration Status register (see Table 19-4 on page 372).
  - If the bridge is a PCI-to-PCI bridge, software should check the 66MHz-Capable bit in the bridge's PCI Secondary Status register (see "Secondary Status Register" on page 565).

Power-Related Issues

Slot Power Requirements

Table 22-5 on page 476 lists the slot power requirements. The maximum power drawn by all supply voltages to a slot may not exceed 25W. Cards that have a range of operating currents, or that have a dynamic or switching load, must guarantee that the peak operating loads never exceed the values shown in Table 22-5 on page 476 (even while the card is turning on). During card turn on, the card must tolerate voltage slew rates within the ranges defined in the table without suffering damage.

Table 22-5: Slot Power Requirements

Supply Voltage (V)	Max Operating Current	Max Card Decoupling Capacitance (uF)	Min Supply Voltage Slew Rate (V/s)	Max supply Voltage Slew Rate (V/s)
+5	5A	3000	25	3300
+3.3	7.6A	3000	16.5	3300
+12	500mA	300	60	33000
-12	100mA	150	60	66000

Card Connected To Device With Separate Power Source

In this case, the card designer must ensure that the user is not exposed to any danger, and that neither the card nor the remote device will sustain any damage if one device is powered for a prolonged period of time while the other is not. The card designer must also ensure that the device's PCI master and target state machine remain reset as long as the PCI RST# signal remains asserted, whether or not the remote device is powered on.

23 Power Management

The Previous Chapter

The previous chapter described the Hot-Plug PCI capability defined by the revision 1.0 PCI Hot-Plug spec. A Hot-Plug capable system permits cards to be removed and installed without powering down the system.

This Chapter

This chapter provides a detailed description of PCI power management as defined in the revision 1.1 *PCI Bus PM Interface Specification*. In order to provide an overall context for this discussion, a description of the OnNow Initiative, ACPI (Advanced Configuration and Power Interface), and the involvement of the Windows OS is also provided.

The Next Chapter

The next chapter provides a detailed discussion of PCI-to-PCI bridge implementation. The information is drawn from the revision *1.1 PCI-to-PCI Bridge Architecture Specification*, dated December 18, 1998.

Power Management Abbreviated "PM" In This Chapter

Throughout this chapter, the author has abbreviated Power Management as "PM" for brevity's sake.

PCI Bus PM Interface Specification—But First...

The *PCI Bus PM Interface Specification* describes how to implement the optional PCI PM registers and signals. These registers and signals permit the OS to manage the power environment of PCI buses and the functions that reside on them.

Rather than immediately diving into a detailed nuts-and-bolts description of the *PCI Bus PM Interface Specification*, it's a good idea to begin by describing where it fits within the overall context of the OS and the system. Otherwise, this would just be a disconnected discussion of registers, bits, signals, etc. with no frame of reference.

A Power Management Primer

Basics of PC PM

The most popular OSs currently in use on PC-compatible machines are Windows 95/98/NT/2000. This section provides an overview of how the OS interacts with other major software and hardware elements to manage the power usage of individual devices and the system as a whole. Table 23-1 on page 480 introduces the major elements involved in this process and provides a very basic description of how they relate to each other. It should be noted that neither the PCI Power Management spec nor the ACPI spec (Advanced Configuration and Power Interface) dictate the policies that the OS uses to manage power. It does, however, define the registers (and some data structures) that are used to control the power usage of PCI functions.

Table 23-1: Major Software/Hardware Elements Involved In PC PM

Element	Responsibility
OS	Directs the **overall system power management**.To accomplish this goal, the OS issues requests to the ACPI Driver, WDM (Windows Driver Model) device drivers, and to the PCI Bus Driver. Application programs that are power conservation-aware interact with the OS to accomplish device power management.
ACPI Driver	Manages configuration, power management, and thermal control of **devices embedded on the system board that do not adhere to any industry standard interface specification**. Examples would could be chipset-specific registers, system board-specific registers that control power planes and bus clocks (e.g., the PCI CLK), etc. The PM registers within PCI functions (embedded or otherwise) are defined by the PCI PM spec and are therefore not managed by the ACPI driver, but rather by the PCI Bus Driver (see entry in this table).

Table 23-1: Major Software/Hardware Elements Involved In PC PM (Continued)

Element	Responsibility
WDM Device Driver	The WDM driver is a **Class driver** that can work with any device that falls within the Class of devices that it was written to control. The fact that it's not written for a specific device from a specific vendor means that it doesn't have register and bit-level knowledge of the device's interface. When it needs to issue a command to or check the status of the device, it issues a request to the **Miniport** driver supplied by the vendor of the specific device. The WDM also doesn't understand device characteristics that are peculiar to a specific bus implementation of that device type. As an example, the WDM doesn't understand a PCI device's configuration register set. It depends on the **PCI Bus Driver** to communicate with PCI configuration registers. When it receives requests from the OS to control the power state of its PCI device, it passes the request to the PCI Bus Driver: • When a request to power down its device is received from the OS, the WDM saves the contents of its associated PCI function's device-specific registers (in other words, it performs a context save) and then passes the request to the PCI Bus Driver to change the power state of the device. • Conversely, when a request to repower the device is received from the OS, the WDM passes the request to the PCI Bus Driver to change the power state of the device. After the PCI Bus Driver has repowered the device, the WDM then restores the context to the PCI function's device-specific registers.
Miniport Driver	**Supplied by the vendor of a device**, it receives requests from the WDM Class driver and converts them into the proper series of accesses to the device's register set.

Table 23-1: Major Software/Hardware Elements Involved In PC PM (Continued)

Element	Responsibility
PCI Bus Driver	This driver is **generic to all PCI-compliant devices**. It **manages their power states and configuration registers**, but does not have knowledge of a PCI function's device-specific register set (that knowledge is possessed by the Miniport Driver that the WDM driver uses to communicate with the device's register set). It receives requests from the device's WDM to change the state of the device's power management logic: • When a request is received to power down the device, the PCI Bus Driver is responsible for saving the context of the function's PCI configuration Header registers and any New Capability registers that the device implements. Using the device's PCI configuration Command register, it then disables the ability of the device to act as a bus master or to respond as the target of transactions. Finally, it writes to the PCI function's PM registers to change its state. • Conversely, when the device must be repowered, the PCI Bus Driver writes to the PCI function's PM registers to change its state. It then restores the function's PCI configuration Header registers to their original state.
PCI PM registers within each PCI function's PCI configuration space.	**The location, format and usage of these registers is defined by the PCI PM spec.** The PCI Bus Driver understands this spec and therefore is the entity responsible for accessing a function's PM registers when requested to do so by the function's device driver (i.e., its WDM).
System Board power plane and bus clock control logic	The implementation and control of this logic is typically system board design-specific and is therefore **controlled by the ACPI Driver** (under the OS's direction).

OnNow Design Initiative Scheme Defines Overall PM

A whitepaper on Microsoft's website clearly defines the goals of the OnNow Design Initiative and the problems it addresses. The author has taken the liberty of reproducing the text from that paper verbatim in the two sections that follow: *Goals*, and *Current Platform Shortcomings*.

Goals

The OnNow Design Initiative represents the overall guiding spirit behind the sought-after PC design. The following are the major goals as stated in an OnNow document:

- The PC is ready for use immediately when the user presses the On button.
- The PC is perceived to be off when not in use but is still capable of responding to wake-up events. Wake-up events might be triggered by a device receiving input such as a phone ringing, or by software that has requested the PC to wake up at some predetermined time.
- Software adjusts its behavior when the PC's power state changes. The operating system and applications work together intelligently to operate the PC to deliver effective power management in accordance with the user's current needs and expectations. For example, applications will not inadvertently keep the PC busy when it is not necessary, and instead will proactively participate in shutting down the PC to conserve energy and reduce noise.
- All devices participate in the device power management scheme, whether originally installed in the PC or added later by the user. Any new device can have its power state changed as system use dictates.

Current Platform Shortcomings

No Cooperation Among System Components. Hardware, system BIOS, operating system, and applications do not cooperate, resulting in the various system components fighting for control of the hardware. This causes erratic behavior: disks spin up when they are not supposed to; screens come on unexpectedly.

Add-on Components Do Not Participate In PM. When a person buys a computer, the hardware in the system typically operates in an integrated power management scheme, and peripherals added by the user or reseller may not be power managed by the system. Traditional power management is no longer sufficient, because it typically does not deal outside the domain of the system board. To meet the OnNow goals, the entire system must function as an integrated power-managed environment, which requires a generalized solution in the operating system.

Current PM Schemes Fail Purposes of OnNow Goals. The power management schemes currently in use focus only on the system board and use only device access information to make decisions about when to power down a device. This approach causes two major problems:

PROBLEM 1. The system cannot be extended and still be fully power managed. The PCMCIA subsystem is a good example of this. The BIOS might know what port the PCMCIA controller is using but cannot determine whether the device currently inserted in the socket is actually busy or not. To fully power-manage PCMCIA, the device driver running the device must be able to indicate when it is really time to power down its device.

PROBLEM 2. There are lost opportunities for extra power management. For example, the operating system knows that the disk I/O is really a paging maintenance operation and should not be considered when trying to determine whether a device is busy. Current power management schemes cannot determine this "user priority" or intent of a particular I/O access. By moving the policy into the operating system, individual devices will be powered down more quickly.

Installing New Devices Still Too Hard.
Microsoft Windows 95 and the Plug and Play initiative have provided an architecture that allows the user to install hardware more easily; however, the task is still not an easy operation for the end use. To install a new device, the user must turn off the computer and open the box. The OnNow PC must be easily extensible by the end user, and any device the user adds must become available without requiring a reboot or restart.

Apps Generally Assume System Fully On At All Times.
Applications that assume this can inadvertently keep the system from entering a lower power state. Also, applications that assume the PC is always On can crash when the PC wakes up after time has passed or devices have been removed.

System PM States

Table 23-2 on page 484 defines the possible states of the overall system with reference to power consumption. The "Working", "Sleep", and "Soft Off" states are defined in the OnNow Design Initiative documents.

Table 23-2: System PM States as Defined by the OnNow Design Initiative

Power State	Description
Working	The system is completely usable and the OS is performing power management on a device-by-device basis. As an example, the modem may be powered down during periods when it isn't being used.

Table 23-2: System PM States as Defined by the OnNow Design Initiative (Continued)

Power State	Description
Sleeping	The system appears to be off and power consumption has been reduced. The sleep levels a system may implement is system design-specific. The amount of time it takes to return to the "Working" state is inversely proportional to the selected level of power conservation. Here are some examples: • The system may keep power applied to main memory, thereby preserving the OS and application programs in memory. The processor's register set contents may also be preserved. In this case, program execution can be resumed very quickly. • The system may copy the complete contents of main memory and the processor's register set contents to disk, and then remove power from the processor and main memory. In this case, the restart time will be longer because memory must restore both before resuming program execution.
Soft Off	The system appears to be off and power consumption has been greatly reduced. It requires a full reboot to return to the "Working" state (because the contents of memory has been lost).
No Power	This state isn't listed in the OnNow Design Initiative documents. The system has been disconnected from its power source.

Device PM States

The OnNow Design Initiative also defines the PM states at the device level. They are listed and defined in Table 23-4 on page 486. Table 23-3 on page 485 presents the same information in a slightly different form.

Table 23-3: OnNow Definition of Device-Level PM States

State	Description
D0	**Device support: Mandatory.** State in which device is on and running. It is receiving full power from the system and is delivering full functionality to the user.

Table 23-3: OnNow Definition of Device-Level PM States (Continued)

State	Description
D1	**Device support: Optional**. Class-specific low-power state (refer to "Device Class-Specific PM Specifications" on page 488) in which device context (see "Definition of Device Context" on page 486) may or may not be lost. If a Bus is in the D1 state, software cannot do anything to the bus that would force devices on that bus to lose context.
D2	**Device support: Optional**. Class-specific low-power state ("Device Class-Specific PM Specifications" on page 488) in which device context (see "Definition of Device Context" on page 486) may or may not be lost. Attains greater power savings than D1. A Bus in the D2 state can cause devices on that bus to lose some context (for example, the bus reduces power supplied to the bus). Devices in D2 must be prepared for the bus to remain in D2 or a higher state.
D3	**Device support: Mandatory**. State in which device is off. Device context is lost. Power can be removed from the device.

Table 23-4: Concise Description of OnNow Device PM States

Device Power State	Power Consumption	Time to Return to D0 State
D0	Highest	NA
D1	< D0	Faster than D2
D2	< D1	Faster than D3
D3	For all intents and purposes, **none**, although there might be some negligible consumption.	Slowest

Definition of Device Context

General. During normal operation, the operational state of a device is constantly changing. Software external to the device (e.g., its device driver, the PCI Bus Driver, etc.) writes values into some of its registers, reads its status, etc. In addition, the device may contain a processor that executes device-specific code to control the device's interaction with the system as well as with an external element such as a network. The state of the device at a given instant in time is defined by (but not limited to) the following:

- The contents of the device's PCI configuration registers.
- The state of the device's IO registers that its device driver interacts with.
- If the device contains a processor, its current program pointer as well as the contents of some of the processor's other registers.

This is referred to as the current *device context*. Some or all of this information might be lost if the device's PM state is changed to a more aggressive power conservation level:

- If the device is placed in the D1 or D2 state, it may or may not lose some of this context information.
- If the device is placed in the D3 state, it will lose its context information.

Assume that a device is placed in a more aggressive power conservation state that causes it to lose some or all of its context information. If the device's context information is not restored when the device is placed back in the D0 state (i.e., fully-operational), it will no longer function correctly.

PM Event (PME) Context. Assume that the OS sets up a modem to wake up the system if the phone rings (in other words, on a Ring Detect) and that the system is then commanded to power down by the OS (e.g., in response to the user depressing the power switch). Remember that "power down" is a relative term within the context of power management. The chipset has power applied and monitors the PME# signal. To support this feature, the modem must implement:

- A PME# (Power Management Event) output signal.
- A PME# output driver enable/disable control bit.
- A PME status bit that indicates whether or not the device asserted PME#.
- One or more device-specific control bits that are used to selectively enable/disable the various device-specific events (such as Ring Detect) that can cause the device to assert PME#.
- Corresponding device-specific status bits that indicate why the device asserted PME#.

It should be obvious that the modem could not wake the system (by asserting PME#) if the logic described in the bullet list also lost power when the device is commanded to enter the D3 (off) state. It wouldn't "remember" that it was supposed to do so or why, would not be enabled to do so, etc. In other words, for the Ring Detect to successfully wake the system, the device's PME context information must not be lost when the device is placed in the D3 state.

Device Class-Specific PM Specifications

Default Device Class Specification. As mentioned earlier in this chapter, the OnNow Design Initiative provides a basic definition of the four possible power states (D0 - through - D3). It also defines the minimum PM states that all device types must implement. The document that provides this definition is the *Default Device Class Power Management spec*. This document mandates that all devices, irrespective of device category, must implement the PM states defined in Table 23-5 on page 488.

Table 23-5: Default Device Class PM States

State	Description
D0	Device is on and running. It is receiving full power from the system and is delivering full functionality to the user.
D1	This state is not defined and not used.
D2	This state is not defined and not used.
D3	Device is off and not running. Device context is assumed lost, and there is no need for any of it to be preserved in hardware. This state should consume the minimum power possible. Its only requirement is to recognize a bus-specific command to re-enter D0. Power can be removed from the device while in D3. If power is removed, the device will receive a bus-specific hardware reset upon reapplication of power, and should initialize itself as in a normal power on.

Device Class-Specific PM Specifications. Above and beyond the power states mandated by the *Default Device Class Specification*, certain categories (i.e., Classes) of devices may require:

- the implementation of the intermediate power states (D1 and/or D2)
- that devices within a class exhibit certain common characteristics when in a particular power state.

The rules associated with a particular device class are found in a set of documents referred to as *Device Class Power Management Specifications*. Currently, Device Class Power Management Specifications exist for the following device classes:

- Audio
- Communications
- Display
- Input
- Network
- PC Card
- Storage

They are available on Microsoft's Hardware Developers' web site.

Power Management Policy Owner

General. A device's PM policy owner is defined as the software module that makes decisions regarding the PM state of a device.

In Windows OS Environment. In a Windows environment, the policy owner is the class-specific driver (i.e., the WDM) associated with devices of that class.

PCI Power Management vs. ACPI

PCI Bus Driver Accesses PCI Configuration and PM Registers

As indicated in Table 23-1 on page 480 and Figure 23-1 on page 490, the PCI Bus Driver understands the location, format and usage of the PM registers defined in the PCI Power Management spec. It therefore is the software entity that is called whenever the OS needs to change the power state of a PCI device (or to determine its current power state and capabilities), or to access its configuration registers. Likewise,

- The IEEE 1394 Bus Driver understands the location, format and usage of the PM registers defined in the 1394 Power Management spec.
- The USB Bus Driver understands the location, format and usage of the PM registers defined in the USB Power Management spec.

Note that a discussion of the 1394 and USB Bus drivers is outside the scope of this book.

ACPI Driver Controls Non-Standard Embedded Devices

There are devices embedded on the system board whose register sets do not adhere to any particular industry standard spec. At boot time, the BIOS reports these devices to the OS via a set of tables (the **ACPI tables**; also referred to as the **namespace**; ACPI stands for Advanced Configuration and Power Interface). When the OS needs to communicate with any of these devices, it calls the ACPI Driver. The ACPI Driver executes a handler (referred to as a **Control Method**) associated with the device. The handler is found in the ACPI tables that were passed to the OS by the BIOS at boot time. The handler is written by the system board designer in a special interpretive language referred to as ACPI Source Language, or **ASL**. The format of ASL is defined in the ACPI spec. The ASL source is then compiled into ACPI Machine Language, or **AML**. Note that AML is not a processor-specific machine language. It is a tokenized (i.e., compressed) version of the ASL source code. The ACPI Driver incorporates an AML token interpreter that enables it to "execute" a Control Method.

A discussion of ACPI is outside the scope of this book. It is only mentioned because the OS uses a combination of ACPI and Bus Driver services (such as the PCI Bus Driver) to manage the system's power and configuration.

Figure 23-1: Relationship of OS, Device Drivers, Bus Driver, PCI Registers, and ACPI

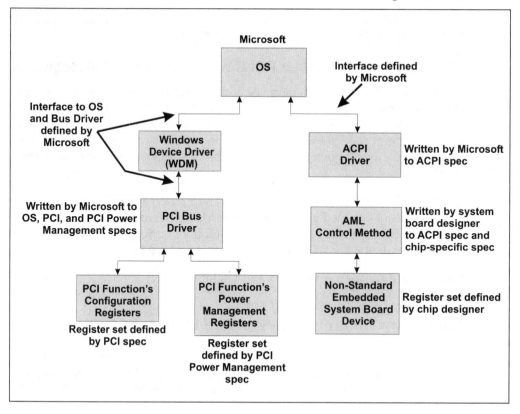

Some Example Scenarios

Figure 23-2 on page 493, Figure 23-3 on page 495, and Figure 23-4 on page 496 illustrate some example PM scenarios. *It should be noted that these illustrations are meant to be introductory in nature and do not cover all possible power state changes.* The examples focus on turning a PCI function Off (from a power perspective), or turning it On. This implies two possible states for a device (D0 and D3). While it's possible a function only has two states, a function may additionally implement other optional, intermediate power states (D1 and/or D2). The possible power states are discussed later in this chapter.

The following are some of the terms used in the illustrations:

- **IO Request Packet, or IRP.** The OS communicates a request to a Windows device driver by issuing an IRP to it. There are different categories of IRPs; for example, a Power IRP is used to request a change in the PM state of a device to or get its current PM state.
- **Windows Driver Model, or WDM**. A device driver written for Windows 98 or Windows 2000 (i.e., Windows NT 5.0) that controls a device or a group of similar devices (e.g., network adapters).
- **General Purpose Event, or GPE**. ACPI-related events. The chipset implements a GPE register which is used to selectively enable or disable recognition of various GPEs. When recognition of a specific GPE is enabled (such as a PM event) and that event occurs, the chipset generates an SCI (System Control Interrupt) to the processor. This invokes the GPE handler within the ACPI Driver which then reads the GPE Status registers in the chipset to determine which GPE caused the interrupt.
- **System Control Interrupt, or SCI**. A system interrupt used by hardware to notify the OS of ACPI events. The SCI is an active low, shareable, level-sensitive interrupt.
- **Control Method**. A Control Method is a definition of how the OS can perform a simple hardware task. For example, the OS invokes a Control Method to read the temperature of a thermal zone. See the definition of ASL. An ACPI-compatible system must provide a minimal set of common Control Methods in the ACPI tables. The OS provides a set of well-defined Control Methods that ACPI table developers can reference in their Control Methods. OEMs can support different revisions of chipsets with one BIOS by either including Control Methods in the BIOS that test configurations and respond as needed or by including a different set of Control Methods for each chipset revision.

- **ACPI Source Language, or ASL**. Control Methods are written in a language called ASL which is then compiled into **AML (ACPI Machine Language)**. AML is comprised of a highly-compressed series of **tokens** that represent the ASL code. The AML code is interpreted and executed by an AML interpreter incorporated within the ACPI Driver.

Scenario—Restore Function To Powered Up State. Figure 23-2 on page 493 illustrates the basic series of actions required when the OS wishes to power up a PCI function that was placed in the powered down state earlier.

STEP 1. It's possible that the OS had turned off Vcc to the devices on the PCI bus and stopped the PCI clock generator that supplies the PCI clock to them. In this case, the OS would issue a Power (i.e., Power Management) IRP to the ACPI Driver requesting that the bus be turned back on. In response, the ACPI Driver would execute the AML code necessary to turn on the PCI clock generator and Vcc to the devices on the bus. When the ACPI Driver has completed this operation, it issues an IRP completion notice back to the OS. If the bus clock and Vcc had not been turned off earlier, this step can be skipped.

STEP 2. The OS issues a Power IRP to the PCI device's WDM requesting that the device be restored to the full power state. The WDM passes the IRP to the PCI Bus Driver.

STEP 3. The PCI Bus Driver writes to the device's PCI PM registers to power up device.

STEP 4. The PCI Bus Driver restores the contents of the device's PCI configuration Header registers and any New Capability register sets that the device implements. This automatically restores the device's PCI configuration Command register enable bits to their original states.

STEP 5. The PCI Bus Driver passes an IRP completion notice back to the WDM.

STEP 6. The WDM restores the content of the device's device-specific IO or memory-mapped IO registers. This causes the device's interrupt enable bit to be restored, re-enabling the device's ability to generate interrupt requests. The device is now ready to resume normal operation.

STEP 7. The WDM returns an IRP completion notice to the OS.

Figure 23-2: Example of OS Restoring a PCI Function To Full Power

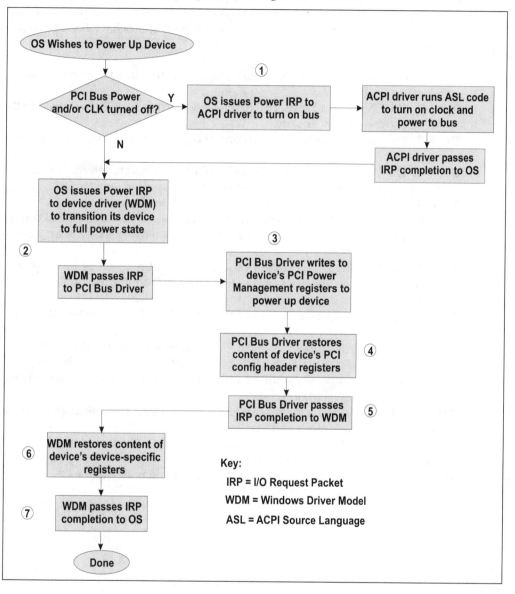

Scenario—OS Wishes To Power Down Bus. Figure 23-3 on page 495 illustrates the basic series of actions required when the OS wishes to power down a PCI bus (i.e., remove its clock and Vcc) to conserve on power. Before doing this, it must first ensure that all device's on that bus have been powered down.

STEP 1. If all of the PCI devices on the target bus are already powered down, skip to step 11.

STEP 2. The OS issues a Power IRP to the device driver (WDM) to transition its device to lowest power state.

STEP 3. The WDM saves the current content of the device's device-specific registers.

STEP 4. The WDM disables the device's ability to generate interrupt requests by clearing its interrupt enable bit in its device-specific register set.

STEP 5. The WDM pass the Power IRP to the PCI Bus Driver.

STEP 6. The PCI Bus Driver saves the current content of the device's PCI config Header registers and any New Capability register sets that it may implement.

STEP 7. The PCI Bus Driver disables the device's ability to act as a master and target by clearing the appropriate bits in its PCI configuration Command register.

STEP 8. The PCI Bus Driver writes to the device's PCI PM registers to set the new power state.

STEP 9. The PCI Bus Driver passes an IRP completion notice to the WDM.

STEP 10. The WDM passes the IRP completion notice to the OS. Steps 2-through-10 are repeated until all PCI devices on the target bus have been placed in the powered down state.

STEP 11. The OS issues a Power IRP to the ACPI driver requesting that it turn off the target bus's clock and Vcc.

STEP 12. The ACPI driver runs the appropriate AML Control Method to turn off the clock and power to the bus.

STEP 13. The ACPI driver passes the IRP completion notice to the OS.

Figure 23-3: Example of OS Powering Down All Functions On PCI Bus and Then the Bus Itself

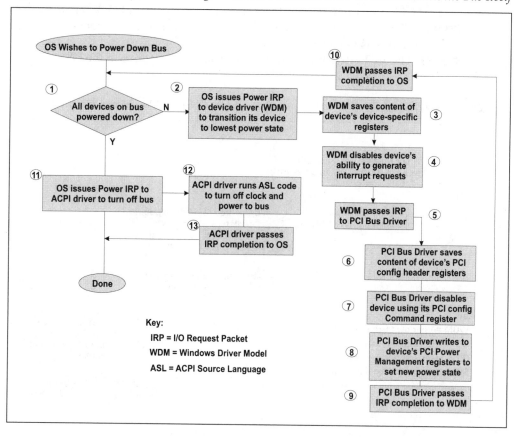

Scenario—Setup a Function-Specific System WakeUp Event.

Figure 23-4 on page 496 illustrates the OS preparing a PCI device so that it will wake up the system when a particular device-specific event occurs.

STEP 1. The OS issues a Power IRP to the device driver (WDM) to enable the device to wakeup the system on a specified event.

STEP 2. The WDM writes to device-specific registers within the device to enable the event that will cause the system to wake up.

STEP 3. The WDM passes the IRP to the PCI Bus driver.

STEP 4. The PCI Bus Driver writes to the function's PCI PM registers to enable its PME# logic.

STEP 5. The PCI Bus Driver returns the IRP completion notice to the WDM.

STEP 6. The WDM returns the IRP completion notice to the OS.

STEP 7. The OS issues a Power IRP to the ACPI driver requesting that the PCI Power Management Event (PME) monitoring logic be enabled to generate an ACPI interrupt (referred to as an SCI, or System Control Interrupt).

STEP 8. The ACPI driver enables the chipset's GPE logic to generate an SCI when PME# is detected asserted.

STEP 9. The ACPI driver returns the IRP completion notice to the OS.

Figure 23-4: OS Prepares a Function To Cause System WakeUp On Device-Specific Event

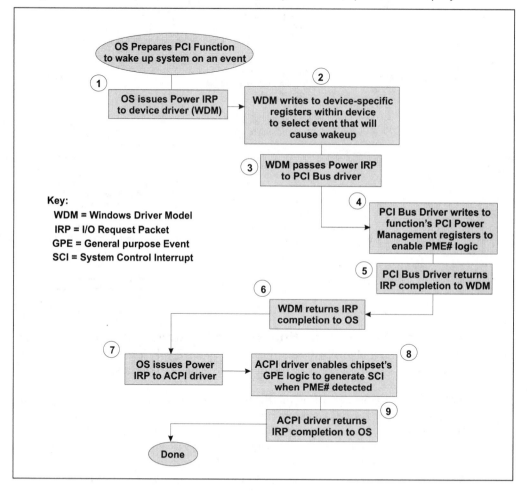

Chapter 23: Power Management

PCI Bus PM Interface Specification

Now that the overall framework of the PM environment has been described, this section begins the detailed description of the *PCI Bus PM Interface Specification*.

Legacy PCI Devices—No Standard PM Method

PCI devices designed before the advent of the *PCI Bus PM Interface Spec* may or may not implement some form of power management. If implemented, the method used to control the device's power state is specific to the device and therefore requires device-specific software to manage it.

PCI devices that do not implement any form of PM logic can only be in one of two possible power states, On (D0) or Off (D3$_{cold}$), and cannot be programmatically switched between the two.

Device Support for PCI PM Optional

It is optional whether or not a PCI device implements power management capability. If it does and was designed after the advent of the PCI Power Management spec, it must be implemented as defined by that spec.

Discovering Function's PM Capability

"New Capabilities" on page 390 describes the New Capabilities registers. This is essentially a linked list of register sets, each of which controls an optional new capability that the PCI function may or may not implement. The Capability ID of the PM register set is 01h. To determine if a PCI function implements the PM registers:

STEP 1. Software **checks** bit 4 (**Capabilities List bit**) of the function's **PCI configuration Status register** (see Figure 23-6 on page 499 and Figure 23-5 on page 498). A one indicates that the Capabilities Pointer register is implemented in the first byte of dword 13d of the function's configuration Header space.

497

STEP 2. The programmer then **reads** the dword-aligned pointer from the **Capabilities Pointer register** and uses it to read the indicated dword from the function's configuration space. This is the first dword of the first New Capability register set.

STEP 3. Refer to Figure 23-7 on page 500. If the first (i.e., least-significant) byte of the dword read contains **Capability ID 01h**, this identifies it as the PM register set used to control the function's power state. If the ID is something other than 01h, then this is the register set for a New Capability other than PM (e.g., AGP or VPD). The byte immediately following the Capability ID byte is the pointer (within the function's configuration space) to the start of the register set for the next New Capability (if there are any additional New Capabilities). 00h indicates there isn't any, while a non-zero value is a valid pointer. As **software traverses the linked-list** of the function's New Capabilities, its PM register set will hopefully be located. A detailed description of the PM registers can be found in "Detailed Description of PM Registers" on page 517.

Figure 23-5: PCI Configuration Status Register

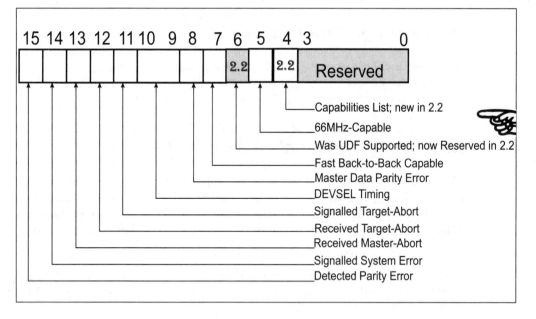

Figure 23-6: PCI Configuration Header Registers

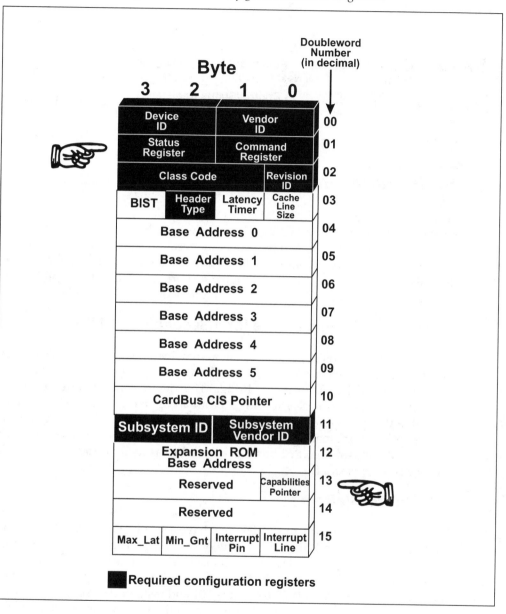

Figure 23-7: PCI Power Management Capability Register Set

31	16	15	8	7	0	
Power Management Capabilities (PMC)		**Pointer to Next Capability**		**Capability ID 01h**		1st Dword
Data Register	**Bridge Support Extensions (PMCSR_BSE)**	**Control/Status Register (PMCSR)**				2nd Dword

Power Management—PCI Bus vs. PCI Function

Just as the OS can manage the PM state of a PCI function, it may also be able to manage the PM state of a PCI bus. In other words, hardware (specifically, the host/PCI bridge or PCI-to-PCI bridges) may permit the PM software to turn off the clock on a PCI bus. It may also allow power to be removed from the devices that reside on a PCI bus. A bridge design may permit one, the other, both or neither of these capabilities. The sections that follow describe PM of a PCI bus.

Bridge—Originating Device for a Secondary PCI Bus

Refer to Figure 23-8 on page 503. A system may include one or more PCI buses and each PCI bus is controlled by a bus bridge. In the figure, PCI bus zero is controlled by the Processor-to-PCI Bridge. This device is also referred to as the Host/PCI bridge, or the North bridge. From a PM standpoint, the bridge that controls a PCI bus is referred to as its *originating device*. The PCI-to-PCI bridge in the figure is the originating device for PCI bus one. Relative to the PCI-to-PCI bridge in the illustration, PCI bus 0 is referred to as its *primary bus*, while PCI bus one is its *secondary bus*.

PCI Bus PM States

Like any other PCI device, the bridge may have a set of PM registers that define the PM capabilities and current PM state of the bridge. The current PM state of the bridge (D0, D1, D2, or D3—refer to "Device PM States" on page 485) also defines the current PM state of the bridge's secondary bus. The possible bus PM states are described in Table 23-6 on page 501 and in Table 23-7 on page 502 (the second table provides the same information as the first, but in a different format).

Table 23-6: Basic Description of PCI Bus PM States

Bus PM State	Description
B0	The **bus** is **fully operational** and ready to host transactions. Bridge support for the B0 PM state is **mandatory**.
B1	Vcc is still applied to all devices on the secondary bus and its PCI CLK is still running. The **bridge is in a light sleep** power conservation state and is not prepared to deal with transactions initiated on its secondary bus. The **bus** is **in an enforced idle state** (FRAME# and IRDY# remain deasserted) and no bus master on the secondary side (including the bridge) is permitted to initiate transactions. The PM software ensures that no transactions will be initiated by placing all functions on the secondary bus into a PM state other than the D0 before placing the bus into the B1 PM state. Bridge support for the B1 state is **optional**.
B2	The bridge is in a deep sleep power conservation state. Vcc is still applied to all functions, but the PCI **CLK** has been **stopped** (in the low state). Bridge support for the B2 state is **optional**.
B3	The bridge has **removed** power (**Vcc**) from all devices on the secondary bus. Obviously, all bridges support the B3 state if the system removes power from the bridge itself. *Whether or not a bridge design supports programmatically placing its secondary bus into this PM state is optional.*

Table 23-7: Bus Power Management (PM) States

Bus PM State	State of Vcc	State of PCI CLK	Permissible PCI Activity on Secondary PCI Bus
B0 (full on)	on	free running	1. Any PCI bus transaction. 2. Function may generate interrupts. 3. Function may assert PME# (if enabled to do so by PME_En bit in PMCSR; see Figure 23-13 on page 521). Also see note following table.
B1	on	free running	Function may assert PME# (if enabled to do so by PME_En bit in PMCSR; see Figure 23-13 on page 521). Also see note following table.
B2	on	Stopped in low state. *Note*: If CLK normally 33.33MHz - 66MHz, RST# must be asserted when frequency changed.	
B3 (full off)	off	NA—no power	

Note: The references to PME# in column four of Table 23-7 refer to the PM Event signal, PME#, and its corresponding enable bit, PME_En. The concept of the PM event was introduced in "PM Event (PME) Context" on page 487 and is described in detail in "Detailed Description of PM Events" on page 529. The PCI bus PM states are discussed in detail in "PCI Bus PM States" on page 500.

Figure 23-8: System Block Diagram

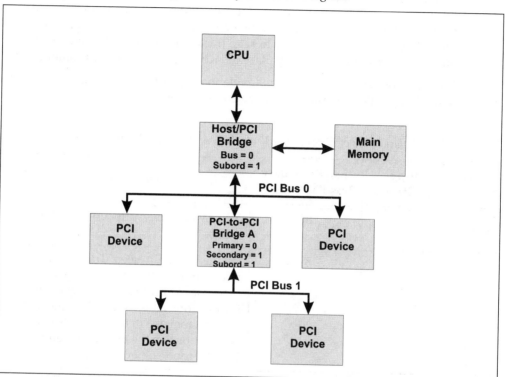

Bus PM State vs. PM State of the PCI Functions On the Bus

Each PCI device may contain between one and eight PCI functions. A function is a PCI logical device. Each function may implement its own set of PM registers that are used to report its PM capabilities and to control its current PM state.

There is a relationship between the bus PM state and the PM state of the functions that reside on that bus: the *bus PM state cannot be in a numerically higher (more aggressively) PM state than the numerically lowest PM state of any of the functions that reside on the bus.* As an example, assume that all of the functions on a PCI bus are in the D0 state and the bus is in the B1 state. This is an illegal combination because functions (PCI bus masters) are not permitted to generate PCI transactions on a bus when the bus is in the B1 state (because the bridge is not prepared to deal with transactions).

Keep in mind that functions are only aware of their own PM state. They are not aware of the PM state of the other functions on the bus or that of the bus itself. Likewise, the bridge is only aware of its own PM state and has no knowledge of the PM states of the functions residing on its secondary bus. In other words, it is the PM software's responsibility to keep track of the current PM states of all PCI buses and functions and to only place devices into supported PM combinations.

Table 23-8 on page 504 describes the relationship between the current PM state of the bridge and the resultant PM state of its secondary bus.

Table 23-8: Relationship of Originating Bridge's PM State to Secondary Bus PM State

If Originating Bridge's PM State is	then Secondary Bus PM State is	Description
D0	B0	No power conservation in effect for bridge or bus.
D1	B1	Bridge is in light sleep. Transactions are not permitted on the secondary bus (because the bridge cannot deal with transactions while in the D1 mode). The PCI bus remains in the Idle state because all functions on the bus have been placed in a PM mode other than D0.
D2	B2	Bridge is in deep sleep and the PCI CLK is stopped on the secondary bus.
$D3_{hot}$ and B2_B3# bit = 1 (see Figure 23-15 on page 527)	B2	PCI **CLK stopped**, but **Vcc still applied** to all PCI devices on secondary bus. The bridge designer can choose to only turn off the CLK but not Vcc when the bridge is programmed to the $D3_{hot}$ state.
$D3_{hot}$ and B2_B3# bit = 0 (see Figure 23-15 on page 527)	B3	PCI **CLK stopped** and **Vcc turned off** to all PCI devices on secondary bus. The bridge designer can choose to turn off the CLK **and** Vcc when the bridge is programmed to the $D3_{hot}$ state.
$D3_{cold}$	B3	PCI CLK stopped and Vcc turned off to all PCI devices on secondary bus.

Bus PM State Transitions

Figure 23-9 on page 505 illustrates the allowable PCI bus PM state transitions. Remember that the PM state of the bus is determined by the current PM state of the bridge that originates the bus (see "Bus PM State vs. PM State of the PCI Functions On the Bus" on page 503).

Figure 23-9: Bus Power Management State Transitions

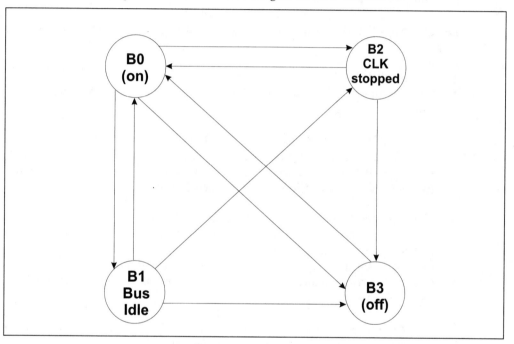

Function PM States

Each PCI function must support the full-on (D0) PM state and the full-off (D3) PM state. The D1 and D2 PM states are optional, as are the PM registers. The sections that follow provide a description of the possible PM states that may be supported by a PCI function.

D0 State—Full On

Mandatory. In this state, no power conservation is in effect and the device is fully-functional. All PCI functions must support the D0 state. Devices designed prior to the advent of the *PCI Bus PM Interface spec* support the D0 state, but they cannot be programmatically switched into and out of this state (unless via a proprietary, non-standard method). There are two flavors of the D0 PM state: D0 Uninitialized and D0 Active. No power conservation is in effect in either of these two states. Table 23-9 on page 507 illustrates the PM policies while in the D0 state.

D0 Uninitialized. A function enters the D0 Uninitialized state in one two ways:

- As a result of the PCI RST# signal being asserted, or
- When commanded to transition from the $D3_{hot}$ to the D0 PM state by software.

In either case, the function exhibits all of the characteristics that it has after detecting RST# asserted. In other words, its registers are all returned to their default states (before the function was configured and enabled by software). The function exhibits the following characteristics:

- It only responds to PCI configuration transactions.
- Its Command register enable bits are all returned to their default states.
- It cannot initiate transactions.
- It cannot act as the target of memory or IO transactions.
- It will not recognize messages delivered via Special Cycle transactions.
- It cannot generate PERR# or SERR#.

D0 Active. Once the function has been configured and enabled by software, it is in the D0 Active PM state and is fully functional.

Table 23-9: D0 Power Management Policies

Bus PM State	Function PM State	Registers and/or State that must be valid	Power	Access Delay	Restore Time	Actions permitted to Function	Actions permitted by Function
B0	Legacy function (D0)	all	full			Any PCI transaction	Any transaction or interrupt.
B0	D0 uninitialized	PME context **	< 10W	none		PCI config transactions.	none
B0	D0 active	all	full			Any PCI transaction.	Any transaction, interrupt, or PME. **
B1-3	D0 active	NA *					

*   This combination of Bus/Function PM states not allowed.

** If PME supported in this state.

D1 State—Light Sleep

Optional. This is a light sleep power conservation state. The function cannot:

- initiate bus transactions
- act as the target of transactions other than PCI configuration transactions. The function's PM registers are implemented in its configuration space and software must be able to access these registers while the device is in the D1 state.
- generate interrupts.

Other characteristics of the D1 state are:

- The function may assert PME# to wake up the system (assuming that it supports the generation of PM events while in the D1 state and has been enabled to do so).
- The function may or may not lose its context in this state. If it does and the device supports the generation of PME#, it must maintain its PME context (see "PM Event (PME) Context" on page 487) while in this state.
- The function must be returned to the D0 Active PM state in order to be fully-functional.

Table 23-10 on page 508 illustrates the PM policies while in the D1 state.

Table 23-10: D1 Power Management Policies

Bus PM State	Function PM State	Registers and/or State that must be valid	Power	Access Delay	Function Restore Time	Actions permitted to Function	Actions permitted by Function
B0	D1	Device class-specific registers and PME context. **	≤ D0 uninitialized	none	Device class-specific	PCI config transactions and transactions permitted by device class PM spec (typically none).	PME. ** Transactions are typically not permitted (but device class spec may permit).
B1				Time necessary to restore bridge to B0 state where it can deal with transactions		none	Only PME. **
B2-B3		NA *					

* This combination of Bus/Function PM states not allowed.

** If PME supported in this state.

D2 State—Deep Sleep

Optional. This power state provides more power conservation than the D1 PM state and less than the $D3_{hot}$ PM state. The function cannot:

- initiate bus transactions
- act as the target of transactions other than PCI configuration transactions. The function's PM registers are implemented in its configuration space and software must be able to access these registers while the device is in the D2 state.
- generate interrupts.

Other characteristics of the D2 state are:

- The function may assert PME# to wake up the system (assuming that it supports the generation of PM events while in the D2 state and has been enabled to do so).
- The function may or may not lose its context (other than its PME# context) in this state. If it does and the device supports the generation of PME#, it must maintain its PME context (see "PM Event (PME) Context" on page 487) while in this state.
- The function must be returned to the D0 Active PM state in order to be fully-functional.

Table 23-11 on page 510 illustrates the PM policies while in the D2 state.

Table 23-11: D2 Power Management Policies

Bus PM State	Function PM State	Registers and/or State that must be valid	Power	Access Delay	Function Restore Time	Actions permitted to Function	Actions permitted by Function
B0	D2	Device class-specific registers and PME context. **	≤ next lower supported PM state or ≤ D0 uninitialized.	200ms see note 1	Device class-specific	PCI config transactions	Only PME. **
B1				Greater of either bus restoration time or 200ms (see note 2).			
B2						none	
B3	D2	NA *					

* This combination of Bus/Function PM states not allowed.

** If PME supported in this state.

NOTE 1. This condition is not typical. It specifies the case where the system software has programmed the function's PowerState field and then immediately decides to change its power state again. Typically, the state transition recovery time will have expired prior to another power state change by software.

NOTE 2. The more typical case where the bus must first be restored to B0 before being able to access the function residing on the bus to request a change of its power state. State transition recovery time begins from the time of the last write to the function's PowerState field. In this case, the bus restoration time is dictated by state transition recovery times incurred in programming the bus's Originating Device to D0 which then transitions its bus to B0. Bus restoration time is typically the deciding factor in access delay for this case.

D3—Full Off

Mandatory. All functions must support the D3 PM state. This is the PM state in which power conservation is maximized. There are two ways that a function can be placed into the D3 PM state:

- Removal of power (Vcc) from the device. This is referred to as the **D3$_{cold}$** PM state. The function could transition into the D3$_{cold}$ state for one of two reasons: if the bus it resides on is placed in the B3 state; or the system is unplugged.
- Vcc is still applied to the function and software commands the function to enter the D3 state. This is referred to as the **D3$_{hot}$** PM state.

The following two sections describe the D3$_{hot}$ and D3$_{cold}$ PM states.

D3$_{Hot}$ State. Mandatory. As mentioned in the previous section, a function is placed into the D3$_{hot}$ PM state under program control (by writing the appropriate value into the PowerState field of its PMCSR register).

The function cannot:

- initiate bus transactions
- act as the target of transactions other than PCI configuration transactions. The function's PM registers are implemented in its configuration space and software must be able to access these registers while the device is in the D3$_{hot}$ state.
- generate interrupts.

Other characteristics of the D3$_{hot}$ state are:

- The function may assert PME# to wake up the system (assuming that it supports the generation of PM events while in the D3$_{hot}$ state and has been enabled to do so).
- The function almost certainly loses its context (other than its PME# context) in this state. If it does and the device supports the generation of PME# while in the D3$_{hot}$ state, it must maintain its PME context (see "PM Event (PME) Context" on page 487) while in this state.
- The function must be returned to the D0 Active PM state in order to be fully-functional.

The function exits the D3$_{hot}$ state under two circumstances:

- If Vcc is subsequently removed from the device, it transitions from D3$_{hot}$ to the D3$_{cold}$ PM state.
- Software can write to the PowerState field of the function's PMCSR register to change its PM state.

When programmed to exit D3$_{hot}$ and return to the D0 PM state, the function performs the equivalent of soft reset and returns to the D0 Uninitialized PM state (but PCI RST# is *not* asserted). Table 23-12 on page 512 illustrates the PM policies while in the D3$_{hot}$ state.

Table 23-12: D3$_{hot}$ Power Management Policies

Bus PM State	Function PM State	Registers and/or State that must be valid	Power	Access Delay	Function Restore Time	Actions permitted to Function	Actions permitted by Function
B0	D3$_{hot}$	PME con-text. **	≤ next lower supported PM state or ≤ D0 uninitialized.	10ms see note 1	Device class-specific	PCI config transactions	Only PME. **
B1				Greater of either bus restoration time or 10ms (see note 2).			
B2						none	
B3	NA *						

* This combination of Bus/Function PM states not allowed.

** If PME supported in this state.

Chapter 23: Power Management

NOTE 1. This condition is not typical. It specifies the case where the system software has programmed the function's PowerState field and then immediately decides to change its power state again. Typically, the state transition recovery time will have expired prior to another power state change by software.

NOTE 2. The more typical case where the bus must first be restored to B0 before being able to access the function residing on the bus to request a change of its power state. State transition recovery time begins from the time of the last write to the function's PowerState field. In this case, the bus restoration time is dictated by state transition recovery times incurred in programming the bus's Originating Device to D0 which then transitions its bus to B0. Bus restoration time is typically the deciding factor in access delay for this case.

D3$_{Cold}$ State. Mandatory. Every PCI function enters the D3$_{Cold}$ PM state upon removal of power (Vcc) from the function. When power is restored, RST# must also be asserted. The function then transitions from the D3$_{Cold}$ state to the D0 Uninitialized state. A function capable of generating a PME from the D3$_{Cold}$ state must maintain its PME context while in this state and when transitioning to the D0 state. Since power has been removed from the function, the function must utilize some auxiliary power source to maintain the PME context. For more information on the auxiliary power source, refer to "3.3Vaux" on page 534.

Table 23-13 on page 513 illustrates the PM policies while in the D3$_{Cold}$ state.

Table 23-13: D3$_{cold}$ Power Management Policies

Bus PM State	Function PM State	Registers and/or State that must be valid	Power	Access Delay	Function Restore Time	Actions permitted to Function	Actions permitted by Function
B0-2		NA *					
B3	D3$_{cold}$	PME context **	No power from bus	NA	Full context restore or boot latency.	Bus reset only.	Only PME. **
B3	Legacy PCI function(D3)	None					None

* Implies device-specific or slot-specific power supplies (outside the scope of the PCI PM spec; see "Hot-Plug PCI" on page 455).

** If PME supported in this state.

Function PM State Transitions

Figure 23-10 on page 514 illustrates the permissible PM state transitions for a PCI function. Table 23-14 on page 515 provides a description of each transition.

Table 23-15 on page 516 illustrates the delays involved in transitioning from one state to another from both a hardware and a software perspective.

Figure 23-10: PCI Function Power Management State Transitions

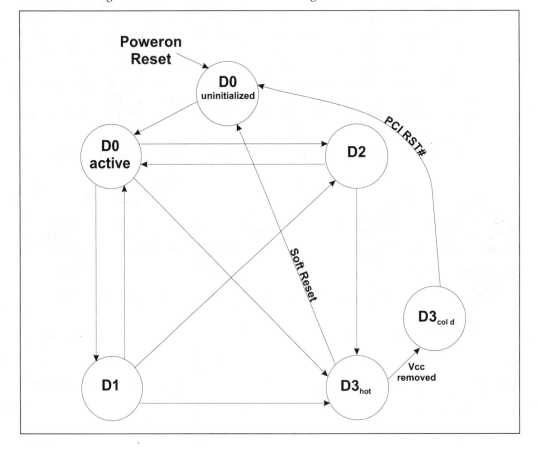

Table 23-14: Description of Function State Transitions

From State	To State	Description
D0 Uninitialized	D0 Active	Occurs under program control when function has been completely configured and enabled by its driver.
D0 Active	D1	Occurs when software writes to the PowerState field in the function's PMCSR register and sets the state to D1.
	D2	Occurs when software writes to the PowerState field in the function's PMCSR register and sets the state to D2.
	D3$_{hot}$	Occurs when software writes to the PowerState field in the function's PMCSR register and sets the state to D3$_{hot}$.
D1	D0 Active	Occurs when software writes to the PowerState field in the function's PMCSR register and sets the state to D0.
	D2	Occurs when software writes to the PowerState field in the function's PMCSR register and sets the state to D2.
	D3$_{hot}$	Occurs when software writes to the PowerState field in the function's PMCSR register and sets the state to D3$_{hot}$.
D2	D0 Active	Occurs when software writes to the PowerState field in the function's PMCSR register and sets the state to D0.
	D3$_{hot}$	Occurs when software writes to the PowerState field in the function's PMCSR register and sets the state to D3$_{hot}$.

Table 23-14: Description of Function State Transitions (Continued)

From State	To State	Description
D3$_{hot}$	D3$_{cold}$	Occurs when the bus's originating device (i.e., the bridge) removes Vcc from the function.
	D0 Uninitialized	Occurs when software writes to the PowerState field in the function's PMCSR register and sets the state to D0.
D3$_{cold}$	D0 Uninitialized	When power (Vcc) is restored, RST# must be asserted to the function at the same time. This causes the function to return to the D0 Uninitialized state.

Table 23-15: Function State Transition Delays

Initial State	Next State	Minimum software-guaranteed delays	Hardware-enforced delays (enforced by Bus's Originating Device)
D0	D1	0	NA
D0 or D1	D2	200µs from new state setting to first access to function (including config accesses).	The bridge must wait at least $\geq$ 16 PCI clocks before PCI clock is stopped.
D0, D1, or D2	D3$_{hot}$	10ms from new state setting to first access to function (including config accesses).	

Table 23-15: Function State Transition Delays (Continued)

Initial State	Next State	Minimum software-guaranteed delays	Hardware-enforced delays (enforced by Bus's Originating Device)
D1	D0	0	NA
D2	D0	200µs from new state setting to first access to function (including config accesses).	
D3_{hot}	D0	10ms from new state setting to first access to function (including config accesses).	
D3_{cold}	D0		

Detailed Description of PM Registers

The *PCI Bus PM Interface spec* defines the PM registers (see Figure 23-11 on page 517) that may be implemented in a PCI function. These registers provide software with information regarding the function's PM capabilities and permit software to control the PM properties of the function. An earlier section ("Discovering Function's PM Capability" on page 497) discussed how software discovers that a PCI function supports PM and therefore implements the PM register set. Since the PM registers are implemented in the PCI function's configuration space, software uses PCI configuration accesses to read and write the PM registers. The sections that follow provide a detailed description of these registers.

Figure 23-11: PCI Function's PM Registers

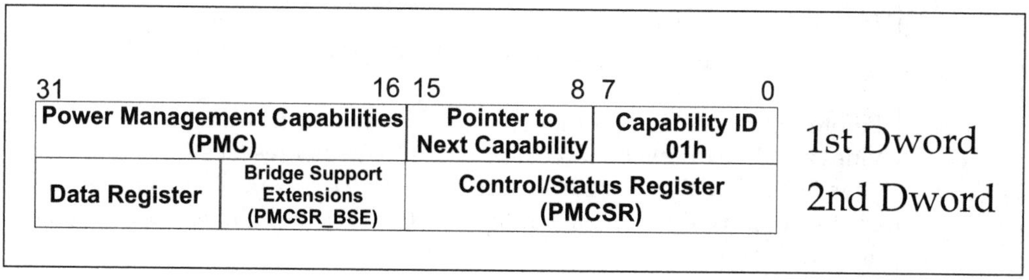

31 16 15 8 7 0	
Power Management Capabilities (PMC)	**Pointer to Next Capability** | **Capability ID 01h**	1st Dword
Data Register | **Bridge Support Extensions (PMCSR_BSE)**	**Control/Status Register (PMCSR)**	2nd Dword

PM Capabilities (PMC) Register

Mandatory for function that implements PM. This 16-bit read-only register is interrogated by software to determine the PM capabilities of the function. Figure 23-12 on page 518 illustrates the register and Table 23-16 on page 518 describes each bit field.

Figure 23-12: Read-Only Power Management Capabilities (PMC) Register

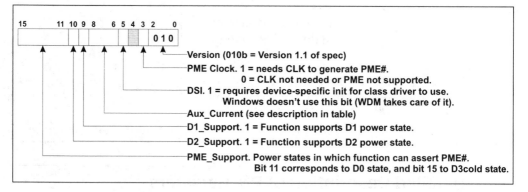

Table 23-16: The PMC Register Bit Assignments

Bit(s)	Description
15:11	**PME_Support** field. Indicates the PM states within which the function is capable of asserting PME# (Power Management Event). 0 in a bit indicates PME# generation is not supported in the respective PM state. **Bit** **Corresponds to PM State** 11 D0 12 D1 13 D2 14 $D3_{hot}$ 15 $D3_{cold}$ (function requires aux power to power PME logic) Before setting bit 15, the function must first determine that the system provides a 3.3Vaux power source (see "Card 3.3Vaux Presence Detection" on page 537). Note that CardBus cards receive their aux power over the card's Vcc pins. Refer to the whitepaper *PCI Style PM Interface Specification for CardBus Cards*.

Table 23-16: The PMC Register Bit Assignments (Continued)

Bit(s)	Description
10	**D2_Support** bit. 1 = Function does not implement the D2 PM state.
9	**D1_Support** bit. 1 = Function does not implement the D1 PM state.
8:6	**Aux_Current** field. For a function that supports generation of PME# from the $D3_{cold}$ state, this field reports the current demand made upon the 3.3Vaux power source (see "3.3Vaux" on page 534) by the function's logic that retains the PME context information. This information is used by software to determine how many functions can simultaneously be enabled for PME generation (based on the total amount of current each draws from the system 3.3Vaux power source and the power sourcing capability of the power source). • If the function does not support PME# generation from within the $D3_{cold}$ PM state, then this field is not implemented and always returns zero when read. • If the function implements the Data register (see "Data Register" on page 524), this field is not implemented and always returns zero when read. The Data register then takes precedence over this field in reporting the 3.3Vaux current requirements for the function. • If the function supports PME# generation from the $D3_{cold}$ state and does not implement the Data register, then the Aux_Current field reports the 3.3Vaux current requirements for the function. It is encoded as follows: **Bit** **8 7 6** **Max Current Required** 1 1 1 375mA 1 1 0 320mA 1 0 1 270mA 1 0 0 220mA 0 1 1 160mA 0 1 0 100mA 0 0 1 55mA 0 0 0 0mA

Table 23-16: The PMC Register Bit Assignments (Continued)

Bit(s)	Description
5	**Device-Specific Initialization (DSI)** bit. A one in this bit indicates that immediately after entry into the D0 Uninitialized state, the function requires additional configuration above and beyond setup of its PCI configuration Header registers before the Class driver can use the function. Microsoft OSs do not use this bit. Rather, the determination and initialization is made by the Class driver.
4	Reserved.
3	**PME Clock** bit. A one in this bit indicates that the function requires the presence of the PCI clock in order to generate PME#. Functions that don't require the clock or that don't generate PME# hardwire this bit to zero.
2:0	**Version** field. This field indicates the version of the PCI Bus PM Interface spec that the function complies with. **Bit** **2 1 0** **Complies with Spec Version** 0 0 1 1.0 0 1 0 1.1

PM Control/Status (PMCSR) Register

Mandatory for function that implements PM. This register is used for the following purposes:

- If the function implements PME capability, this register contains a **PME Status bit** that reflects whether or not a previously-enabled PME has occurred or not.
- If the function implements PME capability, this register contains a **PME Enable** bit that permits software to enable or disable the function's ability to assert the PME# signal.
- If the optional Data register is implemented (see "Data Register" on page 524), this register contains two fields that:
  - permit software to **select** the **information** that can be **read through** the **Data register**;
  - and provide the **scaling factor** that the **Data register value** must be **multiplied by**.
- The register's **PowerState** field can be used by software to determine the current PM state of the function and to place the function into a new PM state.

Figure 23-13 on page 521 and Table 23-17 on page 522 provide a description of the PMCSR bit fields. Note that PME is the abbreviation for Power Management Event. For a detailed discussion of PM Events, refer to "Detailed Description of PM Events" on page 529.

Figure 23-13: Power Management Control/Status (PMCSR) Register

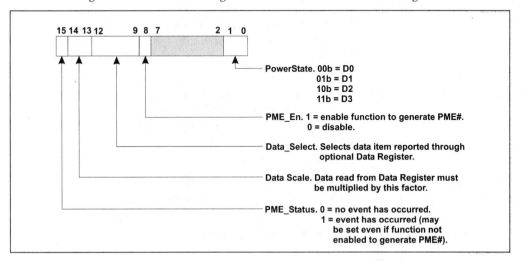

Table 23-17: PM Control/Status Register (PMCSR) Bit Assignments

Bit(s)	Value at Reset	Read/ Write	Description
15	See Description.	Read/Write. To Clear a one bit, write a one to it.	**PME_Status** bit. **Optional**. Only implemented if the function supports PME#, otherwise this bit is always zero. If the function supports PME, this bit reflects whether the function has experienced a PME (even if the PME_En bit in this register has disabled the function's ability to assert PME# in the event of a PME). If set to one, the function has experienced a PME and software clears this bit by writing a one to it. After reset, this bit is zero if the function doesn't support PME from $D3_{cold}$. If the function supports PME from $D3_{cold}$: • this bit is indeterminate at initial OS boot time. • otherwise, it reflects whether the function has experienced a PME. If the function supports PME from $D3_{cold}$, the state of this bit must persist while the function remains in the $D3_{cold}$ state and during the transition from $D3_{cold}$ to the D0 Uninitialized state. This implies that the PME logic must use an aux power source to power this logic during these conditions (see "3.3Vaux" on page 534).
14:13	Device-specific	Read-only	**Data_Scale** field. **Optional**. If the function does not implement the Data register (see "Data Register" on page 524), this field is hardwired to return zeros. If the Data register is implemented, the Data_Scale field is mandatory and must be implemented as a read-only field. The value read from this field represents the scaling factor that the value read from the Data register must be multiplied by. The value and interpretation of the Data_Scale field depends on the data item selected to be viewed through the Data register by the Data_Select field (see description in the next row of this table).

Table 23-17: PM Control/Status Register (PMCSR) Bit Assignments (Continued)

Bit(s)	Value at Reset	Read/ Write	Description
12:9	0000b	Read/Write	**Data_Select** field. **Optional.** If the function does not implement the Data register (see "Data Register" on page 524), this field is hardwired to return zeros. If the Data register is implemented, the Data_Select field is mandatory and is implemented as a read/write field. The value placed in this register selects the data value to be viewed through the Data register. That value must then be multiplied by the value read from the Data_Scale field (see previous row in this table).
8	See Description.	Read/Write	**PME_En** bit. **Optional.** 1 = enable function's ability to assert PME# in the event of a PME. 0 = disable. If the function does not support the generation of PMEs from any power state, this bit is hardwired to always return zero when read. After reset, this bit is zero if the function doesn't support PME from $D3_{cold}$. If the function supports PME from $D3_{cold}$: • this bit is indeterminate at initial OS boot time. • otherwise, it enables or disables whether the function can assert PME# in the event of a PME. If the function supports PME from $D3_{cold}$, the state of this bit must persist while the function remains in the $D3_{cold}$ state and during the transition from $D3_{cold}$ to the D0 Uninitialized state. This implies that the PME logic must use an aux power source to power this logic during these conditions (see "3.3Vaux" on page 534).
7:2	all zeros	Read-only	Reserved

Table 23-17: PM Control/Status Register (PMCSR) Bit Assignments (Continued)

Bit(s)	Value at Reset	Read/ Write	Description
1:0	00b	R/W	**PowerState** field. **Mandatory**. Software uses this field to determine the current PM state of the function (by reading this field) or to place it into a new PM state (by writing to this field). If software selects a PM state that isn't supported by the function, the writes must complete normally, but the write data is discarded and no state change occurs. **1 0** **PM State** 0 0 D0 0 1 D1 1 0 D2 1 1 D3$_{hot}$

Data Register

Optional, read-only. Refer to Figure 23-14 on page 526. The Data register is an optional, 8-bit, read-only register. If implemented, the Data register provides the programmer with the following information:

- Power consumed in the selected PM state. This information is useful in power budgeting.
- Power dissipated in the selected PM state. This information is useful in managing the thermal environment.
- Other, device-specific information regarding the function's operational characteristics. Currently, the spec only defines power consumption and power dissipation information to be reported through this register.

If the Data register is implemented,

- the Data_Select and Data_Scale fields of the PMCSR registers must also be implemented
- the Aux_Current field of the PMC register must not be implemented.

Determining Presence of Data Register. Perform the following procedure to determine the presence of the Data register:

STEP 1. Write a value of 0000b into the Data_Select field of the PMCSR register.

STEP 2. Read from either the Data register or the Data_Scale field of the PMCSR register. A non-zero value indicates that the Data register as well as the Data_Scale and Data_Select fields of the PMCSR registers are implemented. If a value of zero is read, go to step 3.

STEP 3. If the current value of the Data_Select field is a value other than 1111b, go to step 4. If the current value of the Data_Select field is 1111b, all possible Data register values have been scanned and returned zero, indicating that neither the Data register nor the Data_Scale and Data_Select fields of the PMCSR registers are implemented.

STEP 4. Increment the content of the Data_Select field and go to step 2.

Operation of the Data Register. The information returned is typically a static copy of the function's worst-case power consumption and power dissipation characteristics (obtained from the device's data sheet) in the various PM states. This data must be determined in the following test environment:

- **Bus frequency**: 33MHz if the function is not 66MHz-capable; 66MHz if the function is 66MHz-capable.
- **Vcc** = 5.25Vdc or 3.3Vdc (if 5Vdc not supported).
- **Temperature** = 70 degrees Centigrade.

To use the Data register, the programmer uses the following sequence:

STEP 1. Write a value into the PowerState field of the PMCSR register (see "PM Control/Status (PMCSR) Register" on page 520) to select the desired PM state.

STEP 2. Write a value into the Data_Select field (see Table 23-18 on page 526) of the PMCSR register to select the data item to be viewed through the Data register.

STEP 3. Read the data value from Data register.

STEP 4. Multiply the value by the scaling factor read from the Data_Scale field of the PMCSR register (see "PM Control/Status (PMCSR) Register" on page 520).

Multi-Function Devices. In a multi-function PCI device, each function must supply its own power-oriented information and the power information related to their common logic must be reported through function zero's Data register (see Data Select Value = 8 in Table 23-18 on page 526).

PCI-to-PCI Bridge Power Data. A PCI-to-PCI bridge function must only report the power information related to itself. Each PCI function that resides on its secondary bus is responsible for reporting its own power-related data.

Figure 23-14: PM Registers

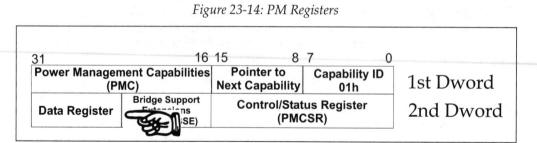

Table 23-18: Data Register Interpretation

Data Select Value	Data Reported in Data Register	Interpretation of Data Scale Field in PMCSR	Units/ Accuracy
00h	Power consumed in D0 state		
01h	Power consumed in D1 state		
02h	Power consumed in D2 state		
03h	Power consumed in D3 state		
04h	Power dissipated in D0 state		
05h	Power dissipated in D1 state	00b = unknown 01b = multiply by 0.1 10b = multiply by 0.01 11b = multiply by 0.001	Watts
06h	Power dissipated in D2 state		
07h	Power dissipated in D3 state		
08h	In a multi-function PCI device, function 0 indicates the power consumed by the logic that is common to all of the functions residing within this package.		

Table 23-18: Data Register Interpretation (Continued)

Data Select Value	Data Reported in Data Register	Interpretation of Data Scale Field in PMCSR	Units/ Accuracy
09h-0Fh. Spec actually shows this as decimal values 9-15. Author has chosen to represent in hex.	Reserved for future use of function 0 in a multi-function device.	Reserved	TBD
08h-0Fh. Spec actually shows this as decimal values 8-15. Author has chosen to represent in hex. *This entry seems to conflict with the previous row in this table. Perhaps it's a spec mistake and should really be 10h-FFh (16d-255d).*	Reserved (single function devices and other functions (greater than function 0) within a multi-function device		

PCI-to-PCI Bridge Support Extensions Register

Mandatory, Read-Only for all bridge devices. Note that the "CSR" in PMCSR_BSE stands for Control/Status Register. Refer to Figure 23-15 on page 527 and Table 23-19 on page 528 for a description of the bits within this register.

Figure 23-15: PCI-to-PCI Bridge Support Extensions (PMCSR_BSE) Register

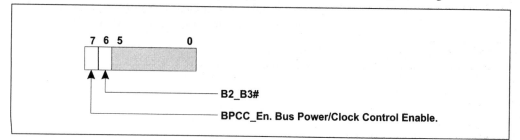

Table 23-19: PMCSR_BSE Register Bit Assignments

Bit(s)	Value at Reset	Description
7	External strap or internally hardwired	**BPCC_En (Bus Power/Clock Control Enable) bit.** When set to one, the current setting of the bridge's PowerState field controls both the bridge's PM state as well as the PM state of its secondary bus. • Setting the bridge's PM state to D2 causes the bridge to turn off the PCI clock to the secondary bus, placing the bus into the B2 PM state. • Transitioning the bridge's PM state from D2 to D3 causes the bridge to enter the $D3_{hot}$ PM state. In this case, whether or not the bridge turns off Vcc to the secondary bus devices is determined by the state of the B2_B3# bit (see next row in this table).
6	External strap or internally hardwired	**B2_B3# (B2/B3 support for $D3_{hot}$) bit.** This bit only has meaning if bit 7 = 1. The state of bit 6 then determines whether the bridge places the secondary bus into the B2 (clock off but Vcc still on) or B3 state (both clock and Vcc turned off) when the bridge is placed in the $D3_{hot}$ PM state. • If this bit = 0, the bridge turns off both the clock and Vcc to the secondary bus devices, thereby placing the secondary bus into the B3 state. • If this bit = 1, the bridge turns off the clock to the secondary bus devices but not Vcc, thereby placing the secondary bus into the B2 state.
5:0	Zero	Reserved.

Detailed Description of PM Events

Two New Pins—PME# and 3.3Vaux

THE PCI 2.2 SPEC DEFINES TWO NEW CONNECTOR PINS ASSOCIATED WITH PM EVENTS: **2.2**

- PME# (PIN A19) IS AN ACTIVE-LOW, SHARED, OPEN-DRAIN SIGNAL THAT A SLEEPING PCI FUNCTION MAY USE TO REQUEST THAT THE OS CHANGE ITS PM STATE IN RESPONSE TO AN EVENT THAT HAS BEEN DETECTED. ONCE RESTORED TO FULL-POWER AND CAPABILITY, THE FUNCTION, UNDER THE DIRECTION OF ITS DEVICE DRIVER, CAN TAKE THE SERIES OF ACTIONS NECESSARY TO SERVICE THE EVENT.
- 3.3VAUX (PIN A14) IS REQUIRED BY A PCI FUNCTION THAT CAN GENERATE A PME WHILE IN THE D3COLD PM STATE (IN OTHER WORDS, VCC HAS BEEN REMOVED FROM THE FUNCTION BY THE BRIDGE).

These two signals are described in the sections that follow.

What Is a PM Event?

As discussed earlier in this chapter, a PCI function may or may not implement PM capability. Assuming that is does, the OS may choose to (or an application program associated with the device may choose to) place the function in a low-power mode to save on energy consumption during periods when the function's capability isn't required. Optionally, the function design may permit the OS to set it up so as to assert the PME# signal upon the occurrence of one or more function-specific events. An example would be setting up a modem to assert PME# upon detection of Ring Detect and then placing the modem in a low-power mode. This would require that device driver use a bit in a device-specific control register (outside the scope of this spec) to enable the Ring Detect event to generate a PME. The driver must also enable the function (i.e., the modem) to assert the PME# signal when the event is detected. The driver accomplished this by setting the function's PME_En bit in its PMCSR register to a one.

Example Scenario

Figure 23-16 on page 531 refers to the following steps:

STEP 1. When a ring is detected (in other words, when a PME-enabled event occurs), the modem asserts the PME# signal to request a change in its power state.

STEP 2. The assertion of PME# is detected by the chipset which alerts the processor in some manner. In an ACPI-compliant system, the chipset will generate an SCI (System Control Interrupt) interrupt to the processor.

STEP 3. This causes the processor to suspend the currently-running program and execute the GPE (General Purpose Event) handler within the ACPI driver.

STEP 4. The GPE handler reads the GPE Status register(s) within the chipset to determine the cause of the SCI. In this case, a status bit is set indicating that someone asserted the PME# signal.

STEP 5. The GPE handler then traverses the PCI bus (or buses) to determine which function or functions previously enabled to generate PME# have asserted PME# (PME# is active-low, shared open-drain signal that can be driven by multiple devices simultaneously). This is accomplished by reading the state of the PME_Status bit in each function's PMCSR register (see "PM Control/Status (PMCSR) Register" on page 520).

STEP 6. After determining which function (or functions) asserted PME#, the handler calls each of their device drivers with a request to return each of their functions to the D0 Active state (or the D0 Uninitialized state if the function was in the $D3_{cold}$ state).

STEP 7. The driver clears the PME_Status bit in the function's PMCSR register (or clears its PME_En bit), thereby causing it to deassert PME#.

STEP 8. Once in the D0 Active PM state, the function is then fully active. The device driver checks its device-specific status to determine the specific event that caused the PME (e.g., the phone is ringing).

STEP 9. The driver then performs the series of actions necessary to handle the event (in the example scenario, it would command the modem to take the phone off hook, etc.).

A basic example of restoring a function to the operational state in the Windows environment can be found in "Scenario—Restore Function To Powered Up State" on page 492.

Figure 23-16: Example Scenario—Ring Detect Generates PME

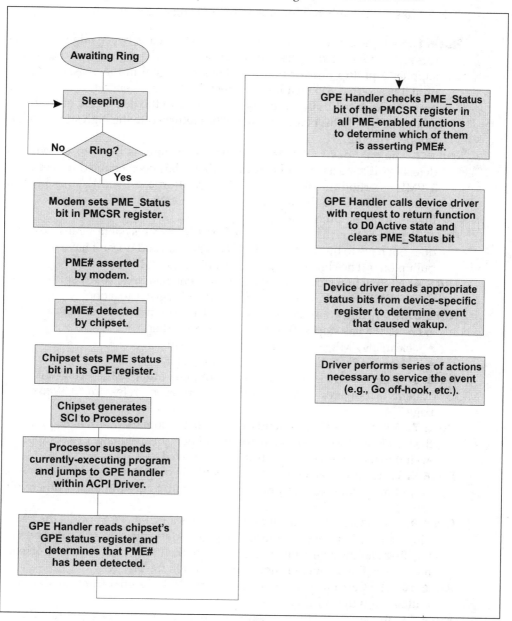

Rules Associated With PME#'s Implementation

This list has been numbered for ease in referencing a specific item:

RULE 1. In a typical system, the PME# signal is bussed between all PCI connectors and is connected to the chipset as an input. The system board designer supplies a pullup resistor that maintains the signal in the deasserted state until it is asserted. When all of the functions that are generating PME# have been serviced, the pullup returns PME# back to the deasserted state. It can take as long as 100ns before the signal has returned to the high state and has stopped ringing.

RULE 2. The only device that treats PME# as an input is the chipset. When it detects PME# asserted, and assuming that it has been enabled to recognize a PME assertion, it sets the GPE (General Purpose Event) status bit that indicates a PME has been detected and generates an SCI (System Control Interrupt) to the processor.

RULE 3. In a system that does not support PME#, the system board designer does not have to bus PME# to all PCI connectors and doesn't have to place a pullup on it. The chipset would not monitor the PME# signal.

RULE 4. No function may assert PME# unless enabled to do so (by software setting its PME_En bit in the function's PMCSR register to a one).

RULE 5. A function continues to assert PME# (even if the event that caused to assert PME# has stopped) until the software either:
- clears its PME_Status bit in its PMCSR register, or
- clears its PME_En bit in its PMCSR register.

RULE 6. Some functions may be capable of generating PME# even WHEN the system is powered off. For more information, refer to "3.3Vaux" on page 534.

RULE 7. A function's PME# circuit design must ensure that a voltage applied to the PME# signal on the system board will not cause damage to a component even if that component's Vcc has been removed.

RULE 8. When power is removed from its PME# output driver, the unpowered output must not present a low-impedance path to ground or any other voltage.

RULE 9. On a PCI add-in card that incorporates a PCI-to-PCI bridge, the PME# pins of functions that reside on the secondary bus are typically bussed together and the signal line is connected to the PME# pin on the add-in connector. The PME# signal is not routed through the bridge.

RULE 10. The CardBus spec requires that the PME# signal from PC Cards be routed through the bridge.

RULE 11. In a system with a large number of functions that can generate PME#, several PME# networks (each with its own pullup resistor) may be created and each of them connected to a separate PME# input on the chipset. The chipset would implement a separate GPE status bit for each input. This would diminish the amount of time that it would take software to discover which functions are asserting PME#.

Example PME# Circuit Design

Figure 23-17 on page 534 is an example PME# circuit presented in the *PCI Bus PM Interface spec*.

The example illustrates a PCI add-in card with multiple functions, a number of which are capable of asserting PME# on the card. Their PME# output drivers are labeled U1 (an open-drain buffer). The outputs of each of their drivers are wire-ORed together and are connected to the drain (D) on the Field Effect Transistor (FET) labeled Q1. The circuit that supplies the Gate (G) to Q1 is designed to keep the Gate turned off if Vcc (labeled as Vsource) has been removed from the card. This isolates the U1 output drivers from the system board's PME# trace and prevents the drivers from incurring possible damage when other components that still have Vcc applied are asserting the system board's PME# trace.

The Vsource may be supplied by a power source separate from the system board such as an on-card battery or an AC/DC adapter. In this case, U2 would still detect the presence of Vsource even if Vcc were removed from the card. As a result, the FET's Gate would be left open, keeping the on-card output drivers connected to the system board's PME# network even when power (i.e., Vcc) has been removed from the card.

Figure 23-17: Example PME# Circuit Design

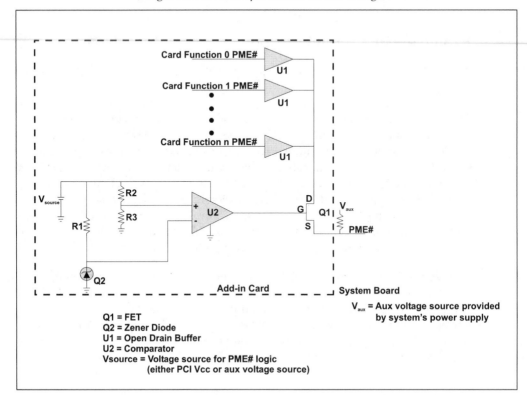

Q1 = FET
Q2 = Zener Diode
U1 = Open Drain Buffer
U2 = Comparator
Vsource = Voltage source for PME# logic
(either PCI Vcc or aux voltage source)

3.3Vaux

Can a Card With No Power Generate PME#? The answer is maybe. This discussion makes the following assumptions:

- Vcc has been removed from the card by the system. In other words, the PCI bus that it resides on has been placed in the B3 state by the bridge that originates the bus. As a result, the function or functions that reside on the card are in the $D3_{cold}$ PM state.
- The card may or may not incorporate an on-card auxiliary power source to keep its PME# logic powered during the power down period.

Now consider the following scenarios:

SCENARIO 1. If the card *doesn't have* an *on-card power source and* the *system* board *doesn't supply* it with an alternate source of power (*3.3Vaux*) to maintain its PME# logic during the power down, then the card *cannot generate PME#* while it is *in the D3$_{cold}$* PM state.

SCENARIO 2. Perhaps the card is designed such that it *doesn't have an on-card power source*, but the *system supplies* it with an alternate source of power (*3.3Vaux*) to maintain its PME# logic during the power down. Unfortunately, however, in this scenario the *card is not designed to take advantage of* the *3.3Vaux* to power its PME# logic. In this scenario, the card *cannot generate PME#* while it is *in the D3$_{cold}$* PM state.

SCENARIO 3. The card is designed *without an on-card power source*, it *can take advantage of 3.3Vaux* if the system supplies it on the 3.3Vaux connector pin, and the *system does supply 3.3Vaux* to it. In this scenario, the card *can generate PME#* while it is *in the D3$_{cold}$* PM state, but only if it is installed in a system that supplies it with 3.3Vaux.

SCENARIO 4. The *card* is designed *with* an *on-card power source* and therefore does not need 3.3Vaux from the system in order to maintain its PME# logic. In this scenario, the card *can generate PME#* while it is *in the D3$_{cold}$* PM state, irrespective of *whether or not* the *system supplies* it with *3.3Vaux*.

Maintaining PME Context in D3$_{cold}$ State.

Continuing an earlier example wherein the OS sets up a modem to generate PME# if the phone rings (in other words, on a Ring Detect), assume that the system is then commanded to power down by the OS (e.g., in response to the user depressing the power switch). To support this feature, the modem must implement:

- A PME# output signal.
- A PME enable/disable control bit (PME_En bit in PMCSR register)
- A PME status bit that indicates whether or not the device caused the wakeup (PME_Status bit in PMCSR register).
- One or more device-specific control bits that are used to selectively enable/disable the various device-specific events (such as Ring Detect) that can cause the device to assert PME#. These bits would be in device-specific registers outside the scope of this spec.
- Corresponding device-specific status bits that indicate why the device asserted PME#. These bits would also be in device-specific registers outside the scope of this spec.

It should be obvious that the modem could not wakeup the system (by asserting PME#) if the logic described in the bullet list also lost power when the device enters the $D3_{cold}$ (powered off) state. It wouldn't "remember" that it was supposed to do so or why, would not be enabled to do so, etc. In other words, for the Ring Detect to successfully wakeup the system, the device's PME context information must not be lost when the device is placed in the $D3_{cold}$ state. This highlights the need for an auxiliary power source whose sole purpose in life is keep the card's PME context logic alive during the period when Vcc has been removed from the function. The 3.3Vaux power pin (A14 on the PCI connector) is intended to serve as this source.

System May or May Not Supply 3.3Vaux. It is optional whether a system board supplies 3.3Vaux to the connectors. However, if the intent of the system board design is to support PMEs generated by functions in the $D3_{cold}$ state, then the system board design must supply 3.3Vaux to the connectors to ensure that these functions can do so.

3.3Vaux System Board Requirements. The following requirements regarding 3.3Vaux must be met. The list has been numbered for ease of reference:

1. A system board design that does not supply 3.3Vaux to the connectors must leave the 3.3Vaux connector pin (A14) unconnected.
2. A system board design that does supply 3.3Vaux must connect it to the 3.3Vaux pin on every PCI connector.
3. Table 23-20 on page 537 defines the DC operating environment that a 3.3Vaux-enabled system must deliver.
4. At a minimum, a system that supplies 3.3Vaux must be capable of fully powering the PME logic on least one PCI slot while the PCI bus is in the B3 state (i.e., clock stopped and Vcc removed). For a four-slot PCI bus, the minimum 3.3Vaux current capacity would be 435mA (one slot enabled to generate PME#—375mA, and three disabled slots—at 20mA each).
5. While the bus is in a state other than the B3 state (i.e., the B0, B1 or B2 state), Vcc is applied to the cards. In this case, the system must be capable of fully powering the PME logic on all slots. In the case of a four slot system, the minimum 3.3Vaux current capacity would be 1.5A (375mA x 4 = 1.5A).
6. A system board design that does supply 3.3Vaux must be capable of delivering up 1.24W (375mA x 3.3Vdc) to each enabled slot.
7. A system board design that does supply 3.3Vaux must be capable of delivering up 66mW (20mA x 3.3Vdc) to each disabled slot.
8. Functions in the D0, D1, D2, or $D3_{hot}$ PM state are unconditionally enabled to draw up to 1.24W from the 3.3Vaux source.

Table 23-20: DC Operating Environment for a 3.3Vaux-Enabled System

Parameter	Minimum	Typical	Maximum	Units
3.3Vaux	3.0	3.3	3.6	Volts
$I_{Max\_Enabled}$	-	-	375, see note 1	mA
$I_{Max\_Disabled}$	-	-	20, see note 2	

NOTE 1. Upper limit when function is in D0, D1, D2, $D3_{hot}$, or is in $D3_{cold}$ with its PME_En bit set to one.

NOTE 2. Upper limit when function is in $D3_{cold}$ and its PME_En bit is cleared to zero.

3.3Vaux Card Requirements. The following requirements regarding 3.3Vaux must be met. The list has been numbered for ease of reference:

1. A PME-enabled card may not draw more than 375mA from the 3.3Vaux supply.
2. A PME-disabled card may not draw more than 20mA from the 3.3Vaux supply.
3. Only cards capable of asserting PME# while in the $D3_{cold}$ PM state are permitted to connect to the connector's 3.3Vaux pin.
4. A card that uses 3.3Vaux must keep the 3.3Vaux and Vcc power planes electrically isolated from each other. In the case of a component that connects to both of these supplies, special care must be taken to keep them separated within the component. When power is removed from Vcc, special care must be taken to ensure that no damage or malfunction occurs whether the component is currently powered or not.

Card 3.3Vaux Presence Detection. A function capable of asserting PME# while in the $D3_{cold}$ state that does not have its own power source (e.g., a battery) must first determine the presence or absence of 3.3Vaux before reporting its support for PME# while in the $D3_{cold}$ state (in bit 15 of the PMC register). A weak pull-down resistor (see Figure 23-18 on page 538) must be implemented on every card to create a logic low reference when installed in a system board that doesn't supply 3.3Vaux. The current consumed by the pull-down must be included in the slot's total 3.3Vaux budget. The function then logically-ANDs this reference level with bit 15 of the PMC register when bit 15 is read by software. A function that normally supports PME# while in the $D3_{cold}$ state would then report that it doesn't support it if it's installed in a slot that doesn't supply 3.3Vaux.

A card that implements both a Vcc (i.e., 3.3V) power plane and a separate 3.3Vaux power plane would not function correctly if installed in a system that doesn't supply any voltage to its 3.3Vaux power plane. The circuit pictured in Figure 23-18 on page 538 automatically sources power to the card's 3.3Vaux power plane from the connector's 3.3Vaux pin (A14) if it detects the presence of a system board 3.3Vaux supply. Conversely, if it detects that 3.3Vaux is not being supplied by the system board, power is automatically routed onto the card's 3.3Vaux power plane from the system's Vcc power source.

Figure 23-18: 3.3Vaux Presence-Detect and Source Selection Logic

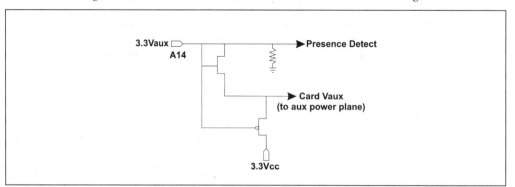

Problem: In B3 State, PCI RST# Signal Would Float. The PCI spec requires that the RST# signal must be asserted whenever the PCI main power rails are out of spec (e.g., when low and ramping up, or low as a result of a power failure). During these problem power periods, the assertion of RST# causes the output buffers within all PCI devices to be placed in the high-impedance state until the power is completely lost. At that point, the entire bus, including RST# is floating.

In a system that implements power management, software may instruct a bridge to place itself into the D3 state and its secondary bus into the B3 state. When the secondary bus enters the B3 state, the CLK is stopped *and the power (Vcc) is removed from the PCI devices that reside on that PCI bus.* In other words, it's a programmable power failure.

Solution. A system board that supplies 3.3Vaux to the card connectors must ensure that the PCI RST# signal remains asserted whenever the bus is in the B3 state. This can be accomplished in one of two ways:

- The system board logic could power the PCI RST# signal's output buffer from an auxiliary power source, or
- A weak pull-down resistor can be placed on the PCI RST# signal to keep it asserted during the B3 powered down period.

When the bus is in the B3 state, PCI functions can then depend on a valid low-to-high transition on RST# to signal when they must return all of their volatile registers to their default states and transition from the $D3_{cold}$ state to the D0 Uninitialized state.

OS Power Management Function Calls

In order to support power management, the OS must implement the basic function call capabilities described in the next three sections.

Get Capabilities Function Call

This function call returns the PM capabilities of a PCI function. This information is obtained from the function's PMC register.

Set Power State Function Call

This function call is used by the OS to change the PM mode from the one that the PCI function is currently in. This is accomplished by writing the appropriate value into the PowerState field of the function's PMCSR register.

Get Power Status Function Call

This function call permits the OS to obtain the present PM state of a PCI function as well as its PM capabilities. This information is obtained by reading from the PowerState field of the function's PMCSR register (to obtain the function's current power state), and by reading from its PMC register (to obtain its capabilities).

BIOS/POST Responsibilities at Startup

In an environment wherein the OS is responsible for managing power, the system BIOS isn't involved in PM but is responsible for basic system initialization before the OS loads and takes over. The system BIOS should include the following capabilities in its POST routines:

1. **During initial power**-up of the platform, the BIOS should ensure that the **chipset masks** off **recognition of** the **PME#** signal (in case a spurious PME occurs before the PME interrupt handler is placed in memory).
2. **During** a **warm boot** (Control-Alt-Del), the BIOS should ensure that the **chipset masks** off **recognition of** the **PME#** signal (in case a device enabled earlier in time to generate a PME# does so during the boot process before the PME interrupt handler is placed in memory).
3. **During** a **warm boot** (Control-Alt-del), the BIOS must **restore all PCI functions to** the **D0** state. There are two ways that this may be accomplished:
    *   Program the PowerState field in every function's PMCSR register to the D0 state. Due to the amount of time this might take, this is not the preferred method.
    *   Cause the chipset to assert the PCI RST# signal to all PCI functions. This is the preferred method.

24 PCI-to-PCI Bridge

The Previous Chapter

The previous chapter provided a detailed description of PCI power management as defined in the revision 1.1 *PCI Bus PM Interface Specification*. In order to provide an overall context for this discussion, a description of the OnNow Initiative, ACPI (Advanced Configuration and Power Interface), and the involvement of the Windows OS was also provided.

This Chapter

This chapter provides a detailed discussion of PCI-to-PCI bridge implementation. The information is drawn from the revision *1.1 PCI-to-PCI Bridge Architecture Specification*, dated December 18, 1998.

The Next Chapter

The next chapter focuses on the ordering rules that govern the behavior of simple devices as well as the relationships of multiple transactions traversing a PCI-to-PCI bridge. It also describes how the rules prevent deadlocks from occurring.

Scaleable Bus Architecture

A machine that incorporates one PCI bus has some obvious limitations. Some examples follow:

- If too many electrical loads (i.e., devices) are placed on a PCI bus, it ceases to function correctly.
- The devices that populate a particular PCI bus may not co-exist together too well. A master that requires a lot of bus time in order to achieve good performance must share the bus with other masters. Demands for bus time by these other masters may degrade the performance of this bus master subsystem.
- One PCI bus only supports a limited number of PCI expansion connectors (due to the electrical loading constraints mentioned earlier).

These problems could be solved by adding one or more additional PCI buses into the system and re-distributing the device population. How can a customer (or a system designer) add another PCI bus into the system? The *PCI-to-PCI Bridge Architecture Specification* provides a complete definition of a PCI-to-PCI bridge device. This device can either be embedded on a PCI bus or may be on an add-in card installed in a PCI expansion connector. The PCI-to-PCI bridge provides a bridge from one PCI bus to another, but it only places one electrical load on its host PCI bus. The new PCI bus can then support a number of additional devices and/or PCI expansion connectors. The electrical loading constraint is on a per bus basis, not a system basis. Of course, the power supply in the host system must be capable of supplying sufficient power for the load imposed by the additional devices residing on the new bus. The system designer could also include more than one host/PCI bridge.

Terminology

Before proceeding, it's important to define some basic terms associated with PCI-to-PCI bridges. Each PCI-to-PCI bridge is connected to two PCI buses, referred to as its primary and secondary buses.

- **Downstream**. When a transaction is initiated and is passed through one or more PCI-to-PCI bridges flowing away from the host processor, it is said to be moving downstream.
- **Upstream**. When a transaction is initiated and is passed through one or more PCI-to-PCI bridges flowing towards the host processor, it is said to be moving upstream.
- **Primary bus**. PCI bus on the upstream side of a bridge.
- **Secondary bus**. PCI bus that resides on the downstream side of a PCI-to-PCI bridge.
- **Subordinate bus**. Highest-numbered PCI bus on the downstream side of the bridge.

Figure 24-1: Basic Bridge Terminology

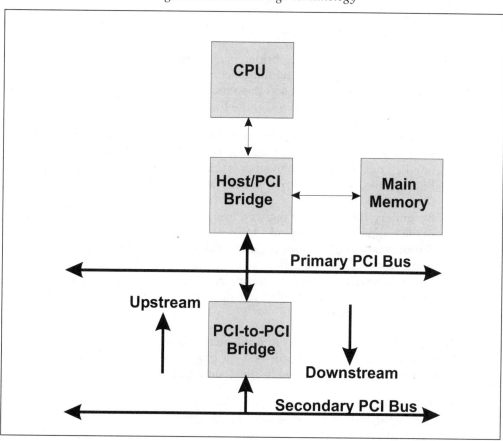

Example Systems

Figure 24-2 on page 545 and Figure 24-3 on page 546 illustrate two examples of systems with more than one PCI bus.

Example One

The system in Figure 24-2 on page 545 has two PCI buses. Bus number one is subordinate to, or beneath, bus number zero. The PCI bus that resides directly on the other side of the host/PCI bridge is guaranteed present in every PCI system and is always assigned a bus number of zero. Since the host/PCI bridge "knows" its bus number, the bridge designer may or may not implement a Bus Number register in the bridge. If the Bus Number register is present, the value it contains could be hardwired to zero, or reset could force it to zero.

It is a rule that each PCI-to-PCI bridge must implement three bus number registers in pre-defined locations within its configuration space. All three registers are read/writable and reset forces them to zero. They are assigned bus numbers during the configuration process. Those three registers are:

- **Primary Bus Number register**. Initialized by software with the number of the bridge's upstream PCI bus. The host/PCI bridge is only connected to one PCI bus, so it only implements a Bus Number register. The host/PCI bridge doesn't have to implement a Secondary Bus Number register (because it is irrelevant).
- **Secondary Bus Number register**. Initialized by software with the number of the bridge's downstream PCI bus.
- **Subordinate Bus Number register**. Initialized by software with the highest numbered PCI bus that exists on the secondary side. If the only bus on the bridge's downstream side is the bridge's secondary bus, then the Secondary and Subordinate Bus Number registers would be initialized with the number of the secondary bus.

The host/PCI bridge only has to implement a Bus Number and a Subordinate Bus Number register. In Figure 24-2 on page 545, the host/PCI bridge's bus number registers are initialized (during configuration) as follows:

- **Bus Number = 0**. The host/PCI bridge's PCI bus is always numbered zero.
- **Subordinate Bus Number = 1**, the number of the highest numbered PCI bus that exists on the downstream side of the bridge. The host/PCI bridge must therefore pass through all configuration read and write transaction requests initiated by the host processor specifying a bus number in the range zero through one.

PCI-to-PCI bridge A has its bus registers initialized as follows:

- **Primary Bus = 0**. This is the number of the PCI bus closer to the host processor.
- **Secondary Bus = 1**. This is the number of the PCI bus on the downstream side of the bridge.
- **Subordinate Bus = 1**. This is the number of the highest-numbered bus that exists on the downstream side of the bridge.

Figure 24-2: Example System One

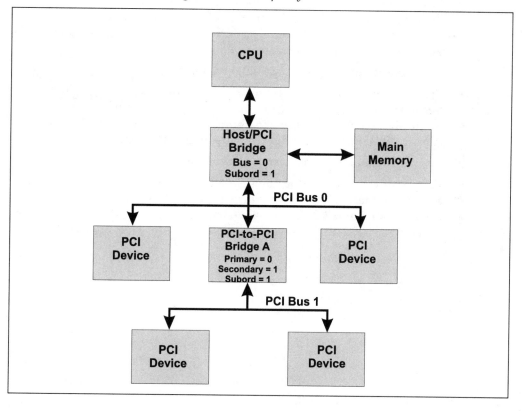

Example Two

Figure 24-3 on page 546 has four PCI buses. During configuration, the host/PCI bridge's bus number registers are initialized as follows:

- **Bus Number = 0**. The host/PCI bridge's PCI bus is always numbered zero.
- **Subordinate Bus = 3**. This is the number of the highest-numbered bus that exists on the downstream side of the host/PCI bridge. The host/PCI bridge must therefore pass through all configuration read and write transaction requests initiated by the host processor specifying a target bus number in the range zero through three.

Bridge A's bus number registers are initialized as follows:

- **Primary Bus = 0**. This is the number of its upstream bus.
- **Secondary Bus = 1**. This is the number of its downstream bus.
- **Subordinate Bus = 1**. The number of the highest-numbered PCI bus on its downstream side (in this case, it's equal to the secondary bus number).

Bridge B's bus number registers are initialized as follows:

- **Primary Bus = 0**. This is the number of its upstream bus.
- **Secondary Bus = 2**. This is the number of its downstream bus.
- **Subordinate Bus = 3**. This is the number of the highest-numbered bus that exists on its downstream side (bus 3 is subordinate to bus 2).

Bridge C's bus number registers are initialized as follows:

- **Primary Bus = 2**. This is the number of its upstream bus.
- **Secondary Bus = 3**. This is the number of its downstream bus.
- **Subordinate Bus = 3**. This is the number of the highest-numbered bus on its downstream side (in this case, the same as secondary bus number).

Figure 24-3: Example System Two

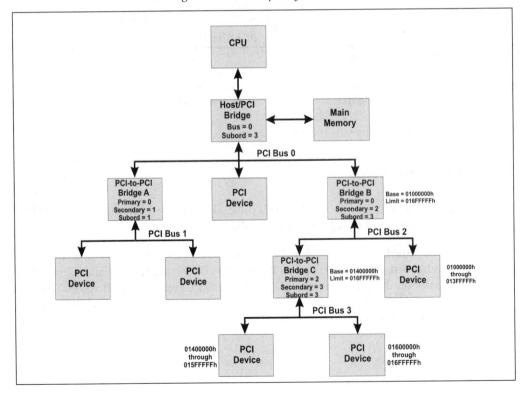

PCI-to-PCI Bridge: Traffic Director

The PCI-to-PCI bridge functions as a traffic coordinator between two PCI buses. Its job is to monitor each transaction that is initiated on the two PCI buses and to decide whether or not to pass the transaction through to the opposite PCI bus. When the bridge determines that a transaction on one bus needs to be passed to the other bus, the bridge must act as the target of the transaction on the originating bus and as the initiator of the new transaction on the destination bus. The fact that the bridge resides between the transaction initiator and the target is invisible to the initiator (as well as to the target).

In addition to determining if a transaction initiated on one bus must be passed through to the other, the bridge also supplies the following functions:

- The bridge monitors SERR# on the secondary bus and passes it to SERR# on its primary bus if it is sampled asserted (see "Handling SERR# on Secondary Side" on page 647).
- The bridge monitors RST# on the primary bus and passes it to RST# on its secondary bus if it is sampled asserted.
- A bridge may incorporate a device ROM that contains its device driver. In this case, the bridge must recognize and permit accesses to the ROM memory.
- A bridge may incorporate a set of device-specific, IO or memory-mapped IO registers that control its own functionality. In this case, it must recognize and permit accesses to these registers.
- A bridge may incorporate a memory buffer. In this case, it must recognize and permit accesses to this memory.

Table 24-1 on page 548 defines the types of transactions that may be detected on a PCI bus and how the bridge handles each of them. "Address Decode-Related Registers" on page 568 provides a detailed description of the address decode mechanisms implemented in a PCI-to-PCI bridge.

Table 24-1: Transaction Types That the Bridge Must Detect and Handle

Transaction Type	Bus Detected On	Action by Bridge
Memory Read	Primary or Secondary	There are five cases: 1. Within memory range to pass through: claim and pass through. 2. Within memory range of bridge's device ROM: claim and permit access to internal ROM; do not pass through. 3. Within memory-mapped IO range to pass through: claim and pass through. 4. Within memory range of bridge's device-specific IO or memory-mapped IO internal registers: claim and permit access to internal register(s); do not pass through. 5. Within range of bridge's internal memory buffer: claim and permit access to internal memory buffer; do not pass through. 6. None of the above: do not pass through and do not claim for internal access.
Memory Read Line (MRL)	Primary or secondary	Same as memory read.
Memory Read Multiple (MRM)	Primary or secondary	Same as memory read.
Memory Write	Primary or secondary	Same as memory read.
Memory Write and Invalidate (MWI)	Primary or secondary	Same as memory read.
IO Read	Primary or secondary	There are three cases: 1. Within IO range to pass through: claim and pass through. 2. Within IO range of bridge's device-specific IO-mapped internal registers: claim and permit access to internal register(s); do not pass through. 3. None of the above: do not pass through and do not claim for internal access.
IO Write	Primary or secondary	Same as IO read.

Table 24-1: Transaction Types That the Bridge Must Detect and Handle (Continued)

Transaction Type	Bus Detected On	Action by Bridge
Type 0 Configuration Read	Primary	If the bridge's IDSEL# input is asserted, perform function decode and claim if target function implemented, otherwise ignore. If claimed, permit access to target function's configuration registers. Do not pass through under any circumstances.
	Secondary	Ignore.
Type 0 Configuration Write	Primary	Same as configuration read.
	Secondary	Ignore.
Type 1 Configuration Read	Primary	There are three cases: 1. Target bus is the bridge's secondary bus: claim and pass through as a Type 0 Configuration Read. 2. Target bus is in the range of subordinate buses that exists behind the bridge (but not equal to the secondary bus): claim and pass through as Type 1 Configuration Read. 3. None of the above: ignore.
	Secondary	Ignore.
Type 1 Configuration Write (not a Special Cycle Request)	Primary	There are three cases: 1. Target bus is the bridge's secondary bus: claim and pass through as a Type 0 Configuration Write. 2. Target bus is in the range of subordinate buses that exists behind the bridge (but not equal to the secondary bus): claim and pass through unchanged as Type 1 Configuration Write. 3. None of the above: ignore.
	Secondary	Ignore.

Table 24-1: Transaction Types That the Bridge Must Detect and Handle (Continued)

Transaction Type	Bus Detected On	Action by Bridge
Type 1 Configuration Write as Special Cycle Request (device = 1Fh, function = 7h and dword = 0)	Primary	There are three cases: 1. Target bus is the bridge's secondary bus: claim and pass through as a Special Cycle. 2. Target bus is in the range of subordinate buses that exists behind the bridge (but not equal to the secondary bus): claim and pass through unchanged as Type 1 Configuration Write. 3. None of the above: ignore.
	Secondary	There are three cases: 1. Target bus is the bridge's primary bus: claim and pass through as a Special Cycle. 2. Target bus is neither the bridge's primary bus nor is it in the range of buses defined by the bridge's secondary and subordinate bus registers: claim and pass through unchanged as Type 1 Configuration Write. 3. Target bus is not the bridge's primary bus, but it is within the range of buses defined by the bridge's Secondary and Subordinate Bus Number registers: ignore.
Special Cycle	Primary or secondary	Do not claim. Ignore. Special Cycles are meaningless to PCI-to-PCI bridges.
Interrupt Acknowledge	Primary or secondary	Ignore.
Dual-Address Cycle (DAC)	Primary	There are three cases: 1. The bridge does not support memory above the 4GB address boundary on secondary side: in this case, the bridge ignores the access. 2. The bridge supports memory above the 4GB address boundary on secondary side, but the system may not have any there: in this case, the bridge ignores the access. 3. The bridge supports memory above the 4GB address boundary on secondary side and the system has programmed the bridge to recognize addresses above 4GB: in this case, the bridge latches the two address packets delivered during the two address phases and decodes. If the address is in range, transaction is claimed and passed through. If out of range, it is ignored.

Table 24-1: Transaction Types That the Bridge Must Detect and Handle (Continued)

Transaction Type	Bus Detected On	Action by Bridge
Dual-Address Cycle (DAC)	Secondary	There are three cases: 1. The bridge supports memory above the 4GB boundary on the secondary side and one or more memory targets do reside above the 4GB boundary on the secondary side. If a DAC is detected on the secondary side and the address is outside the range defined it is claimed and passed through to the primary bus (because the transaction is not addressing memory on the secondary side, so the target must be on the primary side). 2. The bridge supports memory above the 4GB boundary on the secondary side. A DAC is detected on the secondary side and the address is within the range defined for the memory targets that reside above the 4GB boundary on the secondary side of the bridge. The bridge ignores it (because the transaction is addressing a memory target on the secondary side of the bridge). 3. Bridge does not support memory above the 4GB address boundary on the secondary side. *WHEN A DAC IS DETECTED ON THE SECONDARY SIDE, THE BRIDGE MUST CLAIM THE TRANSACTION AND PASS IT THROUGH TO THE PRIMARY BUS. A MASTER ON THE SECONDARY SIDE IS ATTEMPTING AN ACCESS TO MAIN MEMORY ABOVE THE 4GB BOUNDARY, SO THE BRIDGE FORWARDS THE TRANSACTION UPSTREAM TOWARDS MAIN MEMORY. THE 1.0 PCI-TO-PCI BRIDGE ARCHITECTURE SPECIFICATION STATED THAT IT WAS OPTIONAL WHETHER A BRIDGE SUPPORTED THE DAC COMMAND ON EITHER SIDE, WHILE THE 1.1 SPEC STATES THAT BRIDGE SUPPORT FOR THE DAC COMMAND IS OPTIONAL ON THE PRIMARY SIDE, BUT IS MANDATORY ON THE SECONDARY SIDE SO MASTERS ON THE SECONDARY SIDE CAN ACCESS MAIN MEMORY ABOVE THE 4GB BOUNDARY.*

1.1

Latency Rules

As with any other PCI device, the bridge must comply with the master and target latency rules described in the chapter entitled "Master and Target Latency" on page 73. Some special notes:

1.1

- THE BRIDGE MUST HONOR THE MEMORY WRITE MAXIMUM COMPLETION TIME (SEE "MEMORY WRITE MAXIMUM COMPLETION LIMIT" ON PAGE 96) WHEN A MASTER ON EITHER SIDE IS ATTEMPTING TO ACCESS THE BRIDGE'S INTERNAL MEMORY-MAPPED IO REGISTERS OR MEMORY.
- THE BRIDGE MUST HANDLE ALL MEMORY WRITE AND MEMORY WRITE-AND-INVALI-DATE TRANSACTIONS AS POSTED MEMORY WRITES.
- ALL OTHER TRANSACTIONS MUST BE HANDLED AS DELAYED TRANSACTIONS.

Configuration Registers

General

The chapter entitled "Configuration Registers" on page 351 provided a detailed discussion of the configuration registers defined by the specification for inclusion in all PCI devices other than PCI-to-PCI and PCI-to-CardBus bridges. These configuration registers were defined as configuration Header Type 0. This section provides a detailed description of the configuration registers defined by the *PCI-to-PCI Bridge Architecture Specification* for implementation in PCI-to-PCI bridges. This is referred to as configuration Header Type 1 and is illustrated in Figure 24-4 on page 553. It consists of the first 16 dwords of the 64 dword configuration space associated with the bridge. For a discussion of the new SubClass added in the 2.2 spec, refer to "PCI-to-PCI Bridge With Subtractive Decode Feature" on page 622.

This chapter also provides a detailed description of the methods utilized by the bridge to decide what memory and IO transactions to accept and which to ignore.

Chapter 24: PCI-to-PCI Bridge

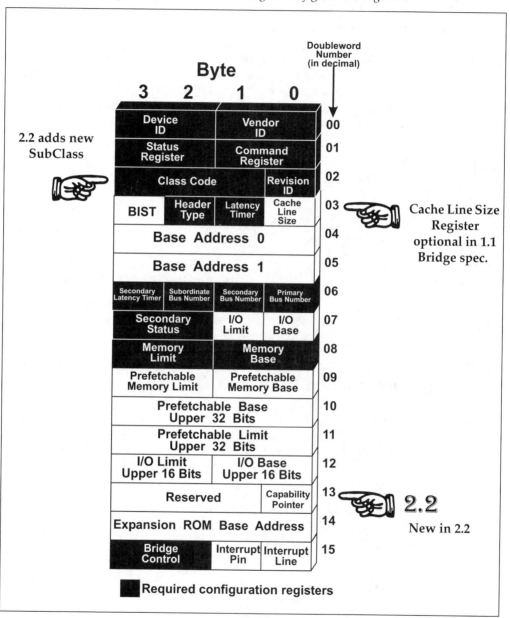

Figure 24-4: PCI-to-PCI Bridge's Configuration Registers

Header Type Register

Mandatory. Location in Header: byte two of dword three. The register is illustrated in Figure 24-5 on page 554. If the device contains other functions in addition to the bridge function, bit seven is set to one; otherwise, bit seven is hardwired to zero. For a single-function device containing a PCI-to-PCI bridge, the Header Type register is hardwired to 00000001b (01h). The Header Type Register of a bridge within a multi-function device would contain 81h. This indicates that dwords 4-through-15 are structured as defined by the Header Type 1 template.

Figure 24-5: Header Type Register

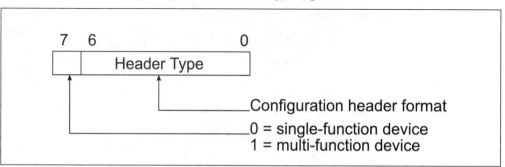

Registers Related to Device ID

Introduction

There are four registers associated with device identification. They are:

- Vendor ID register.
- Device ID register.
- Revision ID register.
- Class Code register.

The sections that follow describe these registers.

Vendor ID Register

Mandatory. Location in Header: bytes zero and one in dword zero. This 16-bit register contains the hardwired Vendor ID and is implemented the same as it is in a non-bridge PCI device. The Vendor ID is assigned by the PCI SIG and is guaranteed to be mutually-exclusive from the IDs issued to other vendors. In combination with the Device ID (and possible the revision ID), the Vendor ID register can be used by a device driver or the OS to "discover" an instance of its associated device. The Vendor ID of FFFFh is reserved and is not used. This is the value returned during a configuration read from a non-existent PCI device (returned to the host processor when the host/PCI bridge experiences a Master Abort due to no assertion of DEVSEL#).

Device ID Register

Mandatory. Location in Header: bytes two and three in dword zero. The 16-bit Device ID register is hardwired with the Device ID chosen by the device vendor. Also see "Vendor ID Register" on page 554.

Revision ID Register

Mandatory. Location in Header: byte zero in dword two. The 8-bit Revision ID register contains the device's hardwired revision number. Also see "Vendor ID Register" on page 554.

Class Code Register

Mandatory. Location in Header: bytes one, two and three in dword two. The three byte Class Code register is implemented in the same manner as it is for a non-bridge PCI device. Figure 24-6 on page 555 illustrates the Class Code register. For a PCI-to-PCI bridge, the Class Code is 06h (bridge), Sub-Class is 04h (PCI-to-PCI bridge), and the Programming Interface Byte may be either:

- 00h = Normal PCI-to-PCI Bridge.
- *01H = PCI-TO-PCI BRIDGE THAT, IN ADDITION TO ITS NORMAL PCI-TO-PCI BRIDGE OPERATIONS, PERFORMS SUBTRACTIVE DECODE ON THE PRIMARY SIDE OF THE BRIDGE. FOR MORE INFORMATION, REFER TO "PCI-TO-PCI BRIDGE WITH SUBTRACTIVE DECODE FEATURE" ON PAGE 622. THIS PROGRAMMING INTERFACE BYTE VALUE WAS ADDED IN THE 2.2 PCI SPEC.* **2.2**

Figure 24-6: Class Code Register

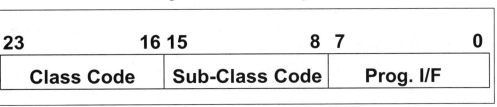

23	16	15	8	7	0
Class Code		Sub-Class Code		Prog. I/F	

Bus Number Registers

Introduction

Each PCI-to-PCI bridge must implement three *mandatory* bus number registers. All of them are read/writable and are cleared to zero by reset. During configuration, the configuration software initializes these three registers to assign bus numbers. These registers are:

- Primary Bus Number register.
- Secondary Bus Number register.
- Subordinate Bus Number register.

The combination of the Secondary and the Subordinate Bus Number registers defines the range of buses that exists on the downstream side of the bridge. The information supplied by these three registers is used by the bridge to determine whether or not to pass through:

- Type 1 configuration reads and writes on the primary side that are to be passed through as a Type 0 configuration access (if the target is on the bridge's secondary bus) or as a Type 1 configuration access (if the target is on a bus subordinate to the bridge's secondary bus).
- Type 1 configuration writes received on either the primary or secondary side that are to be converted to Special Cycles on the specified target bus.

Primary Bus Number Register

Mandatory. Location in Header: byte zero in dword six. The Primary Bus Number register is initialized by software with the number of the bridge's bus that is closer to the host processor. The only reason that this register exists is so the bridge can determine if a Special Cycle Request latched on the secondary side should be converted to a Special Cycle on the primary side.

Secondary Bus Number Register

Mandatory. Location in Header: byte one in dword six. The Secondary Bus Number register is initialized by software with the number of the bridge's downstream bus. This register exists for two reasons:

- When a Special Cycle Request is latched on the primary side, the bridge uses this register to determine if it should be converted to a Special Cycle transaction on the secondary side.

- When a Type 1 Configuration transaction (read or write) is latched on the primary side, the bridge uses this register to determine if the transaction should be converted to a Type 0 Configuration transaction on the secondary bus.

Subordinate Bus Number Register

Mandatory. Location in Header: byte two in dword six. The Subordinate Bus Number register is initialized by software with the number of the highest-numbered bus that exists on the downstream side of the bridge. If there are no PCI-to-PCI bridges on the secondary bus, the Subordinate Bus Number register is initialized with the same value as the Secondary Bus Number register.

Command Registers

Introduction

The PCI-to-PCI bridge designer must implement two required Command registers in the bridge's configuration Header region:

- The Command register is the standard configuration Command register defined by the specification for any PCI device. It is associated with the bridge's primary bus interface.
- The Bridge Control register is an extension to the standard Command register. It is associated with the operation of both of the bridge's bus interfaces.

These two registers are described in the next two sections.

Command Register

Mandatory. The Command register format, pictured in Figure 24-7 on page 558, is the same as that for a non-bridge PCI device. Some of the bits, however, have different effects. Each of the bits are described in Table 24-2 on page 558.

Figure 24-7: Command Register

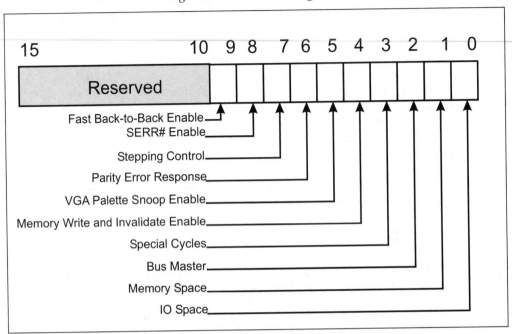

Table 24-2: Command Register Bit Assignment

Bit	Description
0	**IO Space**. When set, the bridge's IO address decoders on its primary side are enabled. When cleared, they are disabled. If cleared, any IO transactions detected on the secondary side are passed through to the primary side and all IO transactions detected on the primary side are ignored. Reset clears this bit.
1	**Memory Space**. When set, the bridge's memory and memory-mapped IO address decoders on its primary side are enabled. When cleared, they are disabled. If cleared, any memory transactions detected on the secondary side are passed through to the primary side and all memory transactions on the primary side are ignored. Reset clears this bit.

Table 24-2: Command Register Bit Assignment (Continued)

Bit	Description
2	**Bus Master**. Control's the bridge's ability to act as a master on the primary side. However, the bridge is always enabled to forward and convert configuration transactions. When cleared, the bridge ignores all memory and IO transactions detected on the secondary side (because it cannot act as a master to pass the transactions through to the primary side). Reset clears this bit.
3	**Special Cycles**. Hardwired to zero (because PCI-to-PCI bridges don't monitor Special Cycles).
4	**Memory Write and Invalidate Enable**. This bit must be implemented as a read/write bit if the bridge is capable of converting posted memory writes (that were received via a Memory Write transaction) into a Memory Write-and-Invalidate (MWI) transaction on the other side of the bridge. The writes would have to be sequential, start on a cache line boundary, and write an entire cache line (or multiple cache lines). If the bridge implements this optional capability, it must also implement the Cache Line Size configuration register as a read/write register. The bridge does not consult this bit to determine if it should pass an MWI received on one side through as an MWI on the other side. The fact that the originating master used the MWI transaction type means that it has met all of the criteria for its usage.
5	**VGA Palette Snoop**. Implementation of this bit is optional. If not implemented, must be hardwired to zero. Reset clears this bit. If implemented, its effects on a PCI-to-PCI bridge are different than on a display adapter. When set, IO writes to 03C6h, 03C8h and 03C9h (including any IO addresses that alias to these addresses) are positively decoded on the primary side and are passed through to the secondary side. If IO writes to these addresses are detected on the secondary side, they are ignored. Also see description of the VGA Enable bit in Table 24-3 on page 561, and "Display Configuration" on page 608.
6	**Parity Error Response**. When set, the bridge takes the normal actions defined by the specification (see "Introduction to PCI Parity" on page 199) when a parity error is detected on the primary side. When cleared, parity errors are ignored, but the bridge must generate proper parity. Reset clears this bit.

Table 24-2: Command Register Bit Assignment (Continued)

Bit	Description
7	**Stepping Control**. Bridges that never use address and/or data stepping hardwire this bit to zero. Bridges that always use stepping hardwire this bit to one. Bridges that permit stepping to be turned on and off under program control implement this as a read/writable bit. If the bit is read/writable, reset sets the bit to one.
8	**SERR# Enable**. Controls the SERR# output driver on the primary bus. When set, the bridge is enabled to generate SERR# on the primary side. When cleared it cannot generate SERR#. Reset clears this bit. For more information, refer to "SERR# Signal" on page 214.
9	**Fast Back-to-Back Enable.** Controls the bridge's ability to utilize Fast Back-to-Back transactions with different targets on the primary bus. A bridge that doesn't support this ability hardwires this bit to zero, otherwise it must be read/writable. Reset clears this bit. For more information, refer to "Fast Back-to-Back Transactions" on page 153.
15:10	**Reserved**. Read-only and must return zero when read.

Bridge Control Register

2.2

Mandatory. The bridge control register is a required extension to the bridge's command register and is associated with operation of both the primary and the secondary sides. Figure 24-8 on page 561 illustrates this register and Table 24-3 on page 561 defines its bit assignment. *BITS 8 - THROUGH - 11 ARE NEWLY-DEFINED IN THE 2.2 SPEC. FOR ADDITIONAL INFORMATION ABOUT THESE BITS, REFER TO "DISCARD TIMER TIMEOUT" ON PAGE 644.*

Figure 24-8: Bridge Control Register

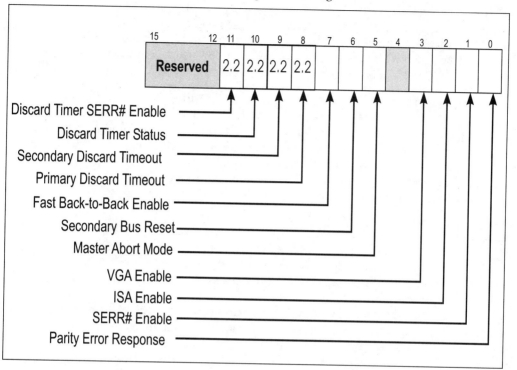

Table 24-3: Bridge Control Register Bit Assignment

Bit	Description
0	**Parity Error Response**. When set, the bridge takes the normal actions defined by the specification when a parity error is detected on the secondary side. When cleared, parity errors are ignored, but the bridge must generate proper parity. Reset clears this bit. For more information, refer to "Introduction to PCI Parity" on page 199.
1	**SERR# Enable.** When set, detection of SERR# asserted on the secondary side causes the bridge to assert SERR# on the primary side (but only if the SERR# Enable bit in the device's Command register is set). When cleared, detection of SERR# on secondary side is ignored. Reset clears this bit. For more information, refer to "SERR# Signal" on page 214.

Table 24-3: Bridge Control Register Bit Assignment (Continued)

Bit	Description
2	**ISA Enable.** When set, bridge only recognizes IO addresses within its assigned IO range that do not alias to an ISA range. For information, refer to the "Effect of Setting the ISA Enable Bit" on page 582. Reset clears this bit.
3	**VGA Enable.** When set, bridge performs positive decode on memory accesses in the range from 000A0000h through 000BFFFFh (the address range of the VGA video frame buffer), and IO addresses associated with the VGA register set (03B0h-03BBh and 03C0h-03DFh—including addresses that alias into these two IO ranges). This bit is qualified by bits zero and one in the Command register. Reset clears this bit. For more information, refer to "Display Configuration" on page 608.
4	**Reserved.** Hardwired to zero.
5	**Master Abort Mode.** Controls the manner in which the bridge responds when it is mastering a transaction on either bus and experiences a Master Abort. For additional information, refer to "Handling Master Abort" on page 641. • **Master Abort Mode = 0** (its default state after RST#)—treats unclaimed accesses (on both sides) in the same manner that the Host/PCI bridge treats unclaimed configuration accesses during initialization time. Any read that experiences a Master Abort returns all ones; any write that experiences a Master Abort completes normally and the data is thrown away. • **Master Abort Mode = 1**—If bridge experiences a Master Abort when passing a transaction to the opposite side, it issues a Target Abort to the originating master (for all reads and non-posted writes). If the bridge experiences a Master Abort while performing a posted-write, it signals SERR# on the primary side (if the SERR# Enable bit in the Command register is set).
6	**Secondary Bus Reset.** When set, the bridge asserts RST# on the secondary bus. When cleared, the secondary bus RST# is deasserted. Irrespective of the state of this bit, secondary bus RST# follows primary bus RST#. The bridge's interface to the secondary bus and all buffers between the two buses are initialized by the assertion of RST# on the secondary bus. Assertion of RST# on the secondary bus, however, does not affect the configuration registers nor the primary bus interface logic. Reset clears this bit.

Table 24-3: Bridge Control Register Bit Assignment (Continued)

Bit	Description
7	**Fast Back-to-Back Enable.** Same as the Fast Back-To-Back Enable bit in the Command register, but it enables/disables bridge's ability to perform Fast Back-to-Back transactions on its secondary bus. For more information, refer to "Fast Back-to-Back Transactions" on page 153.
8	PRIMARY DISCARD TIMEOUT. SELECTS THE NUMBER OF PCI CLOCKS THAT THE BRIDGE WAITS FOR A MASTER ON THE PRIMARY BUS TO REPEAT A DELAYED TRANSACTION REQUEST. THE COUNTER STARTS WHEN THE DELAYED COMPLETION (THE COMPLETION OF THE DELAYED TRANSACTION ON THE SECONDARY INTERFACE) HAS REACHED THE HEAD OF THE UPSTREAM QUEUE OF THE BRIDGE (I.E., ALL ORDERING REQUIREMENTS HAVE BEEN SATISFIED AND THE BRIDGE IS READY TO COMPLETE THE DELAYED TRANSACTION WITH THE ORIGINATING MASTER ON THE PRIMARY BUS). IF THE ORIGINATING MASTER DOES NOT REPEAT THE TRANSACTION BEFORE THE COUNTER EXPIRES, THE BRIDGE DELETES THE DELAYED TRANSACTION FROM ITS QUEUE AND SETS THE DISCARD TIMER STATUS BIT (SEE BIT 10). THE DEFAULT STATE OF THIS BIT AFTER RESET IS 0. • 0 = THE PRIMARY DISCARD TIMER COUNTS 2^{15} PCI CLOCK CYCLES. • 1 = THE PRIMARY DISCARD TIMER COUNTS 2^{10} PCI CLOCK CYCLES. FOR ADDITIONAL INFORMATION, REFER TO "DISCARD TIMER TIMEOUT" ON PAGE 644.
9	SECONDARY DISCARD TIMEOUT. SELECTS THE NUMBER OF PCI CLOCKS THAT THE BRIDGE WAITS FOR A MASTER ON THE SECONDARY BUS TO REPEAT A DELAYED TRANS-ACTION REQUEST. THE COUNTER STARTS WHEN THE DELAYED COMPLETION (THE COMPLETION OF THE DELAYED TRANSACTION ON THE PRIMARY INTERFACE) HAS REACHED THE HEAD OF THE DOWNSTREAM QUEUE OF THE BRIDGE (I.E., ALL ORDERING REQUIREMENTS HAVE BEEN SATISFIED AND THE BRIDGE IS READY TO COMPLETE THE DELAYED TRANSAC-TION WITH THE ORIGINATING MASTER ON THE SECONDARY BUS). IF THE ORIGINATING MASTER DOES NOT REPEAT THE TRANSACTION BEFORE THE COUNTER EXPIRES, THE BRIDGE DELETES THE DELAYED TRANSACTION FROM ITS QUEUE AND SETS THE DISCARD TIMER STATUS BIT (SEE BIT 10). THE DEFAULT STATE OF THIS BIT AFTER RESET IS 0. • 0 = THE SECONDARY DISCARD TIMER COUNTS 2^{15} PCI CLOCK CYCLES. • 1 = THE SECONDARY DISCARD TIMER COUNTS 2^{10} PCI CLOCK CYCLES. FOR ADDITIONAL INFORMATION, REFER TO "DISCARD TIMER TIMEOUT" ON PAGE 644.

2.2

2.2

Table 24-3: Bridge Control Register Bit Assignment (Continued)

	Bit	Description
2.2	10	DISCARD TIMER STATUS. THIS BIT IS SET TO A 1 WHEN EITHER THE PRIMARY DISCARD TIMER (SEE BIT 8) OR SECONDARY DISCARD TIMER (SEE BIT 9) EXPIRES AND A DELAYED COMPLETION IS DISCARDED FROM A QUEUE IN THE BRIDGE. THE DEFAULT STATE OF THIS BIT AFTER RESET MUST BE 0. ONCE SET, THIS BIT REMAINS SET UNTIL IT IS RESET BY WRITING A 1 TO IT. • 0 = NO DISCARD TIMER ERROR • 1 = DISCARD TIMER ERROR FOR ADDITIONAL INFORMATION, REFER TO "DISCARD TIMER TIMEOUT" ON PAGE 644.
2.2	11	DISCARD TIMER SERR# ENABLE. ENABLES OR DISABLES THE BRIDGE'S ABILITY TO ASSERT SERR# ON THE PRIMARY BUS WHEN EITHER THE PRIMARY DISCARD TIMER (SEE BIT 8) OR SECONDARY DISCARD TIMER (SEE BIT 9) EXPIRES AND A DELAYED TRANSACTION IS DISCARDED FROM A QUEUE IN THE BRIDGE. THE DEFAULT STATE IS 0 AFTER RESET. • 0 = DO NOT ASSERT SERR# ON THE PRIMARY BUS ON EXPIRATION OF EITHER THE PRIMARY DISCARD TIMER OR SECONDARY DISCARD TIMER. • 1 = ASSERT SERR# ON THE PRIMARY BUS IF EITHER THE PRIMARY DISCARD TIMER OR SECONDARY DISCARD TIMER EXPIRES AND A DELAYED TRANSACTION IS DISCARDED FROM A QUEUE IN THE BRIDGE. FOR ADDITIONAL INFORMATION, REFER TO "DISCARD TIMER TIMEOUT" ON PAGE 644.
	15:12	Reserved.

Status Registers

Introduction

The bridge contains two required status registers, each of which is associated with one of the buses.

Status Register (Primary Bus)

Mandatory. Refer to Figure 24-9 on page 565. This required register is completely compatible with the Status register definition for a non-bridge PCI device (see "Status Register" on page 371) and only reflects the status of the primary side.

2.2   IF THE CAPABILITIES LIST BIT (BIT 4) IS SET TO ONE, THIS INDICATES THAT THE BRIDGE IMPLEMENTS THE CAPABILITY POINTER REGISTER IN BYTE 0 OF DWORD 13 IN ITS CONFIGURATION HEADER (SEE FIGURE 24-4 ON PAGE 553). FOR A GENERAL DESCRIPTION OF THE NEW

CAPABILITIES, REFER TO "NEW CAPABILITIES" ON PAGE 390. IN SUBSEQUENTLY TRAVERS-
ING THE NEW CAPABILITIES LIST, SOFTWARE MAY DISCOVER THAT THE BRIDGE IMPLEMENTS
THE SLOT NUMBERING REGISTERS. FOR A DESCRIPTION OF THIS FEATURE, REFER TO "CHAS-
SIS AND SLOT NUMBER ASSIGNMENT" ON PAGE 594.

THE UDF BIT (BIT 6) HAS BEEN DELETED IN THE 2.2 SPEC. 2.2

Figure 24-9: Primary Interface Status Register

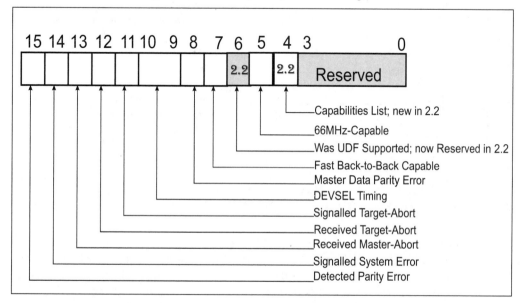

Secondary Status Register

Mandatory. Refer to Figure 24-10 on page 566. With the exception of the Received System Error bit, this required register is completely compatible with the Status register definition for a non-bridge PCI device (see "Status Register" on page 371) and only reflects the status of the secondary side. It should be noted that THE CAPABILITIES LIST BIT (BIT 4) IS NEVER IMPLEMENTED IN THIS REGISTER. 2.2

While bit 14 is the Signaled System Error bit in the primary side Status register, it is the Received System Error bit in the Secondary Status register. When set, this bit indicates that SERR# was detected asserted on the secondary side. Writing a one to it clears the bit, while a zero doesn't affect it. Reset clears this bit.

Figure 24-10: Secondary Status Register

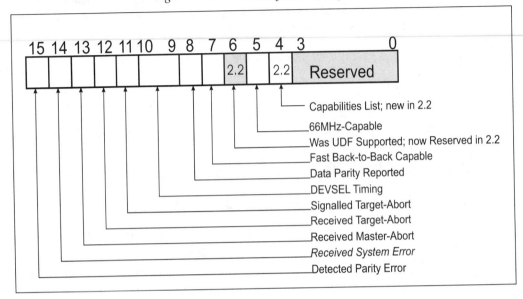

2.2 Introduction To Chassis/Slot Numbering Registers

Assuming that the Capabilities List bit is set in the bridge's primary Status register, the bridge implements the Capabilities Pointer register (see "New Capabilities" on page 390). When software traverses a PCI-to-PCI bridge's linked list of New Capabilities, it may encounter the Slot Numbering registers (if this is the bridge to an expansion chassis).

Figure 24-11 on page 566 pictures the Slot Numbering register set. It consists of the registers described in Table 24-4 on page 567. For additional information, refer to "Chassis and Slot Number Assignment" on page 594.

Figure 24-11: Chassis and Slot Number Registers

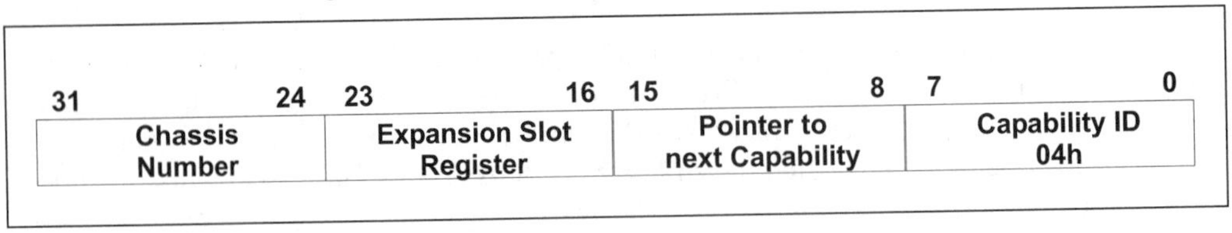

31 Chassis Number 24	23 Expansion Slot Register 16	15 Pointer to next Capability 8	7 Capability ID 04h 0

Table 24-4: Slot Numbering Register Set

Register	Description
Capability ID	**Read-Only. 04h** identifies this as the Slot Numbering register set.
Next Capability Pointer	**Read-Only.** **00h** = Indicates that this is the last register set in the linked New Capabilities list. **Non-zero value** = dword-aligned pointer to the next register set in the linked list.
Expansion Slot	**Read-Only, automatically loaded by hardware after reset.** The configuration software uses the value in this register to determine the number of expansion card slots present on the bridge's secondary PCI bus. The spec doesn't define where the hardware obtains this information. It could read a set of strapping pins on the trailing-edge of RST#, or could obtain the information from a serial EEPROM. For a detailed description of the Chassis and Slot Numbering feature, refer to "Chassis and Slot Number Assignment" on page 594.
Chassis Number	**Read/Write.** The value in this register identifies the chassis number assigned to the PCI add-in card slots on this bridge's secondary bus. At reset time, this register may: • be pre-loaded with 00h, or • be implemented as a non-volatile register that "remembers" the chassis number assigned during a previous platform configuration. For a detailed description of the Chassis and Slot Numbering feature, refer to "Chassis and Slot Number Assignment" on page 594.

Address Decode-Related Registers

Basic Transaction Filtering Mechanism

PCI devices that reside on the downstream side of a PCI-to-PCI bridge may incorporate internal memory (mapped into memory space) and/or an internal, device-specific register set mapped into either IO or memory-mapped IO space. The configuration program automatically detects the presence, type and address space requirements of these devices and allocates space to them by programming their address decoders to recognize the address ranges it assigns to them.

The configuration program assigns all IO devices that reside behind a PCI-to-PCI bridge mutually-exclusive address ranges that are blocked together within a common overall range of IO locations. The PCI-to-PCI bridge is then programmed to pass any IO transactions detected on the primary side of the bridge to the secondary side if the target address is within the range associated with the community of IO devices that reside behind the bridge. Conversely, any IO transactions detected on the secondary side of the bridge are passed to the primary side if the target address is outside the range associated with the community of IO devices that reside on the secondary side (because the target device doesn't reside on the secondary side, but may reside on the primary side).

All memory-mapped IO devices (i.e., non-prefetchable memory) that reside behind a PCI-to-PCI bridge are assigned mutually-exclusive memory address ranges within a common block of memory locations. The PCI-to-PCI bridge is then programmed to pass any memory transactions detected on the primary side of the bridge to the secondary side if the target address is within the range associated with the community of memory-mapped IO devices that reside behind the bridge. Conversely, any memory transactions detected on the secondary side of the bridge are passed to the primary side if the target address is outside the range associated with the community of memory-mapped IO devices that reside on the secondary side (because the target device doesn't reside on the secondary side, but may reside on the primary side).

All memory devices (i.e., regular memory, not memory-mapped IO) that reside behind a PCI-to-PCI bridge are assigned mutually-exclusive memory address ranges within a common overall range of memory locations. The PCI-to-PCI bridge is then programmed to pass any memory transactions detected on the primary side of the bridge to the secondary side if the target address is within the range associated with the community of memory devices that reside behind the bridge. Conversely, any memory transactions detected on the secondary side of the bridge are passed to the primary side if the target address is outside the range associated with the community of memory devices that reside on the secondary side (because the target device doesn't reside on the secondary side, but may reside on the primary side).

The bridge itself may incorporate:

- a memory buffer.
- an IO register set that is used to control the bridge
- a device ROM that contains a device driver for the bridge.

The bridge must incorporate programmable address decoders for these devices.

Bridge Memory, Register Set and Device ROM

Introduction. A PCI-to-PCI bridge designer may choose to incorporate the following entities within the bridge:

- A set of internal, device-specific registers that are used to control the bridge's operational characteristics or check its status. These registers are outside the scope of the PCI specification.
- A memory buffer within the bridge.
- A device ROM that contains a device driver for the bridge.

The register set must be mapped into memory or IO address space (or both). The designer implements one or two Base Address Registers (programmable address decoders) for this purpose.

If there is a device ROM within the bridge, the designer must implement an Expansion ROM base address register used by configuration software to map the ROM into memory space.

Likewise, if the bridge incorporates a memory buffer, the design must include a Base Address Register used to assign a base address to the memory.

Base Address Registers. *Optional. Only necessary if the bridge implements a device-specific register set and/or a memory buffer.* Location in the Header: dwords four and five. It should be obvious that the two Base Address Registers are optional. If the designer doesn't implement any internal, device-specific register set or memory, then these address decoders aren't necessary. These Base Address Registers are used in the same manner as those described for a non-bridge PCI function (see "Base Address Registers (BARs)" on page 378). If implemented, both may be implemented as memory decoders, both as IO decoders, one as memory and one as IO, or only one may be implemented as either IO or memory.

Expansion ROM Base Address Register. *Optional. Only necessary if the bridge implements a bridge-specific device ROM.* Location in the Header: dword 14. This register is optional (because there may not be a device ROM incorporated within the bridge). The format and usage of this register is precisely the same as that described for a non-bridge PCI function (see "Expansion ROM Base Address Register" on page 386).

Bridge's IO Filter

Introduction. *There is no requirement for a bridge to support devices that reside in IO space within or behind the bridge.* For this reason, implementation of the IO decode-related configuration registers is optional.

When the bridge detects an IO transaction initiated on either PCI bus, it must determine which of the following actions to take:

1. **Ignore the transaction** because the target IO address isn't located on the other side of the bridge, nor is it targeting an IO location embedded within the bridge itself.
2. **Claim the transaction** because the target IO address is one of the bridge's internal IO registers. The initiator is permitted to access the targeted internal register and the **transaction is not passed through the bridge**.
3. **Claim the transaction** because the target IO location is located on the other side of the bridge. The **transaction is passed through the bridge** and is initiated on the opposite bus.

The optional configuration registers within the bridge that support this "filtering" capability are:

- **Base Address Registers**. If present, the Base Address Register or registers can be designed as IO or memory decoders for an internal register set or memory.
- **IO Base and IO Limit registers**. If the bridge supports IO space on the downstream side of the bridge, the IO Base register defines the start address and the IO Limit register defines the end address of the range to recognize, claim and pass through to the secondary bus.
- **IO Extension registers** (IO Base Upper 16-Bits and IO Limit Upper 16-Bits registers). If the bridge supports a 4GB (rather than a 64KB) IO address space on the downstream side of the bridge (as indicated in the IO Base and IO Limit registers), the combination of the IO Base plus IO Base Upper 16 Bits registers define the start address, and the combination of the IO Limit plus the IO Limit Upper 16-Bits registers define the end address of the range to recognize, claim and pass to the secondary side.

The sections that follow describe each of these scenarios.

Bridge Doesn't Support Any IO Space Behind Bridge. Assume that a bridge doesn't support any devices that reside in IO space behind the bridge. In other words, it doesn't recognize any IO addresses as being implemented behind the bridge and therefore ignores (doesn't assert DEVSEL#) all IO transactions detected on its primary bus. In this case, the bridge designer does not implement the optional IO Base, IO Limit, or IO Extension registers (i.e., IO Base Upper 16-bits and IO Limit Upper 16-Bits registers).

The bridge ignores all IO transactions detected on the primary bus (other than transactions that may target an optional set of bridge-specific registers contained within the bridge itself).

Any IO transactions detected on the bridge's secondary bus would be claimed and passed through to the primary bus in case the target IO device is implemented somewhere upstream of the bridge.

Bridge Supports 64KB IO Space Behind Bridge. Assume that a bridge is designed to support IO transactions initiated on the primary bus that may target locations within the first 64KB of IO space (IO locations 00000000h through 0000FFFFh) on the secondary bus. It ignores any primary side IO accesses over the 64KB address boundary. In other words, the bridge supports a 64KB IO space, but not a 4GB IO space on the secondary side of the bridge.

In this case, the bridge designer must implement the IO Base and the IO Limit registers, but does not implement the IO Extension registers (i.e., the IO Base Upper 16-Bits and the IO Limit Upper 16-Bits registers).

The IO Base and IO Limit register pair comprise the global IO address decoder for all IO targets that reside on the secondary side of the bridge.

STEP 1. Before the registers are initialized by the configuration software, they are first read from to determine whether they support 64KB or a 4GB of IO space on the secondary side of the bridge. In this scenario, assume that the registers are hardwired to indicate that the bridge only supports a 64KB IO space.

STEP 2. The configuration software then walks the secondary bus (and any subordinate buses it discovers) and assigns to each IO decoder it discovers an exclusive IO address range within the first 64KB of IO space. The sub-ranges assigned to the devices are assigned in sequential blocks to make efficient use of IO space.

STEP 3. The IO Base and Limit register pair are then initialized by the startup configuration software with the start and end address of the IO range that all IO devices that were discovered behind the bridge (on the secondary and on any subordinate buses) have been programmed to reside within. In this case, since the bridge only supports the first 64KB of IO space, the defined range will be a subset of the first 64KB of IO space.

STEP 4. After they have been initialized, these two registers provide the bridge with the start and the end address of the IO address range to recognize.

The bridge only supports the lower 64KB of IO space, but the IO address decoder comprised of the IO Base and Limit registers must perform a full 32-bit IO address decode of address bits [31:0] to determine whether or not to claim (i.e., assert DEVSEL#) an IO access on the primary bus and pass it to the secondary bus.

The format of the IO Base and IO Limit registers are ILLUSTRATED in Figure 24-12 on page 573 and Figure 24-13 on page 573. Both registers have the same format: the upper hex digit, bits [7:4], defines the most-significant hex digit of a 16-bit IO address; the lower hex digit, bits [3:0], defines whether the bridge performs a 16-bit or 32-bit IO address decode. In the scenario under discussion, the lower hex digit of both registers is hardwired with the value 0h, indicating that it performs a 16-bit IO address decode and therefore only supports recognition within the first 64KB of IO space.

Assume that the configuration software programs the upper digit of the IO Base register with the value 2h and the upper digit of the IO Limit register with the value 3h. This indicates that the start of the IO range to recognize is 2000h and the end address is 3FFFh—an 8KB block. As another example, assume that the upper digit in the base and limit registers are both set to 3h. The IO address range to recognize is then 3000h through 3FFFh—a 4KB block. In other words, this register pair defines the start address aligned on a 4KB address boundary, and the size, also referred to as the granularity, of the defined block is in increments of 4KB.

It should be noted that, if there aren't any IO devices on the bridge's secondary side, the IO Limit register can be programmed with a numerically lower IO address than the IO Base register. The bridge will not claim and pass any IO transactions latched on the primary side through to the secondary side, but will claim and pass any IO transactions latched on the secondary side through to the primary side.

Figure 24-12: IO Base Register

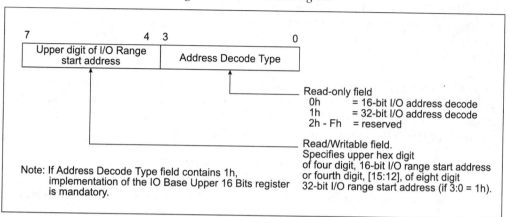

Figure 24-13: IO Limit Register

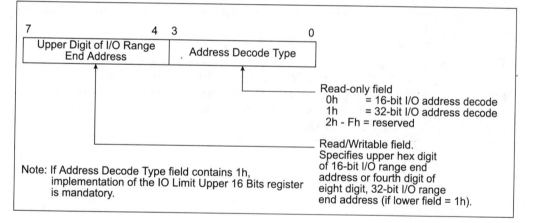

Example. Assume that the IO base is set to 2h and the IO Limit is set to 3h. The bridge is now primed to recognize any IO transaction on the primary bus that targets an IO address within the range consisting of 2000h through 3FFFh. Refer to Figure 24-14 on page 575.

Anytime that the bridge detects an IO transaction on the primary bus with an address inside the 2000h through 3FFFh range, it claims the transaction and passes it through (because it's within the range defined by the IO Base and Limit registers and may therefore be for an IO device that resides behind the bridge).

Anytime that the bridge detects an IO transaction on the primary bus with an address outside the 2000h through 3FFFh range, it ignores the transaction (because the target IO address is outside the range of addresses assigned to IO devices that reside behind the bridge).

Anytime that the bridge detects an IO transaction on the secondary bus with an address inside the 2000h through 3FFFh range, it ignores the transaction (because the target address falls within the range assigned to IO devices that reside on the secondary side of the bridge).

Anytime that the bridge detects an IO transaction on the secondary bus with an address outside the 2000h through 3FFFh range, it claims the transaction and passes it through to the primary side (because the target address falls outside the range assigned to IO devices that reside on the secondary side of the bridge, but it may be for an IO device on the primary side).

Figure 24-14: Example of IO Filtering Actions

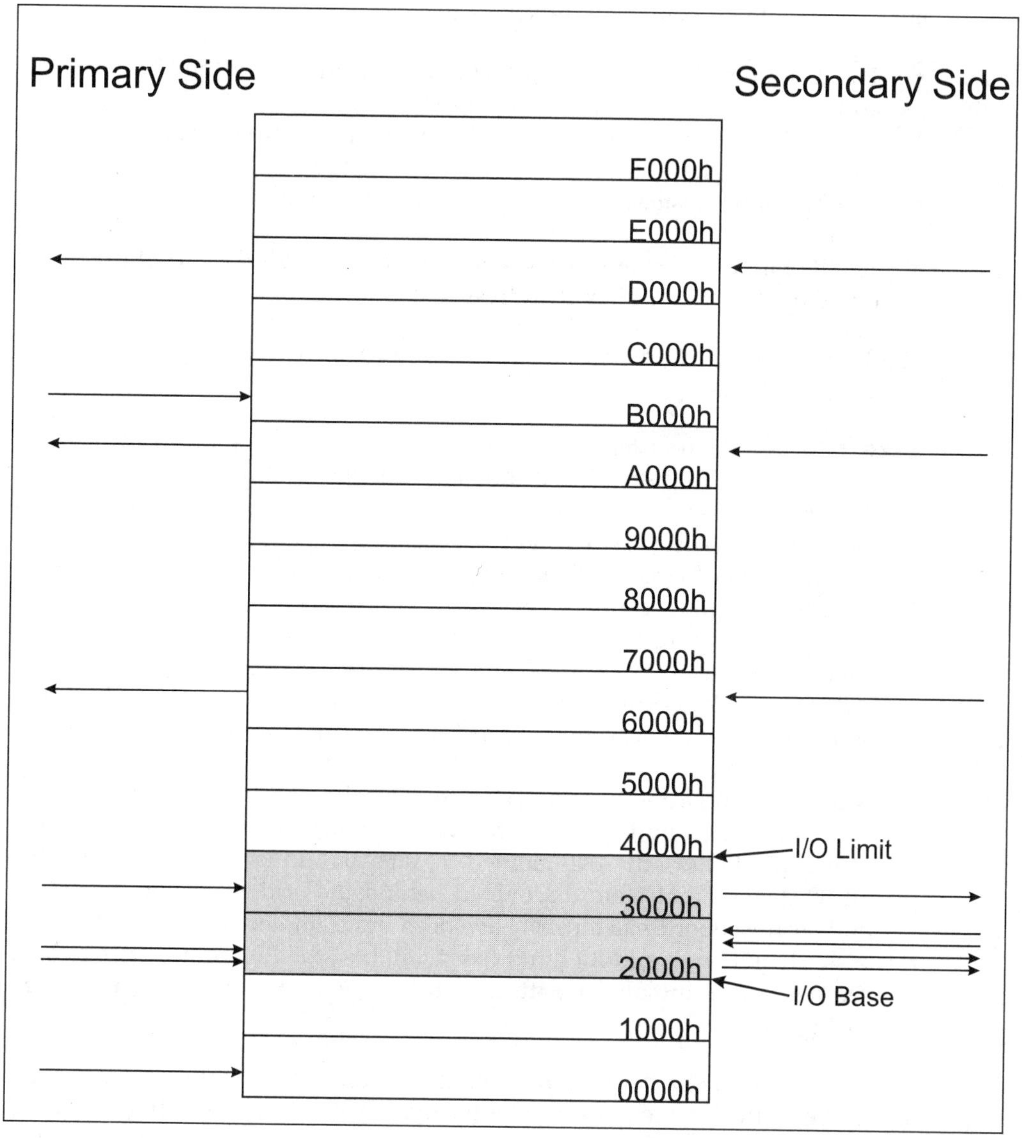

Bridge Supports 4GB IO Space Behind Bridge. Assume a bridge is designed to recognize IO transactions initiated on the primary bus that target locations anywhere within the 4GB of IO space (IO locations 00000000h through FFFFFFFFh) on the secondary bus.

In this case, in addition to the IO Base and the IO Limit registers, the bridge designer must also implement the IO Extension registers—IO Base Upper 16-bits and the IO Limit Upper 16-bits registers.

- The IO Base register is initialized with the fourth digit of the 32-bit start IO address.
- The IO Base Upper 16 bits register is initialized with the fifth through the eight digits of the 32-bit start address of the range.
- The IO Limit register is initialized with the fourth digit of the 32-bit end IO address.
- The IO Limit Upper 16 bits register is initialized with the fifth through the eight digits of the 32-bit end address of the range.

The IO Base and IO Limit register pair comprise an IO address decoder. They are used as follows:

STEP 1. Before the registers are initialized by the configuration software, they are read from to determine if they are capable of supporting a 64KB or a 4GB IO address space behind the bridge. In this scenario, the Address Decode Type field (see "IO Base Register" on page 573) within each of the registers is hardwired (with a value of 1h) to indicate that a 4GB IO space is supported on the secondary side.

STEP 2. The configuration software than walks the secondary bus (and any subordinate buses it discovers) and assigns each IO device that it discovers an exclusive IO address range within the 4GB IO space. The sub-ranges assigned to the devices are assigned in sequential blocks to make efficient use of IO space.

STEP 3. The IO Base and IO Base Extension (i.e., the IO Base Upper 16-bits) register pair is then initialized by the startup configuration software with the upper five digits of the 4KB-aligned, 32-bit start address of the IO range that all IO devices that were discovered behind the bridge (on the secondary and on any subordinate buses) have been programmed to reside within.

STEP 4. The IO Limit and IO Limit Extension (i.e., the IO Limit Upper 16 bits) register pair is initialized with the 4KB-aligned end address of the range that the devices occupy.

In the scenario under discussion, since the bridge supports the entire 4GB IO space, the defined range is a subset of the overall 4GB IO space. After they have been initialized, these four registers provide the bridge with the start and the end address of the IO address range to recognize.

Since the bridge supports the entire 4GB IO space, the IO address decoder comprised of the four registers (Base and Limit registers plus their Extension registers) performs an IO address decode within address bits [31:12] to determine whether or not to pass an IO access detected on the primary bus through to the secondary bus.

The format of the IO Base and IO Limit registers was illustrated earlier in Figure 24-12 on page 573 and Figure 24-13 on page 573. In the scenario under discussion, the lower hex digit of the Base and Limit registers is hardwired with the value 1h, indicating a 32-bit IO address decode, supporting recognition within the entire 4GB IO space. Simply put, the IO Base and IO Limit Upper 16-bits registers are used to hold the upper four digits of the start and end IO address boundaries, respectively.

Assume that the configuration software programs the registers as follows:

- Upper digit of the IO Base = 2h.
- IO Base Upper 16-bits register = 1234h.
- Upper digit of the IO Limit register = 3h.
- IO Limit Upper 16-bits register = 1235h.

This indicates a 72KB range consisting of:

- start of IO range = 12342000h
- end address = 12353FFFh.

As another example, assume the following:

- Upper digit of the IO Base = 3h.
- IO Base Upper 16-bits register = 1234h.
- Upper digit of the IO Limit register = 3h.
- IO Limit Upper 16-bits register = 1234h.

This indicates a 4KB range consisting of:

- start of IO range = 12343000h
- end address = 12343FFFh.

In other words, the four registers define the start address aligned on a 4KB address boundary, and the size of the defined block is an increment of 4KB.

Legacy ISA IO Decode Problem. When the original IBM PC and XT were designed, IBM defined the use of the processor's 64KB IO address space as shown in Table 24-5 on page 578.

Table 24-5: IBM PC and XT IO Address Space Usage

IO Address Range	Reserved For
0000h through 00FFh	256 locations for IO devices integrated on system board.
0100h through 03FFh	768 locations set aside for ISA IO expansion cards.
0400h through FFFFh	Not used.

Initially, IO addresses above 03FFh were not used by ISA IO cards. As shown in Table 24-5 on page 578, the IO address range used by these IO cards was 0100h through 03FFh. The card's IO address decoder inspected a sufficient number of address bits from A9 on down to determine if the IO address is within the range of IO ports implemented on the card. It should be noted, however, that these decoders ignored address bits [15:10].

Within the group of address bits used by expansion IO address decoders, A[9:0], bits A9 and A8 would therefore be one of the following:

- 01b (0100h-01FFh range)
- 10b (0200h-02FFh range)
- 11b (0300h-03FFh range).

When a bus master places any IO address on the address bus with A[9:8] = 01b, 10b, or 11b, an ISA IO expansion card may therefore respond.

As an example, assume that a machine has two ISA IO expansion cards installed. One of them performs an inadequate address decode using A[9:3], but ignoring A[15:10], and has eight registers residing at IO ports 0100h through 0107h. The other card performs a full decode using A[15:2] and has four registers residing at IO ports 1500h through 1503h. Now assume that a bus master initiates a one byte IO read from IO port 1500h. The address placed on the bus is shown in Table 24-6 on page 578.

Table 24-6: Example IO Address

A15	A14	A13	A12	A11	A10	A9	A8	A7	A6	A5	A4	A3	A2	A1	A0
0	0	0	1	0	1	0	1	0	0	0	0	0	0	0	0

The board that occupies the 1500h through 1503h range looks at A[15:2] and determines that the address is within the 1500h through 1503h block. It then looks at A[1:0] and determines that location 1500h is being addressed. The card places the contents of location 1500h on the lower data path (this is an even address) of the ISA data bus.

At the same time, the board that occupies the 0100h through 0107h range looks at A[9:3], a subset of the address seen by the other card's address decoder, and determines that the address appears to be within the 0100h through 0107h block. It then looks at A[2:0] and determines that location 0100h is apparently being addressed. The card places the contents of location 0100h on the lower data path (this is an even address).

Since both cards are driving a byte of data onto the lower ISA data path, SD[7:0], data bus contention is occurring. This results in garbage data and possible hardware damage because two separate current sources are driving the lower data path. The problem occurs because the card residing in the 0100h through 0107h range only looks at A[9:0] and thinks that this address is 0100h. If the card were designed to perform a full address decode using A[15:0], the problem could have been avoided.

Some ISA Drivers Use Alias Addresses To Talk To Card.
Some device drivers associated with legacy ISA IO devices communicate with the IO device using high addresses (above 03FFh) that alias down to the 01xxh, 02xxh, or 03xxh range. Consider the example used in the previous section. The device driver associated with the legacy IO card that owns IO ports 0100h-0107h might perform an IO read from IO address 1500h to read data from IO port 0100h. To be truly compliant with the ISA standard, the system designer must make sure that the driver is able to successfully communicate with the device, even when using alias addresses. This example is carried through to the next section.

Problem: ISA and PCI-to-PCI Bridges on Same PCI Bus.
Refer to Figure 24-15 on page 580. This problem makes the following set of assumptions:

- PCI-to-PCI Bridge A resides on the same PCI bus as an ISA bridge.
- ISA bridges claim transactions using subtractive decode (see "Subtractive Decode (by ISA Bridge)" on page 53).
- The IO Base and IO Limit registers within Bridge A have been programmed to recognize the IO address range 1000h-1FFFh as belonging to the PCI IO devices that reside on the secondary side of Bridge A. However, no PCI device on Bus 1 has been configured to recognize IO address 1500h (because it is an IO address that aliases to legacy ISA IO address 0100h).
- The ISA Enable bit in Bridge A's Bridge Control register is cleared to zero.

- An ISA device driver executing on the processor initiates an IO read from IO address 1500h. Its intention is to read from IO port 0100h in its ISA device.

The transaction is initiated on PCI bus 0 by the Host/PCI bridge and is latched by all agents on PCI bus 0. Using subtractive decode, the ISA bridge waits to see if any other PCI device asserts DEVSEL#. In this case, Bridge A has a hit on the IO range (1000h-1FFFh) defined by its IO Base and Limit registers and asserts DEVSEL# in the Fast, Medium, or Slow Decode time slot. When the ISA bridge detects DEVSEL# asserted by another agent, it ignores the transaction. As a result:

- The IO read from IO address 1500h never appears on the ISA bus and the driver therefore cannot read from its device's port 0100h (which is an alias of port 1500h).
- Bridge A initiates the read from IO address 1500h on PCI bus 1. No PCI address decoder (i.e., BAR register) has been set up to recognize this address, so Bridge A experiences a Master Abort.

Figure 24-15: Problem—ISA and PCI-to-PCI Bridges Reside on Same PCI Bus

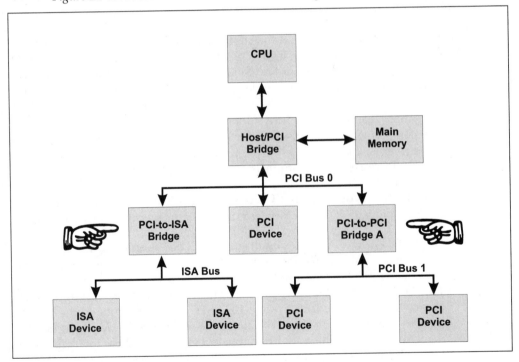

PCI IO Address Assignment. Addresses within the lower 64KB of IO space that are above 03FFh may be assigned to PCI IO decoders as long as address bits [9:8] are always 00b, thus ensuring that the address does not appear to be in the 0100h-01FFh, 0200h-02FFh, or 0300h-03FF ranges. Table 24-7 on page 581 illustrates the acceptable address ranges above 03FFh. Note that "x" can be any hex digit.

Table 24-7: Address Range Assignments Acceptable For PCI Devices

IO Address Range	Usable or Unusable
x000h - x0FFh	Usable by PCI devices. However, this does not include 0000h-00FFh range (because this range is used by embedded system board IO devices such as the Interrupt and DMA Controllers).
x100h - x1FFh	Unusable by PCI devices. Aliases to 0100h - 01FFh.
x200h - x2FFh	Unusable by PCI devices. Aliases to 0200h - 02FFh.
x300h - x3FFh	Unusable by PCI devices. Aliases to 0300h - 03FFh.
x400h - x4FFh	Usable by PCI devices.
x500h - x5FFh	Unusable by PCI devices. Aliases to 0100h - 01FFh.
x600h - x6FFh	Unusable by PCI devices. Aliases to 0200h - 02FFh.
x700h - x7FFh	Unusable by PCI devices. Aliases to 0300h - 03FFh.
x800h - x8FFh	Usable by PCI devices.
x900h - x9FFh	Unusable by PCI devices. Aliases to 0100h - 01FFh.
xA00h - xAFFh	Unusable by PCI devices. Aliases to 0200h - 02FFh.
xB00h - xBFFh	Unusable by PCI devices. Aliases to 0300h - 03FFh.
xC00h - xCFFh	Usable by PCI devices.
xD00h - xDFFh	Unusable by PCI devices. Aliases to 0100h - 01FFh.
xE00h - xEFFh	Unusable by PCI devices. Aliases to 0200h - 02FFh.
xF00h - xFFFh	Unusable by PCI devices. Aliases to 0300h - 03FFh.

Effect of Setting the ISA Enable Bit. Refer to Figure 24-15 on page 580 once again and assume the following set of conditions:

- The IO Base and IO Limit registers within Bridge A have been programmed to recognize the IO address range 1000h-1FFFh as belonging to the PCI IO devices that reside on the secondary side of Bridge A. However, no PCI device on bus 1 has been configured to recognize IO address 1500h (because it is an IO address that aliases to legacy ISA IO address 0100h).
- The ISA Enable bit in Bridge A's Bridge Control register is set to one.
- An ISA device driver executing on the processor initiates an IO read from IO address 1500h. Its intention is to read from IO port 0100h in its ISA device.

This results in the following actions:

- The Host/PCI bridge initiates the IO read from address 1500h and all PCI agents on bus 0 latch the transaction.
- Although IO address 1500h falls within the overall 4KB range of IO addresses (1000h-1FFFh) delimited by Bridge A's IO Base and Limit registers, the bridge ignores any access within the legacy ISA IO alias ranges. Since 1500h is an alias to 0100h, Bridge A will not assert DEVSEL# to claim the transaction.
- When the ISA bridge doesn't see any PCI device assert DEVSEL# in the Fast, Medium, or Slow Decode time slots, the ISA bridge asserts DEVSEL# in the Subtractive Decode time slot.
- The ISA bridge then initiates the IO read from IO address 1500h on the ISA bus. The ISA device supplies the read data from port 0100h to the ISA bridge which supplies it to the Host/PCI bridge which in turn returns it to the processor.

Bridge's Memory Filter

Introduction. *The Memory Base and Limit registers are mandatory (to support memory-mapped IO behind the bridge). The Prefetchable Memory Base and Limit registers (and their extensions) are optional (there is no requirement for a bridge to support prefetchable memory behind the bridge).* The PCI-to-PCI bridge specification recognizes the fact that although both groups are mapped into memory address space, memory devices and memory-mapped IO devices have distinctly different operational characteristics.

A well-behaved memory device always returns the same data from a location no matter how many times the location is read from. In other words, reading from a memory device doesn't in any way alter the contents of memory. This is one of the characteristics of a Prefetchable Memory target. Due to this operational characteristic, it is permissible for a bridge to perform a read-ahead when a master on the primary bus causes the bridge to perform a memory read from a Prefetchable memory target on the secondary bus. Assume that a master initiates a memory read to read a dword from a memory device. The bridge could read the requested dword and go on to prefetch data that hasn't been requested yet into a read-ahead buffer in case the master should ask for that data as well. If the master does request the prefetched data, it can be delivered quickly, yielding better performance. If the master doesn't ask for it, no harm is done and the bridge must discard the data.

A bridge also incorporates a posted-write buffer that quickly absorbs data to be written to a memory device on the other side of the bridge. Since the initiating master doesn't have to delay until the write to the memory device has actually been completed, posting yields better performance during memory write operations. The bridge would ensure that, before any subsequent memory read is permitted to propagate through the bridge, the bridge would flush its posted-write buffer to the memory device.

To summarize, it is permissible to performs prefetches from well-behaved Prefetchable memory targets. The bridge also implements posted-write buffers to expedite the completion of memory writes that must pass through the bridge. An optional set of registers are provided in the bridge's configuration space that permit the configuration software to define the start and end address of the prefetchable memory space that is occupied by well-behaved memory devices behind the bridge.

Memory-mapped IO devices exhibit a different set of operational characteristics. Performing a memory read from a memory-mapped IO location often has the effect of altering the contents of the location. As examples, one of the following may be true:

- The location may be occupied by a memory-mapped IO status port. Reading from the location causes the IO device to deassert any status bits that were set in the register (on the assumption that they've been read and will therefore be dealt with by the device driver). If the read was caused by a prefetch and the prefetched data is never actually read by the device driver, then status information has just been discarded.
- The location may be the front-end of a FIFO data buffer. Performing a read from the location causes the delivery of its current contents and the next data item is then automatically placed in the location by the IO device. The device assumes that the first data item has just been read by the device driver and sets up the next data item in the FIFO location. If the read was caused by a prefetch and the prefetched data is never actually read by the device driver, then the data has just been discarded.

Reads within an area of memory space occupied by memory-mapped IO devices must never result in prefetching by a bridge. A mandatory set of registers are provided that permit the configuration software to define the start and end address of the memory space that is occupied by memory-mapped IO devices that reside on the bridge's secondary side.

Determining If Memory Is Prefetchable or Not. The configuration software determines that a PCI memory target supports prefetching by testing the state of the *Prefetchable* attribute bit in the memory target's Base Address Register (see "Memory Base Address Register" on page 380).

- Prefetchable = 1 indicates that the memory is prefetchable. The memory target must be mapped into Prefetchable memory space using the bridge's Prefetchable Base and Limit configuration registers.
- Prefetchable = 0 indicates that it's not. In this case, the memory target must be mapped into memory-mapped IO space using the Memory Base and Limit registers.

Supports 4GB Prefetchable Memory On Secondary Side. Whether or not a bridge supports Prefetchable memory on the bridge's secondary side is optional. If the designer chooses to support this capability, then the following registers must be implemented to define the start and end address of the memory range occupied by Prefetchable memory devices behind the bridge:

- Prefetchable Memory Base register.
- Prefetchable Memory Limit register.

These two registers are used to define the start (base) and end (limit) address of the memory range. Any address within the lower 4GB can be specified. The start address is 1MB-aligned and the size of the range can be any 1MB increment. If the bridge designer intends to support a 2^{64} prefetchable memory space behind the bridge (in other words, the bridge can perform the Dual Address Command on its secondary side), then the extensions to these two registers must also be implemented:

- Prefetchable Memory Base Upper 32-bits register.
- Prefetchable Memory Limit Upper 32-bits register.

A discussion of these two registers and 2^{64} prefetchable memory support can be found in "Supports > 4GB Prefetchable Memory On Secondary" on page 588. The Prefetchable Memory Base and Limit registers are illustrated in Figure 24-16 on page 586 and Figure 24-17 on page 587. Assuming that the bridge only supports a 4GB (2^{32}) Prefetchable memory space on the secondary side, the lower hex digit of both the Base and Limit registers is hardwired with the value 0h to indicate this to the configuration software. The configuration software then walks the secondary bus and any buses subordinate to the bridge and assigns each Prefetchable memory target a sub-range in a global overall range within the lower 4GB of memory space. After completing the address assignment process, the software then writes the upper three hex digits of the range's start address into the upper three digits of the Base register and the upper three hex digits of the end address into the upper three digits of the Limit register.

As an example, assume that the upper three digits in the two registers are set as follows:

- 123h written into the upper three digits of the Base register.
- 124h written into the upper three digits of the Limit register.

This defines the Prefetchable memory address range as the 2MB range from 12300000h through 124FFFFFh. As another example, assume they are programmed as follows:

- 222h written into the upper three digits of the Base register.
- 222h written into the upper three digits of the Limit register.

This defines the Prefetchable memory address range as the 1MB range from 22200000h through 222FFFFFh.

Figure 24-16: Prefetchable Memory Base Register

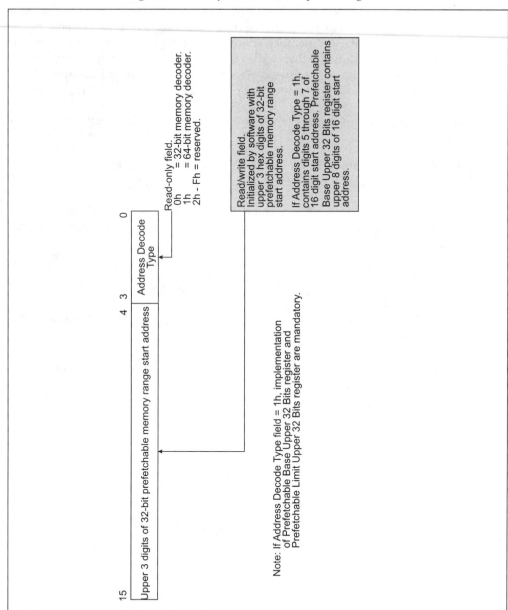

Figure 24-17: Prefetchable Memory Limit Register

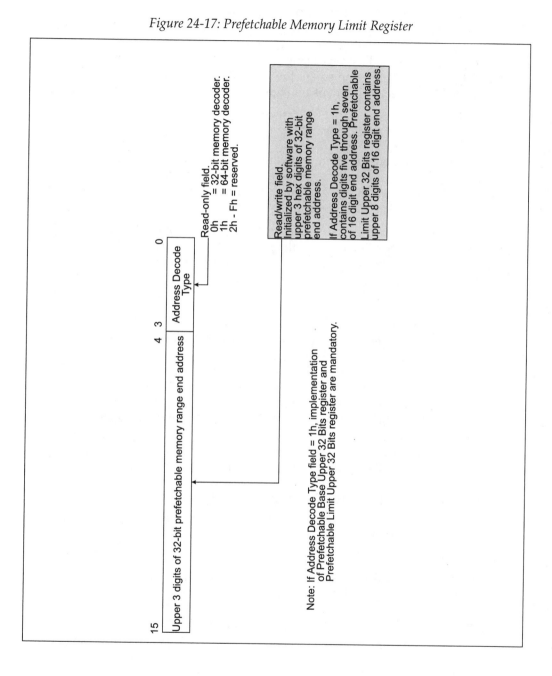

Supports > 4GB Prefetchable Memory On Secondary. If the bridge designer wants the bridge to support 2^{64} prefetchable memory space behind the bridge, this means that the bridge must be capable of initiating memory transactions on the secondary bus using the Dual Address Cycle. In addition, the bridge must not only implement the Prefetchable Base and Limit registers, but also the Base and Limit Extension registers:

- Prefetchable Base Upper 32-bits register.
- Prefetchable Limit Upper 32-bits register.

To inform the configuration software that the bridge can map Prefetchable memory behind the bridge anywhere in 2^{64} memory space, the designer must hardwire the value 1h into the lower hex digit of the Base and Limit registers (see Figure 24-16 on page 586 and Figure 24-17 on page 587).

After the configuration software completes the walk of the bridge's secondary bus and any subordinate buses, the four registers are then initialized with the start and end address of the memory range assigned to the Prefetchable memory targets that were found behind the bridge. The start and end addresses are assigned as follows:

- Upper eight digits of the start address are written to the Prefetchable Memory Base Upper 32-bit register. Next lower three digits of the start address are written to the upper three digits of the Prefetchable Memory Base register. Together, these two registers define the upper 11 digits of the start address. The lower five digits are assumed to be 00000h.
- Upper eight digits of the end address are written to the Prefetchable Memory Limit Upper 32-bit register. The next lower three digits of the end address are written to the upper three digits of the Prefetchable Memory Limit register. Together, these two registers define the upper 11 digits of the end address. The lower five digits are assumed to be FFFFFh.

Rules for Prefetchable Memory. The following rules apply to Prefetchable memory:

RULE 1. Bridge support for Prefetchable memory on its secondary side is optional.

RULE 2. If the bridge does not support Prefetchable memory on its secondary side, the Prefetchable Memory Base and Limit registers must be implemented as read-only registers that return zero when read.

RULE 3. The Prefetchable Memory Base and Limit Upper 32-bits registers only have to be implemented if the bridge supports 2^{64} Prefetchable memory on its secondary side (as indicated by hardwiring the first digit in the Base and Limit registers to a value of 1h).

RULE 4. Bridge can prefetch read data when a memory read initiated on the primary side crosses the bridge within the address range defined by the Prefetchable Memory Base and Limit registers.

RULE 5. Memory transactions are forwarded from the primary to the secondary bus if the address is within the range defined by the Prefetchable Memory Base and Limit registers or that defined by the Memory Base and Limit registers (for memory-mapped IO).

RULE 6. Memory transactions are forwarded from the secondary to the primary bus when the address is outside the ranges defined by the Prefetchable Memory Base and Limit registers and the Memory Base and Limit registers (for memory-mapped IO).

RULE 7. When 2^{64} memory is supported, transactions targeting addresses within the address range specified by the Prefetchable Memory Base and Limit registers (and their extensions) are permitted to cross the 4GB boundary.

RULE 8. The bridge designer may choose not to support the DAC command initiated on the primary side, *BUT MUST SUPPORT IT ON ITS SECONDARY SIDE. PRIOR TO THE 1.1 PCI-TO-PCI BRIDGE SPEC, IT WAS OPTIONAL ON BOTH SIDES. THIS WAS CHANGED TO ENSURE THAT BUS MASTERS ON THE SECONDARY BUS CAN ACCESS MAIN MEMORY ABOVE THE 4GB ADDRESS BOUNDARY.*

1.1

RULE 9. Assume that the bridge supports Prefetchable memory anywhere in 2^{64} memory space on the secondary side, but the configuration software maps all Prefetchable memory behind the bridge below the 4GB boundary. In this case, the upper extensions of the Prefetchable Base and Limit registers must be set to zero and the bridge does not respond to Dual Address Commands initiated on the primary side. Those initiated on the secondary side would be passed to the primary side (in case the initiator is addressing main memory above the 4GB boundary).

RULE 10. Assume that the bridge supports Prefetchable memory anywhere in 2^{64} memory space on the secondary side and that the configuration software maps all Prefetchable memory behind the bridge above the 4GB boundary. In this case, the upper extensions of the Prefetchable Base and Limit registers contain non-zero values and the bridge responds only to Dual Address Commands initiated on the primary side.

RULE 11. Assume that the bridge supports Prefetchable memory anywhere in 2^{64} memory space behind the bridge and that the configuration software maps the Prefetchable memory behind the bridge into a space that straddles the 4GB boundary. In this case, the extension to the Prefetchable Base register is set to zero and the extension to the Limit register contains a non-zero value. When a single-address memory command (in other words, an address below the 4GB boundary) is detected on either side, the bridge compares the address only to the Prefetchable Memory Base register. If the address is equal to or greater than the start address specified in the register, the address is in range. When a Dual Address Command is detected on either side, the bridge compares the lower 32-bits of the address to the Limit register and the Upper 32-bits of the address to the Limit Upper 32-bits register. If the address is equal to or less than the end address specified in the two registers, the address is in range.

RULE 12. The bridge may safely prefetch data when the transaction uses the Memory Read Line or the Memory Read Multiple command.

RULE 13. The bridge may safely convert a Memory Read command to a Memory Read Line or a Memory Read Multiple command, or may turn a single data phase memory read into an extended read burst if the address is within the range specified by the Prefetchable Memory Base and Limit registers.

RULE 14. The bridge may safely prefetch data on the primary bus if the command detected on the secondary bus is a Memory Read Line or a Memory Read Multiple command.

RULE 15. The bridge may be designed to assume that all memory accesses detected on the secondary bus that are passed to the primary bus are Prefetchable. This assumes that the destination of all memory reads traveling upstream is system memory (which is Prefetchable). If a bridge makes this assumption and performs "blind" prefetches, it must implement a device-specific bit in its configuration space that allows this ability to be disabled (in case a problem results from blind prefetching).

RULE 16. Bridges that prefetch must ensure that they do not cross a 4KB address boundary when prefetching. If the bridge were to do so, it may cross the upper boundary (specified by the Prefetchable Limit register) into memory that does not support prefetching.

Bridge's Memory-Mapped IO Filter

Mandatory. The bridge designer is required to implement the Memory Base and Limit registers used to define a memory-mapped IO range. These two registers are used to define a range of memory occupied by memory-mapped IO devices that reside on the secondary side of the bridge. Figure 24-18 on page 591 and Figure 24-19 on page 591 illustrate the Memory Base and Limit registers. The lower digit of each register is hardwired to zero and the upper three digits are used to define the upper three hex digits of the eight-digit start and end addresses, respectively. Note that, unlike the Prefetchable Base and Limit and IO Base and Limit register pairs, there are no Extension registers associated with the Memory Base and Limit register pair. This means that all memory-mapped IO devices in the system must reside in the lower 4GB of memory address space.

As an example, assume that the configuration software has written the following values to the Memory Base and Limit registers:

- The upper three digits of the Memory Base register contain 555h.
- The upper three digits of the Memory Limit register contain 678h.

This defines a 12.4MB memory-mapped IO region on the secondary side of the bridge starting at 55500000h and ending at 678FFFFFh.

Figure 24-18: Memory-Mapped IO Base Register

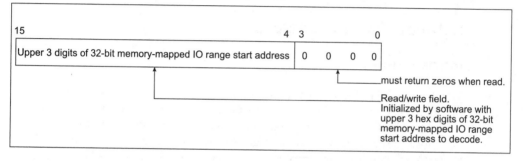

Figure 24-19: Memory-Mapped IO Limit Register

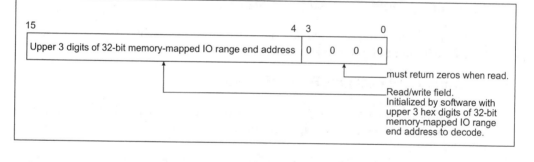

Cache Line Size Register

Mandatory. THIS REGISTER WAS MANDATORY IN THE 1.0 BRIDGE SPEC. IN THE 1.1 SPEC, IT IS ONLY MANDATORY IF A BRIDGE IS DESIGNED TO INITIATE OR FORWARD THE MEMORY WRITE AND INVALIDATE COMMAND OR IF IT SUPPORTS THE BULK MEMORY READ COMMANDS (MEMORY READ LINE AND MEMORY READ MULTIPLE). IF A BRIDGE DOESN'T SUPPORT THESE COMMANDS, THEN THE CACHE LINE SIZE REGISTER IS IMPLEMENTED AS A READ-ONLY REGISTER THAT ALWAYS RETURNS ZERO WHEN READ.

1.1

The format and usage of this register is completely compatible with its definition for non-bridge PCI devices (see "Cache Line Size Register" on page 376). It defines the system cache line size for both sides of the bridge. The value in this register is used by the bridge:

- in determining when it has transferred an entire line when using the Memory Write and Invalidate transaction.
- in determining the cache line size during performance of Memory Read Line and Memory Read Multiple transactions.

Latency Timer Registers

Introduction

The bridge includes an independent Master Latency (i.e., Timeslice) Timer (MLT) for each of its two master interfaces (primary and secondary). The contents of each of these required registers defines the minimum period of time (in PCI clock cycles since FRAME# asserted) that the bridge may continue a burst transaction even if it's preempted (loses its GNT#). For a detailed description of the MLT, refer to "Latency Timer Keeps Master From Monopolizing Bus" on page 78.

Latency Timer Register (Primary Bus)

Mandatory. This required register defines the timeslice when the bridge is acting as the initiator on the primary interface.

Secondary Latency Timer Register

Mandatory. This required register defines the timeslice when the bridge is acting as the initiator on the secondary interface.

BIST Register

Optional. This optional register is fully-compatible with the BIST register definition for non-bridge PCI devices (for a detailed description, see "BIST Register" on page 377).

Interrupt-Related Registers

Only required if the bridge itself generates interrupts. If the bridge is capable of generating an interrupt (to signal a bridge-specific event) on any of the PCI interrupt request pins, then the designer must implement the Interrupt Pin and Interrupt Line registers. The format and usage of these registers are compatible with that of non-bridge PCI devices (see "Interrupt Pin Register" on page 388 and "Interrupt Line Register" on page 388). It should be noted that the IRQ lines from devices on the secondary side do not go through the bridge. If the bridge is located on an add-in card, the interrupt lines from the secondary side PCI devices are connected directly to the interrupt pins (INTA#-INTD#) on the connector (see "Interrupt Support" on page 624). If, on the other hand, the bridge is embedded on the system board, the interrupt lines from the secondary side devices are connected directly to the system board Interrupt Controller or Interrupt Router.

Configuration Process

Introduction

At startup time, the configuration software must (among other things) accomplish the following:

- The bus number registers in all PCI-to-PCI bridges and in the Host/PCI bridge must be initialized to identify the range of buses that reside behind each bridge.
- Using PCI configuration accesses, the configuration software must detect all PCI functions (by reading their Vendor ID registers) and assign mutually-exclusive address ranges to each of their respective IO and memory decoders (i.e., their BAR registers).
- Detect interrupt-driven PCI functions (those that implement the Interrupt Pin register) and program the interrupt routing information into each of their Interrupt Line registers.
- Initialization of the display subsystem on the PCI bus.

Bus Number Assignment

At startup time, the configuration software is only aware of the existence of PCI bus zero. It must build a picture of the bus "tree" that represents the overall system topology. The system startup configuration software must walk the base PCI bus (bus zero) and search for PCI-to-PCI bridges. When a bridge is discovered (using the Class Code register), the software walks the secondary bus in an attempt to discover other bridges. The software proceeds with this process until all PCI buses behind the first PCI-to-PCI bridge have been discovered. As each was discovered, the software assigns it the next sequential bus number and must also go back and update the Subordinate Bus Number registers in each bridge that resides upstream of the bridge (including the Host/PCI bridge).

When a complete picture of the tree branch that extends behind the first PCI-to-PCI bridge has been built, the software searches for other PCI-to-PCI bridges stemming from the first PCI bus and builds pictures of the branch behind each.

The specification does not define in what order bus numbers are assigned and when they are assigned. This is system software-specific. It does, however, dictate that the bus number assigned to each bus that resides behind a PCI-to-PCI bridge must be a value greater than the bridge's secondary bus number and less then or equal to the value placed in its own Subordinate Bus Number register.

2.2 Chassis and Slot Number Assignment

Problem: Adding/Removing Bridge Causes Buses to Be Renumbered

The best way to start this discussion is to illustrate the problem with an example. Assume the following set of conditions:

- The system has several PCI add-in card slots on PCI bus 0.
- There are one or more PCI-to-PCI bridges on PCI bus 0 and one or more of them have add-in card slots on their secondary buses.
- The system was shipped as described in items one and two and no cards have been added or removed.
- Diagnostic software has detected a problem with an add-in card in one of the slots.

Now, the question: *When the software displays a message to identify the bad card to the end user, how will it identify the location of the card slot to the end user?* The software knows the following:

- The PCI bus number that the device resides on.
- Which device number is assigned to the device.

So, let's say that the software identifies the bad boy to the end user by displaying its location using the bus and device numbers and let's say that someone at the factory was nice enough to physically label each card slot using that information (bus and device number). That would work just fine—as long as no one installs or removes a card that has a PCI-to-PCI bridge on it. Remember that the configuration software discovers PCI-to-PCI bridges each time that the machine is restarted and assigns a bus number to each bridge's secondary bus. In other words, if a bus is added or removed, that can change the bus numbers assigned to a number of the buses. *This would result in the labels on the card slots being wrong and the end user wouldn't know it.*

If Buses Added/Removed, Slot Labels Must Remain Correct

As stated in this section's heading, the addition or removal of a bus must not render the physical slot labels incorrect. This requirement highlights that the bus number cannot be used as part of the slot labeling (because it can change). The only exception would be PCI Bus 0 which cannot be removed and always is assigned bus number 0.

Definition of a Chassis

As defined in the 1.1 PCI-to-PCI bridge specification, there are two types of chassis:

- **Main Chassis**—Refer to Figure 24-20 on page 596. These PCI add-in card **slots** are located on PCI Bus 0 and are **not removable**. The PCI **Interrupt Routing Table** (see "Interrupt Routing Table" on page 233) contains entries identifying each of these card slots and relates a slot's bus number/device number to its physical slot label. These card slots do not present a problem in that the physical labeling of the slots is always correct.
- **Expansion Chassis**—Refer to Figure 24-23 on page 601, Figure 24-24 on page 603, and Figure 24-25 on page 605. An Expansion Chassis consists of a group of one or more buses each with card slots and the entire group can be installed in or removed from the system as a single entity. The slots within an expansion chassis are numbered sequentially and are identified by chassis number and slot number.

Figure 24-20: Main Chassis

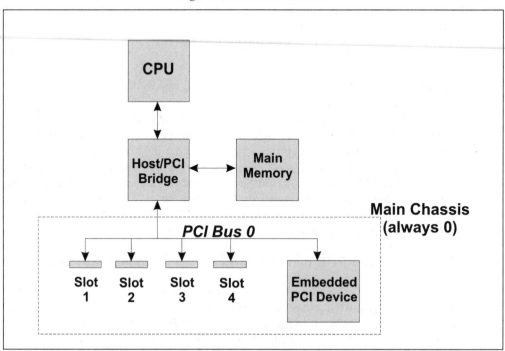

Chassis/Slot Numbering Registers

Introduction. "Introduction To Chassis/Slot Numbering Registers" on page 566 introduced the configuration registers associated with chassis and slot numbering. Figure 24-21 on page 596 pictures these registers and Table 24-8 on page 597 describes them.

The Chassis and Slot Number registers are required for the first bridge in a PCI expansion chassis and for each bridge within an expansion chassis that has expansion slots on its secondary bus.

Figure 24-21: Chassis and Slot Number Registers

31 24	23 16	15 8	7 0
Chassis Number	Expansion Slot Register	Pointer to next Capability	Capability ID 04h

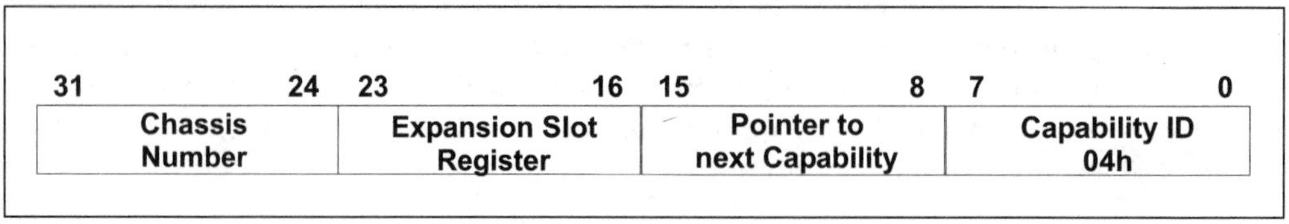

Table 24-8: Slot Numbering Register Set

Register	Description
Capability ID	**Read-Only.** 04h identifies this as the Slot Numbering register set.
Next Capability Pointer	**Read-Only.** **00h** = Indicates that this is the last register set in the linked New Capabilities list. **Non-zero value** = dword-aligned pointer to the next register set in the linked list.
Expansion Slot	**Read-Only, automatically loaded by hardware after reset.** The configuration software uses the value in this register to determine the number of expansion card slots present on the bridge's secondary PCI bus. The spec doesn't define where the hardware obtains this information. It could read a set of strapping pins on the trailing-edge of RST#, or could obtain the information from a serial EEPROM.
Chassis Number	**Read/Write.** The value in this register identifies the chassis number assigned to the PCI add-in card slots on this bridge's secondary bus. At reset time, this register may: • be pre-loaded with 00h, or • may be implemented as a non-volatile register that "remembers" the chassis number assigned during a previous platform configuration.

Slot Number Register (read-only). The Slot Number register is pictured in Figure 24-22 on page 598 and is described in Table 24-9 on page 598. The Slot Number register is preloaded with the indicated information by hardware before the configuration software is executed. As an example, the bridge could sample a set of strapping pins on the trailing-edge of RST# to determine the contents of the Slot Number register. A bridge may implement the Chassis/Slot numbering registers and yet may not have any expansion card slots on its secondary bus (see Bridges A and C in Figure 24-24 on page 603).

Figure 24-22: Slot Number Register

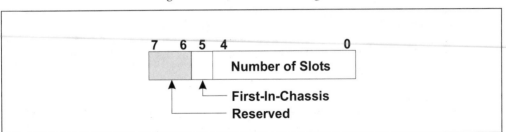

Table 24-9: Slot Number Register Bit Assignment

Bit Field	Description
7:6	**Reserved**. Read-only and must always return zero when read.
5	**First-In-Chassis bit**. This bit must be set to one in the first bridge within each expansion chassis. This is defined as follows: • If there is only one expansion chassis and it contains only one bridge with slots on its secondary side, that bridge is the First-In-Chassis. • If an expansion chassis contains a hierarchy of bridges springing from one parent bridge (see Figure 24-23 on page 601 and Figure 24-24 on page 603), the parent bridge is First-In-Chassis, while the other bridges will have the First-In-Chassis bit cleared to zero. • If an expansion chassis contains more than one bridge and those bridges share the same primary PCI bus (i.e., they are peers; see Figure 24-25 on page 605), the bridge that occupies the lowest Device Number position on the parent primary bus is marked as the First-In-Chassis.
4:0	**Number of Expansion Slots** on bridge's secondary bus. If there aren't any expansion slots on the bridge's secondary bus, this field must be hardwired to zero.

Chassis Number Register (read/write). The configuration software will initialize all bridges within the same chassis with the same Chassis Number and must guarantee that each chassis is assigned a mutually-exclusive Chassis Number. A bridge may implement the Chassis/Slot numbering registers and yet may not have any expansion card slots on its secondary bus (see Bridges A and C in Figure 24-24 on page 603).

The Chassis Number register may be cleared to zero by RST#, or may be non-volatile (i.e., the current contents of the register will survive resets and power cycles). If it is non-volatile, its initial state after the first power up will be zero. When the configuration software detects zero in an expansion Chassis Number register, it must assign a number to it. Zero is not a valid Chassis Number for an expansion chassis because Chassis Zero is reserved for the card slots embedded on the system board.

Some Rules

The following rules must be adhered to:

RULE 1. A bridge within an expansion chassis that implements the Chassis/Slot numbering registers may not use Device Number 0 for any device on its secondary bus.

RULE 2. Card slot 1 is always implemented as Device Number 1 on the bridge's secondary bus, card slot 2 as Device Number 2, etc. Expansion card slots implemented on the bridge's secondary bus must be implemented as Device Number 1 through n, where n = the maximum slot number on the bus. The first slot must always be implemented as Device Number 1 and no holes are permitted (e.g., it would be illegal to implement three card slots as Device Numbers 1, 2 and 4 on the bus).

RULE 3. Any embedded devices on the bridge's secondary bus must have Device Numbers that are greater than that used by the highest slot number implemented on the bridge's secondary bus. As an example, see Device 4 on PCI Bus 1 in Figure 24-23 on page 601.

RULE 4. If there are any embedded bridges on the bridge's secondary bus they must have Device Numbers that are greater than that assigned to all other embedded devices. As an example, see Bridges B (Device 5) and D (Device 6) on PCI Bus 1 in Figure 24-23 on page 601.

Three Examples

Example One. Figure 24-23 on page 601 illustrates a system with one Expansion Chassis connected to the system. This example system has the following characteristics:

- A proprietary card is installed in Slot 1 on PCI Bus 0 (in other words, Slot 1 in Chassis 0). This is *not* a PCI-to-PCI bridge. Rather, it's a special-purpose "repeater" function that buffers and re-drives PCI Bus 0, permitting it to drive a cable to the expansion chassis. This function may or may not implement the Chassis/Slot numbering registers and the bus numbering registers.

- Bridge A is a PCI-to-PCI bridge residing in the expansion chassis at the other end of the cable. From a configuration standpoint, it appears to be another function residing within the Proprietary bridge card. The configuration software assigns Bus Number 1 to Bridge A's Secondary Bus Number register.
- Bridge A implements the Chassis/Slot numbering registers.
- The configuration software determines that the First-in-Chassis bit is set and the Slot Number register indicates that there are three expansion card slots on the bridge's secondary bus. Since they are by definition the first three slots in the expansion chassis and this was the first expansion chassis discovered, they are labelled as Slots 1-3 in Chassis 1. The configuration software assigns Chassis Number 1 to Bridge A's Chassis Number register.
- By looking for valid Vendor IDs, the configuration software determines that slots 1-3 are currently unoccupied.
- Device 4 is not a bridge.
- Device 5 is a bridge (Bridge B) and it implements the Chassis/Slot numbering registers. Its First-In-Chassis bit is cleared (indicating that this is a continuation of Chassis 1) and the Slot Number register indicates that there are two expansion card slots on the bridge's secondary bus. They are therefore physically numbered as Slots 4-5 in Chassis 1. The Chassis Number register is set to 1 by software.
- One of the card slots is occupied by a card with a bridge (Bridge C), but there are no slots on the bridge's secondary bus.
- Bridge D implements the Chassis/Slot numbering registers. It is not the first bridge in the chassis and it's secondary bus has three slots. Since this is a continuation of Chassis 1, its Chassis Number is set to one, and the card slots are labelled as Slots 6-8.

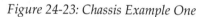

Figure 24-23: Chassis Example One

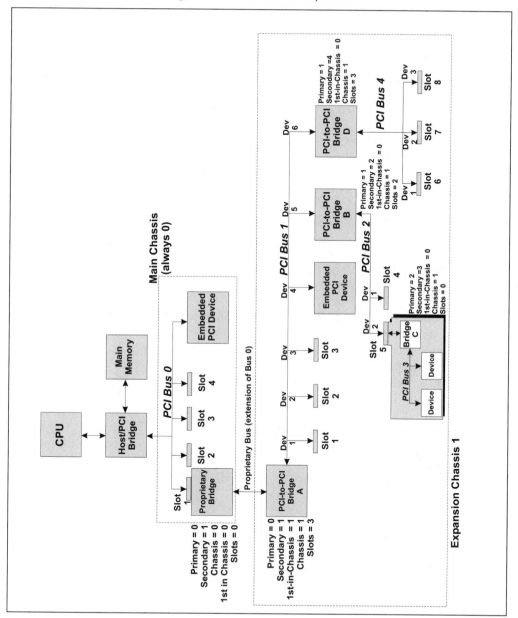

Example Two. Figure 24-24 on page 603 illustrates a system with one Expansion Chassis connected to the system. This example system has the following characteristics:

- A proprietary card is installed in Slot 1 on PCI Bus 0 (in other words, Slot 1 in Chassis 0). This is *not* a PCI-to-PCI bridge. Rather, it's a special-purpose "repeater" function that buffers and re-drives PCI Bus 0, permitting it to drive a cable to the expansion chassis. This function may or may not implement the Chassis/Slot numbering registers and the bus numbering registers.
- Bridge A is a PCI-to-PCI bridge residing in the expansion chassis at the other end of the cable. From a configuration standpoint, it appears to be another function residing within the Proprietary bridge card. The configuration software assigns Bus Number 1 to Bridge A's Secondary Bus Number register.
- Bridge A implements the Chassis/Slot numbering registers.
- The configuration software determines that the First-in-Chassis bit is set and the Slot Number register indicates that there no expansion card slots on the bridge's secondary bus. The configuration software assigns Chassis Number 1 to Bridge A's Chassis Number register.
- Device 4 is not a bridge.
- Device 5 is a bridge (Bridge B) and it implements the Chassis/Slot numbering registers. Its First-In-Chassis bit is cleared (indicating that this is a continuation of Chassis 1) and the Slot Number register indicates that there are two expansion card slots on the bridge's secondary bus. They are therefore physically labelled as Slots 1-2 in Chassis 1. The Chassis Number register is set to 1 by software.
- One of the card slots is occupied by a card with a bridge (Bridge C), but there are no slots on the bridge's secondary bus.
- Bridge D implements the Chassis/Slot numbering registers. It is not the first bridge in the chassis and it's secondary bus has three slots. Since this is a continuation of Chassis 1, its Chassis Number is set to one, and the card slots are labelled as Slots 3-5.

Figure 24-24: Chassis Example Two

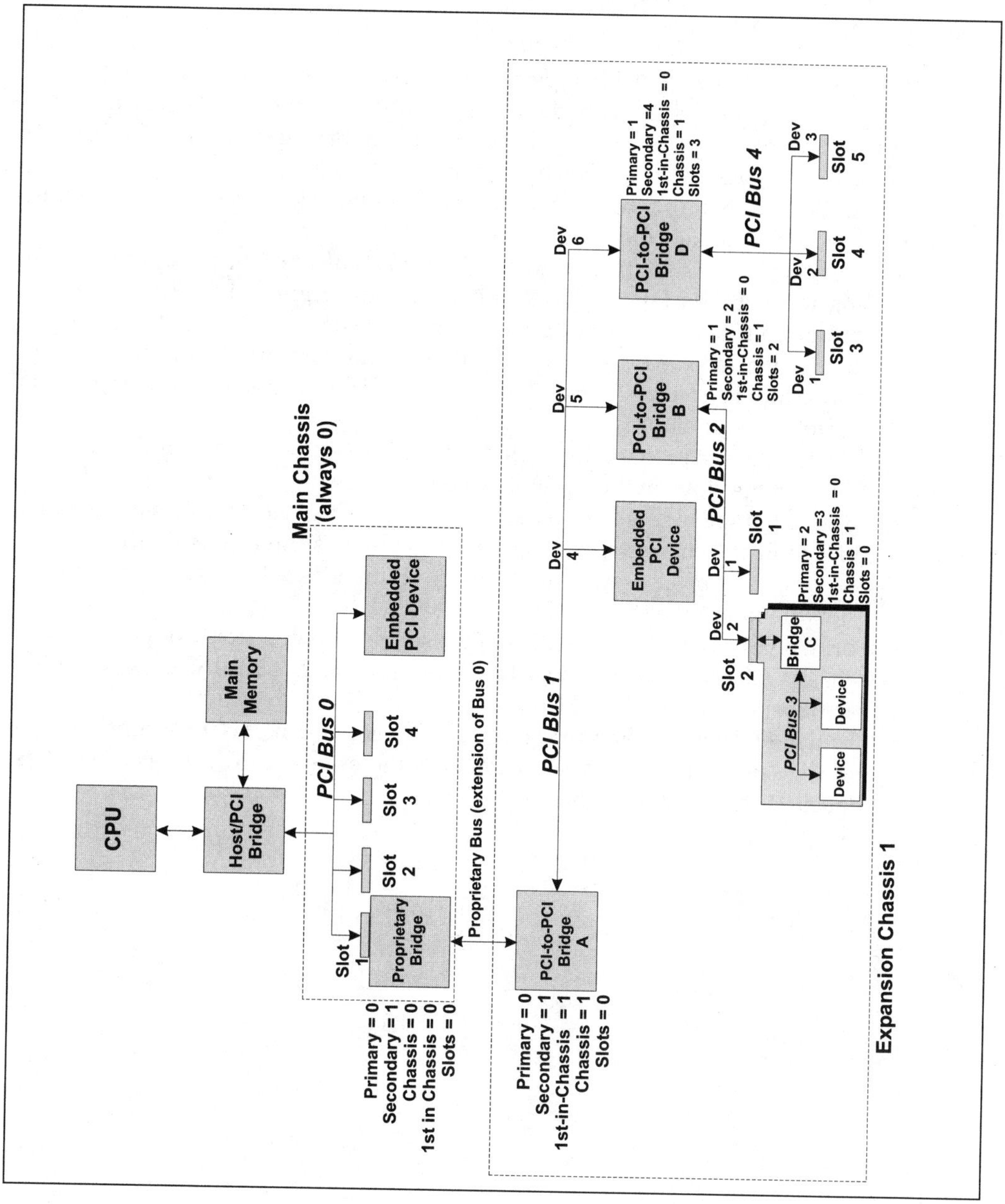

Example Three. Figure 24-25 on page 605 illustrates a system with two Expansion Chassis connected to the system. This example system has the following characteristics:

- A standard PCI-to-PCI bridge resides in Slot 1 in Chassis 0. The configuration software sets its Secondary Bus Number register to 1. This bridge may or may not implement the Chassis/Slot numbering registers. If it does, it doesn't reside in an expansion chassis, so its First-In-Chassis bit is cleared, and its Slot Number register indicates it has zero slots on its secondary bus.
- Device 4 is not a bridge.
- Device 5 is a bridge (Bridge A) and it implements the Chassis/Slot numbering registers. Its First-In-Chassis bit is set (indicating that this is the first bridge in Chassis 1) and the Slot Number register indicates that there are two expansion card slots on the bridge's secondary bus. They are therefore physically labeled as Slots 1-2 in Chassis 1. The Chassis Number register is set to 1 by software.
- One of the card slots is occupied by a card with a bridge (Bridge C), but there are no slots on the bridge's secondary bus.
- Bridge B implements the Chassis/Slot numbering registers. It is not the first bridge in the chassis and it's secondary bus has three slots. Since this is a continuation of Chassis 1, its Chassis Number is set to one, and the card slots are labelled as Slots 3-5.
- Bridge C has the First-In-Chassis bit set, so it is the first bridge in a new chassis. The software sets its Chassis Number to 2. It has two slots and they are labelled as Slots 1-2 in Chassis 2.
- Bridge D is not the first bridge in the current chassis, so it's a continuation of Chassis 2 and its Chassis Number is therefore set to 2. It has three slots labelled as Slots 3-5 of Chassis 2.

Figure 24-25: Chassis Example Three

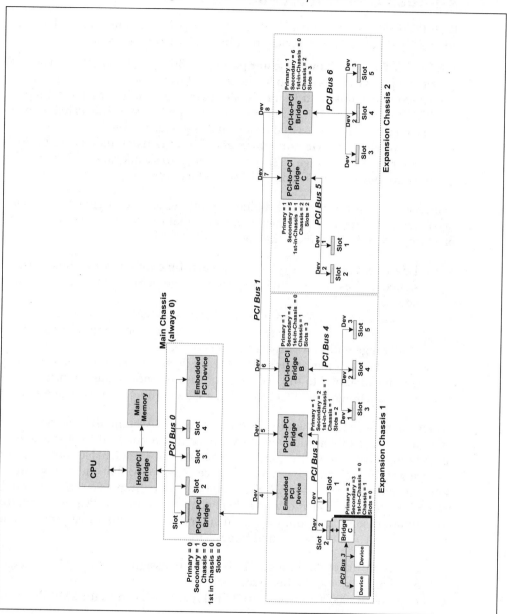

Address Space Allocation

Each PCI-to-PCI bridge contains three register pairs that are used to define the address space allocated to devices residing on its secondary side:

- The **IO Base and Limit register pair** (see "Bridge's IO Filter" on page 570) define IO space allocated to IO devices that reside on its secondary side.
- The **Memory Base and Limit register pair** (see "Bridge's Memory-Mapped IO Filter" on page 590) define memory-mapped IO space allocated to memory-mapped IO devices that reside on its secondary side.
- The **Prefetchable Memory Base and Limit register pair** (see "Bridge's Memory Filter" on page 582) define memory space allocated to Prefetchable memory devices that reside on its secondary side.

Only one address range can be defined for all decoders of a given type (memory-mapped IO, IO, or Prefetchable memory) that reside on the secondary side of a bridge. This implies the following:

- All decoders of a given type within each function on a PCI bus must be assigned address ranges that are grouped together into one overall address range.
- The configuration software then backtracks to that bus's bridge and programs the respective register pair with the start and end address of the overall range within which all decoders of that type reside.
- Ultimately, the range assigned to that register pair encompasses not only the range assigned to the decoders for that secondary bus's functions, but for the functions on all PCI buses that are subordinate to this bridge as well.

As an example, refer to Figure 24-26 on page 607. Assume that the device on PCI bus two is a Prefetchable memory device that requires 4MB of space. Also assume that the two devices on bus three are also Prefetchable memory, one requiring 2MB and the other 1MB of space. Assuming that the configuration software has already assigned the memory space from 00000000h through 00FFFFFFh to system memory and Prefetchable memory on PCI bus zero, the configuration software would assign memory space to the three prefetchable memory devices on buses two and three as follows:

- Locations 01000000h through 013FFFFFh are assigned to the 4MB Prefetchable memory device on bus two.
- Locations 01400000h through 015FFFFFh are assigned to the 2MB Prefetchable memory device on bus three.
- Locations 01600000h through 016FFFFFh are assigned to the 1MB Prefetchable memory device on bus three.

The Prefetchable Memory Base and Limit registers in bridges B and C are programmed as follows:

- The Prefetchable Memory Base register in bridge B is set to the base address of the Prefetchable memory device on bus two: 01000000h.
- The Prefetchable Memory Limit register in bridge B is set to the end address of the range assigned to the last Prefetchable memory device on bus three: 016FFFFFh.
- The Prefetchable Memory Base register in bridge C is set to the base address assigned to the first Prefetchable memory device on bus three: 01400000h.
- The Prefetchable Memory Limit register in bridge C is set to the end address of the range assigned to the last Prefetchable memory device on bus three: 016FFFFFh.

Figure 24-26: Example System

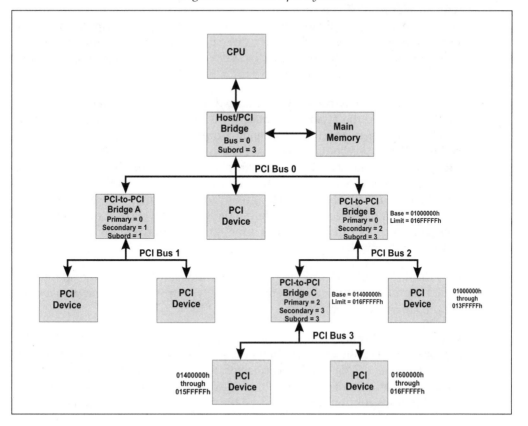

IRQ Assignment

During the discovery process, the startup configuration software also determines which PCI functions are interrupt driven. Each function that indicates that it is interrupt-driven (a value between 01h and 04h hardwired into the device's Interrupt Pin register) also implements an Interrupt Line register. The startup software must write the interrupt routing information into each device's Interrupt Line register. This process is described in "Interrupt Routing" on page 225.

Display Configuration

There May Be Two Display Adapters

Refer to Figure 24-27 on page 610. Assume that a platform has two display adapters installed, but there's only one display. One of the adapters is a VGA-compatible adapter, while the other one supports higher-resolution graphics modes other than those supported by VGA. The PCI spec refers to the other adapter as an Advanced Graphics Adapter, or GFX.

Obviously, the display can only be attached to the connector on one of the two adapters. Each of the adapters contains a Digital-to-Analog Converter (DAC) and the Red, Green, and Blue Gun analog outputs to the display are driven by the DAC. Each DAC contains a set of color palette registers. As each dot (pixel) is to be written onto the display, the graphics adapter supplies a data value to the DAC. This selects an entry in the color palette register set. Each entry contains three values: a red gun value, a green gun value, and a blue gun value. The three values in the selected entry define the voltage level to be driven onto the three gun outputs during that dot time, and therefore define the color and intensity of the pixel.

If the display is only attached to the output connector on one of the adapters, it would seem that only one of them can supply output data to the display and that the other one never could.

Assume that a display is attached to the GFX's display connector and that this display supports both VGA and higher-resolution display modes. No display is attached to the VGA's display connector. Some older DOS applications programs (e.g., games) talk directly to the VGA's register set to control the display. In the Windows environment, however, the driver for the GFX would be used to control the display. In either case, the display output provided by either adapter must end up being driven to the GFX's display connector on the rear-panel. To accomplish this, a VGA pass-through cable connects the video output of the VGA adapter to the other adapter. It should be obvious that in this scenario, any IO write that is performed to the color palette registers must update the GFX's color palette registers.

It is possible, however, that a VGA-capable display unit is attached to the VGA's display connector and another, higher-resolution display is attached to the GFX's display connector. Because software doesn't know which connector the VGA-compatible display is attached to, *any IO write that is performed to the color palette registers must update the color palette registers in both the VGA's and the GFX's DACs.*

If software has enabled the GFX and disabled the VGA, then the VGA's output drivers are disabled and the GFX logic is driving the display data to the GFX's DAC and therefore to the display. On the other hand, if the GFX is disabled and the VGA is enabled, the GFX's output drivers are disabled and the VGA logic is driving the display data to the GFX's DAC and therefore to the display.

Identifying the Two Adapters

The VGA adapter has a Class Code of 03h and a Sub Class Code of 00h. The GFX has a Class Code of 03h and a Sub Class Code of 80h.

The Adapters May Be On Same or Different Buses

Refer to Figure 24-28 on page 611 and Figure 24-29 on page 612.

It was established in the previous section that any IO write that is performed to the color palette registers must update the color palette registers in both the VGA's and the GFX's DACs. The color palette registers are located at the same IO address in both the VGA's and GFX's DACs. There are many different possibilities as to where the two display adapters are located in the machine (in other words, which bus each resides on).

If they are on the same PCI bus and an IO write is performed to the color palette registers, unless something is done to prevent it, both device's would assert DEVSEL# to claim the transaction when an IO read or write is performed to the color palette registers. Obviously, this would present a protocol violation.

If the adapters are on different buses, the bridges between the two buses would have to be programmed so as to ensure that both adapters see the IO write transaction, but only one would actively participate (i.e., assert DEVSEL# and TRDY#) as the target of the transaction.

Solution

The solution consists of the following control bits within VGA adapters, GFX adapters, and PCI-to-PCI bridges:

- The VGA Palette Snoop bit in the display adapter's Command register.
- The VGA Enable bit in the bridge's Bridge Control Register.
- The VGA Palette Snoop bit in the bridge's Command register.

Figure 24-27: VGA and GFX Display Adapters In a System

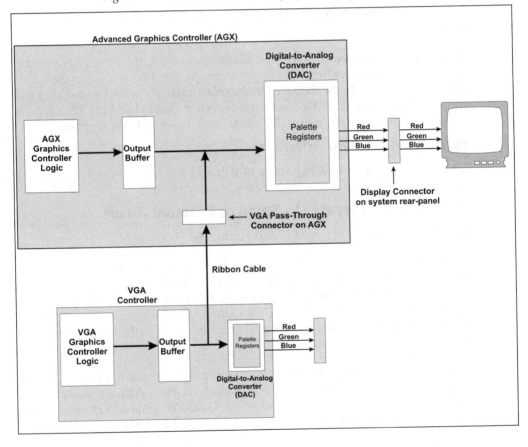

Figure 24-28: Both Adapters on Same Bus

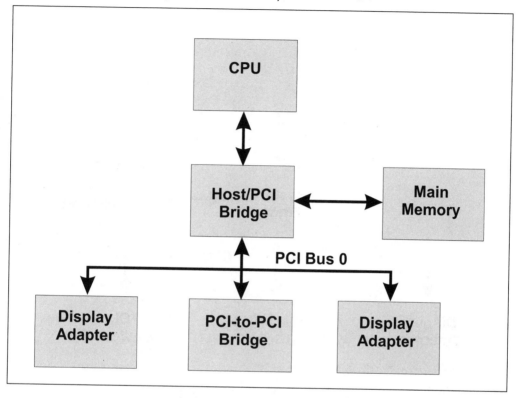

Figure 24-29: Adapters On Different Buses

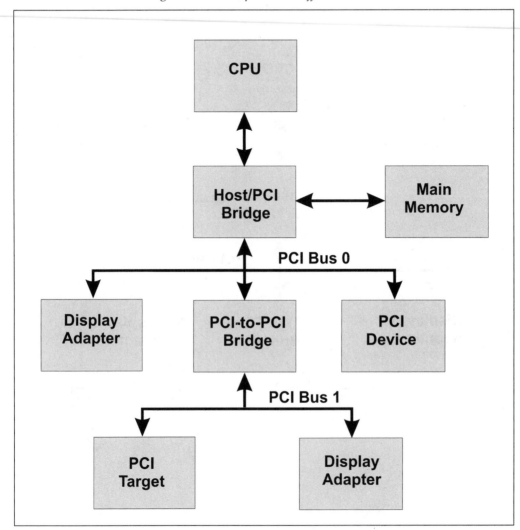

PCI-to-PCI Bridge State After Reset

Reset clears the bridge's VGA Enable bit and its VGA Palette Snoop bit, causing the bridge to **ignore all VGA accesses** initiated on its Primary side. This is the proper setting if neither the VGA nor the GFX is on the bridge's secondary side.

Non-VGA Graphics Controller (aka GFX) After Reset

Reset sets the VGA Palette Snoop bit in its Command register to one. This causes the non-VGA graphics display controller, referred to as a **GFX** in the specification, to:

- snoop all VGA palette register writes.
- ignore all palette register reads.

This is the appropriate setting if the GFX is on the same PCI bus as the VGA or is on the secondary side of a bridge.

VGA Graphics Controller After Reset

Reset clears the VGA Palette Snoop bit in its Command register. The VGA-compatible display controller doesn't snoop VGA palette register writes. Rather, assuming that the configuration software has set the function's IO Space bit in its Command register, the VGA device:

- claims palette register reads.
- claims palette register writes.

This is the appropriate setting if:

- the VGA is the only graphics device.
- the GFX is on the same PCI bus as the VGA.

Effects of Setting VGA's Palette Snoop Bit

When the VGA Palette Snoop bit is set to one, the VGA device:

- decodes and claims palette register reads.
- snarfs palette register writes, but does not claim them.

This is the appropriate setting if the GFX is further downstream in the bus hierarchy than the VGA. It permits the bridge in the path to the GFX to claim the palette register write and pass it to the GFX.

Effects of Clearing GFX's Palette Snoop Bit

When the VGA Palette Snoop bit is cleared to zero, the GFX device:

- decodes and claims palette register writes.
- ignores palette register reads.

This is the appropriate bit setting if the GFX is on the secondary side of a PCI-to-PCI bridge and the VGA is upstream in the bus hierarchy.

Effects of Bridge's VGA-Related Control Bits

A PCI-to-PCI bridge's treatment of VGA accesses initiated on its Primary side is defined by the setting of the following two control bits:

- VGA Palette Snoop bit in its Command register. The default state of this bit after reset is zero.
- VGA Enable bit in its Bridge Control register. The default state of this bit after reset is zero.

Table 24-10 on page 614 defines the effects of the bridge's VGA-related control bits.

Table 24-10: Effects of Bridge's VGA Control Bit Settings

VGA Enable Bit	VGA Snoop Enable Bit	Bridge's Treatment of VGA Accesses Initiated On Its Primary Side
0	0	The bridge **ignores** (i.e., does not claim and pass through) **all accesses** within the memory and IO ranges associated with the VGA device. This includes palette register reads and writes. This is the state when **neither the VGA nor the GFX resides on the bridge's secondary side.**
0	1	The bridge ignores and does not pass through palette register reads. It does, however, claim and pass through palette register writes. This is the setup when the **GFX** resides **on** the bridge's **secondary** side and the VGA is on the Primary side. It ensures that the palette register set within the GFX's DAC receives palette register updates.
1	x	When the VGA Enable bit is set to one, the VGA Palette Snoop bit is ignored. The bridge claims and passes through both palette register reads and writes. This is the setup when the **VGA** device resides **on** the bridge's **secondary** side.

Detecting and Configuring Adapters and Bridges

The sequence that must be utilized to detect and set up all VGA-compatible controllers and non-VGA, GFX controllers is as follows:

STEP 1. Identify the VGA display device to be utilized during the boot process. This is accomplished by first scanning the standard expansion bus (e.g., ISA, EISA or Micro Channel). If the display device is found on the expansion bus, that display is used for the boot process and the initialization sequence has completed. Do not perform the steps that follow. If the VGA device is not found on the expansion bus, scan the PCI bus(es), starting at the bus with the largest bus number. If it is found on a PCI bus, save the bus number for use during the remaining steps in the initialization sequence.

STEP 2. Set the IO Space and Memory Space enable bits in the device's Command register so it can respond to VGA accesses.

STEP 3. Starting at the PCI bus number the boot display device is on, scan the PCI bus hierarchy upstream (towards bus zero). In each PCI-to-PCI bridge detected, set the VGA Enable bit in its bridge control register.

STEP 4. Starting at the PCI bus the boot display device is on, scan the PCI buses downstream (all buses subordinate to this bus) looking for GFXs. Abort the scan when the first instance of a GFX is found. Set the GFX device's IO Space and VGA Palette Snoop Enable bits in its Command register.

STEP 5. Scan back upstream from the bus the GFX is on towards the bus the boot display device resides on. At each PCI-to-PCI bridge encountered, set the VGA Palette Snoop Enable bit in the bridge's Command register.

STEP 6. Finally, set the VGA Palette Snoop Enable bit in the boot display device's Command register.

The PCI-to-PCI bridge specification provides pseudo-code for two procedures that can be used to implement the sequence described above. The two procedures are:

- DisplayInit(). This is the top-level procedure. It has no input parameters and it calls the GFXScanR procedure.
- GFXScanR(BusNum). This procedure scans the buses subordinate to the one the boot display was found on looking for the first instance of a GFX device.

Chapter 12 of the 1.1 PCI-to-PCI bridge specification provides a more detailed discussion of issues related to VGA palette snooping and includes a number of examples.

Configuration and Special Cycle Filter

Introduction

In addition to memory and IO transactions, the PCI-to-PCI bridge must also monitor both buses for configuration transactions. These transactions occur for the following reasons:

- Host/PCI bridge is performing a configuration read or write to access a specific PCI function's configuration registers.
- Host/PCI bridge or another PCI master is performing a special form of the Type 1 configuration write transaction in order to broadcast a message on a specific PCI bus in the system.

Table 24-11 on page 616 defines the various types of configuration reads and writes that may be detected on the bridge's two interfaces and the action to be taken by the bridge. A complete description of the Type 0 configuration transaction can be found in "Type 0 Configuration Transaction" on page 335. A complete description of the Type 1 configuration transaction can be found later in this chapter in "Type 1 Configuration Transactions" on page 620.

Table 24-11: Configuration Transactions That May Be Detected On the Two Buses

Transaction	Bus Detected On	Description
Type 0 configuration read	primary	If the bridge's IDSEL# input is not asserted, ignore. If asserted, perform function decode to determine if target function implemented. If not, ignore. If implemented, assert DEVSEL# and permit access to internal configuration registers or memory.
Type 0 configuration read	secondary	Ignore.
Type 0 configuration write	primary	Same as configuration read.

Table 24-11: Configuration Transactions That May Be Detected On the Two Buses (Continued)

Transaction	Bus Detected On	Description
Type 0 configuration write	secondary	Ignore.
Type 1 configuration read	primary	Compare target bus to bridge's bus number registers. If not equal to Secondary Bus register and not in range defined by Secondary and Subordinate Bus Number registers, ignore. If equal to Secondary Bus Number register, claim and pass through as Type 0 configuration read on secondary. If not equal to Secondary Bus Number, but in range defined by Secondary and Subordinate Bus Number registers, claim and pass through to secondary as Type 1 configuration read as is (no conversion).
Type 1 configuration read	secondary	Ignore.
Type 1 configuration write (not Special Cycle Request)	primary	Same as Type 1 configuration read.
Type 1 configuration write (not Special Cycle Request)	secondary	Ignore.

Table 24-11: Configuration Transactions That May Be Detected On the Two Buses (Continued)

Transaction	Bus Detected On	Description
Type 1 configuration write (Special Cycle Request)	primary	If target bus matches Secondary Bus Number register, claim and convert to Special Cycle on secondary. The write data supplies the message during the data phase. If target bus doesn't match Secondary Bus Number register, but is in the range defined by Secondary and Subordinate Bus Number registers, claim and pass through to secondary unchanged as Type 1 Special Cycle Request. If target bus not secondary and not in range defined by Secondary and Subordinate Bus Number registers, ignore.
Type 1 configuration write (Special Cycle Request)	secondary	If target bus matches Primary Bus Number register, claim and pass through as Special Cycle with write data as message. If target bus is not primary and not in range of buses defined by Secondary and Subordinate Bus Number registers, claim and pass through unchanged as Type 1 Special Cycle Request. If target bus is within range of buses subordinate to secondary, ignore.

Special Cycle Transactions

The Special Cycle transaction is defined in "Special Cycle Command" on page 107. The Host/PCI bridge designer may or may not supply a method that permits the programmer to stimulate the Host/PCI bridge to forward a Special Cycle transaction to a specific PCI bus in the system. Assuming that the Host/PCI bridge designer supports software-generation of Special Cycles, the following sequence causes the Host/PCI bridge to generate a Special Cycle on a specific target bus.

STEP 1. Programmer writes a 32-bit pattern to the Configuration Address Port specifying the target bus number and setting the target device to 1Fh, function to 7h, and dword to 0. The enable bit (bit 31) in the Address Port is set to one.

STEP 2. The programmer then performs either a 16 or a 32-bit write to the Configuration Data Port.

STEP 3. The Host/PCI bridge compares the target bus to the number of its PCI bus (typically 0). If it matches, the bridge generates a Special Cycle on PCI bus 0 and supplies the write data written to the Configuration Data Port as the message. If the target bus is not PCI Bus 0 but is within the range of subordinate buses that exist beyond the bridge, the bridge generates a special form of the Type 1 configuration write transaction that is recognized as a Special Cycle Request by PCI-to-PCI bridges. During the address phase, it drives the contents of the Configuration Address Port (except for bits 31 and [1:0]) onto the AD bus. AD[1:0] is set to 01b, indicating that this is a Type 1 configuration write transaction. During the data phase it drives the data being written to the Configuration Data Port onto the AD bus as the message.

The only devices on a PCI bus that pay attention to a Type 1 configuration transaction are PCI-to-PCI bridges. They test the target bus number supplied in the transaction's address phase to determine whether to ignore the transaction or to pass it through as one of the following:

- Type 0 configuration transaction for a device on its secondary bus.
- Type 1 configuration transaction for a device on a bus subordinate to its secondary bus.
- Type 1 Special Cycle Request that is targeting a subordinate bus.
- Special Cycle transaction on the opposite bus.

When the bus number specified in the Special Cycle Request matches the number of the bridge's opposite bus, that bridge converts the Special Cycle Request into a Special Cycle on the opposite bus. A bus master residing on any PCI bus can utilize this special form of the Type 1 configuration write to force PCI bridges to forward a Special Cycle Request upstream or downstream until it arrives on the target bus.

Type 1 Configuration Transactions

Type 1 configuration accesses (AD[1:0] set to 01b) are ignored by all PCI devices except PCI-to-PCI bridges residing on the PCI bus that the transaction appears on. If the target of a configuration access resides on a PCI bus subordinate to the bus upon which the configuration access is performed, the PCI-to-PCI bridge that connects the two PCI buses must claim and pass the configuration access through to its secondary bus. When a PCI-to-PCI bridge latches a Type 1 configuration access on its primary bus and the target bus is its secondary bus or a bus subordinate to the bridge, it must pass the access through to its secondary bus in one of two forms:

- If the access targets the bridge's secondary bus, it must pass it through as a **Type 0 configuration access**.
- If the access targets a PCI bus that is subordinate to the bridge's secondary bus, it must pass the access through as a **Type 1 configuration access**.

For a complete description of the Type 1 configuration transaction, refer to "Type 1 Configuration Transactions" on page 344.

Type 0 Configuration Access

Type 0 configuration read and write transactions are used to access a PCI function's configuration registers. A complete description of the Type 0 configuration access can be found in "Type 0 Configuration Transaction" on page 335.

When a PCI-to-PCI bridge detects a Type 0 configuration access on its primary side and its IDSEL is sampled asserted, it recognizes that it is the target of the configuration access. It is a read or write of the bridge's configuration registers.

When a PCI-to-PCI bridge detects a Type 1 configuration access on its primary side, it converts the transaction into a Type 0 access on its secondary bus if the following criteria are met:

- Target bus matches the bridge's Secondary Bus Number register.
- Target device number, function number and dword are not 1Fh, 7h and 0h, respectively (this would be a Special Cycle Request).

Assuming that the criteria are met, the bridge converts the transaction into a Type 0 configuration transaction on the secondary bus. When doing so, the bridge must assert IDSEL to the target physical device on its secondary bus. The bridge specification states that the bridge does not implement IDSEL output pins on its secondary side. Rather, the bridge designer must internally decode the target physical device number and assert one upper AD line in the range AD[31:16]. Table 24-12 on page 621 defines the target device number-to-AD signal line mapping mandated in the bridge spec. This imposes a limit of 16 physical devices per secondary PCI bus.

On the secondary PCI bus, the designer must resistively-couple each of these upper AD lines (AD[31:16]) to an IDSEL pin at a separate physical device location on the bus. The designer of a device to be embedded or installed on a PCI bus must never internally couple one of these AD lines to the device's IDSEL pin. This would effectively "hardwire" the device's physical address. If everyone did this, there is the strong probability that two or more devices on the bus would respond to Type 0 configuration accesses.

Table 24-12: Target Device Number-to-AD Line Mapping (for IDSEL assertion)

Target Device	AD Line to Assert in AD[31:16] Field
0	AD16
1	AD17
2	AD18
3	AD19
4	AD20
5	AD21
6	AD22
7	AD23
8	AD24
9	AD25
10d	AD26
11d	AD27

Table 24-12: *Target Device Number-to-AD Line Mapping (for IDSEL assertion) (Continued)*

Target Device	AD Line to Assert in AD[31:16] Field
12d	AD28
13d	AD29
14d	AD30
15d	AD31
16d - 31d	none

Interrupt Acknowledge Handling

A PCI-to-PCI bridge ignores all Interrupt Acknowledge transactions detected on either side (because the system interrupt controller is never placed on a subordinate PCI bus).

2.2 PCI-to-PCI Bridge With Subtractive Decode Feature

PRIOR TO THE 2.2 PCI SPEC, THE ONLY VALID PROGRAMMING INTERFACE VALUE WAS THAT OF A STANDARD PCI-TO-PCI BRIDGE:

- CLASS CODE = 06 (BRIDGE)
- SUBCLASS = 04 (PCI-TO-PCI BRIDGE)
- PROGRAMMING INTERFACE = 00H.

THE 2.2 SPEC HAS ADDED A PROGRAMMING INTERFACE VALUE OF 01H TO INDICATE THAT A PCI-TO-PCI BRIDGE:

- IS 100% COMPLIANT WITH THE 1.1 PCI-TO-PCI BRIDGE SPEC,
- AND, IN ADDITION, ALSO PERFORMS SUBTRACTIVE DECODE (REFER TO "SUBTRACTIVE DECODE (BY ISA BRIDGE)" ON PAGE 53) ON TRANSACTIONS THAT ORIGINATE ON THE PRIMARY BUS.

THE PRIMARY USE OF A PCI-TO-PCI BRIDGE THAT ALSO SUPPORTS SUBTRACTIVE DECODE IS TO SUPPORT A LAPTOP DOCKING STATION WITH AN ISA BUS AND A PCI BUS ON THE BRIDGE'S SECONDARY SIDE.

IF A BRIDGE IMPLEMENTS SUBTRACTIVE DECODE CAPABILITY, IT MUST ALSO IMPLEMENT A DEVICE-SPECIFIC CONFIGURATION BIT (ITS LOCATION IS OUTSIDE THE SCOPE OF THE SPEC) THAT CAN BE USED TO ENABLE OR DISABLE THE BRIDGE'S SUBTRACTIVE DECODE CAPABILITY. THE PROGRAMMING INTERFACE BYTE IN THE BRIDGE'S CLASS CODE CONFIGURATION REGISTER MUST REFLECT THE STATE OF THIS ENABLE/DISABLE BIT. IN OTHER WORDS:

- IF THE ENABLE/DISABLE BIT IS IN THE DISABLED STATE, THE PROGRAMMING INTERFACE BYTE MUST RETURN 00H WHEN READ.
- IF THE ENABLE/DISABLE BIT IS IN THE ENABLED STATE, THE PROGRAMMING INTERFACE BYTE MUST RETURN 01H WHEN READ.

Reset

The RST# signal on the bridge's secondary side is asserted under two conditions (in other words, it's the logical OR of two conditions):

- When RST# is detected asserted on the primary side, the bridge must assert RST# on the secondary side.
- The bridge asserts RST# on the secondary side whenever software sets the Secondary Bus Reset bit in the bridge's Bridge Control register to one.

All PCI-to-PCI bridges are required to take ownership of the secondary bus's AD, C/BE and PAR signals whenever RST# is asserted on the secondary bus. The bridge must drive all of these signals low to keep them from floating during the reset period (otherwise, input buffers connected to the secondary bus would oscillate and draw excessive power). This requirement is independent of the location (inside or outside the bridge) of the secondary bus's arbiter. There isn't a danger of another PCI device on the secondary bus also driving the bus during reset, because reset causes all PCI devices other than the PCI-to-PCI bridge to float their AD, C/BE and PAR outputs.

Arbitration

The PCI-to-PCI bridge designer is not required to provide a PCI bus arbiter for the bridge's secondary bus, but it is strongly recommended that the bridge include the arbiter (it makes sense to do so).

WHEN TRANSACTIONS ON OPPOSITE SIDES OF THE BRIDGE OCCUR SIMULTANEOUSLY AND BOTH REQUIRE A CROSSOVER TO THE OPPOSITE BUS, THE BRIDGE IS NOT REQUIRED TO GIVE ONE INTERFACE PRIORITY OVER THE OTHER. HOWEVER, THE BRIDGE IS REQUIRED TO IMPLEMENT A FAIR ARBITRATION MECHANISM BETWEEN THE INTERFACES. THIS IS DIFFERENT THAN THE 1.0 BRIDGE SPEC WHICH STATED, "THE BRIDGE MUST GIVE PRECEDENCE TO THE PRIMARY SIDE.

1.1

When the bridge designer integrates the secondary bus arbiter into the bridge, the arbiter's operation must adhere to the revision 2.1 specification. These rules are covered in "PCI Bus Arbitration" on page 59.

Interrupt Support

Devices That Use Interrupt Traces

A PCI-to-PCI bridge is not required to route interrupt requests generated (on interrupt pins) by devices on the secondary side through the bridge.

The PCI specification requires that either the system, the device-specific interrupt handler or the device itself (if it has bus master capability) ensure that all posted-write buffers *between the device and host processor* are flushed to memory before interrupts are delivered to the host processor. The author would like to stress at this point that the bridge specification uses the wording *"between the device and its final destination."* "Final destination" is quite vague. The author believes the specification is saying between the device and the device that services the interrupt. That would be the host processor. The device-specific interrupt handler within the device driver must take responsibility for ensuring that this rule is met if it does not "know" that flushing of posted-write buffers is handled by the system board logic or by the device itself.

All posted-write buffers can be flushed by the interrupt handler by performing a read from any location within the device that generated the request. The buffers can be flushed by the device itself (if it has bus master capability) by having the device perform a read from the last memory address it wrote to before generating the interrupt request. Either one of these actions causes all bridges between the device and the host processor to flush all outstanding posted-writes to memory.

The system configuration software has the responsibility of providing interrupt routing information to each interrupt-driven PCI function at startup time. This routing information consists of the system IRQ input the interrupt is routed to on the system interrupt controller. The routing information is used by a device's device driver to determine which entry in the memory-based interrupt table to "hook."

The system configuration software "knows" the signal routing between the interrupt pins on embedded devices and the system interrupt controller. The software writes the IRQ number into the device's Interrupt Line register. Each add-in card connector on a PCI bus must implement the four PCI interrupt pins designated as INTA# through INTD#. If a card implements a PCI-to-PCI bridge and a secondary PCI bus, the bridge specification dictates that the interrupt pins on the secondary bus's PCI functions must be connected to the add-in card's connector interrupt pins as indicated in Table 24-13 on page 625.

Table 24-13: Interrupt Routing on Add-in Card With PCI-to-PCI Bridge

Device On Add-in Bus	Device's INT Pin	Wired To Connector INT Pin
0, 4, 8, 12, 16, 20, 24, 28	INTA#	INTA#
	INTB#	INTB#
	INTC#	INTC#
	INTD#	INTD#
1, 5, 9, 13, 17, 21, 25, 29	INTA#	INTB#
	INTB#	INTC#
	INTC#	INTD#
	INTD#	INTA#
2, 6, 10, 14, 18, 22, 26, 30	INTA#	INTC#
	INTB#	INTD#
	INTC#	INTA#
	INTD#	INTB#
3, 7, 11, 15, 19, 23, 27, 31	INTA#	INTD#
	INTB#	INTA#
	INTC#	INTB#
	INTD#	INTC#

This table does not specify the physical interconnect to the add-in connector for the bridge's interrupt pin (if it implements one). The bridge specification states:

"Assuming that the bridge is a single function device, its interrupt pin must be INTA#."

While that's true, the PCI specification does not define the external interconnect of a function's pin to a trace. By this statement, the writers of the specification are apparently indicating that it should be routed to the INTA# pin on the connector.

Devices That Use MSI

A PCI-to-PCI bridge receives memory writes into its posted memory write buffer. It cannot discern between actual writes to memory versus memory writes generated by PCI functions to cause an interrupt to the processor. In other words, these MSI memory writes (see "Message Signaled Interrupts (MSI)" on page 252) are not treated in a special manner by the bridge.

Buffer Management

A PCI-to-PCI bridge deals with two streams of transactions: those occurring on the primary side and those occurring on the secondary side. As already described in this chapter, a transaction that the bridge latches on either side falls into one of the following categories with reference to the bridge:

1. The bridge ignores it (because it's not targeting the bridge or a device on the other side of the bridge).
2. The bridge must claim it because the initiator is attempting to access one of the bridge's internal registers or memory. The transaction is not passed to the other side.
3. The transaction has been latched on the bridge's primary side and the bridge must claim it and pass it through to the secondary side because the address falls within the IO, memory-mapped IO, or Prefetchable memory windows that the bridge has been configured to recognize as assigned to functions residing on the secondary side.
4. A non-configuration transaction has been latched on the bridge's secondary side and the bridge must claim it and pass it through to the primary side because the address falls outside the IO, memory-mapped IO, or Prefetchable memory windows that the bridge has been configured to recognize as assigned to functions residing on the secondary side.

5. A Type 1 configuration read or write has been latched on the bridge's primary side and it targets a function on the bridge's secondary bus. The bridge must claim it and pass it through as a Type 0 configuration transaction, or as a Special Cycle transaction if it's a Type 1 configuration write that is actually a Special Cycle Request.

6. A Type 1 configuration read or write has been latched on the bridge's primary side and it targets a function on a bus subordinate to the bridge's secondary bus. The bridge must claim it and pass it through as a Type 1 configuration transaction.

7. A Type 1 configuration write has been latched on the bridge's secondary side and it is a Special Cycle Request that targets the bridge's primary bus or a bus number that matches neither the bridge's primary bus or the range of buses on its secondary side. The bridge must claim it and pass it through as a Special Cycle transaction or as a Special Cycle Request.

Transactions other than Memory Write and Memory Write-and-Invalidate are treated as Delayed Transactions by the bridge, while the two memory write commands are typically posted in the bridge. For a detailed discussion of transaction ordering, refer to the chapter entitled "Transaction Ordering & Deadlocks" on page 649.

Handling of Memory Write and Invalidate Command

Assume that a PCI-to-PCI bridge accepts a Memory Write-and-Invalidate command and initiates it on the opposite side of the bridge. Using this command implies a solemn promise to write an entire line (or multiple lines) to memory. The memory target may issue a disconnect before it has accepted the entire line from the bridge. In this case, assuming that the initiating master on the other side has not yet completed sending the write data to the bridge, the bridge can issue a disconnect to the master. The master that was disconnected will resume the transaction as a Memory Write and the bridge will then reinitiate the transaction as a Memory Write to the target and complete writing the entire line to the target. The specification says that no error is generated in this case (because, truly, everything worked just fine).

The Memory Write-and-Invalidate bit must be implemented as a read/write bit if the bridge is capable of converting posted memory writes (that were received via a Memory Write transaction) into a Memory Write-and-Invalidate (MWI) transaction on the other side of the bridge. The writes would have to be sequential, start on a cache line boundary, and write an entire cache line (or multiple cache lines). If the bridge implements this optional capability, it must also implement the Cache Line Size configuration register as a read/write register.

The bridge does not consult this bit to determine if it should pass an MWI received on one side through as an MWI on the other side. The fact that the originating master used the MWI transaction type means that it has met all of the criteria for its usage.

Rules Regarding Posted Write Buffer Usage

For a detailed description of issues related to a bridge's posted memory write buffers, refer to the indicated sections:

- Write Combining—refer to "Combining" on page 94.
- Byte Merging—refer to "Byte Merging" on page 95.
- Collapsing—refer to "Collapsing Is Forbidden" on page 95.
- Transaction Ordering and Deadlocks—refer to "Transaction Ordering & Deadlocks" on page 649.

Multiple-Data Phase Special Cycle Requests

The PCI specification permits the generation of Special Cycle transactions with multiple data phases (see "Multiple Data Phase Special Cycle Transaction" on page 112). If the programmer instructs the host/PCI bridge to perform a multiple-data phase Special Cycle transaction on bus zero, it will work. If, however, the programmer instructs the host/PCI bridge to generate a Type 1 configuration write to forward a multiple data phase Special Cycle transaction to a subordinate bus, problems can occur.

It is permissible for a target to issue a disconnect during a multiple-data phase configuration write. Assuming that this were to occur, the transaction could arrive at the bridge that will perform the conversion to a Special Cycle as a series of single-data phase Type One Special Cycle Requests. This would result in the generation of a series of single-data phase Special Cycle transactions on the target bus, thereby sending the wrong message (no pun intended).

The bridge specification therefore dictates that is illegal to request a multiple-data phase special transaction on any bus other than bus zero.

Error Detection and Handling

General

Like any other PCI-compliant device, the PCI-to-PCI bridge must generate parity, check parity and report parity errors (if enabled to do so) on both buses. The sections that follow describe how the bridge must behave during both the address and data phases of the transaction.

In addition, bridge behavior when handling the following types of conditions is also described:

- Master Aborts
- Target Aborts
- Discard Timer timeout
- SERR# assertion on the secondary bus.

Refer to Figure 24-30 on page 629. The following terms are used in the discussions that follow:

- The **originating bus** is the bus from which the bridge receives a transaction that must cross the bridge.
- The **destination bus** is the bus that the bridge must pass the transaction to.

Figure 24-30: Originating and Destination Buses

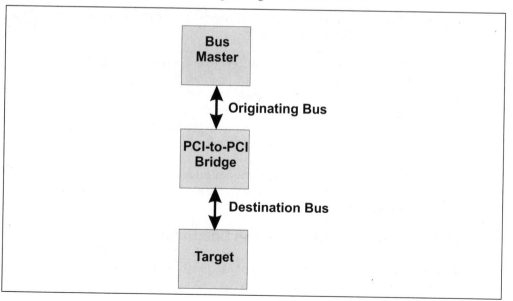

Handling Address Phase Parity Errors

Introduction

The bridge acts as the target of transactions that must cross the bridge. The specification defines how a target must respond to an address phase parity error. If the bridge appears to be the target of a transaction, is enabled to respond to parity errors, and detects an address phase parity error, it may use any of the following methods to terminate the transaction:

1. The bridge may claim the transaction and complete it normally.
2. The bridge may claim the transaction and terminate the transaction with a Target Abort.
3. The bridge may choose not to claim the transaction, thereby letting it terminate with a Master Abort.

The following two sections define the exact response of the bridge to an address phase parity error detected on the primary and secondary sides. In both cases, the bridge is not the master of the transaction. Rather, it has just latched a transaction generated by another master on its primary or secondary side.

Address Phase Parity Error on Primary Side

When the bridge detects an address phase parity error on its primary side, it must take all of the following actions:

1. If the SERR# Enable and the Parity Error Response bits in the Command register are set, assert SERR# on the primary side.
2. If SERR# is asserted, set the Signaled System Error bit in the (primary side) Status register.
3. Set the Detected Parity Error bit in the (primary side) Status register (irrespective of the state of the Parity Error Response bit in the Command register).
4. If the bridge claimed the transaction (i.e., it asserted DEVSEL#) and terminated it with a Target Abort, it must also set the Signaled Target Abort bit in its (primary side) Status register.

Address Phase Parity Error on Secondary Side

When the bridge detects an address phase parity error on its secondary side, it must take all of the following actions:

1. If the SERR# Enable bit is set in the Command register and the Parity Error Response and SERR# Enable bits are set in the Bridge Control register, assert SERR# on the primary side.
2. If SERR# is asserted, set the Signaled System Error bit in the Status register.
3. Set the Detected Parity Error bit in the Secondary Status register (irrespective of the state of the Parity Error Response bit in the Bridge Control register).
4. If the bridge claimed the transaction (i.e., it asserted DEVSEL#) and terminated it with a Target Abort, it must also set the Signaled Target Abort bit in its Secondary Status register.

Read Data Phase Parity Error

Introduction

When a read transaction must cross the bridge, the bridge treats it as a Delayed Transaction and issues a Retry to the originating master. No data is transferred in the first (and only) data phase and there is therefore no possibility of a parity error. The originating master must Retry the transaction identically on a periodic basis until it receives the requested read data from the bridge (or receives a Master Abort or a Target Abort).

The bridge must re-initiate the read on the destination bus, obtain the read data from the target, and deliver the read data to the master. There are three possibilities:

- There isn't a parity error on either bus.
- There is a parity error during the read on the destination side. In this case, the bridge must deliver the corrupted read data and the parity to the originating master.
- There isn't a parity error during the read on the destination side, but there is a parity error during the delivery of the requested data on the originating bus.

Parity Error When Performing Read On Destination Bus

The spec refers to this as a **target completion error**. In other words, the bridge has performed the read on the destination bus and has received corrupted read data from the target. The bridge then takes the following actions:

- Assert PERR# on the destination side if the Parity Error Response bit is set to one in the register associated with the destination bus (Command register for primary side, or Bridge Control register for secondary side).

- If the Parity Error Response bit is set to one in the Command register associated with the destination bus (Command register for primary side, or Bridge Control register for secondary side), set the Master Data Parity Error bit in the destination bus's status register (Status register if primary side, or Secondary Status register if secondary side),
- Set the Detected Parity error bit in the destination side status register.

Parity Error When Delivering Read Data To Originating Master

A read parity error may be detected by the originating master when read data is delivered to it by the bridge. The read data may have been obtained either from an internal bridge register or from a target on the other side of the bridge.

In either case, the master must assert PERR# if enabled to do so by its Parity Error Response bit. The bridge is acting as the source of the read data (and parity). If the read data and parity was obtained from a target on the other side of the bridge, there may or may not have been a read parity error when the bridge read the data from the target. If there was an error, that error is recorded in the bridge's destination side status register, not in its originating side status register. In this case, the bridge must deliver the bad data and parity to the originating master.

Bad Parity On Prefetched Data

When a bridge initiates a read transaction on the destination bus, it must perform the first data phase requested by the originating master and may, in addition, prefetch additional read data into a read-ahead buffer within the bridge (if the read is from prefetchable memory). The bridge is required to check the parity of all data items that it reads, including data that it has prefetched, without knowing if the originating master will actually read all of it. However, the bridge will ultimately only deliver the amount of data actually requested by the master and this may not include any or all of the data that it had prefetched. The error status bits in the bridge's destination side status register reflect any parity errors incurred during the destination side read, including those associated with prefetched data.

When the originating master receives the read data it requested, it obviously only checks parity on that data and has no knowledge of any data prefetched by the bridge.

Write Data Phase Parity Error

General

The following transactions write data to a target:

- Memory Write
- Memory Write and Invalidate
- IO Write
- Configuration Write

When one of these transactions must cross a PCI-to-PCI bridge, the bridge treats them as indicated in Table 24-14 on page 633. As indicated, **memory writes are usually posted, while non-memory writes are always treated as Delayed Write Requests**. The remainder of this section provides a detailed description of parity handling for both Delayed Writes and Posted Writes.

Table 24-14: Parity Error On Writes That Must Cross the Bridge

Transaction Type	Treatment by Bridge
Memory Write and Memory Write and Invalidate	Usually posted in the bridge and completes immediately (i.e., bridge asserts TRDY# to indicate its acceptance of the data). From the master's perspective, the write to memory has been completed. Parity errors could occur at two points in time: 1. A data parity error could occur when the originating master delivers the write data to the bridge on the originating bus. 2. A data parity error could occur when the bridge attempts to write the posted data to the target on the destination bus.

Table 24-14: Parity Error On Writes That Must Cross the Bridge (Continued)

Transaction Type	Treatment by Bridge
IO Write and Configuration Write	Refer to Figure 24-31 on page 634. The bridge must treat it as a **Delayed Write Request**, latching the first data phase write data when IRDY# is sampled asserted (a parity error could occur at this point), and issuing a Retry to the originating master. Upon receipt of the Retry, the originating master must periodically Retry the transaction identically until it has completion (i.e., TRDY# asserted by the bridge). A parity error could occur on any of these Retries. The bridge then arbitrates for ownership of the destination bus and initiates the write to deliver the write data to the target (a parity error could occur at this point). After the data has been written (referred to in the spec as **Target Completion**), the bridge awaits the next Retry by the originating master and then delivers the completion to the master (referred to in the spec as **Master Completion**). A parity error could occur at this point.

Figure 24-31: Delayed IO or Configuration Write Crossing Bridge

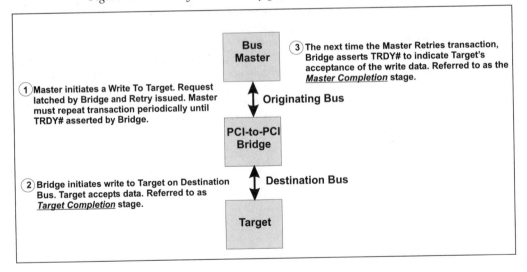

Data Phase Parity Error on IO or Configuration Write

Introduction. As indicated in Table 24-14 on page 633 and Figure 24-31 on page 634, when an IO write or a Configuration Write must cross a PCI-to-PCI bridge, the bridge must treat it as a **Delayed Write Request**, latching the first data phase write data when IRDY# is sampled asserted (a parity error could occur at this point), and issuing a Retry to the originating master.

Upon receipt of the Retry, the originating master must periodically Retry the transaction identically until it has completion (i.e., TRDY# asserted by the bridge). A parity error could occur on any of these Retries.

The bridge then arbitrates for ownership of the destination bus and initiates the write to deliver the write data to the target (a parity error could occur at this point). After the data has been written (referred to in the spec as **Target Completion**), the bridge awaits the next Retry by the originating master and then delivers the completion to the master (referred to in the spec as **Master Completion**). A parity error could occur at this point.

The sections that follow describe parity error handling for parity errors that occur on:

- The initiation and repeat of the **Delayed Write Request** (also referred to as the **Master Request**).
- The initiation of the write on the destination bus (i.e., the **Target Completion**).
- The delivery of the completion the master's final Retry (i.e., the **Master Completion**).

Master Request Error. See step one in Figure 24-31 on page 634. An IO Write or a Configuration Write transaction may be initiated by a master on either side of the bridge and may have to cross the bridge.

If the write is initiated by a master on the primary side of the bridge and the bridge detects a data parity error, it must take the following actions:

Step 1. The bridge asserts TRDY# to indicate that is accepting the data. If the transaction is a write burst (i.e., the master left FRAME# asserted when it asserted IRDY#), the bridge must also assert STOP#.

Step 2. Assuming that the Parity Error Response bit in the bridge's Command register is set, the bridge must report the error to the master by asserting PERR#.

Step 3. The bridge must set the Detected Parity Error bit in its Status register.

STEP 4. The bridge must discard the transaction. In other words, it does not act on the Delayed Write Request by initiating a write on the secondary side of the bridge.

If the write is initiated by a master on the secondary side of the bridge and the bridge detects a data parity error, it must take the following actions:

STEP 1. The bridge asserts TRDY# to indicate that is accepting the data. If the transaction is a write burst (i.e., the master left FRAME# asserted when it asserted IRDY#), the bridge must also assert STOP#.

STEP 2. Assuming that the Parity Error Response bit in the bridge's Bridge Control register is set, the bridge must report the error to the master by asserting PERR#.

STEP 3. The bridge must set the Detected Parity Error bit in its Secondary Status register.

STEP 4. The bridge must discard the transaction. In other words, it does not act on the Delayed Write Request by initiating a write on the primary side of the bridge.

When the Parity Error Response bit is set, the bridge will only pass a Delayed Write Request to the destination bus if a data parity error is *not* detected during the master request.

Target Completion Error. See step two in Figure 24-31 on page 634. Assuming that the bridge latched the Delayed Write Request from the originating bus without a parity error, the bridge will re-initiate the write on the destination bus. If a data phase parity error occurs during the write to the target on the destination bus, the bridge, acting as a faithful messenger, will report the parity error back to the originating master when it next Retries the transaction. The master can then handle the error in an appropriate manner.

There are two possible cases:

CASE 1. When the **bridge performs** a **Delayed Write on** its **primary** side for a master on its secondary side, the target asserts PERR# to the bridge (assuming that the Parity Error Response bit in its Command register is set) if it detects a parity error on the write data sent by the bridge. In response to PERR#, the bridge must take the following actions:
  • set the Master Data Parity Error bit in its Status register.
  • remember that the parity error occurred.

When the originating master Retries the transaction on the originating (secondary) bus, the bridge must assert PERR# (assuming that the Parity Error

Response bit is set in its Bridge Control register) to the master. The bridge does *not* set the Detected Parity Error bit in its Secondary Status register.

CASE 2. When the **bridge performs** a **Delayed Write on** its **secondary** side for a master on its primary side, the target asserts PERR# to the bridge (assuming that the Parity Error Response bit in its Command register is set) if it detects a parity error on the write data sent by the bridge. In response to PERR#, the bridge must take the following actions:
* set the Master Data Parity Error bit in its Secondary Status register.
* remember that the parity error occurred.

When the originating master Retries the transaction on the originating (primary) bus, the bridge must assert PERR# (assuming that the Parity Error Response bit is set in its Command register) to the master. The bridge does *not* set the Detected Parity Error bit in its Status register.

Parity Error On a Subsequent Retry. See steps one and three in Figure 24-31 on page 634. When the originating master first attempted the write transaction, the bridge latched it and issued a Retry to the master. The master must then periodically repeat the transaction identically until it receives a termination other than a Retry from the bridge. It is possible that the bridge might detect a data phase parity error on any one of the master's Retries.

In this case, the bridge must react in the same manner as it would if there were a data parity error on the master's initial attempt of the transaction (see "Master Request Error" on page 635). In other words, it must terminate the transaction on the originating bus (TRDY# and PERR# asserted, and possibly STOP# as well, if the master was attempting a burst write). Since there was a parity error on the repeat of the transaction, it cannot be reliably matched with any previously-received Delayed write Requests. In fact, the bridge must not attempt to match it to one of them. The master will not Retry the transaction again, so, after completing the write on the destination bus, the bridge will end up with an orphan Delayed Write Completion. Ultimately, when the bridge's Discard Timer expires (see "Discard Timer Timeout" on page 644 and "Master Tardy In Repeating Transaction" on page 91), the bridge will throw away the Delayed Write Completion.

It should also be noted that a bridge that is only capable of dealing with one Delayed Transaction at a time is a legal (although low-performance) implementation. In this case, the bridge would not be able to accept any new Delayed Transaction Requests until the Discard Timer expires and it can discard the one it was hung on. However, the bridge must accept any Memory Write or Memory Write and Invalidate transactions into its Posted Memory Write Buffers during the period of time while awaiting the Discard Timer timeout.

Data Phase Parity Error on Posted Write

Introduction. Refer to Figure 24-32 on page 638. Completion of a posted memory write is a two-step process and a parity error may occur in either stage:

STEP 1. The master initiates the Memory **Write** or Memory Write-and-Invalidate transaction **on** the **originating bus** and, when the bridge samples IRDY# and TRDY# asserted, it latches the address and data into its Posted Memory Write Buffer. If the data or Byte Enables were corrupted on the originating bus, the bridge would detect a parity error at this point. From the master's perspective, the transaction has completed.

STEP 2. The bridge initiates the Memory **Write** or Memory Write-and-Invalidate transaction **on** the **destination bus**. When the target samples IRDY# and TRDY# asserted, it latches the write data. If the data or Byte Enables were corrupted on the destination bus, the target would detect a parity error at this point.

Figure 24-32: Posted Write Error Handling

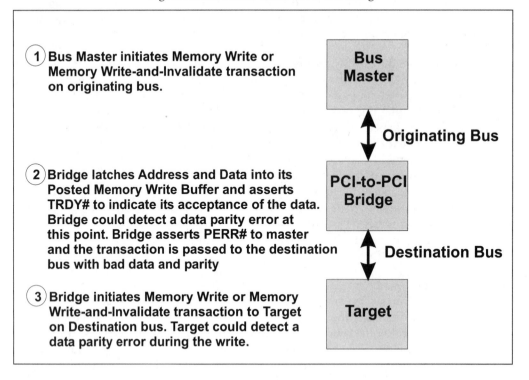

Originating Bus Error—Pass It Along To Target. See steps one and two in Figure 24-32 on page 638. When a bus master initiates a Memory Write or Memory Write-and-Invalidate transaction, it is writing to one of the following:

CASE 1. A memory-mapped IO register internal to the bridge. In this case, the transaction doesn't have to cross the bridge and the bridge, acting as the ultimate target of the transaction, handles the error as described in "Parity Error During Write" on page 210. Remember that the bridge has two sides and a master on either side could attempt to write to its internal registers.

- If the bridge is the target of a memory write on the primary side and it detects a data parity error, it must assert PERR# on the primary side (assuming that the Parity Error Response bit in its Command register is set). It must also set the Detected Parity Error bit in its Status register.
- If the bridge is the target of a memory write on the secondary side and it detects a data parity error, it must assert PERR# on the secondary side (assuming that the Parity Error Response bit in its Bridge Control register is set). It must also set the Detected Parity Error bit in its Secondary Status register.

CASE 2. A memory target on the other side of the bridge. In this case, the bridge's handling of the error is defined in the paragraphs that follow.

When the bridge accepts a memory write with bad parity into its Posted Memory Write Buffer, it asserts PERR# to the originating master (assuming its Parity Error Response bit is set) and must forward the corrupted data and parity to the target on the destination bus. This is necessary because the master doesn't know that it was the bridge rather than the memory target that asserted PERR# to it. It doesn't even know that the bridge exists. Rather, it assumes that the target received the bad data and parity and asserted PERR#. As a result the master may attempt some form of error recovery with the target. If the bridge doesn't transport the bad data and parity to the target, the master may confuse the target by attempting to fix a problem that the target isn't even aware of!

When a memory write transaction originates on the bridge's primary side and the bridge detects bad parity on the write data from the master, the bridge must:

- assert PERR# to the master on the primary side (assuming that the Parity Error Response bit in its Command register is set to one).
- retain the bad parity and data in its Posted Memory Write Buffer.
- set the Detected Parity Error bit in its Status register.

When the bridge initiates the write on the secondary side, the bad data and parity are supplied to the target. Assuming that the Parity Error Response bit in the target's Command register is set to one, the target asserts PERR# to the bridge. When the bridge detects PERR# asserted by the target, it must set the Master Data Parity Error bit in its Secondary Status register.

When a memory write transaction originates on the bridge's secondary side and the bridge detects bad parity on the write data it receives from the master, the bridge must:

- assert PERR# to the master on the secondary side (assuming that the Parity Error Response bit in its Bridge Control register is set to one).
- retain the bad parity and data in its Posted Memory Write Buffer.
- set the Detected Parity Error bit in its Secondary Status register.

When the bridge initiates the write on the primary side, the bad data and parity are supplied to the target. Assuming that the Parity Error Response bit in the target's Command register is set to one, the target asserts PERR# to the bridge. When the bridge detects PERR# asserted by the target, it must set the Master Data Parity Error bit in its Status register.

Destination Bus Error. See step three in Figure 24-32 on page 638. When the bridge initiates the memory write on the destination bus, there are two possible cases:

CASE 1. The bridge received bad data and parity from the master on the originating bus and it passes along the bad data and parity to the target.

CASE 2. The bridge received good data and parity from the master on the originating bus and it is passing it along to the target.

In **Case 1**, the target on the destination bus asserts PERR# (assuming that the Parity Error Response bit in the target's Command register is set to one) upon receipt of the bad data and parity. The bridge detects PERR# asserted by the target. Assuming that the Parity Error Response bit in the appropriate bridge register is set to one (in the bridge's Command register if the target is on the primary side, or in the Bridge Control register if the target is on the secondary side), the bridge must set the Master Data Parity Error bit to one in the appropriate status register (the Status register if the target is on the primary side, or the Secondary Status register if the target is on the secondary side).

In **Case 2**, the bridge received the memory write from the bus master on the originating bus without a parity error, but the target then asserts PERR# when the transaction is attempted on the destination bus. The bridge is forced to take drastic action. As far as the originating master is concerned, the data had been successfully written to the target some time ago. In reality, the bridge took responsibility for delivering the write data to the target, but has now discovered that it wasn't able to do so successfully.

Unfortunately, the bridge must assert SERR# (assuming that the SERR# Enable bit in the bridge's Command register is set to one) on the primary side and set the Signaled System Error bit in its Status register.

Handling Master Abort

When the bridge is acting as the bus master to pass a transaction through to the opposite side, it's possible that the transaction may not be claimed by any target (i.e., it ends in a Master Abort). There are a number of reasons this could occur:

- It is a configuration access during initialization time (starts at removal of RST# and last for 2^{25} PCI clock cycles) and no target occupies the currently-addressed device position on the destination bus. This is not considered to be an error during initialization time because the configuration software is probing all device positions to determine which ones are occupied and which are vacant.
- It is run-time and the software is inadvertently addressing a non-existent PCI device. This is considered to be an error.
- It is run-time and software is addressing a device that should respond but doesn't do so because it is broken.

Table 24-15 on page 642 defines the actions taken by the bridge if a transaction it initiates results in a Master Abort (i.e., DEVSEL# not sampled asserted in the Fast, Medium, Slow, or Subtractive time slots). How the bridge handles a Master Abort depends on the current state of the Master Abort Mode bit in the bridge's Bridge Control register. The default state of this bit is zero after RST# is removed.

Master-Aborts are never reported when they occur during Special Cycle transactions.

Table 24-15: Bridge Action On Master Abort

Master Abort Mode Bit	Transaction Type	Action Taken By Bridge If Transaction Not Claimed
0	Any form of read that is not an exclusive access (i.e., the transaction isn't locked).	When a read ends in a Master Abort on the destination bus, the bridge must **return all ones** to the originating master. No error bits are set.
	Any form of write that is not an exclusive access (i.e., the transaction isn't locked).	When a write ends in a Master Abort on the destination bus, the bridge accepts the write data from the originating master and then **discards** the **data**. No error bits are set.
1	Any form of Delayed Read or Delayed Write.	When the master on the originating bus next Retries the read, the bridge signals a **Target-Abort** to the master. The bridge **also sets** the **Received Master Abort bit** in the Status register associated with the destination bus, as **well as** the **Signaled Target Abort bit** in the Status register associated with the originating bus.
	Locked or un-locked Posted-write.	In this case, the connection with the originating bus master has already been severed, so the bridge must **assert SERR# on** the **primary side** (assuming the SERR# Enable bit is set in its Command register). The originating master may have been performing a burst memory write transaction and the transaction may still be in progress on the originating bus (i.e., the bridge has continued to accept subsequent data phase write data into its Posted Memory Write Buffer). If this is the case, the spec recommends that the bridge terminate the transaction on the originating bus as soon as possible. In addition, the bridge must discard any remaining write data associated with that transaction.

Table 24-15: Bridge Action On Master Abort (Continued)

Master Abort Mode Bit	Transaction Type	Action Taken By Bridge If Transaction Not Claimed
X (don't care)	Locked Delayed Transaction that originates on the primary side of the bridge. Remember that locked transactions can only be passed through a bridge in the downstream direction (i.e., primary to secondary).	Regardless of the state of the Master Abort Mode bit, the bridge must report a **Target Abort** to the originating master when it next repeats its transaction. The bridge **also sets** the **Received Master Abort bit** in the Status register associated with the destination bus, **as well as** the **Signaled Target Abort bit** in the Status register associated with the originating bus. This requirement is necessary to avoid potential deadlock conditions.

Handling Target Abort

Introduction

A bridge acts as the target of a transaction under two circumstances:

CASE 1. The transaction **addresses** a **register or memory within** the **bridge**. The bridge may issue a Target Abort to the initiator if it is broken or if an unsupported combination of byte enables is detected (i.e., the bridge doesn't own all of the bytes to be accessed within the current dword). The spec referred to this a bridge **internal error**. The transaction doesn't cross the bridge. The bridge signals a Target Abort to the master and sets the Signaled Target Abort bit in the Status register associated with the originating bus.

CASE 2. The transaction **addresses** a **target on** the **opposite side of** the **bridge**. The bridge must therefore pass the transaction through the bridge. This case is described in the paragraphs that follow.

When a transaction addresses a target on the other side of the bridge, the manner in which the bridge deals with the transaction depends on the type of transaction:

- Memory Write and Memory Write-and-Invalidate transactions are posted in the bridge and complete immediately.
- Other types of transactions are treated as Delayed Transactions.

When the Delayed or posted transaction is performed on the destination bus, the target may issue a Target Abort to the bridge. The sections that follow describe the bridge's actions.

Target Abort On Delayed Write Transaction

When the bridge is performing a Delayed Transaction on the destination bus, the target may issue a Target Abort to the bridge in the first or a subsequent data phase of the transaction. The following actions must be taken:

- The target sets the Signaled Target Abort bit in its Status register.
- The **bridge sets** the **Received Target Abort bit** in the Status register associated with the destination bus.
- When the originating master Retries the transaction, the **bridge must issue** a **Target Abort to** the **master** in the same data phase that incurred the error on the destination bus.
- The bridge also **sets** the **Signaled Target Abort bit** in the Status register associated with the originating bus.

Target Abort On Posted Write

The bridge absorbs memory writes that must cross the bridge into its Posted Memory Write Buffer. From the perspective of the originating master, the write has already been completed. The bridge has assumed responsibility for delivering the write data to the target. The bridge then performs the writes on the destination bus. The target may issue a Target Abort in the first or a subsequent data phase of the write transaction. In response to the Target Abort, the bridge must:

- **set** the **Received Target-Abort bit** in the Status register associated with the destination bus.
- Assuming that the SERR# Enable bit is set in the Command register, the bridge must also **assert SERR# on** the **primary side and set** the **System Error Signaled bit** in the Status register.

1.1 Discard Timer Timeout

Refer to Figure 24-33 on page 645 and Table 24-16 on page 646. *THE 1.1 BRIDGE SPEC ADDED FOUR BITS IN THE BRIDGE CONTROL REGISTER THAT ARE ASSOCIATED WITH THE PRIMARY AND SECONDARY SIDE DISCARD TIMERS:*

- The Primary and Secondary Discard Timeout bits control the amount of time that the bridge will wait for the originating master to Retry a Delayed Transaction before discarding the Delayed Completion for that transaction.
- The state of the Discard Timer Status bit indicates whether the bridge has discarded any orphan Delayed Completions.
- The Discard Timer SERR# Enable bit controls whether or not the bridge will assert SERR# on the primary side when it discards a Delayed Completion on either side. The SERR# Enable bit in the Command register must also be set to one in order for SERR# to be asserted on the primary side. The bridge must also set the Signaled SERR# bit in the Status register.

Figure 24-33: Bridge Control Register

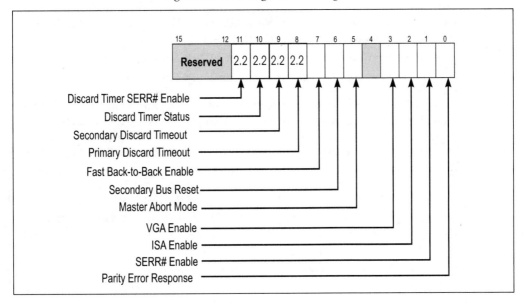

Table 24-16: Bridge Control Register Discard Timer Bits

Bit	Description
8	**Primary Discard Timeout**. Selects the number of PCI clocks that the bridge waits for a master on the primary bus to repeat a Delayed Transaction request. The counter starts when the Delayed Completion (the completion of the Delayed Transaction on the secondary interface) has reached the head of the upstream queue of the bridge (i.e., all ordering requirements have been satisfied and the bridge is ready to complete the Delayed Transaction with the originating master on the primary bus). If the originating master does not repeat the transaction before the counter expires, the bridge deletes the Delayed Transaction from its queue and sets the Discard Timer Status bit (see bit 10). The default state of this bit after reset is 0. • 0 = the Primary Discard Timer counts 2^{15} PCI clock cycles. • 1 = the Primary Discard Timer counts 2^{10} PCI clock cycles.
9	**Secondary Discard Timeout**. Selects the number of PCI clocks that the bridge waits for a master on the secondary bus to repeat a Delayed Transaction request. The counter starts when the Delayed Completion (the completion of the Delayed Transaction on the primary interface) has reached the head of the downstream queue of the bridge (i.e., all ordering requirements have been satisfied and the bridge is ready to complete the Delayed Transaction with the originating master on the secondary bus). If the originating master does not repeat the transaction before the counter expires, the bridge deletes the Delayed Transaction from its queue and sets the Discard Timer Status bit (see bit 10). The default state of this bit after reset is 0. • 0 = the Primary Discard Timer counts 2^{15} PCI clock cycles. • 1 = the Primary Discard Timer counts 2^{10} PCI clock cycles.
10	**Discard Timer Status**. This bit is set to a 1 when either the Primary Discard Timer (see bit 8) or Secondary Discard Timer (see bit 9) expires and a Delayed Completion is discarded from a queue in the bridge. The default state of this bit after reset must be 0. Once set, this bit remains set until it is reset by writing a 1 to it. • 0 = no discard timer error • 1 = discard timer error

1.1   1.1   1.1

Table 24-16: Bridge Control Register Discard Timer Bits (Continued)

Bit	Description
11	**Discard Timer SERR# Enable**. Enables or disables the bridge's ability to assert **SERR#** on the primary bus when either the Primary Discard Timer (see bit 8) or Secondary Discard Timer (see bit 9) expires and a Delayed Transaction is discarded from a queue in the bridge. The default state is 0 after reset. • 0 = do not assert SERR# on the primary bus on expiration of either the Primary Discard Timer or Secondary Discard Timer. • 1 = assert SERR# on the primary bus if either the Primary Discard Timer or Secondary Discard Timer expires and a Delayed Transaction is discarded from a queue in the bridge. The SERR# Enable bit in the Command register must also be set to one in order for SERR# to be asserted on the primary side. The bridge must also set the Signaled SERR# bit in the Status register.

1.1

Handling SERR# on Secondary Side

SERR# is strictly an input to the secondary side of the bridge interface. If the bridge detects SERR# asserted on the secondary side, it must set the Received System Error bit in the Secondary Status register (see Figure 24-35 on page 648).

Refer to Figure 24-34 on page 647. Assuming that the SERR# Enable bit in both the Bridge Control and Command registers are set, the bridge must assert SERR# on the primary side and set the Signaled System Error bit in the Status register. If either bit is cleared, SERR# is not asserted on the primary side and the Signaled System Error bit in the Status register is not set.

Figure 24-34: Policy On Passing Through Secondary SERR# To Primary Side

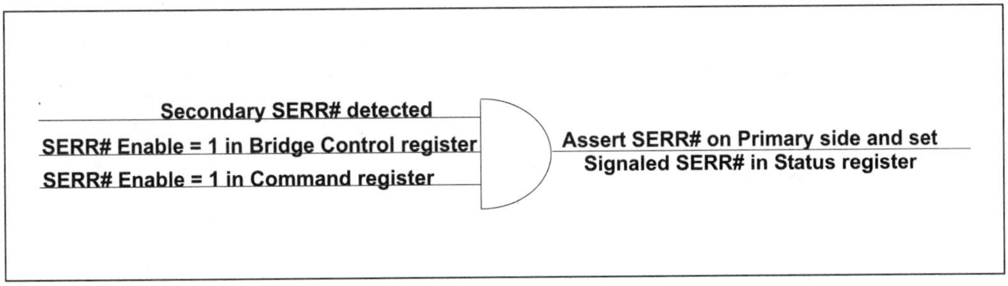

Secondary SERR# detected
SERR# Enable = 1 in Bridge Control register
SERR# Enable = 1 in Command register

Assert SERR# on Primary side and set
Signaled SERR# in Status register

Figure 24-35: Secondary Status Register

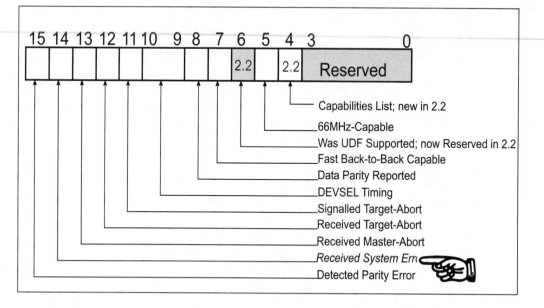

25 *Transaction Ordering & Deadlocks*

The Previous Chapter

The previous chapter provided a detailed discussion of PCI-to-PCI bridge implementation. The information is drawn from the revision *1.1 PCI-to-PCI Bridge Architecture Specification*, dated December 18, 1998.

This Chapter

This chapter focuses on the ordering rules that govern the behavior of simple devices as well as the relationships of multiple transactions traversing a PCI-to-PCI bridge. It also describes how the rules prevent deadlocks from occurring.

The Next Chapter

The next chapter introduces the PCI BIOS specification, revision 2.1, dated August 26, 1994.

Definition of Simple Device vs. a Bridge

Assume that a master incorporates an entity (e.g., a local processor) that performs writes to system memory over the PCI bus. The master can handle the internally-generated memory writes in one of two ways and the method it uses defines it (according to the 2.2 PCI spec) as a simple device or as a bridge:

Simple Device

The 2.2 spec defines a simple device as **any device that does not require outbound write posting.** The internal logic is designed such that it would not be allowed to proceed with any other action (e.g., the update of a status register that can be read by masters external to the device) until the data has actually been written over the PCI bus to the target memory. Generally, devices that do not connect to local CPUs (in other words, devices other than Host/PCI bridges) are implemented as simple devices.

Bridge

The internal logic is designed such that an outbound memory write is posted within a posted memory write buffer in the master's PCI interface and thus, to the internal logic, appears to have been completed. In reality, the write to the target memory location has not yet been performed on the PCI bus. Bridges that connect two buses together (e.g., a PCI-to-PCI bridge) typically exhibit this type of behavior.

Simple Devices: Ordering Rules and Deadlocks

Ordering Rules For Simple Devices

The **target and master state machines** in the PCI interface of a simple device **must be completely independent**. When acting as a target, it must not make the completion of any transaction that targets it (either posted or non-posted) contingent upon the prior completion of any other transaction when it is acting as a master. When acting as the target of a transaction, a simple device is only allowed to issue a retry when treating it as a Delayed Transaction, or for temporary conditions which are guaranteed to be resolved with time (i.e., a temporary in-bound posted memory write buffer full condition).

The required independence of target and master state machines in a simple device implies that a **simple device cannot internally post any outbound transactions**. Consider the following example scenario:

STEP 1. Assume that logic internal to the device performs a write to a memory location in another PCI device.

STEP 2. The write is posted in an outbound posted write buffer within the device's master state machine to be written to memory later.

STEP 3. Assuming (incorrectly) that the data has already been successfully written to the external memory, logic internal to the device then updates an internal status register to indicate that this is so (but it's wrong!).

STEP 4. Another PCI device, external to the PCI device under discussion, then performs a PCI read to read the status register in this device.

STEP 5. If the device, acting as the target of the read transaction, provides the status register contents to the other master, it is lying to the other guy (because it sends a status bit that says the data it thinks is in memory is fresh). In order to tell the other guy the truth, the device only has one option—issue a retry to the other guy and then perform the posted memory write.

This example highlights that the device's master and target state machines are dependent on each other, thereby defining it (according to the 2.2 specs's definitions) as a bridge and not as a simple device.

The simple device must wait until it completes the memory write transaction on the PCI bus (the target memory asserts **TRDY#**, or signals a Master Abort or a Target Abort) before proceeding internally (in the example, assuming that the write doesn't receive a Master or target Abort, updating the status register).

To increase PCI bus performance, **simple devices** are **strongly encouraged to post inbound memory write transactions** to allow memory writes targeting it to complete quickly. How the simple device orders inbound posted write data is design-dependent and outside the scope of the spec.

Simple devices do not support exclusive (i.e., locked) accesses (only bridges do) and do not use the LOCK# signal either a master or as a target. Refer to "Locking" on page 683 for a discussion of the use of LOCK# in bridge devices.

Deadlocks Associated With Simple Devices

The following are two examples of deadlocks that could occur if devices make their target and master interfaces inter-dependent.

Scenario One

STEP 1. Two devices, referred to as A and B, simultaneously start arbitrating for bus ownership to attempt IO writes to each other.

STEP 2. Device A is granted the bus first and initiates its IO write to device B (device B·is the target of the transaction). Device B decodes the address/command and asserts DEVSEL#.

STEP 3. Assume that, when acting as a target, device B always terminates transactions that target it with Retry until its master state machine completes its outstanding requests (in this case, an IO write).

STEP 4. Device B is then granted the bus and initiates its IO write to device A.

STEP 5. If device A responds in the same manner that device B did (i.e., with a Retry), the system will deadlock.

Scenario Two

As described in a later section ("Bridges: Ordering Rules and Deadlocks" on page 652), in certain cases a bridge is required to flush its posting buffer as a master before it completes a transaction as a target. As described in the following sequence, this can result in a deadlock:

STEP 1. A PCI-to-PCI bridge contains posted memory write data addressed to a downstream device (i.e., a device on its secondary side).

STEP 2. Before the bridge can acquire ownership of secondary bus to perform the write transaction, the downstream device that it intends to target initiates a read from main memory (in other words, the read has to cross the bridge from the secondary side to the primary side to get to memory).

STEP 3. To ensure that fresh read data is always received by any read that has to cross a bridge, the bridge ordering rules require that the bridge must flush its posted memory write buffers before the read is allowed to cross the bridge. The bridge must therefore Retry the downstream agent's read.

STEP 4. The bridge then performs the posted write to the downstream device on the secondary bus.

STEP 5. If the downstream device is designed in such a fashion that its target and master state machines are inter-dependent, it will issue a Retry in response to the bridge's posted write attempt and then re-issue its previously-attempted read.

STEP 6. The bus is deadlocked.

Since some PCI-to-PCI bridge devices designed to earlier versions of the PCI spec require that their posted memory write buffers be flushed before starting any non-posted transaction, the same deadlock could occur if the downstream device makes the acceptance of a posted write contingent on the prior completion of any non-posted transaction.

Bridges: Ordering Rules and Deadlocks

Introduction

When a bridge accepts a memory write into its posted memory write buffer, the master that initiated the write to memory considers the write completed and can initiate additional operations (i.e., PCI reads and writes) before the target memory location actually receives the write data. Any of these subsequent operations may end up completing before the memory write is finally consummated. The possible result: a read the programmer intended to occur after the write may happen before the data is actually written.

In order to prevent this from causing problems, many of the PCI ordering rules require that a bridge's posted memory write buffers be flushed before permitting subsequently-issued transactions to proceed. These same buffer flushing rules, however, can cause deadlocks. The remainder of the PCI transaction ordering rules prevent the system buses from deadlocking when posting buffers must be flushed.

Chapter 25: Transaction Ordering & Deadlocks

Bridge Manages Bi-Directional Traffic Flow

Refer to Figure 25-1 on page 653. A bridge manages traffic flow between two buses. In the figure, the processor-to-PCI bridge manages traffic flow between the processor bus and PCI Bus 0, while the PCI-to-PCI bridge manages traffic flow between PCI Bus 0 and PCI bus 1. Although the bridge ordering rules hold true for both types of bridges, this chapter focuses on the ordering of transactions that cross a PCI-to-PCI bridge. The typical PCI-to-PCI bridge incorporates two sets of posted memory write buffers:

- a posted memory write buffer that absorbs memory writes initiated on its primary side that target memory devices residing on the secondary side.
- a posted memory write buffer that absorbs memory writes initiated on its secondary side that target memory devices residing on the primary side.

In addition, the bridge handles transactions other than memory writes initiated on both sides as delayed transactions (see "Delayed Transactions" on page 86).

The PCI 2.2 spec incorporates a set of rules to govern the behavior of the bridge to ensure that operations appear to occur in the correct order (from the programmer's perspective) and to prevent deadlocks from occurring.

Figure 25-1: System With PCI-to-PCI Bridge

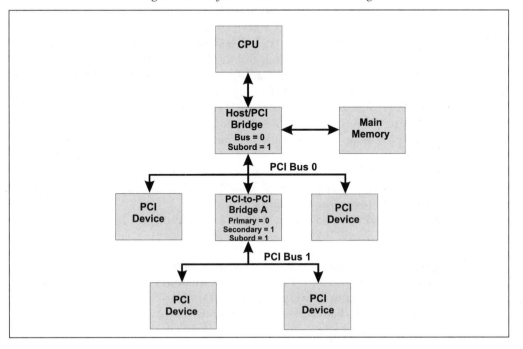

Producer/Consumer Model

The ordering rules defined in the PCI spec ensure that the Producer/Consumer Model works correctly (refer to Figure 25-2 on page 658). The Producer/Consumer model is a common methodology that two bus masters might use to communicate with each other. Consider the following example scenario:

STEP 1. A network adapter begins to receive a stream of compressed video data over the network and performs a burst memory write transaction to place the stream of compressed video data into a **Data buffer** in memory (in other words the network adapter is the **Producer** of the data).

STEP 2. The **Producer** performs a memory write to set an indicator (or **Flag**) in a memory location (or a register) to indicate that the data needs to be processed.

STEP 3. The **Producer** then proceeds to periodically perform a memory read from a **Status** location to see if data processing has been completed by the other bus master (the **Consumer**). This location typically contains zero until the other bus master completes the data processing and writes the completion status into it.

STEP 4. Another PCI master (referred to as the **Consumer**) periodically performs a memory read from the **Flag** location to see if there's any data to be processed. In this example, the other bus master is a video decompressor that will decompress the data and display it.

STEP 5. When it sees that the **Flag** has been set by the **Producer**, it performs a memory write to clear the **Flag** followed by a burst memory read transaction to read the compressed data (it consumes the data; hence the name **Consumer**) from the **Data buffer** in memory.

STEP 6. When it is done consuming the **Data**, the **Consumer** writes the completion status into the **Status** memory location. It then resumes periodically reading the **Flag** location to determine when more data needs to be processed.

STEP 7. The next time that the **Producer** reads the **Status**, it sees that the **Consumer** has completed processing the **Data**. The **Producer** then performs a memory write to clear the **Status** location.

STEP 8. The process then repeats whenever the **Producer** has more data to be processed.

The goal of the ordering rules is that the Producer/Consumer model must work correctly no matter where the **Producer**, the **Consumer**, the **Data** buffer, the **Flag** location, and the **Status** location are located in the system (in other words, no matter how they are distributed on various buses in the system).

Figure 25-2 on page 658 shows an example of where the various entities involved might be located with reference to each other. Table 25-1 on page 655 uses Figure 25-2 on page 658 and provides a detailed description of the activity that occurs during each step of the process. The startup set of assumptions is as follows:

- The **Flag** location contains zero.
- The **Status** location contains zero.

Table 25-1: Detailed Description of Example Producer/Consumer Scenario

Operation	Description
1. A network adapter begins to receive a stream of compressed video data over the network and performs a burst memory write transaction to place the stream of compressed video data into a **Data buffer** in memory (in other words the network adapter is the **Producer** of the data).	The memory write data is absorbed into the posted memory write buffer on the bridge's Bus One side. The data has been accepted by the bridge, but has not yet been written into the **Data** buffer on bus zero.
2. The **Producer** sets an indicator (or **Flag**) in a memory location to indicate that the data needs to be processed.	Since the **Producer** and the **Flag** location are both on Bus One, the transaction doesn't have to traverse the bridge. The data is immediately written into the **Flag** location.
3. The **Producer** then proceeds to periodically perform a memory read from a **Status** location to see if the processing of the **Data** has been completed by the other bus master. This location typically contains zero until the other bus master completes the data processing and writes the completion **Status**.	The **Producer's** read of the **Status** location doesn't have to traverse the bridge and returns a zero value immediately. This tells the **Producer** that the **Consumer** has not yet finished processing the data from the **Data** buffer.

Table 25-1: Detailed Description of Example Producer/Consumer Scenario (Continued)

Operation	Description
4. Another PCI master (referred to as the **Consumer**) periodically performs a memory read from the **Flag** location to see if there's any **Data** to be processed. In this example, the other bus master is a video decompressor that will decompress the data and display it.	The bridge latches the memory read, treats it as a Delayed Read Request (**DRR**) and issues a Retry to the **Consumer**. The **Consumer** begins to periodically Retry the read. In performing the read, the bridge must take the following actions to ensure that the Producer/Consumer Model works correctly: 1. To ensure that the correct read data is obtained, the bridge must flush its posted write buffer going in the same direction as the read. 2. The bridge then performs the memory read from the **Flag** location. The DRR then becomes a DRC (Delayed Read Completion). 3. The bridge flushes any posted memory writes queued up to go to Bus Zero. 4. The bridge delivers the read data to the **Consumer** the next time it retries its read from the **Flag** location.
5. When the **Consumer** sees that the **Flag** has been set by the **Producer**, it performs a memory write to clear the **Flag**.	The memory write is absorbed by the bridge's posted memory write buffer and will be performed at a later time. In other words, the **Flag** is not cleared yet.
6. The **Consumer** then performs a burst memory read transaction to read (or consume) the compressed data from the **Data** buffer in memory.	Since the read doesn't have to traverse the bridge, it is performed and completes immediately.
7. When it is done consuming the **Data**, the **Consumer** writes the completion status into the **Status** memory location.	The memory write is absorbed by the bridge's posted memory write buffer and will be performed at a later time. In other words, the **Status** is not updated yet.

Table 25-1: Detailed Description of Example Producer/Consumer Scenario (Continued)

Operation	Description
8. The **Consumer** then returns to periodically reading the **Flag** location to determine when more **Data** needs to be processed.	The Consumer's next memory read of the **Flag** location has to cross the bridge, so it's treated as a DRR. This causes the previously-queued **Consumer** updates (memory writes) of the **Flag** and **Status** locations to be performed. The **Flag** read is then performed and returns zero. This is given back to the **Consumer** the next time that it Retries the read, telling it that there isn't any additional **Data** to be consumed and processed.
9. The next time that the **Producer** reads the **Status**, it sees that the **Consumer** has completed processing the **Data**.	This read doesn't have to traverse the bridge and takes place immediately.
10. The **Producer** then performs a memory write to clear the **Status** location.	This write doesn't have to traverse the bridge and takes place immediately.
11. The process then repeats whenever the **Producer** has more data to be processed.	

Figure 25-2: Example Producer/Consumer Model

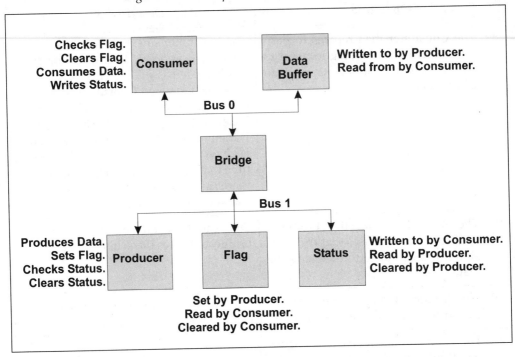

General Ordering Requirements

Only Memory Writes Posted

Bridges implement posted memory write buffers going in both directions through the bridge and memory writes are always posted. Configuration and IO writes are never posted in PCI-to-PCI bridges (optionally, they may be in the host/PCI bridge) and are always handled as Delayed Writes.

Posted Memory Writes Always Complete In Order

As stated earlier, memory writes are always posted in a bridge. When previously-posted writes that are moving in the same direction are subsequently performed on the destination bus, they must always be performed in precisely the same order that they were received. In other words, memory writes are always *strongly-ordered*.

Writes Moving In Opposite Directions Have No Relationship

Memory writes traversing a bridge in opposite directions are like ships passing in the night—they are unaware of each other and that's OK.

Before Read Crosses Bridge, Memory Must Be Sync'd Up

When any type of read must pass through a bridge, the bridge must follow the following procedure:

STEP 1. The read is latched and treated as a Delayed Read Request.

STEP 2. Before performing the read on the destination bus, the bridge must perform all previously-posted memory writes moving in the same direction as the read.

STEP 3. The read can then be performed on the destination bus and be assured of obtaining up-to-date data.

STEP 4. The bridge must then perform all posted memory writes that are moving in the opposite direction and were posted in the bridge prior to the initiation of the read on the destination bus.

STEP 5. The bridge is then permitted to source the read data to the requesting master the next time that it Retries its read transaction.

This procedure ensures:

- that memory on the destination bus is sync'd (i.e., brought up-to-date) before the read is performed on the destination bus and therefore ensures that the read always returns fresh data.
- Additionally, it also ensures that a read of the Flag location (refer to "Producer/Consumer Model" on page 654) will not see the Flag set *before* all of the data written to the Data Buffer has actually arrived.

Posted Write Acceptance Cannot Depend On Master Completion

Description. A bridge must not refuse to accept memory write data into its posted memory write buffer while it's waiting to complete a non-locked transaction as a master on the same bus. If it does, a deadlock may occur (for an example, see "Rule 7—Avoids Deadlock Between Old and New Bridges" on page 667).

A bridge may refuse to accept a memory write for temporary conditions that are guaranteed to be resolved with time (e.g., its posted memory write buffer is temporarily full).

Exception To the Rule—Master Has Locked Target. A bridge can make the acceptance of a memory write transaction as a target contingent on the prior completion of a locked transaction as a master only if the bridge has already established a locked operation with its intended target.

Delayed Transaction Ordering Requirements

The following is a list of requirements that apply to Delayed Transactions:

1. A target that uses Delayed Transactions to achieve the 16 clock first data phase completion limit may be designed to deal with only one Delayed Transaction at a time, or may employ a queueing mechanism so as to support a number of Delayed Transactions outstanding at one time.
2. Only non-posted transactions (i.e., transactions other than posted memory writes) can be handled as Delayed Transactions.
3. A master must repeat any transaction terminated with Retry on the assumption that the target has memorized it and is treating it as a Delayed Transaction.
4. If a Delayed Request is attempted on the destination bus and receives a Retry, the transaction must be Retried periodically until it completes on the destination bus. Before it is attempted on the destination bus, it is only a request and may be discarded at anytime.
5. When a Delayed Request has been completed on the destination bus, it is referred to as a Delayed Completion. The Delayed Completion can only be discarded under the following circumstances:
   - **Case 1**: If it is a read from a prefetchable region (see "What Is Prefetchable Memory?" on page 93). In this case, the read from the target didn't alter the contents of the target, so the data may be discarded.
   - **Case 2**: If the master has not repeated the transaction in 2^{15} clocks. It may then be assumed that the master is not going to repeat the transaction. For more information, refer to "Discard of Delayed Completions" on page 91.
6. On a given side of a bridge, the bridge must accept all memory writes addressed to it as a target, even if it's receiving Retries while attempting to complete a transaction request as a master on the same side.
7. Delayed Requests and Delayed Completions do not have to be performed in any particular order with respect to themselves or each other.
8. Only a Delayed Write Completion can pass a posted memory write. A posted memory write must be given an opportunity to pass everything except another posted memory write.

9. A single master may have any number of transactions terminated with Retry. However, if the master requires one transaction to be completed before another, it cannot attempt the second one on PCI until the first one has completed.

Bridge Ordering Rules

Table 25-2 on page 662 defines the ordering rules that must be adhered to by bridges. When reading the table, please note the following:

- PMW stands for posted memory write.
- DRR and DRC stand for Delayed Read Request and Delayed Read Completion, respectively.
- DWR and DWC stand for Delayed Write Request and Delayed Write Completion, respectively.
- The superscripts represent the Rule numbers.
- A "yes/no" entry means it doesn't matter whether or not the operation just latched is performed before or after the previously-completed operation indicated in the column heading. The Producer/Consumer Model will work correctly either way.
- *THE COLUMN 3 AND 4 ENTRIES IN ROWS 4 AND 5 USED TO READ "YES/NO" IN THE 2.1 SPEC AND HAVE BEEN CHANGED TO "YES" IN THE 2.2 SPEC (AND RULE 6 HAS BEEN ADDED; SEE "RULE 6—AVOIDS DEADLOCK BETWEEN NEW BRIDGES" ON PAGE 666).* **2.2**

The sections that follow provide a detailed explanation of each of the ordering rules. They are referred to by the rule number (shown as superscripts) used in the table.

Table 25-2: Ordering Rules

Transaction just latched	Posted Memory Write	Delayed Request		Delayed Completion	
	PMW Column 1	DRR Column 2	DWR Column 3	DRC Column 4	DWC Column 4
PMW (row 1)	No[1]	Yes[5]	Yes[5]	Yes[7]	Yes[7]
DRR (row 2)	No[2]	Yes/No			
DWR (row 3)	No[3]				
DRC (row 4)	No[4]	YES[6]		Yes/No	
DWC (row 5)	Yes/No				

Rule 1—Ensures Posted Memory Writes Are Strongly-Ordered

A PMW that was just latched may not be performed on the destination bus before a previously-latched PMW moving in the same direction. When PMWs are performed on the destination bus, they must always be performed in the order that they were received. This is referred to as *strong write ordering*.

Rule 2—Ensures Just-Latched Read Obtains Correct Data

A DRR that has just been latched may not be performed on the destination bus before a previously-latched PMW is performed on the destination bus. The memory write might be to the location that the DRR wants to read from and must be performed first in order to ensure that the read obtains the correct data.

Rule 3—Ensures DWR Not Done Until All Posted Writes Done

A DWR that has just been latched may not be performed on the destination bus before a previously-latched PMW is performed on the destination bus. Since the DWR's write was initiated *after* the PMW data was written to the bridge, it must be written to the target on the destination bus *after* the previously-latched PMW data. This ensures strong write ordering. In the Producer/Consumer example, the DWR could be the **Producer's** write to set the **Flag** that indicates the data is all in the **Data** buffer. It wouldn't do to have the **Flag** get set *before* all of the data has actually arrived in the **Data** buffer.

Rule 4—Bi-Directional Posted Writes Done Before Read Data Obtained

Earlier in time, a read that is being treated as a Delayed Read was completed on the destination bus (after posted writes moving in that direction were first flushed) and the bridge has the read data and completion status (i.e., the DRC) ready to give to the originator the next time it retries its request. However, the DRC must not be given to the transaction's originator until all posted write data has been flushed in *both* directions. In other words, before presenting the DRC to its originator, the bridge must first flush any posted writes that are going towards the bus that the originator is on. This is necessary to ensure proper operation of the Producer/Consumer Model.

Refer to Figure 25-2 on page 658. As an example, assume that the read was originated by the **Consumer** to read the **Flag** to see if all of the data is in the **Data** buffer ready to be processed. If the data read from the **Flag** were given to the **Consumer** before all of the data written towards the **Data** buffer by the **Producer** had actually been flushed to the **Data** buffer, the **Consumer** would think that all of the data is in the buffer when in fact it hadn't all arrived yet (it's still posted in the bridge).

Rule 5—Avoids Deadlock Between Old and New Bridges

Essentially, Rule 5 deals with the following scenario:

> At some earlier point in time, the bridge had latched a DRR or DWR, but has not yet initiated the transaction on the destination bus. The bridge then latches a PMW moving in the same direction. **The bridge can perform the just-latched PMW on the destination bus before it initiates the Delayed Read or Write on that bus**. This is necessary to avoid the deadlock described in the paragraphs that follow. The example described uses a DRR, but the same rule applies to DWR.

A deadlock can occur when bridges that support Delayed Transactions (i.e., designed to the 2.1 or 2.2. spec) are transferring data with bridges that do not support Delayed Transactions (i.e., bridges designed to a pre-2.1 version of the PCI spec). Refer to Figure 25-3 on page 665:

1. **Item 1a**—Master 1 starts a read from Target 1. It is passed through Bridge X and is latched by Bridge Y and treated as a DRR. Bridge Y issues a Retry to Bridge X and Bridge X in turn issues a Retry to Master 1.
   Item 1b—In addition, Master 3 starts a read from Target 3. It is passed through Bridge Z and is latched by Bridge Y and treated as a DRR. Bridge Y issues a Retry to Bridge Z and Bridge Z in turn issues a Retry to Master 3.

2. **Item 2a**—Master 4 initiates a burst write to Target 4 and the write data is posted in Bridge Z's posted memory write buffer.
   Item 2b—Master 2 initiates a burst write to Target 2 and the write data is posted in Bridge X's posted memory write buffer.

3. **Item 3a**—Bridge Y attempts its previously-latched Delayed Read and receives a Retry from Bridge Z because Bridge Z must dump its posted memory write buffer to Bridge Y before allowing the Delayed Read to cross Bridge Z.
   Item 3b—Bridge Y attempts its other previously-latched Delayed Read and receives a Retry from Bridge X because Bridge X must dump its posted memory write buffer to Bridge Y before allowing the Delayed Read to cross Bridge X.

4. **Item 4a**—Bridge Z starts dumping its posted write buffer to Bridge Y and Y's buffers become full (because Z's buffers are deeper). Y starts issuing Retries to Z.
   Item 4b—Bridge X starts dumping its posted write buffer to Bridge Y and Y's buffers become full (because X's buffers are deeper). Y starts issuing Retries to X.

5. **Item 5a**—If Bridge Y doesn't dump its posted writes to Bridge X before it's able to complete the read that it keeps re-attempting, the system becomes deadlocked.
   Item 5b—If Bridge Y doesn't dump its posted writes to Bridge Z before it's able to complete the read that it keeps re-attempting, the system becomes deadlocked.

Figure 25-3: Example For Ordering Rule 5

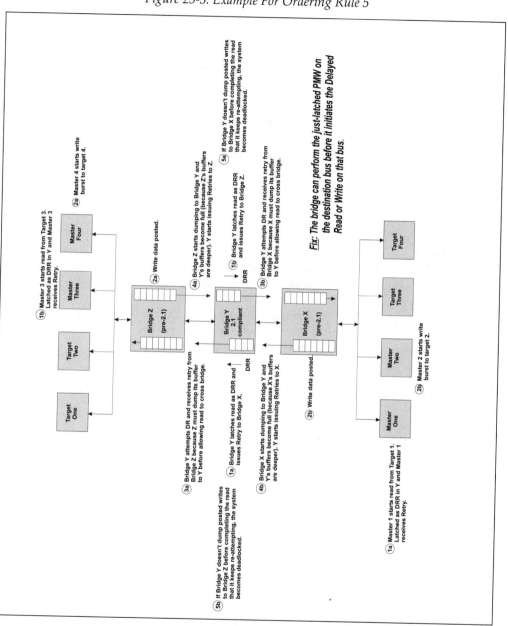

Rule 6—Avoids Deadlock Between New Bridges

THIS RULE WAS ADDED IN THE 2.2 PCI SPEC. A DWC or DRC just latched must be passed to the originating master when the originating master Retries its transaction *without waiting for your own request to complete.*

Consider the example pictured in Figure 25-4 on page 667:

STEP 1. Bus masters X and Y on buses 0 and 2 initiate read or write transactions.

STEP 2. Bridges A and B latch the transactions as Delayed Requests and issue Retries to the respective masters. The masters repeat their respective transactions until they have completion.

STEP 3. As each bridge acquires ownership of bus 1, it attempts the master's transaction. The transaction is latched by the other bridge as a Delayed Request and a Retry is issued.

STEP 4. Each of the two bridges now repeatedly Retries its respective transaction on bus 1 while it awaits completion.

STEP 5. Meanwhile, either bridge acquires ownership of the destination bus (bus 0 or bus 2) and initiates and completes the other bridge's transaction. For example, assume that Bridge A acquires ownership of bus 0 and completes Master Y's transaction. Bridge A now has a Delayed Completion ready to pass back to Bridge B the next time Bridge B Retries its request.

STEP 6. If Bridge A refuses to deliver B's Completion before its able to complete its own outstanding Delayed Request, deadlock occurs.

Figure 25-4: Example For Ordering Rule 6

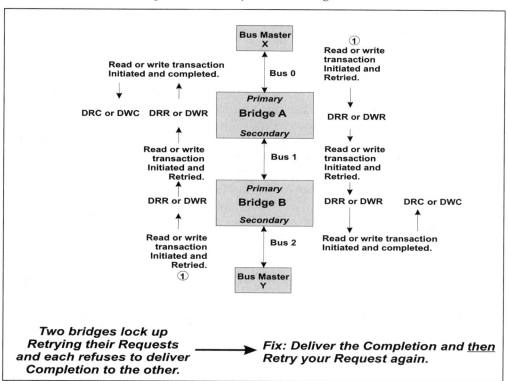

Rule 7—Avoids Deadlock Between Old and New Bridges

To avoid deadlocks, a posted memory write must be allowed to pass a previously-latched Delayed Completion (read or write).

This scenario is similar to the one seen in the example for Rule 5 (Figure 25-3 on page 665) and is illustrated in Figure 25-5 on page 669.

- Bridge Y is 2.1 or 2.2-compliant (it implements posted memory write buffers *and* Delayed Transaction Queues),
- while Bridges X and Z are pre-2.1 bridges (they have posted memory write buffers, but no support for Delayed Transactions).

STEP 1. A DRC sits at the head of the queues in both directions of Bridge Y at the same time. The masters that initiated the reads (Masters One and Three) repeat their transactions on a regular basis. In turn, the old bridges (X and Z) then repeat the transaction to the new bridge.

STEP 2. The old bridges (X and Z) each contain posted write data to be written through Bridge Y.

STEP 3. Each time that the old bridge sees the master repeat the read, it must repeat it to the new bridge, but it cannot do so until it is successful in flushing out all of its posted write data (because the old bridge cannot let a read traverse the bridge until all previously-posted writes have been completed to Bridge Y).

STEP 4. Eventually, the new bridge cannot accept any more posted data from the old bridge because its Posted Write Buffer is full (remember, it's buffer is smaller than the old bridge's buffer).

STEP 5. In addition, the new bridge cannot flush its Posted Write Buffer to the other old bridge until it has successfully delivered the Read Completion to the old bridge (see "Rule 4—Bi-Directional Posted Writes Done Before Read Data Obtained" on page 663). However, the old bridge will not repeat the read until it has successfully completed dumping its posted memory write buffer to Bridge Y.

STEP 6. When this condition exists in both directions, we have a deadlock.

Therefore, when a new bridge has a DRC awaiting the repeat of the DRR by the originating master on one of its interfaces and this prevents it from dumping its posted write buffers through the same interface, the bridge must dump its posted memory writes before it is successful in delivering the Delayed Completion.

The same condition exists when a DWC sits at the head of both queues in Bridge Y.

Figure 25-5: Example For Ordering Rule 7

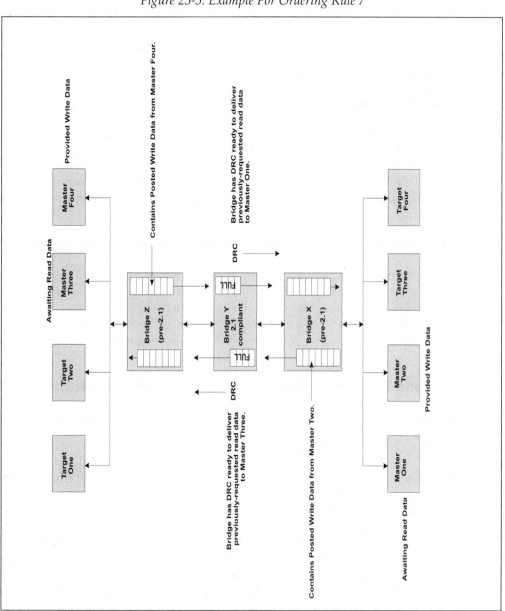

Locking, Delayed Transactions and Posted Writes

A detailed discussion of Locking can be found in the chapter entitled "Locking" on page 683. This section focuses on how locking relates to Delayed Transactions and to posted memory writes.

Lock Passage Is Uni-Directional (Downstream-Only)

A PCI-to-PCI bridge must support the passing of a locked transaction from its primary to secondary side (also referred to as downstream movement), but must not support the passing of a locked transaction from its secondary to primary side (upstream movement). A transaction initiated on the secondary side attempting a lock will be passed through to the primary side, but not as a locked transaction (in other words, LOCK# is ignored).

Once Locked, Bridge Only Permits Locking Master Access

Once a bridge has accepted a locking transaction (i.e., a memory read that uses the LOCK# signal to lock the bridge) and has successfully addressed and locked the target on the secondary bus, the bridge will only accept subsequent transactions from the master that locked it. Transaction requests from all other masters on both buses will receive retries and will not be memorized (i.e., they are not treated as Delayed Transactions).

Actions Taken Before Allowing Lock To Traverse Bridge

If a locked transaction is initiated on the bridge's primary bus and the target resides on the bridge's secondary side, before initiating the locked transaction on the secondary bus the bridge:

- Must perform all previously-posted memory writes (accepted from the primary bus) on the secondary bus.
- With regard to any previously-latched Delayed Requests, before initiating the locked transaction on the secondary bus the bridge may:
    - discard any Delayed Requests previously latched (this causes no harm because the originating masters will repeat the transactions and they can be re-memorized at that time),
    - allow the locked transaction to be performed on the secondary bus before any of the Requests,
    - or complete all previously-latched Requests before passing the locked transaction to the secondary bus.

After Bridge Locked But Before Secondary Target Locked

Until the lock is established on the secondary bus, the bridge is allowed to continue latching transactions initiated on its secondary bus.

After Secondary Target Locked, No Secondary Side Posting

Once the lock has been established on the secondary bus, the bridge cannot accept any posted memory writes initiated on its secondary bus until it has been unlocked by the master that established the lock on its primary side (**FRAME#** and **LOCK#** sampled deasserted on the same rising clock edge).

Simplest Design—Bridge Reserved For Locking Master's Use

In the simplest implementation, once lock is established on the secondary bus, the bridge does not accept any other transactions in either direction except for locked transactions initiated by the master that locked it. The bridge must complete PMWs, DRCs, and DWCs moving toward the primary bus before allowing the locked access to complete on the primary bus. These rules are sufficient for deadlock free operation, but a design may be more or less restrictive as long as it ensures deadlock free operation.

The PCI BIOS

The Previous Chapter

The previous chapter focused on the ordering rules that govern the behavior of simple devices as well as the relationships of multiple transactions traversing a PCI-to-PCI bridge. It also described how the rules prevent deadlocks from occurring.

This Chapter

This chapter introduces the PCI BIOS specification, revision 2.1, dated August 26, 1994.

The Next Chapter

The next chapter provides a detailed description of the PCI locking mechanism that permits an EISA bridge to lock main memory or the host/PCI bridge to lock an EISA memory target.

Purpose of PCI BIOS

The OS (except for the platform-specific micro-kernel), applications programs and device drivers must not directly access the PCI configuration registers, interrupt routing logic (see "Interrupt Routing" on page 225), or the Special Cycle generation logic (see "Software Generation of Special Cycles" on page 329). The hardware methods utilized to implement these capabilities are platform-specific. Any software that directly accesses these mechanisms is therefore, by definition, platform-specific. This can lead to compatibility problems (i.e., the software works on some platforms but not on others).

Instead, the request should be issued to the PCI BIOS. The BIOS is platform-specific. It is implemented in firmware and possibly in the OS's Hardware Abstraction Layer (HAL). The PCI BIOS supplies the following services:

- Permits determination of configuration mechanism(s) supported by the PCI chipset (refer to "Intro to Configuration Mechanisms" on page 321).
- Permits determination of the chipset's ability to generate the PCI Special Cycle transaction under software control and the mechanism(s) used to do so. For more information, refer to "Software Generation of Special Cycles" on page 329.
- Permits determination of the range of PCI buses present in system.
- Searches for all instances of a specific PCI device or a device that falls within a Class.
- Permits generation of the PCI Special Cycle transaction (if the chipset supports its generation under software control).
- Allows caller to get PCI interrupt routing options and then to assign an interrupt line to a device.
- Permits read and write of a device's configuration registers.

OS Environments Supported

General

Different OSs have different operational characteristics (such as the method for defining the usage of system memory and the method utilized to call BIOS services). In systems based on the x86 processor family, the OS executing on a particular platform falls into one of the following three categories:

- Real-mode operating system (in other words, MS-DOS).
- 286 protected mode (God forbid!).
- 386 protected mode. There are two flavors of 386 protected mode:
  - the segmented model (once again, God forbid!).
  - and the flat model.

The PCI BIOS specification defines the following rules regarding the implementation of the PCI BIOS and the software that calls it:

RULE 1. The PCI BIOS must support all of the above-mentioned OS environments.

RULE 2. The BIOS must preserve all registers and flags with the exception of those used to return parameters.

RULE 3. Caller will be returned to with the state of Interrupt Flag bit in the EFLAGs register the same as it was on entry.

RULE 4. Interrupts will not be enabled during the execution of the BIOS function call.

RULE 5. The BIOS routines must be reentrant (i.e., they can be called from within themselves).

RULE 6. The OS must define a stack memory area at least 1KB in size for the BIOS.

RULE 7. The stack segment and code segment defined by the OS for the BIOS must have the same size (16- or 32-bit).

RULE 8. Protected mode OSs that call the BIOS using INT 1Ah must set the CS register to F000h.

RULE 9. The OS must ensure that the privilege level defined for the BIOS permits interrupt enable/disable and performance of IO instructions.

RULE 10. Implementers of the BIOS must assume that the CS for the BIOS defined by the OS is execute-only and that the DS is read-only.

Real-Mode

Real-mode OSs, such as MS-DOS, are written to be executed on the 8088 processor. That processor is only capable of addressing up to 1MB of memory (00000h through FFFFFh). Using four 16-bit segment registers (CS, DS, SS, ES), the programmer defines four segments of memory, each with a fixed length of 64KB. When a program begins execution, each of the four segment registers is initialized with the upper four hex digits of the respective segment's start address in memory.

- The **code segment** contains the currently-executing program,
- the **data segment** defines the area of memory that contains the data the program operates upon,
- the **stack segment** defines the area of memory used to temporarily save values,
- and the **extra data segment** can be used to define another data segment associated with the currently-executing program.

MS-DOS makes calls to the BIOS by loading a subset of the processor's register set with request parameters and then executing a software interrupt instruction that specifies entry 1Ah in the interrupt table as containing the entry point to the BIOS. Upon execution of the INT 1Ah instruction, the processor pushes the address of the instruction that follows the INT 1Ah onto stack memory. Having saved this return address, the processor then reads the pointer from entry 1Ah in the interrupt table and starts executing at the indicated address. This is the entry point of the BIOS.

An alternative method for calling the BIOS is to make a call directly to the BIOS entry point at physical memory location 000FFE6Eh. Use of this method ensures that the caller doesn't have to worry about the 1Ah entry in the interrupt table having been "hooked" by someone else.

286 Protected Mode (16:16)

The BIOS specification refers to this as 16:16 mode because the 286 processor had 16-bit segment registers and the programmer specifies the address of an object in memory by defining the 16-bit offset of the object within the segment (code, data, stack or extra). Although the maximum size of each segment is still 64KB (as it is with the 8088 processor), the OS programmer can set the segment length to any value from one to 64KB in length. When operating in Real Mode, the 286 addresses memory just like the 8088 with the same fixed segment size of 64KB and the ability to only access locations within the first megabyte of memory space.

When operating in Protected Mode, however, the 286 processor addresses memory differently. Rather than containing the upper four hex digits of the segment's physical five-digit start address in memory, the value in the segment register is referred to as a Segment Selector. It points to an entry in a Segment Descriptor Table in memory that is built and maintained by the OS. Each entry in the Segment Descriptor Table contains eight bytes of information defining:

- the 24-bit start physical address of the segment in memory. In other words, the segment start address can be specified anywhere in the first 16MB of memory space.
- the length of the segment (from one byte through 64KB).
- the manner in which the program is permitted to access the segment of memory (read-only, execute-only, read/write, or not at all).

Some OSs (such as Windows 3.1 when operating in 286 mode) use the segment capability to assign separate code, data and stack segments within the 16MB total memory space accessible to each program. Whenever the OS performs a task switch, it must load the segment registers with the set of values defining the segments of memory "belonging" to the current application.

As in the Real Mode OS environment, the BIOS is called via execution of INT 1Ah or by directly calling the industry standard entry point of the BIOS (physical memory location 000FFE6Eh).

386 Protected Mode (16:32)

The 386 processor changed the maximum size of each segment from 64KB to 4GB in size. The 486, Pentium, and P6 family processors have the same maximum segment size as the 386. In addition to increasing the maximum segment size to 4GB, the 386 also introduced a 32-bit register set, permitting the programmer to specify the 32-bit offset of an object within a segment. The segment registers are still 16-bits in size, however. Rather than containing the upper four hex digits of the segment's physical five-digit start address in memory, however, the value in the segment register is referred to as a Segment Selector (when the processor is operating in protected mode). It points to an entry in a Segment Descriptor Table in memory that is built and maintained by the OS. Each entry in the Segment Descriptor Table contains eight bytes of information defining:

- the 32-bit start physical address of the segment in memory. In other words, the base address of the segment can be specified anywhere within the overall 4GB of memory space.
- the length of the segment (from one byte through 4GB).
- the manner in which the program is permitted to access the segment of memory (read-only, execute-only, read/write, or not at all).

Some operating systems (such as Windows 3.1 when operating in 386 Enhanced Mode) use the segment capability to assign separate code, data and stack segments within the 4GB total memory space accessible to each program. Whenever the OS performs a task switch, it must load the segment registers with the set of values defining the segments of memory "belonging" to the current application. In the PCI BIOS specification, this is referred to as 16:32 mode because the 16-bit segment register defines (indirectly) the segment start address and the programmer can use a 32-bit value to specify the offset of the object anywhere in the 4GB of total memory space.

In a 32-bit OS environment, the BIOS is not called using INT 1Ah. In fact, if an applications program attempts to execute an INT instruction it results in a General Protection exception. Rather, the calling program executes a Far Call to the BIOS entry point. This implies that the entry point address is known. A subsequent section in this chapter defines how the BIOS entry point is discovered.

Today's OSs Use Flat Mode (0:32)

A much simpler memory model is to set all of the segment registers to point to Segment Descriptors that define each segment as starting at physical memory location 00000000h each with a length of 4GB. This is referred as the Flat Memory Model. The BIOS specification refers to this as 0:32 mode because all segments start at location 00000000h and have a 32-bit length of FFFFFFFFh (4GB). Since separate segments aren't defined for each program, the OS has the responsibility of managing memory and making sure different programs don't play in each other's space. It accomplishes this using the Attribute bits in the Page Tables.

As stated earlier, in a 32-bit OS environment, the BIOS is not called using INT 1Ah. Rather, the calling program executes a Far Call to the BIOS entry point. This implies that the entry is known. A subsequent section in this chapter defines how the BIOS entry point is discovered.

Determining if System Implements 32-bit BIOS

Before attempting a call to a 32-bit BIOS (such as the PCI BIOS), the 32-bit OS must first determine if the desired 32-bit BIOS is present and what its entry point is. The BIOS specification states that the OS must scan the physical memory area from 000E0000h through 000FFFF0h looking for the 16-byte data structure defined in Table 26-1 on page 678. This data structure must be aligned on a 16-byte address boundary.

Table 26-1: 32-Bit BIOS Data Structure

Offset	Size	Description
0	4 bytes	ASCII signature "_32_". The left-most underscore is stored at offset 0, while the right-most is stored at offset 3.
4	4 bytes	32-bit entry point of the 32-bit BIOS Service Directory Program. The service directory program can be called to determine what services (such as PCI BIOS services) are offered by the 32-bit BIOS. The author thinks of this as the BIOS librarian because it keeps track of what BIOSs are implemented and where they are located in memory.
8	1 bytes	Revision level (i.e., the layout) of this data structure (currently 00h).
9	1 bytes	Data structure length in 16-byte increments. As currently-defined, the data structure is 16 bytes long, so this field contains 01h.
Ah	1 bytes	Checksum of all bytes in data structure. Sum must add up to 00h.
Bh	5 bytes	Reserved and must be zero.

Determining Services 32-bit BIOS Supports

Now that the existence and entry point of the 32-bit Service Directory Program (the BIOS Librarian) has been established, the OS may interrogate it to determine if the 32-bit BIOS specifically implements the PCI BIOS. This is accomplished by calling the entry point and supplying the following as input parameters:

- **EAX = Service Identifier.** To determine if the indicated service (in this case, the PCI BIOS service) is supported by the 32-bit BIOS, the Service Directory Program performs a lookup based on the four byte **Service Identifier** (see "Determining if 32-bit BIOS Supports PCI BIOS Services" on page 679) supplied by the caller in the EAX register.
- **BL = Service Directory Function Identifier.** The only one currently defined is 00h, which directs the Service Directory Program to search for the Service Identifier provided in the EAX register. The upper three bytes of EBX are reserved and must be cleared to zero.

Upon return from the call to the Service Directory Program, the register set contains the following values:

- AL contains 00h if the specified service exists, 80h if the specified service isn't present, or 81h if the Function Identifier supplied in BL isn't implemented.
- EBX contains the physical start address of the indicated BIOS service.
- ECX contains the length of the indicated BIOS service.
- EDX contains the indicated BIOS service entry point. This is an offset from the start address returned in EBX.

Determining if 32-bit BIOS Supports PCI BIOS Services

The service identifier for the PCI BIOS services consists of the ASCII string "$PCI", specified in EAX as 49435024h. Assuming that the Service Directory Program call indicates that the PCI BIOS exists, the PCI BIOS may then be called by performing a Far Call to the entry point returned in the EDX register. Before calling the PCI BIOS, the OS must define the BIOS's code and data segments as encompassing the physical address range returned in EBX and ECX. The code and data segments must have the same start address. The OS must set up the BIOS's privilege level to permit IO operations and it must define a stack area for the BIOS that is at least 1KB in size. BIOS writers must assume that the OS defines the code segment as execute-only and the data segment as read-only.

Calling PCI BIOS

As stated earlier in this chapter, the 16-bit PCI BIOS is called by either executing an INT 1Ah instruction or directly by calling the PCI BIOS at physical memory location 000FFE6Eh. The 32-bit BIOS is called by performing a Far Call.

In both cases, the caller must first load the required request parameters into the processor's register set. On entry,

- the AH register must contain the PCI function ID of B1h.
- The AL register must contain the PCI sub-function identifier.

Table 26-2 on page 681 identifies the input parameters for the various types of PCI function calls. On exit, the state of the carry flag indicates the general success or failure of the call. The BIOS specification contains a detailed description of each of these function calls. Since they are clearly described in the specification, duplication of that information is not contained in this chapter.

PCI BIOS Present Call

Prior to calling the PCI BIOS, AH is set to B1h (ID of the PCI BIOS) and AL to 01h. On return, the register set contains the following values:

- EDX contains the ASCII character string " PCI", with DL = "P", DH = "C", the byte above DH = "I", and the upper byte of EDX set to the ASCII space character.
- AH = 00h.
- AL contains the information in Figure 26-1 on page 681.
- BH = BIOS major version in BCD.
- BL = BIOS minor version in BCD.
- CL = the number of the last PCI bus in the system.
- Carry bit is cleared if BIOS present, set if it's not.

The programmer is only assured that the PCI BIOS is present if EDX, AL and the carry flag contains the indicated information.

Figure 26-1: AL Contents After BIOS Present Call

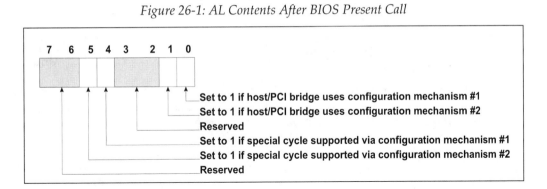

Table 26-2: PCI BIOS Function Request Codes

Function Request	AH Value	AL Value
PCI function ID.	B1h	
Test for PCI BIOS present.	B1h	01h
Find PCI device using Vendor ID/Device ID. Can find all instances of a device in the system using the device's Vendor and Device IDs as search criteria. If an instance of the device is found, the physical location is returned (Bus, Device and Function numbers). These values can then be used as input parameters to the configuration read and write BIOS functions to access the device's configuration registers.	B1h	02h
Find PCI class code. Can find all instances of devices in the system with the indicated Class Code using the specified Class Code as search criteria. If an instance of the device is found, the physical location is returned (Bus, Device and Function numbers). These values can then be used as input parameters when making PCI BIOS function callas to request configuration read and write accesses to the device's configuration registers. As an example of usage, this function would be used to scan for a VGA-compatible interface to be used as the boot display device.	B1h	03h

Table 26-2: PCI BIOS Function Request Codes (Continued)

Function Request	AH Value	AL Value
Generate Special Cycle Transaction. Used to generate a PCI Special Cycle transaction to send the programmer-specified message to all devices on the indicated bus. Note that this function is not implemented if the chipset does not support generation of Special Cycle transactions under software control.	B1h	06h
Read configuration byte.	B1h	08h
Read configuration word.	B1h	09h
Read configuration doubleword.	B1h	0Ah
Write configuration byte.	B1h	0Bh
Write configuration word.	B1h	0Ch
Write configuration doubleword.	B1h	0Dh
Get Interrupt Routing Options. Used to discover the manner in which interrupts from PCI devices can be routed to system interrupt request lines. Routing information is returned in a data structure that identifies the IRQ routing information for each PCI device or slot. This data structure has the same format as that of the "Interrupt Routing Table" on page 233 (in fact, it's the same table). Note that neither this function call nor the one in the next row of this table are supported if the chipset does not implement a programmable interrupt router.	B1h	0Eh
Set (assign) PCI interrupt. Used to route a device's PCI interrupt request line to the specified system interrupt request line.	B1h	0Fh

27 *Locking*

The Previous Chapter

The previous chapter introduced the PCI BIOS specification, revision 2.1, dated August 26, 1994.

This Chapter

This chapter provides a detailed description of the PCI locking mechanism that permits an EISA bridge to lock main memory or the host/PCI bridge to lock an EISA memory target.

The Next Chapter

The next chapter describes the issues that differentiate CompactPCI from PCI. This includes mechanical, electrical and software-related issues. CompactPCI is presented as described in the 2.1 CompactPCI specification. PMC devices are also described.

2.2 Spec Redefined Lock Usage

2.2

THIS CHAPTER HAS BEEN RENAMED AND REWRITTEN TO REFLECT A MAJOR CHANGE IN THE 2.2 SPEC. IN THE EARLIER VERSIONS OF THE SPEC IT WAS PERMISSIBLE FOR A PCI MASTER TO ISSUE A LOCKED TRANSACTION SERIES TO LOCK A PCI MEMORY TARGET. BUS MASTERS ARE NO LONGER ALLOWED TO ISSUE LOCKED TRANSACTIONS AND A PCI MEMORY TARGET MUST NO LONGER HONOR A REQUEST TO LOCK ITSELF. These are the basic rules that define use of the locking mechanism:

RULE 1. Only the **host/PCI bridge** is now **permitted to initiate** a locked transaction series on behalf of a processor residing it.

RULE 2. A **PCI-to-PCI bridge** is **only** permitted to **pass** a **locked transaction from** its **primary to secondary side**. In other words, the bridge only passes through locked transactions that are moving outbound from the processor towards an expansion bus bridge further out in the hierarchy (e.g., an EISA bridge).

RULE 3. An **expansion bus bridge** (such as a PCI-to-EISA bridge) **acts as** the **target** of locked transactions and can optionally initiate them when targeting main memory behind the host/PCI bridge. For this reason, the host/PCI bridge must honor LOCK# as an input from the EISA bridge.

RULE 4. LOCK# is implemented as an sustained tri-state **input** pin **on** a PCI-to-PCI bridge's **primary** side and as a sustained tri-state **output** pin **on** its **secondary** side.

RULE 5. The first transaction of a locked transaction series must be a memory read (to read a memory semaphore).

Scenarios That Require Locking

General

The following sections describe the only circumstances under which the PCI locking mechanism may be used.

EISA Master Initiates Locked Transaction Series Targeting Main Memory

If a PCI-to-EISA bridge is present in the system, there may be a master on the EISA bus that attempts locked transaction series with main memory. In this case, the EISA master may start a transaction on the EISA bus that targets main memory and it may assert the EISA LOCK# signal. In this case, the PCI-to-EISA bridge would have to initiate a PCI memory transaction with the PCI LOCK# signal asserted. This is permissible.

However, if the bridge is not on the PCI bus that is also connected to the host/PCI bridge, although the transaction will be successful in addressing main memory, it will not be successful in locking it. The transaction generated by the EISA bridge will make it through a PCI-to-PCI bridge, but not with LOCK# asserted. This is because PCI-to-PCI bridges only pass a lock through from the primary to the secondary side of the bridge, and not in the opposite direction.

In order to successfully lock main memory, the PCI-to-EISA bridge must be located directly on the same PCI bus that the host/PCI bridge is attached to. The EISA bridge's assertion of the PCI LOCK# signal is then directly visible to the host/PCI bridge.

Processor Initiates Locked Transaction Series Targeting EISA Memory

It is possible that an EISA device driver uses a memory semaphore that resides in memory on an EISA card. If this is the case, when the processor executing the driver code initiates a locked Read/Modify/Write operation to read and update the semaphore, the host/PCI bridge must utilize the PCI locking mechanism (as defined later in this chapter) to lock the EISA bus when performing the accesses on the PCI and EISA buses.

Possible Deadlock Scenario

Refer to Figure 27-1 on page 687. A deadlock can occur under the following circumstances:

Clock 1. The processor initiates an 8-byte read from the PCI memory-mapped IO target on Bus One.

Clock 2. To service the request, the host/PCI bridge initiates a PCI burst memory read transaction to perform a two data phase read from the 32-bit PCI memory-mapped IO target.

Clock 3. The memory-mapped IO target resides on the other side of a PCI-to-PCI bridge, so the PCI-to-PCI bridge acts as the target of the transaction. It initiates a burst memory read from the memory-mapped IO target on Bus One.

Clock 4. The memory-mapped IO target transfers the first dword to the PCI-to-PCI bridge, but then issues a disconnect to the bridge without transferring the second dword. The disconnect could have been because the target could not access the second dword within eight PCI clock cycles.

Clock 5. The PCI-to-PCI bridge in turn issues a disconnect to the host/PCI bridge.

Clock 6. Before the host/PCI bridge can re-initiate the memory read to get the second dword from the memory-mapped IO device, the PCI-to-PCI bridge accepts posted memory write data that must be written to main memory (which is behind the host/PCI bridge) from the bus master on its secondary side.

Clock 7. The host/PCI bridge then reinitiates its memory read transaction to fetch the second dword. The PCI-to-PCI bridge receives the request, memorizes it, issues a retry to the host/PCI bridge and treats it as a Delayed Read Request.

Clock 8. As per the transaction ordering rules, the PCI-to-PCI bridge cannot allow the memory read to cross onto the secondary side until it has flushed any previously-posted memory writes that are going towards its secondary side. This is to ensure that the read receives the correct data.

Clock 9. After any posted writes are completed on its secondary side, the bridge performs the memory read to obtain the second dword from the memory-mapped IO device on its secondary side. If the host/PCI bridge should retry the read request, it receives a retry.

Clock 10. The PCI-to-PCI bridge now has the requested dword in a buffer. It cannot allow the host/PCI bridge's read to complete, however, until it has first performed any previously-posted memory writes to main memory. In other words, a read is not allowed to complete on its originating bus until all previously-posted writes moving in both directions have been completed.

Clock 11. When the PCI-to-PCI bridge attempts to perform the memory write to main memory, the host/PCI bridge issues a retry to it (because it will not accept any write data for main memory until the second half of its outstanding PCI memory read completes).

The result is a deadlock. Every time that the host/PCI bridge re-initiates its read request it receives a retry from the PCI-to-PCI bridge. In turn, the PCI-to-PCI bridge receives a retry each time that it attempts to dump its posted memory write buffer to memory.

This dilemma is **solved by having the host/PCI bridge start the initial memory read as a locked transaction** (in case the target resides behind one or more PCI-to-PCI bridges). *It is a rule that a PCI-to-PCI bridge must turn off write posting until a locked operation completes.* In the scenario just described, the bridge will not accept any posted write data on its secondary side until the entire read has completed and LOCK# has been deasserted.

Figure 27-1: Possible Deadlock Scenario

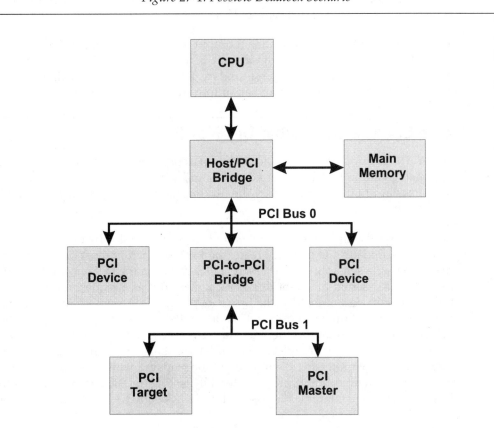

PCI Solutions: Bus and Resource Locking

LOCK# Signal

The PCI bus locking mechanism is implemented via the PCI LOCK# signal. There is only one LOCK# signal and only one master on a PCI bus can use it at a time (*and that master must be the host/PCI bridge or the secondary side interface of a PCI-to-PCI bridge*). This means that only one master may perform a locked transaction series during a given period of time. The LOCK# signal is a sustained tri-state signal. As with all PCI sustained tri-state signals, the system board designer (or add-in card designer if the PCI bus resides on an add-in card) is required to provide a pullup resistor on the LOCK# signal. When not in use, the state of LOCK# is therefore deasserted.

- LOCK# is both an input to and an output from the host/PCI bridge.
- LOCK# is an input to the primary side of a PCI-to-PCI bridge.
- LOCK# is an output from the secondary side of a PCI-to-PCI bridge.
- LOCK# is both an input to and an output from a PCI-to-EISA bridge

Bus Lock: Permissible but Not Preferred

When a PCI bridge initiates a locked transaction series, the bus arbiter can optionally sample LOCK# asserted and could refuse to grant the bus to any other master until so instructed by the bus master (by its release of the LOCK# signal).

PCI permits this implementation wherein LOCK# is sampled by the arbiter. The PCI bridge initiates the memory read (the first transaction must be a memory read—to read a semaphore) and asserts LOCK#. When the PCI bus arbiter samples LOCK# asserted by the bridge, it recognizes this as a request for exclusive bus ownership. Assuming that the first data phase of the memory read transaction completes normally (no Target Abort or Retry issued by the target), the bridge may assume that no other bus master will be able to access the addressed memory target until it completes the update of the semaphore (with a subsequent memory write). After completion of the read and while the requester (the processor, or an EISA bus master) is internally testing the state of the semaphore it read, the bridge continues to assert the LOCK# signal (even though it's not currently using the bus).

While LOCK# remains asserted, the arbiter ignores PCI bus requests from all masters other than the bridge that established the lock. The arbiter knows which master established the lock because each master has a dedicated REQ#/GNT# signal pair and it knows which master asserted LOCK# when it was granted bus ownership.

When the master that established the lock later requests ownership of the PCI bus again to perform the memory write to update the semaphore, the arbiter grants it the bus (in all probability, it had probably parked ownership on that master). The bridge performs the memory write and then releases the LOCK# signal when it returns the bus to the idle state. This instructs the arbiter to cease the bus lock. It also instructs the memory target to unlock itself. A PCI target (a PCI-to-PCI bridge, EISA bridge, or possibly a host/PCI bridge) that is locked unlocks itself whenever it detects FRAME# deasserted with LOCK# deasserted.

In the event that the master reads the semaphore and determines that it has already been set to a non-zero value by another master, it just ceases to assert the LOCK# signal (and the target—and any bridges that the transaction had to traverse—unlocks itself when it detects FRAME# and LOCK# deasserted).

The bus lock implementation impedes other masters from using the PCI bus to prevent anyone from accessing the small area of the memory target that the semaphore resides in. For this reason, this approach is considered to be less than optimal. The next section describes the preferred approach, resource locking.

Resource Lock: Preferred Solution

Introduction

The PCI bus implements a signal (LOCK#) that a bridge uses to prevent the problems described earlier. When the final access of the locked transaction series has been completed, the bridge indicates that it no longer requires exclusive ownership of the target by deasserting LOCK# when it returns the bus to the idle state. During the locked period, non-exclusive accesses (those that do not require use of the LOCK# signal) are permitted to occur on a locked PCI bus (as long they do not have to cross a locked PCI-to-PCI bridge). No accesses are permitted to cross a locked bridge.

Determining Lock Mechanism Availability

There is only one PCI LOCK# signal line and it may only be used by one device at a time. If a bridge wishes to use the LOCK# signal to reserve a target for exclusive access, it must first determine that the LOCK# signal is not already in use by another master. This is accomplished in the following manner:

- Do not assert REQ# if LOCK# is currently asserted.
- If FRAME# and LOCK# are sampled deasserted, the locking resource is available. The bridge may assert its REQ#.
- While waiting for GNT#, the bridge must continue to monitor LOCK#. If LOCK# is sampled asserted, the bridge deasserts its REQ# (because another master has already started using LOCK#).
- When the bridge samples bus idle (FRAME# and IRDY# deasserted) and LOCK# deasserted, it has acquisition of the bus and of the LOCK# signal. It may start the first transaction of its locked transaction series.

The same rules apply for establishing a bus lock.

Establishing Lock

Figure 27-2 on page 692 illustrates the process of gaining exclusive ownership of a target. The access that establishes the lock on the target (in other words, the first transaction of the locked transaction series) must be a memory read. The specification states that the bridge may only access the target that it has locked (no other targets) for the duration of the locked transaction series. This rule exists to ensure that the bridge accomplishes its locked transaction series in an expeditious fashion so as to have minimal impact on other masters that may need to use the locking mechanism or that may need to cross a locked bridge.

Assume that a bridge wishes to perform a locked transaction series. When the bridge has established that the LOCK# signal is not currently in use (see "Determining Lock Mechanism Availability" on page 689) by another bridge, it asserts REQ# to the arbiter to request access to the bus. While waiting for the grant (GNT#), the bridge must continue to monitor the LOCK# signal. If LOCK# is sampled asserted, another master has gained ownership of LOCK# and the bridge must deassert REQ# until LOCK# is available.

CLOCK 1. Assuming that the bridge has acquired ownership of the bus (its GNT# is asserted and the bus is idle), the bridge initiates the transfer at the start of clock one by asserting FRAME#, leaving LOCK# deasserted to request the lock (this sounds contradictory, but continue reading), and driving the address and command type (memory read) onto the AD bus and the Command/Byte Enable lines, respectively.

CLOCK 2. The target latches the address and command and samples LOCK# deasserted at the rising-edge of clock two. It proceeds with the address decode.

THE bridge asserts LOCK# during clock two to instruct the target to stay locked after this transaction completes.

THE bridge asserts LOCK# at the rising-edge of clock two to maintain the lock past the end of this transaction.

FRAME# is deasserted because the bridge is ready (IRDY# asserted) to complete the last (and only) data phase of the transaction.

CLOCK 3. The target decodes the address and asserts DEVSEL# and TRDY# during clock three (medium speed decoder). It also "remembers" that LOCK# was sampled deasserted at the end of the address phase. This instructs the target to lock itself. In fact, the target will only lock itself if the first data phase of the transaction completes successfully (the lock is formally established at the successful completion of the first data phase). If the first data phase doesn't complete successfully (for example, the target issues a Retry because it cannot complete the access yet), the bridge has not gained exclusive ownership of the target. It must terminate the transaction, release LOCK#, and try again later.

CLOCK 4. At the rising-edge of clock four, the first (and only) data item is available for transfer (IRDY# and TRDY# are asserted) and the bridge reads the data from the target. The successful completion of the data phase formally establishes the target lock. In this example, the bridge was only transferring one data item, so the transaction is terminated during clock four (IRDY#, DEVSEL# and TRDY# are deasserted).

CLOCK 5. The bridge continues to assert LOCK# to indicate that LOCK# is now in use. The target samples LOCK# asserted and FRAME# deasserted on the rising-edge of clock five. This target is now locked and cannot be accessed by any other master. While the lock is in force, if it's a PCI-to-PCI bridge it will not accept any transaction requests from either side except from the master that locked it. The target remains locked until it samples LOCK# and FRAME# deasserted on a rising-edge of the clock.

The EISA bridge is the only device capable of establishing a lock on main memory and, in order to do this, the EISA bridge must be located on the PCI bus that is attached directly to the host/PCI bridge. This is because PCI-to-PCI bridges will not pass a lock upstream towards main memory.

At a minimum, the memory controller locks the 16 byte-aligned memory block that was addressed in the address phase. The main memory controller can be designed to lock anything from the paragraph (16 byte block) that contains the semaphore up to the entire memory target. The optimum would be to lock just the paragraph. Other masters that don't require the locking mechanism could then successfully access locations outside the bounds of the locked region while the lock is still in force. If the target of the locked transaction series is beyond a PCI-to-PCI bridge or an EISA bridge, the bridge is locked.

When a target (or a portion of it) has been locked, the target must only permit the master that established the lock to access the locked device (or region, if it's main memory). Any attempt by any other master to access the locked device or main memory region must result in a Retry to the master.

Figure 27-2: Establishing the Lock

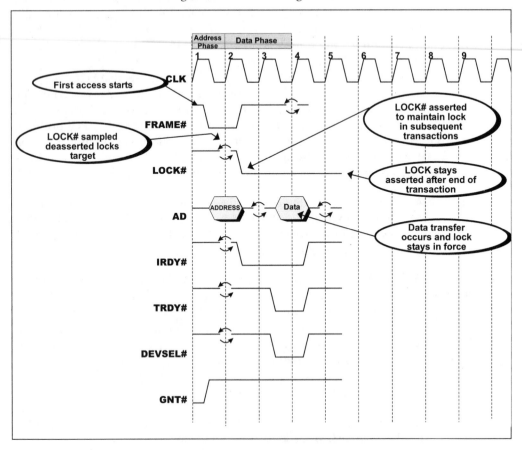

Locked Bridge Cannot Accept Accesses From Either Side

A locked bridge cannot accept any new transaction requests (exclusive or non-exclusive) from either side **except from the master that owns** the LOCK# signal **on** the **primary side** of the bridge.

Unlocked Targets May Be Accessed by any Master On Same PCI Bus

During the period of time that a target is locked, masters that don't require use of the locking signal (to perform a locked transaction series) can successfully acquire the bus and perform transfers with unlocked targets (including unlocked portions of main memory if the master is on the same PCI bus as the host/PCI bridge). A locked target refuses (Retries) access attempts within its locked area that are initiated by other masters, but permits access attempts by the master that locked it.

Access to Locked Target by Master Other than Owner: Retry

Figure 27-3 on page 694 illustrates an attempt by a master other than the one who locked it to access a locked target. The master performing this bus transaction is not performing a locked transaction series, so it is not required to sample LOCK# prior to assuming bus ownership. The illustration shows the LOCK# signal being held asserted by the master that locked the target.

CLOCK 1. The current master initiates the transfer attempt at the start of clock one by asserting FRAME# and driving the address and the command onto the AD and Command/Byte Enable buses, respectively. The LOCK# signal is still asserted by the master that read the semaphore from memory at an earlier point in time.

CLOCK 2. The target latches the address, command and the state of the LOCK# signal at the rising-edge of clock two and begins the address decode.

THE initiator deasserts FRAME# during clock two, indicating that the last (and only) data phase is in progress.

CLOCK 3. When the target decodes its address, it asserts DEVSEL# in clock three to claim the transaction.

IT has also determined that the master attempting to access it is not the one that locked it. The master that locked it would have demonstrated its control of the LOCK# signal by deasserting LOCK# during the address phase. The locked target must therefore reject the access by issuing a Retry to the current master. STOP# is asserted along with DEVSEL#, and TRDY# stays deasserted. This combination indicates that the initiator is to stop the transaction on the current data phase (STOP# asserted) with no data transferred (TRDY# deasserted) and that the initiator is to Retry the transaction again later (DEVSEL# asserted, indicating that it's not a Target Abort).

CLOCK 4. When the initiator samples STOP# and DEVSEL# asserted and TRDY# deasserted at the rising-edge of clock four, it terminates the transaction without a data transfer and will re-attempt the access later. For more information on retry, refer to "Retry" on page 189.

THE initiator then deasserts IRDY#, returning the bus to the idle state.

THE target deasserts STOP# and DEVSEL#.

Figure 27-3: Attempted Access to a Locked Target

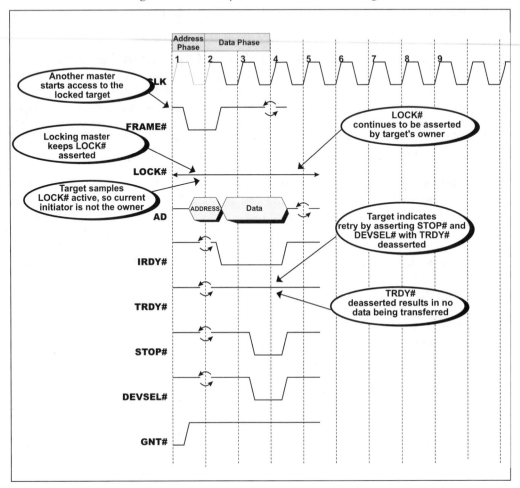

Continuation and/or End of Locked Transaction Series

Figure 27-4 on page 696 illustrates the continuation and/or the end of a locked transaction series. In this example, a bridge had accessed the target earlier (to perform a read) and locked it for its exclusive use (LOCK# was left asserted by the bridge when it ended the earlier access). When the locking bridge gains bus ownership again (GNT# asserted by the arbiter and the bus is idle), it starts the next access in the locked series.

CLOCK 1. At the start of the transaction (the rising-edge of clock one), the initiator asserts FRAME# and deasserts LOCK#. It deasserts LOCK# to reestablish its lock on the target and identify itself as the target's owner.

CLOCK 2. The target latches the address, command and the state of the LOCK# signal at the end of the address phase (on the rising-edge of clock two) and begins the address decode.

UPON decoding the address and asserting DEVSEL#, the target locks itself again (because LOCK# was sampled deasserted at the end of the address phase).

DURING clock two, the initiator reasserts LOCK# to continue the lock through the end of this transaction. If the initiator left LOCK# deasserted during the transaction and the target were to issue a Retry for some reason, the master has lost control of the target. In other words, after the master terminated the transaction (due to the Retry), the target would sample FRAME# and LOCK# deasserted, instructing the target to unlock itself.

CLOCK 3. The data is written into the memory semaphore (or is accepted into an intervening bridge's posted memory write buffer) at the rising-edge of clock three when TRDY# and IRDY# are both sampled active.

THE initiator and target release IRDY# and TRDY#, respectively.

IF the master must maintain the lock on the target for one or more additional accesses, it continues to assert LOCK# after the end of the transaction.

IF, on the other hand, the master has completed its locked series of accesses to the target, it releases LOCK# at the end of the current transaction. When the target samples FRAME# and LOCK# both deasserted (on clock four in the example), it clears its lock.

Figure 27-4: The Final Transaction of the Series and Release of Lock

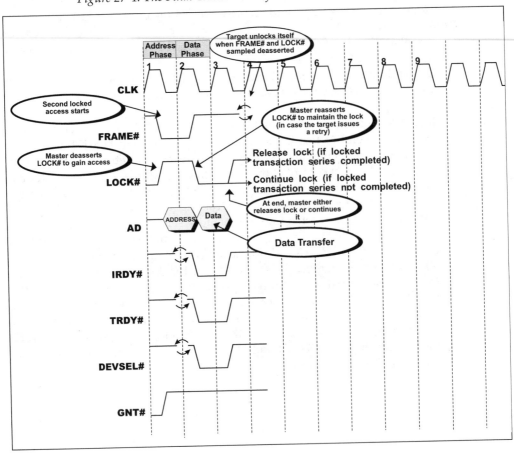

Use of LOCK# with 64-bit Addressing

Locking works the same with Dual-Address Command (DCA) transactions as those that use a single address phase. LOCK# is deasserted during the first address phase and asserted during the second.

Locking and Delayed Transactions

For additional information regarding locking and Delayed Transactions, refer to "Locking, Delayed Transactions and Posted Writes" on page 670.

Summary of Locking Rules

Implementation Rules for Masters

Any master that implements locking capability must adhere to the following rules:

RULE 1. The master may only access a single target for the duration of the lock. This rule exists to force masters to expeditiously return a locked resource to the available state.

RULE 2. The first transaction of a locked transactions series must be a memory read (to read the semaphore from memory).

RULE 3. Lock must be asserted during the clock immediately following the address phase and must be kept asserted after the transaction has concluded (in order to keep the target locked).

RULE 4. The LOCK# signal must be deasserted if the first data phase ends in a Retry. In this case, the master has not locked the target. Other masters can successfully access it.

RULE 5. LOCK# must be deasserted whenever a transaction is terminated by a target abort (in any data phase). This basically indicates that the target is broken or can never complete the access.

RULE 6. LOCK# must also be deasserted if the transaction is terminated by a Master Abort (no target has responded).

RULE 7. LOCK# must be deasserted for at least one idle cycle between consecutive locked transaction series.

Implementation Rules for Targets

PCI memory targets that support locking must adhere to the following rules:

RULE 1. The target of a transaction locks itself when LOCK# is sampled deasserted at the end of the address phase and is then asserted in the clock immediately following the address phase.

RULE 2. Once a target is locked, the target must remain locked until it samples both FRAME# and LOCK# deasserted regardless of how the transaction is terminated.

RULE 3. During the locked period, a bridge is not allowed to accept any new requests on either side (primary or secondary) unless the request is initiated by the owner of LOCK#.

28 CompactPCI and PMC

The Previous Chapter

The previous chapter provided a detailed description of the PCI locking mechanism that permits an EISA bridge to lock main memory or the host/PCI bridge to lock an EISA memory target.

This Chapter

This chapter describes the issues that differentiate CompactPCI from PCI. This includes mechanical, electrical and software-related issues. CompactPCI is presented as described in the 2.1 CompactPCI specification. PMC devices are also described.

Why CompactPCI?

The CompactPCI specification was developed by the PICMG (PCI Industrial Computer Manufacturer's Group) and defines a ruggedized version of PCI to be used in industrial and embedded applications. With regards to electrical, logical and software functionality, it is 100% compatible with the PCI standard. The cards are **rack mounted** and use standard Eurocard packaging. CompactPCI has the following features:

- Standard Eurocard dimensions (complies with the IEEE 1101.1 mechanical standard).
- HD (High-Density) 2mm pin-and-socket connectors (IEC approved and Bellcore qualified).
- Vertical card-orientation to ensure adequate cooling.
- Positive card retention mechanism.
- Optimized for maximum high shock and/or vibration environments.
- Front panel can implement front access IO connectors.
- User-defined IO pins defined on rear of the card.
- Standard chassis with multiple vendors.

- 100% compatible with standard PCI hardware and software components.
- Staged power pins to facilitate hot swap cards.
- Eight card slots per chassis (versus four in the typical PC platform).

CompactPCI Cards are PCI-Compatible

CompactPCI cards must comply with all design rules specified for 33MHz PCI by the PCI 2.1 specification. The CompactPCI specification defines additional requirements and/or limitations that pertain to CompactPCI implementations.

Basic PCI/CompactPCI Comparison

With respect to the PCI standard, CompactPCI exhibits the characteristics introduced in Table 28-1 on page 700.

Table 28-1: CompactPCI versus Standard PCI

Item	Description
Compatibility	From both software and hardware perspectives, CompactPCI is currently 100% compatible with the 2.1 PCI spec. It has not yet been updated to reflect the 2.2 PCI spec.
Passive backplane environment	No active logic.
Connector	Shielded, 2mm-pitch, 5-row connectors defined by IEC 917 and IEC 1076-4-101. This gas-tight, high-density, pin-and-socket connector is available from multiple vendors (e.g., AMP, Framatome, Burndy, and ERNI). It exhibits low inductance and controlled impedance, crucial for PCI signaling. The connector's controlled impedance minimizes unwanted signal reflections, enabling CompactPCI backplanes to implement up to eight connectors, rather than upper limit of four imposed in normal PCI. It incorporates an external metal shield for RFI/EMI shielding purposes. Staged power and ground pins are included to facilitate hot swap implementations in the future.

Table 28-1: CompactPCI versus Standard PCI (Continued)

Item	Description
Number of cards	One system card and up to seven peripheral cards.
Card type	Two Eurocard form factors: small (3U); and large (6U).
User-defined IO signal pins	Permits passage of user-defined IO signals to/from the back plane through edge-connectors.
Hot swap capable	In the future.
Signal set is superset of standard PCI	Some signals added for non-PCI functions.
Responsible SIG	PICMG (PCI Industrial Computer Manufacturer's Group).
Modularity	Ruggedized backplane, rack-mount environment.
Signal termination	For increased signal integrity and more slots than standard PCI.
Legacy IDE support	Two edge-triggered interrupt pins defined to support primary and secondary legacy IDE controllers.

Basic Definitions

Standard PCI Environment

In a standard PCI implementation, the following elements are typically all embedded on the system board:

- the host processor(s).
- main memory.
- the host/PCI bridge.
- PCI bus arbiter.
- system interrupt controller.
- embedded PCI devices (e.g., SCSI controller, Ethernet controller, video adapter).
- PCI card-edge connectors.
- the PCI/ISA bridge.

The end-user adds functionality to the system by installing additional PCI adapter cards into the card-edge connectors. These cards can be strictly targets, or may have both target and bus master capability. In order to upgrade base system characteristics such as the host processor type or the host/PCI bridge, the end-user is forced to swap out the system board. This is a major cost item. In addition, the user must also remove the PCI adapter cards from the old system board and install them in the new one.

CompactPCI is implemented in a more modular fashion, consisting of a passive-backplane with a system board slot and up to seven peripheral slots to install PCI adapter cards. The sections that follow describe the backplane, system card and peripheral cards.

Passive Backplane

A typical passive backplane is pictured in Figure 28-1 on page 704 and contains no active logic. It provides the elements listed in Table 28-2 on page 702.

Table 28-2: Passive Backplane Elements

Element	Description
System slot	One system slot to accept a system card. Implemented with between one and five male connectors numbered P1-through-P5.
Peripheral slots	Up to seven peripheral slots to accept cards that act strictly as targets or as both a target and bus master. Implemented with between one and five male connectors numbered P1-through-P5.
Staged pins	Staged pins to facilitate hot swap of CompactPCI cards.
Connector keying	Appropriate connector keying for either a 5Vdc or 3.3Vdc signaling environment.
32-bit PCI bus	The 32-bit PCI bus interconnects the system slot and peripheral slots.
PCI clock distribution	PCI clock distribution from the system slot to the peripheral slots.

Table 28-2: Passive Backplane Elements (Continued)

Element	Description
Interrupt signals	Interrupt trace distribution to the system slot from the peripheral slots.
REQ#/GNT# signal pairs	REQ#/GNT# signal pairs between the arbiter on the system card and the peripheral slots.
Rear-panel IO connectors	Optionally, through-the-backplane rear-panel IO connectors that route non-PCI signals/buses through the backplane to rear-panel IO connectors.
Rear-panel IO transition boards	Rear-panel IO transition boards may be installed in a rear rack and connected to the non-PCI signals.
Modular power supply connector	Optionally, a modular power supply connector for rack installation of a modular power supply.
64-bit PCI extension signals	Optionally, the 64-bit PCI extension signals (AD[63:32], C/BE[7:4]#, PAR64).
Geographical addressing pins	In a 64-bit implementation, a set of pins that a 64-bit card (and, optionally, a 32-bit card) may interrogate to determine which physical slot it is installed in.

Figure 28-1: Typical CompactPCI Backplane

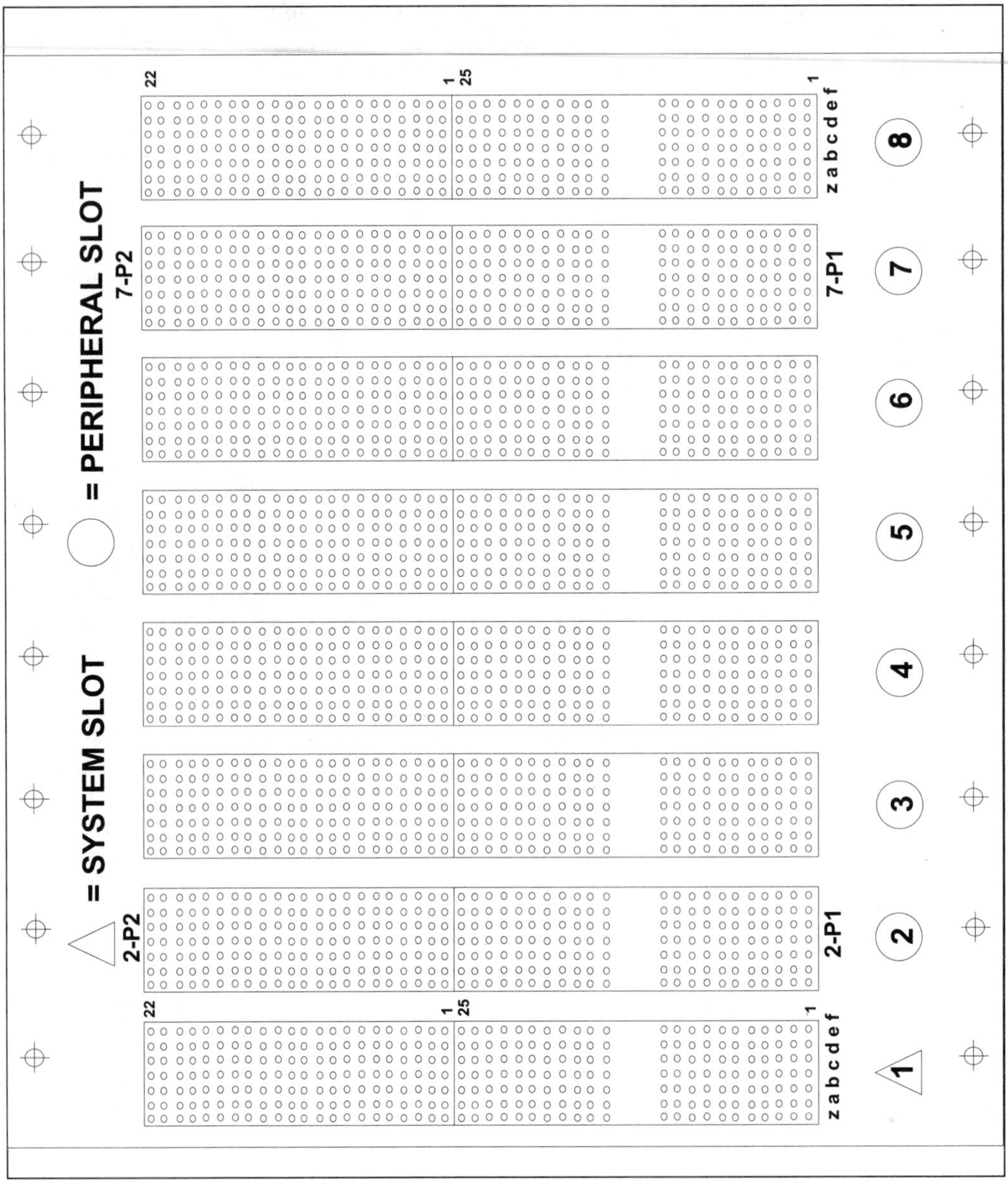

Compatibility Glyphs

As illustrated in Figure 28-1 on page 704, a symbol (referred to as a compatibility glyph) must be displayed directly beneath each of the backplane connectors. The Δ symbol indicates the system card connector, while the O indicates a peripheral card connector. The number within the glyph indicates the physical number of the connector on the backplane. A definition of physical versus logical slot numbering can be found in "Physical Slot Numbering" on page 705.

Definition of a Bus Segment

A CompactPCI backplane may implement one or more CompactPCI bus segments. Each bus segment represents a separate PCI bus and consists of:

- One system slot.
- One or more (up to seven) peripheral slots.

Physical Slot Numbering

The physical slot number of a card slot identifies the position of the slot on the backplane. Backplane slots are numbered from one through N (where N is the number of the last slot on the backplane), with physical slot one located in the top left corner of the backplane (as viewed from the front side of the backplane). As an example, on a backplane that implements 16 slots, starting in the top left corner the slots would be physically numbered as slots 1-through-16. The physical number of each slot must be displayed within its respective compatibility glyph (see Figure 28-1 on page 704).

Logical Slot Numbering

The physical slot number identifies the physical position of the slot on the overall backplane, whereas the logical slot number identifies the slot's location within a specific bus segment (i.e., a specific PCI bus). In addition, it identifies a specific connector within that slot position. The slot label uses the format *x-Pn*, where *x* represents the slot position on a PCI bus (one-through-eight) and *Pn* represents the connector designation (each slot consists of one or more connectors labeled as P1 through P5). As an example, in Figure 28-1 on page 704, connector P1 in logical slot seven is labeled as "7-P1."

As another example, on a backplane that implements two CompactPCI bus segments of eight slots each, the slots are physically numbered as 1-through-16. However, connector P2 on the second slot within the last eight physical slots is numbered as:

- physical slot number 10 (the connector's **P** number is not relevant to the physical slot number).
- logical slot number 2-P2.

Connector Basics

A CompactPCI card implements one or more female connectors, numbered J1-through-J5, that are used to interface with the backplane connectors. There are two sizes of CompactPCI cards, referred to as 3U and 6U cards, with the 3U card being the smaller of the two. Two connectors, J1 and J2, can be placed on a 3U card, while up to five connectors, J1-through-J5, can be placed on a 6U card. Correspondingly, each backplane slot position implements between one and five male connectors, numbered P1-through-P5. Table 28-3 on page 706 describes the basic usage of the five possible connectors.

Each connector row consists of seven pins, labelled A-through-F, plus row Z. Rows Z and F are used as ground pins to be attached to connector shields, while rows A-through-E are the signal pins.

Table 28-3: Basic Connector Usage

Card Connector	Corresponding Backplane Connector	Usage
J1	P1	Contains all of the **32-bit PCI signals**. Required on all backplane slots as well as on all cards. J1/P1 implements connector keying.

Table 28-3: Basic Connector Usage (Continued)

Card Connector	Corresponding Backplane Connector	Usage
J2	P2	1. **On a system card**, J2 contains the **PCI clock signals and the REQ#/GNT# signal pairs** for each peripheral card slot. J2 is therefore required on the system card and the backplane system slot must implement P2. 2. It is **required** that system and peripheral cards that implement the **64-bit** extension must implement J2. 3. **Backplanes that support** the **64-bit** extension must implement P2 (contains 64-bit extension and geographical addressing pins). 4. **32-bit** CompactPCI **cards that support rear-panel IO may implement J2** (contains the rear-panel IO signal pins). Optionally, rear-panel IO may be routed through J3, J4, J5 or any combination thereof (on a 6U card). 5. **32-bit backplanes that support rear-panel IO may implement P2** (contains rear-panel IO pins and may optionally also contain geographical addressing pins).
J3-J5	P3-P5	May be used on 6U cards that support rear-panel IO. May be used on 6U backplanes that support rear-panel IO.

A 32-bit card may implement rear-panel IO signals on any combination of J2-through-J5. A 64-bit card may implement rear-panel IO signals on any combination of J3-through-J5 (on a 6U card).

Introduction to Front and Rear-Panel IO

Front-Panel IO

A CompactPCI system consists of a rack with a series of cards installed. The cards interface with the CompactPCI backplane bus via connector J1 (and J2 if a 64-bit card). In addition, each card may interface to external devices via connectors located on its front panel.

Rear-Panel IO

Optionally, the card designer may use some of a card's rear connectors to route non-PCI signals (e.g., the ISA bus) to the backplane. These are referred to as rear-panel IO signals.

- A 32-bit CompactPCI card may implement rear-panel IO via the rear-panel IO pins on connector J2 (and possibly connectors J3-through-J5 if it's a 6U card).
- A 64-bit CompactPCI card may implement rear-panel IO via the rear-panel IO pins on connectors J3-through-J5 (if it's a 6U card).

The backplane typically routes the rear-panel IO signals supplied via any combination of a slot's P2-through-P5 directly through the backplane to a matching set of connectors on the rear-side of the backplane board. In other words, the backplane interfaces to a card rack on both its front and rear sides. Rear-panel IO transition cards may be installed in the rear card cage slots to interface with the rear-panel IO signals to/from the corresponding CompactPCI cards.

Introduction to CompactPCI Cards

Figure 28-2 on page 709 illustrates a typical CompactPCI card. The card illustrated is a 3U (i.e., small form factor) card implementing both J1 and J2 (refer to "Connector Basics" on page 706), indicating that it is one of the following:

- A system card (either 32-bit or 64-bit). All system cards must implement J2 to carry the PCI clock and bus request/bus grant signal pairs. If it is a 32-bit system card, it may also route rear-panel IO signals to the backplane via J2.
- A 32-bit peripheral card with rear-panel IO implemented via J2.
- A 64-bit peripheral card that may also implement rear-panel IO via J2.

Figure 28-2: Example CompactPCI Card

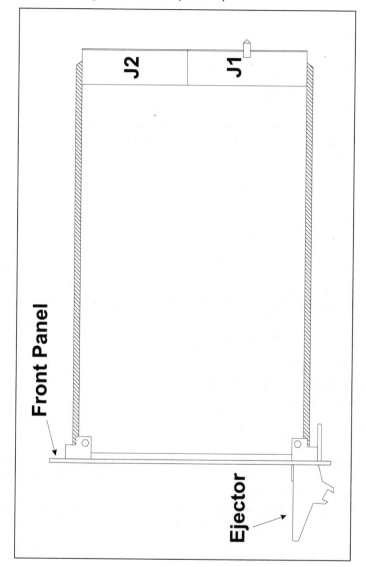

System Card

General

As mentioned earlier, the system card contains:

- **Host processor(s)** and associated support logic.
- **Main memory.** Main memory could reside on a peripheral card, but the host/PCI bridge must then be architected to permit the processor's caches to cache from PCI memory. This complicates system design and negatively affects performance (due to delays for snooping). The authors are not aware of any chipsets that currently support caching from PCI memory.
- **Host/PCI bridge.** This is the bridge between the host processor bus and the backplane's PCI bus.
- **PCI bus arbiter** for use by bus master peripheral cards installed in other slots on the bus segment.
- **IDSEL decoder** necessary for device selection during type 0 configuration transactions initiated by the host processor and targeting peripheral cards residing on the same bus segment as the system card.
- **System interrupt controller** interfaced to the PCI interrupt request signals (INTA#-through-INTD#). In addition, the system board may also interface to the **legacy IDE interrupt request signals**, INTP and INTS, treating them as positive edge-triggered interrupt request lines (rather than active-low, level-sensitive request signals as is the case with the PCI interrupt request signals INTA#-through-INTB#).
- **PCI clock generator.**
- Reset logic responsible for issuing reset to all devices that reside on the CompactPCI bus segment.

Although it isn't a rule, the CompactPCI specification recommends that the system slot be physically placed on either end of the bus segment (rather than in another position in the segment). All testing and verification performed by the PICMG assumes this configuration. Other configurations are permitted but must be verified by testing to validate that the electrical specification is met.

The slot rail for the system slot must be red in color, providing a vivid visual cue to the user that it is the system slot.

32-bit System Card

The system card may be implemented as either a 32-bit or 64-bit PCI implementation. In either case, both the J1 and J2 connectors must be implemented (because J1 carries the 32-bit PCI signals while J2 carries the 64-bit extension signals as well as the PCI clock and bus request/bus grant signals). A 32-bit system card must implement connectors J1 and J2, but may or may not implement rear-panel IO signals. If it does, the rear-panel IO signals may be implemented on any combination of J2-through-J5.

64-bit System Card

As is the case with a 32-bit system card, the 64-bit system card must implement connectors J1 and J2. If it also implements any rear-panel IO signals, they may be implemented on any combination of J3-through-J5 (if it's a 6U card).

ISA Bus Bridge

The system card may or may not contain a PCI/ISA bridge. If it does, the ISA bus signals would be routed to the backplane via the rear-panel IO pins on connectors J2, J3, J4 or J5, or could be routed to a front-panel connector. Alternatively, a PCI-to-ISA bridge can be located on a peripheral card with the ISA bus signals routed to the front panel or via back-panel IO pins.

Peripheral Cards

Peripheral cards can only be installed in peripheral card slots. A peripheral card may act a simple PCI target or may also have PCI bus master capability.

32-bit Peripheral Cards

A 32-bit peripheral card with no rear-panel IO only implements connector J1 (the 32-bit portion of the PCI bus), while one that uses rear-panel IO implements J1 plus any combination of J2-through-J5 to carry the rear-panel IO signals.

64-bit Peripheral Card

A 64-bit peripheral card implements connectors J1 (the 32-bit portion of the PCI bus) and J2 (which carries the 64-bit PCI extension), while one that uses rear-panel IO implements J1 and J2 plus any combination of J3-through-J5 (if it's a 6U card) to carry the rear-panel IO signals.

Design Rules

Connectors

General

The connectors used on the cards and backplane are shielded, 2mm-pitch, 5-row connectors defined by IEC 917 and IEC 1076-4-101. This gas-tight, high-density, pin-and-socket connector is available from multiple vendors (e.g., AMP, Framatome, Burndy, and ERNI). It exhibits low inductance and controlled impedance, crucial for PCI signaling. The connector's controlled impedance minimizes unwanted signal reflections, enabling CompactPCI backplanes to implement up to eight connectors, rather than the upper limit of four imposed in standard PCI. It incorporates an external metal shield for RFI/EMI shielding purposes. Staged power and ground pins are included to facilitate hot swap implementations (refer to "Hot Swap Capability" on page 751).

CompactPCI cards implement female connectors on the rear. When the card is installed in the backplane, they mate with the slot's male connectors located on the backplane.

Pin Numbering (IEC 1076 versus CompactPCI)

To permit connectors to start at the bottom of the card and "grow" upward from J1/P1 through J5/P5, CompactPCI connector pin numbering is intentionally different than the connector manufacturer's numbering.

Each IEC 1076-4-101 connector consists of 25 pin rows. The 3U CompactPCI card has 100mm of space available for the placement of the J1 and J2 connectors. J1 is implemented via a full 25 row connector. When a 3U card requires J2 as well, however, the J2 connector must be cut down in size by three rows (to 22 rows) to physically fit on the card. Rather than start the numbering of J2 with row 4 (because the first three pin rows were removed), the decision was made to number connector pins from bottom-to-top, the reverse order from that specified in IEC 1076. Table 28-4 on page 713 illustrates the difference between the CompactPCI and IEC 1076 pin numbering schemes.

Table 28-4: CompactPCI Connector Pin Numbering versus IEC 1076 Pin Numbering

Connector	CompactPCI Pin Numbering	IEC 1076 Pin Numbering
J1/P1 and J4/P4	Bottom row is 1. Rows 12-14 keying area (in J1/P1, not in J4/P4). Row 25 is at top.	Bottom row is 25. Rows 12-14 are keying area. Row 1 is at top.
J2/P2 and J5/P5	Bottom row is 1. Row 22 is at top.	Bottom row is 22. Row 1 is at top.
J3/P3	Bottom row is 1. Top row is 19.	Bottom row is 19. Top row is 1.

Connector Keying

Card keying is implemented on the J1 connector (see "32-bit PCI Pinout (J1/P1)" on page 714) to ensure that the card cannot be installed 180 degrees out. Also refer to "5V and 3.3V Cards" on page 713 and "Universal Cards" on page 714.

5V and 3.3V Cards

As with standard PCI, the signaling environment on the backplane may be either 5V or 3.3V. The signaling environment is defined by the voltage used by the host/PCI bridge on the system card. In order to ensure correct operation, only cards with 5V PCI buffer/drivers must be installed into a backplane that uses a 5V signaling environment. Conversely, only cards with 3.3V PCI buffer/drivers must be installed into a backplane that uses a 3.3V signaling environment.

It is the responsibility of the backplane designer to install a color-coded keying plug into the P1 connector's keying area (rows 12-14). A Cadmium Yellow plug must be used in a 3.3V backplane's P1 connector keying area, while a Brilliant Blue plug must be used in a 5V backplane's P1 connector keying area.

It is the responsibility of the system card/peripheral card designer to provide the appropriate keying on the card. If the card implements strictly 3.3V buffer drivers, then the Cadmium Yellow keying plug must be used. If the card implements strictly 5V buffer drivers, then the Brilliant Blue keying plug must be used.

Universal Cards

There is no such thing as a universal backplane. By definition, the backplane is keyed as either a 3.3V or a 5V signaling environment. However, a card's buffer/ drivers may be implemented so that they can operate at either 5V or 3.3V. If this is the case, a color-coded keying plug must not be used on the card. This permits the card to be installed into either a 3.3V or 5V backplane. The card's buffer/drivers utilize the power supply voltage supplied by the backplane on the connector's V(IO) pins (see "32-bit PCI Pinout (J1/P1)" on page 714 and "64-bit PCI Pinout (J2/P2)" on page 716).

32-bit PCI Pinout (J1/P1)

Table 28-5 on page 715 defines the pinout for connector J1/P1. The following notes refer to the notations within the table:

NOTE 1. Not used on system or peripheral cards

NOTE 2. Observation: Some manufacturers of top connector shields use every other ground pin while others use every ground pin. Note that some shield connections mate at approximately the same time as medium length signal pins.

NOTE 3. The V(IO) pins are either 3.3V or 5V (depending on backplane implementation). See "5V and 3.3V Cards" on page 713 and "Universal Cards" on page 714.

NOTE 4. M66EN is defined as ground for 33MHz PCI backplane implementations. On 66MHz systems, M66EN is bussed to all slots.

NOTE 5. Originally a long pin used for early hot swap capable cards. See "Hot Swap Capability" on page 751.

NOTE 6. Originally a long pin used as a card select for hot swap implementations. See "Hot Swap Capability" on page 751.

NOTE 7. These pins accommodate those specified as reserved pins by the PCI specification. Although the PCI specification defines these pins as no-connects, bus segments shall bus these signals to all connectors.

Table 28-5: Connector J1/P1 Pinout

Pin	Z[1]	A	B	C	D	E	F[2]
25	GND	5V	REQ64#	ENUM#	3.3V	5V	GND
24	GND	AD[1]	5V	V(IO)[3]	AD[0]	ACK64#	GND
23	GND	3.3V	AD[4]	AD[3]	5V	AD[2]	GND
22	GND	AD[7]	GND	3.3V	AD[6]	AD[5]	GND
21	GND	3.3V	AD[9]	AD[8]	M66EN[4]	C/BE[0]#	GND
20	GND	AD[12]	GND	V(IO)[3]	AD[11]	AD[10]	GND
19	GND	3.3V	AD[15]	AD[14]	GND	AD[13]	GND
18	GND	SERR#	GND	3.3V	PAR	C/BE[1]#	GND
17	GND	3.3V	SDONE	SBO#	GND	PERR#	GND
16	GND	DEVSEL#	GND	V(IO)[3,5]	STOP#	LOCK#	GND
15	GND	3.3V	FRAME#	IRDY#	GND[6]	TRDY#	GND
14-12	Keying Area						
11	GND	AD[18]	AD[17]	AD[16]	GND	C/BE[2]#	GND
10	GND	AD[21]	GND	3.3V	AD[20]	AD[19]	GND
9	GND	C/BE[3]#	IDSEL	AD[23]	GND	AD[22]	GND
8	GND	AD[26]	GND	V(IO)	AD[25]	AD[24]	GND
7	GND	AD[30]	AD[29]	AD[28]	GND	AD[27]	GND
6	GND	REQ#	GND	3.3V	CLK	AD[31]	GND
5	GND	BRSVP1A5[7]	BRSVP1B5[7]	RST#	GND	GNT#	GND
4	GND	BRSVP1A4[7]	GND	V(IO)	INTP	INTS	GND
3	GND	INTA#	INTB#	INTC#	5V	INTD#	GND
2	GND	TCK	5V	TMS	TDO	TDI	GND
1	GND	5V	-12V	TRST#	+12V	5V	GND

64-bit PCI Pinout (J2/P2)

J2/P2 must be implemented under the following circumstances:

- 64-bit extension implemented.
- System card slot and system card must implement J2/P2 because the PCI arbitration signals (bus request and grant) and the PCI clock signals are implemented on J2/P2.
- A 32-bit slot that implements rear-panel IO on J2 (see "Rear-Panel IO Pinouts" on page 718).

Table 28-6 on page 717 defines the pinout for connector J2/P2. The following notes refer to the notations within the table:

NOTE 1. Not used on system or peripheral cards

NOTE 2. Observation: Some manufacturers of top connector shields use every other ground pin while others use every ground pin. Note that some shield connections mate at approximately the same time as medium length signal pins.

NOTE 3. The V(IO) pins are either 3.3V or 5V (depending on backplane implementation). See "5V and 3.3V Cards" on page 713 and "Universal Cards" on page 714.

NOTE 4. These pins accommodate those specified as reserved pins by the PCI specification. Although the PCI specification defines these pins as no-connects, bus segments shall bus these signals to all connectors.

NOTE 5. GA[4:0] shall be used for geographic addressing on the backplane. Each backplane connector in a CompactPCI system has a unique encoding. For more information, see "Geographical Addressing" on page 745.

NOTE 6. The shaded pins in the table are implemented only on the system slot.

NOTE 7. Note that backplane clock routing in the CompactPCI 2.1 specification only supports clocks CLK[4:0]. CLK[6:5] provided by a system card are left unconnected on the backplane.

NOTE 8. Boards designed to CompactPCI specification version 1.0 are not required to connect these grounds and may claim compatibility.

NOTE 9. System cards shall provide a mechanism to connect the REQ#/GNT# signal pairs from any of the seven peripheral slots to the arbiter.

NOTE 10. Connector P2C2 (SYSEN#) is grounded at the system slot only. Remaining slots must leave it unconnected. Cards that will only operate in the system slot must ground this pin, while cards that can operate the system or a peripheral slot must provide a local pull-up to V(IO).

Table 28-6: Connector J2/P2 64-bit PCI Pinout (also used for 32-bit System Card)

Pin	Z[1]	A	B	C	D	E	F[2]
22	GND	GA4[5]	GA3[5]	GA2[5]	GA1[5]	GA0[5]	GND
21	GND	CLK6[6,7]	GND[6,7]	RSV	RSV	RSV	GND
20	GND	CLK5[6,7]	GND[6,7]	RSV	GND[8]	RSV	GND
19	GND	GND[6,7]	GND[6,7]	RSV	RSV	RSV	GND
18	GND	BRSVP2A18[4]	BRSVP2B18[4]	BRSVP2C18[4]	GND[8]	BRSVP2E18	GND
17	GND	BRSVP2A17[4]	GND[8]	PRST#[6]	REQ6#[6,9]	GNT6#[6,9]	GND
16	GND	BRSVP2A16[4]	BRSVP2B16[4]	DEG#[6]	GND[8]	BRSVP2E16	GND
15	GND	BRSVP2A15[4]	GND[8]	FAL#[6]	REQ5#[6,9]	GNT5#[6,9]	GND
14	GND	AD[35]	AD[34]	AD[33]	GND	AD[32]	GND
13	GND	AD[38]	GND	V(IO)[3]	AD[37]	AD[36]	GND
12	GND	AD[42]	AD[41]	AD[40]	GND	AD[39]	GND
11	GND	AD[45]	GND	V(IO)[3]	AD[44]	AD[43]	GND
10	GND	AD[49]	AD[48]	AD[47]	GND	AD[46]	GND
9	GND	AD[52]	GND	V(IO)[3]	AD[51]	AD[50]	GND
8	GND	AD[56]	AD[55]	AD[54]	GND	AD[53]	GND
7	GND	AD[59]	GND	V(IO)[3]	AD[58]	AD[57]	GND
6	GND	AD[63]	AD[62]	AD[61]	GND	AD[60]	GND
5	GND	C/BE[5]#	GND	V(IO)[3]	C/BE[4]#	PAR64	GND
4	GND	V(IO)[3]	BRSVPP2B4	C/BE[7]#	GND	C/BE[6]#	GND
3	GND	CLK4[6]	GND[6]	GNT3#[6]	REQ4#[6]	GNT4#[6]	GND
2	GND	CLK2[6]	CLK3[6]	SYSEN#[6,10]	GNT2#[6]	REQ3#[6]	GND
1	GND	CLK1[6]	GND[6]	REQ1#[6]	GNT1#[6]	REQ2#[6]	GND

Rear-Panel IO Pinouts

When J2/P2 is used to route rear-panel IO signals, it is defined as illustrated in Table 28-7 on page 718. This configuration is only used for peripheral cards that implement rear-panel IO on J2/P2. System cards must define J2/P2 as illustrated in Table 28-6 on page 717. The following notes refer to the notations within the table:

NOTE 1. Not used on system or peripheral cards.

NOTE 2. Observation: Some manufacturers of top connector shields use every other ground pin while others use every ground pin. Note that some shield connections mate at approximately the same time as medium length signal pins.

NOTE 3. GA[4:0] may be used for geographic addressing or rear-panel IO on the backplane. If geographic addressing is used, each backplane slot in a CompactPCI system has a unique encoding. For more information, see "Geographical Addressing" on page 745.

Table 28-7: Connector J2/P2 Rear-Panel IO Pinout (note: BP(IO) = back-panel IO)

Pin	Z[1]	A	B	C	D	E	F[2]
22	GND	GA4[3]	GA3[3]	GA2[3]	GA1[3]	GA0[3]	GND
21	GND	BP(IO)	BP(IO)	BP(IO)	BP(IO)	BP(IO)	GND
20	GND	BP(IO)	BP(IO)	BP(IO)	BP(IO)	BP(IO)	GND
19	GND	BP(IO)	BP(IO)	BP(IO)	BP(IO)	BP(IO)	GND
18	GND	BP(IO)	BP(IO)	BP(IO)	BP(IO)	BP(IO)	GND
17	GND	BP(IO)	BP(IO)	BP(IO)	BP(IO)	BP(IO)	GND
16	GND	BP(IO)	BP(IO)	BP(IO)	BP(IO)	BP(IO)	GND
15	GND	BP(IO)	BP(IO)	BP(IO)	BP(IO)	BP(IO)	GND
14	GND	BP(IO)	BP(IO)	BP(IO)	BP(IO)	BP(IO)	GND
13	GND	BP(IO)	BP(IO)	BP(IO)	BP(IO)	BP(IO)	GND
12	GND	BP(IO)	BP(IO)	BP(IO)	BP(IO)	BP(IO)	GND
11	GND	BP(IO)	BP(IO)	BP(IO)	BP(IO)	BP(IO)	GND
10	GND	BP(IO)	BP(IO)	BP(IO)	BP(IO)	BP(IO)	GND

Table 28-7: Connector J2/P2 Rear-Panel IO Pinout (note: BP(IO) = back-panel IO) (Continued)

Pin	Z[1]	A	B	C	D	E	F[2]
9	GND	BP(IO)	BP(IO)	BP(IO)	BP(IO)	BP(IO)	GND
8	GND	BP(IO)	BP(IO)	BP(IO)	BP(IO)	BP(IO)	GND
7	GND	BP(IO)	BP(IO)	BP(IO)	BP(IO)	BP(IO)	GND
6	GND	BP(IO)	BP(IO)	BP(IO)	BP(IO)	BP(IO)	GND
5	GND	BP(IO)	BP(IO)	BP(IO)	BP(IO)	BP(IO)	GND
4	GND	BP(IO)	BP(IO)	BP(IO)	BP(IO)	BP(IO)	GND
3	GND	BP(IO)	BP(IO)	BP(IO)	BP(IO)	BP(IO)	GND
2	GND	BP(IO)	BP(IO)	BP(IO)	BP(IO)	BP(IO)	GND
1	GND	BP(IO)	BP(IO)	BP(IO)	BP(IO)	BP(IO)	GND

System and Peripheral Card Design Rules

Card Form Factors

General. CompactPCI cards come in two form factors consistent with the Eurocard industry standard:

- The 3U card measures 100mm by 160mm (see Figure 28-3 on page 720).
- The 6U card measures 233.35mm by 160mm (see Figure 28-4 on page 722).

3U Cards. 3U cards have the following characteristics:

- 100mm by 160 mm by 1.6mm thick
- 2mm connector (IEC-1076-4-101)
- 32-bit PCI implemented on J1
- J2 may be used for the 64-bit extension, rear-panel IO or system slot functions (PCI clock signals and bus request/grant signals).
- Row F is attached to the backplane's ground plane and is routed to the connector shield on the part of the connector away from the card surface.
- Row Z (attached to the backplane's ground plane and normally intended for attachment to the connector's lower shield) isn't present on connectors J1 and J2 on system or peripheral cards.

Figure 28-3: 3U Card Form Factor

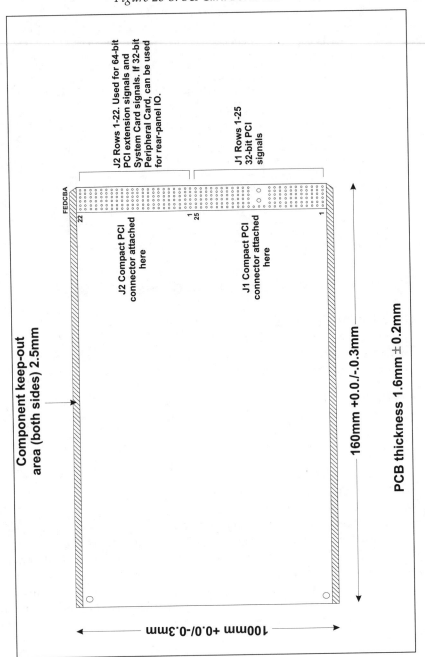

6U Cards. 6U cards have the following characteristics:

- 233.35mm by 160mm.
- 1.6mm thick.
- 32-bit PCI implemented on J1.
- May also implement connectors J2-through-J5.
- J2 may be used for the 64-bit extension, rear-panel IO or system slot functions (PCI clock signals and bus request/grant signals).
- J3-through-J5 may be used for rear-panel IO.
- Row F is attached to the backplane's ground plane and is routed to the connector shield on the part of the connector away from the card surface (i.e., the top side of the connector).
- Row Z (attached to the backplane's ground plane and normally intended for attachment to the connector's lower shield) isn't present on connectors J1 and J2 on system or peripheral cards.

Figure 28-4: 6U Card Form Factor

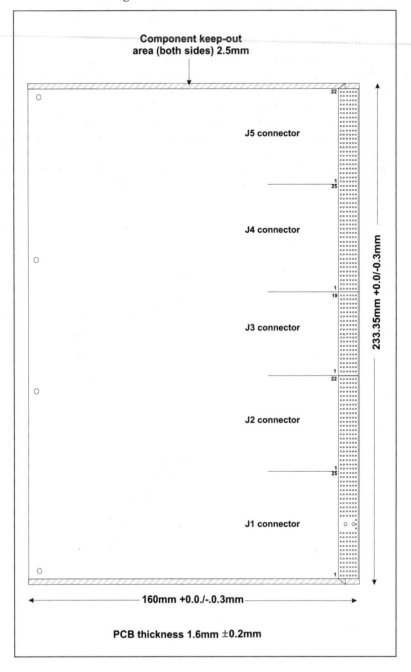

Non-PCI Signals

The signals listed in Table 28-8 on page 723 exist in CompactPCI, but not in PCI. In other words, the CompactPCI signal set is a superset of the PCI signal set.

Table 28-8: CompactPCI Superset Signals

Signal(s)	Description
PRST#	**Push Button reset**. Supplied from the backplane, this signal may be used to reset the system card, which may then in turn reset the bus segment by asserting the PCI reset signal, RST#. The system card must provide a pull-up resistor on PRST# and is responsible for debouncing the signal.
DEG#	Power supply **derating** signal. DEG# may be used as a power supply output. When asserted, it indicates that the power supply is beginning to derate its power output. Backplanes that implement a modular power supply connector shall connect DEG# to the backplane's DEG# signal line.
FAL#	Power supply **fail** signal. FAL# may be used as a power supply output. When asserted, it indicates that the supply has failed. Backplanes that implement a modular power supply connector shall connect FAL# to the backplane's FAL# signal line.
SYSEN#	**System slot enable**. A card may only have system card functionality, or may be capable of functioning as a peripheral card when installed in a non-system slot. When a card that can operate in either type of slot is installed in a slot, it uses this input from the backplane to enable (when asserted) or disable (when deasserted) its system slot functionality. It is the backplane designer's responsibility to ground the SYSEN# signal at the system slot position and to leave it disconnected at the peripheral slot SYSEN# pins. The card designer must include a pull-up on SYSEN# to keep SYSEN# deasserted when the card is installed in a peripheral slot.

Table 28-8: CompactPCI Superset Signals (Continued)

Signal(s)	Description
ENUM#	System **enumeration**. On the backplane, this optional open-drain signal is bussed to the ENUM# pin on P1 of all slot positions on the bus segment. It acts as an output from all peripheral slots and as an input to the system card. ENUM# must be asserted by a hot swap-capable card immediately after insertion and during removal. ENUM# is terminated with a pull-up resistor on the system card. When asserted by a peripheral card, the system card interrupts the processor, causing it to execute an interrupt service routine that enumerates the currently-installed peripheral cards to determine whether a card has been installed or removed. If a card has been removed, the resources (e.g., memory range, IO range, interrupt line, etc.) that were previously allocated to it by the configuration software are deallocated and made available as free resources. If a card has been added, the configuration Header registers for each PCI function on the card are interrogated to determine their resource requirements. The configuration software then allocates resources to each PCI function on the card and enables the devices for normal operation.
GA[4:0]	**Geographical addressing**. Refer to "Geographical Addressing" on page 745.
INTP and INTS	Primary and secondary legacy IDE interrupt request lines. Refer to "Backplane Routing of Legacy IDE Interrupt Request Lines" on page 744.

System Card Implementation of IDSELs

Refer to "IDSEL Routing" on page 741.

Resistors Required on a Card

Series Resistors Required at the Connector Pin. The signals listed in Table 28-9 on page 725 shall be series-terminated on the CompactPCI card at the connector interface with a $10\Omega \pm 5\%$ series-terminating resistor. If used, the optional signals indicated in Table 28-10 on page 725 must also include a termination resistor on the card at the connector. The stub termination resistor minimizes the effect of the stub on each card to the CompactPCI backplane.

The resistor shall be placed within 15.2mm (0.6 inches) of the signal's connector pin. This length shall be included in the overall permissible stub length specified in "Peripheral Card Signal Stub Lengths" on page 727.

Table 28-9: Series-Terminating Resistors Required (at the Connector) on Each Card

Signal(s)	Description
AD[31:0]	Lower 32 bits of the address/data bus.
C/BE[3:0]#	Lower four bits of the command/byte enable bus.
PAR	Even parity bit for AD[31:0] and C/BE[3:0]#.
FRAME#	Frame signal.
IRDY#	Initiator Ready.
TRDY#	Target Ready.
STOP#	Stop.
LOCK#	Lock.
IDSEL	Initialization Device Select.
DEVSEL#	Device Select.
PERR#	Parity Error.
SERR#	System Error.
RST#	Reset.

Table 28-10: Series-Terminating Resistors Required on Card only if Signal Used

Signal(s)	Description
INTA#, INTB#, INTC#, INTD#	PCI interrupt request lines.
SBO#	Snoop BackOff.
SDONE	Snoop Done.
AD[63:32]	Upper 32-bits of the address/data bus.
C/BE#[7:4]	Upper four bits of the command/byte enable bus.

Table 28-10: Series-Terminating Resistors Required on Card only if Signal Used (Continued)

Signal(s)	Description
REQ64#	Initiator request for a 64-bit transfer.
ACK64#	Target's indication that it supports 64-bit transfers (issued in response to detection of REQ64# asserted by the initiator).
PAR64	Even parity bit for AD[63:32] and C/BE[7:4]#.

Resistor Required at Peripheral Card's REQ# Driver Pin. Peripheral cards that use REQ# (i.e., bus master cards) should provide a series-terminating resistor at the driver pin (not a stub termination resistor at the connector).

Resistor Required at Each System Card Clock Driver Pin. On the system card, a series-terminating resistor (value determined by the output characteristics of the clock buffer) is required at the driver for the CLK signal provided to each slot.

Resistor Required at System Card's GNT# Driver Pin. Each system card's GNT# output must be series-terminated at the driver.

Placement of Pull-Ups on System Card. Some signals require pull-ups on the system card. The pull-up resistor value for a 5V signaling environment is 2KΩ typical (1.0KΩ min and 3.0KΩ max). For a 3.3V signaling environment the typical pull-up value is 5.1KΩ (2.7KΩ min and 8.2KΩ max). These values assume nine loads (two on the system card and one each on the seven peripheral slots). The pull-up resistor must be placed on the in-board side of the stub termination resistor.

System Card Pull-Ups Required on REQ64# and ACK64#. The system card must include a pull-up resistor on REQ64# and ACK64# (whether or not it has 64-bit capability). This ensures that other 64-bit cards will not see floating REQ64# and ACK64# signals. Also see "64-bit Cards in 32-bit Add-in Connectors" in the chapter entitled "The 64-bit PCI Extension."

Bus Master Requires Pull-Up on GNT#. Unlike standard PCI, CompactPCI requires that each bus master must include a 100KΩ pull-up resistor on its GNT# input to prevent a floating level if GNT# isn't driven by the system card.

Decoupling Requirements

Each CompactPCI card must include decoupling capacitors as specified in the CompactPCI specification (refer to the electrical requirements section of the specification).

Peripheral Card Signal Stub Lengths

32-bit and 64-bit Stub Lengths. The trace stub length for all 32-bit and 64-bit signals on peripheral cards must be less than or equal to 38.1mm (1.5 inches). The stub length is measured from the connector pin through the stub or series-terminating resistor (see "Resistors Required on a Card" on page 724) to the pin of the PCI device.

Clock Stub Length. The trace stub length on peripheral cards must be 63.5mm ± 2.54mm (2.5 inches ± 0.1 inches) and must only drive one input on the card.

System Card Stub Lengths

32-bit and 64-bit Stub Lengths. The trace stub length for all 32-bit and 64-bit signals on system cards must be less than or equal to 63.5mm (2.5 inches). The stub length is measured from the connector pin through the stub or series-terminating resistor (see "Resistors Required on a Card" on page 724) to the pin of the PCI device.

Clock Routing. The total permissible clock skew from the clock input pin of a PCI device on one card to the clock input of the device in the next backplane slot cannot exceed 2ns (at 33MHz). System card clock routing must accommodate up to 1.2ns of backplane skew (minimum versus maximum number of slots and various loading configurations).

The system card **must** provide separate clocks to each of the CompactPCI connector pins used to deliver the clocks to the peripheral card slots (CLK[4:0]). It **should** also supply two additional clocks to the CLK[6:5] connector pins (although current backplanes do not route these signals, future backplanes may use them to support hot swap capability). The routing of all of the clock traces (CLK[6:0]) must be such that all trace stub lengths are the same.

PCI devices that reside locally on the system card must be provided a clock that is delayed to accommodate the maximum clock skew imposed by the backplane (.8ns), but must not exceed the maximum permissible clock skew of 2ns. This means that up to 800ps (.8ns) of skew is allowed for on-card clock distribution (this includes the clock buffer's internal skew).

Signal Loading

Peripheral Card Signal Loading. A peripheral card must connect only one load to each PCI signal on the connector.

System Card Signal Loading. The system card may present up to two electrical loads to each bus signal. However, there must be only one stub-termination resistor per signal. This rule reflects the reality that most PCI chipsets (consisting of a host/PCI bridge and a PCI/ISA bridge) impose two electrical loads on each PCI signal.

Card Characteristic Impedance

The characteristic impedance range of on-card signal traces must be $65\Omega \pm 10\%$. This impedance only includes the impedance of the on-card trace.

Connector Shielding

The on-card connector shield must cover the top of the connector, providing a low-impedance return path for ground between the card and the backplane. This shield is connected to the connector's row F pins (i.e, ground). The connector lower side shield is not required. If present, it must not project into the guaranteed inter-card area (i.e., the interboard separation plane).

Front Panel and Front Panel IO Connectors

As illustrated in Figure 28-5 on page 729, each CompactPCI card has a front panel. A front panel has the following characteristics:

- Compliant with the IEEE 1101.1 (for flat panels) or IEEE 1101.10 (for EMC panels; EMC = Electro-Magnetically Compatible).
- If a card's front-panel implements IO connectors, the connector shells should use metallized shield connectors for EMI/RFI protection. The shell should be electrically connected to the IO front panel plate through a low-impedance path.
- The front panel plate is connected to earth ground and is isolated from logic ground.
- Ejector/injector handles compliant with IEEE 1101.10 shall be used. 3U cards implement one handle, while 6U cards implement two handles. Filler panels (for empty slots) do not require handles.
- The card's front panel shall display the appropriate glyph indicating what type of slot (system or peripheral) it must be installed in. A card that can be installed in either slot type must display both glyphs superimposed on each other.

Figure 28-5: Example Card Front Panel

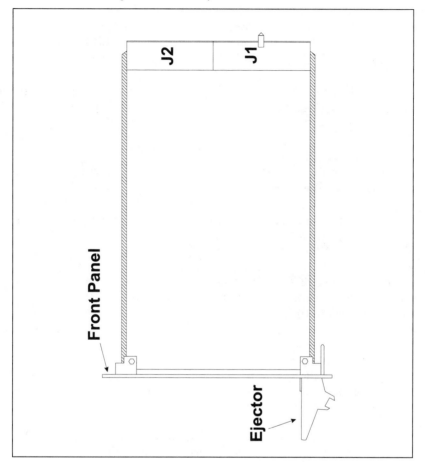

Backplane Design Rules

General

Backplanes come in two form factors:

- The 3U backplane accepts only 3U cards.
- The 6U backplane may accept either 3U or 6U cards.

The backplane portion of the specification is based on simulations performed by PICMG on a 33MHz CompactPCI bus segment and assumes the following characteristics:

- CompactPCI bus segment consists of up to eight slots (one system slot and up to seven peripheral slots) arranged in a linear manner.
- The system slot is physically located on either end of the segment.
- The center-to-center slot connector spacing is 20.32mm (0.8 inches).
- If more than eight slots are required, a PCI-to-PCI bridge must be utilized to bridge to another CompactPCI bus segment.
- As stated earlier (see "Compatibility Glyphs" on page 705), each slot must be marked with the appropriate glyph (system or peripheral). The physical slot number (see "Physical Slot Numbering" on page 705) must be displayed within the glyph.
- Each slot must display its logical slot number (see "Logical Slot Numbering" on page 705).
- Depending on system design requirements, clock speed, termination networks, etc., the ends of a backplane may be physically extended. When extended, however, the end dimensions shall be an increment of 5.08mm (thereby permitting modular construction of backplanes and racks).

3U Backplane

Figure 28-6 on page 731 illustrates a 3U backplane without a modular power supply connector. The backplane must implement both P1 and P2 in the system slot (to connect to the full 32-bit PCI bus plus the PCI clock and bus request/ grant signal lines). Connector implementation on the peripheral slots shall be as follows:

- If 64-bit operation is supported, both P1 and P2 must be implemented.
- If 64-bit operation is not supported but rear-panel IO is supported, both P1 and P2 must be supported.

Figure 28-7 on page 732 illustrates a 3U backplane that implements a modular power supply (see "Power Connections" on page 735) connector.

6U Backplane

Figure 28-8 on page 733 illustrates a typical 6U backplane. As with the 3U backplane, it may also be implemented with a modular power supply connector (see Figure 28-7 on page 732).

Figure 28-6: 3U Backplane

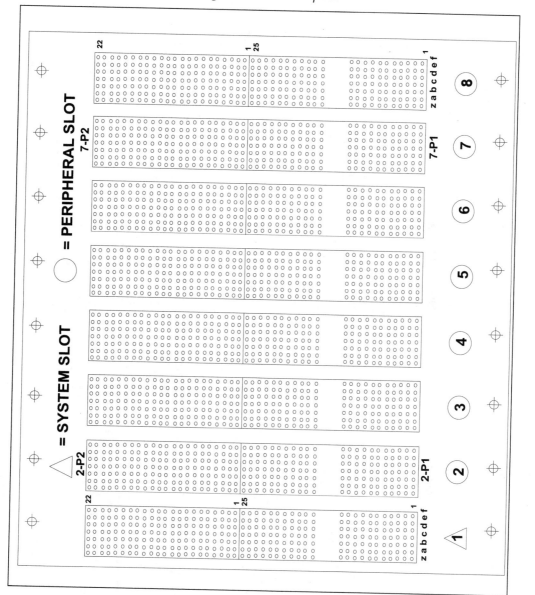

Figure 28-7: 3U Backplane with Modular Power Connector

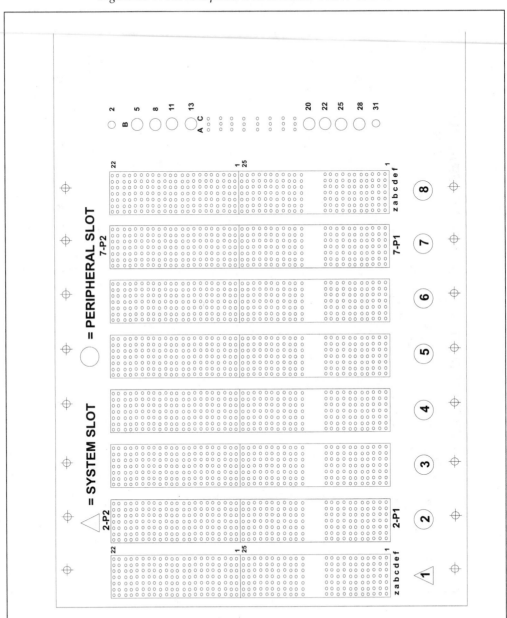

Figure 28-8: Typical 6U Backplane

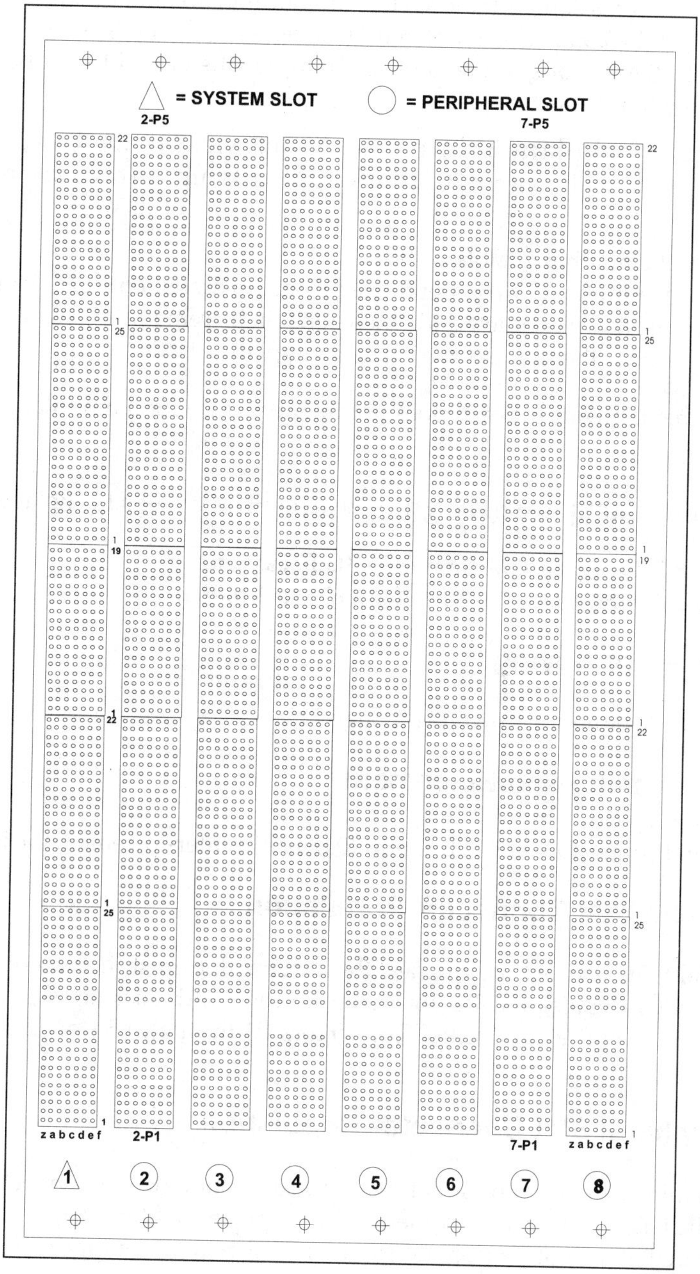

Dimensions

As stated earlier, the model tested by PICMG assumes up to eight connectors in a linear progression with the system slot located on either end. The slot connectors have 20.32mm (0.8 inch) center-to-center spacing. The ends of the backplane to the left of slot one and to the right of slot eight may be extended in 5.08mm increments.

Overall Backplane Width. The overall width of the backplane is therefore: Overall width = (n x 20.32mm) + (R x 5.08mm) + (L x 5.08mm) + 4.08mm, where

- n = the number of slots
- R = the number of right-end extensions (in increments of 5.08mm)
- L = the number of left-end extensions (in increments of 5.08mm)
- 4.08mm = the first interboard spacing plane width

Note that the width shown does not include space for a modular power supply connector.

Overall Backplane Height. The overall height of a backplane is:

- 128.7mm, +0mm, -0.3mm for a **3U backplane**.
- 262.05mm, +0mm, -0.3mm for a **6U backplane**.

Connector Keying

Refer to "Connector Keying" on page 713.

Slot Spacing and Placement

The slot connectors have 20.32mm (0.8 inch) center-to-center spacing.

System Slot Connector Population

On both 3U and 6U backplanes, the system slot must include both P1 (for the 32-bit PCI signals) and P2 (for the arbitration and clock signals). The 6U backplane may optionally include connectors P3-through-P5 (for rear-panel IO signals).

Peripheral Slot Connector Population

At a minimum, each peripheral slot must include the P1 connector (for the 32-bit PCI signals). If a peripheral slot supports 64-bit PCI, P2 must also be included. If a 32-bit peripheral slot on a 3U backplane supports rear-panel IO, it will include P2. If a 32-bit peripheral slot on a 6U backplane supports rear-panel IO, it may include any combination of P2-through-P5. If a 64-bit peripheral slot on a 6U backplane supports rear-panel IO, it may include any combination of P3-through-P5.

Power Distribution

Power Specifications. Backplanes must provide separate power planes for 3.3V, 5V, +12V, -12V and ground. If V(IO) is configurable as 3.3V or 5V, then a separate power plane must be dedicated to V(IO). Table 28-11 on page 735 defines the power requirements.

Table 28-11: Power Specifications

Mnemonic	Description	Nominal Value	Tolerance	Maximum Ripple
5V	+5Vdc	5.0V	±5%	50mV[1]
3.3V	+3.3Vdc	3.3V	±5%	50mV[1]
+12V	+12Vdc	12.0V	±5%	50mV[1]
-12V	-12Vdc	-12.0V	±5%	50mV[1]
GND	Ground			

Note (1): Measurement should be made at full load at 20MHz bandwidth with a 22μf and .1μf capacitor located at the measurement point.

Power Connections. Either of two methods of connecting the power supply to the backplane may be provided:

- Power terminals.
- Modular power supply connector.

Figure 28-9 on page 738 illustrates the modular power supply connector (type IEC 603-2) mandated by the 1.0 CompactPCI specification. Table 28-12 on page 736 describes its pinouts. The 2.1 specification has been revised to permit modular power supply connectors other than this type. The modular connector permits installation use of a rack-mounted modular power supply. The female connector is located on the backplane.

DEG# and FAL# Interconnect. Backplanes that provide a modular power supply connector must provide connections for the DEG# and FAL# signals described in Table 28-12 on page 736. The DEG# and FAL# signals from the modular power supply connector must be connected to the system slot connector's DEG# and FAL# pins.

Power Decoupling. Refer to the CompactPCI specification for information on backplane power decoupling.

Table 28-12: IEC 603-2 Modular Power Supply Connector

Pin	Staging	Mnemonic	Description
			Column A
A13	EL (extra length)	SP	Spare
A14	EL	INH#	**Inhibit.** May be used to turn off the power supply's outputs. Due to its longer pin, has precedence over the EN# signal. Typically connected to on/off switch.
A15	EL	ISH	**Current Share.** May be used between multiple power supplies for load balancing. Not required for single power supply systems.
A16	EL	5S-	**5V sense minus.** Must be connected to the center of the power plane for accommodating power distribution losses. Required for all modular power supplies.
A17	EL	5S+	**5V sense plus.** Must be connected to the center of the power plane for accommodating power distribution losses. Required for all modular power supplies.
A18	EL	3.3V	+3.3Vdc
A19	EL	+12V	+12Vdc
A20	EL	-12V	-12Vdc
			Column B
B2	SL (standard length)	ACL	**AC line.** Not required for DC input power supplies.
B5	SL	ACN	**AC neutral.** Not required for DC input power supplies.
B8	-	-	no pin.
B11	EL	CG	Chassis ground.
B13	SL	3.3V	+3.3Vdc
B14	SL	3.3V	+3.3Vdc
B15	SL	3.3V	+3.3Vdc

Table 28-12: IEC 603-2 Modular Power Supply Connector (Continued)

Pin	Staging	Mnemonic	Description
B16	SL	3.3V	+3.3Vdc
B17	SL	3.3V	+3.3Vdc
B18	SL	3.3V	+3.3Vdc
B19	SL	+12V	+12Vdc
B20	SL	-12V	-12Vdc
B22	EL	5V	+5Vdc
B25	EL	GND	Ground
B28	EL	+DC	+ DC input
B31	EL	-DC	- DC input
Column C			
C13	SL	EN#	**Enable signal**. May be used to turn on the power supply's outputs. Used in conjunction with INH# signal. Typically connected to ground to enable power supply after other signals on longer pins have made contact.
C14	SL	DEG#	**Derate signal**. DEG# may be used as a power supply output. When asserted, it indicates that the power supply is beginning to derate its power output. Backplanes that implement a modular power supply connector shall connect DEG# to the backplane's DEG# signal line.
C15	SL	FAL#	**Supply fail signal**. FAL# may be used as a power supply output. When asserted, it indicates that the supply has failed. Backplanes that implement a modular power supply connector shall connect FAL# to the backplane's FAL# signal line.
C16	SL	3.3V	+3.3Vdc
C17	SL	3.3V	+3.3Vdc
C18	SL	3.3V	+3.3Vdc
C19	SL	+12V	+12Vdc
C20	SL	-12V	-12Vdc

Figure 28-9: Modular Power Supply Connector

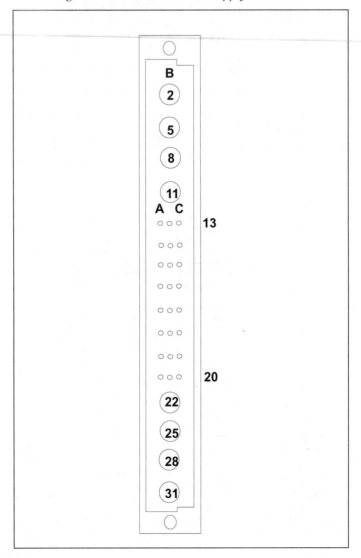

Chapter 28: CompactPCI and PMC

Signaling Environment

Refer to "5V and 3.3V Cards" on page 713.

Clock Routing

As stated in the PCI specification, the maximum permissible device-to-device (not card-to-card) PCI clock skew is 2ns. The system slot card must drive five clock lines, CLK[4:0] onto the backplane for distribution to the clock pins on up to seven peripheral slots. Additionally, the system card should also drive clocks to the system slot's CLK[6:5] pins. As of the 2.1 CompactPCI specification, the backplane is only required to route CLK[4:0], not CLK[6:5]. Their routing and usage is addressed in the *CompactPCI Hot Swap Specification*. For additional information, refer to "Separate Clock Lines Required" on page 752.

8-Slot Backplane. For an 8-slot backplane, the distribution of CLK[4:0] from the system slot to the peripheral slots is defined in Table 28-13 on page 739. It is evident in the table that the CLK0 pin on the system slot P1 connector is fanned out to the CLK pins on peripheral slots four and five. Likewise, the CLK1 pin on the system slot P2 connector is fanned out to the CLK pins on peripheral slots two and three. To minimize signal reflections, the fanout must be accomplished as indicated in Figure 28-10 on page 740.

The trace routing on the backplane for each of the clocks for slots 6-through-8 must match within 50mm (2 inches). No trace routed to slots 6-through-8 may exceed 185mm (7.3 inches) in length. The shared clocks (CLK0 and CLK1) connected to logical slots 4-5 and 2-3 respectively, must be shorter than or equal to 83.8mm (3.3 inches).

Table 28-13: System Slot-to-Peripheral Slot Clock Distribution (8-slot backplane)

System Slot		Peripheral Slot		
Pin Name	Pin Number	Logical Slot Number	Pin Name	Pin Number
CLK0	P1:D6	4	CLK	P1:D6
		5	CLK	P1:D6
CLK1	P2:A1	2	CLK	P1:D6
		3	CLK	P1:D6

Table 28-13: System Slot-to-Peripheral Slot Clock Distribution (8-slot backplane) (Continued)

System Slot		Peripheral Slot		
Pin Name	Pin Number	Logical Slot Number	Pin Name	Pin Number
CLK2	P2:A2	6	CLK	P1:D6
CLK3	P2:B2	7	CLK	P1:D6
CLK4	P2:A3	8	CLK	P1:D6

7-Slot Backplane. For a 7-slot backplane, only slots two and three need to share CLK0.

The trace routing on the backplane for each of the clocks for slots 4-through-7 must match within 50mm (2 inches). No trace routed to slots 4-through-7 may exceed 185mm (7.3 inches) in length. The shared clock (CLK0) connected to logical slots two and three must be shorter than or equal to 83.8mm (3.3 inches).

Backplane with Six or Fewer Slots. A backplane with six or fewer slots provides each slot with a dedicated clock.

The trace routing on the backplane for each of the clocks must match within 50mm (2 inches). No trace may exceed 185mm (7.3 inches) in length.

Figure 28-10: Shared Clock Distribution for Slots 2 and 3 and Slots 4 and 5

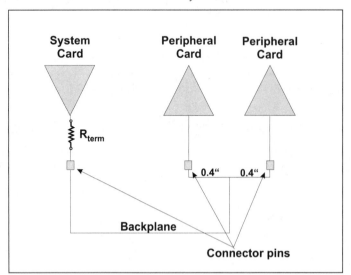

Chapter 28: CompactPCI and PMC

Characteristic Impedance

The characteristic impedance range of backplane signal traces must be 65Ω ±10%. This impedance only includes the impedance of the trace (i.e., backplane without connectors or boards installed).

8-Slot Termination

Simulations performed by the PICMG indicate that the 10ns maximum propagation delay (at 33MHz) is violated under the following circumstances:

- 8-slot backplane
- strongest PCI buffer allowed is used
- system slot occupied
- one peripheral slot (slot two) occupied.

To address this problem, fast Schottky diode signal termination (reference Texas Instruments 74S1053 diode array) must be added to the end of the backplane furthest away from the system slot. This is illustrated in Figure 28-11 on page 741.

Figure 28-11: PCI Signal Diode Termination

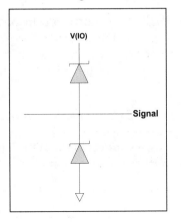

IDSEL Routing

Background. During Type 0 configuration transactions, the system card's host/PCI bridge decodes the target physical PCI package number (i.e., the CompactPCI card) and must assert IDSEL only to the target logical slot during the address phase of the transaction.

In CompactPCI, the host/PCI bridge decodes the target package number specified by the programmer and selects one of the upper address lines to place a logic one on. Address lines AD[31:11] are not used during a Type 0 configuration transaction. Table 28-14 on page 742 indicates the required mapping of target card to AD lines.

Table 28-14: Mapping Target Card to Upper AD Lines

Target Logical Slot	One Placed on:
2	AD[31]
3	AD[30]
4	AD[29]
5	AD[28]
6	AD[27]
7	AD[26]
8	AD[25]

Backplane AD/IDSEL Interconnect. In order for the logic one on the respective AD line to get to the associated slot's IDSEL pin, the backplane designer must connect the respective AD trace to the slot's IDSEL pin at the connector with the shortest possible trace length. The interconnect is defined in Table 28-15 on page 742.

Table 28-15: AD Line-to-IDSEL Interconnect

AD Line	Must connect to the IDSEL pin on slot:
AD[31]	2
AD[30]	3
AD[29]	4
AD[28]	5
AD[27]	6
AD[26]	7
AD[25]	8

REQ#/GNT# Routing

The PCI bus arbiter resides on the system card and is connected to each of up to seven peripheral slots via the REQ[6:0]#/GNT[6:0]# signal pairs. The REQ# (P1:A6) and GNT# (P1:E5) pins on the system card connector are used as REQ0# and GNT0#. Table 28-16 on page 743 defines the REQ#/GNT# signal routing on the backplane.

The specification states that it is a requirement that the system slot on any backplane must support the "full-complement of REQ#/GNT# signals." On the other hand, it states that the system card should (not must) support seven pairs of REQ#/GNT# signals for a system in which there are seven peripheral card bus masters. In the event that the system card does not support the seven pairs, the pairs that it does support must be configurable (e.g., configuring a REQ#/GNT# signal router on the system card under software control) so that a bus master can be supported in any slot.

Table 28-16: REQ#/GNT# Backplane Signal Routing

System Card		is Routed on the Backplane to		
Signal	Pin	Logical Slot Number	Signal	Pin
REQ#	P1:A6	2	REQ#	P1:A6
GNT#	P1:E5	2	GNT#	P1:E5
REQ1#	P2:C1	3	REQ#	P1:A6
GNT1#	P2:D1	3	GNT#	P1:E5
REQ2#	P2:E1	4	REQ#	P1:A6
GNT2#	P2:D2	4	GNT#	P1:E5
REQ3#	P2:E2	5	REQ#	P1:A6
GNT3#	P2:C3	5	GNT#	P1:E5
REQ4#	P2:D3	6	REQ#	P1:A6
GNT4#	P2:E3	6	GNT#	P1:E5
REQ5#	P2:D15	7	REQ#	P1:A6

Table 28-16: REQ#/GNT# Backplane Signal Routing (Continued)

System Card		is Routed on the Backplane to		
Signal	Pin	Logical Slot Number	Signal	Pin
GNT5#	P2:E15	7	GNT#	P1:E5
REQ6#	P2:D17	8	REQ#	P1:A6
GNT6#	P2:E17	8	GNT#	P1:E5

Interrupt Line Routing

Backplane Routing of PCI Interrupt Request Lines. Table 28-17 on page 744 defines the backplane's routing of the PCI interrupt request lines, INTA#-through-INTD#. This rotating pattern provides dedicated interrupt request lines to the first four peripheral slots (logical slots 2-through-5), assuming that each card uses just its INTA# pin (i.e., a single PCI function generates requests on the INTA# pin or multiple PCI functions share the card's INTA# pin). The rotating pattern repeats itself after slot four. This interrupt routing is consistent with that specified in the PCI-to-PCI bridge specification issued by the PCI SIG. This allows compliant bridging from PCI bus 0 to a CompactPCI bus segment. For a detailed description of PCI interrupts, refer to the chapter entitled "Interrupt-Related Issues."

Table 28-17: Backplane Routing of PCI Interrupt Lines

	Logical Slot 1	Logical Slot 2	Logical Slot 3	Logical Slot 4	Logical Slot 5	Logical Slot 6	Logical Slot 7	Logical Slot 8
INTA#	INTA# on A3	INTB# on B3	INTC# on C3	INTD# on E3	INTA# on A3	INTB# on B3	INTC# on C3	INTD# on E3
INTB#	INTB# on B3	INTC# on C3	INTD# on E3	INTA# on A3	INTB# on B3	INTC# on C3	INTD# on E3	INTA# on A3
INTC#	INTC# on C3	INTD# on E3	INTA# on A3	INTB# on B3	INTC# on C3	INTD# on E3	INTA# on A3	INTB# on B3
INTD#	INTD# on E3	INTA# on A3	INTB# on B3	INTC# on C3	INTD# on E3	INTA# on A3	INTB# on B3	INTC# on C3

Backplane Routing of Legacy IDE Interrupt Request Lines. A system may contain a legacy (i.e., ISA-style) IDE disk controller (referred to as the primary IDE controller) that uses the ISA method to generate interrupt requests. In other words, rather than generating a request by placing a logic low on an interrupt request line, a low-to-high transition is generated. Since this method is antithetical to the PCI interrupt request methodology, a legacy IDE controller must use a dedicated interrupt request line. If a second IDE controller is also present (referred to as the secondary IDE controller), it requires its own dedicated interrupt request line as well.

The CompactPCI specification defines two pins on the system card connector, INTP and INTS, that are reserved for use by primary and secondary legacy IDE controllers. The system card must route INTP to the IRQ14 input on the interrupt controller and INTS to the IRQ15 input.

The backplane designer is required to bus the INTP and INTS pins on the P1 connector of each peripheral slot to the INTP and INTS pins, respectively, on the system slot P1 connector.

Non-PCI Signals

Refer to Table 28-8 on page 723.

Geographical Addressing

Some backplanes provide information to a card (via the geographical addressing pins on P2) that identifies which physical card slot the card is installed in. This is referred to as the "geographic address" of the card. Cards that support JTAG multi-drop can use this information as a unique address. The ability of a card (either 32-bit or 64-bit) to read its geographical address from the backplane is optional. The ability of a backplane to supply this information is dictated by the following rule set:

- It is required that a backplane support geographical addressing via the geographical addressing pins on P2 if it implements the 64-bit PCI extension on P2.
- It is optional that a backplane support geographical addressing via the geographical addressing pins on P2 if it implements rear-panel IO on P2.

The geographic address of a slot must be identical to its physical slot number (see "Physical Slot Numbering" on page 705). It is supplied to a slot via the GA[4:0] connector pins on P2. The backplane encodes a "one" on a GA pin by leaving it unconnected and a "zero" by attaching it to ground. Table 28-18 on page 746 defines the GA encoding. As indicated, the GA codes of 0 and 31 are reserved for future use. This permits a backplane to identify up to 30 physical slots via the GA encoding.

Table 28-18: Backplane's Geographical Address Encoding

Physical Slot Number	GA[4] (P2:A22)	GA[3] (P2:B22)	GA[2] (P2:C22)	GA[1] (P2:D22)	GA[0] (P2:E22)
0 (Reserved)	GND	GND	GND	GND	GND
1	GND	GND	GND	GND	Open
2	GND	GND	GND	Open	GND
3	GND	GND	GND	Open	Open
4	GND	GND	Open	GND	GND
5	GND	GND	Open	GND	Open
6	GND	GND	Open	Open	GND
7	GND	GND	Open	Open	Open
8	GND	Open	GND	GND	GND
9	GND	Open	GND	GND	Open
10	GND	Open	GND	Open	GND
11	GND	Open	GND	Open	Open
12	GND	Open	Open	GND	GND
13	GND	Open	Open	GND	Open
14	GND	Open	Open	Open	GND
15	GND	Open	Open	Open	Open
16	Open	GND	GND	GND	GND
17	Open	GND	GND	GND	Open
18	Open	GND	GND	Open	GND
19	Open	GND	GND	Open	Open
20	Open	GND	Open	GND	GND
21	Open	GND	Open	GND	Open
22	Open	GND	Open	Open	GND
23	Open	GND	Open	Open	Open
24	Open	Open	GND	GND	GND
25	Open	Open	GND	GND	Open

Table 28-18: Backplane's Geographical Address Encoding (Continued)

Physical Slot Number	GA[4] (P2:A22)	GA[3] (P2:B22)	GA[2] (P2:C22)	GA[1] (P2:D22)	GA[0] (P2:E22)
26	Open	Open	GND	Open	GND
27	Open	Open	GND	Open	Open
28	Open	Open	Open	GND	GND
29	Open	Open	Open	GND	Open
30	Open	Open	Open	Open	GND
31 (reserved)	Open	Open	Open	Open	Open

Backplane 64-bit Support

Backplane support for 64-bit PCI is optional. The following rules apply:

1. If the backplane supports 64-bit PCI, the system slot must implement both P1 and P2 (see Table 28-6 on page 717).
2. Each peripheral slot position that supports 64-bit PCI will also implement P1 and P2 on the backplane.
3. A backplane that supports 64-bit PCI will bus the PCI 64-bit extension signals to P2 on the system slot and P2 on all 64-bit peripheral slots.
4. Backplanes that support 64-bit PCI will bus the REQ64# and ACK64# signals to P1 on all 64-bit slots and will supply a single pull-up resistor on each of these two signal lines.
5. Any 32-bit PCI slots will supply pull-up resistors on the REQ64# and ACK64# pins of P1 at the slot.

For additional information regarding the requirement for pull-ups on REQ64# and ACK64#, as well as a detailed discussion of 64-bit PCI, refer to "64-bit Cards in 32-bit Add-in Connectors" in the chapter entitled "The 64-bit PCI Extension."

Treatment of SYSEN# Signal

The backplane designer must ground the SYSEN# signal at the system slot and leave it unconnected at the peripheral slots. For additional information, refer to Table 28-8 on page 723.

Treatment of M66EN Signal

M66EN is defined as ground for 33MHz PCI backplane implementations. On future 66MHz systems, M66EN will be bussed to all slots and will have a pull-up resistor (almost certainly on the system card).

Rear-Panel IO Transition Boards

Rear-panel IO transition cards install in rear-panel connectors on the rear side of the backplane (in other words, the backplane services two racks, one on the front and one on the rear). They are used to gain access to rear-panel IO signals presented to the backplane by CompactPCI cards installed in the front rack. Figure 28-12 on page 750 illustrates a rear-panel IO transition card. Transition cards may or may not contain active components (i.e., logic). If active components are present, they may receive power either via rear-panel IO pins used for this purpose or from the backplane.

Dimensions

Rear-panel IO transition cards may be either the 3U (height = 100mm) or 6U (height = 233.35mm) form factor in height and are typically 80mm in depth. Their design is defined by IEEE P1101.11. Depths other than 80mm are permitted.

Connectors Used for Rear-Panel IO

1. The system slot may route rear-panel IO signals via any combination of P3-through-P5.
2. 32-bit peripheral slots may route rear-panel IO via any combination of P2-through-P5.
3. 64-bit peripheral slots may route rear-panel IO via any combination of P3-through-P5.

Other Mechanical Issues

The same rack rails, card guides, EMC support, ESD support, keying, alignment pin hole, and injector/extractor comb should be used as on the front rack except for the card guide's depth (typically 80mm).

The same front panel, handles, keying, alignment pin, EMC, and ESD mechanics should be used as on front panel CompactPCI cards.

Orientation Relative to Front-Panel CompactPCI Cards

Rear-panel IO transition cards are "in-line" with the front panel CompactPCI cards, resulting in the transition card's front panel being a mirror-image of the CompactPCI card's front panel. The top handles are on the bottom, the bottom handles on top, and slot keying holes and hole labels in both the card guides and front panels are upside down relative to the front boards and card guides.

Connector Pin Labeling

The transition card should use the same pin labeling sequence as the front CompactPCI cards with the pin numbering increasing from the bottom to the top of the connectors (resulting in a mirror image of the front card's layout). As a result, pin A1 is the same on the front cards, transition card, and on the backplane.

Connector P2 Rear-Panel IO Pinout

Refer to Table 28-7 on page 718. Note that the GA[4:0] pins may be used for either rear-panel IO or geographic addressing.

Figure 28-12: Rear-Panel IO Transition Card

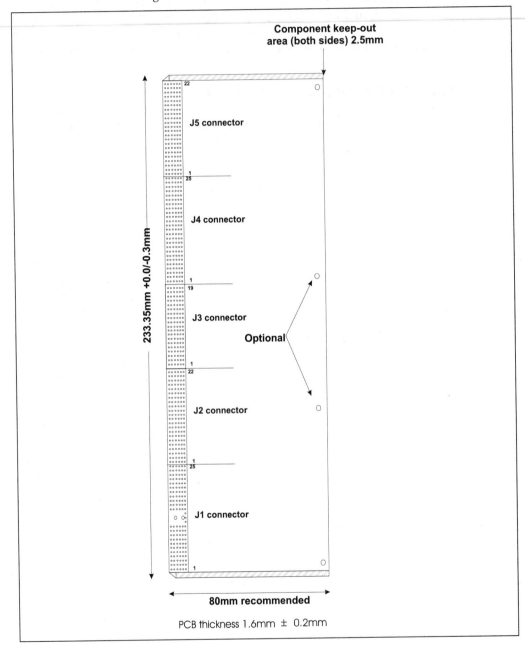

Chapter 28: CompactPCI and PMC

Hot Swap Capability

The industry organization (PICMG) that manages the CompactPCI spec released a separate *CompactPCI Hot-Swap Spec* on Aug. 17, 1998. It is extremely similar to the *Hot-Swap PCI spec* (refer to "Hot-Plug PCI" on page 455), differing in the following basic respects:

- the backplane is passive and, unlike Hot-Swap PCI wherein the card isolation logic resides on the system board, the isolation logic is on the adapter card.
- the logic that powers the card up is located on the adapter card rather than on the backplane.

Both of these changes were necessary because the CompactPCI backplane is passive, containing no active logic. If they had taken an approach that placed the card isolation and power control logic on the backplane rather than on the card, some systems would support hot swap while others wouldn't.

ENUM# Signal Added In CompactPCI 2.1 Spec

This is the System Enumeration signal. On the backplane, this optional open-drain signal is bussed to the ENUM# pin on P1 of all slot positions on the bus segment. It acts as an output from all peripheral slots and as an input to the system card. ENUM# must be asserted by a hot swap-capable card immediately after insertion and during removal. ENUM# is terminated with a pull-up resistor on the system card. When asserted by a peripheral card, the system card interrupts the processor, causing it to execute an interrupt service routine that enumerates the currently-installed peripheral cards to determine whether a card has been installed or removed. If a card has been removed, the resources (e.g., memory range, IO range, interrupt line, etc.) that were previously allocated to it by the configuration software are deallocated and made available as free resources. If a card has been added, the configuration Header registers for each PCI function on the card are interrogated to determine their resource requirements. The configuration software then allocates resources to each PCI function on the card and enables the devices for normal operation.

Electrical Insertion/Removal Occurs In Stages

Card Insertion Sequence

When a card is installed, the physical insertion sequence occurs as follows:

- The longest pins, power and ground, make contact first. Logic on the card begins to precharge all of the PCI signal pins to 1Vdc. This done to minimize the energy transfer between the card's buffers and the backplane PCI bus signals.
- The medium-length PCI signal pins make contact. At this point, they have already been precharged to the 1Vdc level.
- Finally, the short BD_SEL# pin makes contact, informing the on-card logic that the card is now firmly-seated. The on-card logic completes the power-up of the on-card logic.

Card Removal Sequence

When a card is removed, the sequence is reversed:

- The shortest pin, BD_SEL#, breaks contact first. This tells the on-card logic to pre-condition all of the PCI signal lines to minimize the effects of the removal on the system power supply.
- By the time the medium-length PCI signal pins break contact, they have been conditioned to have minimal effect on the backplane's PCI bus signals.
- Finally, the longest pins, power and ground, break contact, and power is removed from the card.

Separate Clock Lines Required

Testing revealed that the typical Compact PCI Clock distribution model that uses one Clock trace for two slots (see "System Slot-to-Peripheral Slot Clock Distribution (8-slot backplane)" on page 739) is unacceptable. It is a requirement that the backplane **must supply** a **separate Clock trace to each slot**. The two-slot distribution model caused unacceptable amounts of jitter on the Clock line when one of the two cards that share the Clock line is hot-swapped.

Three Levels of Implementation

Basic Hot-Swap

This is the most basic implementation of CompactPCI hot-swap and is extremely similar to PCI hot-swap. The end user must interact with the OS via the console to inform it of imminent card insertion or removal.

Installing a New Card. The following steps must be accomplished when installing a new card:

STEP 1. Using the console, the user informs the OS that a new card will be installed in a slot.

STEP 2. As the card is inserted, it encounters staged power and ground pins (see "Electrical Insertion/Removal Occurs In Stages" on page 752). When it is fully-seated, the card has been automatically power up.

STEP 3. The end user informs the system that the card is present.

STEP 4. The hot-swap handler informs the OS that a new card is present and the OS performs bus enumeration (see "Introduction" on page 309) to determine the resources required by the new card.

STEP 5. The OS programs the device's PCI configuration registers to assign resources to it.

STEP 6. The OS then loads the appropriate device driver and calls its initialization code.

STEP 7. The device driver's initialization code finishes the setup of the card (see "Step 7: OS Loads and Call Drivers' Initialization Code" on page 243) and brings it on-line.

Removing a Card. This involved the same steps as installing a card, only in reverse order:

STEP 1. Using the console, the user warns the OS that a card will be removed.

STEP 2. The **OS commands** the device's **driver to quiesce**. In other words, the driver must stop using the card. In addition, either the driver or the software utility would clear the device's PCI configuration Command register (see "Command Register" on page 368) to disable the device.

STEP 3. The OS removes the driver from memory.

STEP 4. The OS deallocates the resources that were assigned to the functions on the card.

STEP 5. The OS informs the end user (via the console) that the card can be removed.

STEP 6. The end user removes the card (see "Card Removal Sequence" on page 752).

Full Hot-Swap

Full Hot-Swap capability builds on top of Basic Hot-Swap. A microswitch is attached to the card's injector/ejector mechanism. This eliminates the step wherein the user must use the console to warn the OS about the upcoming card install/remove event. When a new card is installed or removed, the switch changes state before the card begins to engage or disengage. This gives the OS advance warning that a card is being installed or is about to be removed. When a card is being installed, the processor is interrupted when the card asserts the ENUM# signal to the host/PCI bridge, invoking the Hot-Plug Service. The card is then enumerated and configured, and a device driver is loaded. The OS calls the driver's init (i.e., initialization) code entry point and the init code finished the setup of the card and brings it on-line.

High-Availability Hot-Swap

High-Availability Hot-Swap builds on top of Full Hot-Swap. It requires the implementation of point-to-point RST# and isolation signals (over the backplane) between the System Card and each Peripheral card slot. This permits the OS to automatically isolate a card that fails. It can then bring a replacement card (that is already installed) on-line to take the place of the failed card.

Telecom-Related Issues Regarding Connector Keying

The 2.1 CompactPCI specification contains a statement indicating that the Telecom Interest Subcommittee (TISC) has requested defined keying for connector J4/P4 and for front panel connectors. The base CompactPCI 2.1 specification only mandates keying for connector J1/P1. The expanded key definition will prevent non-telecom cards from being inadvertently installed in a Telecom-specific backplane. This key definition is not available at this time.

PCI Mezzanine Cards (PMC)

Small Size Permits Attachment to CompactPCI Card

PCI cards designed to the 2.1 PCI standard will not fit on VME, CompactPCI and other types of Eurocards. They mount vertically and are 107mm in height and either 312mm (64-bit card) or 175mm (32-bit card) in depth. The basic, or single PMC card dimensions are 75mm in height by 150mm in depth with a 10mm stacking height above the host card that it is connected to. The PMC double card measures 150mm by 150mm.

Specifications

The Common Mezzanine Card (CMC) standard, IEEE P1386, defines the mechanics for the mezzanine card and its connector interface to the host card (e.g., CompactPCI). Associated child specifications further define the hardware/software interface to the host card environment. The PMC standard, IEEE P1386.1, references the PMC specification relative to the mechanical issues and the 2.1 PCI specification for the electrical, functional and software issues.

Stacking Height and Card Thickness

Refer to Figure 28-13 on page 755. The stacking height of a PMC card is defined as the distance between the component side of the host card (e.g., CompactPCI card) and the component side of the PMC card (which faces the component side of the host card). This distance is 10mm. The maximum PMC component height is 4.7mm, resulting in an air gap of .6mm. The combined height of the PMC card above the stacking height consists of the card's thickness plus the height of components on its opposite side. This can be no more than 3.5mm. The overall thickness of the PMC card's component area is therefore 8.2mm (4.7mm plus 3.5mm).

Figure 28-13: PMC Card Side View

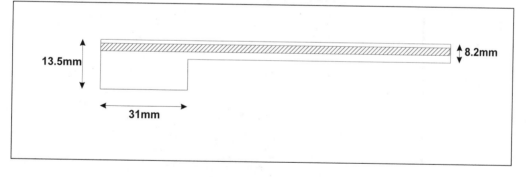

PMC Card's Connector Area

Refer to Figure 28-13 on page 755. The maximum height for the PMC card's connector area is 13.5mm. The area of the host card under the connector area must be non-conductive and component-free.

Front-Panel Bezel

The host card's front panel must provide a 71.8mm x 13.2mm opening for PMC mounting.

The PMC Connector

The PMC card uses a modified version of the Molex 1mm surface-mount connector. It has 64 pins, is 36mm in length and 10mm in height. On a single-size PMC card (75mm in width), two connectors (designated as P1 and P2) can be mounted side-by-side. This (128 pins) is sufficient to carry the 32-bit PCI signals plus power and ground. 64-bit PCI would require the addition of a third connector designated as P3. A fourth connector, P4 can be used for rear-panel IO signals (on either a 32-bit or 64-bit PMC card).

Figure 28-14: PMC Card Connectors and View when Mounted on Host Card

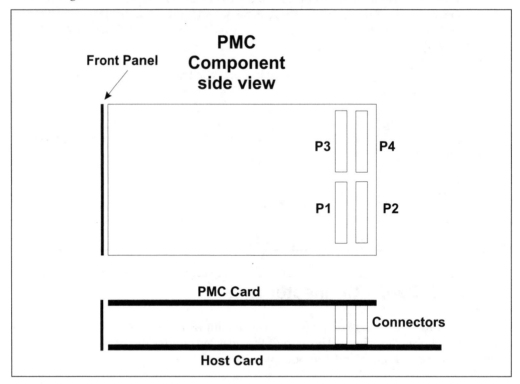

Mapping PMC Rear-Panel IO to 3U Rear-Panel IO

Table 28-19 on page 757 defines the mapping of the 64-pin PMC J4 (User IO) connector to the CompactPCI 3U card's J2 rear-panel IO connector. All references to UD are user-defined pins and can be used for any purpose.

Table 28-19: PMC P4 Connector (User IO) to 3U CompactPCI J2 (Rear-Panel IO)

CompactPCI J2 Pin	F	E	D	C	B	A
22	GND	UD	UD	UD	UD	UD
21	GND	UD	UD	UD	UD	UD
20	GND	UD	UD	UD	UD	UD
19	GND	UD	UD	UD	UD	UD
18	GND	UD	UD	UD	UD	UD
17	GND	UD	UD	UD	UD	UD
16	GND	UD	UD	UD	UD	UD
15	GND	UD	UD	UD	UD	UD
14	GND	5V	5V	3.3V	3.3V	3.3V
13	GND	PMC J4-1	PMC J4-2	PMC J4-3	PMC J4-4	PMC J4-5
12	GND	PMC J4-6	PMC J4-7	PMC J4-8	PMC J4-9	PMC J4-10
11	GND	PMC J4-11	PMC J4-12	PMC J4-13	PMC J4-14	PMC J4-15
10	GND	PMC J4-16	PMC J4-17	PMC J4-18	PMC J4-19	PMC J4-20
9	GND	PMC J4-21	PMC J4-22	PMC J4-23	PMC J4-24	PMC J4-25
8	GND	PMC J4-26	PMC J4-27	PMC J4-28	PMC J4-29	PMC J4-30
7	GND	PMC J4-31	PMC J4-32	PMC J4-33	PMC J4-34	PMC J4-35
6	GND	PMC J4-36	PMC J4-37	PMC J4-38	PMC J4-39	PMC J4-40
5	GND	PMC J4-41	PMC J4-42	PMC J4-43	PMC J4-44	PMC J4-45
4	GND	PMC J4-46	PMC J4-47	PMC J4-48	PMC J4-49	PMC J4-50
3	GND	PMC J4-51	PMC J4-52	PMC J4-53	PMC J4-54	PMC J4-55

Table 28-19: PMC P4 Connector (User IO) to 3U CompactPCI J2 (Rear-Panel IO) (Continued)

CompactPCI J2 Pin	F	E	D	C	B	A
2	GND	PMC J4-56	PMC J4-57	PMC J4-58	PMC J4-59	PMC J4-60
1	GND	PMC J4-61	PMC J4-62	PMC J4-63	PMC J4-64	V(IO)

Mapping PMC Rear-Panel IO to 6U Rear-Panel IO

Table 28-20 on page 758 defines the mapping of the 64-pin PMC J4 (User IO) connector to the CompactPCI 6U card's J3 and J4 rear-panel IO connectors. Table 28-21 on page 759 defines the mapping of the 64-pin PMC J4 (User IO) connector to the CompactPCI 6U card's J3 rear-panel IO connector.

Table 28-20: Mapping PMC P4 Connector (User IO) to 6U CompactPCI J3 and J4 (Rear-Panel IO)

CompactPCI Connector	F	E	D	C	B	A
J4-9	GND	GND	GND	GND	GND	GND
J4-8	GND	PMC J4-1	PMC J4-2	PMC J4-3	PMC J4-4	PMC J4-5
J4-7	GND	PMC J4-6	PMC J4-7	PMC J4-8	PMC J4-9	PMC J4-10
J4-6	GND	PMC J4-11	PMC J4-12	PMC J4-13	PMC J4-14	PMC J4-15
J4-5	GND	PMC J4-16	PMC J4-17	PMC J4-18	PMC J4-19	PMC J4-20
J4-4	GND	PMC J4-21	PMC J4-22	PMC J4-23	PMC J4-24	PMC J4-25
J4-3	GND	PMC J4-26	PMC J4-27	PMC J4-28	PMC J4-29	PMC J4-30
J4-2	GND	PMC J4-31	PMC J4-32	PMC J4-33	PMC J4-34	PMC J4-35
J4-1	GND	PMC J4-36	PMC J4-37	PMC J4-38	PMC J4-39	PMC J4-40
J3-19	GND	PMC J4-41	PMC J4-42	PMC J4-43	PMC J4-44	PMC J4-45
J3-18	GND	PMC J4-46	PMC J4-47	PMC J4-48	PMC J4-49	PMC J4-50
J3-17	GND	PMC J4-51	PMC J4-52	PMC J4-53	PMC J4-54	PMC J4-55
J3-16	GND	PMC J4-56	PMC J4-57	PMC J4-58	PMC J4-59	PMC J4-60

Table 28-20: Mapping PMC P4 Connector (User IO) to 6U CompactPCI J3 and J4 (Rear-Panel IO) (Continued)

CompactPCI Connector	F	E	D	C	B	A
J3-15	GND	PMC J4-61	PMC J4-62	PMC J4-63	PMC J4-64	V(IO)
J3-14	GND	5V	5V	3.3V	3.3V	3.3V

Table 28-21: Mapping PMC P4 Connector (User IO) to 6U CompactPCI J3 (Rear-Panel IO)

CompactPCI Connector	F	E	D	C	B	A
J3-14	GND	5V	5V	3.3V	3.3V	3.3V
J3-13	GND	PMC J4-1	PMC J4-2	PMC J4-3	PMC J4-4	PMC J4-5
J3-12	GND	PMC J4-6	PMC J4-7	PMC J4-8	PMC J4-9	PMC J4-10
J3-11	GND	PMC J4-11	PMC J4-12	PMC J4-13	PMC J4-14	PMC J4-15
J3-10	GND	PMC J4-16	PMC J4-17	PMC J4-18	PMC J4-19	PMC J4-20
J3-9	GND	PMC J4-21	PMC J4-22	PMC J4-23	PMC J4-24	PMC J4-25
J3-8	GND	PMC J4-26	PMC J4-27	PMC J4-28	PMC J4-29	PMC J4-30
J3-7	GND	PMC J4-31	PMC J4-32	PMC J4-33	PMC J4-34	PMC J4-35
J3-6	GND	PMC J4-36	PMC J4-37	PMC J4-38	PMC J4-39	PMC J4-40
J3-5	GND	PMC J4-41	PMC J4-42	PMC J4-43	PMC J4-44	PMC J4-45
J3-4	GND	PMC J4-46	PMC J4-47	PMC J4-48	PMC J4-49	PMC J4-50
J3-3	GND	PMC J4-51	PMC J4-52	PMC J4-53	PMC J4-54	PMC J4-55
J3-2	GND	PMC J4-56	PMC J4-57	PMC J4-58	PMC J4-59	PMC J4-60
J3-1	GND	PMC J4-61	PMC J4-62	PMC J4-63	PMC J4-64	V(IO)

Appendix A

Glossary
of
Terms

Access Latency. The amount of time that expires from the moment a bus master requests the use of the PCI bus until it completes the first data transfer of the transaction.

AD Bus. The PCI address/data bus carries address information during the address phase of a transaction and data during each data phase.

Address Ordering. During PCI burst memory transfers, the initiator must indicate whether the addressing sequence will be sequential (also referred to as linear) or will use cacheline wrap ordering of addresses. The initiator uses the state of AD[1:0] to indicate the addressing order. During I/O accesses, there is no explicit or implicit address ordering. It is the responsibility of the programmer to understand the I/O addressing characteristic of the target device.

Address Phase. During the first clock period of a PCI transaction, the initiator outputs the start address and the PCI command. This period is referred to as the address phase of the transaction. When 64-bit addressing is used, there are two address phases.

Agents. Each PCI device, whether a bus master (initiator) or a target is referred to as a PCI agent.

Arbiter. The arbiter is the device that evaluates the pending requests for access to the bus and grants the bus to a bus master based on a system-specific algorithm.

Arbitration Latency. The period of time from the bus master's assertion of REQ# until the bus arbiter asserts the bus master's GNT#. This period is a function of the arbitration algorithm, the master's priority and system utilization.

Atomic Operation. A series of two or more accesses to a device by the same initiator without intervening accesses by other bus masters.

Base Address Registers. Device configuration registers that define the start address, length and type of memory space required by a device. The type of space required will be either memory or I/O. The value written to this register during device configuration will program its memory or I/O address decoder to detect accesses within the indicated range.

BIST. Some integrated devices (such as the i486 microprocessor) implement a built-in self-test that can be invoked by external logic during system start up.

Bridge. The device that provides the bridge between two independent buses. Examples would be the bridge between the host processor bus and the PCI bus, the bridge between the PCI bus and a standard expansion bus (such as the ISA bus) and the bridge between two PCI buses.

Bus Access Latency. Defined as the amount of time that expires from the moment a bus master requests the use of the PCI bus until it completes the first data transfer of the transaction. In other words, it is the sum of arbitration, bus acquisition and target latency.

Bus Acquisition Latency. Defined as the period time from the reception of GNT# by the requesting bus master until the current bus master surrenders the bus and the requesting bus master can initiate its transaction by asserting FRAME#. The duration of this period is a function of how long the current bus master's transaction-in-progress will take to complete.

Bus Concurrency. Separate transfers occurring simultaneously on two or more separate buses. An example would be an EISA bus master transferring data to or from another EISA device while the host processor is transferring data to or from system memory.

Bus Idle State. A transaction is not currently in progress on the bus. On the PCI bus, this state is signalled when FRAME# and IRDY# are both deasserted.

Bus Lock. Gives a bus master sole access to the bus while it performs a series of two or more transfers. This can be implemented on the PCI bus, but the preferred method is resource locking. The EISA bus implements bus locking.

Bus Master. A device capable of initiating a data transfer with another device.

Bus Parking. An arbiter may grant the buses to a bus master when the bus is idle and no bus masters are generating a request for the bus. If the bus master that the bus is parked on subsequently issues a request for the bus, it has immediate access to the bus.

Byte Enable. I486, Pentium™ or PCI Bus control signal that indicates that a particular data path will be used during a transfer. Indirectly, the byte enable signal also indicates what byte within an addressed doubleword (or quadword, during 64-bit transfers) is being addressed.

Cache. A relatively small amount of high-speed Static RAM (SRAM) that is used to keep copies of information recently read from system DRAM memory. The cache controller maintains a directory that tracks the information currently resident within the cache. If the host processor should request any of the information currently resident in the cache, it will be returned to the processor quickly (due to the fast access time of the SRAM).

Cache Controller. See the definition of **Cache.**

Cache Line Fill. When a processor's internal cache, or its external second level cache has a miss on a read attempt by the processor, it will read a fixed amount (referred to as a line) of information from the external cache or system DRAM memory and record it in the cache. This is referred to as a cache line fill. The size of a line of information is cache controller design dependent.

Cache Line Size. See the definition of **Cache Line Fill.**

CacheLine Wrap Mode. At the start of each data phase of the burst read, the memory target increments the doubleword address in its address counter. When the end of the cache line is encountered and assuming that the transfer did not start at the first doubleword of the cache line, the target wraps to start address of the cacheline and continues incrementing the address in each data phase until the entire cache line has been transferred. If the burst continues past the point where the entire cache line has been transferred, the target starts the transfer of the next cache line at the same address that the transfer of the previous line started at.

CAS Before RAS Refresh, or CBR Refresh. Some DRAMs incorporate their own row counters to be used for DRAM refresh. The external DRAM refresh logic has only to activate the DRAM's CAS line and then its RAS line. The DRAM will automatically increment its internal row counter and refresh (recharge) the next row of storage.

CBR Refresh. See the definition of **CAS Before RAS Refresh.**

Central Resource Functions. Functions that are essential to operation of the PCI bus. Examples would be the PCI bus arbiter and "keeper" pullup resistors that return PCI control signals to their quiescent state or maintain them at the quiescent state once driven there by a PCI agent.

Claiming the Transaction. An initiator starts a PCI transaction by placing the target device's address on the AD bus and the command on the C/BE bus. All PCI targets latch the address on the next rising-edge of the PCI clock and begin to decode the address to determined if they are being addressed. The target that recognizes the address will "claim" the transaction by asserting DEVSEL#.

Class Code. Identifies the generic function of the device (for example, a display device) and, in some cases, a register-specific programming interface (such as the VGA register set). The upper byte defines a basic class type, the middle byte a sub-class within the basic class, and the lower byte may define the programming interface.

Coherency. If the information resident in a cache accurately reflects the original information in DRAM memory, the cache is said to be coherent or consistent.

Commands. During the address phase of a PCI transaction, the initiator broadcasts a command (such as the memory read command) on the C/BE bus.

Compatibility Hole. The DOS compatibility hole is defined as the memory address range from 80000h - FFFFFh. Depending on the function implemented within any of these memory address ranges, the area of memory will have to be defined in one of the following ways: Read-Only, Write-Only, Read/Writable, Inaccessible.

Concurrent Bus Operation. See the definition of **Bus Concurrency**.

Configuration Access. A PCI transaction to read or write the contents of one of a PCI device's configuration registers.

Configuration Address Space. x86 processors possess the ability to address two distinct address spaces: I/O and memory. The PCI bus uses I/O and memory accesses to access I/O and memory devices, respectively. In addition, a third access type, the configuration access, is used to access the configuration registers that must be implemented in all PCI devices.

Configuration CMOS RAM. The information used to configure devices each time an ISA, EISA or Micro Channel™ machine is powered up is stored in battery backed-up CMOS RAM.

Configuration Header Region. Each functional PCI device possesses a block of two hundred and fifty-six configuration addresses reserved for implementation of its configuration registers. The format, or usage, of the first sixty-four locations is predefined by the PCI specification. This area is referred to as the device's configuration header region.

Consistency. See the definition of **Coherency**.

Data Packets. In order to improve throughput, a PCI bridge may consolidate a series of single memory reads or writes into a single PCI memory burst transfer.

Data Phase. After the address phase of a PCI transaction, a data item will be transferred during each data phase of the transaction. The data is transferred when both TRDY# and IRDY# are sampled asserted.

Deadlock. A deadlock is a condition where two masters each require access to a target simultaneously, but the action taken by each will prevent the desired action of the other.

Direct-Mapped Cache. In a direct-mapped cache, the cache is the same size as a page in memory. When a line of information is fetched from a position within a page of DRAM memory, it is stored in the same relative position within the cache. If the processor should subsequently request a line of information from the same relative position within a different page of memory, the cache controller will fetch the new line from memory and must overwrite the line currently in the cache.

Dirty Line. A write-back cache controller has cached a line of information from memory. The processor subsequently performs a memory write to a location within the cache line. There is a hit on the cache and the cache line is updated with the new information, but the cache controller will not perform a memory write bus cycle to update the line in memory. The line in the cache no longer reflects the line in memory and now has the latest information. The cache line is said to be "dirty" and the memory line is "stale." Dirty is another way of saying "modified."

Disconnect. A very slow access target may force a disconnect between accesses to give other initiators a chance to use the bus. This is known as a disconnect. If the current access is quite long and will consume a lot of bus time, the target signals a disconnect, completes the current data phase, and the initiator terminates the transaction. The initiator then arbitrates for the bus again so that it may re-initiate the transaction, continuing the data transfer at the point of disconnection.

DOS Compatibility Hole. See the definition of **Compatibility Hole**.

DRAM controller. The DRAM controller converts memory read or write bus cycles on the host or PCI bus to the proper sequence of actions on the memory bus to access the target DRAM location.

EISA. Extension to Industry Standard Architecture. The EISA specification was developed to extend the capabilities of the ISA machine architecture to support more advanced features such as bus arbitration and faster types of bus transfers.

Exclusive Access. A series of accesses to a target by one bus master while other masters are prevented from accessing the device.

Expansion ROM. A device ROM related to a PCI function. This ROM typically contains the initialization code and possibly the BIOS and interrupt service routines for its associated device.

Functional PCI Devices. A PCI device that performs a single, self-contained function. Examples would be a video adapter or a serial port. A single, physical PCI component might actually contain from one to eight PCI functional devices.

Hidden bus arbitration. Unlike some arbitration schemes, the PCI scheme allows bus arbitration to take place at the same time that the current PCI bus master is performing a data transfer. No bus time is wasted on a dedicated period of time to perform an arbitration bus cycle. This is referred to as hidden arbitration.

Hidden Refresh. If a DRAM controller uses the memory bus to perform DRAM refresh when the system is currently accessing a device other than DRAM memory, this is referred to as hidden refresh. Refreshing DRAM in this fashion doesn't impact system performance.

Hierarchical PCI Buses. When one PCI bus is subordinate to another PCI bus, they are arranged in a hierarchical order. A PCI-to-PCI bridge would interconnect the two buses.

Hit. Refers to a hit on the cache. The processor initiates a memory read or write and the cache controller has a copy of the target line in its cache.

Host/PCI Bridge. A device that provides the bridge between the host processor's bus and a PCI bus. The bridge provides transaction translation in both directions. It may also provide data buffering and/or a second-level cache for the host processor.

Idle State. See the definition for the **Bus Idle State**.

Incident-Wave Switching. See the definition of **Class I Driver**.

Initiator. When a bus master has arbitrated for and won access to the PCI bus, it becomes the initiator of a transaction. It then starts a transaction, asserting FRAME# and driving the address and command onto the bus.

Interrupt Acknowledge. The host ix86 processor responds to an interrupt request on its INTR input by generating two, back-to-back interrupt acknowledge bus cycles. If the interrupt controller resides on the PCI bus, the host/PCI bridge translates the two cycles into a single PCI interrupt acknowledge bus cycle. In response to an interrupt acknowledge, the interrupt controller must send the interrupt vector corresponding to the highest priority device generating a request back to the processor.

Interrupt Controller. A device requiring service from the host processor generates a request to the interrupt controller. The interrupt controller, in turn, generates a request to the host processor on its INTR signal line. When the host processor responds with an interrupt acknowledge, the interrupt controller prioritizes the pending requests and returns the interrupt vector of the highest priority device to the processor.

Level-Two, or L2, Cache. The host processor's internal cache is frequently referred to as the primary, or level-one cache. An external cache that attempts to service misses on the internal cache is referred to as the level-two cache.

Line. See the definition of **Cache Line Fill**.

Line Buffer. If a device has a buffer that can hold an entire line of information previously fetched from memory, the buffer is frequently referred to as a line buffer.

Linear Addressing. If a PCI master initiates a burst memory transfer and sets AD[1:0] equal to a 00b, this indicates to the addressed target that the memory address should be incremented for each subsequent data phase of the transaction.

Local Bus. Generally, refers to the processor's local bus structure. An example would be the 486's bus structure.

Look-Through Cache Controller. A cache controller that resides between its associated processor and the rest of the world is referred to as a look-through cache controller. Look-through cache controllers are divided into two categories: write-through and write-back.

Master Abort. If an initiator starts a PCI transaction and the transaction isn't claimed by a target (DEVSEL# asserted) within five PCI clock periods, the initiator aborts the transaction with no data transfer.

Master Latency Timer. Each bus master must incorporate a Latency Timer, or LT. The LT benefits both the current bus master and any bus master that may request access to the PCI bus while the current bus master is performing a transaction. The LT ensures that the current bus master will not hog the bus if the PCI bus arbitrator indicates that another PCI master is requesting access to the bus. Looking at it from another point of view, it guarantees the current bus master a minimum amount of time on the bus before it must surrender it to another master.

Master-Initiated Termination. The LT count may have expired and the transaction continued without preemption by the arbitrator (removal of its grant) because no other PCI master required the bus. Another bus master may then request and be granted the bus while the current master still has a transaction in progress. Upon sensing the removal of its grant by the arbitrator, the current bus master must initiate transaction termination at the end of the current data transfer with the target. This is referred to as master-initiated termination.

Memory Read Command. The PCI memory read command should be used when reading less than a cache line from memory.

Memory Read Line Command. This PCI command should be used to fetch one complete cache line from memory.

Memory Read Multiple Command. This command should be used to fetch multiple memory cache lines from memory. When this command is used, the target memory device should fetch the requested cache line from memory. When the requested line has been fetched from memory, the memory controller should start fetching the next line from memory in anticipation of a request from the initiator. The memory controller should continue to prefetch lines from memory as long as the initiator keeps FRAME# asserted.

Memory Write Command. The initiator may use the PCI memory write or the memory write and invalidate command to update data in memory.

Memory Write and Invalidate Command. The memory write and invalidate command is identical to the memory write except that it transfers a complete cache line during the current transaction. The initiator's configuration registers must allow specification of the line size during system configuration. If, when snooping, the cache/bridge's write-back cache detects a memory write and invalidate issued by the initiator and has a snoop hit on a line marked as dirty, the cache can just invalidate the line and doesn't need to perform the flush to memory. This is possible because the initiator is updating the entire memory line and all of the data in the dirty cache line is therefor invalid. This increases performance by eliminating the requirement for the line flush.

Message. An initiator may broadcast a message to one or more PCI devices by using the PCI Special Cycle command. During the address phase, the AD bus is driven to random values and must be ignored. The initiator does, however, use the C/BE lines to broadcast the special cycle command. During the data phase, the initiator broadcasts the message type on AD[15:0] and an optional message-dependent data field over AD[31:16]. The message and data are only valid during the clock after IRDY# is asserted. The data contained in, and the timing of subsequent data phases is message dependent.

Miss. Refers to a miss on the cache. The processor initiates a memory read or write and the cache controller does not have a copy of the target line in its cache.

Multi-Function Devices. A physical PCI component may have one or more independent PCI functions integrated within the package. A component that incorporates more than one function is referred to as a Multi-Function Device.

Non-Cacheable Memory. Memory whose contents can be altered by a local processor without using the bus should be designated as non-cacheable. A cache somewhere else in the system would have no visibility to the change and could end up with stale data and not realize that it no longer accurately reflects the contents of memory.

Packets. See the definition of **Data Packets**.

Page Register. The upper portion of the start memory address for a DMA transfer is written to the respective DMA channel's Page register. The contents of this register is then driven onto the upper part of the address bus during a DMA data transfer.

Parking. See the definition of **Bus Parking**.

PCI. See the definition of **Peripheral Component Interconnect.**

Peer PCI Buses. PCI buses that occupy the same ranking in the PCI bus hierarchy (with respect to the host bus) are referred to as peer PCI buses.

Peripheral Component Interconnect (or PCI). Specification that defines the PCI bus. This bus is intended to define the interconnect and bus transfer protocol between highly-integrated peripheral adapters that reside on a common local bus on the system board (or add-in expansion cards on the PCI bus).

Physical PCI Device. See the definition of **Functional PCI Devices.**

Point-To-Point Signals. Signals that provide a direct interconnect between two PCI agents. An example would be the REQ# and GNT# lines between a PCI bus master and the PCI bus arbiter.

Posted-Write Capability. The ability of a device to "memorize" or post a memory write transaction and signal immediate completion to the bus master. As long as there is room in the posted-write buffer, this permits the bus master to complete memory writes with no wait states. After posting the write and signalling completion to the bus master, the device will then perform the actual memory write.

Preemption. Preemption occurs when the arbitrator removes the grant from one master and gives it to another.

Prefetching. Fetching a line of information from memory before a bus master requests it. If the master should subsequently request the line, the target device can supply it immediately. This shields the master from the slow access time of the actual target memory.

Primary Bus. The bus closest to the host processor that is connected to one side of an inter-bus bridge.

Reflected-Wave Switching. The output drivers commonly implemented in highly-integrated components fall into the class II category. They take advantage of the reflected-wave switching characteristic common to high-speed transmission lines and printed circuit traces in order to achieve the input logic thresholds. When a class II output driver transitions a signal line from a logic low to a high, the low-to-high transition is rather weak and only achieves half of the voltage change required to cross the logic threshold. This transition wavefront is transmitted along the trace and is seen sequentially by the input of each device connected to the line. When the wavefront gets to the end of the transmission line, it is reflected back along the trace, effectively doubling the voltage change and thereby boosting the voltage change past the logic threshold. As the wave passes each device's input, the new valid logic level is detected.

Reserved Bus Commands. Several of the PCI bus command codes are reserved for future use. Targets should ignore reserved bus commands.

Resource Lock. The PCI bus implements a signal, LOCK#. It allows a master (a processor) to reserve a particular target for its sole use until it completes a series of accesses to the target. The master then indicates that it no longer requires exclusive access to the target. One of the nice features of the PCI bus is that it permits other masters to use the bus to access targets other than the locked target during the period that a master has locked access to a particular target.

Retry. If a target cannot respond to a transaction at the current time, it will signal "retry" to the initiator and terminate the transaction. The initiator will respond by ending the transaction and then retrying it later. No data transfer takes place during this transaction. An example of the need for a retry would be if the target is currently locked for exclusive access by another initiator.

SCSI. Small Computer System Interface. A bus designed to offload block data transfers from the host processor. The SCSI host bus adapter provides the interface between the host system's bus and the SCSI bus.

Secondary Bus. The bus further from the host processor that is connected to one side of an inter-bus bridge.

Sideband Signals. A sideband signal is defined as a signal that is not part of the PCI bus standard and interconnects two or more PCI agents. This signal only has meaning for the agents it interconnects.

Single-Function Devices. A physical PCI component may have one or more independent PCI functions integrated within the package. A component that incorporates only one function is referred to as a Single-Function Device.

Slave. Another name for the target being addressed during a transaction.

Snooping. When a memory access is performed by an agent other than the cache controller, the cache controller must snoop the transaction to determine if the current master is accessing information that is also resident within the cache. If a snoop hit occurs, the cache controller must take an appropriate action to ensure the continued consistency of its cached information.

Soft-Encoded Messages. The first two message codes, 0000h and 0001h, are defined as SHUTDOWN and HALT. Message code 0002h is reserved for Intel device-specific messages, while codes 0003h - through - FFFFh are reserved. Questions regarding the allocation of the reserved message codes should be forwarded to the PCI SIG. Also see the definition of **Message**.

Special Cycle Command. See the definition of **Message**.

Special Interest Group, or SIG. The PCI SIG manages the specification.

Speedway. Intel performed over 5000 hours of simulations in order to establish the best possible layout of the PCI bus on a high-frequency system board. The result is the Speedway (trademarked by Intel) definition. This layout may be used for up to ten physical PCI components operating at speeds up to 33MHz.

Stale Information. See the definition of **Dirty Line**.

Standard Form Factor. Also referred to as the long card form factor, the standard form factor defines a PCI expansion board that is designed to fit into existent desktop machines with ISA, EISA or Micro Channel™ card slots.

Streaming Data Procedures. Advanced bus cycle types implemented on the more advanced Micro Channel machines.

Subordinate Bus Number. The subordinate bus number configuration register in a PCI-to-PCI bridge (or a host/PCI bridge) defines the bus number of the highest-numbered PCI bus that exists behind the bridge.

Subtractive Decode. The PCI-to-expansion bus bridge is designed to claim many transactions not claimed by other devices on the PCI bus. If the bridge doesn't see DEVSEL# asserted by a PCI target within four PCI clock periods from the start of a transaction, the bridge may assert DEVSEL# to claim the transaction and then pass the transaction onto the standard expansion bus (such as ISA, EISA or the Micro Channel).

Tag SRAM. The high-speed static RAM used as a directory by a cache controller.

Target. The PCI device that is the target of a PCI transaction initiated by a PCI bus master.

Target Latency. Defined as the period of time until the currently-addressed target is ready to complete the first data phase of the transaction. This period is a function of the access time for the currently-addressed target device.

Target-Abort. If the target detects a fatal error or will never be able to respond to the transaction, it must signal a target-abort (using the STOP# signal). This will cause the initiator to end the transaction with no data transfer and no retry.

Target-Initiated Termination. Under some circumstances, the target may have to end a transfer prematurely. The following are some examples. A very slow access target may force a disconnect between accesses to give other initiators a chance to use the bus. This is known as a **disconnect**. If the current access is quite long and will consume a lot of bus time, the target signals a disconnect, completes the current data transfer, and the initiator terminates the transaction. The initiator then arbitrates for the bus again so that it may re-initiate the transaction, continuing the data transfer at the point of disconnection. If a target cannot respond to a transaction at the current time, it will signal **retry** to the initiator and terminate the transaction. The initiator will respond by ending the transaction and then retrying it. No data transfer takes place during this transaction. An example of the need for a retry would be if the target is currently locked for exclusive access by another initiator. If the target detects a fatal error or will never be able to respond to the transaction, it may signal a **target-abort**. This will cause the initiator to end the transaction with no data transfer and no retry.

Turn-Around Cycle. A turn-around cycle is required on all signals that may be driven by more than one PCI bus agent. This period is required to avoid contention when one agent stops driving a signal and another agent begins.

Type One Configuration Access. The type one access is used to configure a device on a lower-level PCI bus (in a system with hierarchical PCI buses).

Type Zero Configuration Access. The type zero access is used to configure a device on the PCI bus the configuration access is run on.

Utility Bus. The utility bus is located on the system board and is a buffered version of the standard expansion bus (ISA, EISA or the Micro Channel). Devices such as the keyboard controller, CMOS RAM, and floppy controller typically reside on the utility bus. This bus is also frequently referred to as the X-bus.

Vendor ID. Every PCI device must have a vendor ID configuration register that identifies the vendor of the device.

VESA. The Video Electronics Standards Association, or VESA, is a consortium of add-in card manufacturers tasked with developing standards for PC device interfacing.

VESA VL Bus. This is the local bus standard developed by the VESA consortium.

Video Electronics Standards Association (VESA). See the definition of **VESA**.

Video Memory. Memory that is dedicated to the storage of the video image to be scanned out to the display device.

VL bus. See the definition of **VESA VL Bus**.

VL Type A Local Bus. This is the direct-connect version of the VESA VL bus. For more information, refer to chapter two.

VL Type B Local Bus. This is the buffered version of the VESA VL bus. For more information, refer to chapter two.

Wait State. A delay of one PCI clock period injected into a PCI data phase because either the initiator (IRDY# deasserted), the target (TRDY# deasserted), or both are not yet ready to complete the data transfer.

Write Miss. The processor initiates a memory write and the cache controller does not have a copy of the target memory location within its cache.

Write-Back Cache. The write-back cache controller is a variant of the look-through cache controller. When the processor initiates a memory write bus cycle, the cache controller determines whether or not is has a copy of the target memory location within its cache. If it does, this is a write hit. The cache controller updates the line of information in its cache, but does not initiate a memory write bus cycle to update the line in DRAM memory. This permits processor-initiated memory writes to complete with no wait states. The cache line is now dirty and the memory line is stale. The cache controller will not flush its dirty lines to memory until later. In the event of a miss, the data is written to memory.

Write-Through Cache. The write-through cache controller is a variant of the look-through cache controller. When the processor initiates a memory write bus cycle, the cache controller determines whether or not is has a copy of the target memory location within its cache. If it does, this is a write hit. The cache controller updates the line of information in its cache, and also writes it through to DRAM memory. This ensures that the cache and DRAM memory are always in sync. In the event of a miss, the data is written to memory.

X-Bus. See the definition of **Utility Bus**.

Index

Index

Index

Index

Index

Index

The PC System Architecture Series

The PC System Architecture Series is a crisply written and comprehensive set of guides to the most important PC hardware standards. Each title illustrates the relationship between the software and hardware, and thoroughly explains the architecture, features, and operation of systems built using one particular type of chip or hardware specification.

MindShare, Inc. is one of the leading technical training companies in the computer industry, providing innovative courses for dozens of companies, including Intel, IBM, and Compaq.

> *"There is only one way to describe the series of PC hardware and architecture books written by Tom Shanley and Don Anderson: INVALUABLE."*
> —*PC Magazine*'s "Read Only" column

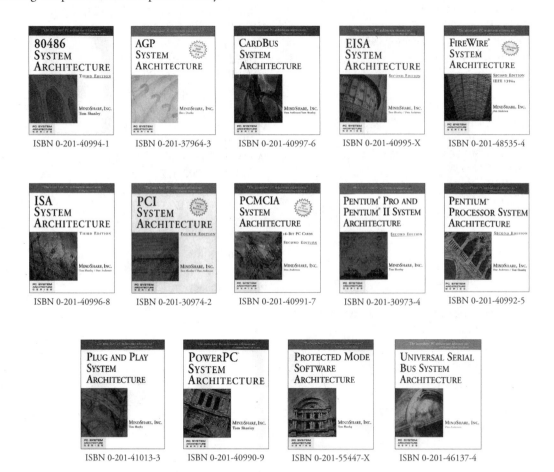

ISBN 0-201-40994-1

ISBN 0-201-37964-3

ISBN 0-201-40997-6

ISBN 0-201-40995-X

ISBN 0-201-48535-4

ISBN 0-201-40996-8

ISBN 0-201-30974-2

ISBN 0-201-40991-7

ISBN 0-201-30973-4

ISBN 0-201-40992-5

ISBN 0-201-41013-3

ISBN 0-201-40990-9

ISBN 0-201-55447-X

ISBN 0-201-46137-4

http://www.awl.com/cseng/series/mindshare/

◆ Addison-Wesley